READINGS
IN
INTELLECTUAL HISTORY
The American Tradition

READINGS
IN
INTELLECTUAL HISTORY
The American Tradition

C. K. McFarland

HOLT, RINEHART AND WINSTON, INC.
New York Chicago San Francisco Atlanta Dallas Montreal Toronto London Sydney

PREFACE

"Writing intellectual history," the late William B. Hesseltine once complained, "is like trying to nail jelly to the wall." Other political and diplomatic historians agree. But students of United States intellectual history and American studies vigorously disagree. Throughout the twentieth century—and especially since the death of Vernon L. Parrington in 1930—they have indeed nailed jelly to the wall. Their numbers include such eminent scholars as Loren Baritz, Henry Steele Commager, Alan Heimert, John Higham, Perry Miller, Stow Persons, George W. Pierson, and Henry Nash Smith, and their works represent significant contributions to the American intellectual tradition.

The selections in this book have been chosen to meet the need for supplementary readings in courses on United States intellectual history and American studies. They are arranged to emphasize topics and problems to which instructors generally give considerable attention. Because of the predominance of history and literature majors in these classes, it is important for students to become acquainted with the major ideas and interpretations of prominent scholars available in numerous journals. These articles provide a knowledge and understanding of the field that will greatly aid the perceptive student. The thirty-two essays are of unusually high competence. They help explain the origin and development of the American mind.

In spite of the value of this rich and provocative literature, instructors are reluctant to assign articles to their classes. Many college and university libraries do not have complete collections of the nine journals from which the readings in this book have been taken. More often, however, it is impossible for the large number of students attracted to the study of the American intellectual tradition to gain access to the volumes. Consequently, they do not become familiar with material on historiography and methodology. This book provides both.

Readings in Intellectual History: The American Tradition has been designed as an independent volume. Its subheadings are "The Development of a Field," "The American Puritans," "The American Enlightenment," "The Transcendentalists," "The American West," "The Idea of Progress," "The Meaning of Democracy," and "The National Character." The articles were reprinted here by permission of the authors and the publishers. Obvious typographical errors in the original articles have been corrected, but the articles have not been revised. Brief notes identify the authors and list their major publications, which students should be encouraged to use for additional reading.

C. K. McF.

CONTENTS

PART 5
The American West

PART 6
The Idea of Progress

PART 7
The Meaning of Democracy

PART 8
The National Character

READINGS
IN
INTELLECTUAL HISTORY
The American Tradition

Fritz Glarner "Relational Painting"   Massachusetts Historical Society

PART 1

THE DEVELOPMENT
OF A FIELD

Introduction

The development of United States intellectual history as an academic field began during the late nineteenth century when a number of prominent scholars became convinced that history was more than past politics and diplomacy. Moses Coit Tyler, John Bach McMaster, and Henry Adams earnestly searched for a more accurate description of the American tradition. The German concept of *Kulturgeschichte* and the "new history" publicized by James Harvey Robinson and others officially inaugurated intellectual history.

Arthur M. Schlesinger, Sr. introduced a course entitled the "Social and Cultural History of the United States" at the State University of Iowa in 1922, the first course of its kind in any college. But it was not until the publication of *Main Currents in American Thought* (3 vols., 1927–1930) by Vernon L. Parrington that United States intellectual history gained a permanent position in the college curriculum. Since then, and especially since World War II, the history of the American intellectual tradition has become one of the most popular courses on the college campus.

The first article by Arthur A. Ekirch, Jr. presents an excellent survey of intellectual history. The essay begins with a discussion of the late nineteenth-century reaction against traditional and "scientific" history. The author cites major writers who describe the evolution of intellectual history.

The essay by Robert Allen Skotheim analyzes the two major traditions that characterize intellectual historians during the twentieth century. The dominant trend, represented by Charles A. Beard, Vernon L. Parrington, and Merle Curti, was reformist and progressive. By the 1930's this interpretation was challenged by such writers as Samuel Eliot Morison, Perry Miller, and Ralph Henry Gabriel who were more sympathetic toward Puritanism and the "democratic faith." Contemporary intellectual historians often reflect one of these dominant trends.

The last two selections discuss the problems of methodology. Rush Welter states that every student of intellectual history must solve the dilemma between the internal and external approach, between the thought of men and its influence on society, and that intellectual historians should examine the thought of the people as well as the ideas of the philosophers. John Higham presents an evaluation of the internal and external approaches and of the relationship of intellectual history to other disciplines. A realization of these problems provides a fascinating challenge to students of United States intellectual history.

AMERICAN INTELLECTUAL HISTORY

Arthur A. Ekirch, Jr.[*]

I

The development of American intellectual history as a field of study is relatively recent. Its rise in large part stems from the reaction of the late nineteenth century to the kind of history that was devoted almost exclusively to the study of past politics and wars. But, if intellectual history is thus comparatively new as a scholarly methodology, a proper concern for the affairs of the mind is almost as old as recorded history. As far back as ancient Greece man expressed his ideas about nature and the gods, and even our primitive ancestors probably tried to work out some sort of rationalization or explanation of their role in the world about them. Later, under the guiding concept of the idea of progress, the philosophers of the eighteenth-century Enlightenment began to arrange some of man's ideas in an orderly historical sequence.

In our own time there has been an increasing number of excellent surveys of specific bodies of thought—histories of philosophy, literature, education, or political theory, for example. There have also been significant studies of the place of the intellectuals as a distinct class in society. Intellectual history, however, is more than the chronicle of the systematic thought of a particular scholarly discipline or of the ideas of an elite group. It does, indeed, try to cover political, social, economic, religious, and philosophical thought, but it also attempts to deal with these subjects in their historical setting. In other words, it proposes to treat ideas in relation to their environment, or to their climate of opinion. It may embrace, therefore, the history of institutions—the schools, churches, libraries, and museums—which help support the life of the mind. Moreover, the intel-

*ARTHUR A. EKIRCH, JR. (1915–   ) is a Professor of History at the State University of New York at Albany. His publications include The Idea of Progress in America, 1815–1860 (1944), The Decline of American Liberalism (1955), and The American Democratic Tradition (1963). Reprinted by permission of the author and the American Historical Association's Service Center for Teachers of History, Washington, D.C., 2nd ed., 1967, pp. 1–33.

2

lectual historian is interested in individuals who formulate and disseminate ideas and in those less well-defined, speculative ideas that may perhaps better be called opinions or concepts and which may be held more strongly by the common man than by the philosopher. It should be noted, too, that an understanding of the thought of an age involves such complex problems as the causes and effects of ideas and their relationships to the individuals holding them.

The intellectual historian is likewise faced by such especial difficulties as trying to determine the origins and to account for the popularity and spread of certain ideas. Many concepts, particularly those of a philosophical or ideological character—nature, progress, nationalism, for example—are so important, and yet so vague, that they require intensive analysis of their internal structure or meaning. The scholar who follows this approach may be unable at the same time to pursue the more traditional role of the intellectual historian in setting forth the general climate of opinion or spirit of the age. But, unlike the philosopher who values ideas irrespective of their social setting, the intellectual historian is committed to the study of ideas in their wider relationships. This does not mean that he neglects the ideas themselves, but in his analysis of the meaning, importance, and interconnections of various bodies of thought, he is ever mindful of both the historical background and subsequent influence of the ideas that he treats.

As the above definition of its varied meanings, problems, and responsibilities indicates, intellectual history is an extremely comprehensive and ambitious kind of scholarly discipline. Indeed, it is sometimes so broad and diffuse as to be virtually synonymous with a history of culture. But, although admittedly general in its scope, intellectual history differs from cultural history by reason of its primary emphasis on man's thoughts and writings. At the same time, despite certain common interests, intellectual history does not try to duplicate literary criticism with its stress on style and structure and its concern with symbols and myths. A classic example of this type of work, which continues to inspire scholars, is F. O. Matthiessen's *American Renaissance* (1941). Thus the intellectual, in contrast to the literary or cultural, historian usually devotes less attention to art, music, or literature in the sense of *belles lettres*, although he does not, of course, exclude ideas related to the fine arts. Perhaps intellectual history can be most simply and easily defined as the broad, and yet systematic, study of man thinking.

Because its approach is newer than that of some of the other ways of looking at history, a number of scholars have written interpretive essays which help one to appreciate the meaning and scope of intellectual history. The interested teacher will find it useful to read the Introductions in Crane Brinton's *Ideas and Men* (1950) and Merle Curti's *Growth of American Thought* (1943). Both authors see the main task of the intellectual historian as one of analyzing ideas in terms of their historical framework or environment. His own book, Curti points out, is really a survey of ideas in the sense of being a history of social thought, while Brinton writes that the main job of intellectual historians "is to try to find *the relations between the ideas of the philosophers, the intellectuals, the thinkers, and the actual way of living of the millions who carry the tasks of civilization*" (p. 7). At one end of his spectrum, Brinton says, the intellectual historian "comes close to being a philosopher, or at least a historian of philosophy and at the other end he comes close to being a social historian, or just a plain historian, concerned with the daily lives of human beings" (p. 9).

The place of ideas in historical writing has also been treated by a number of younger historians including John Higham, who has published several important articles on the subject. Most pertinent is his "The Rise of American Intellectual History" (*American Historical Review*, LVI [1951], 453–471), which gives a bibliographical survey of some of the classic works in the field. More recently, Rush Welter has argued very cogently that there should be a greater distinction between the history of ideas and intellectual history—"between the historical examination of ideas as ideas apart from questions of their social origin or their social influence, and the pursuit of ideas in their relationships to events" ("The History of Ideas in America: An Essay in Redefinition," *Journal of American History*, LI [1965], 599).

The internal approach to the study of ideas has been particularly popular among scholars trained in the multidisciplinary area of American studies. But, despite keen insights and novel techniques, such a method—with a primary emphasis on literary and philosophical analysis—is not without certain dangers. By its refined distinctions and complex modes of reasoning, it sometimes carries the treatment of ideas beyond the range of history and the social and public concerns of the historian. It may also result in works so abstract that they are of limited value as history. It is probably significant, too, that no intellectual historian governed by this approach to the study of ideas has as yet been able to achieve a comprehensive, synthetic account of American thought.

Still another way of dealing with intellectual history is by studying the role of intellectuals and intellectualism in American thought. Richard Hofstadter's *Anti-intellectualism in American Life* (1963) is the most ambitious and successful effort to treat this subject historically. From the vantage point of contemporary anti-intellectualism, Hofstadter shows how, in the past, evangelical religion, democratic politics, practical business, and progressive education have each, in certain important respects, been hostile to the life of the mind. He

concludes that the intellectual in American society, like his counterpart in Europe, has oscillated uneasily between the poles of alienation and conformity—between radical social protest and national consensus.

II

In terms of formal studies, American intellectual history is hardly more than a generation old. Yet, it would be unfair not to point out that earlier writers also made contributions which led in the direction of what we now understand as intellectual history. Some of the colonial New England clergy, including the famous and prolific Cotton Mather, in their sermons and annalistic accounts of events attempted to analyze and interpret historically the thought as well as the activity of their time. Later, George Bancroft and others of the more philosophic and literary historians of the Middle Period also exhibited a concern with American ideas and ideology.

Following the Civil War, two trends in American historiography affected the development of intellectual history as a separate discipline. First, American scholars wrote about the intellectual history of Europe, particularly in regard to the conflict of science and religion. And second, despite the continued emphasis on history as past politics, a few historians began to explore the possibilities of social or cultural history. By the close of the 1880's, Moses Coit Tyler, John Bach McMaster, and Henry Adams had already published important volumes that devoted some attention to those aspects of American life hitherto largely neglected by their fellow historians.

For the generation before World War I, this growing interest in non-political history was put into the framework of an academic discipline for the first time by James Harvey Robinson. Robinson, who John Higham points out, "did more than anyone else in his day to promote the study of intellectual history," began in 1904 to teach at Columbia University a notable course on the subject as it pertained to Europe. What Robinson called the "new history" was a revolt against the older scientific history and its preoccupation was past politics. It was also an attempt through the study of social life and thought to write history that had a greater contemporary interest and meaning. As defined by Robinson, the new history ideally should include "every trace and vestige of everything that man has done or thought since first he appeared on earth" [*The New History* (1912), p. 1]. Robinson's doctrine of the new history, reinforced by the German concept of *Kulturgeschichte*, and by the growth of progressivism and pragmatism in the United States, furnished the final necessary background for the writing of the initial systematic accounts of American intellectual history.

The *annus mirabilis* that signified the coming of age of American intellectual history was 1927. In that year there appeared Charles and Mary Beard's *Rise of American Civilization*, the first two volumes of Vernon L. Parrington's *Main Currents in American Thought*, and the initial volumes in the series called *A History of American Life*, edited by Arthur M. Schlesinger and Dixon Ryan Fox. All of these works reflected strands of thought that had merged to make up the new history of the twentieth century. Schlesinger and Fox had been students of James Harvey Robinson at Columbia, and Charles Beard had been a colleague, collaborator, and friend of Robinson. Parrington's outlook, though dominated by the populism and progressivism of his native West, was also affected by the currents of the new history. Parrington admired Beard's early attempts at an economic interpretation of American history, and he was also influenced by the similar studies of his associate and friend at the University of Washington, J. Allen Smith.

To his own field of American literature, Parrington applied such tenets of the new history as a critical and realistic judgment and an emphasis upon social and historical background. Despite such promising pioneer studies as the literary histories of Moses Coit Tyler, *Main Currents in American Thought* was the first real work of synthesis in the intellectual history of the United States. Although Parrington ignored a number of subjects now regarded as important to intellectual history—science and theology, for example—he was the first American scholar to knit together in a broad historical survey *belles lettres* and American social, economic, and political thought. Frankly Jeffersonian in his sympathies, his guiding principle was the growth and decline of democratic liberalism in the United States. He accordingly was troubled by what he termed "the rise of the coercive state in America." Although the Civil War and mounting industrialization exerted the chief pull in this direction, Parrington saw its beginnings in the weakening of the Jeffersonian agrarian tradition.

Modern literary scholars no longer find Parrington's interpretations and esthetic judgments satisfactory, and his work has been termed "a noble ruin." But to students of history, even more than to students of literature, *Main Currents* remains a forceful, stimulating, provocative survey and interpretation of American social and political thought. In his own time, and in large part since, Parrington stands almost alone among intellectual historians in the wide range of the literary materials and historical sources that he was able to weave together in a classic synthesis. Beginning with the Puritans and the English influence on American colonial thought, Parrington passed on to the liberalizing influences that he discerned in the American and French Revolutions. From the adoption of the Constitution to the coming of the Civil War, he traced the conflict between the

Hamiltonian-Federalist or Whig, and the Jeffersonian-Jacksonian positions. A final third volume, published in its unfinished state the year after Parrington's death in 1929, was a scathing analysis of the decline of American liberalism in the midst of the materialistic forces generated by the Civil War and expanding industrialism.

Although neither the Beards' *Rise* nor *A History of American Life* can compare with *Main Currents* as a synthesis of American intellectual history, each of these works is superior to Parrington's in some respects. The Beards, in their attempt to write a reasonably complete history of American civilization, included the whole sweep of politics and culture in a two-volume survey. With a greater degree of success than any other American historians, they were able to integrate the many facets of history into one connected narrative. The chapters dealing with social and cultural history include valuable discussions of American literature and thought, but, except for the concept of progress, the Beards devoted scant attention to abstract ideas. And their history is also much more concerned with what Americans did, and why, than with their thought.

A History of American Life, though its volumes contain useful chapters on education, religion, science, literature, and the arts, is primarily a social history with little in the way of a unifying thesis or general interpretation. The series as a whole faced some of the same problems of organizing materials that had beset McMaster, but the footnotes and the critical bibliographies appended to each volume pointed out the variety of materials that the intellectual historian can profitably use.

III

In the generation that has passed since the publication of the Beards' and Parrington's major works, American intellectual history has achieved maturity and become an important part of American historical writing. Over these years large numbers of monographs devoted to wide areas of national experience, as well as notable syntheses of the field, have been published. Only a portion of this rich literature can be surveyed, for, although the tenor and emphasis of intellectual history has shifted in the last decade, there is no sign that either popular interest or scholarly work in this field is diminishing.

The period of the Second World War with its increasing concern over ideological issues and conflict seems especially to have encouraged the study of ideas. The 1940's, more than any other single decade, witnessed the publication of works that deal systematically with intellectual history. Of these new histories, the most important and inclusive is Merle Curti's *The Growth of American Thought* (1943) which, like Parrington's *Main Currents*, won a Pulitzer Prize. Still the best survey of its subject, the Curti book is encyclopedic in the wide range of materials that it covers. Popular concepts as well as scientific and philosophical ideas are treated, with the chapters organized chronologically and topically around dominant patterns of social thought. On the whole, less attention is given to individual thinkers and to formal philosophy than to the varied uses to which ideas were put and to the social purposes that they served. Two dominating ideals which, Curti believes, helped shape the American mind and modify the European intellectual heritage were the growth of nationalism and a broader popular democracy. He also stresses in terms of their influence on American thinking the interactions between traditional individualism and increasing collectivism.

Curti's instrumentalist approach to intellectual history is in line with the precepts of the new history and the philosophy of John Dewey. While the balanced judgments and wealth of detail in the *Growth* sometimes make difficulties for the reader, the skillful ordering and sophisticated interpretation of the diffuse and complex materials have insured the book a first place in its field. Not least among the scholarly values of the book are the immense numbers of individual thinkers and original writings that are cited and placed in their social and historical setting. An additional conspicuous merit is the extensive critical bibliography which surveys a good part of the monographic literature pertaining to the intellectual history of the United States.

Published three years before Curti's book, Ralph H. Gabriel's *The Course of American Democratic Thought* (1940) is quite different in its approach. Selective rather than systematic or encyclopedic, the Gabriel volume contains an intensive analysis of the ideas of a limited number of prominent American thinkers, including Emerson and Thoreau, Calhoun, Whitman, William Graham Sumner, Frederick Jackson Turner, Josiah Royce, William James, and Oliver Wendell Holmes, Jr. Within the framework of an intellectual history of the United States since 1815, Gabriel has sought out those ideas that seem best to illustrate the various facets of the American experience, and which provide the basic foundations of the national democratic tradition. In his treatment, American confidence in the importance and capabilities of the free individual mind emerges as one of the major themes of the nation's democracy. Also stressed are religious influences and the parallels of the Christian and American democratic beliefs. "In the United States the democratic faith and evangelical Protestantism grew up side by side" (p. 28). On the other hand, despite the promise of the title, *The Course of American Democratic Thought* pays little attention to democracy in the sense of either political theory or the political process. Thoughtful and well written, despite its rather loosely organized ar-

rangement of materials, Gabriel's work has achieved a place, along with Curti's and Parrington's, as one of the classics of American intellectual history.

Both the Gabriel and Curti volumes are also significant for the way in which they have defined and encouraged the study of American intellectual history. Gabriel at Yale and Curti at Smith, Columbia, and Wisconsin have offered courses in intellectual history or American studies. The publication of their books, in turn, has stimulated the teaching of similar courses in other institutions, often by their own former graduate students. Thus, in contrast to their predecessors in the field who generally had not taught American history or American intellectual history, Gabriel and Curti by their own writings and through their graduate seminars have been able to inspire a whole generation of scholarship.

Two later works by younger men, which, like the Curti and Gabriel books, attempt a general survey and synthesis of American intellectual history are *Society and Thought in America* (2 vols., 1950–1952), by Harvey Wish, and *American Minds* (1958), by Stow Persons. Wish's volumes make an effort to integrate social and intellectual history. Although the result is more successful in regard to social history, ideas are not neglected. Reader interest is stimulated by the selection of key individuals as focal points for many of the topical chapters, even though this biographical approach is sometimes lost in the actual writing. The Wish volumes provide more general material than the other intellectual histories, and they contain illustrations that help make unusually attractive books.

In the Preface, Persons describes his work as "an introduction to the history of American thought. It does not attempt to be encyclopedic in its coverage of the subject. . . . Its purpose is to describe the principal focal concentrations of ideas, or 'minds,' that have determined the profile of American intellectual life during its historical development." The five "minds" that Persons subjects to detailed study and analysis include colonial religion, the early American nationalism of the Enlightenment, mid-nineteenth century democracy, later naturalistic patterns of thought in the social sciences, and the contemporary neo-democratic mind. Democratic theory runs as a connecting thread through the various American minds, and, like many of his fellow historians, Persons seems to see a change in American ideals as the United States moved from an individualistic to a more collectivist and paternalistic pattern of society. Assuming more knowledge on the part of the reader than is the case in Wish's volumes, Persons' book is most valuable for its careful examination of a group of selected major ideas and thinkers. In this and other respects, it resembles Gabriel's *Course of American Democratic Thought* more than Curti's *Growth of American Thought*.

IV

In addition to the Curti and Gabriel books, the decade of the 'forties also saw the beginning or completion of a number of works that deal comprehensively with certain parts of intellectual history. To their earlier volumes in *The Rise of American Civilization*, Charles and Mary Beard added a conclusion entitled *The American Spirit* (1942). Using the concept of civilization as their theme, they summarized the thought of a wide variety of American writers who had concerned themselves with this idea. The Beards were particularly interested in the interaction of thought and political activity, devoting special attention to both economic and foreign policy. Their point of view indicated some pessimism over the effects which, they feared, war and totalitarianism would have on traditional American ideals. Although *The American Spirit* has neither the outstanding synthetic nor the literary qualities of the first two

volumes of *The Rise of American Civilization*, its heavy quotation from original materials almost turns a stylistic defect into a virtue by providing the interested reader with a useful source-book in intellectual history.

Characterized by the same kind of lengthy quotation is Herbert W. Schneider's *A History of American Philosophy* (1946). Although there has been no lack of textbook surveys of the history of philosophy, Schneider's study is unique in the way in which it fits philosophical ideas into the framework of American history. As his elaborate scholarly bibliographies testify, Schneider is more familiar than most philosophers with the general literature of American history. He is able to document effectively the degree of interest and support which Americans have accorded to philosophical ideas, and he treats these ideas in terms both of the thought of leading American philosophers and of their more popular expression. Major subjects covered by Schneider include Puritanism, the Enlightenment, nationalism and democracy, religious orthodoxy versus transcendentalism, evolutionary theory, and the modern philosophies of idealism and pragmatism. Underlying much of American philosophy was the interplay between religious ideas of the Christian tradition and secular concepts derived from the eighteenth-century Enlightenment. Although the Enlightenment produced no systematic formal philosophy in America, Schneider believes "it contains the heart of our heritage as a people and our deepest tie to the rest of humanity." He sees, therefore, "an increasing and nostalgic return among American philosophers to the memory of those great days, and no American thinker who is more than a professor can refrain from occasional thoughtful wishing for the utility and freedom which philosophy then enjoyed" (pp. 35–36).

Most ambitious of all the attempts by a single author to deal comprehensively with a major area of American thought is Joseph Dorfman's *The Economic Mind in American Civilization* (5 vols., 1946–1959). This work, to which the term encyclopedic easily applies, justifies its title by surveying the history of American economic ideas within their broader historical and social setting. "In America as elsewhere," Dorfman explains in the Preface to his first volume, "economic thought is an integral part of culture. Its richness and the reach of its relevance can be appreciated fully only when it is treated in its natural habitat of practical affairs and intellectual endeavor. It grows by constant cross-breeding with other species of learning and speculation. Since in the final analysis men's minds may be read most clearly in their actions, the practical ambitions and political interests of the molders of economic thought must constantly be kept in view by those who seek to understand what successive generations have put into the public record."

For the most part the *Economic Mind* is organized biographically with systematic analyses of each individual's economic thought and his relationship to the dominant economic trends and ideas of his time. The volumes include not only formal academic concepts, but also the economic and financial ideas found in political, labor, and radical writings. The vast scope of the study makes it most interesting to specialists, but the more general student of intellectual history can also profit from much of the material, as well as from the exceptionally rich citation of original and monographic literature that is appended in the bibliographical notes.

While Dorfman and Schneider managed their broad subjects single-handedly, over fifty scholars collaborated to produce the three-volume *Literary History of the United States* (1946). From colonial times to the present, all major authors and important literary and intellectual trends are surveyed, with historians, as well as professors of English and literary critics, contributing chapters. Throughout the work an effort is made to interrelate American literature with its historical background. As the editors point out in their "Address to the Reader," American literature, perhaps more than the literature of other peoples, in its great variety expresses the many aspects of the American experience. Some of the chapters devoted to general subjects, in contrast to the ones concerned with particular authors, are more interesting from the standpoint of intellectual history. For example, Gilbert Chinard in "The American Dream" analyzes early Utopian literature and thought, Henry Nash Smith describes "The Widening of Horizons" following the Civil War, while Ralph Gabriel, Merle Curti, and Henry Steele Commager contribute important sections summarizing the dominant ideas in American literature around the turn of the century. The third volume of the *Literary History* is devoted entirely to a bibliography, including sources as well as monographs and standard works of literary and historical criticism.

Complementary to the *Literary History of the United States* and to other systematic accounts of American thought written in the decade of the 'forties, is the interesting and useful volume *Art and Life in America* (1949), by Oliver W. Larkin. Few intellectual historians are able to devote to the fine arts the same kind of understanding or attention that they give to the history of ideas, but as students of American civilization they recognize the important part that the graphic arts, for example, have played in American thought and society. Better than previous histories of painting or the fine arts generally, Larkin's work provides the student of history with a good summary of American accomplishment in the fields of painting, architecture, and sculpture. The material is organized in harmony with the major chronological divisions of American history, and Larkin is able to see the interrelations in the world of ideas and art. Thus he shows that the American Revolution, Jeffersonian and Jacksonian democracy, the "chromo civilization" after the Civil War, progressivism, economic depression, and finally world war all influenced in some way American artistic expression as well as American thinking. Even modern abstract art, sometimes criticized for evading the realities of social conflict, can be considered, Larkin notes, as "the inevitable product of a society in turmoil and confusion" (p. 459).

Not least of the merits of the Larkin work are the profuse illustrations that brighten almost every page and provide the intellectual historian with a convenient introduction and catalogue of the visual arts. There is also a detailed bibliography with many useful references to scholarly articles in the art journals and magazines.

V

Paralleling the number of important works in which some phase of American intellectual history is surveyed from colonial times to the present, there have been many useful and significant studies in intellectual history that are confined to a limited subject or a shorter chronological period. Any discussion of this vast monographic literature must be highly selective with, indeed, long lists of valuable books going unmentioned.

Appropriately enough, in view of their contributions to American thought, the New England Puritans have attracted much attention from intellectual historians. Especially impressive have been the writings of Samuel Eliot Morison, Perry Miller, and Ralph Barton Perry, respectively professors of history, literature, and philosophy at Harvard, which, rather naturally, has been a center for the study of the Puritan way of life.

Harvard College, founded in 1636 to educate Puritan youths and train some of them for the ministry, long dominated the intellectual life of the Massachusetts Bay Colony, and the history of the college is, therefore, almost an intellectual history of New England, or even of early America. Morison's multi-volume account of the founding and development of the college, despite its great value to scholars, is too specialized and detailed for the needs of most teachers. But some of Morison's other writings, particularly his *Puritan Pronaos: An Intellectual History of New England in the Seventeenth Century* (1935), provide valuable studies of how Puritans contributed to the life of the mind. In frontier America the necessary concentration on making a living entailed the risk of stifling those Renaissance cultural traditions which had been a part of the English settlers' intellectual heritage. Although the Puritans had little esthetic appreciation of the fine arts in the sense of the Elizabethan drama or of ceremonial church music, their great emotional drive helped to keep humanist values alive, especially insofar as education and the classics were concerned. Not only Harvard College and their common and grammar schools, but also printing, bookselling, and private libraries, Morison points out, testified to the Puritans' intellectual interests. Their complex theology and scholarly sermons were evidences of learning; and, in addition, the Puritans also wrote some enduring verse and history and took a circumspect interest in natural science.

Morison's defense of the quality of the Puritans' intellectual life and interests has been expounded upon with much greater detail, and with exceptionally full attention to theology, in the important writings by his Harvard colleague, Perry Miller. Some of the material in Miller's scholarly studies of the New England mind is available in more popular form in his biographies of Roger Williams and Jonathan Edwards, as well as in some of his articles and collections of sources.

Most useful is the critical introduction to the anthology *The Puritans* (1938), which he published with Thomas H. Johnson. Here Miller and Johnson assert that "Any inventory of the elements that have gone into the making of the 'American mind' would have to commence with Puritanism. . . . Among these factors Puritanism has been perhaps the most conspicuous, the most sustained, and the most fecund. Its role in American thought has been almost the dominant one. . . . Without some understanding of Puritanism, it may safely be said, there is no understanding of America" (p. 1). The selections chosen by Miller and Johnson, which include a wide range of Puritan writings—history, religion, and government, as well as diaries, letters, sermons, and poetry—give a picture of the varied nature of Puritan thinking, not all of which was as austere as later critics have alleged. Biographical sketches of the Puritan writers and an analysis of their works help to make the anthology valuable to the student.

The Puritans, frequently condemned as religious fanatics and as intolerant, narrow-minded, and anti-democratic in their political and social thought, have also been defended as staunch individualists who, by their doctrines of the religious covenant and congregationalism, helped to pave the way for a later American democracy. *Puritanism and Democracy* (1944), by Ralph Barton Perry, traces the history and also develops the linkage of these two concepts. Writing in the midst of a World War II concern over the totalitarian threat to American ideology, Perry attacked those relativist interpretations of history which saw no fundamental enduring values in Puritanism and democracy. While he did not overlook flaws in the Puritans' way of life, Perry at the same time praised them for their moral qualities, their devotion to work and duty, and for the way their separatism and congregationalism provided a model for a democratic political organization.

He points out that "The deepest bond between Puritanism and democracy was their common respect for the human individual irrespective of his place in any ecclesiastical, political, social, economic, or other institution. This individualism, with its far-reaching implications, modified every difference of method and doctrine" (p. 192).

In completing his analysis of the making of the American mind, Perry turned in the other half of his book to the study of the democratic idea and its expression. Critical of the school of thought that interpreted the Declaration of Independence as merely the rationalization or apology for the American cause in the Revolution, Perry maintains rather that "The Declaration of Independence contains the essential ideas of American democracy, and has remained its creed and standard throughout the years of its subsequent development" (p. 130). Thus the merit of the Declaration, in addition to the way it invoked the natural rights philosophy in behalf of American rights, was that it stated fundamental political and philosophical truths of enduring importance. Though the organization of the Perry book is at times confusing, it is a stimulating analysis of the ideals which form a substantial part of the American heritage.

Singled out for criticism by Perry, though he also noted that it was the best book on the subject, was Carl Becker's *The Declaration of Independence* (1922). Becker, along with Charles Beard, was an advocate of the historical relativism that Perry so strongly deplored. Although Becker wrote widely and with increasing interest in intellectual history, it is *The Declaration of Independence*, one of his earlier books, that is probably the most pertinent to American intellectual history. Becker subtitled his volume "A Study of the History of Political Ideas," and, along with a valuable account of the antecedents, authorship, text, and literary qualities of the Declaration, he wrote what may be called an intellectual history or biography of Jefferson's famous masterpiece. To Becker it was of little importance whether the natural rights philosophy summarized in the Declaration was true or false. More noteworthy was the justification and inspiration it provided Americans as a manifesto of their cause. The great merit of Becker's volume is the historical perspective it affords in relating the Declaration of Independence to the political thinking and general climate of opinion of the eighteenth century.

VI

Broader in scope than the works of Becker and the historians of New England Puritanism are several books, selected from among many, that attempt to deal in a comprehensive way with the intellectual life of early America. In *Seeds of Liberty: The Genius of the American Mind* (1948), Max Savelle has written an informative survey of the major categories of American thought for the period around the middle of the eighteenth century. Savelle describes and analyzes colonial culture with chapters on political, social, and economic thought as well as on colonial art, music, education, religion, and patriotism. Although the study shows the changes and development in colonial thinking, the topical organization of Savelle's book is most valuable for its systematic coverage of each separate area of American thought on the eve of the Revolution. Thus *Seeds of Liberty* provides a good over-all view of what might be called the American Enlightenment in the period before colonial thinking was compressed into the mould of a rising political and cultural nationalism.

It is the thesis of Michael Kraus' *The Atlantic Civilization* (1949) that this American Enlightenment influenced intellectual life in the Old World as well as in the New. "The conventional interpretation which pictures America as the terminal in the transit of European civilization needs to be broadened," he asserts, "to include the idea of a return trip. America did much to give greater substance to such concepts as political and religious freedom, economic opportunity, and humanitarian ideals; and she hurried the Western World to the realization of them" (pp. vi-vii). Kraus presents in rich detail the cultural contrasts between Europe and America in the eighteenth century, the colonial conflict between nascent ideas of nationalism and cosmopolitanism, and the popular image of America as the Utopian ideal of the Western World.

Unlike the Kraus and Savelle volumes, Clinton Rossiter's *Seedtime of the Republic* (1953) is devoted primarily to the political aspects of early American intellectual life. In tracing the evolution of the tradition of political liberty in colonial and Revolutionary America, Rossiter stresses the influence of religious and economic liberalism. He sees the origins of American democracy in ideas more than in material forces. *Seedtime of the Republic*, as its author acknowledges, owes much to the earlier works by Tyler and Parrington. But in retracing this ground Rossiter has also judiciously summarized the research of many modern scholars whose studies are cited in the full and valuable bibliographic notes.

One of the more recent efforts to write an intellectual history for the whole of the period from Jamestown to the American Revolution is Louis B. Wright's *The Cultural Life of the American Colonies* (1957). This volume, which chronologically is the first of several in the *New American Nation Series* that deal primarily with cultural life, is too brief an account to cover adequately such a broad subject. Wright, however, is the author of a number of scholarly studies bearing on colonial history, and his book accordingly is valuable as a synthesis of his work and that of others. In contrast to Rossiter, who minimizes physical and institutional forces, Wright declares that agriculture shaped colonial life and thought.

Economic opportunity and fluid social classes encouraged independent thinking and a zeal for education. One of the great merits of colonial culture, Wright asserts, was its diversity, which stemmed in large part from the mixture of races and religions among the settlers. A surprising amount of colonial literature endured, and in architecture and the decorative arts colonial taste could also compete with Europe. Scientific interests, then as later, were utilitarian, but the New World contributed much to intellectual life in the stimulus that it offered to all kinds of scientific observation and speculation. On the eve of their Revolution, Wright concludes, the colonies "were less remote in mind and spirit from the rest of the world than were some of the more isolated counties of England" (p. 251).

Of the Founding Fathers, Thomas Jefferson was the towering intellectual figure who has attracted the attention of numerous historians. A useful introduction to the social and intellectual environment in which Jefferson's thought matured is Russel B. Nye's *The Cultural Life of the New Nation* (1960). Nye's chapters provide summaries, of early American thinking in respect to science, the idea of progress, religion, education, art, literature, and nationalism. In a specific effort to recapture the intellectual milieu in which Jefferson and his circle of friends lived and exercised their influence, Daniel J. Boorstin's *The Lost World of Thomas Jefferson* (1948) explores the philosophical side of his thinking. Boorstin is the author of a number of distinctive, topical and somewhat impressionistic works which interpret American life very broadly in terms of its pragmatic experience. In like manner, he analyzes Jefferson's practical adaptation of the concepts of the eighteenth-century Enlightenment in regard to nature, God, and the equality of the human species as well as his ideas on morals, science, and politics. Boorstin also points out the continuing implications of Jefferson's ideas for the modern American mind.

The Jeffersonian Tradition in American Democracy (1935), by Charles M. Wiltse, studies Jefferson's political philosophy in scholarly detail, covering the intellectual heritage in England and colonial America and treating Jefferson's importance for both individualistic and social democracy. A complementary work with a somewhat broader approach is Adrienne Koch's *Jefferson and Madison* (1950). The social and political thought of the two men is analyzed for the half-century of their successful collaboration from the close of the Revolution to Jefferson's death. No other pair of American statesmen, the author writes in her Preface, "had a more pervasive philosophy of democracy, a firmer faith in human intelligence, or a more progressive view of the American experiment as a 'workshop of liberty.'"

What history made of Jefferson, beginning with his reinstatement after 1826 by the Jacksonians, is the subject of Merrill D. Peterson's *The Jefferson Image in the American Mind* (1960). A study in both historiography and intellectual history, Peterson's book treats the concepts of democracy, history, and union in their relationships to Jefferson and his image. By his thorough account of Jefferson's varying historical reputation down to the period of its modern revival, Peterson illuminates an important facet of American thought.

VII

In the world of ideas, the cosmopolitan thinking of Jefferson and his circle was followed by the nationalism of the nineteenth century. It is not surprising, therefore, that a number of intellectual historians have concerned themselves with ideas closely allied to the theme of a rising American nationality. Despite this interest, no historian has yet accomplished for the United States the kind of definitive studies that Carlton Hayes and Hans Kohn have produced on the idea of nationalism in Europe. Kohn and some younger scholars have attempted brief accounts of American nationalism, but the most perceptive interpretation from the standpoint of intellectual history is Merle Curti's *The Roots of American Loyalty* (1946).

Including both nationalism and patriotism in his definition of loyalty, Curti shows how Americanism was born in the colonial period, tried in the crisis of the Civil War, and then gradually reconstructed, only to be tried anew in the world crises of the twentieth century. Loyalty to the nation involved an appreciation of both geography and history, as well as the adoption of American patriotism by the new peoples emigrating to the United States. Loyalty, as Curti shows, has often meant more than an unquestioning patriotism, and the radical reformers who opposed such national policies as war and slavery, for example, usually couched their criticisms in terms of a higher loyalty and patriotism to what, they believed, was the true national destiny of the United States. Thus in time of crisis, or when various class, race, or sectional interests were at stake, a patriotic loyalty to the nation might become confused or lead to a kind of mass hysteria at odds with traditions of cultural nationalism. "In the public mind," according to Curti, "it is often hard to say whether a specific action is loyal or disloyal. Men are prone to confuse their private interest and larger patriotism, and the line between the two spheres is hazy" (p. 145).

Among the slogans and symbols of American nationalism and patriotism, to which Curti's *Roots* devotes some attention, none was more popular in the nineteenth century than the concept of manifest destiny—the idea that the United States was an ocean-bound republic destined to move across the continent from the Atlantic to the Pacific Ocean, and even beyond. Of the various studies of the ideology of national expansionism, Albert Weinberg's *Manifest Destiny* (1935) is by far the most comprehensive. On the basis of elaborate research in scattered sources, Weinberg shows the varied ways the American people justified their spread westward. Geography, the material forces of a growing population, and natural right, Americans believed, made it inevitable that they should assume the white man's burden and carry on a political mission of democratic regeneration for lands and peoples less favored. When challenged, the United States invoked the doctrine of self-defense and in the twentieth century took over the responsibilities of an international police power and world leadership.

Often associated in the American mind with the doctrine of manifest destiny as an essential justification of American expansionism was the idea of progress. This concept, which impressed itself upon the thinking of both philosophers and the common man, was the subject of widespread American attention throughout the nineteenth century. A detailed exposition of the various facets of the early American faith, which became almost a secular religion, is provided in Arthur Ekirch's *The Idea of Progress in America, 1815–1860* (1944). Ekirch's study is written within the framework of Merle Curti's emphasis on the social history of ideas, and the purpose of this work is to examine a great variety of sources, rather than to analyze thoroughly the more philosophical ideas of a few selected thinkers. The author shows how the belief in progress was derived from science, theology, American natural resources, and political democracy. Reformers identified progress with the success of their particular causes, of which education was the most important, while conservatives called for progress in the sense of a gradual change or evolution. Thus the concept of progress became "the most popular American philosophy, thoroughly congenial to the ideas and interests of the age" (p. 267).

America's obvious nineteenth-century success as a nation, fulfilling almost every dream of political and material progress, made it possible for a select number of thinkers to assert the primacy of spirit over matter and to turn the most vital part of the American mind from statecraft to literature. This interpretation of Loren Baritz is a part of his study of the ideas and myths which have contributed to the concept of Americans as a chosen people. In *City on a Hill* (1964), Baritz attempts a fusion of American politics, theology, and literature through an intensive analysis of the ideas of such key figures as John Winthrop, Jonathan Edwards, John Adams, John Taylor of Caroline, Emerson, and Melville. Although unsatisfactory as a synthesis of early American thought, Baritz's work provides a deeper understanding of the philosophies of Puritanism, the Enlightenment, and Transcendentalism.

For the Middle Period, Roy H. Pearce's scholarly study, *The Savages of America* (1953), shows how the Indians, long regarded as stubborn obstacles to progress, forced Americans "to reconsider what it was to be civilized and what it took to build a civilization" (p. ix). Thus the Red Man became a symbol of the tensions in the opposed ideas of civilization and savagism. It is Pearce's thesis that the white man, in the midst of his changing attitudes toward the Indians from the time of the first Virginia settlements to the middle years of the nineteenth century, learned much from the aboriginal first Americans. Just as the idea of progress grew to be an article of American faith, "so did the idea of savagism from which it took substance and to which it gave strength" (p. 49).

An explanation of why the South offered only a qualified affirmation to the otherwise generally enthusiastic American acceptance of the idea of progress is provided in Clement Eaton's *Freedom of Thought in the Old South* (1940). In the change in southern thinking that took place between the worlds of Thomas Jefferson and John C. Calhoun, Eaton sees the key to the intellectual history of the Old South. The liberalism and freedom of thought that characterized the mind of the aristocrats of Jefferson's day were subverted by the South's growing need to defend its peculiar institution of slavery. Moulded by plantation life, menaced by the fear of servile insurrection and by the reality of widespread illiteracy, the South increasingly turned to the harsh conservative leadership of figures like Calhoun. Freedom of speech, press, religion, and thought were accordingly severely modified by the two great taboos in southern life—criticism of slavery and heterodoxy in religion.

Still among the most useful of the many works that attempt to interpret the mind of the antebellum South is William S. Jenkins' *Pro-Slavery Thought in the Old South* (1935). Beginning with a detailed account of early American thinking in regard to slavery, Jenkins summarizes the development of the various arguments which southerners used to justify their civilization. Finally, to support its defense of slavery on social, economic, moral, and historical grounds, the South evolved an elaborate theory of the merits of a slave versus a free society.

VIII

The way both the conservatives of the Old South and the radical abolitionists of the North became highly emotional in their respective defense and criticism of slavery illustrates the significance of the non-rational elements in men's minds, with which the intellectual historian also has to deal. Both Gabriel in his *Course of American Democratic Thought* and Curti in his *Roots of*

American Loyalty show the importance to American patriotism of such symbols as the Constitution and the myths that have sometimes enveloped it. Weinberg's *Manifest Destiny* in the same way demonstrates the extent of aroused national feelings in connection with territorial expansion westward. The role of the American West, considered as both symbol and myth, is the subject of an original and provocative study by Henry Nash Smith. His *Virgin Land* (1950) traces the history of the frontier in terms of the popular American conceptions of its place and influence. Smith points out in his Preface, however, that in his analysis of the varied representations of the collective American image of the West, his purpose is not "to raise the question whether such products of the imagination accurately reflect empirical fact."

American ideas of the West were often more romance than reality. To Jefferson and his followers the back-country was the Arcadia and guarantee of an agrarian society, while Thomas Hart Benton identified it with a future American imperial destiny. The most popular figures in American folklore were a part of the West—Daniel Boone, Leatherstocking, Kit Carson, and Buffalo Bill. In the belief that the West was the Garden of the World, the American people saw the frontier as the escape valve or Utopian solution for all ills and problems. In a final chapter Smith treats Turner's frontier hypothesis as the most influential piece of historical writing about the West and attempts to put its main ideas within the intellectual framework of his own study. Like other scholars, Smith sees a dilemma in Turner's association of American democracy with the frontier. Since the westward march of population across the continent had caused the free land to disappear, "What then was to become of democracy?" (p. 257). To Smith and others it seemed clear that the older agrarian tradition of the nineteenth

century no longer provided the answers to this twentieth-century problem.

Intimately related to concepts of the frontier and of the West is the theme of man and nature in the United States and the conflict between the older American agrarian dream and the rise of the city. A pioneer work exploring three centuries of changing American attitudes, Hans Huth's *Nature and the American* (1957) stresses the esthetic and literary influences that led to the conservation movement. Handsomely illustrated, the book documents the American appreciation of the generous natural beauty of the nation's landscape. Romantic nostalgia for an environment and a pastoral ideal fast vanishing before a developing technology is the subject of Leo Marx's interpretive study, *The Machine in the Garden* (1964). By using selected examples drawn mostly from literary sources in the Middle Period, Marx depicts the often ambivalent American views of nature and machinery. Broader in scope, though less detailed than the Marx and Huth volumes, Arthur Ekirch's *Man and Nature in America* (1963) offers a comprehensive summary of the views of those scientists and philosophers who have believed that the future of the world and of man depends on the achievement of a more equable balance between the constructive and destructive forces of civilization.

Implicit in much of the American thinking about nature has been an aggressive hostility toward an urban way of life. In *The Intellectual Versus the City* (1962), Morton and Lucia White demonstrate that fear of the city has been a common reaction of American intellectuals, writers, and artists from the time of Franklin and Jefferson and the New England transcendentalists to Frank Lloyd Wright and a number of modern philosophers and social scientists. This powerful anti-urban tradition reflects in large part the continuing American dreams of the older, nineteenth-century agrarian society but it also gives an insight into the role of the city in contemporary life and thought.

IX

Many of the problems associated with the varying American attitudes toward the environment took on a new urgency after the turn of the century. For example, Frederick Jackson Turner's assertions of the significance of the close of the frontier can be placed in the broader perspective of the general changes taking place in American society. Thus Henry Steele Commager in *The American Mind* (1950) writes:

> The decade of the nineties is the watershed of American history. As with all watersheds the topography is blurred, but in the perspective of half a century the grand outlines emerge clearly. On the one side lies an America predominantly agricultural. . . , an America on the whole self-confident, self-contained, self-reliant, and conscious of its unique characters and of a unique destiny. On the other side lies the modern America, predominantly urban and industrial; inextricably involved in world economy and politics; troubled with the problems that had long been thought peculiar to the Old World; experiencing profound changes in population, social institutions, economy, and technology; and trying to accommodate its traditional institutions and habits of thought to conditions new and in part alien (p. 41).

Commager's work, which is not a detailed chronicle of American thought, serves, nevertheless, as an admirable introduction to the recent intellectual history of the United States. The emphasis is on literature and the social sciences, but there is also attention to religion and architecture. Many of the chapters dealing with broad areas of American thought are made more readable by being focussed on individuals—John Fiske and evolution, William James and pragmatism, for example. The major ideas, though given systematic treatment, are also related to the historical environment. Especially valuable, in addition to the attention paid American novelists, are the chapters which summarize developments in each of the social sciences. A final chapter effectively compares the character of the twentieth- and the nineteenth-century American.

Among the major intellectual trends which contributed to Commager's interpretation of the turn of the century as a watershed in American history was the breakdown of the older absolutes in American thought under the pressures generated by the doctrine of evolution. Along with its obvious importance in the area of the natural sciences, Darwinian evolution also had great significance for the social sciences. Although this role of Darwinism in American intellectual history has had increasing scholarly attention, one of the most useful and stimulating works is still Richard Hofstadter's *Social Darwinism in American Thought, 1860–1915* (1944). After a brief summary of the impact of *The Origin of Species* upon American scientists and theologians, Hofstadter turns to his main task of analyzing "the more general adaptation of Darwinism and related biological concepts to social ideologies" (p. vii).

Under the influence of Herbert Spencer and William Graham Sumner, many Americans saw in the biological doctrines of the struggle for survival a justification for their own philosophy of individualism and laissez faire. At the same time a number of reformers and sociologists believed that evolution indicated the possibility of man controlling his environment through conscious planning and effort. Thus Darwinian evolution had both a conservative and radical import. A major influence in the currents of thought that led to pragmatism and the Progressive Era, it also served as a rationale for racism and imperialism.

Currents of change and reform in which the older patterns of the American mind were being transformed under the impact of evolution and pragmatism are the subject of *Social Thought in America: The Revolt Against Formalism* (1949), by Morton G. White. Despite its ambitious title, White's book is more a case study than a systematic survey of the ideas of a selected group of Americans who deeply influenced their particular scholarly disciplines. White examines closely the leading concepts and key philosophical views of Charles Beard, John Dewey, Oliver Wendell Holmes, Jr., James Harvey Robinson, and Thorstein Veblen. All were to some extent progressives who played major roles in breaking down the conventional modes of thinking in their respective fields—and this White sees as "the revolt against formalism." The new history and its economic interpretation, empiricism in law and philosophy, progressive education, and radical economic theory all played their part in the transformation of American thought along progressive lines. Despite the disastrous effects of World War I, White notes that a liberal ideology rose to "its highest level of publication and popularity" in the 1920's. But for the most part, as Veblen complained, the positive ideas that came out of the revolt against formalism could not be put into effect—"just yet" (pp. 201–202).

Somewhat unfairly, White indicts his select group of American intellectuals for their failure to provide a workable philosophy to succeed the older absolutes that their negative criticisms had so largely destroyed. "Unfortunately," he writes, "they were unable to set limits to this revolt against rigidity and sometimes they allowed it to run wild. . . . The twenties marked the end of this reign of terror. But the result, I fear, was Thermidor and not freedom" (p. 241). Nevertheless, the

American social thought of the future, White concludes, will be built on the work of those thinkers who, like Beard, Dewey, Holmes, Robinson, and Veblen, attacked the older formalized absolutes of their time.

Shedding further light on White's select group of intellectuals, Henry F. May's *The End of American Innocence* (1959) dates the cultural revolution of the twentieth century from the years immediately preceding the First World War. May emphasizes the naive innocence as well as the amoral, questioning, relativistic, and rebellious spirit of much of American thinking in the Progressive Era. He concludes, "The American culture of 1912 fell into pieces not because it was attacked but because attack, combined with the challenge of events, brought to light its old inadequacies. Since this happened, American civilization has been less happy, less unanimous, and more precarious" (pp. 397–398).

X

From Puritanism to the pragmatic revolt of the twentieth century, a wide variety of subjects has been scrutinized by the intellectual historians of our generation. But in the course of the latter half of this century, the need for new works of synthesis and interpretation, as well as scholarly monographs, will no doubt continue. Although it seems true that most of the major areas of American thought have already received attention, there are still some gaps to be filled—for example, the lack of comprehensive histories of educational and scientific thought.

Despite valuable recent studies of education in American culture, with particular attention to progressive education, academic freedom, and higher education, Merle Curti's older work, *The Social Ideas of American Educators* (1935), remains the most sweeping survey of educational thought.

After a chapter on colonial education, Curti covers the impact of the American Revolution and early nationalism on educational theory and practice. Along with a detailed analysis of "the interiors" of the ideas of individual educators from Horace Mann and Henry Barnard to William James and John Dewey, topical chapters call attention to the education of women and Negroes, the place of the South and industrialism, and post-World War I patterns. It is Curti's conclusion that, despite the leaders who, beginning with Jefferson, looked to education as a means of democratic reform, "most educational spokesmen have aligned themselves with the established order and have asked for support from the dominant classes on the ground that they were protecting those classes from possible or even probable danger . . ." (p. 583).

Useful as supplements to Curti's *Social Ideas* are Lawrence A. Cremin's comprehensive account of the progressive movement in American education, entitled *The Transformation of the School* (1961), and *Popular Education and Democratic Thought in America* (1962), by Rush Welter. Cremin treats the educational ideas of John Dewey and his associates as a part of a broad humanitarian effort to apply the promise of American life and the ideals of democratic government to the school system in the face of the new, and often puzzling, changes of an industrial-urban civilization. Carrying this theme backward in time, Welter explores the interrelations of popular public education and democratic political thought from the Jacksonian Period to the Progressive Era. He concludes that the preservation of democratic institutions depends on the reality and practice of democratic education.

By all odds the most glaring omission in the writings on American intellectual history is an account of scientific thought, or even a good history of science, as distinct from invention, in the United States. The familiar practical bent of American scientists has, of course, resulted in

great achievements in technology, but an interest and degree of accomplishment in pure science have not been completely lacking. That this is true is suggested in A. Hunter Dupree's *Science in the Federal Government* (1957). Broader in scope than its title indicates, Dupree's volume is, as yet, the best substitute for a comprehensive history of American scientific thought. The federal government's interest in science was sparked originally by the bequest which resulted in the founding of the Smithsonian Institution. The federal government also encouraged and supported various types of scientific inquiry—notably exploring expeditions to the South Seas, geological surveys, and research in agriculture, conservation, medicine and public health, and potential war weapons. Although the United States government in the nineteenth century did not directly honor its scientists or give much financial support to their work, such outstanding figures as Alexander Dallas Bache, Charles Henry Davis, Joseph Henry, and John Wesley Powell spent most of their scientific careers in the civil service. By the twentieth century, as Dupree makes clear, the federal government's expanding role in science became a matter of concern as well as of pride.

Until recently the lack of a history of scientific thought was matched by the equal need for a history of American religious thought. Despite the publication of a number of significant studies of the relations of church, state, and education in the United States, and of the impact of industrialism upon the life and thought of the churches, no scholar attempted a synthesis of religious ideas and influence. Now this omission has been filled in part by the collective efforts of a number of distinguished authors in the four-volume *Religion in American Life* (1961), edited by James Ward Smith and A. Leland Jamison. Two separate volumes constitute a definitive "Critical Bibliography" compiled by Nelson R. Burr in collaboration with the editors. *Religion in American Life* is another achievement in the *Princeton Studies in American Civilization*, a series in which such subjects as foreign influences, socialism, and evolution in American life have been treated. With full recognition of the diversity of the American religious pattern, the editors of *Religion in American Life* include chapters that cover the story of the small sects as well as the larger denominations—Protestant, Catholic, and Jewish. The emphasis, however, is upon religious thought and theology rather than upon individual church bodies, and the significance and relationship of religion to politics, education, literature, and the fine arts is also treated analytically. Although the work is somewhat uneven, it is a most useful source for reference and information.

XI

It is natural that intellectual historians should reflect current concerns in their choice of subjects for investigation. Thus the historic role of American vis-à-vis Europe, and American ideas about race and minority groups, have attracted recent attention. Cushing Strout's *The American Image of the Old World* (1963) and Howard Mumford Jones's *O Strange New World* (1964), covering the European image of the United States, are complementary works of unusual interest. Both books show how the varying ideas of another continent influenced the domestic scene in America and Europe, and each volume relies on a wide sampling of political and literary evidence to support its thesis. Jones's work, intended as the first volume in a history of American culture, includes useful chapters on the radical republican thinking of the American Revolution and on the happy influence of the American landscape. Strout, in the conclusion of his study, shows that much of the nationalism in the traditional American view

of Europe has been modified since World War II. He observes that even the "Cold War has itself ironically tended to reduce the differences between its giant antagonists. Russia has imitated American nuclear technology and economic aid to underdeveloped countries, and America has added to a modest welfare state a massive military-industrial complex" (p. 274).

Of the many discussions of race relations in the United States, Thomas F. Gossett's *Race: The History of an Idea in America* (1963) comes closest to being a definitive treatment of changing American concepts. Early anthropological theories with respect to the Indian and Negro are examined, and Gossett contends that the race prejudice against the latter grew into undisguised hatred, in the North as well as in the South, only after the Civil War. Gossett also discusses the more modern manifestations of Anglo-Saxon prejudice directed against immigrant groups. He concludes, "Racism, the most serious threat to the idea of equality before the law and to the individual development of one's own capabilities, is now on the defensive as it has never been before. With the proper resolution, it can be changed from a major to a minor problem of our national life" (p. 459). In support of Gossett's book, William Stanton's *The Leopard's Spots* (1960) provides a detailed scholarly survey of scientific attitudes toward race in the United States before the Civil War.

The Negro's role in American history, the subject of much recent attention, is treated in terms of ideas by August Meier's *Negro Thought in America, 1880–1915* (1963). Pointing out that he must necessarily deal with the most favored classes of Negroes who were articulate, Meier covers the influence of Booker T. Washington and the "divided mind" of his successors. From the mixed heritage of Reconstruction to the deteriorating position of the Negro on the eve of the First World War, Meier turns in the concluding chapter of his book to "The Social and Intellectual Origins of the New Negro."

As the major gaps in American intellectual history thus become filled, it may be that the future of the field as an academic and popular subject will be devoted increasingly to the publication of specialized monographs and biographies of individual ideas and thinkers. Or intellectual history may turn still another corner and answer the criticisms of those who have argued the need for a more systematic and disciplined methodology. Meanwhile the records and sources, many of which have been assembled in excellent anthologies, as well as the scholarly secondary literature, should ensure ample reading materials for the interested student and teacher.

THE WRITING OF AMERICAN HISTORIES OF IDEAS: TWO TRADITIONS IN THE XXTH CENTURY

*Robert Allen Skotheim**

The two groups of historians of ideas in the United States during the XXth century to be discussed here were foreshadowed by two pioneer scholars of the late 1800's, Moses Coit Tyler and Edward Eggleston. "There is but one thing more interesting than the intellectual history of a man," wrote Tyler (1835–1900) in the first book announcing itself a history of American ideas, *A History of American Literature, 1607–1765* (1878), "and that is the intellectual history of a nation."[1] Two decades later, as he began *The Literary History of the*

[1] (2 vols., New York, 1897), I, 5. Originally published in 2 vols. in 1878, as was the revised edition of 1897, to which citations cited here refer. There are two one-volume editions: Ithaca, 1949, and New York, 1962.

*ROBERT ALLEN SKOTHEIM (1933–   ) is an Associate Professor of History at the University of Colorado. His publications include American Intellectual Histories and Historians *(1966),* Historical Scholarship in the United States and Other Essays *(1967), and* The Historian and the Climate of Opinion *(1969). Reprinted by permission of the author and the* Journal of the History of Ideas, *Vol. 25, No. 2 (April, 1964), 257–278.*

American Revolution, 1763–1785 (1897), Tyler asserted that the "Revolution was pre-eminently a revolution caused by ideas, and pivoted on ideas."[2] He attributed to thought an exceedingly strong, if not virtually autonomous causal power in human affairs.

Tyler's belief in the majesty of human thought was accompanied by his celebration of specific ideas, people, and times. Writing during the late XIXth century in the United States—"a grinning and flabby age," he said—Tyler looked back with nostalgia at the intellectual virility of Puritan and revolutionary heroes. Puritan New England was "a thinking community; an arena and mart for ideas; its characteristic organ being not the hand, nor the heart, nor the pocket, but the brain."[3] And Tyler, former theology student, one-time Congregational minister, and later to be ordained Episcopal priest, championed the fact that Puritan intellectuality was fastened to religious ends. "The result was tremendous," he wrote. "Never were men more logical or self-consistent in theory and in practice. Religion, they said, was the chief thing; they meant it; they acted upon it."[4] That "wonderful epoch," as revealed by "the mind of New England," was best seen in Puritan sermons, Tyler thought, but it was natural that they should go unappreciated by a modern "age that lacks the faith of that period, its grip, its mental robustness."[5]

The American revolutionary period similarly revealed, according to Tyler,

> for all who choose to see, the magestic operation of ideas, the creative and decisive play of spiritual forces in the development of history, in the rise

and fall of nations, in the aggregation and division of races.[6]

He was excited by the revolutionary years, when "the very brain of man seems to be in armor." Tyler saw the revolutionary years much the same way many later Americans would view the mid-XXth century, as

> an epoch in which nearly all that is great and dear in man's life on earth has to be argued for, as well as to be fought for, and in which ideas have a work to do quite as pertinent and quite as effective as that of bullets. . . .[7]

A conviction as to the significance of ideas in man's past may be a prerequisite for a historian of ideas, and Tyler's conviction no doubt contributed to his writing the first American history of ideas. But he expressed not merely a general belief that thought was sometimes influential: he asserted, as the quotations above suggest, that ideas were causally decisive in history, and further, he clearly indicated sympathy for certain ideas and intellectual tempers.

Tyler focused upon the writings of leading religious, political, and, most of all, literary figures in the colonies. In this investigation of "elite" spokesmen, he pursued literary questions of style and artistic worth as well as those of intellectual content. This dual focus simply reflected the fact that Tyler was pioneering in the history of American literature at the same time as he was pioneering in the history of ideas. From the perspective of later historians of ideas, Tyler's work—particularly his first two volumes—necessarily lacks a consistency of focus on ideas.

[2] (2 vols., New York, 1941), I, 8. Originally published in 2 vols. (New York, 1897).
[3] A History of American Literature, 1607–1765, I, 98.
[4] Ibid., 101.
[5] Ibid., 192.
[6] The Literary History of the American Revolution, I, viii.
[7] Ibid., I, 6, 9.

Moses Tyler's interpretation of ideas was not shared by the second American to pioneer in writing the history of his country's ideas—Edward Eggleston (1837–1902). Eggleston, who dealt with a wide range of ideas in his two volumes on colonial America, *The Beginners of a Nation* (1896) and *The Transit of Civilization: From England to America in the Seventeenth Century* (1900), found ideas to be significant, but in a strikingly different way from Tyler.[8] Indeed, the differences between Eggleston's and Tyler's interpretation of ideas foreshadowed two divergent tendencies in the writing of many major American histories of ideas during the XXth century. Eggleston did not find Puritanism to be an admirable intellectual temper, and its ideas were interesting primarily, he thought, as a reflection of the inhumane, unenlightened backwardness of the XVIIth century. Modern science, not traditional religion, drew Edward Eggleston's sympathy.[9] "A Kempis may rest where he is," wrote Eggleston, "I would rather walk in wide fields with Charles Darwin."[10] He viewed his own intellectual development just as he saw American history itself, as a gradually achieved emancipation from archaic superstition. Puritanism's "false and harsh ideals" were "sufficient condemnation" of the XVIIth century and of the Puritan, in Eggleston's eyes.

Eggleston did not deny the causal importance of XVIIth-century thought however. He opened *The Transit of Civilization* by speaking of "national characteristics," meaning "seminal ideas received in childhood, standards of feeling and thinking and living handed down from one overlapping generation to another." In other words, ideas were most responsible for making the national character what it was, and gradual alteration of "fundamental notions" produced "the difference between the character of a nation at an early epoch and that of the same people in a later age."[11] For Eggleston no less than for Tyler, it was this intellectual character which decisively influenced colonial behavior. Eggleston did not deny the causal power of XVIIth century ideas—he simply regretted it. The ideas which he discussed were characterized ordinarily as incorrect or morally wrong and as causing bad behavior. Witchcraft, for example, "was part of what we may call the fixed intellect of the age," and Eggleston emphasized the Salem trials as a revealing expression of XVIIth-century ideas in action.[12] Constant medical blood letting, to take another instance of intellectual ignorance causing harmful acts, stemmed from lack of scientific knowledge in the colonies. Again, the aristocratic conception of life led to undemocratic discrimination and inequity in colonial law, religion, and social relations.

In addition to disagreeing with Tyler as to the good or ill effect of XVIIth-century ideas, Eggleston differed from Tyler also as to what ideas he described. Eggleston did not, as did Tyler, look solely to the intellectual or literary elite, but instead emphasized a more popular mind. He investigated ideas concerning astronomy or astrology, medicine, manners, property, education, language, and folk-literature in *The Transit of Civilization*. This democratizing or diversifying of the subject matter of the history of thought was an important development in method, and later scholarship in

[8] (*New York, 1896*), *quotations cited here refer to 4th ed.* (*New York, 1899*); (*New York, 1900*), *quotations cited here refer to* (*Boston, 1959*).

[9] *Eggleston was a Protestant minister, as was Tyler, prior to turning historian, but Eggleston by 1880 called himself an unbeliever. See Charles Hirschfeld. "Edward Eggleston: Pioneer in Social History,"* Historiography and Urbanization, *Eric Goldman, ed.* (*Baltimore, 1941*), *199.*

[10] *Eggleston, "Books that Have Helped Me,"* Forum, *III (1887), 586.*

[11] The Transit of Civilization, *1.*
[12] Ibid., *23.*

these diverse areas can be viewed as harvests in research areas first located and plowed by Eggleston.

That Eggleston saw his written histories of ideas as part of his social philosophy was suggested by his presidential address to the American Historical Association in 1900. He implored historians to broaden their vision beyond the traditional range of wars and politics, not merely for the sake of variety, nor merely to tell a fuller story of the past, but in order to influence the future along lines he considered "enlightened" and "civilized." Eggleston wanted to hasten the coming of a "scientific" outlook, "rationalism," and pacifism. Politics, he wrote, as if thinking of Tyler's celebration in two volumes of the American Revolution, "likes to call itself patriotism." But, continued Eggleston in the vein of a *philosophe*,

> what is patriotism? It is a virtue of the half-developed. Higher than tribal instinct and lower than that great world benevolence that is to be the mark of coming ages.[13]

Edward Eggleston was as interested in the past generally, and in the history of thought specifically, as was Moses Coit Tyler. Eggleston, like Tyler, attributed causal significance to ideas, and he had his heroes and his favorite bodies of belief. But Eggleston was most excited by possibilities for the future, possibilities suggested by modern science, religious skepticism, and the belief that, for example, war could be "educated out" of mankind. Obviously, then, he sympathized with different aspects of America's intellectual past from those which most attracted Tyler. Eggleston dwelled on the XVIIth century, but it was because he wished to expose its foolishness. Implicit in the

exposè was a championing of ideas which the century opposed. But more than that, from the perspective of later historians of ideas, he pioneered in describing new and diverse areas of colonial activity, because in these diverse expressions of the popular mind lay the opportunities for "progress" and "enlightenment."

James Harvey Robinson (1863–1936) systematized and extended Eggleston's rationale for studying the history of ideas, although Robinson's rôle for American intellectual historiography remained that of a publicist rather than that of a publishing scholar. Robinson explicitly argued, in *The New History* (1912), that the history of ideas could help reform the contemporary world. "The history of thought is one of the most potent means of dissolving the bonds of prejudice," wrote Robinson, because it shows how man's traditional beliefs—"the bonds of prejudice"—"have arisen in conditions quite alien to those of the present."[14] "Only a study of the vicissitudes of human opinion," he continued, "can make us fully aware of this and enable us to readjust our views so as to adapt them to our present environment."[15] Robinson's religious skepticism, his admiration for modern science, and his egalitarianism, echoed Eggleston's views, and Robinson's faith in the developing social sciences brought a new weapon to "the career of conscious social readjustment upon which mankind is now embarked," as it seemed to him during the progressive era.[16] Even more than Eggleston, Robinson enunciated the "enlightened" direction to be taken by reform-minded histories of ideas.

Robinson celebrated "creative thought," "that peculiar species of thought which leads us to change our mind," which "has raised man from

---

[13] Annual Report of the American Historical Association, 1900 (*Washington, 1901*), 40.

[14] The New History (*New York, 1912*), 130, 102.
[15] Ibid., *103.*
[16] Ibid., *130.*

his pristine, subsavage ignorance and squalor to the degree of knowledge and comfort which he now possesses."[17] With the help of "creative thought," wrote Robinson in *The New History*, the "abolition of poverty and disease and war, and the promotion of happy and rational lives" could be achieved.[18] Robinson concluded:

> The reformer who appeals to the future is a recent upstart, but it is clear enough today that the conscious reformer who appeals to the future is the final product of a progressive order of things.[19]

The reformist historian of ideas, according to Robinson, was to demonstrate that old, outworn beliefs, unfitted to reformist plans, had originated and developed in old environments now replaced by new environments which demand new ideas. "We are," he argued, "in constant danger of viewing present problems with obsolete emotions and of attempting to settle them by obsolete reasoning." "This is one of the chief reasons," he said, "why we are never by any means perfectly adjusted to our environment."[20]

Explicitly, Robinson was here celebrating the power of human thought. But implicitly, he was introducing a new element which undercut the causal significance of ideas. This new element was the implicit emphasis Robinson placed upon the power of the non-intellectual environment to mold ideas. Man's thought developed as part of his attempt to cope with his environment, and Robinson urged upon the historian of ideas the study of the relation between thought and the physical and social environment. To study ideas in relation to their non-intellectual environment, he exhorted historians to absorb

> those discoveries that are being made about mankind by anthropologists, economists, psychologists, and sociologists—discoveries which during the past fifty years have served to revolutionize our ideas of the origin, progress, and prospects of our race.[21]

Robinson hoped that a better understanding of the physical, economic, social, and psychological factors in the environment would help the historian understand the formation of human thought. No explicit emphasis was placed by Robinson on the determinism implicit in his environmental interpretation, but the deterministic implication was nonetheless present, and it would be developed by later historians who wrote the kinds of histories of ideas for which Robinson called.

It was thus Robinson's reliance upon the emergent social sciences which marked his writings, as well as his elaboration of the reformist uses of histories of ideas. As Eggleston had broadened the scope of Tyler's literary and political subject matter to include a more diversified and more "popular" or more "democratic" body of source materials, so Robinson further broadened the scope of the history of thought by looking to the social sciences for guidance.

Robinson's younger friend and Columbia colleague, Charles Beard (1874–1948), explored at length in his historical writings the relation between beliefs and their non-intellectual environments. Beard developed into a specifically economic interpretation of ideas what had been only an implication of Robinson's, namely, that thought is formed by social environmental influences.

Beard's most famous study, *An Economic Inter-*

[17] *Robinson*, The Mind in the Making (*New York, 1921*), 49.

[18] The New History, 247.

[19] Ibid., *264*.

[20] Ibid., *22–23*.

[21] Ibid., *24*.

pretation of the Constitution of the United States (1913), was written as a corrective to traditional historical accounts lacking "analysis of determining forces" in the environment which were responsible for the ideas which appeared in the Constitution. He argued that since "the primary object" of any government was

> the making of the rules which determine the property relations of members of society, the dominant classes whose rights are thus to be determined must perforce obtain from the government such rules as are consonant with the larger interests necessary to the continuance of their economic processes.[22]

Thus, said Beard at the outset of his examination of economic factors behind the ideas which went into the Constitution, it followed that:

> The social structure by which one type of legislation is secured and another prevented—that is, the constitution—is a secondary or derivative feature arising from the nature of the economic groups seeking positive action and negative restraint.[23]

He then attempted to show a correlation between property holding and political beliefs, or more precisely, certain types of property holding and certain kinds of political beliefs. One chapter out of eleven, roughly six per cent of the total pages, was devoted to "The Political Doctrines of the Members of the Convention," and the purpose of the entire volume was to "explain" the brief chapter on political beliefs.

Beard's *Economic Origins of Jeffersonian Democ-*

racy (1915)[24] pushed the economic interpretation of the Constitution's formation into the period culminating in the Jeffersonian election victory of 1800. Beard in this volume devoted more attention to an analysis of the ideas of specific individuals, however, and there were separate chapters on the political ideas of John Taylor, Thomas Jefferson, and John Adams. In this respect, *Economic Origins* took at least a small step in the direction of *The Rise of American Civilization* (1927) in which Beard, in addition to applying an economic interpretation to the entire course of American history, for the first time widened the scope of his subject matter beyond politics to include, in one-third of the total pages, treatment of social and intellectual life.[25] As a rule, Beard portrayed the development of ideas as influenced by non-intellectual, predominantly economic, environmental factors, just as he had done in his earlier studies of political opinion. While discussing the Glorious Revolution of 1688, for example, he wrote that religious ideas were brought into the XVIIth-century controversy as a "defense mechanism" by "men who were engaged in resisting taxes." "All that was reasonable enough," he added, "but the historian need not tarry long with the logical devices of men in action."[26] Again, describing an argument defending the economic *status quo* during the late 1800s, Beard interpreted the belief as little more than rationalizing environmental economic pressures:

> The capitalist system, in which the plutocracy flourished, like every other social organism, had to evolve a scheme of defense and, as things turned out, the task of justifying to man his own handiwork fell mainly to the economists in the

---

[22] An Economic Interpretation of the Constitution (*New York, 1913*), *quotations cited here refer to* (*New York, 1935*), *10, 13.*

[23] Ibid., *43.*

[24] (*New York, 1915*).

[25] (*2 vols., New York, 1927*), *chaps. IV, X, XVI of I, chaps. XXV, XXX of II.*

[26] Ibid., *I, 31.*

universities that sprang up like mushrooms as the gilded age advanced.[27]

But Beard had not altogether forsaken Robinson's and Eggleston's faith in the causal power of certain "enlightened" thought. For instance, when Beard discussed the reformist arguments attacking the economic *status quo* of the same late XIXth century, no reference was made to environmental factors; rather, these reform ideas were simply signs that

> social criticism had crept into scholarship. Indeed, university teachers were openly proclaiming that science had nothing to do with bolstering up or assailing any social order; its business, they said, was the search for truth.[28]

Beard gave extended treatment (over seven pages) to only one idea in *The Rise*, but it was to the idea of progress, and to it he attributed great causal power. Synthesizing modern scientific thought and democratic reform ideas, the belief in progress was called by Beard "the most dynamic social theory ever shaped in the history of thought."[29] Like Robinson, who had called the concept of progress "the greatest single idea in the whole history of mankind,"[30] Beard minimized environmental origins of the idea and maximized the idea's autonomy when discussing it.

Beard's occasional celebration, in *The Rise*, of the creative causal power of reform ideas and modern scientific thought was consistent with Robinsonian views. But it was during the 1930's accompanying the emergence of totalitarianism

in Europe, that Beard began to place greater emphasis upon the causal importance of human thought. "Interests, both psychological and material, change under the impacts of ideas," he wrote in 1937, and "to employ a figure, ideas march, divide, and come into conflict with themselves, with or without relation to the world of external events."[31] Introducing J. B. Bury's *The Idea of Progress* in 1932, Beard said that the "world is largely ruled by ideas, true and false." An "idea contains within itself a dynamic power to move individuals and nations, to drive them in the direction of effecting the ends and institutions implicit in it."[32]

One reason why ideas had to be accorded an importance, continued Beard in 1932, was because of the necessity for preserving constitutional government:

> Constitutional and democratic government is impossible unless the significance of ideas is recognized. It is founded on the assumption that all social conflicts will be fought out within the framework set by the fundamental law through the exchange of ideas. To government by opinion there is no other alternative except government by violence.[33]

In addition to arguing explicitly here that ideas are important because they are the means by which differences are resolved constitutionally, Beard was also celebrating thought by his implicit commitment to an idea, or value—that of constitutional and democratic government. This emphasis in 1932 contrasted dramatically with his statement

[27] Ibid., II, 429.
* *Quotations cited here refer to 1930 one-volume edition—Ed.*
[28] Ibid., II, 430–431.
[29] Ibid., II, 443.
[30] The New History, 247.
[31] *Beard and Vagts, "Currents of Thought in Historiography,"* American Historical Review, XLII, (April, 1937) 479, 461.
[32] *"Introduction" to J. B. Bury*, The Idea of Progress (New York, 1932), ix, x.
[33] Ibid., x.

in 1913 that "the rules of fundamental law" embodied in the Constitution were designed simply "to secure the property of one group against the assaults of another," even if the contrast of emphasis does not amount to an explicit contradiction.

To some extent, then, Charles Beard during and after the 1930's qualified his environmental interpretation of thought. But his celebration of the idea of progress in the 1920's, as well as his championing of non-totalitarian beliefs during the era of totalitarianism, suggest that Beard had a dual interpretation of ideas, and this duality continued during and after the 1930s.

Beard's two major histories of ideas, published in the 1930s and 1940s, illustrate his interpretation of the rôle of thought. *The Idea of National Interest* (1934) investigated one concept in the history of American foreign relations. Beard presented two conflicting policies of national interest, one an agrarian Jeffersonian belief, and the other a commercial Hamiltonian concept. It was clear, to Beard, that this conflict of (mainly economic) interest provoked the conflict of policies. "Public policies," he wrote, "are not abstractions":

> They are the products of concrete experiences with concrete economic phenomena, such as the production and exchange of American commodities, the acquisition of material sources and markets abroad.[34]

By contrast, *The American Spirit: A Study of the Idea of Civilization in the United States* (1942) was essentially a celebration of domestic reform thought:

> This idea of civilization . . . embraces a conception of history as a struggle of human beings in the world for individual and social perfection—for

the good, the true, the beautiful—against ignorance, disease, the harshness of physical nature, the forces of barbarism in individuals and in society.[35]

One component of the idea of civilization, the belief in individual freedom, "was a creed of seasoned strength," and "had been one of the major forces in American civilization as fact."[36] Beard traced American contributions to the reformist "idea of civilization" from Thomas Jefferson to John Dewey (like Eggleston, Beard saw little contribution to enlightened thought by the Puritans). When Beard interpreted ideas primarily as outgrowths of environmental factors in this volume, the ideas were usually ones for which Beard had little sympathy;[37] he attributed causal force to ideas only when he was sympathetic to those ideas.

So Beard's basically environmental interpretation of human thought was joined with a Robinsonian willingness to attribute causal power to certain particularly attractive ideas. Regardless of Beard's sympathies, however, he did not linger long in analyzing any ideas. He discussed, for more than two or three pages each in his last history of ideas, the "ideas of civilization" expressed by approximately fifty thinkers. The volume's index listed roughly 200 other individuals whose ideas were more briefly discussed. His characteristic technique, even in dealing with thought he admired and to which he granted considerable autonomy, was to sketch ideas on the run, so to speak, rather than to settle down with them in a detailed analysis.

Carl Becker (1873–1945) published less history of any kind than did Charles Beard, and Becker

[34] *(New York, 1934), 112.*

[35] *(New York, 1942), 672.*

[36] Ibid., *333.*

[37] *See* ibid., *for example, where Beard remarks that the post-Civil War idea of "individualism" was a belief which was used "especially in relation to economic activities and vested rights."*

devoted himself to fewer studies of American opinion specifically. Yet Becker's influence upon American historians of thought was probably greater than Beard's.

Becker appeared to share many reformist attitudes concerning society during the early 1900s—his latest biographer characterizes him as subscribing to the "Progressive faith"[38]—although Becker remained always somewhat detached and aloof. He also shared Robinson's and Beard's interest in the relation between thought and its environment and, like them, he minimized over the years the importance of thought on certain occasions and maximized its importance at other times.

Becker's most outstanding contributions stemmed from his conviction that the environment decisively influenced ideas. But he emphasized intellectual as well as non-intellectual factors in making up the environment, and when he wrote histories of thought he focused almost exclusively upon ideas rather than upon non-intellectual environmental components—as Beard often did. Becker showed that a historian of ideas could believe that given ideas were virtually determined by their environments, and yet go on studying those ideas in detail. Becker's famous development of the "climate of opinion" concept in the European study, *The Heavenly City of the Eighteenth-Century Philosophers* (1932), was matched by his earlier study of a climate of opinion, *The Declaration of Independence: A Study in the History of Political Ideas* (1922).[39] He analyzed those "instinctively held preconceptions" expressed implicitly and explicitly in the Declaration, and he traced the literary composition of the document in considerable detail. He paid little attention to non-intellectual environmental determinants, even

though he made clear his view that environmental conditions had provoked the expression of the ideas in the Declaration of Independence:

> When honest men are impelled to withdraw their allegiance to the established law or custom of the community, still more when they are persuaded that such law or custom is too iniquitous to be longer tolerated, they seek for some principle more generally valid, some "law" of higher authority, than the established law or custom of the community.[40]

"The latest fashion among psychologists and philosophers," wrote Becker approvingly in 1913, "seems to be to regard the individual intelligence, not as an instrument suited to furnish an absolute test of objective truth, but rather as a tool pragmatically useful in enabling the individual to find his way about in a disordered objective world." Consequently, he concluded:

> one may conveniently regard the general intellectual activity of any period—the common ideas and beliefs, the prepossessions and points of view—as having had its origin in practical interests, and as deriving its validity from the service it renders in solving the problems that grow out of community life.[41]

Becker conceived this resultant climate of opinion crucial not only to an understanding of history but crucial as well to an understanding of the writing of history, for historians also were enveloped by the climates of their times. The "historical work that is most characteristic of any time," he wrote, "may be regarded as embodying an interpretation of the past in terms of present

---

[38] *Burleigh Taylor Wilkins*, Carl Becker (*Cambridge, Mass., 1961*), *92.*

[39] (*New Haven, 1932*); (*New York, 1922*), *quotations cited here refer to 1958 Vintage ed.*

[40] The Declaration of Independence, 277.

[41] *"Some Aspects of the Influence of Social Problems upon the Study and Writing of History,"* American Journal of Sociology, *XVIII*, (*March, 1913*), 641–42.

social interests." Naturally, then, XIXth-century historians viewed the past differently from early XXth-century historians who were, he said, influenced by "a revival of faith in the possibility of social regeneration":

> Out of the wreck of old creeds, [he said in 1913] there is arising a new faith, born of science and democracy, almost the only vital conviction left to us—the profound belief, namely, in progress; the belief that society can, by taking thought, modify the conditions of life, and thereby indefinitely improve the happiness and welfare of all men.[42]

Thus he agreed that the new reform histories had contemporary relevance, as Eggleston, Robinson, and Beard had urged, but Becker explicitly placed these new histories in their own climate of opinion. His view of the writing of history made historiography—the history of history—part of the history of ideas, and from this perspective several studies of the writing of American histories have been carried out in the middle 1900s.

Encroaching totalitarianism apparently modified Becker's emphasis upon environmental determinism of thought, just as it did Beard's. Ideas have a significance, a life of their own, Becker began to say in the late 1930s, as independent causal agents, including acting as standards of value. In articles written separately, and published in *New Liberties for Old* (1941), Becker wrote of the core of humane values which

> have a life of their own part from any particular social system or type of civilization. They are the values which, since the time of Buddah and Confucius, Solomon and Zoroaster, Plato and Aristotle, Socrates and Jesus, men have commonly employed to measure the advance or the decline

of civilization, the values they have celebrated in the saints and sages whom they have agreed to canonize.[43]

Thus Becker, like Beard, celebrated the vitality of beliefs which he cherished in the face of a threatening totalitarianism during the World War II era. But Becker had always magnified the significance of the history of ideas, even while maximizing an environmental determinism of thought, for he emphasized the influence of intellectual as well as non-intellectual components of the environment, and he described ideas at length without particular reference to non-intellectual factors.

The first attempt to cover virtually the entire chronological sweep of American ideas was made by Vernon Louis Parrington (1871–1929), whose *Main Currents in American Thought* (2 vols., 1927; inc., posthumous vol. 3, 1930) resembled in various ways the writings of Eggleston, Robinson, Beard, and Becker. Parrington's volumes formed a more distinguished American history of ideas than any of those written by his predecessors, and are deserving of detailed analysis here, but I have recently discussed Parrington's work at considerable length elsewhere, and problems of space forbid repetition of that discussion.[44] But it must at least be noted that Parrington's attribution of autonomy to ideas he liked, combined with his

---

[42] Ibid., *641, 663.*

[43] (*New Haven, 1941*), *149–50. Cushing Strout has made conclusions similar to those presented here concerning modifications in Beard's and Becker's views, during this period, of the rôle of ideas. See* The Pragmatic Revolt in American History: Charles Beard and Carl Becker (*New Haven, 1958*), *105, 127–130.*

[44] *See Robert A. Skotheim and Kermit Vanderbilt, "Vernon Louis Parrington: The Mind and Art of a Historian of Ideas,"* Pacific Northwest Quarterly, *53, (July, 1962), 100–113. See also Skotheim, "Environmental Interpretations of Ideas by Beard, Parrington, and Curti,"* Pacific Historical Review, *XXXIII (February, 1964), 35–44.*

environmental interpretation of ideas he did not like, was similar to the interpretations of ideas expressed by Robinson, Beard, and Becker.

Parrington's *Main Currents* received the highest number of historians' votes as the "most preferred" American history published between 1920 and 1935, in a poll reported in the *Mississippi Valley Historical Review* in 1952. In the same poll, Merle Curti's *The Growth of American Thought* was selected as the "most preferred" work appearing between 1936–1950.[45] It was fitting that a survey singling out Parrington should also have picked Curti, for both expressed a similar reformist outlook and a similar view of the character of ideas in history. Curti (1897–   ), like his predecessors discussed above, alternately emphasized the decisive importance of the (usually non-intellectual) environment in forming human thought, and the independent causal importance of ideas. Echoing their reformist hopes also, Curti drew on a common background as he became a most prolific American historian of ideas. The background included a sympathy for the emergent social sciences as he broadened the subject matter of the history of ideas to include the intellectual component in virtually all human activity.

To mention Curti's books even briefly is to indicate the nature of his reformist social philosophy, his conception of ideas in history, and the breadth of his interests. Curti's earliest work in the 1920s and 1930s was concerned almost entirely with pacifist ideas and peace movements. His doctoral dissertation became, in 1929, *The American Peace Crusade, 1815–1860; Bryan and World Peace* was published in 1931; *Peace or War: The American Struggle, 1636–1936*, came out in 1936.[46]

These books were sympathetic to the pacifist ideas they described and it was obvious that Curti portrayed pacifism's fate in the past at least partly in order to increase the understanding and possible success of peace movements in the future. Pacifist ideas were presented as beliefs which could operate as creative instruments to change the world by "determining" future behavior. Pacifism developed, according to Curti, "a body of brilliant arguments against war," giving increasing attention, "for example, to the wastefulness of war and to the burdens it inflicted on the working class."[47] Curti explained the failure of these pacifist ideas to prevail historically not on the grounds that they were defeated by opposing ideas of great causal force, but rather by unfavorable environmental conditions which supported "irrational," "rationalizing" pro-war opinions. Among various factors in the environment, Curti came to stress by 1936 the economic in particular:

> peacemakers have not adequately fought the economic forces that make for war. . . . In short, while individual capitalists have sincerely desired peace, war has been functional to the capitalistic system itself.[48]

Thus Curti revealed, in his early histories, a belief in the potential causal power of some ideas (pacifism), but also an environmental interpretation, particularly economic, of other ideas (opposition to pacifistic beliefs).

Curti's sympathy for pacifist ideas was but part of an overall reform outlook, and from the middle thirties on, Curti's publications broadened their focus. *Social Ideas of American Educators* (1935)[49] stressed the relation between the ideas of educators

[45] *John Caughey, "Historians' Choice: Results of a Poll on Recently Published American History and Biography,"* MVHR, *XXXIX,* (*September, 1952*) 289–302.
[46] (*Durham, N. C.*), (*Northampton, Mass.*), (*New York*).
[47] The American Peace Crusade, *225.*
[48] Peace or War: The American Struggle, *307, 308.*
[49] (*New York, 1935, 1959*).

and the American social and economic system. *The Growth of American Thought* (1943), Curti's synthesis of virtually all areas of intellectual life, was organized, like Beard's *The American Spirit* and Parrington's *Main Currents*, in terms of the conflict between reform ideas which looked forward in history and anti-reform ideas which looked backward. Like Beard's *The American Spirit*, *The Growth of American Thought* was a book for free men in an era of totalitarianism, as well as a historical Bible for reformers. It was a statement of what Americans had achieved, and it seemed to Curti—as it had come to seem also to Beard and Becker when totalitarianism threatened the United States—that Americans had developed ideas and institutions which were particularly good, even of virtually "absolute" value.

> As war crept closer [Curti wrote, ending his 1943 volume], always against the wish of the great majority of the American people, as step by step aid was given to the democracies resisting the totalitarian onslaught, a larger number of men and women, both among the intellectual leadership and the rank and file, realized that fascism menaced much that Americans had long held precious. The traditional American love of individual freedom, opposition to regimentation, devotion to fair play and the doctrine of live and let live, and above all, loyalty to the ideal of a moral law— these values seemed clearly jeopardized.[50]

Thus Curti emphasized the significance of traditional American humane values generally in the World War II era as he had stressed earlier the importance of pacifism specifically.

The greatest emphasis in *The Growth of American Thought*, however, and the one which became a Curti trademark, was the importance attributed to the social environment in forming ideas. Curti was the latest, of course, in a line of historians emphasizing the importance of the social environment in the development of thought, but he most consciously attempted to describe that environment itself and at the same time to describe the ideas which came out of it. Curti explicitly contrasted his method with that of a detailed analysis of the content and structure of thought without regard to the environment. As he said of *The Growth of American Thought*, "It is thus not a history of American thought but a social history of American thought, and to some extent a socioeconomic history of American thought."[51] This method of describing "the functional or instrumental nature of intellectual activities" rather than probing the "interiors" of ideas was thus, for Curti, associated with his overall emphasis upon the influence of the environment.[52]

The writings of these historians of ideas—Eggleston, Robinson, Beard, Becker, Parrington, Curti—represented the dominant tradition during most of the first half of the XXth century in the United States. Possibly too heterogeneous a group of historians to be characterized as a "tradition" (the similarities rather than the differences among them are necessarily emphasized in this brief overview), yet the writings of these scholars shared, first, a view of society: a blend of sympathy for social reform, and admiration for modern science as opposed to traditional religions. Second, these reformist historians shared a belief in the power of certain ideas, though not all ideas, to act as independent, and powerfully influential, causal agents in history. Insofar as they saw thought as the mere creature of a non-intellectual environment, it was frequently thought for which the

---

[50] The Growth of American Thought (*New York,* 1943), 751.

[51] Ibid., *vi.*

[52] *Quotations from Curti's preface to the 1951 edition of* The Growth, *xviii.*

reformist had little sympathy. An environmental interpretation of ideas thus did not hopelessly undercut their interest in ideas, because they always retained a conviction that certain ideas had independent causal force. These characteristics had not appeared in any histories before Edward Eggleston's—there were no earlier histories of ideas of course except Tyler's—and these characteristics have not appeared in the same pervasive intensity in American histories of ideas written since World War II. The similar characteristics of their writings thus may be sufficient to lump these historians together, despite the fact that some expressed historical relativism, and some did not; some described ideas at length and in great detail, and some sketched more briefly a greater number of ideas; the specifics of some historians' desired social and intellectual reforms differed from others, as did the degree of faith possessed by each scholar that the reforms could be realized. Most important of all, finally, these historians' writings spanned more than a half century and the times not only changed generally, but, specifically, the craft of writing history was altered with decades of research and specialization.

Although the reformist historians of ideas dominated the first portion of the XXth century, they were not altogether unchallenged. As Moses Tyler's histories stood in contrast to Edward Eggleston's, so the dominant reformist histories of ideas stood in contrast to those of Samuel Eliot Morison, Perry Miller, and Ralph Gabriel. Samuel Eliot Morison (1887–   ), not exclusively nor even most significantly a historian of ideas, nevertheless made important contributions during the late 1920s and 1930s to the development of a description and assessment of American intellectual experience similar to Moses Tyler's and different from that given by Eggleston, Robinson, Beard, Becker, Parrington, and Curti. Morison's studies of Puritan life and ideas, including *Builders of the*

Bay Colony (1930), *The Founding of Harvard College* (1935), *Harvard College in the Seventeenth Century* (1936), and *The Puritan Pronaos* (1936), all revealed a strong Tylerlike sympathy and admiration for Puritanism.[53] During the 1920s and 1930s Morison felt compelled, he wrote in the 1950s, "to counteract the disparaging" accounts written concerning colonial New England culture.[54] His sympathetic view of the Puritans rested in part on his conviction that they took the life of the mind seriously and lived it successfully:

> What is not sufficiently known or appreciated is this: puritanism not only did not prevent, but stimulated an interest in the classics, belles-lettres, poetry, and scientific research. Neither pioneer hardships nor other restrictions were ever so great as to prevent the burgeoning of genuine intellectual life in that series of little beachheads on the edge of the wilderness, which was seventeenth-century New England.[55]

This conviction as to the quality of Puritan intellectual life was accompanied by a conviction that Puritan ideas were the most important factors in early New England history: "the dynamic force in settling New England was English puritanism desiring to realize itself."[56] The specific religious doctrine of Puritanism was not in itself particularly appealing to Morison, but he was attracted by the fact that religion and ideas were taken seriously by the Puritans. "After three hundred years," he wrote, "it no longer seems to be so important

[53] (*Boston, 1930*), (*2 vols., Cambridge, 1935*), (*Cambridge, 1936*), (*New York, 1936, republished with slight revisions as* The Intellectual Life of Colonial New England, *New York, 1956*), *quotations cited here refer to* (*Ithaca, 1960*).
[54] The Intellectual Life of Colonial New England, *v.*
[55] Ibid., *4.*
[56] Ibid., *7.*

what sort of religious faith the puritans had, as that they had faith."[57] Puritanism carried the early New Englanders to success despite unfriendly environmental conditions. "Nature seemed to doom Massachusetts to insignificance," he commented, "with a tithe of the bounty that Nature grants more favored lands, the Puritan settlers made their land the most fruitful not only in things of the Spirit, but in material wealth."[58]

Morison's celebration of the power of ideas was accompanied by a celebration of Puritanism, and it was joined with a marked criticism of certain "modernist" currents supported by reformist historians. From the 1930s on, he attacked "progressive education," as opposed to traditional classical education, and he explicitly criticized Beard's and Curti's deprecatory treatment of Puritan education.[59] Morison, unlike Beard, Becker, Parrington, and Curti, did not express during the 1920s and 1930s any sympathy for an economic interpretation of past wars nor any sympathy for pacifism. Later, in the 1940s, Morison became the official United States Naval historian for the Second World War, and published criticisms of historians—particularly Beard—who since the First World War had "ignored wars, belittled wars, taught that no war was necessary and no war did any good," and whose "Zeal against war did nothing to preserve peace."[60]

In 1950, in his presidential address to the American Historical Association, Morison made his most explicit statement of his ideological position.

He argued that totalitarianism had demonstrated the necessity for appreciation of the traditional American values and beliefs, because it was those ideas or values which caused Americans to oppose totalitarianism. By contrast, he said, those persons during the 1920s and 1930s who had emphasized the influence of the environment in determining thought had contributed to an erosion of belief and "American spiritual unpreparedness for World War II."[61] Despite Morison's glorification of the rôle of thought in human affairs, his own Puritan scholarship comprised an investigation of colonial institutions (schools) and genres of intellectual activity (verse, historical writings), rather than an analysis of the content and structure of ideas. Detailed analysis of Puritan ideas was to be done by Morison's younger Harvard colleague, Perry Miller. Miller (1905–63) expressed a conception of the nature of ideas in history similar to Morison's, and Miller showed great respect for Puritan ideas, although he emphasized even more than did Morison that "respect for them is not the same as believing in them."[62] Part of Miller's respect for the Puritans stemmed from the fact that these New England colonists took their theological concepts and intellectual life seriously. He was critical of scholars who did not consider ideas as seriously as did the New Englanders:

> historians are apt to slide over these [theological] concepts in a shockingly superficial manner simply because they have so little respect for the intellect in general. I have difficulty imagining that anyone can be a historian without realizing that history itself is part of the life of the mind; hence I have been compelled to insist that the mind of man is the basic factor in human history.[63]

[57] Builders of the Bay Colony, *129.*

[58] The Maritime History of Massachusetts, 1783–1860 (*Boston, 1921*), 7.

[59] The Puritan Pronaos, *64–65,* The Intellectual Life of Colonial New England, *67.*

[60] "*Faith of an Historian,*" American Historical Review, *LVI,*(*January, 1951*), 266, 267.

[61] Ibid., *267.*

[62] Errand Into The Wilderness (*Cambridge, 1956*), *ix.*

[63] Ibid.

Miller's written histories implemented his theoretical statements as to the significance of thought by examining ideas independently of possible environmental determinants. Opening his study of the Puritan mind, in 1933, he wrote that "I have attempted to tell of a great folk movement with an utter disregard of the economic and social factors."[64] He continued, with obvious facetiousness and derision:

> I lay myself open to the charge of being so very naive as to believe that the way men think has some influence upon their actions, of not remembering that these ways of thinking have been officially decided by modern psychologists to be generally just so many rationalizations constructed by the subconscious to disguise the pursuit of more tangible ends.[65]

In *Orthodoxy in Massachusetts, 1630–1650* (1933) and *The New England Mind: The Seventeenth Century* (1939), which traced the growth and climax of Puritanism, Miller executed an unprecedented analysis of Puritan epistemology, natural philosophy, rhetoric, literary style, ideas of government, and theory of human nature, as well as theology. "I assume," he wrote, "that Puritanism was one of the major expressions of the Western intellect, that it achieved an organized synthesis of concepts which are fundamental to our culture, and that therefore it calls for the most serious examination."[66]

Miller continued to analyze the components of Puritan thought as he traced Puritanism's decline in *The New England Mind: From Colony to Province*

(1953), but he for the first time joined with this analysis an emphasis upon the non-intellectual environment's influence in altering the old Puritanism. In contrast to his former statements deprecating attention paid by historians to social and economic factors in studies of ideas, Miller wrote of colonial New England as a "laboratory" demonstrating the relation between ideas and their environment. Indeed, he believed "profoundly that the story herein recounted is chiefly valuable for its *representative* quality" as a "case history of the accommodation to the American landscape of an imported and highly articulated system of ideas."[67] It was the story "of a society which was founded by men dedicated, in unity and simplicity, to realizing on earth eternal and immutable principles," but which, according to Miller, "progressively became involved with fishing, trade and settlement."[68] By emphasizing the environment in his explanation of the decline of Puritan thought, and of the corresponding rise of new XVIIIth-century ideas, Miller in a sense did just the opposite of Beard, Parrington, and Curti. They emphasized the environmental factors which contributed to the rise of Puritanism, and they tended to minimize environmental factors in the decline of Puritan ideas and the rise of Enlightenment thought. Miller argued symptomatically, that the proper characterization of the late 1600s and early 1700s was not "a growth of toleration, but rather a shedding of the religious conception of the universe, a turning toward a way of life in which the secular state, even when embodied in a provincial corporation, has become central."[69] So even when Miller stressed the importance of non-intellectual influences in the development of

[64] Orthodoxy in Massachusetts, 1630–1650 (*Cambridge, 1933*), *quotations cited here refer to* (*Boston, 1959*), *xi.*
[65] Ibid.
[66] The New England Mind: The Seventeenth Century, *viii.*

[67] The New England Mind: From Colony to Province (*Cambridge, 1953*), *x.*
[68] Ibid., *40.*
[69] Ibid., *171.*

ideas, the resulting written history differed from those of the reformist scholars.

Although Perry Miller had in recent years moved out of the colonial period, his most important work remains his studies of Puritanism. The historian who first extended to XIXth- and XXth-century-studies of ideas the tendencies expressed by Tyler, Morison, and Miller, was Ralph Gabriel (1890–   ). Gabriel's writings since the 1920s have searched for the beliefs which have decisively structured American life traditionally, which were threatened during the 1920s and 1930s, and which survived in strengthened form as they helped guide Americans during mid-XXth-century totalitarian crisis. Markedly respectful toward religion, Gabriel asserted its continuing relevance to the contemporary world. "It is the problem of religion," he wrote in the debunking 1920s, "to deal with adjustments of human life to the infinite mysteries."[70] Moreover, he attributed considerable causal significance to religious ideas in the development of American political and social thought. John Calvin's thought, for example, was credited for contributing to American constitutionalism, evangelical protestantism was held mainly responsible for "taming" the "crude, turbulent, and godless" frontier, and, further, "religion" was called "the most powerful drive behind the humanitarian movements" of the pre-Civil War period.[71]

Gabriel emphasized the close relationship between religion and humane American values or ideas as part of his attempt to locate, during and after the 1920s, beliefs which Americans had traditionally expressed. Convinced that ideas decisively influenced human affairs, and persuaded that the beliefs Americans agreed upon were more fundamental than those upon which they were divided, Gabriel searched areas of apparent disagreement in order to find an underlying consensus. Just as he found certain humane values stemming from religious thought more important than various religious differences, so he concluded that modern science had confirmed historic humane values of Americans rather than destroyed them. Admitting that the modern natural and social sciences had eroded many old certainties in all fields of knowledge, Gabriel noted particularly the threatening effect which the environmental interpretation of thought had upon the accepted validity of traditional beliefs:

> the rise of the biological and social sciences had made it extremely difficult for the mid-twentieth-century man to define the good save in terms of a particular culture, while at the same time the emphasis on the relativity of standards of values had lowered the prestige of all ideals and ethical principles. Among these was the idea of human dignity and the importance of the individual.[72]

But, argued Gabriel, science was itself dependent upon the existence of a free society which guaranteed the integrity of the individual:

> the hope of the present world is to be found in the fact that science itself, which is the ultimate source of power in the modern age, is by a strange paradox founded on an ethical code that is absolute and universal. Science requires freedom for the investigator.[73]

"These principles of dependence on reason, of

[70] From Gabriel's Foreword to a collection of essays, Gabriel, ed. Christianity and Modern Thought (*New Haven, 1924*), *xi.*

[71] The Course of American Democratic Thought (*New York, 1940*), *30, 33, 161.*

[72] "*Democracy: Retrospect and Prospect,*" American Journal of Sociology, *XLVIII (Nov., 1942), 416.*

[73] Ibid., *417.*

individual freedom, of individual honesty and responsibility, and of mutual co-operation belong," continued Gabriel, "in a larger frame of reference. . . . They are a twentieth-century statement in naturalistic terms of the standards of value that were the core of the democratic pattern as it was established in America at the end of the eighteenth century."[74]

Thus, the traditional humane beliefs of Americans were significant sources of authority in the XXth century, as they had been in the past. Emergent totalitarianism in the 1930s tragically increased the necessity that Americans recognize the validity of their traditional values, according to Gabriel, for they had to take a stand. It was against this background of rising totalitarianism and the questioning of old traditions, that Gabriel published *The Course of American Democratic Thought* (1940). The traditional "democratic faith," which he traced, was not identical with the "eternal" humane values of a free society and the dignified individual within a free society, about which Gabriel was so concerned at mid-XXth century, but he was convinced that the "democratic faith" included these humane values within it. He manifested a distinct sympathy, if not nostalgia, for the mid-XIXth-century America which had "that mental peace and that sense of security which comes to the man who feels he has planted his feet upon the eternal rock."[75] Gabriel unfavorably contrasted the intellectual uncertainty of the mid-XXth century with the certainty of a hundred years earlier. "The absolution of the nineteenth century which expressed itself in the theory of the moral law is out of fashion in our America," he wrote. "Faith in the eternal character of right and wrong is in retreat before the advance of the pragmatic ethics of expediency."

"But," he said, "the retreat has not yet ended and while it continues, modern Americans are confused. The bitter fruit of their confusion is a sense of intellectual and of social insecurity."[76] It was not clear to Gabriel, in 1940, whether the "democratic faith" would survive the challenges of new knowledge, on the one hand, and totalitarianism on the other.

The American reaction to totalitarianism in the military efforts of the Second World War (Gabriel's writings had opposed pacifism since the 1920s[77]), and the explicit reassertion of dedication to "absolute" values by many Americans, furnished Gabriel with a cheering answer to his doubts and questions. Americans had come to realize, he declared after World War II, that their society was based upon certain humane beliefs or ideals which had a validity or truth of virtually universal applicability:

> Americans who had insisted that relativism provides the only realistic approach to ethics discovered that a philosophy of ethical relativism made any American criticism of genocide as practiced by the Nazis within their jurisdiction irrelevant.[78]

---

[74] Ibid., *418*.

[75] The Course of American Democratic Thought, *19*.

[76] Ibid., *18–19*.

[77] *Gabriel, like Morison, consistently argued that war had been an important and frequently noble and purposeful part of American experience. In the 1920s, when Curti was publishing his first history of American peace movements, Gabriel was the joint author of two pictorial histories of American wars, one significantly entitled* In Defense of Liberty (*New Haven, 1929*). *Gabriel argued that war was rooted in "the fact of human conflict," whereas he thought pacifism was based upon too optimistic a conception of human nature. See William Wood and Gabriel,* The Winning of Freedom (*New Haven, 1925*), *1.*

[78] *"Thomas Jefferson and Twentieth-Century Rationalism,"* Virginia Quarterly Review, *XXVI* (Summer, *1950*), *331.*

Totalitarianism had perhaps an equally decisive effect upon American historians of ideas by contributing to their belief in the significance of ideas in human affairs. Those historians who had earlier espoused social interpretations of thought seemed to modify their espousals in the era of totalitarianism, and historians who had earlier declared the primacy of thought in history seemed later to feel confirmed in those declarations. By the 1950s, the influence of the non-intellectual environment in developing ideas appeared to be minimized, rather than maximized, by American historians.

There seems to have occurred, in fact, a convergence of the two traditions, in more respects than one. A striking example of the convergence after World War II was that the large-scale histories of ideas published by two legatees of the opposing "traditions," Henry Steele Commager (1902–   ) and Stow Persons (1913–   ), the former a self-styled Parringtonian and the latter a student and follower of Ralph Gabriel, revealed more similarities than differences.[79] Both histories expressed a clear, yet restrained sympathy for historic social reform, a quiet acceptance of social and cultural influences upon ideas coupled with primary emphasis upon the power of thought and the responsibility of the individual for his beliefs, and finally, both books revealed a deep concern for traditional American ideas in contrast to totalitarianism. Within this mid-XXth-century convergence of older groupings, younger historians of ideas are charting new courses to new destinations.

[79] *See Henry Steele Commager*, The American Mind (*New Haven, 1950*), *Stow Persons*, American Minds (*New York, 1958*).

THE HISTORY OF IDEAS IN AMERICA: AN ESSAY IN REDEFINITION

*Rush Welter**

Even the most cursory examination of recent historical writing will reveal that intellectual history has become a full-fledged branch of American scholarship. Students of American life and institutions have taken its virtues for granted, much as earlier scholars took for granted the virtues of diplomatic, political, and social history, and they have explored both the main currents of American thought and a number of the particular ideas or intellectual configurations which have characterized that thought. Their undertaking has also acquired a rudimentary critical apparatus. Thanks to such writers as John Higham and Roy H. Pearce, R. W. B. Lewis and John W. Ward, scholars have begun to acknowledge the assumptions that underlie any attempt to examine American ideas in their historic setting. Nor have they stopped with making their methodological assumptions more explicit. Recognizing that a discipline is defined at least as much by the questions it does not seek to answer as by those it does, they have also begun to consider what the historical examination of ideas cannot accomplish. In short, American intellectual history flourishes both as a scholarly commitment and as a self-conscious scholarly enterprise, and we need no longer either justify its existence or apologize for its naiveté.

Nevertheless, the discipline confronts an almost intolerable intellectual dilemma, which its practitioners have been unable to resolve satisfactorily. That dilemma originates in a distinction between internal and external approaches to ideas: between the historical examination of ideas as ideas apart from questions of their social origin or their social influence, and the pursuit of ideas in their relationships to events. Pursuing internal intellectual history, scholars have also tended to lay primary emphasis on major philosophical concepts, on

*RUSH WELTER (1923–   ) is a Professor of the History of American Civilization at Bennington College. His publications include "The Idea of Progress in America: An Essay in Ideas and Method" (1955), and Popular Education and Democratic Thought in America (1962). Reprinted by permission of the author and the Journal of American History, Vol. 51, No. 4 (March, 1965), 599–614.

literary and philosophical techniques of analysis, on the study of ideas for their own sake. Pursuing external intellectual history, they have stressed the content of popular beliefs, sociological and ideological modes of analysis, description rather than close study of public opinion. But they have seldom attempted both, and discussions of the discipline have come increasingly to assume that its works cannot and should not attempt to achieve more than one kind of knowledge of ideas.

Even the vocabulary with which scholars discuss their work has been affected by this assumption: it has become customary to assign scholarly works in the field either to "the history of ideas" or to "intellectual history" according to whether they practice internal or external analysis.[1] This terminological distinction points to methodological difficulties that are inherent in any attempt to choose between the two halves of the discipline. Usually a work in the history of ideas is just that: an extended analysis of a single idea or cluster of ideas in its successive formulations, treating it in virtual isolation from other aspects of history. Such analysis is often in a strict and unfortunate sense "internal" to the ideas under consideration; it reads as if historic change could be reduced to changes in the content of ideas, which it examines in essentially philosophical terms. On the other hand, a work in intellectual history usually assumes the preeminence of the general historic process, and it treats the ideas it deals with as functions of that process. In other words, intellectual history attempts the study of history-in-general in its specifically intellectual aspects, and in an equally unfortunate sense it is disinclined to examine ideas except in terms external to them.

Obviously, these distinctions cut to the heart of the discipline. Hence they cast doubt on the significance of its achievements; one hardly knows how to evaluate them, to use them, or to imitate them. The difficulties are clearly apparent in the writings of Higham, who has been at once a most prolific and a most thoughtful commentator on the history of ideas.[2] Higham argued in 1954 that there are several different kinds of intellectual history, each of which has peculiar strengths and weaknesses, and suggested that American scholars must choose among them because they cannot employ all of them simultaneously. By 1961, however, Higham felt that there was only one

___

[1] *The distinction goes as far back as the American originators of the discipline: Arthur O. Lovejoy habitually spoke of "the history of ideas," and James Harvey Robinson advocated "intellectual history." But until recently it was not clear how basic the distinction might be. Among recent proponents of the history of ideas are R. W. B. Lewis and Roy H. Pearce, whose work clearly reflects their commitment to internal rather than external analysis of ideas even though they are also critical of the Lovejoy approach. At the same time Franklin L. Baumer and R. Richard Wohl are explicitly devoted to intellectual history both as a term and as a definition of their responsibilities. By the same token, we find differences in method as well as in title between Stow Persons and Merle Curti in their comprehensive treatments of American thought: the one deals with "American Minds: A History of Ideas," the other with "The Growth of American Thought."*

There are scholars who do not observe this distinction in their writings, among them John Higham, who uses the term "intellectual history" to describe an approach that I would assign to "the history of ideas." But even their practice may be significant. At any rate, Higham has generally sought to discover an approach to ideas that would have the virtues of both elements of the discipline; hence it is understandable that he should not make the usual distinction of terms. More important, the fact that some scholars still use the two terms interchangeably gives us hope that intellectual history may remain

one discipline rather than two, if only we can resolve its dilemmas.

[2] *In the absence of a satisfactory term to identify the discipline without aligning myself with one or the other of its two main branches, I shall use "the history of ideas" and "intellectual history" interchangeably.*

plausible choice, at least for this generation of historians. Writing in the *American Quarterly* he committed himself and those who would follow him to the internal study of ideas. Yet the essay in which he developed this position was unusually complex and difficult, and it offered almost as many objections to the intellectual history practiced by philosophers and literary critics (who tend to pursue the internal relationships among ideas) as it did to that practiced by social and cultural historians (who tend to see ideas in their external relationships).[3] The process of defining the discipline by dividing it in half has raised at least as many questions as it has answered.

In his 1961 essay, Higham suggests that one way out of the dilemma is to pursue the "spirit of an age." The search for this phenomenon, which has also attracted the interest of historians of European thought, has two major virtues. First, it calls attention to the connecting links between European and American thought, which have more often been assumed than explored by American historians. Second, it focuses investigation on concepts so fundamental to our culture that they can neither be ignored as intellectual events nor be exhausted by philosophical analysis. But it still represents a radical choice between alternatives rather than a resolution of conflicting claims to the historian's attention, for it eliminates from his consideration all ideas that are not so pervasive as to be virtually universal in a nation or a culture. Nor can such a choice be an entirely happy one. Granted that universal ideas may be more funda-

mental or more important than other ideas in explaining the history of a society, we have no warrant for deciding a priori that they are the only kinds of ideas that deserve close historical analysis.[4]

Moreover, any attempt to discover the spirit of an age tends to commit historians to another a priori distinction. This is most clearly apparent in H. Stuart Hughes' recent study of the social concepts that have reshaped the thought of Western Europe. Focusing his attention on "pristine" ideas, "the fund of ideas available at any particular time to men who have received a superior general education," which are also "the ideas that eventually will inspire . . . governing élites," Hughes relegates the study of public opinion to history understood as "retrospective cultural anthropology."[5] Similarly, Higham distinguishes between intellectual history, properly understood, and the study of social psychology. There are differences as well as similarities between these perspectives, for Hughes identifies the spirit of an age exclusively with its pristine ideas, whereas Higham leaves room for the systematic analysis of any pervasive attitude. Yet the distinction each makes between intellectual history and a behavioral science seems to imply that historians should assign a method of analysis according to their estimates of the intel-

---

[4] *The quest for the spirit of an age also seems to echo Hegelian historicism, which historians of ideas have all they can do to escape. For example, the Hegelian reading of history treats historic phenomena as reflections of a higher philosophic reality; in embracing contradictory ideas and conflicting events its dialectic only fixes them more firmly in their assigned places. Furthermore, Hegelian assumptions press historians to visualize history in heroic terms, which suggest in turn a predisposition toward great or heroic ideas. Both tendencies seem to me to interfere with objective analysis of the role of ideas in history.*

[5] H. Stuart Hughes, Consciousness and Society: The Reorientation of European Social Thought, 1890–1930 (*New York, 1958*), 10.

---

[3] Higham, "*Intellectual History and Its Neighbors,*" Journal of the History of Ideas, *XV* (*June, 1954*), *339–47;* "*American Intellectual History: A Critical Appraisal,*" American Quarterly, XIII (*Summer Supplement, 1961*), *219–33. See also Higham, "The Rise of American Intellectual History,*" American Historical Review, *LVI* (*April, 1951*), *453–71.*

lectual significance or the aesthetic value of the ideas they deal with. Because popular attitudes are less systematic or less interesting than major philosophical concepts, both arguments suggest, they are worthy of examination only in terms of anthropology or of social psychology.

At the same time, proponents of the study of American popular thought themselves bear a major responsibility for the present tendency to assign their discipline to one of the behavioral sciences. As Higham has pointed out, American intellectual history developed very largely out of the New History, which was characterized by biases in favor of the common man, social reform, and the pragmatic nature of ideas. The discipline that resulted could hardly have been anything but descriptive, eclectic, and social-scientific: ideas were visualized as levers for social change, and their internal structure and philosophical significance meant far less than their social context and instrumental importance. Therefore historians of popular thought in the United States have tacitly accepted the inferior status that philosophical historians of ideas ascribe to common beliefs, although they have not conceded that popular ideas were historically insignificant.[6]

In short, the most basic tendencies of American intellectual history have been divisive and even destructive of the discipline. Nevertheless, in recent years scholars in American Studies have developed a mode of analysis that seems to offer new hope of reconciling, even of synthesizing, these disparate approaches to the history of ideas. This is the method of symbolic analysis, which focuses on intellectual configurations that apparently enlisted emotional as well as intellectual loyalty. Instead of reducing historic beliefs to their cognitive elements by a process of philosophical dissection, proponents of this approach have sought to examine complexes of thought and emotion. Yet they have also treated them as ideas, in that they have neither reduced them to by-products of historic events nor submerged them in the spirit of their age. Rather, they have sought to identify both the separate elements and the broader reach of such American themes as the belief in a bountiful West, the idea of the savage

---

[6] *One of the most striking instances of the way in which historians of popular thought have accepted an inferior role is the work of R. Richard Wohl. Distinguishing between "aristocratic" and "plebeian" intellectual history, Wohl insisted that the historians of plebeian thought had made egregious blunders in interpreting their raw materials and challenged them to limit both their questions and their methods of analysis to the approaches that the behavioral sciences had developed. Meanwhile he thought that "aristocratic" historians of ideas (that is, historians of "aristocratic" ideas) might continue to pursue their time-honored craft.*

Wohl's untimely death cut short his attempts to apply the behavioral sciences to the study of popular thought, but perhaps Thomas C. Cochran's study of the attitudes of business leaders indicates the direction it would have taken. That study is a meticulously objective account of what leading railroad men wrote each other on a variety of topics that are interesting to students of entrepreneurial history, and it has the defects of its virtues. Employing the techniques of content analysis, it pursues the ideas businessmen expressed as if they were discrete units of opinion without either structure or intellectual context, and it concludes that they tended to reflect and even to rationalize immediate pragmatic decisions. Undoubtedly the conclusion is warranted by the evidence and valid so far as it goes, but its ultimate effect is to suggest that alternative techniques of analysis must be followed if we are to understand ideas as components of thought.*

On these points see R. Richard Wohl, "Intellectual History: An Historian's View," The Historian, XVI (Autumn, 1953), 62–77, and "The 'Rags to Riches Story': An Episode of Secular Idealism," in Reinhard Bendix and Seymour Lipset, eds., Class, Status and Power: A Reader in Social Stratification (Glencoe, 1953), 388–95; Thomas C. Cochran, Railroad Leaders, 1845–1890: The Business Mind in Action (Cambridge, 1953).

Indian, the myth of the American Adam, and the charismatic appeal of Andrew Jackson.[7] Both in their choice of subject matter and in their method of handling it they have done much to extend the scope of intellectual history.

At the same time, symbolic analysis of this sort has failed to convince a good many experienced historians of its relevance to their discipline. Nor is this fact an indictment merely of their professional conservatism, for in most respects the examination of symbolic materials has not solved so much as restated methodological problems that affect other approaches to historic ideas.

In the first place, the proponents of symbolic analysis tend to seek out essentially literary themes even when they apply it to works that were not primarily imaginative. In part, their literary preoccupations may be attributed to the fact that the symbolic approach to ideas derives very largely from literary criticism. Hence it seems likely that those who employ it will broaden the scope of their inquiries as they continue to examine historic materials. But their preoccupations also represent an all but inescapable corollary of the attempt to use symbols as the raw materials of historical study. By definition, a symbol is ambiguous and multidimensional; indeed, its virtues lie in its richness of meaning. Hence ideas or concepts that have proved congenial to the literary imagination in the past because of their richness of meaning can be expected to attract a disproportionate atten-

tion from scholars who seek to study symbolic expression. More simply, those who focus their attention on symbols will always be tempted to govern their inquiries by aesthetic rather than historic criteria.[8]

Be it noted that this is a methodological rather than a substantive criticism, albeit one grounded in reflections on current work in American Studies. Clearly, there can be no objection to recognizing and analyzing concepts like the myth of the garden, the ideas of savagism and civilization, or the Paradox of the Fortunate Fall when they seem to have occupied an important place in our thought. But literary ideas hardly constitute the only elements of belief a people shared, and they may even have been conventions that disguised rather than manifested more basic convictions.[9] At the very least their importance must be

---

[7] *These themes are treated in Henry Nash Smith,* Virgin Land: The American West as Symbol and Myth *(Cambridge, 1950); Roy H. Pearce,* The Savages of America: A Study of the Indian and the Idea of Civilization *(Baltimore, 1953); R. W. B. Lewis,* The American Adam: Innocence, Tragedy, and Tradition in the Nineteenth Century *(Chicago, 1955); Charles Sanford,* The Quest for Paradise: Europe and the American Moral Imagination *(Urbana, 1961); John William Ward,* Andrew Jackson: Symbol for an Age *(New York, 1955).*

[8] *It seems likely that they will also be tempted to trace themes that are universal in the literature of Western Europe, if only because established literary models were powerful in American literature and can serve as a comparative basis for detailed examination of American expression. Certainly the major studies undertaken to date seem to reflect this tendency; of those listed only Ward's study pursues an indigenous American phenomenon.*

I trust it is clear that in criticizing the symbolic approach to historic documents I do not intend to deny that all thought and expression are symbolic. What is at issue here is the syllogism that runs: (1) All thought is symbolic; (2) Literature is preeminently a symbolic medium; (3) Therefore, literary symbols are our most promising vehicle for the historic understanding of American thought.

[9] *In an ingenious article, Bernard Bowron, Leo Marx, and Arnold Rose have argued that recurrent literary metaphors may well reveal covert or unarticulated attitudes in a society. While their essay suggests a novel way of using literary documents as historical evidence, it is by definition limited to identifying and analyzing only a handful of the ideas that characterized a culture. See "Literature and Covert Culture,"* American Quarterly, *IX (Winter, 1957), 377–86.*

established, not simply assumed, if we are to treat them as significant historic phenomena. Therefore, unless we can develop a way of fitting the symbolic study of documents to other kinds of inquiry, it is likely to remain almost as limited in its relevance as the purely philosophical approach it seeks to replace.

Pursued simply on the basis described, the study of literary symbols would remain a frankly internal method of analysis, enriched but not greatly altered by its interest in the affective aspects of ideas. However, its proponents have suggested that in analyzing complexes of thought and emotion they also illuminate a causal relationship between ideas and events. Drawing in various degrees and in various ways on the New Criticism, psychoanalytic theory, the study of myth, and cultural anthropology, they argue that pervasive symbolic expressions represent the ways in which any people confronts its experience; hence historic American symbols indicate how the American people understood themselves and organized their lives. By this means such writers move from a scholarly interest in ideas that were tinged with emotion to an assertion, implicit when not explicit, that the ideas they are interested in influenced historic developments.[10]

10 *This assertion is implicit and tentative in* Virgin Land; *it becomes increasingly explicit, not only in* The Savages of America *and* The American Adam, *but also in critical essays written by their authors. See R. W. B. Lewis, "Spectroscope for Ideas,"* Kenyon Review, *XVI (Spring, 1954), 313–22, and three essays by Pearce: "A Note on Method in the History of Ideas,"* Journal of the History of Ideas, *IX (June, 1948), 372–79; "The American Adam* and the *State of American Studies,"* Journal of Higher Education, *XXVII (Feb. 1956), 104–06; and "American Studies as a Discipline,"* College English, *XVIII (Jan., 1957), 179–86. Of the works that I am especially concerned with here,* Andrew Jackson: Symbol for an Age *is least, and* The

The ideas they study may well have influenced history; except for the doubts that their literary orientation raises, the possibility is not at issue here. But there is grave difficulty in the fact that analysis undertaken on these general suppositions tends to pass over the crucial question of how any given idea was related to events. The proposition that symbolic constructs can be influential offers no real warrant, either for asserting that a specific symbol was influential or for attributing specific consequences to its presence. Indeed, there is a good deal of hortatory speculation at the bottom of most of these studies, which tend to adopt the vocabulary but not the methodological precision of the behavioral sciences. They have suggested a number of possibilities for investigation, but not developed a mode of analysis that will persuade readers who are not already predisposed to accept their conclusions.

Finally, scholars who favor symbolic analysis may overcome their predilection for literary subject matter and close the other gaps in their method by developing a more scientific grasp of the emotional significance of symbolic material. In doing so, however, they are likely to find themselves in the anomalous position of adopting working assumptions that support a narrow definition of the history of ideas. Refinements borrowed from the behavioral sciences may well extend the scope of literary analysis, but they will also reinforce rather than challenge the assumption, implicit in so many works of intellectual history, that ideas are best understood in terms external to them. At best, a behavioral approach to symbolic materials is likely to treat the intellectual content of those materials as a secondary phenomenon; at worst, it may be expected to reduce intellectual

Quest for Paradise *most, inclined to attribute influence to its symbol.*

history to a history of affects.[11] In either case it will tend unnecessarily to restrict our conception of the role ideas may have played in our history.

These observations bear with particular force upon the psychoanalytic approach to historic documents, which has long attracted the interest of literary critics and which begins to attract the interest of historians. By definition, psychoanalytic theory supports the belief that expressed ideas were overt manifestations of subconscious emotional processes. But this means that the historian who employs it in the study of ideas must begin by seeking to comprehend those ideas in terms of a reality that was external to them, equating their content with their emotional functions and their emotional functions with their emotional origins. No more than economic determinism is emotional determinism likely to direct his attention to ideas as ideas once he has used it to explain their origins.

This is not to say that every attempt to employ psychoanalytic categories in historical research is useless; the work Stanley Elkins has begun on the social psychology of slavery indicates its value.[12]

But it does suggest that the psychoanalytic apparatus may be more useful in understanding events than in examining ideas. Not only does it threaten to introduce the genetic fallacy into the study of ideas; it also establishes the subconscious rather than consciousness as the focus of historical inquiry, and this is a contradiction in terms. Whereas the historian who undertakes to explain a train of events may well visualize it in terms of emotional projections or emotional compensations, the historian who is interested in establishing the place an idea occupied or the role it played cannot be satisfied with evaluating its subconscious significance. The difficulty with psychoanalytic theory, so far as intellectual history is concerned, is not that it is implausible but that it is non-intellectual.

In short, neither the literary nor the psychoanalytic approach to the history of ideas solves problems that are inherent in the traditional methodological distinction between the internal and the external analysis of ideas. Yet no one would deny the significance of what various scholars have achieved even when handicapped by unresolved methodological difficulties; they are nearer to understanding the history of American thought than they were ten or twenty years ago. What is needed now is a mode of analysis that will overcome problems that have weakened even the best work in the field by assigning all that has already been accomplished places in a conceptual scheme less biased and less restrictive than any of the schemes that have been used thus far. The remainder of this essay is devoted to sketching such a conceptual framework. Little that it says may seem new, while much may seem superfluous, but it seeks to state and in some degree

[11] *Richard E. Sykes points up the dangers of confusing the affective with the intellectual content and significance of ideas in "American Studies and the Concept of Culture: A Theory and Method,"* American Quarterly, *XV (Summer Supplement, 1963), 253–70. However, he goes on to argue that the historic study of culture is an adequate objective in its own right, and that the historian neither can nor should make himself responsible for stating how the society which shared a culture actually functioned. Plausible as his contention is when seen in the framework of modern logical theory, it surrenders the traditional objectives of the intellectual historian too easily. In effect, Sykes would escape from the difficulties that beset any attempt to understand ideas in relationship to other phenomena by denying that the historian should seek to establish their larger context. His reflections eventuate in an appeal for the content analysis of symbolic materials.*

[12] *Elkins,* Slavery: A Problem in American Institutional and Intellectual Life *(Chicago, 1959).*

to explicate a series of methodological assumptions that will serve to draw together most of the conflicting strains of American intellectual history. The author hopes to show thereby how we may make use of both pristine and popular thought, both internal and external analysis, in the historical treatment of ideas.

The first of these assumptions has already become apparent in the foregoing criticisms of recent tendencies in the field: intellectual history must begin with the study of ideas understood in intellectual terms. Even if a scholar suspects that a belief he is interested in reflected ulterior motives or combined emotional and cognitive elements, the only way he can identify its sources or gauge its emotional significance is to establish its intellectual content. More generally, ideas are the necessary starting point and subject matter of his inquiry, and he cannot hope to deal with them adequately unless he recognizes that fact.

Second, ideas are interesting because they were held by men in groups.[13] It may be assumed that the people who lived in a given society shared certain intellectual dispositions, also that in some respects they differed among themselves in their attitudes toward their common experience. Historians will normally choose particular groups or certain kinds of attitudes for analysis, but the general concept of shared attitudes is worth articulating because it provides equally for a study of the spirit of an age and for a study of ideas that were held by some but not all members of a society. It also leaves room for the possibility that different social groups may have held different attitudes toward identical historic phenomena, and it calls attention to the fact that while the number and importance of the individuals who held an idea may be irrelevant to its philosophical standing they are directly relevant to the significance it may have had in a given historic situation.

Third, ideas are promising subjects of historical analysis because they represent the intellectual devices by means of which a social group dealt with the events it experienced. The proposition is tautological in that "intellectual devices" and "ideas" are virtually synonymous; but it has the merit of stressing the fact that although the historian must begin by examining ideas as ideas, he is interested in them because he believes that men used them. A scholar may profitably spend a lifetime in tracing the successive appearances of a given idea or cluster of ideas without explicitly asking how its presence affected the ways in which those who shared it acted in the world. Yet the very step of making the inquiry would seem to imply that the idea was important beyond itself, and (for that matter) it is difficult to justify the study of ideas as a branch of historical study unless some external significance is attached to its objects. Granted that not every historian of ideas can find time and means to pursue them in terms of their practical significance, the discipline as a whole requires a way of viewing its subject matter that will carry investigation beyond even the most exacting analysis of opinions or beliefs. The concept of intellectual devices hardly solves the problems of research, but it should help to make them more apparent.[14]

---

13 *It is not necessary to settle the difficult question of what properly constitutes a group in order to appreciate the general relevance of this proposition. Nevertheless, it may be worth noting that the proposition makes room equally for the group defined as a body of men with identical "objective" interests and for the group defined in terms of shared attitudes. This dual possibility might spare us the pressure intellectual historians sometimes feel to equate the attitudes they study with "objective" considerations like economic interest.*

14 *Talcott Parsons has commented on both the promise and the difficulties of this kind of enterprise in "The Role of Ideas in Social Action,"* Essays in Sociological Theory Pure and Applied *(Glencoe, 1949), 151–65.*

Nevertheless, the assertion that ideas should be visualized as practical devices cannot be permitted to reduce them to mere adjuncts of politics or economics, as some historians have supposed. There is no good reason for denying that ideas seem to arise in particular socio-economic contexts or that they often serve particular interests, although it is more difficult to demonstrate these connections than many writers have believed.[15] But one must also bear in mind the likelihood that, whatever their origins, ideas played an autonomous part in defining the terms in which groups conceived their experience. Even the historian who assumes that ideas always reflect the interests and motives of those who share them must still discover which ideas his group possessed or employed. Once he recognizes the fact that a group did not employ every idea that might conceivably have served their purposes, not to mention the possibility that some of the ideas they did employ may have served them badly, he is on the verge of admitting that the ideas they employed were significant historic phenomena in their own right.[16] The fourth proposition comes down to an assertion that in examining ideas as intellectual devices one cannot afford to treat them simply as reflections of the circumstances in which they flourished.

Fifth, the historic significance of any given idea must be treated as a question to be explored during the course of the attempt to study it in its historic context. No formula that automatically assigns ideas "influence" in history, no research that restricts itself to concepts that were so fundamental that they *must* have been influential, can suffice for this purpose. Instead, the historian of ideas must trace the consequences that followed from the use of certain ideas as carefully as the political or economic historian traces the consequences of the events in which he is interested. The methodological difficulties that this proposition entails are immense; they can be solved only by developing techniques of analysis that parallel (not simply imitate) the techniques employed by more traditional historians. But the responsibility must be accepted if the intellectual historian is to achieve results that are as persuasive in their way as the results that other types of historians have achieved.[17]

Sixth, the historical analysis of ideas should proceed by substantially the same methods whether the historian devotes himself to popular thought or to fundamental philosophical concepts. True, philosophical and literary works of great merit are more likely than lesser writings to reward intensive internal investigation, while lesser writings may be expected to suffer from intellectual obscurities that invite external explanation. But the attempt to understand ideas as intellectual devices requires that documentary materials of all kinds be understood so far as possible in the same terms. The fact that men or women of great intelligence and perception saw the world in a complex and sophisticated way, whereas persons of lesser stature saw it less complexly, may be highly significant;

[15] *On this point, see especially Robert K. Merton, "The Sociology of Knowledge," Social Theory and Social Structure (Glencoe, 1957), 457–88.*

[16] *By the same token, the scholar who derives the ideas of a group or a generation from its predecessors has not exhausted his responsibilities as historian. If a generation adopted less than the whole range of ideas on which it might have drawn, it thereby committed itself to a distinct way of viewing its experience—hence to one that may be assumed to have had distinct consequences, whether broad or narrow.*

[17] *I trust it is clear that I do not claim to have solved the difficult methodological problems that confront any attempt to employ this general proposition in actual research. Rather, I think that we must restate our working assumptions in very general terms before we can decide what techniques of research are appropriate.*

it does not indicate that the ideas laymen used to organize their experience can be understood in terms peculiar to them as laymen. Nor does it indicate that popular ideas can be dealt with by measuring their irrational or emotional components instead of their intellectual content. Unless the historian studies popular ideas in the same terms that he employs in studying sophisticated concepts he cannot even attempt to judge whether they were simple or complex, nor what their irrational or affective components may have been.

Recognition of this fact has apparently led some historians to contemplate investigating the dissemination of major intellectual concepts. But while study of the dissemination of pristine ideas represents an important aspect of intellectual history, it cannot take the place of the study of popular ideas themselves. It may be true that ordinary men think with ideas that have trickled down to them from above; it does not follow that they think only with ideas that have passed down in terms that may be understood by appreciating their philosophical origins. The seventh proposition is an extension and an epitome of all the rest: if the concept of intellectual devices holds any promise it is because it recommends the analysis of historically significant ideas wherever they appeared and whatever form they took.

To a considerable extent, the approach that is proposed here deprecates the psychologically oriented analysis of ideas. In this sense it may be said to defend intellectual history from some of its enthusiasts—not by denying the relevance of emotions to historiography, nor by refusing to examine documents for their affective overtones, but by insisting that ideas as well as emotions have played a part in history, and that the historian of ideas must examine the intellectual content of any attitudes he deals with. Nevertheless, one branch of psychology may both help to clarify and help to validate what is suggested here. At least it seems

appropriate to suggest ways in which certain theoretical formulations may make us more sure-footed in our explorations without forcing us to substitute psychological for historical analysis of ideas.

These theoretical formulations are to be found in the transactional psychology that first came to prominence at the turn of the century, and they may best be understood by reference to the writings of John Dewey. Although Dewey's theories of human conduct have not significantly influenced research in psychology, his basic conceptions still stand as our most comprehensive model for understanding human thought as thought rather than as a datum of psychological behaviorism or of depth psychology. Once scholars have recognized the possibilities his psychology holds as a model for the study of intellectual history they should be able to adjust it to the demands of their discipline.

There are two major statements of Dewey's psychology that answer to the historian's needs. The first is his paper "The Reflex Arc Concept in Psychology," which appeared in the *Psychological Review* in 1896. Here Dewey praised contemporary experimental psychologists for criticizing the fallacies of the introspectionist school of mental philosophy, but he also took them to task for adhering to the traditional philosophical dualism between sensation and idea in postulating that human actions consist of muscular "responses" to sensory "stimuli" mediated through the mind. Instead he insisted that stimulus, idea, and response—the three categories into which experimental psychologists divided human activity—obscured the "fundamental psychic unity" of experience. For example, a muscular "response" to some sort of visual "stimulus" in the environment depends in the first instance on a positive act of seeing. At the same time, that response will also be controlled by a continuous activity of seeing, which will in turn be purposive and therefore selective. Meanwhile the whole operation of seeing-and-responding will be informed by previous experience gained through previous "responses" to comparable "stimuli." In short, he held there *is* no reflex arc, but a continuous and even circular process of experiencing and augmenting experience.[18]

In this early paper Dewey's sole target was the philosophical assumptions made by a school of psychologists who were in the process of converting study of the psyche from a philosophical to a laboratory enterprise. Thirty-four years later Dewey showed that the same concept of psychic unity might also serve to limit the claims of depth psychology, which had already become a prominent competitor for public attention. In "Conduct and Experience" he reiterated his criticisms of experimental psychology, now fully committed to behaviorism, for neglecting the role individual activity plays in shaping experience; but he went on to suggest that, in reasserting the psychic role of the individual, introspective psychologists had also repeated the traditional philosophical mistake of assigning "experience" entirely to the individual psyche. Rather, he said, behaviorists and introspectionists alike must keep constantly in mind that they are working with a series of actions that takes place in a changing environment. If there is no "stimulus" as such and no "response" as such there is also no "experience" as such; each function is part of a continuous conscious activity that is constantly changing in content.[19]

One need not accept Dewey's strictures on either behavioral or introspective psychology in order to appreciate the uses his theory may have for the intellectual historian. However inadequate it may be in explaining the full range of mental phenomena, it provides a model for the study of ideas that does not deprive them of their intellectual content. On the one hand, it accepts the assumption, compatible with behavioral psychology, that external events influenced human thought; but it rejects the belief that we can understand that thought simply by understanding the events. On the other hand, it accepts the assumption, compatible with introspective psychology, that human beings "thought" with their emotions; but it rejects the belief that we can understand what they thought simply as a manifestation of internal emotional experience.[20]

At the same time, the model also suggests a middle way between those who would study intellectual phenomena in virtual isolation from

bility for being "scientific" in Dewey's sense, historians of ideas may well ponder the question whether in dealing with ideas they have not been satisfied with identifying subject matter rather than understanding it.

20 *In* Human Nature and Conduct (*New York, 1922*), *33–34, 86–87, Dewey explicitly criticizes psychoanalytic theory for its introspective character.*

I have used Dewey's analysis as my model because it poses the key issues so economically. However, other writers have developed essentially psychological formulations that serve both to extend and to strengthen Dewey's argument.

For brief accounts of these theories, see Anselm Strauss, ed., The Social Psychology of George Herbert Mead (*Chicago, 1956*); *David Krech and Richard S. Crutchfield,* Theory and Problems of Social Psychology (*New York, 1948*); *Ernst Cassirer,* The Myth of the State (*New Haven, 1946*), *3–49; Cassirer,* An Essay on Man: An Introduction to a Philosophy of Human Culture (*New Haven, 1962*); *Kenneth E. Boulding,* The Image: Knowledge in Life and Society (*Ann Arbor, 1956*).

18 *Dewey, "The Reflex Arc Concept in Psychology,"* Psychological Review, *III (July, 1896), 357–70.*

19 *Dewey, "Conduct and Experience," in Carl Murchison, ed.,* Psychologies of 1930 (*Worcester, 1930*), *409–22. Dewey also laid stress on the proposition that while introspection may serve to identify the subject matter of psychology it cannot provide us with a scientific understanding of the phenomena it identifies. Even without accepting a responsi-*

their surroundings and those who would study them as if they were little more than byproducts of the life process. More simply, it mediates between internal and external methods of analysis. If ideas are important in history, the model suggests, it is because men held them and put them to use; if intellectual history has meaning, it is because men acted in the light of their thoughts as well as their interests or their emotions. Recognizing both the pressure of events and the pressure of emotions on the actions of mankind, the historian of ideas may yet devote his main efforts to understanding the ways in which intellectual habits and intellectual inventions shaped historic developments by setting the terms in which groups or generations of men conducted their lives.

In short, the model offers a way of overcoming the cleavage between the history of ideas and intellectual history, as these two fields of scholarship have come to be distinguished from each other, by inviting us to study the history of intelligences. Whether or not we use the term is unimportant so long as we recognize the scholarly purpose it identifies. Nor can we stop with using the term; it will still be incumbent on us to develop detailed methods of analysis and methods of proof that will carry conviction outside the ranks of intellectual historians. But redefining our responsibilities in these terms may enable us to attempt a coherent understanding of our intellectual history, whereas defining them in other terms has not.

At the very least, the conceptual scheme sketched here seems to address itself to many of the problems this essay has discussed. In the first place, it dispenses with the presumption that only fundamental or universal ideas are important to historians. Instead, it suggests that the importance of any given idea is a matter for examination in the transactions of its time. More than this, the concept either of intellectual devices or of intelligences should permit us to recognize popular thought and philosophical doctrine, rational judgments and irrational attitudes, time-honored stereotypes and intellectual innovations, wisdom and folly, as equally the subject matter of intellectual history.

Again, the scheme suggests that if we focus our attention on ideas in use we may be able to free ourselves from the debilitating effects of the distinction that has arisen between internal and external analysis of ideas. Furthermore, working in terms either of intellectual devices or intelligences, we should be able to avoid the fallacy of assuming that when an idea has been traced to its origins it has been understood as an historic phenomenon, for we may be reminded that what a generation thought was far more important in determining the way they dealt with events than whence they had derived it. Reorienting our efforts is likely to involve us in immense problems or research, but at least we have reason to hope that if we can solve them our results will be significant.

Finally, the scheme points to a single general method for examining any sort of idea in its historic setting, one which assigns meaning to the whole range of special techniques of analysis that historians have employed in dealing with ideas but does not permit any of them to monopolize our attention. In all these respects it may help to resolve the dilemmas that presently affect the history of ideas in America.

INTELLECTUAL HISTORY AND ITS NEIGHBORS

*John Higham**

The writing of intellectual history has been the work of many hands, and we have come to do it from all the points of the academic compass. Philosophers, literary scholars, historians and others have converged upon one another, bringing their various interests, backgrounds and methods to a common task for which they were not initially trained. It is, then, an interdisciplinary enterprise on which they have entered, and intellectual history exhibits the marks of any such enterprise in our day: the blessings of effervescence and the curse of confusion. Along with an exhilarating sense of pioneering and the joy of smashing through conventional walls come the perplexities of understanding just what is going on.

In studying intellectual history, as in conducting a foreign policy, one may adopt a variation on one of three attitudes. The expansionist point of view, extending over new terrain the claims of the academic homeland, may breed a good deal of jostling and rivalry as representatives of established disciplines claim competing spheres of influence over intellectual history. Isolationists may venture abroad without realizing that they have done so—and pursue their separate ways through the tumult while steadfastly ignoring it. Proponents of collective security may inspire one another and borrow from one another, sometimes to the extent of entering into formally cooperative arrangements as in the American Studies programs. The dangers of academic isolation or expansion are evident enough. Those of cooperation should not get out of sight. In trying to fuse insights and procedures derived from unlike disciplines, intellectual historians may lose a sense of direction; they may exchange customary means

*JOHN HIGHAM (1920–   ) is the Tyler University Professor at the University of Michigan. His publications include "The Rise of American Intellectual History" (1951), "Beyond Consensus: the Historian as Moral Critic" (1962), The Reconstruction of American History (1962), and History (1965). Reprinted by permission of the author and the Journal of the History of Ideas, Vol. 15, No. 3 (June, 1965), 599–614.

of analysis for formulas of the lowest common denominator which answer all questions and clarify none. At the risk of imposing my own kind of imperialism on intellectual history I want to suggest that until it assumes another name or character it forms a branch of history. Whatever else it involves, it deserves from students of every academic persuasion a central allegiance to the aims and methods of historical study. I propose, at any rate, to appraise the dimensions of intellectual history and its relations to other disciplines from the vantage-point of its historical foundations.

I assume that history characteristically reports particular and unique human experiences in an attempt to elucidate their connections through time. Above all the historian wants to know why a sequence of happenings took place as it did. To find out, he links those specific experiences one to the other with the aid of appropriate generalizations. He does not, like the scientist, move away from particulars toward a system of general, verifiable concepts; nor does he, like the artist, move into particulars to disclose the values inherent in them. The historian moves between particular experiences to learn how one begot another. But to establish these relationships he employs both the values of the artist and the inclusive propositions of the scientist; in his hands tested constructs and untestable values become functional to a narrative task.

Intellectual history differs from other varieties simply because it has a distinctive subject-matter. It concentrates on experiences occurring inside men's heads. It centers on man's inner experiences, the experiences which he has in thinking. Many other disciplines, of course, share an interest in man as a thinking being, but they concern themselves either with one kind of thinking or with thinking in general. Intellectual history is unlimited in scope, but it should respect the historian's method. It deals with all sorts of thoughts but deals with them discretely, in terms of their genetic relations in time and place.

The historian's concern with ideas in all their specific variety compels a close and precise attention to the documents which reveal them; and this practical condition in turn has often encouraged misunderstanding of the permissible range of intellectual history. Partly because the most discriminating and readily available documents are produced by highly articulate people, intellectual historians have tended to write mostly about the thoughts which circulate among intellectuals. Meanwhile a substantial, perhaps a preponderant part of the academic world relegates to social history the study of the moods and beliefs of the man in the street, reserving for intellectual history the study of high-level ideas.[1] To define the field in this limited sense is to miss much of its complexity and significance. At least by construing it narrowly we run the risk of pre-judging its affiliations and character. Intellectual history may (though it need not in any single instance) embrace simple attitudes in simple or complicated people as well as systematic knowledge and speculation. It includes Little Orphan Annie as well as Adam Smith. I am not of course proposing our absorption in men's trivial reactions to the passing scene. History is selective; it looks for the bolder contours on the landscape of the past. In examining the mental landscape the intellectual historian selects the relatively enduring ideas which sway a considerable number of people over a period of some time; but he may select them from the comics as well as from the philosophers.

[1] *Evidence of the vogue of this distinction among professional historians is in T. C. Cochran, "A Decade of American Histories,"* Pennsylvania Magazine of History and Biography, *73 (1949), 154–55; W. T. Hutchinson in* American Historical Review, *58 (1952), 126.*

Whether he deals in popular myths or in metaphysics, the intellectual historian must perform the historian's task of relating the particular inner happenings which interest him to a context of other happenings which explain them. Here a quest for definition grows more difficult. What kind of other happenings? What type of context? Where should the connective generalizations serviceable to intellectual history lead? These questions have given rise to two rather distinct answers which amount almost to two different conceptions of the discipline. In one view the connections lead outward to an external context of events and behavior. Intellectual history becomes an investigation of the connections between thought and deed. Crane Brinton expressed a version of this approach in emphasizing as intellectual history's primary task the uncovering of relations between what a few men write or say and what many men actually do.[2] On the other hand a second school has insisted principally on establishing the internal relationships between what some men write or say and what other men write or say. This kind of intellectual history directs attention away from the context of events in order to enlarge and systematize the context of ideas. It seeks the connections between thought and thought.

The distinction between an internal and an external history of thinking is, I believe, widely appreciated, although the proponents of each have seldom ventured into explicit controversy beyond an appeal for emphasis.[3] Having had little debate,

we have only begun to assess the respective ramifications and consequences of each approach. Yet such assessment must precede an adequate understanding of the nature of intellectual history and its place in the spectrum of knowledge, for the two approaches contain their own underlying assumptions, lead to different disciplinary affiliations, and suggest contrasting objectives.

Hardly anyone today would argue the total wrong-headedness of either the internal or the external view of intellectual history. Indeed many scholars seem increasingly concerned with combining the two. The difficulties involved in any real merging of them, however, are far more than technical. At bottom each approach expresses a fundamental philosophical commitment. Often accepted implicitly, one commitment or the other directs scholarship more than scholars realize. They may refuse a categorical choice; they may work under the tensions of a divided allegiance. But they can hardly serve two masters with equal loyalty. The issue lies between two ways of conceiving the human mind; and entangled in each is a divergent view of human nature.

A primary interest in the outward links between thought and deed presupposes the notion that mind at its best or most characteristic is functional. Mind makes its mark by serving the practical needs of the workaday world. The relations between thinking and the concrete circumstances of life acquire importance in the light of the functionalist's respect for the utility of the mind as an instrument of survival. At the same time a functional orientation supplies a rough yardstick for measuring the historical significance of ideas. The

[2] *Crane Brinton*, Ideas & Men: The Story of Western Thought (*New York, 1950*), 7.

[3] *Merle Curti's* The Growth of American Thought (*New York, 1942*) *brought the distinction I am making clearly into view; see p. vi. Arthur O. Lovejoy has ably defended his own internal approach in* "Reflections on the History of Ideas," *this* Journal, *I (1940), 3–23. I have also*

profited from the attack on this position in Bert J. Loewenberg, The History of Ideas: 1935–1945; Retrospect and Prospect (*New York, 1947*), 13–18. *And I am especially indebted to the stimulus of Professor Curti's interest in this whole issue.*

test is action, and the importance of an idea approximates that of the deeds associated with it. By this criterion, for example, a persuasive propagandist like Tom Paine might loom larger in history than a frustrated genius like Henry Adams.

On the other hand the internal approach to intellectual history rests upon quite different assumptions. A concern with the inner affinities and structures among ideas neglects functional criteria. Instead, the historian assumes that mind at its best or most characteristic reaches beyond practical needs to create a world of values and achievements which have their own excuse for being. The mind pursues objectives somehow "higher" (or at least more noteworthy) than survival, and in place of the yardstick of action one must apply some internal standard to measure its most significant output. The logical consistency of a sequence of thought, the elaboration of a world view, the achievement of a reverberating insight, or the power of an idea to bear further intellectual fruit—these become the norms of an intellectual history pledged to the sheer creative vitality of the human mind.

Parenthetically it is worth noting that the theories of the intellectual process at issue here point toward even vaster alternatives. A view of the mind calls forth a view of human nature. If the mind creates in ways that are neither bound by nor referable to the demands of an external environment—if ideas have a life of their own—then human nature bursts and transcends the patterns of the natural world around it. If, on the other hand, mind interests us as an agent of bio-social adaptation, we tend to assimilate human nature to an encompassing system of nature.

Without venturing to cope with the whole problem of the nature of man, it is easy to see objections to either conception of the mind as a controlling principle in historiography. Functional presuppositions are chargeable with devaluing mind. By reducing thought to a series of responses

to situations, the functionalist treats it as merely auxiliary to the main business of life. He tends to neglect what his standards cannot appraise—the inner "go," the spontaneity, or the qualitative richness of mental phenomena. He can tell us little about the persistence of an intellectual heritage after the environment has grown hostile to it; still less can he account for the quite impractical ways in which the mind seems to pour forth religious and artistic symbols.[4]

The dualistic assumptions behind the internal history of thought create contrary difficulties. These assumptions tend to divorce thinking from doing and to confine it within categories that have no reference to the world of material circumstance. A separation from events forces an increased degree of subjectivity on intellectual history, since all the elements in the story are then intangibles. With the aid of publishers' records we can trace the circulation of books, but we can never with the same precision trace the circulation of ideas. We can observe the meeting of two armies and know that the destiny of an idea hangs upon their encounter, but we can never quite so clearly see the meeting of two ideas. Furthermore the notion that mind has its own distinctive and superior goals involves an intellectualistic bias. Ideas capable of the most subtle or systematic articulation become the center of attention and are endowed with special potency. Intellectual history narrows to the history of intellectuals, and among the products of thought literature and philosophy assume a privileged status. Carried far enough, the same bias leads to a sweeping assertion of the primacy of ideas in history, just as a functionalist bias ultimately debases ideas into passive echoes of events.

If no student of ideas can escape some preference for one or the other of these two positions, surely

[4] S. K. Langer, Philosophy in a New Key (*New York, 1948*), *24–33.*

all can profit from the fullest understanding of the possibilities as well as the limitations inherent in each. For such understanding the professional historian has a strategic location. His discipline lies between and to some extent bridges the gulf separating the humanities from the social sciences. Now the intellectualism of the internal approach appears most typically and completely in humanistic scholarship, while the functionalism of the external view is characteristic of the social sciences. The distinction certainly is not sharp nor is the correspondence exact, for too many cross-currents have blown between them to permit the humanities or social sciences to follow entirely separate ways. Literary scholars like Vernon L. Parrington, deriving stimulus from social scientists, have weighted intellectual history with a functional emphasis, while an occasional writer on the other side of the fence—like the psychoanalyst Erich Fromm—has made fruitful use of humanistic insights.[5] Still, in their main thrust the humanities and social sciences have diverged.[6] The former look toward the qualitative exploration of an inner world of values and imagination. The latter, seeking quantitative measurements of human phenomena, tend to objectify ideas and values into forms of behavior. And the internal study of intellectual history has developed particularly within the value-oriented humanities, just as the external history of thinking has benefited especially from the behavioral emphasis of the social sciences. Perhaps historians—without final allegiance to either domain—can see further into the oppor-

tunities of intellectual history by learning from the example of each.

Among the branches of history the intellectual one lies closest to the humanities and has received the most encouragement from them. (On the other hand, economic history with its wealth of measurable data has probably felt the impact of the social sciences more than any other branch, while having the least contact with the humanities.) Certainly the humanities have influenced the writing of intellectual history far more directly than have the social sciences. Perhaps the most central contribution has come from philosophy, which is the critic of abstractions. In its rôle as one of the humanities, philosophy seeks to harmonize and clarify the most basic and general propositions involved in value judgments. It is hard to see how an internal analysis of thought can proceed without some philosophical training. From it we receive skill in definition, in discriminating meanings, in detecting assumptions, in formulating issues. These abilities come into constant play in intellectual history because the factual units with which it principally deals are not events which we can observe directly but rather ideas and sentiments which we must define in order to know. An internal history of the connections between ideas obviously calls for especially close philosophical scrutiny. A few philosophers such as Arthur O. Lovejoy have made important advances in the writing of intellectual history by demonstrating ways of grasping the underlying unities which run through many diverse provinces of thought. Other philosophers have worked in the history of philosophy, which differs from intellectual history by interesting itself more in the logical implications of doctrines than in their genetic relationships. By and large the philosophers' overriding interest in abstractions has kept them from contributing as much in substance as in method. Relatively few philosophical scholars do justice to history's concrete particularity. It is significant

[5] *Vernon L. Parrington*, Main Currents in American Thought, *3 vols.* (*New York, 1927–30*); *Erich Fromm,* Escape from Freedom (*New York, 1941*).

[6] *I refer to American scholarship, the divergence being much more noticeable here than in Europe, where a positivistic tradition has not had so commanding an influence over the social sciences. See E. K. Francis, "History and the Social Sciences: Some Reflections on the Re-integration of Social Science,"* Review of Politics, *XIII (1951), 354–74.*

that a philosopher's proposal to trace the history of liberal social thought in modern America should turn out instead as an analytical critique of five men.[7]

Literary scholars have more than made up for the aloofness of most philosophers. Intellectual history, written chiefly from an internal point of view, has become a leading concern in departments of literature. Relying heavily on philosophy and history, these scholars have resurrected many of the movements of thought which have supported and pervaded literary achievements. The distinctive contribution which the best students of literature make is not, I think, the analytical precision characteristic of the best philosophical inquiry. Rather it is a sense of the imaginative and emotional overtones in the history of thought. The literary scholar should have an ear sensitive to the resonances of ideas. If he has, he can communicate the passions and aspirations woven through them. He can add an internal dimension to intellectual history by capturing the fusion of thought and feeling. His studies, however, often leave historians unsatisfied by adapting intellectual history to the purposes of literary criticism. One who feels a primary obligation to sharpen aesthetic judgments will naturally employ intellectual history as a means of vivifying literary documents instead of using all documents as means of understanding why men thought and felt the way they did.

The humanities, then, tend to celebrate the finer products of mind, and in doing so they bring to a focus all of the characteristic consequences of an internal approach: a sensitivity to qualitative distinctions, an exaltation of creative thought, an appreciation of subjective criteria for judging it, a restricted sphere of interest and a limited body of materials. How different the prevailing temper in the social sciences! There an attempt to describe the uniformities in human affairs leads to an ideal of quantitative measurement. There the subjective categories appropriate to value judgments are rejected for principles derived from observations of how men behave.[8] There a respect for the molding force of social controls replaces the humanistic emphasis on creative thinkers. There scholars struggle with massive data to interpret the life of the mass of mankind. In so far as he studies ideas, therefore, the social scientist wants to learn how numbers of people put them to work within a larger pattern of living. His stress on quantity, objectivity, and behavior will lead to external analysis.

Few social scientists take much interest in the past, and fewer have contributed directly to intellectual history, though we should remember such notable exceptions as Tawney and Weber. The ideals of social science have, however, gradually filtered into the historical profession and there have exerted a somewhat roundabout influence on intellectual studies. Although each of the social disciplines deserves separate appraisal, I want simply to mention three general ways in which we can profit from more direct contact with them.

First, the social sciences may yet teach us something about how to count. Certainly statistical analyses are much more difficult with historical than with contemporary data, and the difficulty increases the further into the past one goes. Even with voluminous records we can probably never count ideas but only certain outward tokens of

---

[7] M. G. White, Social Thought in America: The Revolt Against Formalism (*New York, 1949*).

[8] *Humanists, of course, vigorously dispute the claim of many social scientists to the possession of a more objective kind of knowledge. Quite possibly the conclusions attainable in the humanities are no less objective than those reached in the social sciences, but the latter have been more insistent on developing techniques of objective analysis. The humanities must employ such subjective concepts as evil, will, etc., and do not shrink from doing so.*

intellectual life. But any advance toward mathematical precision should clearly seem desirable to those who value exact knowledge. Who knows, for example, what new light a statistical historian might cast on changing attitudes by counting the appearance of certain "loaded" words or phrases in nineteenth-century magazines?

Quantification works better for large aggregations than for small ones, and the social scientist typically deals with large ones—with crowds and classes and age groups and cultures. We need to study his procedures if we are going to fulfill the whole range of intellectual history. The internal analysis of the humanist applies chiefly to the intellectual elite; it has not reached very far into the broad field of popular thought. The blunter, external approach of the social sciences leads us closer to the collective loyalties and aspirations of the bulk of humanity.

Finally the social sciences offer us a multitude of tentative generalizations and classifications which can enrich our interpretive schemes if we use them cautiously. Very likely few principles of human affairs are exactly applicable outside of the historical epoch which conceived them, but since we bring our own notions and hunches to the past in any case, we may well find, in social science, hypotheses which discipline the historical imagination. These fields can guide us especially in formulating generalizations which connect thought and behavior, for the social sciences—in contrast to the humanities—have lavished attention on functional problems. For example, one of the shrewdest definitions of an intellectual has been provided by an economist in behavioral terms.[9]

So far I have tried to show how two types of intellectual history, each shaped by a characteristic assumption about the mind, draw aid and stimulus from the two realms of knowledge in which those

assumptions find a natural locus. But this is not an end to the matter. For all of its interdisciplinary affiliations intellectual history, like any historical enterprise, must fulfill its own objectives and move toward its own goals. Here the internal-external dichotomy presents a final face. In my view intellectual history confronts within the field of history two different tasks, each related to one of the two approaches in question. On the one hand, intellectual history needs to develop a viable degree of autonomy as a branch of history. It needs a more coherent form and structure of its own in order to escape subordination to other disciplines and a subordinate place among the fields of history. This self-fulfillment must come largely through clarification of the causal connections between ideas. It depends, therefore, principally on internal analysis.

Intellectual history has a second task exactly the reverse of autonomy: a task of synthesis. The history of thought must contribute what it can to the organization and understanding of history as a whole. In some sense all human activity has a mental component, and intellectual history is displaying increasing usefulness as an integrative tool. This synthetic objective is approachable by studying the causal linkage of ideas with political, social, and economic events. It depends ultimately on external analysis.

Now that my argument is complete I fear that I have made too much of it. In the practice of historians the line of cleavage is hardly ever absolute. Most historians take some account of both perspectives and of both objectives. Their work gains subtlety through a skillful blend, just as the two types of intellectual history advance through mutual interaction. The difference, then, is one of emphasis. But the emphasis is basic. At some point in his thinking or research each scholar must choose. He can choose with sophistication if he appreciates the values sacrificed no less than the advantages gained.

[9] *J. Schumpeter*, Capitalism, Socialism and Democracy (*New York, 1942*), 147.

John Foster "Richard Mather"   Whitney Museum of American Art

PART 2

THE AMERICAN PURITANS

Introduction

The student of the American intellectual tradition begins his search for the earliest expressions of the national mind with the religious dissenters who settled in New England during the first half of the seventeenth century. Intellectual historians have viewed the Puritans both as the forerunners of capitalism and democracy and as intolerant and authoritarian Calvinists. In spite of conflicting interpretations most scholars agree with Perry Miller and Thomas H. Johnson (*The Puritans*, 1938) that "without some understanding of Puritanism . . . there is no understanding of America."

The article by Alan Heimert discusses two of the most controversial issues in American historiography, the Puritans and the frontier. He maintains that the Puritans originally came to the New World not to subdue the wilderness but to propagate the gospel. Soon after their arrival, however, they were confronted by the magnetic force of the wilderness. By 1700 the challenge of the frontier had caused significant changes in Puritan thought and practice.

The frontier was not the only factor that threatened Puritan orthodoxy. Perry Miller skillfully describes important but almost imperceptible religious changes occurring between the first and second generations of Puritans. At the Synod of 1662 it was decided that baptized children could be members of the church even though they were unregenerate. This decision transformed Congregationalism from a religious utopia to a legalized order. According to the Congregationalists, religion was confined to inner consciousness.

Robert Middlekauff analyzes the Puritan inner consciousness as it was motivated by the duality of religious emotion, or piety, and the mind, or intellect. The ideal of emulating Christ tempered Puritan psychological responses as the thought of Cotton Mather (1663–1728) and his friend Samuel Sewall (1652–1730) illustrates.

In the last selection John E. Van de Wetering describes the impact of Newtonian science on the American Puritans. Their responses to science are explained by the writings of Thomas Prince (1687–1758) who naturalized God and placed science at the service of religion. The reconciliation of science and religion "despiritualized" God, but it paved the way for the acceptance of science and rationalism during the eighteenth century.

PURITANISM, THE WILDERNESS, AND THE FRONTIER

Alan Heimert*

The notion of subjugating an American wilderness had no place in the aspirations of the English religious dissenters who came to New England in the years after 1620. John Robinson's last letter to the Leyden emigrants charged them to preserve their ecclesiastical polity.[1] Ten years later John Cotton assured Winthrop's company of God's favor for "that which hath beene a maine meane of peopling the world, and is likely to be of propagating the Gospell."[2] But he spoke of no American wilderness; like Thomas Hooker he gathered evidence that the Lord would imminently withdraw from England.[3] Peopling the world and propagating the gospel were parts of the general Protestant purpose of carrying the fruits of the Reformation to the New World. The Massachusetts Bay group left with a more particular aim in mind, that example contained in the "city set on a hill" of Winthrop and Peter Bulkeley. But no one attached significance to their wilderness-destination, certainly nothing comparable to the animism which overcame Puritan thinking about the wilderness in the course of the century. Their concept of the American "wilderness," we must conclude, was not, as it were, carried to America on

[1] *Alexander Young, editor,* Chronicles of the Pilgrim Fathers . . . (*Boston, 1844*), *91–96. Winthrop also conceived the perfection of polity the most important goal with which to charge his companions. See his lay sermon, "A Modell of Christian Charity,"* The Winthrop Papers (*Boston, 1931*), *II, 282–295.*

[2] *John Cotton,* God's Promise to His Plantation (*1630*), *reprinted in* Old South Leaflets, *No. 53.*

[3] The Danger of Desertion . . . (*London, 1641*). See *also Robert C. Winthrop,* Life and Letters of John Winthrop (*Boston, 1864*), *I, 309 ff.*

ALAN HEIMERT (1928–   ) is a Professor of English at Harvard University. His publications include A Nation So Conceived (*1963*), *and* Religion and the American Mind, from the Great Awakening to the Revolution (*1966*). *Reprinted by permission of the author and the* New England Quarterly, *Vol. 26, No. 3 (September, 1953), 361–382.*

the *Mayflower* or the *Arbella*, but came out of that wilderness itself.

For the Puritans America was to be "the good Land," as Winthrop put it, a veritable Canaan. The Atlantic, if not the Red, was their "vast Sea," and the successful conclusion of their voyage, the end of their tribulations, their emergence from the "wilderness."[4] In justifying their removal, Cotton drew this same parallel of the Jews leaving Egypt.[5] Even if we discount the promotional aspects of *Mourt's Relation* and Higginson's *New-England's Plantation*, the inference is inescapable that these colonists were not prepared for the "thicke Wood"[6] which they found, for a country "wilde and overgrowne with woods."[7] If this were the promised land—and Winthrop could write that "here is sweet air, fair rivers, and plenty of springs, and the water better than in England"[8]—the task of building Zion proved greater than had been foreseen. Very soon Winthrop was writing of "unexpected troubles and difficulties" in "this strange land, where we have met with many troubles and adversities," until he could "discern little difference between it and our own."[9] Plagues, water shortages, famines, miserable climate, and hardships of every kind came between

the emigrants and their objectives. By 1643 Roger Williams could write of the American wilderness as a "cleere resemblance of the world; where greedie and furious men persecute and devour the harmlesse and innocent, as the wild beasts pursue and devoure the Hinds and Roes."[10] Whatever is personal to Williams in this passage, enough remains to indicate the distance travelled from the days of Winthrop's "good Land."

Out of these conditions and the various reactions to them was shaped the Puritan conception of the "West." One such response was removal from the original settlements into adjacent areas. Plymouth, "by reason of ye straightnes and ye barrennes of ye same," was, as Bradford complained, especially embarrassed by such withdrawals.[11] Adverse comment and efforts to check this movement on the part of the leadership of the Old Colony and Massachusetts Bay reflect the other (for our purposes) crucial element in New England thought. That part of the New England mind which partook of an inheritance from the Middle Ages, from Aristotle and scholasticism, held that society was an organism and not an aggregate of individuals and that the public good was to be achieved by cohesiveness and coöperation, by being "knitt together in this worke as one man." This conception, doubly significant by virtue of the special form it took in their social thought, dominated the Puritan attitude toward expansion and the frontier. Plymouth sought to hold its people together, to be sure, both for "ye better improvement of ye generall imployments" and "for more saftie and defence."[12] But to

[4] "*A Modell of Christian Charity*," Winthrop Papers, II, 295.

[5] God's Promise, 3. *As warrant for their appropriation of Indian land, the Plymouth settlers invoked the entrance of the Jews into Canaan*, "*where the land lay idle and waste, and none used it.*" Mourt's Relation . . . , *edited by H. M. Dexter (Boston, 1865), 146–148.*

[6] *Francis Higginson*, New-England's Plantation . . . (Salem, Mass., 1908), 23.

[7] Mourt's Relation, *135. The colonists were not totally oblivious to New England's discommodities. See John White,* The Planters Plea . . . , *edited by M. H. Saville (Rockport, Mass., 1930), 23–33.*

[8] *Winthrop*, Life and Letters, *II, 43.*

[9] *Winthrop*, Life and Letters, *II, 38, 43, 48, 59.*

[10] A Key into the Language of America (*London,* 1643), 107.

[11] *William Bradford*, History of Plymouth Plantation (Boston, 1856), 425.

[12] *Bradford*, History of Plymouth Plantation, *168. See also p. 316.*

Bradford the departures suggested something far more ominous. The prosperity brought with the immigration of the 1630's was as much a "hurte" as a "benefite," for, with an increase in the demand for food:

> there was no longer any holding them togeather but now they must of necessitie go to their great lots. . . . By which means they were scattered all over ye bay, quickly, and ye towne, in which they lived compactly till now, was left very thine, and if this had been all, it had been less, though to much: but ye church must also be divided, and those yt lived so long togeather in Christian and comfortable fellowship must now part and suffer many divisions.

When legislation failed to check these dispersions, Bradford feared that it meant "ye ruine of New-England, at least of ye churches of God ther, & will provock ye Lords displeasure against them."[13]

The Bay, though able to regulate such defections, was found wanting by reason of the "barrenes of the lande, and the coldness of the ayre in winter." Lord Say and Sele advised Winthrop that God had evidently intended New England as only a way-station to the true new Canaan of the West Indies.[14] But the great withdrawal was to the Connecticut valley, its most notable participants being the Cambridge flock and their leader. This the Bay leaders sought to frustrate, both with land concessions and with a number of pointed arguments. Their departure would weaken the economy and expose the settlements to Indians. "Being knit to us in one body," the group should not depart. For lastly, though by no means of least importance, "the removing of a candlestick is a great judgment, which is to be avoided."[15] We should not interpret this opposition as a mere pious façade hiding an economic reality, if indeed the two realms were thus separable at that time. As late as 1642, Winthrop was concerned by the dangers brought on by these splinterings, bewailing the number of those who sought the "liberty of removing for outward advantages." Those who "confederate together in civil and church estate," he insisted, "implicitly at least, bind themselves to support each other."[16] This was the social convenant of the Congregational way, an easy corollary of the whole federal theology. As Perry Miller has shown, the covenant was the Puritans' method of infusing static medieval conceptions with a voluntaristic note.[17] Yet the same principle which justified the break with the established church and society of England appeared through the century, reflecting, and partially causing, opposition to further separations within the ranks of American Puritanism. The words of Winthrop and Bradford indicate that, until 1640, the orthodox mind was unable to equate even tentative penetration of the interior with the purposes of the Lord.

The migration to the Connecticut valley actually represents the earliest of the great American land-manias, focusing on one of the three interior

---

[13] *Bradford,* History of Plymouth Plantation, *302–304. He thought his opinion was verified by the earthquake of 1638, which occurred just as another removal was being discussed, "as if ye Lord would herby show ye signes of his displeasure, in their shaking a peeces & removals one from another."*

[14] *Winthrop,* Life and Letters, *II, 425.*

[15] Winthrop's Journal "History of New England," 1630–1649, *edited by James K. Hosmer (New York, 1908),* I, 132–133.

[16] Winthrop's Journal "History of New England . . . ," *II, 83–84.*

[17] *In this section, as throughout the essay, I am heavily indebted to Perry Miller's* The New England Mind: The Seventeenth Century *(New York, 1939), Book III.*

Canaans[18] which so fascinated seventeenth-century New England, the only one which they were to occupy. The personal motives of Hooker and Cotton[19] cannot obscure the fact that Connecticut appeared to be the answer to a long-standing hope of the disappointed. At the very moment of landing, Bradford expected to ascend eventually some "Pisgah, to vew from the wilderness a more goodly cuntrie,"[20] and Higginson, for all his lavish promoting of the Salem region, betrayed his discomfort with its "thicke Wood" and took final refuge in a rumor that "about three miles" away "a man may stand on a little hilly place, and see divers thousands of acres of ground as good as need be."[21] The petition of Hooker's group posited both the "fruitfulness and commodiousness" of Connecticut and "the strong bent of their spirits to remove thither."[22] Similarly some men of Plymouth had a "hankering mind after it,"[23] and not much later Davenport was "much taken with the fruitfulness" of what came to be New Haven.[24] With the valley's reputation extending to the whole southwest, it is little wonder that the colonists welcomed an epidemic among the Indians that made of it the "Lords wast" and undertook a war to prove it so.

Yet, particularly for those who actually observed it, the valley proved unequal to its assigned role. Both the rascal Underhill and Thomas Mor-

ton agreed that "if you would know the garden of New England, then you must glance your eye upon the Hudson's river."[25] To the first arrivals merely one river whose "secrets" they planned to seek out, the Hudson was, to Nathaniel Morton in 1669, "a place far more commodious, and the soil more fertile" than the erstwhile Canaan of Connecticut.[26] In 1680 William Hubbard similarly belittled the Connecticut valley, remarking that the earlier generation had found that its previous "fame, peradventure, did not a little outdo its real excellency," declaring the Hudson area to be "The most fertile and desirable tract of land in all the southerly part of New England."[27]

If the Hudson valley was coveted, it was hardly a "wast" and not easy of possession; the region beyond it, however, might profitably absorb the interest of New England. Winthrop recorded his knowledge of a "great lake," where the Potomac, Connecticut, and Hudson were supposed to take their rise, the area of the great beaver trade.[28] Four decades later, Hubbard was still confused as to the precise geography but wise enough to convert a 1644 trading expedition into an attempted discovery of the "Great Lakes."[29] For in 1677 Daniel Gookin had already envisioned the western country to be what Bradford and Higginson had

[18] *Those who settled insisted, in familiar language, that it had been tendered them by Providence, "it being the Lords wast, and for ye presente altogeather voyd of inhabitants."* Bradford, History . . . , 340–341.

[19] *Isabel M. Calder, "John Cotton and the New Haven Colony,"* New England Quarterly, III (1930), 82–94.

[20] *Bradford,* History of Plymouth Plantation, 78–79.

[21] *Higginson,* New England's Plantation . . . , 23.

[22] *Winthrop,* Journal, I, 132.

[23] *Bradford,* History of Plymouth Plantation, 339.

[24] *Winthrop,* Journal, I, 265.

[25] *"Newes from America: or a New and Experimental Discoverie of New England,"* in History of the Pequot War, *edited by Charles Orr (Cleveland, 1897), 64;* The New English Canaan, *edited by C. F. Adams (Boston, 1883), 245.*

[26] *Young,* Chronicles, 256, *and William Wood,* New Englands Prospect *(1634), edited by Charles Deane (Boston, 1865), 1;* Nathaniel Morton, New England's Memorial . . . (Boston, 1855), 22.

[27] A General History of New-England, from the Discovery to MDCLXXX (Boston, 1848), 1305, 666.

[28] Journal, *I, 110.*

[29] General History, 442.

sought and what others had mistaken the Connecticut valley for. Assuming that "this place is a good climate, and probably not only very fertile, . . . but . . . otherwise furnished with furs and other desirable things," he offered a program for "a full and perfect discovery of this vast lake, or part of the sea."[30] New England's hunger was not thus satisfied until after 1800; but if the notion of a promised land to the westward was, even within the seventeenth century, increasingly divested of its Old Testament framework and the Puritan disposition to identify this earthly Canaan with the country east of the Berkshires, the attitude represented by the Connecticut mania remained in the mind of even the likes of Cotton Mather.

In these early years, the new Connecticut society differed neither ecclesiastically[31] nor in social ideals: "Many of them," wrote Brewster of the Massachusetts group which contended with Plymouth for possession of the valley, "look at that which this river will not afford, excepte it be at this place which we have, namely, to be a great towne, and have a commodious dwelling for many togeather."[32] Indeed in 1654 Edward Johnson stoutly denied any divergence, defending the New England federation. Though the valley was more open to Indian attack, "Yet are the Massachusetts far from deserting them, esteeming them highly so long as their Governments maintain the same purity in religion with themselves."[33] Though the peculiar circumstances of the exodus from Cambridge did leave a somewhat bitter

memory, Johnson could publish, as an example to the world, this identity of congregational polity and purpose, though a hundred miles apart, of the New England communities.[34] This conception of a whole people marching as one with each other, and with God, erecting myriad congregational churches throughout New England, supplies the grandeur of Johnson's *Wonder-Working Providence*, an uneven work which has nevertheless inspired one critic to laud it as "the first classical narrative of the American overland trek toward the setting sun."[35] That such could be his major theme suggests that the previous restraints on expansion could be safely relaxed as immigration strengthened the Bay, that the settlement of new towns in the "Inland country" was now a benefit and no longer jeopardized the success of the colony.[36]

But more importantly, it reflected a subtle and crucial change in the purposes of the New England venture. Even Davenport had not erected expansion into a positive virtue of such magnitude, his best offer being a tentative assertion that his New Haven colony might divert "the thoughts and intentions of such in England as intended evil against us, whose designs might be frustrate by our scatterings so far."[37] Hooker's group merely invoked a Dutch menace.[38] But now Winthrop's "city on a hill" had given way to "the service of our Lord Jesus Christ, to re-build the most glorious

the English Planting in the Yeere 1628 untill the Yeere 1652 . . . , *reprinted under its better-known running title*, The Wonder-Working Providence of Sions Saviour in New England, *edited by J. F. Jameson (New York, 1910),* 219.

[34] *Johnson,* Wonder-Working Providence, *106, 239.*

[35] *Harold S. Jantz,* The First Century of New England Verse *(Worcester, 1944), 240.*

[36] *Johnson,* Wonder-Working Providence, *111.*

[37] *Winthrop,* Journal, *I, 265.*

[38] *Winthrop,* Journal, *I, 132.*

[30] *Daniel Gookin, "Historical Collections of the Indians in New England," in* Collections of the Mass. Hist. Soc., *first series, I, 141–227, 158 (1792).*

[31] *Perry Miller, "Thomas Hooker and the Democracy of Early Connecticut," New England Quarterly, IV (1931), 663–712.*

[32] *Bradford,* History of Plymouth Plantation, *339.*

[33] *Edward Johnson,* A History of New England. From

Edifice of Mount Sion in a Wilderness."[39] If this was, in major part, a symptom of a changing European scene and the failure and disruption of international Calvinsim, the imputation of divine assistance for those who "populate this howling Desart" reflects American experience as well. The new vision was a response to the "greatest difficulties, and sorest labours"[40] which the colony had suffered, subjections which underlay the transition from Higginson's depiction of the wilderness to that of Roger Williams. In 1642 Thomas Shepard, citing the "straits, the wants, the tryalls of God's people," argued that the Lord must have indeed had a great "Worke" in mind "so as to carry out a people of his owne from so flourishing a State, to a wilderness so far distant."[41] This was a minor point in Shepard's defense of New England[42] from charges of weakhearted flight from England. Johnson's work is therefore the first full-dress exposition of the new interpretation given to New England's mission. Instead of the promised land, America had become the wilderness itself through which the generation of Jacob, as he would have it, was forced to pass before entering Canaan, "the Lord being pleased to hide from the Eyes of his people the difficulties they are to encounter withall in a New Plantation, that they might not thereby be hindred from taking the worke in hand."[43] The methods of the Lord, as well as His purposes, of course, had to be reinterpreted in light of experience, and they too were subtly naturalized.

That the subjection of the wilderness was now divinely commissioned did not, however, transform the Puritan into a lonely axe-and-plow pioneer. Even the Indian policy allowed no solitary missionary preceding civilization into the forest; Eliot did not go unto the Indians but brought them into his towns, civilizing them that they might be Christianized.[44] That with which the Puritans sought to replace the wilderness was a "garden." Yet both Fenwick, enjoying "the primitive imployment of dressing a garden," and Bradford, in whose verses roots and herbs, which "in

---

39 *Johnson*, Wonder-Working Providence, *52.*

40 *Johnson*, Wonder-Working Providence, *115.*

41 A Defence of the Answer made unto the Nine Questions or Positions . . . (*London, 1648*), *5–6.*

42 *Nathaniel Ward's* The Simple Cobbler of Aggawam in America . . . , *edited by Lawrence C. Wroth* (*New York, 1937*), *was similarly motivated. Replying that it was really the tolerating English Puritans who had betrayed the old faith, he also denied that his people had* "swarmed into a remote wilderness to find elbow-roome for our phanatick Doctrines and practices" (*p. 3*). *The identification of their liberty with the American wilderness was, of course, easy enough for the Puritans. Cotton Mather,* Magnalia Christi Americana (*Hartford, 1820*), *I, 11. They also noticed that the likes of Gorton set up in the* "fag-end of the world" (*Magnalia, II, 437*), *that libertines generally fled* "unto a dissolute corner of the land" (*Magnalia, II, 351*), *and that Quakerism,* "that great Choakweed *of the Christian and Protestant religion,*" *took* "Root in the Borders" *of the country. Cotton Mather,* Quakerism Display'd and George Keith Detected . . . (*Cambridge, 1691*), *1. For those who looked to the wilderness, the Puritan reply was a reaffirmation of the orthodox polity.* (*See Morton's* Memorial, *98–99.*) *As they saw it only* "Wild creatures" *would* "ordinarily love the liberty of the Woods." *William Hubbard,* Narrative of the Troubles with the Indians in New-England, *edited by S. G. Drake* (*Roxbury, 1865*), *I, 287. Liberty to the Puritan meant Christian or civil, or covenant liberty, and was not to be otherwise defined. Perhaps because the notion of a freedom outside society was so foreign to their ideals, there was no elaborate association of liberty with the wilderness in the Puritan mind.*

43 *Johnson*, Wonder-Working Providence, *11.*

44 *Thomas Shepard, in* The Clear Sunshine of the Gospel . . . (*New York, 1865*), *asked* (*p. 4*) "what more hopefull way of doing them good than by inhabitation in such Townes. . . ."

gardens grow," prove the wilderness conquered, intended to limit their meaning to a mere pattern of tillage.[45] The "garden," a sustained metaphor in Samuel Danforth's 1648 poem, was the entire culture which had been transplanted:[46]

> A skillful Husband-man he was, who brought
>   This matchless plant from far; & here hath
>   sought
>   A place to set it in; & for it's sake
>   The wilderness a pleasant land doth make.

Johnson's celebration continues in this vein: "This constant penetrating further into this wilderness" meant, for him, not only "Bridges" and "frequented wayes" through "the wild and uncouth woods" but, most importantly, a goodly number of congregational churches and towns.[47] Cotton Mather's representation of New England, late in the century, as "The Almost only *Garden*, which our Lord Jesus has in the vast continent of America,"[48] shows how persistently the Puritans refused to identify the garden which they sought or attained with a mere untamed and unchurched paradise, however lush, fertile, or rolling its acres might be.

"The wild boars of the Wilderness" which Mather saw threatening his garden commonwealth still connoted the unsubdued, but he and his generation had come to look on the "wilderness' as something more than the habitat of pagan and papist. Certain obvious sources of this later conception of the wilderness are to be found without, at this point, tracing its elaboration from a merely descriptive term to an intellectual formulation of wider signification. John Higginson's 1663 sermon, in which he credits God for the New England "garden," a "pleasant land" of "towns and fields, . . . habitations and shops,"[49] can be read as a mere extension of the logic of Johnson's argument. But the animus of his address betrays the vast difference. Though he was, to be sure, attributing to God's favor the "great increase in blessings" which his contemporaries enjoyed, he, like Michael Wigglesworth, whose narrative poem, *God's Controversy with New England*,[50] was published the preceding year, was reminding a back-sliding people that they who sought the blessings without the favor would soon be without both. In urging a return to the faith which had brought success to their ancestors, this later generation tended to magnify their exemplary achievements. The jeremiad produced the filiopietism of "God sifted a whole nation that he might send choice Grain over into the Wilderness,"[51] but it also resulted in an awesome caricature of that wilderness. "The Hazzards they run," intoned Cotton Mather, "and the difficulties they encountered with, in subduing a Wilderness, cannot easily be expressed in a large Tract."[52] They came, went another memorial, to "an *uninhabited Wilder-*

[45] Hutchinson Papers (*Albany, 1865*), I, 121; "*A Descriptive and Historical Account of New England in Verse; from a MS*," Collections, *Mass. Hist. Soc., first series, III, 77–84 (1704)*.

[46] "*An Almanack for the Year of Our Lord 1648*," in K. B. Murdock (editor). Handkerchiefs from Paul . . . (*Cambridge, 1927*), 104. *In the "Epistle to the Reader" of* The Clear Sunshine of the Gospel, "*garden*" *and* "*wilderness*" *are studiously used in contrasting the rising of the faith in America with its decline in England.* (N.p.)

[47] *Johnson*, Wonder-Working Providence, *234*.

[48] *Cotton Mather*, The Present State of New England (*Boston, 1690*), 37.

[49] *Higginson*, The Cause of God and his people in New-England (*Cambridge, 1663*), *10–11*.

[50] Proceedings, *Mass. Hist. Soc., first series, XII, 83–93 (1873)*.

[51] *William Stoughton*, New-Englands True Interest . . . (*London, 1670*), 16.

[52] A Brief Relation of the State of New England . . . (*London, 1689*), 4.

ness, where they had Cause to Fear the *Wild Beasts, and Wilder Men,*"[53] and both Mathers chronicled the Plymouth settlement as a "Flock of sheep amidst a Thousand Wolves."[54] The first generation used neither the Old Testament nor Luther to record their experiences in such extravagant fashion. Perhaps later incidents convinced these writers that their ancestors' wilderness was this frightening, but it is also possible that a belief in the terror of their fathers' predicament colored their perceptions of the contemporary wilderness.

That wilderness suddenly came to life again in the form of King Philip's uprising, which left its mark on New England's thinking. As they saw it, nature itself seemed to contrive with the Indians to work the destruction of the colonists, the Indians withholding from battle until "they should have the leaves of trees and *Swamps* to befriend them," and, when pursued, making their escape "into the deserts."[55] Unfamiliarity with the terrain, together with the Indians' being, so they thought, "so light of Foot that they can run away where they list," through inaccessible "Boggs, rocky Mountains, and Thickets,"[56] accounted for

some disasters. Even more, however, were consequences of the colonial military methods. Ambushes, of course, were suffered;[57] as was the calamity reported by Increase Mather: "Our Men when in that hideous place, if they did but see a Bush stir, would fire presently, whereby it is verily feared they did sometimes unhappily shoot Men instead of Indians."[58] The Puritan reaction was unvaried; the Indian tactics were denounced as "stealth," cowardice, and withal quite unfair and the Indians as "being like Wolves, and other beasts of Prey."[59] William Hubbard, though knowing the results of the traditional discipline, still branded as a "gross Mistake" one captain's "wrong notion":[60]

> about the best Way and Manner of fighting with the Indians . . . *viz.* that it were best to deal with the Indians in their own Way, *sc.* by skulking behind Trees, and taking their Aim at single Persons. . . .

Cotton Mather, in the *Magnalia,* defended that captain for his "successes" but still lauded the others for their "conduct."[61] The new era only fully emerged when Captain Church triumphantly laid his victories to his use of the "Indian custom" of marching "thin and scattered."[62] Meanwhile, that such experiences recurred through the last sorrowful decade of the century explains some of the fury of 1704 despatching of parties "into the

---

53 *Cotton Mather, "The Deplorable State of New England . . . ,"* Collections, *Mass. Hist. Soc., fifth series, VI, 97*–131*, 99* (1879).*

54 *Increase Mather,* A Relation of the Troubles which have hapned in New-England . . . , *edited by S. G. Drake as* Early History of New England *(Albany, 1864), 78; Cotton Mather, Magnalia, II, 427.*

55 *Increase Mather,* A Brief History of the Warr with the Indians in New-England, *edited by S. G. Drake as* The History of King Philip's War *(Boston, 1862), 103; Benjamin Church,* Entertaining Passages Relating to Philip's War . . . , *reprinted as* The History of the Great Indian War . . . *(New York [1845]), 56.*

56 *"A New and Further Narrative of the State of New-England, by N[athaniel] S[altonstall], 1676," in* Narratives of the Indian Wars, 1675–1699, *edited by C. H. Lincoln (New York, 1913), 77 ff.*

57 *See "Captain Thomas Wheeler's Narrative . . . ,"* Collections, *New Hampshire Hist. Soc., II, 7–8 (1827).*

58 Brief History, *62.*

59 *"A New and Further Narrative,"* Narratives of the Indian Wars . . . , *89. The council ordered any Indian found "sculking in our Towns or Woods" to be shot.*

60 Narrative of the Troubles, *I, 99, 113.*

61 *II, 515. See also his* Souldiers Counselled & Comforted . . . *(Boston, 1690), 3–4.*

62 Entertaining Passages, *108.*

Desert, in places almost inaccessible, if possible, to find out those bloody Rebels in their obscure Recesses under covert of a vast hideous Wilderness (their manner of living being much like that of the Wild Beasts of the same)."[63] Yet similar incidents in the Pequot war had only served to attach the adjective "hideous" to swamps;[64] more than this, even together with ancestor-worship, produced this later conception of the wilderness.

In the second half of the century Puritan attention was being drawn to the frontiers, particularly during the war years. Johnson's chants of praise for the "Inland townes," however, gave way to concern for the character of their inhabitants. Orthodox opinion of the outlying settlements, reflecting the dominant social conceptions, was critical of those who appeared to be abandoning the church militant. This was expressed, among other ways, as invective against those who followed the "evil manners of the Indians."[65] The Puritans had their own ideas as to how the wilderness, like the Indians, was to be conquered, and if their criticism of those who became "too like unto the Indians" in neglecting family order or worship[66] now seems ludicrous, perhaps all for which they can be justly condemned is an inability, given their social ideals, to fight two of the good fights at once.

As regards the war itself, however, that the commonwealth was simply guilty of over-expansion was inconceivable to the Puritans; the war was a divine rebuke to New England.[67] That its worst ravages were on the frontiers was not, to them, merely fortuitous. In the "scattering Plantations," Hubbard explained, "many were contented to live without, yea, desirous to shake off all Yoake of Government, both sacred and civil," adopting "the Manners of the Indians they lived amongst."[68] Increase Mather claimed to have foreseen their fate, in having discerned that "they were a scattered people, and such as had many of them Scandalized the Heathen, and lived themselves too like the Heathen, without any *Instituted Ordinances*."[69] Yet both limited such remarks to "some of the Southern, and all the Eastern Parts" of New England,[70] which had, of course, never been regarded as true members of the union of the Godly.

Though providence was not invoked to account for the disasters in the west, there is reason to believe that the reforming synod of 1679, when, in a list of sinful conditions to be extirpated, it inveighed "against that practice of setling Plantations without any ministry amongst them,"[71] was referring to that area directly. In 1642 Winthrop had questioned the worldly ambitions of those who went to the interior,[72] and Johnson observed "an overweaning desire . . . after Medow-land" on their part. But, he quickly added, "though these people are laborious in gaining the goods of this life, they are not unmindful of the chief end

[63] "*Address of Council and Assembly, July 12, 1704,*" in Collections, *Mass. Hist. Soc., fifth series, IV, 92* (1879).*

[64] John Mason, "*An Epitome or Brief History of the Pequot War,*" in History of the Pequot War, *44 ff.*

[65] Magnalia, *II, 576.*

[66] Necessity of Reformation with the Expedients subservient thereunto asserted; . . . Agreed upon by the . . . Synod . . . (*Boston, 1679*), 5.

[67] *Increase Mather,* Brief History, *224, 47.*

[68] Narrative of the Troubles, *II, 256–257.*

[69] Brief History, *88–89.* Cf. *Hubbard,* Narrative of the Troubles, *II, 85, and, for a later but like opinion,* Magnalia, *II, 499, 574. For background on the "providential historians" I have relied on Kenneth B. Murdock,* Literature and Theology in Colonial New England (*Cambridge, 1949*), *chap. 3, and, on Hubbard, Murdock's "William Hubbard and the Providential Interpretation of History,"* Proceedings, *Amer. Antiq. Soc., Vol. 52, 15–37 (1949).*

[70] *Hubbard,* Narrative of the Troubles, *II, 257.*

[71] Necessity of Reformation, *7.*

[72] Journal, *II, 83, 84.*

of their coming hither."[73] Undoubtedly these settlers were among the first, if not the only ones, who had forgotten that New England was a plantation of religion, not of trade. But a consciousness of something radically amiss in the "Out-Plantations" did not come, as it did by implication in Nicholas Noyes's 1698 demand for "more vigilancy and care" among them,[74] until the end of the century. Then the indictment, compiled under the synodical rubrics by Cotton Mather, quickly comprehended all the sins of Maine: "some woful villages in the skirts of the Colony, beginning to live without the *means of grace* among them,"[75] over-weening worldly avarice,[76] and selling liquor to the Indians instead of gospellizing them.[77] "Be sure," was his admonition, "your Sin will find you out, as that of your *Brethren* in the East has done *Them*, and their Trading Houses."[78]

F. J. Turner[79] has characterized Mather's diatribes as little more than the carpings of an orthodox east against a healthily-independent west. Yet Turner himself showed the frontier town's re-

sponsibility for implementing the Indian policy, and Mather's position, as we have seen, faithfully engrossed Puritan social ideals. Mather's plea for the west was clearly more complex than Turner saw reason to admit; for, whatever the temperament of Cotton Mather, he was as concerned for these plantations, lest they be damned by an indignant God, as for the remainder of the commonwealth. Nor was this a mask for some seething sectional bitterness; each pamphlet arraigning the frontier in these years can be matched with dozens from the pens of Mather and Benjamin Colman rebuking the dissolute coastal towns in similar terms. Solomon Stoddard, the valley pope, moreover, could both attack the degenerate metropolis and seriously ask if God were not disappointed with the New England frontier.[80] The fact that the frontier was departing from the ranks of the godly was related to New England's sectionalism in a much more subtle manner.[81]

The remarkableness of Mather's arguments cannot, however, be appreciated without returning to the development of the Puritan conception of the "wilderness" in the second half of the century. Neither swamp warfare nor the invocation of ancestral heroism offer the full explanation. This latter, indeed, was merely ancillary to the Puritans' attention to history in their jeremiads. Even in the days of the founders, the covenant theology was commonly buttressed with reference to Jewish history, between which nation and their own the Puritans saw an uncommon similarity. An early use of Biblical imagery pertinent to the American scene was Winthrop's 1642 allusion, in dramatizing the need for social unity, to "such as come to-

[73] Wonder-Working Providence, *234–235*.

[74] New-Englands Duty and Interest, To be an Habitation of Justice (*Boston, 1698*), 83–84. *After Philip's War, Hubbard did lay the disasters in the west, not to providence, but at least to the tactical advantage the Indians enjoyed from these areas being overrun with scrub-wood, a consequence, as he saw it, of "the Inhabitants being everywhere apt to engross more Land into their Hands than they were able to subdue."* Narrative of the Troubles, I, 169.

[75] Magnalia, *I, 59*.

[76] A Letter to the Ungospellized Plantations . . . (*Boston, 1702*), 10.

[77] A Monitory and Hortatory Letter to those English who Debauch the Indians . . . (*Boston, 1700*), 8.

[78] A Monitory and Hortatory Letter . . . , 15.

[79] *"The First Official Frontier of the Massachusetts Bay,"* Publications, *Colonial Soc. of Mass.*, XVII, 250–271 (*1915*).

[80] Questions Whether God is not Angry . . . (*Boston, 1723*).

[81] *On the relation of the godless frontier to Stoddard's proto-Presbyterianism, see Perry Miller, "Solomon Stoddard,"* Harvard Theological Review, XXIX, *277–330 (1941)*.

gether in a wilderness, where there are nothing but wild beasts and beastlike men."[82] The "garden" verses all relied on such a communal covenant, and Bradford's recollections (ca. 1650) of thoughts of "salvage & brutish men, which range up and downe," deterring some in the Leyden deliberations and "a hidious & desolate wilderness, full of wild beasts & willd men" confronting them on arrival indicate his struggle to demonstrate the existence of such a covenant by patterning Plymouth's history after that of Israel.[83] Shepard also wrote in this vein, but the "worthiest Worke" of Johnson was its first successful elaboration.

Just as the social covenant evolved from "a mere adjunct of the Covenant of Grace" into a "self-sufficient principle" and ultimately "a dominant idea in the minds of social leaders in Massachusetts and Connecticut,"[84] the comparison with the Jews in the wilderness came to be in part divorced from the national covenant itself and took on a metaphorical existence of its own. The advantage of the covenant was that prosperity could be attributed to God and the over-greedy rebuked without impugning the fruits of their wilderness-labors, yet allowing for God's withdrawal, accounting for his controversy as well as His favor. If Abraham's seed had been consigned to yet another wilderness, so might these latter-day children of Israel. If the God of Higginson and Wigglesworth could say of New England that he had turned "an howling wilderness . . . into a fruitful paradise," and, beginning with Nathaniel Morton, each succeeding memorialist insist that it had indeed been made a "pleasant Land,"[85] the

post-war synod was not so sure as to the appropriate comparison. "It was a great and high undertaking of our fathers. . . . A parallel instance not to be given, except that," and here they hesitated, "of our Father Abraham from Ur of the Chaldees, or that of his Seed from the land of Egypt."[86] For Hubbard the war was enough proof that his nation was neither, as the first settlers had surmised, the successful occupants of Canaan, nor as Johnson suggested, "Jaacobites," but the generation of Esau:[87]

> For ever since they forsook their fathers' houses and the pleasant heritage of their ancestors they have by solemn providence been ordered, not into the fields where the mandrakes grew . . . , but rather into the barren wilderness and remote deserts. . . .

So far as it referred to the actual Indian peril, this extension of the sojourn had substantial meaning. What happened, however, is that crop failures, sea disasters, droughts, and every other ill that New England flesh was heir to were imputed to a "*wilderness*-condition."[88] The partial reality of the Indian wars may have made this myth more credible, but the real wilderness was reclothed in more appalling garments when interpreted through the myth. New England, moreover, was never again certain that it had been brought into the promised land; for all its celebration of the society's achievements, the *Magnalia* frequently questions whether this later wilderness had been

---

[82] Journal, II, 83–84.

[83] History, 24–25, 78.

[84] *Perry Miller*, The New England Mind, 478.

[85] New-Englands Memorial, 6; *Increase Mather*, A Relation of the Troubles, 62–63; Necessity of Reforma-

tion, *Epistle, n.p.;* Stoughton, New-Englands True Interest, 13–14; C. Mather, A Brief Relation, 5 and Magnalia, I, 74. *The adjective "howling," of course, merely represents a closer accommodation to the Pentateuch.*

[86] Necessity of Reformation, *Epistle, n.p.*

[87] General History, x–xi.

[88] Magnalia, I, 10.

overcome. Each new lapse of faith and each succeeding catastrophe strengthened the doubts. A
frenzied urgency was given to conquering the
wilderness, for on this the ultimate success or
failure of the whole society was assumed to depend. Perhaps such fervid imagery as this (from
a volume, be it noted, on witchcraft) helped
create, in an area for which the reality of a wilderness was no longer immediately relevant, an
image so portentous that the popular imagination
was never liberated from it:[89]

> The Wilderness through which we are passing to
> the Promised Land is all over fill'd with Fiery fly-
> ing serpents. But, blessed be God, none of them
> have hitherto so fastened upon us to confound us
> utterly! All our way to Heaven lies by *Dens of
> Lions* and the *Mounts of Leopards;* there are incred-
> ible droves of Devils in our way

The implications of such typological[90] thinking
in the realm of social salvation were matched by
equally significant ones for the individual in his
relation to the wilderness. If calamities were seen
as "Thorns" visited by an angry deity, "Why,"
it was asked, "may not God, as well as Gideon,
teach the Men of *Succoth,* and of other places, by
the *Briers and Thorns of the Wilderness?*"[91] The
wilderness now had a moral purpose, and Cotton
Mather, writing of "a continual *temptation* of the
devil," explicitly alluded to Christ.[92] Moving,
without rigorous logic, among the various Biblical

parallels, the piety of Richard Mather was explained by the truth that trials of faith might "be
expected" in a wilderness.[93] Cotton Mather contended that New England's faith was the greater
because it was more often tried in "*desarts* full of
dismal circumstances,"[94] and affirmed generally
"that a *wilderness* was a place where temptation
was to be met withal."[95] This did not, of course,
mean that the individual was automatically redeemed or even ennobled by mere contact with
the vernal wood, but that its vicissitudes could try
his faith and that success in the struggle might be
a mark of grace.

Cotton Mather tested this possibility in his
commentary on the Indian captives and found the
analogies of both Testaments verified by a convenient reality.[96] It is this conception that explains
his hope that the frontier inhabitants might, in
the threatened war, "get all Possible and *Eternal
Good* by the *Evil*" they would meet (a possibility,
he insisted, likely only if the proper church ordinances were observed)[97] and account for the
startling, but neglected, first sentences of his
Frontiers Well-Defended:[98]

> An Address is now making to a people, who
> ought on some Great Accounts, to be the *best
> People* in the Land. It is unto YOU, O our dear
> Brethren, who are a people Exposed to inexpress-
> ible *Hazards* and *Sorrows* by your being in the
> Exposed <u>Frontiers</u> of the Land.

---

[89] Cotton Mather, The Wonders of the Invisible World
(*Boston, 1693*), 63.

[90] *For the function of "types" in Puritan literary practice,
see Perry Miller's introduction to Edwards' Images or Shadows of Divine Things* (*New Haven, 1948*).

[91] Narratives of the Indian Wars, *46;* Hubbard, Narrative of the Troubles, *I, 290, 254.*

[92] Magnalia, *II, 426; cf.* Hubbard, General History, *96.*

[93] *Increase Mather, "The Life and Death of Mr. Richard
Mather,"* Collections Dorchester Antiq. and Hist. Soc., No.
3 (*Boston, 1850*), 76.

[94] Magnalia, *I, 10, 49.*

[95] Magnalia, *II, 67.*

[96] Good Fetch'd out of Evil . . . (*Boston, 1706*), *36, 38.*

[97] Frontiers Well-Defended . . . (*Boston, 1707*), *5–6.*

[98] Frontiers Well-Defended, *3.* [*Double underlining in
the text indicates bold Gothic print in the original.*]

This hypothesis, by which Mather helped to explain the unique development of New England, thus made virtue a partial function of a "*Wilderness*-condition." If the definition of such virtue had changed in two generations, the Puritan's notion of God's special interest in a wilderness people was thereby reaffirmed.

All the ideas which we have been tracing fed into the apocalyptic visions which possessed many Puritan social leaders near the turn of the century. This chiliasm, yet another effort to revive the faith, depended on the increasingly easy identification with the Jews. If convertibility of the Indians was an essential factor, it was, more significantly, to New England's interest "*To be an Habitation of Justice.*" If the Indians were the devil's children, then America would "be the head Quarters of *Gog* and *Magog*" and even "hell itself." "This is worse and worse still," cried Nicholas Noyes, "But may be something alleviated by an opposite Conjecture."[99]

> For there are others that ask why it may not be the New Jerusalem, or part of it? These Opinions are as wide apart from one another, as Heaven is from Hell. I count it sufficient to set them one against the other; without saying which is the widest from the Truth. Only, Who of an American . . . had not rather (if it may stand with the counsel of God) that it should be the New Jerusalem, then the Old Tophet.

As early as 1684 Samuel Sewall had asked "why the Heart of America may not be the seat of the New Jerusalem."[100] Assured that the Indians were of Jacob's posterity, he concluded that America *would* be the site, fixing its location somewhere in Mexico, though the beauties of Plum Island gave him final assurance.[101] But Cotton Mather, who could opine that the "last conflict with antichrist" would be to the "westward,"[102] based his argument on a more spacious geographical knowledge. Somewhere in "the brave Countries and Gardens, which fill the *American Hemisphere*," would be the Holy City in AMERICA; a *City*, the *Street* Whereof will be *Pure* Gold."[103] Though something of a restatement of the visions of Winthrop and Johnson, this latest and most spectacular western New Jerusalem would lie beyond the confines of New England. The hope of those who now looked for a final divine judgment to rescue them from a darker moral wilderness, their utopia served only to assuage the doubts of a society no longer able to judge itself with any certainty.

The refractions in Puritan thought of their wilderness-experience left one explicit legacy to the eighteenth century. "That the discourse comes forth in such homely dresse and course habit," Thomas Hooker wrote, "the reader must consider, It comes out of the wildernesse."[104] "Wilderness dress" remained an appealing pose for practitioners of the plain style,[105] but a new major

99 *Nicholas Noyes*, New Englands True Interest, 44, 74–75. *Increase Mather was one who believed that "God has not seen to take pleasure in the American world, so as to fix and settle his Glory therein."* Ichabod (*Boston, 1702*), 64–65.

100 "*Diary of Samuel Sewall, 1674–1729,*" Collections, *Mass. Hist. Soc., fifth series, V, 58 (1878–1882)*.

101 Phaenomena quaedam Apocalyptica . . . (*Boston, 1697*), 2, 59.

102 Magnalia, I, 302.

103 Theopolis Americana . . . (*Boston, 1710*), 43; cf. Magnalia, II, 97.

104 A Survey of the Summe of Church-Discipline . . . (*London, 1648*), preface.

105 *Daniel Gookin, "An Historical Account of the Doings and Sufferings of the Christian Indians . . . ,"* Archeologica Americana, II, 430, (1836).

theme emerged from the second generation's applying to their ancestors the description of John the Baptist's converts, "They came not into the wilderness to see soft raiment."[106] Said Samuel Danforth of their habit: "Delicate and costly Apparel is to be expected in Princes Courts, and not in wilde Woods and Forrests." Admitting that his own generation had re-entered "pleasant Cities and Habitations," he could still say of "the affection of Courtly Pomp and Gallantry" in his own day, "How much more intolerable and abominable is excess of this kinde in a Wilderness."[107] Though the older Puritan objection was not forgotten—Cotton Mather thought "finery" both "inviting unto *sensualities*" and "disagreeable to a *wilderness*"[108]—these latter-day metaphorical conceptions lent double support to such denunciations as Stoddard's of Boston fashions as "demeanor not becoming a wilderness state" and those of Noyes and Sewall against the wearing of wigs,[109] hastening the process which began

with Danforth in 1663 and eventuated in the eighteenth-century apotheosis of American homespun.

Both a century of colonizing experience and the religious nature of New England fed into the Puritan attitudes toward the wilderness. A realistic appraisal dictated the change in identification of the physical setting from a promised land to a wilderness. But only the Judaizing disposition of the Puritan mind accounts for the acceleration of that process and for the dark conclusion that New England was perhaps a permanent and hideous wilderness. Their difficulties in the wilderness served to reinforce the Puritans' belief that they were the chosen of God and to countenance an expectation that the New Jerusalem would lie in America. Subduing the wilderness quickly became an exalted calling for the Puritan; later new graces were imputed to the now-harrassed occupants of the frontier. Indeed, only an intense consciousness of covenant obligations kept the Puritan from making the frontiersman the particular avatar of all the American wilderness-virtues. As the belief emerged that those who lived in a wilderness should excel in simplicity, there had appeared by 1700 a large reservoir of concepts and values congenial to later American thinkers.

---

[106] *Samuel Danforth*, A Brief Recognition of New-Englands Errand into the Wilderness (*Cambridge, 1671*), 3. Necessity of Reformation, *Epistle*.

[107] Brief Recognition, *17*. Cf. Connecticut Colonial Records, *II, 283 (1676)*.

[108] Magnalia, *I, 111*.

[109] *Solomon Stoddard*, The Way for a People to Live Long in the Land that God Hath given them (*Boston, 1703*); W. C. Ford, "*Samuel Sewall and Nicholas Noyes on Wigs*," Publications, *Colonial Soc. of Mass., XX, 109–128 (1920)*.

THE HALF-WAY COVENANT

*Perry Miller**

Among a vast array of safe assertions, safest of all are wide generalizations concerning the abiding qualities of a nation or a people. While historical principles which seem universally applicable invite deserved suspicion, yet any rule not too good to be true gathers strength by surviving the exceptions which "prove" it. We should have no fears, for instance, that a lack of contradictory testimony will ever compel us to abandon our ancient belief that the English are a pragmatic race, with an innate propensity for compromise and a congenital aversion to clear thinking—that they prefer always to muddle through with muddled logic. To this good platitude a host of convenient exceptions clamor for attention, and of these the conduct of Englishmen in the early and middle seventeenth century is surely the most gratifying.

Up and down the land were men with utopias in their brains and the voice of God in their ears. Whatever else can be said of these worthies, it must be generally agreed that all in their several fashions comprehended the meaning of "thorough." Puritan and prelate alike were prepared to make of their ideals a Procrustian bed upon which society would be stretched or hacked to fit the predetermined dimensions, and both were sublimely indifferent to what might be the practical consequences. Strafford would make an Anglican satrapy of Catholic Ireland, and Laud would do likewise with Presbyterian Scotland; the Scotch in turn would fasten the solemn league and covenant upon the English, and the Massachusetts-Bay Company would bend the wilderness to a Bible commonwealth. Much of the character of American Puritanism is to be attributed

*PERRY MILLER (1905–1963) was Professor of American Literature at Harvard University. His publications include Orthodoxy in Massachusetts (1933), The New England Mind (1939), and Errand Into the Wilderness (1956). Reprinted by permission of the New England Quarterly, Vol. 6, No. 4 (December, 1933), 676–715.

to its having been formulated by Englishmen in a day when too many Englishmen were behaving themselves in a manner which Britons have usually considered bad form. Of all examples of this un-English *a priori-ism*, New England Congregationalism is probably the most extreme.

It should be added, however, that the most spectacular form in which this quality of preconception was manifested in New England was not that which is most often singled out for comment and disparagement. The notion that Biblical ethics should dominate the life of a community was indeed an important item in the New England creed, but it was not the central doctrine, nor was it peculiar to the new world. The fate of such diverse persons as Servetus and Mary Stuart is a reminder that the notion was not unfamiliar to Geneva and Scotland. But the sanguine colonials went far beyond this elementary stage and dedicated themselves to an even more rigorous program, which they called Congregationalism. They had accepted Protestant theology. Very well then, they would conform their world to that theology. For a century Protestant reformers had preached regeneration and faith; New Englanders would make regeneration and faith the touchstones of an ecclesiastical and even of a political system. In this spirit they dared to make a deduction which Calvin had explicitly declared was inadmissible,[1] they dared to assume that if there was any truth in predestination, then the predestined elect could be distinguished in the flesh from the predestined reprobate. Upon this conclusion they proceeded to act. They turned over the government of the churches to congregations made up exclusively of the regenerate. They reasoned, with flawless logic, that saints, being sanctified, needed no supervision of bishops or classical bodies, that the Word of

God was for them sufficient check upon their portion of human depravity. Up to this time no orthodox Protestants had contemplated putting the principle of salvation by faith into anything like so extensive a practice. Compared with the blithe assurance of the New England divines, Luther and Calvin appear downright skeptics; they would have recoiled in horror at the prospect of giving any groups of human beings, even hand-picked groups of the evidently righteous, such breath-taking powers as those of electing their own ministers and enjoying local ecclesiastical autonomy.

The marvel is that this super-logical system actually worked. There were slight modifications, but the essential idea was completely carried out. After overriding antinomianism, expelling Roger Williams, circumventing Dr. Child, and crushing the Quakers, the clergy and magistrates could boast with pardonable pride that in all the world New England alone had succeeded in living up to the Word of God, and at that when the Word had been most exactly interpreted. And then, at this very moment of satisfaction, events threatened to get out of hand. The ministers confronted what Artemus Ward would have called "a darned uncomfortable reality" to which it seemed that they had to make concessions, or else the whole system would go to pot. The problem came, as problems generally do, from an unexpected quarter—not from any frontal attack, which they could have withstood, nor from an outburst of heresy, which they had demonstrated they were competent to deal with, but from the simple fact that time moved on and that even the chosen people of God married and had the customary issue. It was their children, and then their children's children, who by doing nothing but allowing themselves to be born constituted a threat to the marvellous perfection of New England Congregationalism.

[1] *Ernest Troeltsch*, The Social Teaching of the Christian Churches (*New York, 1931*), I, 598.

It was not that the original theory had failed to provide for these children. The Bible taught that churches were to consist only of visible saints, of adults who had experienced regeneration, but it also declared, in passages too numerous to mention, that whenever God extended the covenant of grace to His saints, He included their "seed" in the grant. On such authority Congregationalists had provided for the baptism of the children of church-members, and for no other children whatsoever, as a symbol that God had taken them into the covenant. Of course, everybody assumed that these baptized children would grow up to become somehow saints themselves; whereupon their own children could be baptized, and so *ad infinitum*. Thus, the theory had confidently expected, the churches would be perpetuated through the ages by a continual and unfailing succession of the elect.

The fault lay not in a lack of provision or foresight. It was rather that the provision was not of the right sort, that what was foreseen was precisely what did not happen. Incredible though it might be, there were a vast number of the second generation who were earnest and sober and had immaculate reputations, who sincerely desired to partake of the Lord's Supper, but who, try as they might, "could not come up to that experimental account of their own regeneration, which would sufficiently embolden their access to the other sacrament."[2] And when we reflect that at almost their earliest opportunity, they generally became parents themselves, not once but frequently, we can understand how the problem of an ecclesiastical status for the descendants of the original saints did "come on with some importunity and impetuosity."[3] In 1646 the General Court summoned a

synod to frame a platform of discipline; it had various motives, but the most insistent was a fear that unless the question of baptism were settled, the various apprehensions of the matter then rampant would "begett such differences as will be displeasing to the Lord, offensive to others, and dangerous to ourselves."[4] At the Cambridge gathering the subject was warily introduced, discovered to be "difficultly circumstanced"—which is putting it mildly—and dropped with unanimous alacrity. But within a very few years Puritan fecundity made it impossible to stall any longer. At the suggestion of Connecticut an assembly of divines met at Boston in 1657, drew up a statement which at once caused a furor and divided New England into two violently opposed theological camps. In 1662 an official synod was found necessary, and the conclusions of this body, reached after a stormy session by a majority of about seven to one, were promulgated as the official opinion of the churches.

The issue in these gatherings was simplicity itself: "The children of the parents in question, are either children of the covenant, or strangers from the covenant."[5] The unregenerate heirs of what Cotton Mather called the "good old generation" had to be frankly kept in the churches or else turned out. On this crucial point the ministers had no mind to compromise, and the simple truth of the matter is that they did not. In spite of the label which their solution has borne ever since, there really was no "half-way." In no uncertain tones the majority responded in the affirmative. Baptized children were held to be members, even if unregenerate. This membership was qualified and hedged about, it was distinguished from "full"

[2] *Cotton Mather*, Magnalia Christi Americana (*Hartford, 1855*), II, 277.

[3] *Cotton Mather*, Magnalia Christi Americana (*Hartford, 1855*), II, 98.

[4] Records of Massachusetts, *II, 155; III, 70–73.*

[5] [*Jonathan Mitchel*], Propositions Concerning the Subject of Baptism and Consociation of Churches. . . . (*Cambridge, 1662*), 12.

membership which entitled to communion, but it remained essentially membership, and as such gave the baptized members the right to present their own children for baptism.

There is not the slightest obscurity about the motives for this decision. If the constrictive operation of the polity had been permitted to force the posterity of the saints outside the pale, then presently the whole community would be left "at a loose end without the Discipline of Christ, the Means to prevent sin, or to reduce them to Repentance unto life."[6] Since "even the children of the godly" were making a "woful proof," Ezekiel Rogers in 1658 trembled to think what would "become of this glorious work that we have begun, when the ancient shall be gathered to their fathers."[7] Intrusions of irreligion and apostasy would be bound to emanate from so large a number ejected beyond the limits of control. "Church-way for the good of these there is none, if they be not under Church-government and Discipline."[8] Damned or saved, the children had to be made subject to the watch and ward of the church, or the Bible commonwealth was ruined.

To the modern mind motives as good as these might be deemed sufficient, and we may pardonably wonder what all the pother was about. But unhappily the seventeenth-century mind did not work in this fashion. It was not that New Englanders considered the gaining of happiness or the satisfaction of ulterior motives sinful; they de-cidedly approved of getting what one wanted if one could. But in their scheme worldly profit was incidental to serving the will of God. To aim merely at the continued prosperity of the churches would be in their view to put the cart before the horse. A church system had been decreed once and for all in the Bible. To patch up the divine constitution in response to some mere mechanical urgency was to make "innovation," most heinous of sins and of crimes. Biblical polity did not depend upon sociological considerations, but solely upon the immutable decree of God. The New England fathers had known this when, rather than sacrifice one jot or iota of that polity, they had betaken themselves to the wilderness. The synod could not get away with its doctrine unless it could somehow show that it had enacted "no Apostacy from the first Principles of New England, nor yet any declension from the Congregational way,"[9] but only "a progress in practising according thereunto, as the encrease of the Churches doth require."[10] If baptized but unregenerate persons were members, then somebody had to prove that the idea had been implicit in the system from its very origins.

Nor was this all. New Englanders had a theology as well as a polity. The leaders of Massachusetts and Connecticut had always insisted upon their complete doctrinal concord with the reformed churches of the world. They had accepted without reservation that system of thought which in its main outlines was the creed of English Puritanism and which is generally, though somewhat loosely, spoken of as Calvinism. To prove this the synod at Cambridge in 1648 had enthusiastically endorsed the *Confession of Faith* which

[6] *John Allin*, Animadversions upon the Antisynodalia Americana (*Cambridge, 1664*), 6.

[7] *Cotton Mather*, Magnalia, I, 413.

[8] *Richard Mather*, A Defence of the Answer and Arguments of the Synod met at Boston in the Year 1662 (*Cambridge, 1664*), 18. Jonathan Mitchel's An Answer to the Apologetical Preface Published in the Name and Behalf of the Brethren that Dissented in the Late Synod, *was issued together with Mather's pamphlet under one title-page.*

[9] *Increase Mather*, The First Principles of New England, Concerning the Subject of Baptisme And Communion of Churches (*Cambridge, 1675*), A_4, verso.

[10] *Allin*, Animadversions, 5.

the Westminster assembly had just published. Heresy was as black a sin as innovation, and the synod of 1662 could not issue its *Propositions* without first reassuring the world that these did no violence to the inherited theology.

To generalize about this theology has ever been a dangerous undertaking, and nowadays is certainly a thankless one. Engaging as one may find the labyrinthine involutions of this creed outworn, inflicting them too heavily upon the reader would be like boring a guest with a favourite cross-word puzzle. But considering the fashion in which the New England intellect operated, one must notice certain features of that primitive philosophy in order to trace the history of this movement. A moderately extensive reading of New England authors suggests the thought that the predestinarian aspect of its theology has been rather overemphasized. Popular impressions to the contrary, it is not altogether accurate to declare that New Englanders interpreted their creed to require complete passivity of man in the face of an absolute and arbitrary God. They were not given over irreparably to fatalism and paralysis of the spirit.[11] True, they did conceive the cosmos to be pure determinism, and they did hold that the sole moving force therein was the will of God, a will unfettered by aught but the divine pleasure. True, they did believe that when God saved a man, He did it out of His lofty condescension, "without any fore-sight of Faith or good Works, or perseverance in either of them or any other thing in the Creature, as Conditions or Causes moving him thereunto, and all to the praise of his glorious Grace."[12] So, until a man experienced effectual calling, he did dwell in impotency of spirit, pros-

trate before God, unable either to lift or to wish to lift a finger for his own salvation. To this extent there can be no doubt that Calvinism succeeded in stifling human effort and initiative, but even so it did not entirely suppress them. Even among the unconverted, New Englanders understood that a certain activity, or at least semblance of activity, could go on: the unregenerate could be offered the "means" of conversion. The Gospel and its ordinances, the ministry and the sacraments, could be held out as an inducement to sinners. The clergy were "Ambassadors" of Christ, and their "great business is to make the offers of, and invite sinful Men to embrace Reconciliation with God, through Christ."[13] Of course, these sinful men could make no response, logically they could not be supposed even to make sense out of what was preached to them, until the spirit came to their assistance. Until then they might have ears but they would hear not. "The power to discern the excellency of the Truth, and so to approve and embrace it, and to chuse and close with Christ . . . must come from a superior agent; because in doeing it, the blind mind must be illuminated, and the rebellious heart subdued."[14] But then no one could tell in advance where the superior agent, like lightning, would strike. The only thing to do was continually to stand by, offering the means of conversion to all the unregenerate. Any one of them might suddenly discover himself able to take advantage of his opportunities. None of them could therefore be deprived of a chance. The clergy would sleep ill of nights if they faltered in offering the objective means of grace, not only in spite of, but in the very midst of human inability.

---

11 Cf. *Frank Hugh Foster*, A Genetic History of New England Theology.

12 *Williston Walker*, The Creeds and Platforms of Congregationalism (*New York, 1903*), 371.

13 *Samuel Willard*, A Complete Body of Divinity (*Boston, 1726*), 431.

14 *Samuel Willard*, A Complete Body of Divinity (*Boston, 1726*), 427.

Once the soul became infused with the regenerating spirit, the whole situation was gloriously changed. As soon as the sinner had authentically experienced effectual calling, justification, and adoption, he was freed. Then he could, he inevitably would, commence to strive against sin and the flesh. He was no longer a supine recipient of grace; he was a warrior penetrated with the active spirit of Christ. The *Westminster Confession,* which New England synods endorsed in 1648 and in 1680, emphasized again and again that a sinner translated to a state of grace was a man emancipated from natural bondage to sin, who could, albeit imperfectly, will to do good. He had not only a choice but a duty "to give all diligence to make his calling and election sure."[15] He was voluntarily to coöperate with the divine spirit in striving for sanctification, saving faith, good works, and true repentance. Best of all, the church could exhort and incite him. As long as natural man could contribute positively nothing to his own salvation, so Samuel Willard wrote, then it must be that "a Christians real work begins, when he is Converted."[16]

Thus we can perceive that the existence of these recalcitrant children posed a delicate theological problem. Because they could not even in "the judgment of charity" be accounted saints, they had then to be held incapable of spiritual exertions. What could be the use of exhorting them to moral conduct or making them memorize a catechism? Even if they did the things which God had commanded, they would not do them with a heart purified by faith and their deeds would be of no avail. Good works done by the unregenerate "cannot please God, nor make a man meet to receive grace from God."[17] But though the church could not undertake to convert the children, there was no impropriety in its offering them the "means" of conversion. A great many of them were expected to be ultimately chosen; they had all therefore to be constantly called, and called as loudly as possible. The seed of believers "are successively in their Generations to be trained up for the Kingdome of Heaven," to which "the Elect number shall still be brought in the way of such means."[18] The difficulty was that mere providing of means could not be permitted to become anything more. Opening chances to those who might some day utilize them was one thing, but evangelizing among those who betrayed no signs of a circumsized heart was quite another. The merely baptized could not be treated as though elected nor expected to behave as if regenerate. The temptation was great to demand regenerate actions from sinners, to transform, unwittingly but none the less sinfully, "means" into goads, opportunities into provocations. If their concern for the future led the clergy to push or entice the baptized into actions to which they knew men could really be aroused only by the divine summons, they would make a ghastly mockery of the Congregational principle of regenerate membership.

The majority report in the synod of 1662 has so often been indicted by church historians for being the initiation of precisely such a treason, and that indictment has become so much the accepted verdict, that some further explanation is necessary. The principle of regenerate membership presents at least as many difficulties as any other Puritan conception. It was based upon a postulate, upon a belief in the reality of a supersensual realm in which a converted individual could encounter a definite series of spiritual expe-

[15] *Walker,* Creeds and Platforms, *385.*
[16] *Willard,* Complete Body of Divinity, *503.*
[17] *Walker,* Creeds and Platforms, *384.*

[18] Propositions Concerning the Subject of Baptism, A_3, recto.

riences. In the Congregational plan, before a man became a member of the church militant, he must have had these experiences, he must have become by divine election a member of the church triumphant. This meant that in the inner recesses of his soul there must have been engendered a new life, he must have undergone a subjective, incomprehensible, but recognizable transformation. Upon the foundation of this subjective experience was reared the objective church; correlated with the spiritual realm, with the emotional life, was the ecclesiastical realm, the organized system. The external church was not primarily an evangelical organization to carry the gospel to the heathen, but a brotherhood for the cultivation and intensification of grace in those who already had it. It was designed, as we have just seen, to offer "means" to those who were some day to be converted, but its more important function was to direct the already converted towards larger achievements in the way of sanctification, repentance, and saving faith. The greatest of the early prophets of Congregationalism, William Ames, who was a master among other things of the Aristotelian terminology, defined the "essential" form of the true church to be invisibility, the "accidental" form to be visibility: "the accidental forme is visible, because it is nothing else then an outward profession of inward Faith."[19] As Thomas Hooker expressed it with less jargon, "the Covenant of Grace is ever included and presupposed in the Covenant of the Church."[20] The organization followed upon the fact that certain persons were predestined to salvation; the ecclesiastical realm assumed the previous occurrence of conversion in the spiritual, and without maintaining that as-

sumption the whole theory of Congregationalism would have collapsed.

To make an assumption is easy. To maintain it in the presence of facts is to invite trouble. The trouble here was that this spiritual realm remained a closed book to human comprehension. God alone could know with certainty what happened there. We, poor creatures, could merely follow the motions of the spirit from afar, and endeavor to read the language of the spirit as it was translated in the language of sense. Naturally we would make mistakes. Hence Congregationalists hovered always upon the verge of an exciting predicament: they created an ecclesiastical system based upon the objective reality of election, and at the same time recognized that in practical life it was impossible to be absolutely certain just who was elected and who was not. They desired the membership of their churches to approximate as closely as possible to the membership of the church invisible. But they could discover no method for guaranteeing that the two realms would be more than remotely identical. So the best they could do was to go upon evidences, to pass no judgment upon the thing-in-itself, but to be concerned with its attributes. He who *seemed* regenerate must for practical purposes be treated as such. The individual was to search for faith within the trackless hinterland of the soul, but it remained his own problem to establish his sincerity. The church wished only to know what evidences justified its accepting the individual into the ecclesiastical realm on the assumption that he had probably already been received into the spiritual.

Thus Congregational theorists had progressively recognized that the ecclesiastical realm was based, properly speaking, not upon the *terra incognita* of actual faith and regeneration, but upon externalities, upon evidences, upon probabilities. Whether we were members of the invisible church, said Hooker, "we for the present doe not know: and

[19] *William Ames*, The Marrow of Sacred Divinity (*London, 1643*), 137–138.

[20] A Survey of the Summe of Church Discipline (*London, 1648*), Part III, 24.

its certain, you can neither see, nor know, for truth of grace is invisible to man."[21] We judged on the basis of actions and professions, as best we might, but in the end we called him a Christian who stood up under such fallible tests as we could devise.

> The Profession is to be judged of by Men who cannot know the Heart, but must judge according to Appearances. . . . God hath put it into the hands of Men to dispense the Gospel-Ordinances, and hath told them who are the Subjects, and by what Rule they are to determine them, and that is by their Profession, or outward demeanure of themselves.[22]

The two realms overlapped, but they would always remain separate and distinct. "There is a twofold Dispensation of the Covenant of God in his visible Church," wrote John Allin in reply to President Chauncy; there is the "Inward, Spiritual, and Saving Dispensation of the Covenant to such as truly Believe, and perform the conditions of the Covenant," but quite a different matter is the other dispensation, "Outward and visible, by which the Lord bestows upon his Church, and all the members thereof, the outward Priviledges of the Covenant, his Ordinances, and Means of Grace."[23]

Specific individuals who presented instances either of notorious unregeneracy or of conspicuous holiness caused no confusion between the dispensations. He who in every respect conducted himself as a man of God could safely be supposed truly elect; whereas an equally obvious limb of Satan was presumably not among the saved. But by no means were all persons such clear-cut cases of black or white. As time went on, the divines kept finding a surprising number who did not fit readily into either category. Some who were far from vicious were yet not ostensibly regenerate, and many who seemed in some respects to be called were in other respects palpably deficient. Worse than that, some who gave the most convincing exhibitions, who made "a more than ordinary profession of religion," came to bad ends, created "prodigious and astonishing scandals."[24] It did the bewildered clergy no good to pray to God for an answer to the enigma; no answer was forthcoming, nor could one be expected. God knew His own mind, and He had made no pledge to reveal accurately the secret transactions of the spiritual realm. Congregationalists had undertaken a mighty task: they had set out to embody the infinite will of God in a finite church. They had admitted from the beginning that there might be discrepancies, but when these became too flagrant, they put on a bold face and determined to save their own consistency in default of their parishioners' sincerity. They had aspired to capitalize the hidden energies of conversion, but when they perceived how hidden those energies were, they made shift to be content with evidences. More and more the clergy dodged the responsibility, took refuge in the reflection that the life of the spirit was beyond human ken. It was not their fault if their technique of examination worked injustices or was sometimes inadequate.

> To make a person a Member of the visible Church, the matter is not whether he hath Faith and Grace really, or not; if he hath such qualification as the Rule of the Word accepteth for Faith in the visible Church, we can go no further.[25]

---

[21] A Survey of the Summe of Church Discipline (*London, 1648*), *Part I, 37.*

[22] *Willard*, Complete Body of Divinity, *854.*

[23] *Allin*, Animadversions, *18–19.*

[24] *Cotton Mather*, Magnalia, *II, 493.*

[25] *Allin*, Animadversions, *25.*

It was enough if a man seemed to possess the qualifications; the clergy declared him as good a Christian as any, unless later on he gave overwhelming evidence to the contrary. To say church-members were regenerate, said John Cotton, was to speak of what "they ought to be *de jure* . . . rather then what they are, or are want to be *de facto*."[26] Evidence, not reality, was the bailiwick of the churches, and their evaluation of evidence was confessedly faulty. Clearly they would frequently admit some who would seem satisfactory but who would be in God's eyes reprobate, who were, in short, hypocrites. "It is clearer then the day, that many who are inwardly . . . the children of the *Devil*, are outwardly, or in respect of outward Covenant, the children of God."[27] To this anomalous conclusion the fathers of New England themselves had come, quite independently of the problem of children. They had already made it a part of the Congregational tradition by 1662.

Into the ecclesiastical realm, the fellowship of the evidently righteous, a person could get admitted in one of two ways. The first was to make a personal profession of faith and regeneration before the congregation. Hypocrites could do this, yet it still was the most reliable method for detecting the elect. Any one who passed this inspection became for official purposes one of the chosen, and therefore was entitled to all the privileges of the church, especially the communion. Hence the Lord's Supper came to be the crucial link between the spiritual and the ecclesiastical realms. Everybody agreed that the sacrament should be confined to those who not merely had private assurance of salvation, but who could offer public evidence,

who could show "historical faith," blameless lives, and the ability "to examine themselves and to discern the Lords body." The most stalwart advocates of the half-way covenant were as much resolved as their opponents that satisfactory personal confession should be a prerequisite to partaking of the communion, because that ceremony was instituted, "not for regeneration, but for nourishment and confirmation" of those already regenerate.[28]

The second way was baptism. Because the ecclesiastical realm was not necessarily identical with the spiritual, God by His arbitrary fiat could, if He so pleased, set up another standard besides visible holiness. As New Englanders read the Bible, they found that He would permit no heathen to come in before making a profession, but that after an erstwhile heathen became converted He counted that man's children among His flock. There was, possibly, very little rhyme or reason in this entailing of the covenant, but there was no getting around it. So the children were baptized. But of infants nothing could be demanded, not even evidences. They became church members solely and simply because God so ordered it, and for no better reason. Presumably He would some day elect them. Apparently He desired them in the church, where the means of conversion could be set before them. "Others hear the word, but these in outward Covenant enjoy it by Covenant, and promise; and hence these in the first place, and principally, are sought after by these meanes."[29] To most of the children, it was believed, God would not say, "If thow

---

[26] A Defence of Mr. John Cotton From the Imputation of Selfe Contradiction (*Oxford, 1658*), 71.

[27] *Thomas Shepard*, The Church-Membership of Children and their Right to Baptisme (*Cambridge, 1663*), 1–2.

[28] *Richard Mather*, A Disputation Concerning Church-Members and their Children, in Answer to XXI Questions. . . . (*London, 1659*), 17. MS. in *The American Antiquarian Society, Worcester, Massachusetts.*

[29] *Shepard*, The Church-Membership of Children, 3–4.

believest thow shalt be saved," but instead, "I will enable to believe;" they would have the means "unless they refuse in resisting the means," and even if they refused, God would probably be especially patient with them:

> . . . he will take away this refuseing heart from among them indefinitely, so that though every one cannot assure himself, that he will do it particularly for this or that person, yet every one, through this promise, may hope and pray for the communication of this grace, and so feel it in time.[30]

Thus the normal development of the baptized child ought to cause no trouble. At the age of discretion he would discreetly reveal signs of regeneration, be taken into full membership, and seated at the Lord's Supper. In that case the church would have to regard him as having been chosen in the divine mind from all eternity. Had it been able to decipher his destiny at birth, it would have received him into full standing at once. For obvious reasons that had been impossible, but there had been good grounds to presume that he would grow in grace and become saved; therefore he had to be considered as having been a legitimate member of the ecclesiastical realm even in his probationary period. He had made progress in his ability to furnish evidences, but he had not come from non-membership into membership. He had been included within the church covenant at birth by the explicit statement of God and now his inclusion was simply made good. *Ergo*, the child had been a true member from the very day of his baptism.

That much was clear. But any system of education has to reckon with abnormal children. Abnormality was expressed in this case by a growing up without a concomitant ability to prove regeneration. What should the church do with such intractable youths? How should it account for them? Whom should it blame? The only certainty was that they could not be allowed to approach the communion table, but that still left much to be determined. For example, did every member necessarily have to be a communicant? If so, the children who did become regenerate had not been members before their conversion. Then where was the point in baptism at all? That way anabaptist madness lay. But if all baptized children were held to be members, could those who failed to make the expected progress be thrown out of the fold when they came of age on the grounds that they had secured no foothold in the spiritual realm, when the two realms were held to be altogether separate, when happenings within the spiritual realm were unfathomable by man, and when every one acknowledged that beyond a doubt many who were received into the church were a stench in the nostrils of God? In determining who should participate in the ecclesiastical system, was the blanket promise of God to extend the covenant to the seed of believers less valid evidence than that offered by the individual through his own profession, when all evidence at best was purely presumptive and apt to be fallacious? It was the core of Calvinistic theology that God saved men by His arbitrary condescension, but what if in one case He did it through contact with the individual and in another through the parent, without apparently touching the individual at all? Such a prospect would even seem a challenge to the faith of a people who believed that the Deity customarily performed His wonders in mysterious ways. In fact, in their minds it might take on a decided tinge of probability as they reflected that the danger of getting hypocrites into the church was about as great one way as the other. But on the

[30] *Shepard*, The Church-Membership of Children, 5–6.

other hand, if these children continued to flood the churches, would not that be the end of Congregationalism in New England? Congregationalism, we must recollect, was based on the theory that church-members were at least evidently regenerate. About these unfortunates not even a supposition could be made. Could this system, founded as it had been upon the attributes of sincere religion, continue in existence at all when a great percentage of the generations who were to perpetuate it obviously and conclusively failed to acquire any such attributes?

The dissenters at the synod of 1662, ably represented by President Chauncy, John Davenport, Increase Mather, and Nicholas Street, found the last question unanswerable. They decided that if the system was to survive, it could not stomach baptized but unregenerate children, no matter who their parents were. The churches might indeed be founded upon appearances, but nevertheless these were appearances of spiritual realities. Children who grew up unable to muster any such manifestations should get no better treatment than any other incapable persons. So far as the world could judge, they were essentially unbelievers; they might not have committed open immoralities, but they would have shown their true colors by "neglecting the means of Grace, or non-manifestations of making profession of the Faith, and the fruits thereof."[31] If the adult children could not manage a personal and immediate confederation, said Davenport, they were in a state of sin, they were naturally incapable of good, and in their hearts "these despise the Church of God."[32] Thus, though they may have been members during their minority, when they came of age and

made no professions, "then they do not retain their Membership which they had in minority."[33] They were automatically to be expelled. The dissenters waxed so hot upon this point that they actually insinuated that the children were in some fashion responsible for not having made a better showing. They declared their failure made them *felones de se*. Davenport argued that the children had been pledged to God in their infancy, whereby they had become "engaged and excited the more to give themselves to God in Christ . . . not by constraint but willingly;" consequently they had only themselves to blame if their sinful hearts did not surrender. Amusingly enough, Davenport went on to say that such a willing surrender to Christ would have had to come about "through the operation of God working Faith in their hearts, by the Spirit, who is a voluntary Agent, and therfore likened to the wind which bloweth where it listeth." But though his reasoning was a trifle confused, Davenport came to an unequivocal conclusion: "The Church must make a difference of children grown up, where God makes a difference . . . and receive oneely such whom Christ receiveth."[34] Here the dissenters took their stand, and demanded that the churches of New England unchurch the helpless children, expel the grandchildren, and consign the lot of them to everlasting torments. And the dissenters, it should be remembered, were still Englishmen.

The majority of the divines recognized that the dissenters' position was sincerely taken, but they felt that it was altogether too rash and precipitous. They had an armory of careful theorizing to draw upon, and they were grateful to the fathers who had meticulously distinguished and divided the

[31] *Charles Chauncy*, Anti-Synodalia Scripta Americana (*London, 1662*), 24.

[32] *John Davenport, Another Essay for Investigation of the Truth (Cambridge, 1663), 45.*

[33] *Davenport, Another Essay for Investigation of the Truth, Increase Mather in Preface, A$_2$, recto.*

[34] *Davenport, Another Essay for Investigation of the Truth, 6.*

realms of the spirit and the church. They had no mind to minimize the epistemological speculations which already had brought home the impossibility and the danger of identifying manifestations of regeneration with the thing itself. The minority were zealous, the majority more circumspect. A machinery was needed for rationalizing the pursuit of a practical objective in terms of a divinely preordained system, and they saw that the way to achieve it was to interpret the whole problem as pertaining only to the realm of organization. They remained within the letter of Congregational tradition by the strange device of insisting that the spirit was not concerned, that the issue was not whether the children "have true Faith, or not, in the act or habit, so they have such qualifications as God accepts of, to receive their persons into his Covenant, and to be Members of the Body of Christ." If they had the qualifications, "this sufficeth, though they have no Faith or Grace really."[35] The church realm was, at best, one of probabilities, and God alone specified how the probabilities should be gauged; therefore if He said that simply by being the progeny of church-members persons were fit to become members, that would constitute good qualification. It was enough to warrant their formal, legal inclusion within the group, enough to invest them with evident righteousness, with "federal holiness," if not with inner virtue. To treat them as confederated believers and to keep them within the church did not mean, Thomas Shepard had written,

> . . . that they are alwaies in inward Covenant, and inward Church-Members, who enjoy the inward, and saving benefits of the Covenant, but that they are in external, and outward Covenant, and therefore outwardly Church-Members, to

[35] *Allin*, Animadversions, *25.*

whom belongs some outward privileges of the Covenant for their inward and eternall good.[36]

Hence the synod boldly determined that "meer membership" was its province, a matter quite distinct from ability to make professions, "as in the children of the Covenant, that grow up to years is too often seen."[37] Children could not inherit a right to Heaven or to the communion table, but they could succeed to citizenship in a body politic. "Only the confederation, not the condition or conversation of the Parent is imputed to the Child."[38] The church as a society was concerned only with the legality of their title within the corporate group; if they did not profit by the opportunities it offered for becoming genuine converts, that was their loss. They might secure no standing in the church triumphant, but they would lose none in the church militant. If they did not prove regenerate,

> . . . we may say their Covenant and Church-relation is as none in respect of any Spiritual saving benefit to their souls . . . and yet it can no more be said, that in respect of their Church-relation and external visible state, they are not in the Church . . . then in other particulars it can be said, that they are not . . . baptized.[39]

Just as soon as membership was defined in these terms, as being a formal relationship to a specific commonwealth, a number of interesting consequences followed. In a commonwealth an individual had to be either completely a member or none whatsoever. No one could be half citizen and half alien. He might be a good member or a bad one, he might be entitled to communion or

[36] *Shepard,* The Church-Membership of Children, *2.*
[37] Propositions Concerning the Subject of Baptism, *11.*
[38] *Increase Mather,* First Principles, *19.*
[39] *Richard Mather,* A Defence of the Answer, *33.*

not, but once in, he was altogether in, "Even as a childe of the family is not so perfect to do the work, and enjoy all the Priviledges of the Family, as a grown person is, but yet he is as perfectly a Member of the Family as a grown man."[40] The difference between a non-communicating and a communicating member was not a distinction of kind, but merely one of the methods by which each had entered the compact. One was a citizen by birth, the other had been naturalized. "The Free-grace of God in his Covenant, extended both to Parent and Childe. . . . The way of entring into this Covenant on mans part is onely a differing *modus* or manner of Covenanting with God."[41] Once the essential membership of the children was thus established, the thing clearly could be extended through the generations; the grandchildren were members by the same token. Adults who had not been baptized and had been reared outside the church could not be admitted to the covenant until examined for the visible signs of piety,

> . . . yet this concerns not the Parents of the children here spoken of, because they are not now to be admitted into the Covenant and Church membership, but are therein already, and have been long afore now, even from their minority or birth.[42]

The whole dispute, as the apologists persisted in viewing it, had nothing to do with the admission of adults through personal profession; it was only concerned "About persons already in the Church, and Baptized, whether in such, the grounds of Baptizing their seed, be Faith and Grace made visible in some manner, or their Interest in the Covenant?"[43] Through "interest in the covenant"

these children obtained only a political and not necessarily a religious status; therefore political maxims applied to their condition. It was already a platitude of Puritan political dogma that a compact was irrevocable as long as both parties lived up to it. Therefore, unless these children and grandchildren broke the compact of federal holiness by some overt act of scandal, how in God's name could they be dropped from the society? The idea of their becoming *felones de se* was absurd. A church-member "cannot be outed, till God out him."[44] "In Admitting Members into the Church," said John Allin, "we justly work for such positive Qualifications as the Word of God requireth," but once we have determined that certain persons have the qualifications, either by virtue of their own profession or by virtue of their parentage, then "to cast out such as are *Regularly admitted*, we must have positive Impenitency in sin."[45]

This much of its doctrine the synod attained merely by accentuating already accepted opinions concerning the necessarily objective character of a corporate church. Thus it managed to enter the substance of its decision without apparently doing violence to the inherited theology or creating innovations in the discipline. Indeed, the distinguishing mark of the *Propositions* might be said to be precisely too rigorous a consistency, too ingenious a fidelity to tradition and creed. It has been noted that there was a marked trend towards formalism in the New England of the forties and fifties, but the resolution in 1662 of the status of children on the grounds solely of visibility put a finishing touch to the transformation of Congregationalism from a religious Utopia to a legalized order. Religion was practically confined to the

[40] *Allin*, Animadversions, *28.*
[41] *Allin*, Animadversions, *29.*
[42] *Richard Mather*, A Defence of the Answer, *30.*
[43] *Allin*, Animadversions, *22.*

[44] *Jonathan Mitchel*, An Answer to the Apologetical Preface (*Cambridge, 1664*), *12. See* note 8.
[45] *Allin*, Animadversions, *19.*

inner consciousness of the individual. He alone needed to be concerned about the assurances of election. The churches were pledged, in effect, not to pry into the genuineness of any religious emotions, but to be altogether satisfied with decorous semblances. The apologists concentrated upon the letter of the law, and so solved their problem without noticeably renovating the divine scheme, but they did so at the cost of ignoring the spirit. This came out most clearly when they drew a lengthy analogy between the rite of baptism and the Old Testament rite of circumcision. They refused altogether to recollect that Israel had been a tribe first and a church only secondarily, and that conversion as a basis for membership was utterly foreign to the spirit of Judaism. Even though the Jewish church was "National," argued Richard Mather, while ours is "Congregational," still in each church the covenant runs to members and their seed; "now as well as then, if the Parents continue in covenant, the Children do so also, and so are part of the Church."[46] If an increase of hypocrites had threatened the churches even when men became members only through profession, how much greater was the threat when generation after generation could continue in church compact with confessedly no more grounds to distinguish them from the heathen than the negative virtue of avoiding open scandal! Thomas Shepard had foreseen this possibility, and the synodalists confessed they perceived it too, for they published his letter in 1663:

God knowes what Churches we may have of them, even heaps of hypocrites, and prophane persons, for I know not what can give us hope of their not apostatizing, but only Gods promise to be a God to them, and to preserve them.[47]

[46] *Richard Mather*, A Defence of the Answer, *56.*
[47] *Shepard*, The Church-Membership of Children, *15.*

This was a melancholy prospect for good Christians to contemplate. It is not surprising that at this point the apologists betrayed an uneasy sense that perhaps they had gone too far; and they turned once more for reassurances to logic, which generally worked such wonders in the seventeenth century. Was it after all necessary, they mused, to assume that baptized children who lived and died soberly and morally within the church were damned just because they had undergone no emotional convulsion? If, for instance, a baptized child experienced effectual calling on his twentieth birthday, he was considered to have been all along a legitimate member of the church. But another who did not have the experience until his fortieth year still enjoyed his membership on trust every bit as legitimately for a score of years longer. Now it was conceivable that this one, instead of living to become obviously regenerate at forty, might be cut off at thirty-nine. If God had chosen him, would not God save him anyway? And since no one could even begin to comprehend what went on in the realm of spirit, and since that realm had been divorced completely from the physical world, might not some men become truly regenerate without ever anybody in this world suspecting it, least of all themselves? There might exist a sort of state of grace half-way between demonstrable reprobation and demonstrable regeneration in which men would become saved, as it were, subconsciously. The half-way members, baptized but not communicating, actually might be construed as the worldly embodiment of this intermediate condition. The apologists knew that at this point they skated upon very thin ice indeed. They were dangerously close to pleading for some species of "Universal Baptism Grace," to declaring that baptism was not a means of grace but a vehicle—which Davenport pointed out was a damnable error of the Arminians. Strangely enough, Richard Mather, one of the older generation, handled the notion most daringly. He did not say baptism made children regenerate, but he did go so far as to assert that baptized children who grew up respectable but unconverted need not be pronounced to lack "the very being of Faith." May there not, he asked, be real saving grace "even there where the exercise of it is much wanting? . . . Notwithstanding all this weakness, there may be the being and truth of the thing in such Souls." Even though the children did not have the ability to examine themselves, as required by the Lord's Supper, yet they "are in a latitude of expression to be accounted visible believers" because "Being in covenant and baptized, they have Faith and Repentance indefinitely given to them in the Promise, and sealed up in Baptism . . . which continues valid, and so a valid testimony for them, while they do not reject it."[48] "Surely," Jonathan Mitchel pleaded, suddenly shifting from ecclesiastical metaphysics to *argumentum ad hominem,*

> . . . the Lord does not make so light a matter of his holy Covenant and seal . . . as to enter into a solemn Covenant with Children, take them into his Church, and seal up their taking in before Men and Angels, and then let them goe out so. easily, or drop off we know not how.[49]

One strange and—for the future—pregnant result of having made the realm of spirit a mystery undecipherable to man seems to be here revealing itself almost immediately: New Englanders had practically surrendered the attempt to make positive assertions concerning the real workings of predestination, they had decided that election was an impenetrable "secret with God"; then, paradoxically, they began to prefigure the operations of the decree in a more lively and human fashion than when their imaginations had been weighed down by their original respect for authentic evidences. Once the realm of spirit and the eternal decrees of God were decided to be unintelligible to the flesh, they became susceptible of description in terms of human emotions. The perennial anthropomorphic tendency of the race reasserted itself in the statement that God's attitude toward the baptismal covenant would "surely" be influenced by men's standards of justice. To proclaim the divine mind incomprehensible might become in reality the first step for projecting humanity into it. Samuel Willard, an earnest exponent of the synod's doctrine, would shortly be expressing the orthodox opinion of New England when he wrote:

> We conceive of Gods decrees in a rational way, or according to the manner of men in their purposing and decreeing, in which we design one thing for another; hence first one thing and then another . . . because else we could entertain no conceptions at all about this glorious mystery, but must be wholly ignorant of it.[50]

But in 1662 these were yet undeveloped implications. For the moment the immediate effect was the supplying of a program by which the churches could treat the children as something better than passive onlookers. The children were only formal members, but members of any sort could be incited to good works. Should they by any chance happen to be regenerate without even knowing it, their good deeds would be acceptable to God. In any event they could be disciplined by church censure and excommunication, though they never on earth achieved the ability to warrant

---

48 *Shepard,* The Church-Membership of Children, *51–52, 13.*

49 *Shepard,* The Church-Membership of Children, *15.*

50 *Willard,* Complete Body of Divinity, *255.*

"full" membership. As members of a body politic they were subject to its legislation.

> Baptism leaves the baptized . . . in a state of subjection to the authoritative teaching of Christs Ministers, and to the observation of all his commandments . . . and therefore in a state of subjection unto Discipline . . . otherwise Irreligion and Apostacy would inevitably break into Churches, and no Churchway left by Christ to prevent or heal the same; which would also bring many Church-members under that dreadful judgement of being let alone in their wickedness.[51]

As a purely ecclesiastical matter, baptism was "in the Nature of a Covenant . . . a Mutual Obligation between two Parties upon terms;" to the baptized, therefore, it ought to be "as a strong bond upon them, carefully to keep it;" it would "be a Witness against them, if they violate it."[52] Since there had been shown to be "no certain, but only a probable connexion between federal Holyness . . . and Salvation," persons could be required to become federally holy without implying that they were required to undertake their own conversion. The baptized had promised to do their best on the ecclesiastical plane; they could always be reminded what a compact they had entered into,

> . . . and by what promise of gratitude they have likewise obliged themselves unto obedience to God. . . . And they are seriously to be exhorted . . . that they abide in that Covenant of peace, and endeavour to fulfill that obligation, by mortifying sin, and setting upon newness of life, and that they do this freely, and sincerely.[53]

The response which the baptized were expected to make to these exhortations was institutionalized by the synod in a ceremony called "owning the baptismal covenant." This rite comes the nearest to being an innovation of anything the synod proposed, and it was what earned for the whole doctrine the sobriquet of "halfway"; yet the establishment of this ritual was simply a gesture necessary to the thinking which had reached the point we have described. The children were members of the church, they had accepted a covenant by becoming baptized, and were to live up to their pledge. When they came of age and desired to have their own infants baptized, the churches would need some overt sign that they had done and would continue to do their duty. They could not make a full profession of faith, for they still lacked "ability," but they could acknowledge their ecclesiastical obligations. They could pledge obedience, make a formal agreement with the church, which at the same time was understood to imply no profession of any Christian experience.[54] They could make "an orderly and Church profession of our Faith . . . in an Ecclesiasticall way," if not in a spiritual way.[55] The objectives of the visible church would be obtained if the baptized fulfilled their contract, voluntarily pledged a continuation of their endeavors, and put themselves under discipline. As for the objectives of the invisible church—well, by owning the covenant the children offered evidence of a sort, they demonstrated they had enough freedom of will to undertake at least ecclesiastical responsibilities, and that was something more than impotent passivity. Who could say what this might really mean?

[51] Propositions Concerning the Subject of Baptism, *10.*

[52] *Willard*, Complete Body of Divinity, *848, 855.*

[53] *Quotation from Chemnitus, printed in Shepard*, Church-Membership of Children, A_1, verso.

[54] *Leonard Bacon, "Historical Discourse," in* Contributions to the Ecclesiastical History of Connecticut (*New Haven, 1861*), 21.

[55] A Disputation Concerning Church-Members, *15.*

If Faith be taken for the grace of Faith in the heart, why may they not be said to have Faith in this sense also, seeing it is required of them, that besides their understanding the Doctrine of Faith, and their professing their Assent thereto, that they must also not be Scandalous in Life, but solemnly own the Covenant. . . . And does not this imply some beginning of Faith? Can persons have all these Qualifications, and yet for this be utterly destitute of the grace of Faith? . . . And in as much as men have neither Faith, nor any thing that good is by Nature, therefore they that have it may be said to be converted to it.[56]

The church could confidently risk working with this material. It could not only require the children to own this covenant in order to have their off-spring baptized, it could even take the initiative: "It is the duty of the Church to call upon them for the performance thereof."[57] The apologists had traveled a difficult dialectical road, and it is to be suspected some of them made a wry face when they had to swallow such stuff as the analogy between baptism and circumcision; but they emerged with their objective gained and their scruples laid at rest. The theology of New England remained as deterministic as it had been, the structure of the ecclesiastical system was not disturbed; yet the churches possessed a clear-cut program for keeping youth within bounds. They had grounds upon which they could meet the problem and do something about it.

The success of the majority on the score of practical effectiveness overwhelmed the dissenters. On the whole the minority argued the matter with a finger logic and certainly with a greater concern for the sincerities. They riddled the apologists' picture of a state of grace that could not become evident, they recognized the ridiculousness of setting out to separate the sheep from the goats and then including a number of goats because, although they did not look like it, they might possibly be sheep. "The Children in question," said President Chauncy, "are in a state of Neutrality for the present;" that was the best that could be said of them, but all such in the final analysis "Christ accounts to be against him."[58] The dissenters clearly saw through the parallel between circumcision and baptism: "the similitude runs not upon four feet."[59] They perceived that "owning the covenant" was an affair of the head and not of the heart—that devils, if necessary, could go through with it. To cause unregenerate persons to profess subjection was, as they saw it, to embody a contradiction in terms; "it is but an obligation to an impossibility; neither can there be obedience without faith."[60] Unless the churches preserved healthy faith against contagion by lopping off unhealthy tissue, the dissenters predicted a future of decay. They forecast that the churches would become prevaded with pharisaism.

It is apparent unto all what a corrupt masse of Unbelievers shall by this change throng into the fellowship of Gods People, and the children of strangers, uncircumcised in heart, shall be brought into Gods Sanctuary to pollute it.[61]

But all these excellent arguments were not powerful enough to compensate for the crucial weakness in the dissenters' position: by ruling out the oncoming host of baptized but unregenerate children as *felones de se* they would have reduced the

---

[56] *Richard Mather, quoted in Increase Mather*, First Principles, *14.*

[57] A Disputation Concerning Church-Members, *20.*

[58] *Chauncy*, Anti-Synodalia, *34.*

[59] *Chauncy*, Anti-Synodalia, *14.*

[60] *Chauncy*, Anti-Synodalia, *31.*

[61] *Chauncy*, Anti-Synodalia, *10.*

churches to a wraith. They argued that if persons were admitted without due regard for spiritual fitness "the application of Church-Censures to them, will be disregarded and slighted by them,"[62] but they could suggest no method for dealing with such persons. And yet they, too, confessed that if children were not put under watch and government, the regime would not survive. To the apologists this was enough; "the whole Cause was given up in that Proposition."[63] So the ultimate moral would seem to be that though our seventeenth-century forbears would do nothing without proofs from Holy Writ, yet as between one array of proofs and another, they could find it convenient to choose that which was the more compatible with their mundane interests.

The truth of this observation is aptly illustrated by the history of Increase Mather. To him the rigorous position of the dissenters had at first seemed more attractive, and he had entered the lists against his father, writing the preface for old John Davenport's *Another Essay*. But soon after, largely through the ministrations of Jonathan Mitchel, he came to realize that though the dissenting position might be theologically right, it was ecclesiastically all wrong. Whereupon he came over to the other side with such a vehemence that he soon out-apologized the apologists. He pushed to extremes every argument he had formerly opposed. He refused to acknowledge that the question could be anything but an ecclesiastical affair. "That Faith which giveth right to Baptism . . . *as to us* is not invisible faith. But the visibility of faith is that which we must proceed upon."[64] Accepting this doctrine wholly, Mather

quoted Mitchel to inform his former allies that they had been headed up an ecclesiastical blind-alley. "In the way your self and some others go, the bigger half of the people in this Country will in a little Time be unbaptized."[65] When he had been in the opposition, he had implied that the New England experiment had better fail utterly than survive by transforming its character; thereafter, he seems to have decided that the idealistic position was too quixotic, that the cause of religion was bound up with the continuation of the New England regime in any circumstances. It would be, he now agreed, "subversive to Religion," it would be "absurd," that a people "of a more reformed temper then ordinarily the world hath known . . . should so soon be the body of them unbaptized, as if they were not a Christian, but an Heathen People."[66] As soon as the standard of the synod was taken up by this practical and dynamic man, the intricacies of theological rationalization became a bit superfluous. Once Increase Mather had made up his mind, he brushed aside all the debate, *pro* and *con*, in which his elders had indulged; and, with the instincts of a statesman rather than a theologian, placed his greatest emphasis upon an out-and-out emotional appeal, an argument decidedly *ad hominem*:

> There are many godly Souls in *New-England*, that the great motive which prevailed with them to come into this wilderness, was that so they might leave their Children under the Government of Christ in his Church. . . . Have we for our poor Childrens sake in special, left a dear and pleasant Land, and ventured our Lives upon the great waters, and encountered with the difficulties and

[62] *Davenport*, Another Essay, *34*.

[63] *Allin*, Animadversions, *34*.

[64] *Increase Mather*, A Discourse Concerning the Subject of Baptisme (*Cambridge, 1675*), *9*.

[65] *Mitchel, in Increase Mather*, First Principles, *Appendix, 5*.

[66] First Principles, *Appendix, 5*.

miseries of a wilderness, and doth it at last come to this, that they have no more Advantages as to any *Church care* about them, then the *Indians* and *Infidels* amongst whom we live? O this is sad![67]

Sad indeed, and the synod of 1662, with its provision of a half-way arrangement for baptized but unregenerate church-members, preserved Massachusetts and Connecticut from such a fate. But it preserved "church care" for "our poor Children" at the cost of interpreting it to mean care for only their ecclesiastical well-being. Yet I can not altogether sympathize with the church historians who have unanimously condemned the synod for having guided Congregationalism into compromise and legalism. The leaders of the day faced their task manfully and intelligently, they brought to bear upon it all the learning and insight of their generation. The fault, if it can be called a fault, lay not in themselves but in their stars. They were committed by their inheritance and their characters to the well-nigh hopeless task of bolstering up a system founded on the courageous but ill-considered conviction that the wayward, subjective mysteries of regeneration could be institutionalized in an ecclesiastical system. All over Christendom the intricate, top-heavy structures of Reformation theology were sagging; the

age was turning away from them to more comfortable, if less logical, views; it was groping toward the greater simplicity and utility which were to characterize the eighteenth century. The divines were unwittingly caught between a dying age and one striving to be born, and the halfway covenant controversy is simply the New England counterpart to what was taking place in other guises throughout the western world. It is conceivable that had there existed in Boston at the time some great religious and philosophical mind, some Jonathan Edwards, let us say, enough in advance of his day to proclaim that the emotional life should not be strangled in the coils of an ecclesiastical system, such a mind might have profited by the experience of the preceding decade, remodeled the system and infused it with a revivified faith. But no Edwards appeared. Instead, a man paced forth from the ranks of the dissenters to become, as much as any, the leader of New England orthodoxy for at least the next thirty years, and he was a statesman and a politician before he was a theologian or a priest. He embodied the decision already reached by the majority of the clergy when he assumed leadership in the name of the doctrines of externality, of visibility, of formalism. It was only when the churches had gone the limit in these directions that either Edwards or the rationalists could abandon the preoccupation with polity and get back to the first principles of religion itself.

[67] *Increase Mather*, A Discourse Concerning the Subject of Baptisme, *30–31.*

PIETY AND INTELLECT IN PURITANISM

*Robert Middlekauff**

What the Puritans knew as common sense about the mind has survived to be enshrined by historians as a theory of psychology. Puritans grew up thinking of the mind in terms of the faculties, such as "reason" and "will." Today we recognize that the Puritans had accepted the faculty psychology, a theory much older than they were. We have long since rejected this theory and have exhausted several others; yet we have not managed to divest ourselves of its vocabulary nor have we shaken off its underlying assumptions. Like the Puritans we still describe the mind's functioning with the familiar terms reasoning and willing. And, like them, we separate thought and feeling and ascribe a duality to the mind.

The assumption that the mind is a duality has proved especially important in the interpretation of Puritanism. If the Puritan mind was a duality the problem is one of establishing the relationship of the two parts—the religious emotion, or piety, and the ideas that historians agree informed the mind. Historians have approached this question with the familiar suppositions that emotion somehow produces ideas or, phrased in another way, that religious ideas are the articulations of piety. This proposition seems to defy more explicit statement and it does not exclude a second assumption, which may appear to be in conflict with it, that piety and intellect were historically in opposition to one another. Both assumptions may contribute to a disposition among historians of Puritanism to think of the psychic process in mechanistic terms—in this case as entailing "movement" from feeling to thought. Both hold that the mind was duality; and both imply that piety and intellect were separate.

With its descriptions of images shuttling back and forth among the faculties, the traditional

*ROBERT MIDDLEKAUFF (1929–   ) is an Associate Professor of History at the University of California. His publications include Ancients and Axioms (1963) and "A Persistent Tradition: the Classical Curriculum in 18th Century New England" (1961). Reprinted by permission of the author and the William and Mary Quarterly, Vol. 22, No. 1 (January, 1965), 457–470.

Puritan psychology had obvious mechanistic overtones. If historians have found much of the old language antiquated, they have insensibly made use of the notion of a mechanical movement in which piety somehow yielded intellect. This view pervades Perry Miller's *New England Mind* where it is summed up in a splendid metaphor: "The emotional propulsion was fitted into the articulated philosophy as a shaft to a spear-head."[1] And Alan Simpson, declaring that Miller has told us too much about the Puritan mind and not enough about the Puritan's feelings, reveals a similar mode of thinking: "If the seventeenth-century Puritan, with his formal training in scholasticism, usually tries to give a rational account of his faith, it is the stretched passion which makes him what he is. They are people who suffered and yearned and strived with an unbelievable intensity; and no superstructure of logic ought to be allowed to mask that turmoil of feeling."[2]

The use of terms such as "superstructure," which have mechanical connotations and the conception of the mind as a duality operating on a sequential basis, with emotion first in the sequence, gives the psychic process a deceptive neatness. These mechanical terms, after all, are abstractions which may establish relationships but they do not convey a state of mind. Rather they seem to suggest that emotions may be understood as any mechanical force can, perhaps even as uniformities. In this notion piety is an entity whose inception and expression parallel the action of any physical force.

Perhaps we cannot avoid thinking of the mind as a duality. The idea is embedded in our vocabulary, and we can in fact make meaningful distinctions between emotion and thought. But if

we must acknowledge that thinking and feeling are different modes of the psychic process, perhaps we should give full importance to their connections, for these two modes do not exist apart from one another. Whatever else it is, the psychic process is not simply the sum of thinking and feeling; it is in some peculiar way their interaction. Men think within some emotional disposition and feel in a context that in part has been ordered by thought.

Perhaps, too, we should consider the possibility that creativity in the relationship of Puritan intellect and emotion may have arisen in the intellect. Puritanism, after all, offered an explicit philosophy covering all aspects of human existence. This philosophy defined man's place in the world with absolute clarity: it told him who he was and what he might become; and it told him what God expected of him.

But if man's fate was clear, the fate of individuals was not. In its doctrines of predestination and election, Puritanism offered a man the assurance that his future had been decided. But it gave him no infallible indication of the nature of the decision. All he could know with absolute certainty was that God in his justice had predestined some men for salvation and others for damnation.

These ideas reinforced a bent towards self-awareness in men eager to determine whether or not they were of the elect. Puritanism achieved the same result in yet another way—by explicitly demanding a self-consciousness that made a man aware of his emotions and sensitive to his attitudes towards his own behavior. It accomplished this by describing in elaborate detail the disposition of a godly mind. Sin, it taught, might be incurred as surely by attitudes as by actions. In the process of performing his religious duties a man might sin if his feelings were not properly engaged. Prayer, for example, was commanded of every Christian; but prayer without inward strain, even agony, is mere "Lip-labour," a

[1] *Perry Miller*, The New England Mind: The Seventeenth Century (*New York, 1939*), 67.

[2] *Alan Simpson*, Puritanism in Old and New England (*Chicago, 1955*), 21.

formality that offends God.[3] Prayer for spiritual blessings without faith that those blessings will be granted implies a doubt of God's power and is equivalent to unbelief. Ordinary life, too, must be lived in a Christian habit of mind. A man getting his living in a lawful calling, though staying within the limits imposed by the state, might nevertheless violate divine imperatives by overvaluing the creatures, as Puritans termed excessive esteem for the things of this world. The "*manner of performance*," a Puritan divine once said, was the crucial thing in fulfilling the duties imposed by God.[4]

Puritanism thus bred a deep concern about a state of mind. The norms of good thought and feeling were clear, and every Puritan felt the need for effort to bring his consciousness into harmony with these norms. The most familiar figure among Puritans is the tormented soul, constantly examining his every thought and action, now convinced that hell awaits him, now lunging after the straw of hope that he is saved, and then once more falling into despair. He wants to believe, he tries, he fails, he succeeds, he fails—always on the cycle of alternating moods.

Consider, for example, Cotton Mather. By his own account he seems to have been completely at the mercy of his emotions: his *Diary* reverberates with his groaning, sighing, and panting after the Lord. From youth until death, his spirit fluctuated from despair to ecstasy. Between these

emotions lay a vast number of others but for Cotton Mather few brought peace and repose.

If Mather's piety was more intense than most—in part because his familial heritage and his conception of his profession were unusual—its sources were similar to that of other Puritans. Mather lived in a world of ideas where God reigned, and man, diseased with sin, craved His dispensation. Only the Lord could save man and the Lord made His decisions about man's fate without consulting anyone. Man, helpless and sinful, did not deserve to be consulted. Evoking a world of uncertainty, these ideas engendered an anxiety in him that could be eased only by a conviction that he was somehow acceptable to God.

Cotton Mather never questioned the view of himself and of the world that these conceptions imposed. His description of himself would have satisfied any Puritan, for any Puritan would have recognized himself in it. All his life Cotton Mather accused himself of sin that rendered him indescribably filthy. He was a "vile" sinner, "feeble and worthless," suffering, he once told the Lord, from spiritual "diseases . . . so complicated, that I am not able so much as distinctly to mention them unto thee; much less can I remedy them."[5] He employed these terms in describing himself when he was an adolescent, apparently in the midst of an agonizing crisis of the soul. He survived this crisis and though years later he sometimes appeared complacent, he never lost his sense of sin. As an old man he confessed in a characteristic way his "Humiliation for my . . . Miscarriages" and called himself "as tempted a Man, as any in the World."[6]

The classic Puritan failures, idleness and waste, did not often contribute to his anxiety. He knew that he was rarely idle, that the little money he

[3] *Increase Mather*, A Discourse Concerning Faith and Fervency in Prayer . . . (*Boston, 1710*), 82.

[4] *Increase Mather*, Practical Truths Tending to Promote the Power of Godliness . . . (*Boston, 1682*), 200. *See also Urian Oakes*, New-England Pleaded With . . . (*Cambridge, Mass., 1673*), 11–13; *Urian Oakes*, A Seasonable Discourse Wherein Sincerity and Delight in the Service of God is Earnestly Pressed Upon Professors of Religion . . . (*Cambridge, Mass., 1682*), 4–5, 9, 17; *William Stoughton*, New-Englands True Interests . . . (*Cambridge, Mass., 1670*), 20–25.

[5] *Cotton Mather*, Diary of Cotton Mather (*New York, [1957?]*), I, 5, 9.

[6] *Mather*, Diary, I, II, 483.

earned was not squandered; and he indulged in no false contrition on these scores. But he did recognize in himself pride and sensuality, the habits of mind that Christians had always considered evil.[7]

Mather's anxiety arose when he found himself unable always to bring his behavior and his state of mind into harmony with his ideas. A true Christian, he knew, was humble—not swelled with pride. A true Christian did not prize this world: he was to live in it and he was to give his best but at the same time the attention of his heart should be fastened upon God. Mather was pained by his failure to live up to this ideal. In his pride and in his sensuality, he disappointed both the Lord and himself. Falling short of the divine imperative rendered him ugly in the sight of God: truly Cotton Mather was a filthy creature.[8]

This conception of himself must certainly have helped induce the massive anxiety he endured for so long. From an early age Cotton Mather had learned of his sin; and by the time he reached maturity he did not have to be reminded of it, though he reminded himself often. After a few years of life he seems not to have required the specific accusation of sin to experience the unease; it probably was always there—a part of his consciousness or not far from it. The most trivial incident could set his fears in motion. When he had a toothache he asked: "Have I not sinned with my *Teeth?* How? By sinful, graceless excessive *Eating.* And by evil Speeches, for there are *Literae dentales* used in them?"[9]

The doctrine of predestination intensified Mather's anxiety. Mather knew that God, in a moment of power and justice, had resolved the eternal fates of all men. He knew too that all men were sinners deserving damnation; only those selected by the Lord would escape a punishment all merited. God had made His choice, nothing could be done to alter it, for predestination was a fact, not a theory.

He responded to this knowledge in several ways. Occasionally he achieved resignation, resolving "to resign all my Conserns unto Him, *without whom not* a little Bird falls unto the Ground." But more frequently he felt compelled to inventory his soul, to tabulate his worth. His *Diary* in one sense is an extended ledger of his merit and his failings. He longed to discover that the balance was on the side of his election.[10]

Just as conventional Puritan ideas about human nature and predestination evoked Mather's feeling about himself, so other related ideas helped him to cope with his anxiety. One set of ideas incited another: Cotton Mather was a sinful, helpless soul, but he could take comfort from the knowledge that God used the sinner for His own purposes. God chose him, Cotton Mather, for his vileness and used him for divine purposes. The choice demonstrated God's power: even a wretch like himself could be used in the Lord's work. In this way when Mather recognized the fact of his sin he was disconsolate and then when he remembered the power of the Lord to use even a vile sinner his anxiety was converted to joy. It was wonderful but the Lord worked in wonderful ways.[11]

Received ideas about God stimulated strong emotion. He longed for the Lord's blessing, begged for His aid, and strained to think, act, and feel in ways he imagined would earn His favor. "My highest Acquisition," Mather wrote in his *Diary,* "I will reckon to bee, a Likeness unto God. To *love* that which *God* loves, and *hate* that which God hates; to be *holy as God is holy.* . . . O That

[7] *See, for example, Mather,* Diary, *I, 15, 79–80, 224–225, 475.*

[8] *Mather,* Diary, *I, 24, 38, 62, et passim.*

[9] *Mather,* Diary, *I, 24.*

[10] *Mather,* Diary, *I, 60.*

[11] *Mather,* Diary, *I, 8–12, et passim.*

I may be conformable unto the *communicable* Attributes of God; and agreeable unto his *Incommunicable*."[12]

He would be like Christ. This idea proved to be physically useful in a life filled with abuse from the external world. As the world grew increasingly hostile to Mather's values, he rejoiced in his suffering: "Yea, a Conformity to Him, in Sufferings, Injuries, Reproaches from a malignant World, makes me, even to rejoice in those Humiliations." He should not sorrow at attacks by evil men—had not evil men attacked Christ? He should glory in their abuse, for they were Satan's agents, and their enmity made him more like Christ.[13]

This mechanism did not always operate with perfection. Robert Calef's "Libel" nine years after the outbreak of witchcraft at Salem left Mather with an anger that smoldered. The best that Mather's attempt to "imitate and represent the Gentleness of my Savior" could achieve was a temporary "sweet calm" seven years after Calef's attacks.[14]

He was more successful in handling his emotions when he faced a twenty-year-old widow who set her cap at him after the death of his first wife in December 1702. The young widow informed him in February 1703 that she had long valued his ministry and now wanted to share his life. The "highest Consideration" in her desire for marriage with Cotton Mather, she told him, "was her eternal Salvation, for if she were mine, she could not but hope the Effect of it would be, that she should also be Christ's." Mather was delighted—and suspicious; he clearly found her sexually exciting—she was of a "Comely Aspect," he said—but her reputation was not unblemished.[15]

During the next two months he writhed in a confusion marked by desire and despair. He wanted the woman but he feared that her flattering offer was a snare laid by the Devil, who had long plotted to destroy Cotton Mather. He needed the comfort of his family and friends but they, evidently fearing that he was about to make a fool of himself, refused to listen to him talk of the widow. He would like to have had Boston's sympathy in his suffering but all he was likely to get—he sensed—was disapproval. Family, friends, the community, all proved interested but unwilling to come to his aid. The widow was hardly more helpful: when he warned her of the difficulty of life with a man who spent much of his time in fasting and praying, she replied that his way of living was precisely what had attracted her to him.[16]

Through his confusion Mather realized that neither his friends nor his family could help him. But within two weeks after the young widow approached him, the way out of his dilemma began to appear. In mulling over what to do Mather decided that he would have to be especially gentle. He admitted to himself that the girl's physical appeal "causes in me a mighty Tenderness" toward her; and of course good breeding demanded that she be treated with respect. "But Religion, above all, obliges me, instead of a rash rejecting her Conversation, to contrive rather, how I may imitate the Goodness of the Lord Jesus Christ, in His Dealing with such as are upon a Conversion unto Him." The problem was to find a Christ-like solution. Within three weeks he was to decide that rejection of the widow was a Christ-like action.[17]

During these three weeks his family and the community urged him toward action by impressing their disapproval upon him. They told him

---

[12] *Mather*, Diary, *I, 61.*

[13] *Mather*, Diary, I, 515.

[14] *Mather*, Diary, I, 172.

[15] *Mather*, Diary, I, 457.

[16] *Mather*, Diary, I, 458.

[17] *Mather*, Diary, I, 467.

that bad company was often at the house of the widow's father, presumably visiting her. What was more frightening was a "mighty Noise" around the town that he was courting the widow. The rumor was false; all he aimed at—he told himself—was "conformity to my Lord Jesus Christ, and Serviceableness to Him, in my Treating of her."[18]

Cotton Mather could not bear to have his name besmirched, and he craved the approval of the community. But he could not reject the widow simply because Boston was outraged at his courtship. He would rebuff the widow but he would not be moved by "popular Slanders." Rather he discovered when he made his decision that he was moved "purely, by a religious Respect unto the Holy Name of the L[ord] Jesus Christ, and my Serviceableness to his precious Interests; which I had a Thousand Times rather dy, than damnify." His decision in fact was a victory, a victory over "Flesh and Blood," and suggested that he was regenerate. The girl was his "sacrifice" to Christ.[19]

The language Mather employed to describe this brief episode suggests how Christian values enabled him to act: the whole affair is cast into a conventional Christian form. He—the servant of the Lord—is tempted; he is denied resort to the ordinary comfort supplied by family and friends; his enemies in the community revile him. But strengthened by his conception of conforming to Christ, he disregards his enemies, overcomes the promptings of the flesh, and acts, sacrificing what is dear to him in the service of the Lord.

Phrasing his action in sacrificial terms eased the agony of rejecting in yet another way. His last entry in the *Diary* about the widow conveys a sense of the violence of his inner struggle. "I struck my Knife, into the Heart of my Sacrifice, by a Letter to her Mother." It also suggests that rejec-

tion in these terms, especially in the use of the word "knife" and the action described by the phrase "stuck my Knife, into the Heart," released at least some small portion of his sexual urges.[20]

Christian ideas, for example the imperative to conform to Christ which had saved him from disaster in this extraordinary affair, also affected Cotton Mather in less spectacular ways. Problems of ordinary scale seemed less annoying when one considered Christ's responses to similar ones. Was his salary insufficient and was he reduced to wearing rags? Poverty presented the temptations of uncharitable anger and self-pity, but he resisted them. Christ's condition in the world had been distinguished by poverty and Christ was robbed of his garments. Why then should Cotton Mather complain of a poverty that left him and his children in want? "Anything that makes my Condition resemble His, tis acceptable to me!" Besides he had another, more desirable kind of garment, the robe of Christ's righteousness. The Lord had also used him to help clothe the poor. He gave from his own purse to the needs of the poor; he was honored by the Lord as "the happy Instrument of cloathing other people." This knowledge, he reported, left him "cheerful"; humiliation was banished, and he was strengthened to the point that he resolved to bear his trials with "the Frames of true, vital, joyful, Christianity."[21]

Not even Cotton Mather could keep the divine model constantly in mind; he, like most Puritans, sometimes experienced periods of "deadness," periods when neither ideas of sin nor of God could evoke emotional responses. This paralysis of thought and feeling never lasted long for it gradually built up anxiety until he was desperately searching for revived spirits. When in "an idle Frame of Soul," he found himself "filled with *Fears*, that the Spirit of God was going to take a

18 *Mather, Diary, I, 470.*
19 *Mather, Diary, I, 473–474.*
20 *Mather, Diary, I, 474.*
21 *Mather, Diary, I, II, 4–5.*

sad *Farewell* of mee." In this state he would begin to pray. But his prayers were usually not answered immediately; the lethargy continued and he would find himself unable to believe in God. This feeling might persist for as long as a week, though he usually managed to dispel it in a few days. Horror and confusion filled these days; hope and joy returned only after Mather succeeded in completely humbling himself.[22] Following this state, which was reminiscent of the stage of humiliation in the conversion process, Mather began to feel hope once more. Hope arose when he found himself able to believe that the Lord would heed his plea if only he really believed. After all, God wanted to help him, and would; but he had to trust the Lord.

Although Cotton Mather did not ever comprehend the workings of his psyche, he did understand to some extent that his ideas might affect his emotions. The relationship of thought and feeling appeared most clearly in the case of a "particular faith." A particular faith was a promise given by God about future events. It was not given to everyone, rather "but *here* and *there*, but *now* and *then*, unto those whom a *Sovereign* GOD shall Please to Favour with it." All Christians of course may receive general reassurance when praying but a particular faith is granted only to a chosen few who approach the Lord with a specific request. The favored believer who goes to the Lord with his request receives, after strenuous prayer, assurance that he will get his wish. "The Impression is born in upon his mind, with as clear a Light, and as full a Force, as if it were from Heaven *Angelically*, and even *Articulately* declared unto him."[23]

Convinced that the particular faith came from

without, Mather insisted that "the Devout Believer cannot cause himself to Believe *What* and *When* he will"; but the fact is that he developed in the particular faith a technique to induce belief and feeling. At the same time he described the change wrought by a particular faith: the believer's feelings were altered. For example, he was sad and anxious before he pleaded for reassurance from God; afterwards, he lost his sadness and anxiety and his spirits revived. This was the theory; Cotton Mather's *Diary* reveals that he achieved the ideal in practice. He used such words as "afflatus" and "raptures" in describing his renewed feelings; at times his ecstasy became indescribable. More often his anxiety dropped away, and he found himself full of confidence and even joy. Not surprisingly he also felt physically rejuvenated.[24]

A typical experience with a particular faith occurred in April 1700 when he was to deliver the Thursday lecture, an important occasion when a minister strove to give his best. On this day he found himself "tired, and spent, and faint; especially with torturing Pains in my *Head*." Surely, he reasoned, on a day when he was to do work "to glorify my Lord Jesus Christ," the Lord would help him. And so he prayed for a particular faith—and received it: "I felt a wonderful Force from Heaven, strengthening, and assisting, and enlarging of mee."[25]

Psychologically, the conception of a particular faith was a way of expressing man's dependence upon God. Man required reassurance of the Lord's favor; to obtain it he must grasp the immensity of God's power in contrast to his own helplessness. Once he achieved this sense, usually after a prolonged period of humbling himself, the Lord might choose to speak. Man did not

---

[22] See Mather, Diary, I, 7–12, *an early example of "deadness."*

[23] Cotton Mather, Parentator . . . (Boston, 1724), 189–190.

[24] Mather, Parentator, *189;* Mather, Diary, I, 343, 355, 400, et passim.

[25] Mather, Diary, I, 344.

coerce the Lord, yet the Lord's response came only after man's extended plea. The answer confirmed God's power.[26]

Cotton Mather's inner life was peculiar and, in several ways, unique. His was a psychology of the extreme. If his peers felt a deep piety, he ached for union with Christ. When they were complacent, he was self-righteous. If they were filled with a mild dread, he was tormented by agonizing visions. If they enjoyed contemplating the divine, he experienced raptures. They gained reassurance by praying to the Lord, he received direct communication from an angel.

Samuel Sewall, a friend of Cotton Mather, lived a life in no way extravagant but one which revealed almost as clearly as Mather's, the role of Puritan ideas in creating piety. Like Mather, Sewall recognized that man was sinful and helpless and that only the Lord could save him. Like Mather, Sewall craved God's love; and he too wished to make his life conform to Christ's as closely as possible.[27]

Sewall did not comment on these convictions extensively or on any of the great ideas of Puritanism. Rather his ideas were masked by a life of placid success. There was his work, which followed an upward course after his marriage to the daughter of wealthy John Hull, and a long period as a Superior Court judge and a councillor, two positions he filled with dignity and skill. There was his service to family and friends and to his church which he performed with loving concern. And there was his interest in New England, an interest that propelled him into beliefs that some of his sophisticated contemporaries considered absurd: opposition to wigs, for example, and to the keeping of Christmas.[28]

The record of this life is set down in Sewall's *Diary*. It is a record largely unadorned by reflection, containing little more than his notes on his actions and the events of his world. Even dreadful accidents such as this one of August 10, 1686, stand unremarked: "Ridd to Braintrey in Company of Mr. Pain, and Mr. Joseph Parson, and home agen. 'Tis said a Groton Man is killed by 's cart, Bowells crushed out; and a Boy killed by a Horse at Rowley; foot hung in the Stirrup and so was torn to pieces; both about a week ago."[29] In Cotton Mather's feverish *Diary* such episodes were improved for all they were worth.

Sewall's emotional detachment was probably as great as the spare entries in the *Diary* indicate. His piety burned slowly and evenly throughout his life: it rarely flared as Cotton Mather's often did. Although Sewall knew that he should love God and reproached himself when he felt deadness to God's claims, neither his sense of sin nor his belief in divine power left him deeply anxious.[30]

Despite the absence of intensity in feeling, Puritan ideas patterned Sewall's responses in the approved way. In Sewall's uncomplicated mind ideas were applied simply and literally—in contrast to Cotton Mather's intricate, even tortured, use. They served to suppress doubt and inquiry and to provide reassurance that things were what

---

[26] *I have learned much from Perry Miller's account of Mather's use of the idea of a particular faith in* The New England Mind: From Colony to Province (*Cambridge, Mass., 1953*), *403–404. See also Cotton Mather,* Magnalia Christi Americana . . . (*London, 1702*), *Bk. IV, Pt. II, Chap. I.*

[27] *Samuel Sewall,* Diary of Samuel Sewall, 1674–1729 (*Massachusetts Historical Society,* Collections, *5th Ser., V–VII* [*Boston, 1878–82*]), *I, 46–47; II, 98, 212; III, 200.*

[28] *Sewall,* Diary, *I, passim. For a modern account see Ola Elizabeth Winslow,* Samuel Sewall of Boston (*New York, 1964*).

[29] *Sewall,* Diary, *I, 146.*

[30] *For an example of "deadness," see Sewall,* Diary, *II, 189.*

they seemed to be, that God's universe was ordered and reliable. The lines that attitudes and emotions and behavior should follow were clear— God had traced them in the Scriptures, and Sewall never doubted for a moment that he, or one of Massachusetts's ministers, could follow them out to the Lord's satisfaction. Even the meaning of death, the worst that the world offered, was comprehensible, or at least man could know all he required about it in this life. Death should not become the occasion of wracking grief, or of philosophical speculation. Death was an affliction sent by God to make the living aware of their sin and to prepare them for their own ends. And death contained the promise of union with Christ. Sewall fronted death hundreds of times and though when relatives or close friends died he felt a grief we would recognize as a sense of loss, his emotions assumed other forms in response to his ideas. When a son died he told himself that God had chosen this way of humbling him; he had overvalued his son; his son had become an "Image" to him.[31] The death of his first wife prompted the reflection that "God is teaching me a new Lesson; to live a Widower's Life"; the death of his second left him "ashamed of my Sin."[32] In all these notions there was the assurance that death was a "righteous sentence upon one's self" and that it led ultimately to conformity to Christ.[33] This elaborate rationale controlled emotion, and made it supportable.

Emotional reactions to ordinary events were no less patterned by Puritan ideas. When he reacted, Sewall's response invariably reflected his conviction that all things occurred through the workings of Providence. Happenings in the world around

him drew his comment because he detected God's hand in them. Almost any incident could move him to connect the seemingly trivial to the divine: one day a child's ball clogged a rain spout on the roof causing a leak into a room; Sewall tried to clear the drain and failing put his servant to it. When the ball was poked out Sewall reflected, "Thus a small matter greatly incommodes us; and when God pleases 'tis easily removed." Spilling a can of water, he remarked "that our Lives would shortly be spilt."[34]

Long before Sewall's time making such connections became a Puritan convention. We are most familiar with it in the Puritan penchant for allegory. Cotton Mather, who made more out of the technique than anyone else in New England, saw in it a grand means of stimulating piety. "Daily spiritualizing," as he called it, could be done by anyone, in contrast to a particular faith which was reserved for a qualified few.[35]

The process served Sewall and Puritans like him in a manner they did not comprehend: it routinized their emotions. Savoring the divine was the end the technique proposed to make habitual, but the beginning point had to be the concrete and the immediate. This world must be pondered before the next was approached; and this world, as Sewall's record indicates, was endlessly intriguing. The shift to cosmic meaning was made but too often in perfunctory and spiceless terms. This world remained so fascinating that, instead of a renewed piety, Puritans found that they were still prone to complacency and even deadness in the

---

[31] *Sewall, Diary, II, 114.*

[32] *Sewall, Diary, III, 144, 256.*

[33] *Sewall, Diary, II, 212. See also Sewall, Diary, III, 172, 176.*

[34] *For the comment on the ball see Sewall, Diary, II, 388; for the comment on the spilled water, 404.*

[35] *Cotton Mather's Diary is filled with his attempts at daily spiritualizing. See also his Winter Meditations. Directions How to Employ the Liesure [sic] of the Winter for the Glory of God . . . (Boston, 1693); Agricola, Or, the Religious Husbandman . . . (Boston, 1727).*

face of the Lord's claims. The irony of such experience eluded Puritan ministers who had insisted that in a well-disposed mind the intellect must "frame, and shape, and mould" the emotions.[36] Ruminations on the things of the world were supposed to yield a new spirit, not a growing preoccupation with the creatures.

The failure did not arise from the convention but from the emotional framework in which it was exercised. Sewall and those Puritans who in their complacency resembled him were not fully self-conscious. They had not learned to examine every thought and every feeling for godliness. They had forgotten that sin inhered in attitude as well as in behavior. In their unthinking conformity to creed they were "secure," to use the seventeenth-century word that described an absence of tension.

Different as they were from Cotton Mather, men like Sewall were hardly less Puritan. Both types of Puritan felt what their ideas instructed them to feel. In both the intellect's application of a highly articulated moral code displaced certain kinds of emotion. At times raw, spontaneous feeling burst through—Mather's seething anger at Calef provides one such instance. But most of the time such spontaneity was absent: the model of what a Christian should be and how he should think and feel was too clear to escape. Even love of one's wife had to be carefully controlled: it should not become so absorbing as to divert one's attention from God. Knowing how they were supposed to respond as Christians, Puritans, at some level of their being, transmuted raw feeling into feeling sanctioned by their code.

The experience of Mather and Sewall suggests the great range in the quality of the emotional lives of Puritans. In these two men even the periods of "deadness" must have differed in tone.

Yet both recognized deadness as a state of mind and both felt guilty while they endured it. And in each of them the Puritan conception of man served first to intensify the feeling and then to stimulate the guilt that enabled them to dispel it. Whatever the variation in quality of the feeling of each in these, and similar, periods, the process of emotional development was the same. This process involved a complex interaction of thought and feeling initiated by traditional Puritan ideas.

If this peculiar relationship of piety and intellect existed in Puritans as different as Mather and Sewall were, it probably should be regarded as one of the determinants of Puritan character. Certainly the Puritan was not born with a peculiar emotional bias, nor was his character defined somehow more basically by emotion than by intellect. If "stretched passion" made the Puritan what he was, ideas did much to evoke and control that passion. The traditional notion of the mind as a duality has obscured the connections of emotion and intellect and of the unity of the psychic process itself. This process was incredibly complex; and the interplay of ideas and feelings in Puritans can never be wholly reconstructed. This should not deter us from making the attempt, however. Once it is made, I suspect that it will reveal the pre-eminence of the intellect in Puritan mind and character.[37]

36 Oakes, New-England Pleaded With, 11.

37 For other examples of Puritans whose minds reveal the relationship of piety and intellect discussed in this article see John Hull, "The Diaries of John Hull," in American Antiquarian Society, Transactions and Collections, III (Worcester, 1857), 109–316; M. G. Hall, ed., "The Autobiography of Increase Mather," in Amer. Antiq. Soc., Proceedings, N.S., LXXI (Worcester, 1962), 271–360; Edmund S. Morgan, ed. "The Diary of Michael Wigglesworth," in Colonial Society of Massachusetts, Publications, XXXV (Boston, 1951), 311–444; Winthrop Papers (Boston, 1929———). John and Margaret Winthrop's letters in volumes I and II are especially revealing.

GOD, SCIENCE, AND THE PURITAN DILEMMA

*John E. Van De Wetering**

The precise nature of the impact of Newtonian science on American Puritanism has been elusive.[1] But in the career of one typical, eighteenth-century clergyman, Thomas Prince (1687–1758), the complex, sometimes contradictory threads appear in a microcosm that dispels much of that confusion. Trained appropriately at Harvard when the impact of the new science was being felt, and with some limited educational experience at Gresham College, London, Prince moved for several years among the dissenters of the Mother Country. When he returned to Massachusetts he assumed an important New England pastorate, the Old South in Boston, and he became a leading member of the influential Mather faction. As a man of orthodox religious convictions, with a fine, modern education and with the cosmopolitanism gained from his several years in England, Prince is a nearly perfect New England Puritan to examine for the impact of science on theology.

Thomas Prince absorbed the new science. Like all clergymen who accepted the new knowledge,

[1] *Theodore Hornberger,* Scientific Thought in the American Colleges, 1638–1800 *(1945), 82, stated that conflict between science and theology began to appear between 1690 and 1740. Perry Miller,* The Puritan Mind: From Colony to Province *(1953), 445, claimed that the sense of conflict appeared only later in the age of Jonathan Edwards. Miller insisted, in fact, that the Puritans were sublimely confident in their use of science, and he placed Prince among those who accepted the new science and used it with great confidence for theological purposes. Hornberger (p. 83), placed Prince among those who "constitute a break in the line of development of scientific rationalism." Herbert W. Schneider,* The Puritan Mind *(1930), 47, minimized the role of science in the lives of the Puritan intelligentsia, for which he was taken to task by Theodore Hornberger, "Puritanism and Science," the* New England Quarterly, *X, 503–515 (1937).*

JOHN E. VAN DE WETERING (1927–   ) is Chairman of the Department of History at the University of Montana. His publications include "Thomas Prince's Chronological History" (1961), and "The Christian History of the Great Awakening" (1966). Reprinted by permission of the author and the New England Quarterly, Vol. 38, No. 4 (December, 1965), 494–507.

he wished to use it for theological ends. But the self-sufficient, mechanical universe of Newton offered the church a dilemma. In the harmonious, ordered cosmos of the New Physics, there was little room for the Deity to exercise a direct influence. The world of science was self-sustaining and beautifully contained, but the world of religion was dependent upon an immanent God whose dreadful and immediate presence must always be felt in the operations of Nature. How then could God's identity be maintained within a mechanical universe and in such a way as to affect the daily lives of all men? Prince solved this problem by insisting that God functioned as the constantly present force behind the systematic patterns in the physical universe. He exclaimed over the intricate order of the natural world and said that back of all the harmonies was a consistently active force, God. God served to maintain the network of involved motions by His own persistent activity, and as such was a permanent participant in the operations of Nature. God's hand was behind the simplest fluttering of a leaf to the ground, and behind the most complex displacements of an earthquake.

In explanations such as these lay the error of Prince and of the Puritans. Prince accepted the naturalist emphasis that was being fostered by the science of his age, and he chose, therefore, to accentuate God's natural identity over His spiritual identity. Prince, in dealing with the question of God's immediacy, concentrated upon establishing a place for Him in the natural world rather than the supernatural. Accordingly, Prince shifted his clerical concerns from Heaven to Earth, and he brought God with him. What was truly needed by the Puritan clergy was not a place for the Deity in the confined and lawful world of Nature, but a place for Him deliberately outside Nature, where His powers could transcend the limiting impositions of law, and where His activities depended more upon His will than upon His order.

Apparently Prince was enchanted with the world of natural philosophy.[2] He had listened attentively and regularly to the Gresham lectures in Medicine given by the famous Doctor Woodward, and to the addresses in astronomy offered by a "mr. Harris," probably John Harris, author of *Lexicon Technicum*, and later secretary of the Royal Society.[3] Moreover, once back in Boston, he heard of no official objections to his application of science to theology from his pulpit and in the press. Indeed, Cotton Mather had pronounced his blessing upon Newtonian science soon after Prince had been graduated from Harvard, so that its consistency with orthodoxy was official and the lingering doubts of those who feared the new science were stilled.

Prince, and the Puritans like him who worked the details of scientific explanation into their theological disquisitions, opened the world of science to thousands of Puritans.[4] Those who filled the churches of New England heard from their ministers of the Newtonian system that verified the existence of the Almighty. The apparent ease with which Prince and the Puritans accepted advances in science came from the terms in which Newton and others offered their discoveries to the world. The scientists believed that they were finding objective reality, but beyond the discoverable remained the provinces of God. Newton, as a deeply religious man, offered his declaration of faith in the second edition of the *Principia* where

[2] *See Perry Miller*, The New England Mind: From Colony to Province (*1953*), *for the clerical emphasis placed on science by this generation. See especially, 444–445 for Miller's discussion of Prince in this connection.*

[3] *Thomas Prince, Ms., Journal, Nov. 28, 1710.*

[4] *I. Bernard Cohen*, Franklin and Newton (*1956*), *207, said that Benjamin Franklin, for example, learned some of his earliest science from the sermons of Cotton Mather.*

he insisted that fate could never have produced the regularity seen in Nature.[5] Colin MacLaurin, an old-world academic scientist, summarized the attitude that made science acceptable to Prince. Natural philosophy, he said, was to be valued because it formed a foundation for natural religion and moral philosophy: "To study is to search into his workmanship: every new discovery opens to use a new part of his scheme."[6]

The essence of this new age of science was wedded, then, to classical theology in a way that delighted the Puritan soul. Over and over, the clergy would view the miraculous scheme of God as the scientists were discovering it, and exclaim with pleasure as each new detail rendered the Natural Order more exquisitely intricate. There was an uneasiness, nevertheless, revealed in Prince's work that was indicative of the threats that science had begun to offer his religion. Prince worried about God's direct and constant presence in this Newtonian universe, and his concern to keep God before the individual drove him to act on this matter.

The immediate presence of God had to be preserved, it seemed, and as proof of this immediacy, Prince used the obvious order of the universe for what he hoped would be an advantage for theology. The very existence of an ordered universe offered conclusive proof of God's immediate and continual presence, "For all these curious and well adjusted Systems do intirely hold together and perform their Operations by virtue of certain new and prodigious Forces inspired every where in the same proportion into every Particle of Matter, when once remov'd out of its proper

Place, to reduce and keep it there again. Let but the minutest Atom thro'out this mighty Frame of Being . . . [leave its course] it will immediately receive a new and amazing Force to turn it back into its due Point of Distance; and even there will be a constant Power exerted, in such a certain measure, to preserve it from wandering or being easily driven away."[7] Puritans had always sought an ordered universe. Now, on the basis of scientific authority, Prince suggested an extension of that God-given order to society, and in an election sermon in 1728, the context of which was political, Prince said, "by such means as these the Regulation of this lower World is kept from Age to Age, and without them all things would quickly run into the last Confusion."[8]

God's immediate and constant power and presence were thus established in all realms by one who obviously feared His removal from the daily lives of the congregation. But it was not enough for Prince to claim with Newton that the unity and regularity of Nature proved God's presence, for that only guaranteed God's initial and motivative role. The real problem for Prince rested with an explanation of motion that would assure God's continual action in the universe. For his solution he turned to Aristotle, insisting, "For material substances are plainly unintelligent, unvoluntary, unconscious, un-self-active, un-self-moving, things, and are only subject to be moved by some other Kind of Agent. . . ."[9] Prince always turned to this point as the crucial proof for God's constant presence. If God could remain the mover of

[5] *George S. Brett*, "*Newton's Place in the History of Religious Thought*," Sir Isaac Newton, 1727–1927 (*1928*), *264.*

[6] *Colin MacLaurin*, An Account of Sir Isaac Newton's Philosophical Discoveries (*1748*), *3.*

[7] *Thomas Prince*, Civil Rulers Raised up by God to Feed His People . . . (*1728*), *13.*

[8] *Thomas Prince*, Civil Rulers Raised up by God to Feed His People . . . (*1728*), *13.*

[9] *Thomas Prince*, The Natural and Moral Government and Agency of God, in Causing Droughts and Rains . . . (*1750*), *10.*

unintelligent matter, His continuing action would be sustained. Prince clung to the Aristotelean notion which demanded that every effect have its cause. At the same time he delighted in the modern science which rested on the Galilean premise that motion was a state and needed no causal agent. Prince's application of such terms as "unconscious" and "unintelligent" to material substance revealed the influence of his classical training, but more important it reflected his need for a constantly present and active Almighty. Within a Newtonian framework of natural law, Prince placed his Aristotelean God. It was an unhappy situation. Aristotle's God was no more personal or immediate than was Newton's, and although He had more function as the Constant Mover, He was clearly bound by His own law. Prince had designed no God of free will primarily, but a God whose paramount office was to maintain the neat mechanism He had created. The major error Prince made was in emphasizing this natural role for God. Moreover, the cleric insisted that the idea of natural law be amplified to apply to the dynamics of society as well as Nature.

Prince constructed a very carefully contrived relationship between natural and moral law, expecting by this to extend God's direct influence to society from Nature, where presumably He was already actively involved. The universe for Prince remained anthropocentric, so that natural law, or natural government as he came to call it, complemented moral law, or God's moral government. If moral law could be demonstrated with the mathematical precision of natural law, then religion's involvement in government could be justified in the terms of the new science. In such a way, religion could be "proved" by the most modern methods. For Prince, the "Natural end of God is . . . to effect us, [but] his moral end is to . . . correct us . . ."[10] and in every act of nature,

he sought this dual function. For, if one could explain the incident of rain as God's blessing, or the occasion of lightning as God's vengeance, then the truth of God's ultimate correctional role could be established from the truth of the mechanics of nature.

Prince first made the essential distinction between moral and substantive matter; man the moral, and the rest of God's work the natural. Both forms were directed by God, but all of the natural or unintelligent matter was guided by the natural laws of God, the laws that the new science had uncovered. Man, because of his peculiar position as the principal creation and only intelligent creature of God, was governed by moral law. Prince saw this moral law as an accommodation of all of God's operations to the moral nature of man, for whom the earth was created. Man's moral obligations to God came, in turn, from God's gift of life and the material world. Hence, the natural government of God, or the laws of nature, functioned in a set manner according to God, for the benefit or punishment of man. The effect of such acts of nature, although the acts themselves were a function of the natural government of God, became part of the moral government. All natural acts, then, were moral as well as natural with respect to man.[11]

The moral and natural governments could have been supported by Scripture, but since Prince's object on this occasion was scientific, he simply reminded his audience of this fact without the usual Scriptural citations. The accommodation of God's natural government to His moral government made the study of "Natural Philosophy" a study of "Divinity," he claimed. But in reality, he had reversed his order and

10 *Thomas Prince*, The Natural and Moral Government and Agency of God, in Causing Droughts and Rains . . . (*1750*), *31*.

11 *Thomas Prince*, Civil Rulers Raised up by God to Feed His People . . . (*1728*), *13*.

made the study of "Divinity" a study of "Natural Philosophy" for even when he spoke of God as functioning in His moral role, God was revealed as little more than the keeper of the established order. "And if we strictly search into the Natural State and Course of things in these lower worlds, we may clearly see the careful, constant, wise, and mighty action of the invisible God in every part of the perceptible creation, to preserve it in its proper State and Order."[12]

By implication, moral law appeared as regular and automatic as did natural law. On the surface one might conclude that Prince was moving down the path to Deism with such arguments.[13] In fact, the Deists were objects of great concern to Prince and he constantly warned against the hazards of their materialism.[14] The Deists had talked of God the Clockmaker who had created the laws of nature and then stepped back to observe their operation. Prince, on the other hand, attempted to refute what he considered Deism's evil and disruptive influence by insisting that the hand of God could never be removed from the system of natural law. In short, Prince considered natural law to be the direct result of God's persistent activity, and he answered any objections to his arguments in direct scientific terms.

Sadly for Prince's concerns, it was unnecessary to resort to science. He could have maintained his theological position through Scripture as had been done for centuries and as would continue to be done. He might have approached science in terms of its methods rather than its substance as later Protestant thinkers would do, and have thus saved himself the need for a clumsy defense. But he, like others, was entranced with the new learning. He did not merely wish to abstract from science its cold and sensible method. He wished to embrace the new wealth of material knowledge that enchanted his imagination and enlarged his physical world. Moreover as a Puritan clergyman and member of the intellectual elite, he was accustomed to dealing with all branches of human knowledge. Accordingly, he justified his involvement with science for his congregations in order to deal with it from the pulpit. On one occasion, he explained:

> And here I desire you not to think, I am going to give you a Lecture on meer Philosophy; unless you call the wondrous Government and Agency of God . . . Philosophy. No! I am going to treat on a noble subject of Divinity; viz. in the wise, mighty, and constant operations of God–to rescue some of you from that Branch of Atheism we are exceedingly inclined to by Nature, . . ."[15]

Once he had merged theology and science through the unity of natural and moral government, he was free to discuss science in practically any fashion. He did just that. In 1749, for example, Prince preached on "The Natural and Moral Government and Agency of God, in causing Droughts and Rains." Clearly his concern was scientific, not theological, for he dedicated it to the Royal Society, and he may have hoped to crown his career with membership as Cotton Mather had done. The work was studded with

[12] *Thomas Prince*, Civil Rulers Raised up by God to Feed His People . . . (1728), *12–13.*

[13] *As an illustration of the deistic tendencies inherent in such thinking, see, Theodore Hornberger, "Cotton Mather's Interest in Science," American Literature, 6 (1934), 419. See also, Theodore Hornberger, "Samuel Johnson of Yale," New England Quarterly, VIII (1935), 378–397, for a discussion of Samuel Johnson's escape from deism through a doctrine of the immediacy of God, but with Berkeleyan overtones.*

[14] *John Erskine (editor),* Six Sermons by the Late Thomas Prince . . . , *125.*

[15] *Thomas Prince*, The Natural and Moral Government and Agency of God, in Causing Droughts and Rains . . . , *4–5.*

scholarly allusions and serious attempts at originality. In the best scientific tradition of his age he drew heavily from Newton's *Opticks*.[16] Before he had finished, he cited as well, Halley, Boyle, Harris, Gradley, the Oxford astronomer, and Prince's old Harvard textbook, Morton's *Compendium*. In this instance at least, his inclinations proved themselves to be more scientific than religious.

The ultimate tragedy for the band of orthodox Puritans like Prince occurred when they did, indeed, try to fuse their science most directly with moral preaching. The result was too often bad science and a lost moral. The most dramatic instance of this sort involved Prince in a dispute with John Winthrop, Hollis professor of Natural Philosophy at Harvard, over the nature of earthquakes.

In 1756, New England was shaken by a severe earthquake, and Prince rushed into print with a revised edition of a sermon he had first published in 1727. He now added an appendix that reflected his latest reading in science, and suggested a new possibility as an explanation for earthquakes. He had read of Franklin's work with electricity, and his proof suggested that electricity was the chief agent of lightning and thunder. This new information in no way invalidated Prince's original assumption that earthquakes were caused by a combination of "sulphurous, nitrous, mineral, watery, and airy substance . . . ," but he now felt that electricity, as one of the mightiest agents in the world, was "so extreamly subtil as to pierce thro' the most solid Iron . . ."[17] and acted as a means to excite the various elements to action. Electricity

had caught Prince's fancy so completely that he tended to apply it in some manner to all of nature's phenomena. He said that it surrounded all things, and that it moved about within the earth as it did above. As in clouds, he said, electricity traveled about in different "parties" until it came within striking distance of another such party, and then a shock resulted in proportion to the total amount of electricity present. Prince's underlying point in this description was the affirmation of the immediate presence of God as the moving and directing agent behind the motions of electricity. Whoever observed this process, he insisted, must see God's sure hand at work, for the two parties of electricity came together as "intelligent beings," as if they knew the composition of the other and acted accordingly.[18] After all, he contended, mere material substances knew nothing of distance, kinds, and quantities.

Since Franklin's work had succeeded in explaining the nature of electricity, lightning rods had become familiar devices in Boston and other cities as precautions against fire. Prince thought now that his new theory of earthquakes raised a significant question about the advisability of these new devices. The rods directed lightning harmlessly into the ground, but if lightning were so successfully directed along this course, might not the rods be constantly conducting the ever-present electricity from the air into the ground to add to the volume stored there? If so, the more lightning rods the greater the electrical charge in the ground, and the more electricity underground, the greater the possibility for the excitement of the elements that produced the earthquakes. "And therefore it seems worthy of Consideration whether any Part of the Earth being fuller of this Terrible Substance, may not be more exposed to

16 *I. B. Cohen*, Franklin and Newton *(1956), 114 ff., illustrates the importance of the* Opticks *for eighteenth-century amateur scientists.*

17 *Thomas Prince*, Earthquakes, the Works of God and Tokens of His Just Displeasures . . . *(1755), appendix, 20.*

18 *Thomas Prince*, Earthquakes, the Works of God and Tokens of His Just Displeasures . . . *(1755), appendix, 21.*

more shocking Earthquakes."[19] In short, "The more points of Iron are erected around the Earth . . ." the more earthquakes of great intensity.[20] Prince then drew the inevitable conclusion and the classic description of God's use of Nature to teach morality:

> O! there is no getting out of the mighty Hand of God . . . yea it may grow more fatal; and there is no Safety anywhere, but in his almighty Friendship . . . and by heartily Repenting of every Sin. . . .[21]

Actually Prince's sermon had done nothing to bring an active God closer to his audience. On the contrary, he had explained the extraordinary occurrence of an earthquake in extremely natural terms, and had suggested that possibly a man-made device, the lightning rods, was responsible for the terrible earthquakes. In that light, God's appearance as moral governor, became almost irrelevant, and in his attempt to correlate God's moral law with His natural law, Prince was clearly more interested in deliberating upon the natural aspects. His most urgent message in this sermon was to remove the lightning rods from Boston and not to remove the sin from one's soul. But 1756 was not 1727, and Prince's obvious emphasis on natural phenomena offered a challenge to technology and gained him a new kind of audience.

The earthquake had occurred on the eighteenth of November, and Prince's revised treatise was published on December fifth. In the intervening period, on November twenty-sixth, John Winthrop of Harvard, had devoted a lecture to his own explanation of earthquakes.[22] Prince's attack on applied science in the name of theology brought forth Winthrop's scientific wrath from the quiet of a Harvard professorship to the forum of the Boston press. Winthrop wrote to the Boston *Gazette* to express his surprise at finding so many mistakes in so few lines of Prince's appendix, and was particularly distressed by the threat Prince offered to sound scientific advance. "It is as much our duty to secure ourselves against the effects of lightning as against those of rain, snow, and wind, by the means God has put in our hands," he commented.[23] He then pointed out the fallacy of Prince's claim that the quake had been singularly intense in the Boston area, by suggesting that the reason for its apparent intensity was due to the large number of brick houses.[24]

[22] *John Winthrop,* A Lecture on Earthquakes; Read in the Chapel of Harvard-College, in Cambridge, N. E., November 26th 1755. . . . *More than any of his predecessors, Winthrop brought the weight of the new experimental method to his scholarly, scientific research; he observed sunspots through an eight-foot telescope, wrote papers for the Royal Society on the transits of Mercury, conducted laboratory demonstrations in electricity and magnetism, and suggested that earthquakes occurred in undulatory formations in the earth's crust, generating oscillating motions to objects on the surface. He has justly been called by Frederick E. Brasch, Newton's critical disciple, and has been characterized as a scientist with a practical bent who remained an interpretor of Newtonian philosophy rather than a creative thinker in his own right. See, Frederick E. Brasch, "Newton's First Critical Disciple in the American Colonies," Sir Isaac Newton, 1727–1927.*

[23] *Quoted in Eleanor M. Tilton, "Lightning Rods and Earthquakes, 1755,"* New England Quarterly, *XIII (1940), 86.*

[24] *Quoted in Eleanor M. Tilton, "Lightning Rods and Earthquakes, 1755,"* New England Quarterly, *XIII (1940), 89.*

[19] *Thomas Prince,* Earthquakes, the Works of God and Tokens of His Just Displeasures . . . *(1755), appendix, 23.*

[20] *Thomas Prince,* Earthquakes, the Works of God and Tokens of His Just Displeasures . . . *(1755), appendix, 23.*

[21] *Thomas Prince,* Earthquakes, the Works of God and Tokens of His Just Displeasures . . . *(1755), appendix, 23.*

Prince's reply was evasive. He said that basically no disagreement existed between the two, only a difference in emphasis that followed logically from their different positions.[25] He was, nonetheless, annoyed by Winthrop's sarcasm, and reminded the young professor that the experience of age demanded respect. (Winthrop had been a freshman at Harvard in 1727 when Prince had written his original earthquake sermon.) Winthrop's reply was far from the respectful letter of younger to elder that Prince had maintained he deserved. The scientist asked how they could possibly have a basic agreement when Prince insisted that "points" intensified earthquakes. He continued in the tone of bitter irony that had irritated Prince in the first letter. "Had I known of this learned sermon in season, I might have adorned my discourse with another illustrious name, besides those of Newton, Boyle etc. . . . But alas! so scanty was my knowledge, that some weeks had passed . . . before I saw, or so much as heard of his sermon. . . ."[26] Prince's purpose, said Winthrop, was obviously to introduce a new proof of God's continual agency, "A just and noble design in his complex character of Philosopher and Divine."[27] To do this, however, Prince need not have offered a new supposition concerning the causes of earthquakes, Winthrop explained, since all phenomena of nature offered such proof. Prince's explanation in terms of sulphurous, nitrous, and other such substances would still have served his purpose, Winthrop went on, although it would not have been so "surprising."[28] The

scientist offered the cleric no quarter as a natural philosopher, and barely granted his scientific explanation the dignity of a quick refutation. Prince was suddenly challenged by the new age he had so fervently embraced. A young "specialist" now confronted him with precise knowledge and denied him the right to speculate within the scientific province with only a clergyman's experience.

Prince's response was a withdrawal from the dispute. He excused Winthrop's treatment of him, and concluded with a feeble attempt at humor, misplaced in his otherwise austere public record. He suggested that the Massachusetts assembly allow Winthrop a hundred pounds a year out of respect to his illustrious forefathers, and for the pursuit of science, and he remarked that if this suggestion should excite others to act on the proposal he would be most happy to have served both his country and the professor.[29] Winthrop replied briefly in the March first *Gazette*. Apparently angered by Prince's last letter, he complained, "tho' I can by no Means think of myself fairly treated, even in this last letter, yet I willingly suppress at present, the Remarks that naturally offer themselves upon it . . . my answer to Mr. Prince's sermon did not proceed from a Desire of Victory, but of Truth and Justice."[30] This parting shot closed the dispute, but for many years there remained some reticence among the townspeople to avail themselves of the use of "points."

Prince doubtless had not intended a direct threat against science. He wanted only to suggest additional evidence for God's immediate presence, and he was probably thrilled with the possibilities of his own speculations. Prince had, after all, accepted and used the science of his generation and had regarded it as part of one's intellectual equipment. As a well-trained scholar, Prince was

---

[25] *Quoted in Eleanor M. Tilton, "Lightning Rods and Earthquakes, 1755," New England Quarterly, XIII (1940), 90.*

[26] A Letter to the Publisher of the Boston Gazette . . . inserted in Said Gazette, on the 26th of January, 1756.

[27] A Letter to the Publisher of the Boston Gazette . . . inserted in Said Gazette, on the 26th of January, 1756.

[28] A Letter to the Publisher of the Boston Gazette . . . inserted in Said Gazette, on the 26th of January, 1756.

[29] *Boston* Gazette, *Feb. 23, 1756.*

[30] *Boston* Gazette, *March 1, 1756.*

infatuated with the new knowledge opened by the Newtonians. But as a theologian and active clergyman, he was obligated to reconcile his theology with the new science so that Newtonianism might serve religion. Indeed, he was certain that such a reconciliation constituted the most accurate picture of God's world. In his endeavors, Prince made one crucial error. He failed to see the real nature of the threat that science offered theology, that of a decisive shift of attention to the physical world and away from the spiritual. Prince met and used the new science from a scientist's frame of reference rather than from a cleric's point of view. He sought God in the mundane world of natural law, and the God he found was, understandably, a mechanical God. Increasingly, over the years, Prince looked for and found his Deity on Earth rather than in Heaven. First, God was the Force behind all motion in the physical world, and then He was the maker of moral as well as physical law. In both cases, the paramount function of the Almighty was to contain the order that the scientists had uncovered. God's activity was to make certain that the atoms were pushed to their correct places, to guarantee the mainte-nance of the natural sequences as discovered by science. Even morality had become natural. When Prince accepted this scientific framework and concentrated upon placing God firmly within it, he succeeded in tying God to His own law, and limiting the major proportion of His activities to the natural pattern. In a sense, then, Prince unwillingly and unconsciously did the same thing as the Deists whom he hated and feared. He emphasized the natural functions of God. Having seen the problem of modern science as the removal of God from the immediate care of the universe, Prince deliberately cemented God in that universe and created a very scientific sort of Deity in the process. Finally, as Prince involved the Almighty more and more in the direct operations of Nature, it was only logical that Prince himself become increasingly involved in science. The "proof" of God had come more and more to rest on arguments relating to natural phenomena. When Prince found himself intellectually subdued in this area, as occasioned by his polemic with Winthrop, he found that he could no longer defend his God or his religious position as he had in the past.

Robert Edge Pine and Edward Savage "Congress Voting Independence"　　Historical Society of Pennsylvania

PART 3

THE AMERICAN ENLIGHTENMENT

Introduction

The eighteenth century in America as well as Europe was the Age of Enlightenment. Established ideas of the previous century—mercantilism, monarchy, and uniformity—were displaced by laissez faire, natural law, and reason. The American Enlightenment did not produce a group of intellectuals comparable to the *philosophes*, and it was tremendously influenced by the activities of European intellectual leaders. Yet, the American experience was unique. The spacious wilderness and the absence of a static caste system encouraged an emphasis on the perfectability of man and the belief in progress. These ideas significantly altered the American intellectual tradition.

Bernard Bailyn questions the validity of older interpretations of the Enlightenment which viewed the American Revolution as a natural culmination of enlightened ideas. He maintains that social and political changes such as religious toleration, representative government, and the right to life, liberty, and property, already were matters of fact. The intellectual currents of the Enlightenment merely legitimized and organized the existing conditions.

Gerald Stourzh examines the life of Benjamin Franklin (1706–1790) to dramatize the transition from the Puritan past to the Age of Enlightenment. He believes that Franklin was not so much the "child of the Enlightenment" as has been generally accepted. Although Franklin accepted many enlightened ideas, he did so only with major qualifications. He was also a "child of New England Puritanism."

William H. Nelson discusses American thought during the post-Revolutionary era. Like Bailyn, he maintains that the major social and political changes were realities before the Revolution. The events of 1776 may have signaled the beginning of a new era, but the truly revolutionary attitudes appeared during the formation of constitutional government, not during the war for independence.

Adrienne Koch analyzes the ideas of prominent leaders in the new American government. Thomas Jefferson is presented as the epitome of the enlightened man while Alexander Hamilton barely qualifies as a philosopher-king. John Adams and James Madison are ranked somewhere between Jefferson and Hamilton. The essay is especially important for its attention to the influence of European thought on the American Enlightenment.

113

POLITICAL EXPERIENCE AND ENLIGHTENMENT IDEAS IN EIGHTEENTH-CENTURY AMERICA

Bernard Bailyn*

The political and social ideas of the European Enlightenment have had a peculiar importance in American history. More universally accepted in eighteenth-century America than in Europe, they were more completely and more permanently embodied in the formal arrangements of state and society; and, less controverted, less subject to criticism and dispute, they have lived on more vigorously into later periods, more continuous and more intact. The peculiar force of these ideas in America resulted from many causes. But originally, and basically, it resulted from the circumstances of the prerevolutionary period and from the bearing of these ideas on the political experience of the American colonists.

What this bearing was—the nature of the relationship between Enlightenment ideas and early American political experience—is a matter of particular interest at the present time because it is centrally involved in what amounts to a fundamental revision of early American history now under way. By implication if not direct evidence and argument, a number of recent writings have undermined much of the structure of historical thought by which, for a generation or more, we have understood our eighteenth-century origins, and in particular have placed new and insupportable pressures on its central assumption concerning the political significance of Enlightenment thought. Yet the need for rather extensive rebuilding has not been felt, in part because the architecture has not commonly been seen as a whole—as a unit, that is, of mutually dependent parts related to a central premise—in part because the damage has been piecemeal and uncoordinated: here a beam destroyed, there a stone dislodged, the inner supports only slowly weakened and the balance only gradually thrown off. The edifice still stands,

*BERNARD BAILYN (1922–   ) is Winthrop Professor at Harvard University. His publications include New England Merchants in the 17th Century (1955), Pamphlets of the American Revolution (1965), and The Ideological Origins of the American Revolution (1967). Reprinted by permission of the author and the American Historical Review, Vol. 67, No. 2 (January, 1962), 339–351.

mainly, it seems, by habit and by the force of inertia. A brief consideration of the whole, consequently, a survey from a position far enough above the details to see the outlines of the over-all architecture, and an attempt, however tentative, to sketch a line—a principle—of reconstruction would seem to be in order.

A basic, organizing assumption of the group of ideas that dominated the earlier interpretation of eighteenth-century American history is the belief that previous to the Revolution the political experience of the colonial Americans had been roughly analogous to that of the English. Control of public authority had been firmly held by a native aristocracy—merchants and landlords in the North, planters in the South—allied, commonly, with British officialdom. By restricting representation in the provincial assemblies, limiting the franchise, and invoking the restrictive power of the English state, this aristocracy had dominated the governmental machinery of the mainland colonies. Their political control, together with legal devices such as primogeniture and entail, had allowed them to dominate the economy as well. Not only were they successful in engrossing landed estates and mercantile fortunes, but they were for the most part able also to fight off the clamor of yeoman debtors for cheap paper currency, and of depressed tenants for freehold property. But the control of this colonial counterpart of a traditional aristocracy, with its Old World ideas of privilege and hierarchy, orthodoxy in religious establishment, and economic inequality, was progressively threatened by the growing strength of a native, frontier-bred democracy that expressed itself most forcefully in the lower houses of the "rising" provincial assemblies. A conflict between the two groups and ways of life was building up, and it broke out in fury after 1765.

The outbreak of the Revolution, the argument runs, fundamentally altered the old regime. The Revolution destroyed the power of this traditional aristocracy, for the movement of opposition to parliamentary taxation, 1760–1776, originally controlled by conservative elements, had been taken over by extremists nourished on Enlightenment radicalism, and the once dominant conservative groups had gradually been alienated. The break with England over the question of home rule was part of a general struggle, as Carl Becker put it, over who shall rule at home. Independence gave control to the radicals, who, imposing their advanced doctrines on a traditional society, transformed a rebellious secession into a social revolution. They created a new regime, a reformed society, based on enlightened political and social theory.

But that is not the end of the story; the sequel is important. The success of the enlightened radicals during the early years of the Revolution was notable; but, the argument continues, it was not wholly unqualified. The remnants of the earlier aristocracy, though defeated, had not been eliminated: they were able to reassert themselves in the postwar years. In the 1780's they gradually regained power until, in what amounted to a counterrevolution, they impressed their views indelibly on history in the new federal Constitution, in the revocation of some of the more enthusiastic actions of the earlier revolutionary period, and in the Hamiltonian program for the new government. This was not, of course, merely the old regime resurrected. In a new age whose institutions and ideals had been born of revolutionary radicalism, the old conservative elements made adjustments and concessions by which to survive and periodically to flourish as a force in American life.

The importance of this formulation derived not merely from its usefulness in interpreting eighteenth-century history. It provided a key also for understanding the entire course of American politics. By its light, politics in America, from the very beginning, could be seen to have been a dialectical process in which an aristocracy of wealth and power struggled with the People, who, ordinarily ill-organized and inarticulate, rose upon provocation armed with powerful institutional and ideological weapons, to reform a periodically corrupt and oppressive polity.

In all of this the underlying assumption is the belief that Enlightenment thought—the reforming ideas of advanced thinkers in eighteenth-century England and on the Continent—had been the effective lever by which native American radicals had turned a dispute on imperial relations into a sweeping reformation of public institutions and thereby laid the basis for American democracy.

For some time now, and particularly during the last decade, this interpretation has been fundamentally weakened by the work of many scholars working from different approaches and on different problems. Almost every important point has been challenged in one way or another.[1] All argu-

ments concerning politics during the prerevolutionary years have been affected by an exhaustive demonstration for one colony, which might well be duplicated for others, that the franchise, far from having been restricted in behalf of a borough-mongering aristocracy, was widely available for popular use. Indeed, it was more widespread than the desire to use it—a fact which in itself calls into question a whole range of traditional arguments and assumptions. Similarly, the Populist terms in which economic elements of prerevolutionary history have most often been discussed may no longer be used with the same confidence. For it has been shown that paper money, long believed to have been the inflationary instrument of a depressed and desperate debtor yeomanry, was in general a fiscally sound and successful means—

---

[1] *Recent revisionist writings on eighteenth-century America are voluminous. The main points of reinterpretation will be found in the following books and articles, to which specific reference is made in the paragraphs that follow:* Robert E. Brown, Middle-Class Democracy and the Revolution in Massachusetts, 1691–1780 (*Ithaca, N. Y., 1955*); E. James Ferguson, *"Currency Finance: An Interpretation of Colonial Monetary Practices,"* William and Mary Quarterly, X (*Apr., 1953*), 153–80; Theodore Thayer, *"The Land Bank System in the American Colonies,"* Journal of Economic History, XIII (*Spring, 1953*), 145–59; Bray Hammond, Banks and Politics in America from the Revolution to the Civil War (*Princeton, N. J., 1957*); George A. Billias, The Massachusetts Land Bankers of 1740 (*Orono, Me.,* 1959); Milton M. Klein, *"Democracy and Politics in Colonial New York,"* New York History, XL (*July, 1959*), 221–46; Oscar and Mary F. Handlin, *"Radicals and Conservatives in Massachusetts after Independence,"* New England Quarterly, XVII (*Sept., 1944*), 343–55; Bernard Bailyn, *"The Blount Papers: Notes on the Merchant 'Class' in the Revolutionary Period,"* William and Mary Quarterly, XI (*Jan., 1954*), 98–104; Frederick B. Tolles, *"The American Revolution Considered as a Social Movement: A Re-Evaluation,"* American Historical Review, LX (*Oct., 1954*), 1–12; Robert E. Brown, Charles Beard and the Constitution: A Critical Analysis of "An Economic Interpretation of the Constitution" (*Princeton, N. J., 1956*); Forrest McDonald, We the People: The Economic Origins of the Constitution (*Chicago, 1958*); Daniel J. Boorstin, The Genius of American Politics (*Chicago, 1953*), and The Americans: The Colonial Experience (*New York, 1958*). References to other writings and other viewpoints will be found in Edmund S. Morgan, *"The American Revolution: Revisions in Need of Revising,"* William and Mary Quarterly, XIV (*Jan., 1957*), 3–15; and Richard B. Morris, *"The Confederation Period and the American Historian,"* ibid., XIII (*Apr., 1956*), 139–56.

whether issued directly by the governments or through land banks—not only of providing a medium of exchange but also of creating sources of credit necessary for the growth of an underdeveloped economy and a stable system of public finance for otherwise resourceless governments. Merchants and creditors commonly supported the issuance of paper, and many of the debtors who did so turn out to have been substantial property owners.

Equally, the key writings extending the interpretation into the revolutionary years have come under question. The first and still classic monograph detailing the inner social struggle of the decade before 1776—Carl Becker's *History of Political Parties in the Province of New York, 1760–1776* (1909)—has been subjected to sharp criticism on points of validation and consistency. And, because Becker's book, like other studies of the movement toward revolution, rests upon a belief in the continuity of "radical" and "conservative" groupings, it has been weakened by an analysis proving such terminology to be deceptive in that it fails to define consistently identifiable groups of people. Similarly, the "class" characteristic of the merchant group in the northern colonies, a presupposition of important studies of the merchants in the revolutionary movement, has been questioned, and along with it the belief that there was an economic or occupational basis for positions taken on the revolutionary controversy. More important, a recent survey of the writings following up J. F. Jameson's classic essay, *The American Revolution Considered as a Social Movement* (1926), has shown how little has been written in the last twenty-five years to substantiate that famous statement of the Revolution as a movement of social reform. Most dramatic of all has been the demolition of Charles Beard's *Economic Interpretation of the Constitution* (1913), which stood solidly

for over forty years as the central pillar of the counterrevolution argument: the idea, that is, that the Constitution was a "conservative" document, the polar opposite of the "radical" Articles of Confederation, embodying the interests and desires of public creditors and other moneyed conservatives, and marking the Thermidorian conclusion to the enlightened radicalism of the early revolutionary years.

Finally, there are arguments of another sort, assertions to the effect that not only did Enlightenment ideas not provoke native American radicals to undertake serious reform during the Revolution, but that ideas have never played an important role in American public life, in the eighteenth century or after, and that the political "genius" of the American people, during the Revolution as later, has lain in their brute pragmatism, their successful resistance to the "distant example and teachings of the European Enlightenment," the maunderings of "garret-spawned European illuminati."

Thus from several directions at once have come evidence and arguments that cloud if they do not totally obscure the picture of eighteenth-century American history composed by a generation of scholars. These recent critical writings are of course of unequal weight and validity; but few of them are totally unsubstantiated, almost all of them have some point and substance, and taken together they are sufficient to raise serious doubts about the organization of thought within which we have become accustomed to view the eighteenth century. A full reconsideration of the problems raised by these findings and ideas would of course be out of the question here even if sufficient facts were now available. But one might make at least an approach to the task and a first approximation to some answers to the problems by isolating the central premise concerning the relationship between Enlightenment ideas and political experience and reconsidering it in view of the evidence that is now available.

Considering the material at hand, old and new, that bears on this question, one discovers an apparent paradox. There appear to be two primary and contradictory sets of facts. The first and more obvious is the undeniable evidence of the seriousness with which colonial and revolutionary leaders took ideas, and the deliberateness of their efforts during the Revolution to reshape institutions in their pattern. The more we know about these American provincials the clearer it is that among them were remarkably well-informed students of contemporary social and political theory. There never was a dark age that destroyed the cultural contacts between Europe and America. The sources of transmission had been numerous in the seventeenth century; they increased in the eighteenth. There were not only the impersonal agencies of newspapers, books, and pamphlets, but also continuous personal contact through travel and correspondence. Above all, there were Pan-Atlantic, mainly Anglo-American, interest groups that occasioned a continuous flow of fresh information and ideas between Europe and the mainland colonies in America. Of these, the most important were the English dissenters and their numerous codenominationalists in America. Located perforce on the left of the English political spectrum, acutely alive to ideas of reform that might increase their security in England, they were, for the almost endemically nonconformist colonists, a rich source of political and social theory. It was largely through nonconformist connections, as Caroline Robbins' recent book, *The Eighteenth-Century Commonwealthman* (1959), suggests, that the commonwealth radicalism of seventeenth-century England continued to flow

to the colonists, blending, ultimately, with other strains of thought to form a common body of advanced theory.

In every colony and in every legislature there were people who knew Locke and Beccaria, Montesquieu and Voltaire; but perhaps more important, there was in every village of every colony someone who knew such transmitters of English nonconformist thought as Watts, Neal, and Burgh; later Priestley and Price—lesser writers, no doubt, but staunch opponents of traditional authority, and they spoke in a familiar idiom. In the bitterly contentious pamphlet literature of mid-eighteenth-century American politics, the most frequently cited authority on matters of principle and theory was not Locke or Montesquieu but *Cato's Letters*, a series of radically libertarian essays written in London in 1720–1723 by two supporters of the dissenting interest, John Trenchard and Thomas Gordon. Through such writers, as well as through the major authors, leading colonists kept contact with a powerful tradition of enlightened thought.

This body of doctrine fell naturally into play in the controversy over the power of the imperial government. For the revolutionary leaders it supplied a common vocabulary and a common pattern of thought, and, when the time came, common principles of political reform. That reform was sought and seriously if unevenly undertaken, there can be no doubt. Institutions were remodeled, laws altered, practices questioned all in accordance with advanced doctrine on the nature of liberty and of the institutions needed to achieve it. The Americans were acutely aware of being innovators, of bringing mankind a long step forward. They believed that they had so far succeeded in their effort to reshape circumstances to conform to enlightened ideas and ideals that they had introduced a new era in human affairs.

And they were supported in this by the opinion of informed thinkers in Europe. The contemporary image of the American Revolution at home and abroad was complex; but no one doubted that a revolution that threatened the existing order and portended new social and political arrangements had been made, and made in the name of reason.

Thus, throughout the eighteenth century there were prominent, politically active Americans who were well aware of the development of European thinking, took ideas seriously, and during the Revolution deliberately used them in an effort to reform the institutional basis of society. This much seems obvious. But, paradoxically, and less obviously, it is equally true that many, indeed most, of what these leaders considered to be their greatest achievements during the Revolution—reforms that made America seem to half the world like the veritable heavenly city of the eighteenth-century philosophers—had been matters of fact before they were matters of theory and revolutionary doctrine.

No reform in the entire Revolution appeared of greater importance to Jefferson than the Virginia acts abolishing primogeniture and entail. This action, he later wrote, was part of "a system by which every fibre would be eradicated of antient or future aristocracy; and a foundation laid for a government truly republican." But primogeniture and entail had never taken deep roots in America, not even in tidewater Virginia. Where land was cheap and easily available such legal restrictions proved to be encumbrances profiting few. Often they tended to threaten rather than secure the survival of the family, as Jefferson himself realized when in 1774 he petitioned the Assembly to break an entail on his wife's estate on the very practical, untheoretical, and common ground that to do so would be "greatly to their [the petitioners'] Inter-

est and that of their Families." The legal abolition of primogeniture and entail during and after the Revolution was of little material consequence. Their demise had been effectively decreed years before by the circumstances of life in a wilderness environment.

Similarly, the disestablishment of religion—a major goal of revolutionary reform—was carried out, to the extent that it was, in circumstances so favorable to it that one wonders not how it was done but why it was not done more thoroughly. There is no more eloquent, moving testimony to revolutionary idealism than the Virginia Act for Establishing Religious Freedom: it is the essence of Enlightenment faith. But what did it, and the disestablishment legislation that had preceded it, reform? What had the establishment of religion meant in prerevolutionary Virginia? The Church of England was the state church, but dissent was tolerated well beyond the limits of the English Acts of Toleration. The law required nonconformist organizations to be licensed by the government, but dissenters were not barred from their own worship nor penalized for failure to attend the Anglican communion, and they were commonly exempted from parish taxes. Nonconformity excluded no one from voting and only the very few Catholics from enjoying public office. And when the itinerancy of revivalist preachers led the establishment to contemplate more restrictive measures, the Baptists and Presbyterians advanced to the point of arguing publicly, and pragmatically, that the toleration they had so far enjoyed was an encumbrance, and that the only proper solution was total liberty: in effect, disestablishment.

Virginia was if anything more conservative than most colonies. The legal establishment of the Church of England was in fact no more rigorous in South Carolina and Georgia: it was considerably weaker in North Carolina. It hardly existed at all in the middle colonies (there was of course no vestige of it in Pennsylvania), and where it did, as in four counties of New York, it was either ignored or had become embattled by violent opposition well before the Revolution. And in Massachusetts and Connecticut, where the establishment, being nonconformist according to English law, was legally tenuous to begin with, tolerance in worship and relief from church taxation had been extended to the major dissenting groups early in the century, resulting well before the Revolution in what was, in effect if not in law, a multiple establishment. And this had been further weakened by the splintering effect of the Great Awakening. Almost everywhere the Church of England, the established church of the highest state authority, was embattled and defensive— driven to rely more and more on its missionary arm, the Society for the Propagation of the Gospel, to sustain it against the cohorts of dissent.

None of this had resulted from Enlightenment theory. It had been created by the mundane exigencies of the situation: by the distance that separated Americans from ecclesiastical centers in England and the Continent; by the never-ending need to encourage immigration to the colonies; by the variety, the mere numbers, of religious groups, each by itself a minority, forced to live together; and by the weakness of the coercive powers of the state, its inability to control the social forces within it.

Even more gradual and less contested had been the process by which government in the colonies had become government by the consent of the governed. What has been proved about the franchise in early Massachusetts—that it was open for practically the entire free adult male population—can be proved to a lesser or greater extent for all the colonies. But the extraordinary breadth of the franchise in the American colonies had not

resulted from popular demands: there had been no cries for universal manhood suffrage, nor were there popular theories claiming, or even justifying, general participation in politics. Nowhere in eighteenth-century America was there "democracy"— middle-class or otherwise—as we use the term. The main reason for the wide franchise was that the traditional English laws limiting suffrage to freeholders of certain competences proved in the colonies, where freehold property was almost universal, to be not restrictive but widely permissive.

Representation would seem to be different, since before the Revolution complaints had been voiced against the inequity of its apportioning, especially in the Pennsylvania and North Carolina assemblies. But these complaints were based on an assumption that would have seemed natural and reasonable almost nowhere else in the Western world: the assumption that representation in governing assemblages was a proper and rightful attribute of people as such—of regular units of population, or of populated land—rather than the privileges of particular groups, institutions, or regions. Complaints there were, bitter ones. But they were complaints claiming injury and deprivation, not abstract ideals or unfamiliar desires. They assumed from common experience the normalcy of regular and systematic representation. And how should it have been otherwise? The colonial assemblies had not, like ancient parliaments, grown to satisfy a monarch's need for the support of particular groups or individuals or to protect the interests of a social order, and they had not developed insensibly from precedent to precedent. They had been created at a stroke, and they were in their composition necessarily regular and systematic. Nor did the process, the character, of representation as it was known in the colonies derive from theory. For colonial Americans, representation had none of the symbolic and little of the purely deliberative qualities which, as a result of the revolutionary debates and of Burke's speeches, would become celebrated as "virtual." To the colonists it was direct and actual: it was, most often, a kind of agency, a delegation of powers, to individuals commonly required to be residents of their constituencies and, often, bound by instructions from them—with the result that eighteenth-century American legislatures frequently resembled, in spirit if not otherwise, those "ancient assemblies" of New York, composed, the contemporary historian William Smith wrote, "of plain, illiterate husbandmen, whose views seldom extended farther than to the regulation of highways, the destruction of wolves, wild cats, and foxes, and the advancement of the other little interests of the particular counties which they were chosen to represent." There was no theoretical basis for such direct and actual representation. It had been created and was continuously reinforced by the pressure of local politics in the colonies and by the political circumstances in England, to which the colonists had found it necessary to send closely instructed, paid representatives—agents, so called—from the very beginning.

But franchise and representation are mere mechanisms of government by consent. At its heart lies freedom from executive power, from the independent action of state authority, and the concentration of power in representative bodies and elected officials. The greatest achievement of the Revolution was of course the repudiation of just such state authority and the transfer of power to popular legislatures. No one will deny that this action was taken in accordance with the highest principles of Enlightenment theory. But the way had been paved by fifty years of grinding factionalism in colonial politics. In the details of prerevolutionary American politics, in the complicated maneuverings of provincial politicians

seeking the benefits of government, in the patterns of local patronage and the forms of factional groupings, there lies a history of progressive alienation from the state which resulted, at least by the 1750's, in what Professor Robert Palmer has lucidly described as a revolutionary situation: a condition

> . . . in which confidence in the justice or reasonableness of existing authority is undermined; where old loyalties fade, obligations are felt as impositions, law seems arbitrary, and respect for superiors is felt as a form of humiliation; where existing sources of prestige seem undeserved . . . and government is sensed as distant, apart from the governed and not really "representing" them.

Such a situation had developed in mid-eighteenth-century America, not from theories of government or Enlightenment ideas but from the factional opposition that had grown up against a succession of legally powerful, but often cynically self-seeking, inept, and above all politically weak officers of state.

Surrounding all of these circumstances and in various ways controlling them is the fact that that great goal of the European revolutions of the late eighteenth century, equality of status before the law—the abolition of legal privilege—had been reached almost everywhere in the American colonies at least by the early years of the eighteenth century. Analogies between the upper strata of colonial society and the European aristocracies are misleading. Social stratification existed, of course; but the differences between aristocracies in eighteenth-century Europe and in America are more important than the similarities. So far was legal privilege, or even distinction, absent in the colonies that where it existed it was an open sore of festering discontent, leading not merely, as in the case of the Penn family's hereditary claims to tax exemption, to formal protests, but, as in the case of the powers enjoyed by the Hudson River land magnates, to violent opposition as well. More important, the colonial aristocracy, such as it was, had no formal, institutional role in government. No public office or function was legally a prerogative of birth. As there were no social orders in the eyes of the law, so there were no governmental bodies to represent them. The only claim that has been made to the contrary is that, in effect, the governors' Councils constituted political institutions in the service of the aristocracy. But this claim—of dubious value in any case because of the steadily declining political importance of the Councils in the eighteenth century—cannot be substantiated. It is true that certain families tended to dominate the Councils, but they had less legal claim to places in those bodies than certain royal officials who, though hardly members of an American aristocracy, sat on the Councils by virtue of their office. Councilors could be and were removed by simple political maneuver. Council seats were filled either by appointment or election: when appointive, they were vulnerable to political pressure in England; when elective, to the vagaries of public opinion at home. Thus on the one hand it took William Byrd II three years of maneuvering in London to get himself appointed to the seat on the Virginia Council vacated by his father's death in 1704, and on the other, when in 1766 the Hutchinson faction's control of the Massachusetts Council proved unpopular, it was simply removed wholesale by being voted out of office at the next election. As there were no special privileges, no peculiar group possessions, manners, or attitudes to distinguish councilors from other affluent Americans, so there were no separate political interests expressed in the Councils as such. Councilors joined as directly as others in the factional disputes of the time, associating with groups of all sorts, from minute

and transient American opposition parties to massive English-centered political syndicates. A century before the Revolution and not as the result of anti-aristocratic ideas, the colonial aristocracy had become a vaguely defined, fluid group whose power—in no way guaranteed, buttressed, or even recognized in law—was competitively maintained and dependent on continuous, popular support.

Other examples could be given. Were written constitutions felt to be particular guarantees of liberty in enlightened states? Americans had known them in the form of colonial charters and governors' instructions for a century before the Revolution; and after 1763, seeking a basis for their claims against the constitutionality of specific acts of Parliament, they had been driven, out of sheer logical necessity and not out of principle, to generalize that experience. But the point is perhaps clear enough. Major attributes of enlightened polities had developed naturally, spontaneously, early in the history of the American colonies, and they existed as simple matters of social and political fact on the eve of the Revolution.

But if all this is true, what did the Revolution accomplish? Of what real significance were the ideals and ideas? What was the bearing of Enlightenment thought on the political experience of eighteenth-century Americans?

Perhaps this much may be said. What had evolved spontaneously from the demands of place and time was not self-justifying, nor was it universally welcomed. New developments, however gradual, were suspect by some, resisted in part, and confined in their effects. If it was true that the establishment of religion was everywhere weak in the colonies and that in some places it was even difficult to know what was orthodoxy and what was not, it was nevertheless also true that faith in the idea of orthodoxy persisted and with it belief in the propriety of a privileged state religion. If, as a matter of fact, the spread of freehold tenure qualified large populations for voting, it did not create new reasons for using that power nor make the victims of its use content with what, in terms of the dominant ideal of balance in the state, seemed a disproportionate influence of "the democracy." If many colonists came naturally to assume that representation should be direct and actual, growing with the population and bearing some relation to its distribution, crown officials did not, and they had the weight of precedent and theory as well as of authority with them and hence justification for resistance. If state authority was seen increasingly as alien and hostile and was forced to fight for survival within an abrasive, kaleidoscopic factionalism, the traditional idea nevertheless persisted that the common good was somehow defined by the state and that political parties or factions—organized opposition to established government—were seditious. A traditional aristocracy did not in fact exist; but the assumption that superiority was indivisible, that social eminence and political influence had a natural affinity to each other, did. The colonists instinctively conceded to the claims of the well-born and rich to exercise public office, and in this sense politics remained aristocratic. Behavior had changed—had had to change—with the circumstances of everyday life; but habits of mind and the sense of rightness lagged behind. Many felt the changes to be *away from*, not *toward*, something: that they represented deviance; that they lacked, in a word, legitimacy.

This divergence between habits of mind and belief on the one hand and experience and behavior on the other was ended at the Revolution. A rebellion that destroyed the traditional sources of public authority called forth the full range of advanced ideas. Long-settled attitudes were jolted and loosened. The grounds of legitimacy suddenly shifted. What had happened was seen to have been good and proper, steps in the right direction. The glass was half full, not half empty; and to complete the work of fate and nature, further thought must be taken, theories tested, ideas applied. Precisely because so many social and institutional reforms had already taken place in America, the revolutionary movement there, more than elsewhere, was a matter of doctrine, ideas, and comprehension.

And so it remained. Social change and social conflict of course took place during the revolutionary years; but the essential developments of the period lay elsewhere, in the effort to think through and to apply under the most favorable, permissive, circumstances enlightened ideas of government and society. The problems were many, often unexpected and difficult; some were only gradually perceived. Social and personal privilege, for example, could easily be eliminated —it hardly existed; but what of the impersonal privileges of corporate bodies? Legal orders and ranks within society could be outlawed without creating the slightest tremor, and executive power with equal ease subordinated to the legislative: but how was balance within a polity to be achieved? What were the elements to be balanced and how were they to be separated? It was not even necessary formally to abolish the interest of state as a symbol and determinant of the common good; it was simply dissolved: but what was left to keep clashing factions from tearing a government apart? The problems were pressing, and the efforts to solve them mark the stages of revolutionary history.

In behalf of Enlightenment liberalism the revolutionary leaders undertook to complete, formalize, systematize, and symbolize what previously had been only partially realized, confused, and disputed matters of fact. Enlightenment ideas were not instruments of a particular social group, nor did they destroy a social order. They did not create new social and political forces in America. They released those that had long existed, and vastly increased their power. This completion, this rationalization, this symbolization, this lifting into consciousness and endowing with high moral purpose inchoate, confused elements of social and political change—this was the American Revolution.

REASON AND POWER IN BENJAMIN FRANKLIN'S POLITICAL THOUGHT

Gerald Stourzh*

Perhaps no period of modern history has been more a victim of generalization than the Age of Enlightenment. The worship of reason and progress and belief in the essential goodness and perfectibility of human nature are most commonly associated with the 18th century climate of opinion. Many of the stereotypes which have been applied to it have automatically been transferred to Benjamin Franklin. Already to contemporaries of his old age, Franklin seemed the very personification of the Age of Reason. Condorcet, who had known Franklin personally, summed up his description of Franklin's political career as follows: "In a word, his politics were those of a man who believed in the power of reason and the reality of virtue."[1] In Germany, an admirer was even more

[1] Oeuvres du Marquis de Condorcet, eds. A. Condorcet O'Connor and M. F. Arago, 2nd ed., 12 vols. (Paris, 1847–49), Vol. 3, p. 420.

*GERALD STOURZH is a member of the Department of History at the University of Vienna. His publications include Readings in American Democracy (1967). Reprinted by permission of the author and the American Political Science Review, Vol. 47, No. 4 (December, 1953), 1092–1115.

enthusiastic: "Reason and virtue, made possible through reason alone, consequently again reason and nothing but reason, is the magic with which Benjamin Franklin conquered heaven and earth."[2] This is also the judgment of posterity. F. L. Mott and Chester E. Jorgensen, who have so far presented the most acute analysis of Franklin's thought and its relationship to the intellectual history of his time, do not hesitate to call him "the completest colonial representative" of the Age of Enlightenment.[3] Unanimous agreement seems to exist that Franklin was "in tune with his time."[4]

This essay will attempt to show that these generalizations, instead of illuminating the essence of Franklin's moral and political philosophy, tend rather to obscure some of the mainsprings of his thought and action. Our investigation rests upon the assumption that man's understanding of politics is inseparable from his conception of human nature. Consequently, this reappraisal of Franklin's political thought will subject his views on human nature to close scrutiny; it is hoped that this procedure may lead to a rejection of some of the cliches to which he has fallen victim.

[2] Georg Forster, *"Erinnerungen aus dem Jahre 1790,"* in *"Kleine Schriften,"* Georg Forsters saemmtliche Schriften, *ed. by his daughter, 9 vols. (Leipzig, 1843), Vol. 6, p. 207.*

[3] Benjamin Franklin, Representative Selections with Introduction, Bibliography, and Notes, *eds. F. L. Mott and Chester E. Jorgenson (New York, 1936), p. xiii.*

[4] Carl Becker, review of the Franklin Institute's *Meet Dr. Franklin, in* American Historical Review, *Vol. 50, p. 142 (Oct., 1944). Cf. Henry Steele Commager's statement that it was the faith in reason which gave unity to Franklin's life. "Franklin, the American," review of Carl Van Doren's* Benjamin Franklin, *in* New York Times Book Review, *Oct. 9, 1938, p. 1. Charles A. Beard explicitly referred to Franklin as an outstanding example of American writers on progress. Introduction to J. B. Bury,* The Idea of Progress *(New York, 1932), p. xxxvii.*

I. The "Great Chain of Being"

Many of the notions which are commonly applied to the 18th century, such as the belief in progress and in the perfectibility of human nature, are significant chiefly with respect to the currents of thought and action related to the American and French Revolutions, and do little to deepen our understanding of earlier developments. So it is to the first half of the 18th century that we must now turn. We are prone to overlook the extraordinary difference in age which separated Franklin from the other Founding Fathers of the Republic. Franklin was born in 1706, twenty-six years before Washington, twenty-nine years before John Adams, thirty-seven years before Jefferson, thirty-nine years before John Jay, forty-five years before James Madison, and fifty-one years before Alexander Hamilton.

Franklin's fame as a social and natural philosopher rests mainly on the achievements of his middle and late years. One needs to remember, however, that he was a moral philosopher long before he became a natural philosopher and before he advised his fellowmen how to acquire wealth.[5] At the age of twenty-two, he formed a "club for mutual improvement,"[6] the Junto, where great emphasis was laid on moral or political problems. Whether self-interest was the root of human action, whether man could attain perfection, whether "encroachments on the just

[5] *Even after having achieved world-wide fame as a natural philosopher, he observed that we deserve reprehension if "we neglect the Knowledge and Practice of essential Duties" in order to attain eminence in the knowledge of nature. The* Writings of Benjamin Franklin, *ed. Henry Albert Smyth, 10 vols. (New York, 1905–7), Vol. 4, p. 22. (Hereafter cited as* Writings.)

[6] Autobiography, Writings, *Vol. 1, p. 22.*

liberties of the people"[7] had taken place—all these things were matters of discussion at Franklin's club. Already at the age of nineteen, during his first stay in London, he had printed his first independent opus, *A Dissertation on Liberty and Necessity, Pleasure and Pain*.[8] This piece showed that no trace was left of his Presbyterian family background. The secularization of his thought had been completed.[9] Gone were the Puritan belief in revela-

tion and the Christian conception of human nature which, paradoxically, included the notion of the depravity of man, as well as of his uniqueness among all created beings.[10] Franklin's *Dissertation* shows that he was thoroughly acquainted with the leading ideas of his time. The early decades of the 18th century were characterized by the climate of opinion which has been aptly called

---

[7] *James Parton*, Life and Times of Benjamin Franklin, *2d ed., 2 vols. (Boston, 1897), Vol. 1, p. 160. See also* Writings, *Vol. 2, p. 89. The authors who so far have most closely scrutinized Franklin's political thought do not see the relevance of many of the younger Franklin's remarks on human nature, arbitrary government, or the nature of political dispute to his concept of politics. See M. R. Eiselen, Franklin's Political Theories (Garden City, N. Y., 1928), p. 13; R. D. Miles, "The Political Philosophy of Benjamin Franklin," unpub. diss. (Univ. of Michigan, 1949), p. 36; Benjamin Franklin, Representative Selections (cited in note 3), p. lxxxii. The most recent work in this field, Clinton Rossiter's "The Political Theory of Benjamin Franklin,"* Pennsylvania Magazine of History and Biography, *Vol. 76, pp. 259–93 (July, 1952), pays no attention to Franklin's conception of human nature and his attitude towards the problem of power and the ends of political life. Rossiter's contention (p. 268) is that Franklin "limited his own thought process to the one devastating question: Does it work?, or more exactly, Does it work well?" Franklin, however, like everybody else, had certain ends and goals in view, and the question "Does it work?" is meaningless without the context of certain basic desiderata.*

[8] *This little work has been omitted in the Smyth edition of Franklin's writings, because "the work has no value, and it would be an injury and an offence to the memory of Franklin to republish it."* Writings, *Vol. 2, p. vi. It is, however, reprinted as an appendix to Parton, op. cit., Vol. 1, and has since been republished independently with a bibliographical note by Lawrence C. Wroth (New York, 1930).*

[9] *See Herbert Schneider, "The Significance of Benjamin Franklin's Moral Philosophy,"* Columbia University Studies in the History of Ideas, *Vol. 2, p. 298 (1918).*

[10] *In his* Autobiography, *Franklin acknowledges his debt to Shaftesbury and Collins for becoming "a real doubter in many points of our religious doctrine."* Writings, *Vol. 1, p. 244. The question of Franklin's attitude toward the great moral philosophers and of their influence upon him is considerably more difficult to determine than the same question with regard to John Adams or Thomas Jefferson. With the exception of authors named in the* Autobiography, *comments on books Franklin read are extremely rare. His library has not been preserved; there is, however, a list of books known to have been in Franklin's library at the time of his death (compiled by Dr. George Simpson Eddy in Princeton University; photostat in the library of the American Philosophical Society in Philadelphia). See also Mr. Eddy's article, "Dr. Benjamin Franklin's Library,"* Proceedings of the American Antiquarian Society, *new series, Vol. 34, pp. 206–26 (Oct., 1924). Except for comments in some English pamphlets, there exist nothing like the voluminous marginal notes of John Adams and Jefferson. Also he was not able to keep up a correspondence like Adams' or Jefferson's, discussing great problems from the perspective of a long life in retirement after the great events of their lives had taken place. Immersed in public business almost until his death, Franklin does not seem to have had much time left over for reading. Benjamin Rush told John Adams that "Dr. Franklin thought a great deal, wrote occasionally, but read during the middle and later years of his life very little." October 31, 1807, in Benjamin Rush,* The Letters of Benjamin Rush, *ed. L. H. Butterfield, 2 vols. (Princeton, 1951), Vol. 2, p. 953. For a compilation of the authors with whom Franklin was acquainted, see Lois Margaret MacLaurin, Franklin's Vocabulary (Garden City, N.Y., 1928), Ch. 1, and Benjamin Franklin, Representative Selections (cited in note 3), p. lv.*

"cosmic Toryism."[11] Pope's *Essay on Man* and many pages of Addison's *Spectator*—both of which Franklin admired—most perfectly set forth the creed of a new age. Overshadowing everything else, there was joy about the discoveries of the human mind, which had solved the enigma of creation:

> Nature and Nature's Laws lay hid in Night:
> GOD said, *Let Newton be!* and all was Light.[12]

The perfection of that Great Machine, the Newtonian universe, filling humanity with admiration for the Divine Watchmaker, seemed to suggest that this world was indeed the best of all possible worlds. Everything was necessary, was good. Pope's "Whatever is, is right," is the key phrase of this period. The goodness of the Creator revealed itself in His giving existence to all possible creatures. The universe "presented the spectacle of a continuous scale or ladder of creatures, extending without a break from the worm to the seraph."[13] Somewhere in this "Great Chain of Being," to use a favorite phrase of the period,[14]

there must be a place for Man. Man, as it were, formed the "middle link" between lower and higher creatures. No wonder, then, that Franklin chose as a motto for his *Dissertation* the following lines of Dryden:

> Whatever is, is in its Causes just,
> Since all Things are by Fate; but purblind Man
> Sees but a part o' th' Chain, the nearest Link,
> His Eyes not carrying to the equal Beam
> That poises all above.[15]

The consequences of the conception of the universe as a "Great Chain of Being" for Franklin's understanding of human nature are highly significant. To be sure, man had liberated himself from the oppression of Original Sin, and in his newly established innocence he hailed the Creator and praised the Creation. But if the depravity of human nature had been banished, so had man's striving for redemption, man's aspiration for perfection. There was nothing left which ought to be redeemed. Indeed, in the new rational order of the universe, it would not seem proper to long for a higher place in the hierarchy of beings. Man's release from the anguish of Original Sin was accompanied by a lowering of the goals of human life. "The imperfection of man is indispensable to the fullness of the hierarchy of being." Man had, so to speak, already attained the grade of perfection which belonged to his station. From the point of view of mortality, then, what this amounted to was a "counsel of imperfection—an ethics of prudent mediocrity."[16]

Quiet contentment with, and enjoyment of, one's place in the Great Chain of Being must have

11 *Basil Willey*, The Eighteenth Century Background (*London, 1940*), *Ch. 3, passim.*

12 *Pope's epitaph intended for Newton's tomb.*

13 *Willey, op. cit., pp. 47–48.*

14 *See A. O. Lovejoy*, The Great Chain of Being (*Cambridge, Mass., 1936*). *This brilliant analysis of that complex of ideas has been applied to Franklin only once, although it offers important clues for an understanding of Franklin's conception of human nature. Arthur Stuart Pitt in "The Sources, Significance, and Date of Franklin's 'An Arabian Tale,'"* Publications of the Modern Language Association, *Vol. 57, pp. 155–68 (March, 1942), applies Lovejoy's analysis to one piece of Franklin's and does not refer to relevant writings of Franklin's youth in which this idea may also be found. Pitt's article is valuable in pointing out the sources from which Franklin could have accepted the idea directly, namely Locke, Milton, Addison, and Pope.*

15 *Parton*, Life and Times of Benjamin Franklin (*cited in note 7*), *Vol. 1, p. 605.*

16 *Lovejoy, op. cit., pp. 199, 200.*

been a comforting creed for the wealthy and educated classes of the Augustan Age:

> Order is Heav'n's first law; and this confest,
> Some are, and must be, greater than the rest,
> More rich, more wise.[17]

This was not the optimism of progress, which we usually associate with the eighteenth century. It was an optimism of acceptance;[18] for the rich and complacent, the real and the good seemed indeed to coincide.

Not so for Benjamin Franklin. Late in his life, in 1771, he referred to "the poverty and obscurity in which I was born and bred." His innate desire for justice and equality, his keen awareness of existing conditions of injustice and inequality, finally his own experience of things which he could not possibly call just or good—for instance, he tells us that his brother's "harsh and tyrannical treatment of me might be a means of impressing me with that aversion to arbitrary power that has stuck to me through my whole life"[19]—all this contravened the facile optimism of the Augustan Age.

Franklin, indeed, accepted the cosmological premises of his age (as witness the above quoted motto of the *Dissertation*). But his conclusions make the edifice of "Cosmic Toryism"—so imposing in Pope's magnificent language—appear a mockery and an absurdity. Franklin's argumentation was simple enough: God being all-powerful and good, man could have no free will, and the distinction between good and evil had to be abolished. He also argued that pain or uneasiness was the mainspring of all our actions, and that pleasure was produced by the removal of this uneasiness. It followed that *"No State of Life can be happier than the present, because Pleasure and Pain are inseparable."* The unintentional irony of this brand of optimism cannot be better expressed than in young Franklin's conclusion:

> I am sensible that the Doctrine here advanc'd, if it were to be publish'd, would meet with but an indifferent Reception. Mankind naturally and generally love to be flatter'd: Whatever sooths our Pride, and tends to exalt our Species above the rest of the Creation, we are pleas'd with and easily believe, when ungrateful Truths shall be with the utmost Indignation rejected. "What! bring ourselves down to an Equality with the Beasts of the Field! With the *meanest* part of the Creation! 'Tis insufferable!" But, (to use a Piece of *common* Sense) our *Geese* are but *Geese* tho' we may think 'em *Swans;* and Truth will be Truth tho' it sometimes prove mortifying and distasteful.[20]

The dilemma which confronted him at the age of nineteen is characteristic of most eighteenth-century philosophy: "If nature is good, then there is no evil in the world; if there is evil in the world, then nature so far is not good."[21]

Franklin cut this Gordian knot by sacrificing "Reason" to "Experience." He turned away from metaphysics for the quite pragmatic reason that his denial of good and evil did not provide him with a basis for the attainment of social and individual happiness:

[17] *Alexander Pope, "An Essay on Man," Epistle 4, in* Selected Works, *Modern Library ed. (New York, 1948), p. 127.*

[18] *Willey, op. cit., p. 56.*

[19] Autobiography, Writings, *Vol. 1, pp. 226, 247 (n.1).*

[20] *Parton, op. cit., Vol. 1, p. 617.*

[21] *Carl Becker,* The Heavenly City of the Eighteenth Century Philosophers *(New Haven, 1932), p. 69.*

Revelation had indeed no weight with me, as such; but I entertain'd an opinion that, though certain actions might not be bad *because* they were forbidden by it, or good *because* it commanded them, yet probably these actions might be forbidden *because* they were bad for us, or commanded *because* they were beneficial to us. . . . [22]

To achieve useful things rather than indulge in doubtful metaphysical speculations, to become a doer of good—these, then, became the principal aims of Franklin's thought and action.[23]

This fundamental change from the earlier to the later Enlightenment—from passive contemplation to improvement, from a static to a dynamic conception of human affairs—did contribute to the substitution of the idea of human perfectibility for the idea of human perfection—a very limited kind of perfection, as we have seen; but it was by no means sufficient to bring about the faith in the perfectibility of human nature. Something else was needed: proof that "social evils were due neither to innate and incorrigible disabilities of the human being nor the nature of things, but simply to ignorance and prejudices."[24] The associationist psychology, elaborating Locke's theory of the malleability of human nature, provided the basis for the expansion of the idea of progress and perfectibility from the purely intellectual domain into the realm of moral and social life in general. The Age of Reason, then, presents us with a more perplexing picture than we might have supposed.

Reason, after all, may mean three different things: reason as a faculty of man; reason as a quality of the universe; and reason as a temper in the conduct of human affairs.[25] We might venture the generalization that the earlier Enlightenment stressed reason as the quality of the Newtonian universe, whereas the later Enlightenment, in spite of important exceptions, exalted the power of human reason to mold the moral and social life of mankind.[26] Franklin's "reason," as we shall see presently, is above all a temper in the conduct of human affairs.

This discussion is important for a correct understanding of Franklin's position in the center of the cross-currents of the Age of Enlightenment. The fact that the roots of his thought are to be found in the early Enlightenment is not always realized, or, if realized, not always sufficiently explained. Julian P. Boyd, in his introduction to Carl Becker's biographical sketch of Franklin, states that Franklin and Jefferson believed "that men would be amenable to rational persuasion, that they would thereby be induced to promote their own and their fellows' best interests, and that, in the end, perfect felicity for man and society would be achieved."[27] These ideas are certainly suggestive of the later Enlightenment, and appear to be more applicable to Jefferson than to Franklin. Carl Becker himself asserts, somewhat ambiguously and with undue generalization, that Franklin

[22] Autobiography, Writings, *Vol. 1, p. 296. See also* Writings, *Vol. 7, p. 412.*

[23] *See* Writings, *Vol. 1, p. 341; Vol. 2, p. 215; Vol. 3, p. 145; Vol. 9, p. 208; Vol. 10, p. 38.*

[24] *Bury,* The Idea of Progress (*cited in note 4*), p. 128.

[25] *This distinction is Roland Bainton's. See his "The Appeal to Reason and the American Revolution," in* The Constitution Reconsidered, *ed. Conyers Read (New York, 1938), p. 121.*

[26] *Cf. A. O. Lovejoy's statement: "The authors who were perhaps the most influential and the most representative in the early and mid-eighteenth century, made a great point of reducing man's claims to 'reason' to a minimum." " 'Pride' in Eighteenth Century Thought," in* Essays in the History of Ideas (*Baltimore, 1948*), p. 68.

[27] *Carl Becker,* Benjamin Franklin (*Ithaca, 1946*), p. ix.

"was a true child of the Enlightenment, not indeed of the school of Rousseau, but of Defoe and Pope and Swift, of Fontenelle and Montesquieu and Voltaire."[28] There is little evidence that this school prophesied the achievement of perfect felicity for man and society.

Bernard Mandeville, a personal acquaintance of Franklin, joined the chorus of those who proclaimed the compatibility of human imperfection and the general harmony. "Private Vices, Public Benefits" was the subtitle of his famous *Fable of the Bees*, which Franklin owned and probably read. Mandeville's paradoxical doctrines must have been a powerful challenge to Franklin's young mind. "The Moral Virtues," Mandeville asserted in terms reminiscent of Machiavelli, "are the Political Offspring which Flattery begot upon Pride." While arguing that men are actuated by self-interest and that this self-interest promotes the prosperity of society as a whole, Mandeville maintains a rigorous standard of virtue, declaring those acts alone to be virtuous "by which Man, contrary to the impulse of Nature, should endeavour the Benefit of others, or the Conquest of his own Passions out of a Rational Ambition of being good."[29]

By making ethical standards so excessively rigorous, Mandeville rendered them impossible of observance, and indirectly (though intentionally) pointed out their irrelevance for practical life. The very rigor of his ethical demands in contrast to his practical devices suggests that Mandeville lacked "idealism." This was not the case with Franklin. The consciously paradoxical Mandeville could offer no salvation for the young Franklin caught on the horns of his own dilemma. Shaftesbury, Mandeville's *bête noire*—whose works were already familiar to Franklin—had a more promising solution. In his *Inquiry Concerning Virtue or Merit* (1699), Shaftesbury had asserted that man by nature possesses a faculty to distinguish and to prefer what is right—the famous "moral sense."

Franklin's option for Shaftesbury was made clear from his reprinting two dialogues "Between Philocles and Horatio, . . . concerning Virtue and Pleasure" from the *London Journal* of 1729 in the *Pennsylvania Gazette* of 1730. In the second dialogue, reason was described as the chief faculty of man, and reasonable and morally good actions were defined as actions preservative of the human kind and naturally tending to produce real and unmixed happiness. These dialogues until recently have been held to be Franklin's own work; however, a reference in the *Autobiography* to a "Socratic dialogue" and "a discourse on self-denial," traditionally interpreted as concerning the two dialogues between Philocles and Horatio, recently has been shown to concern two pieces published in the *Pennsylvania Gazette* of 1735. The first piece is a dialogue between Crito and Socrates, never before correctly attributed to Franklin, in which he asserted that the "SCIENCE OF VIRTUE" was "of more worth, and of more consequence" to one's happiness than all other knowledge put together; in the second piece, a discourse on self-denial, Franklin combated the (Mandevillean) idea that "the greater the *Self-Denial* the greater the Virtue." Thirty-three years later, Franklin was still following Shaftesbury when he exhorted: "Be in general virtuous, and you will be happy." However, we shall see later that Franklin, in the last analysis, was not as far removed from Mandeville's pessimism as these cheerful views would suggest. His was a sort of middle position between

28 Ibid., *p. 31.*
29 *Bernard Mandeville,* The Fable of the Bees, *ed. F. B. Kaye, 2 vols. (Oxford, 1924), Vol. 1, pp. 48–49, 51. Franklin owned Mandeville's work, according to a list in the Mason-Franklin Collection of the Yale University Library. He was introduced to Mandeville during his first stay in London.* Writings, *Vol. 1, p. 278.*

Mandeville's "realism" and Shaftesbury's "idealism."[30]

II. The Idea of Progress

The restraining influence of the idea of the Great Chain of Being retained its hold on Franklin after his return to a more conventional recognition of good and evil. In his "Articles of Belief" of 1728 he said that "Man is not the most perfect Being but one, rather as there are many Degrees of Beings his Inferiors, so there are many Degrees of Beings superior to him."[31] Franklin presented the following question and answers to the discussions in the Junto:

Can a man arrive at perfection in his life, as some believe; or it it impossible, as others believe?

Answer. Perhaps they differ in the meaning of the word *perfection.* I suppose the perfection of any thing to be only the greatest the nature of the thing is capable of. . . .

If they mean a man cannot in this life be so perfect as an angel, it may be true; for an angel, by being incorporeal, is allowed some perfections we are at present incapable of, and less liable to some imperfections than we are liable to. If they mean a man is not capable of being perfect here

as he is capable of being in heaven, that may be true likewise. But that a man is not capable of being so perfect here, is not sense. . . . In the above sense, there may be a perfect oyster, a perfect horse, a perfect ship; why not a perfect man? That is, as perfect as his present nature and circumstances admit.[32]

We note here the acknowledgment of man's necessarily "imperfect" state of perfection. However, it is striking to see that Franklin refused to employ this theory as a justification of the status quo. Within certain bounds, change, or progress for the better, was possible. Many years later, Franklin was to use exactly the same argument in the debate on the status of America within the British Empire. A pro-English writer had presented the familiar argument of "Cosmic Toryism" (and of conservatism in general, of course): "To expect perfection in human institutions is absurd." Franklin retorted indignantly: "Does this justify any and every Imperfection that can be invented or added to our Constitution?"[33]

This attitude differs from the belief in moral progress and perfectibility. There are, however, some passages in Franklin's later writings, better known than the preceding ones, which seem to suggest his agreement with the creed of moral progress and perfectibility. Two years before his death, looking with considerable satisfaction upon the achievements of his country and his own life, he explained to a Boston clergyman his belief in "the growing felicity of mankind, from the improvements in philosophy, morals, politics"; he

---

[30] *The proof that the two dialogues between Philocles and Horatio were not written by Franklin and the identification of the two other pieces have been furnished by Alfred O. Aldridge, "Franklin's 'Shaftesburian' Dialogues Not Franklin's: A Revision of the Franklin Canon,"* American Literature, *Vol. 21, pp. 151–59 (May, 1949). See also* Writings, *Vol. 1, p. 343; Vol. 2, pp. 168–69. The discourse on self-denial is printed in* The Complete Works of Benjamin Franklin, *ed. John Bigelow, 10 vols. (New York, 1887–88), Vol. 1, pp. 414–17. The last quote, written in 1768, is in* Writings, *Vol. 5, p. 159.*

[31] Writings, *Vol. 2, p. 92; see also Vol. 10, p. 124 and note 14, above.*

[32] The Works of Benjamin Franklin, *ed. Jared Sparks, 10 vols. (Boston, 1836–40), Vol. 2, p. 554.*

[33] *Franklin's marginal notes in* [Matthew C. Wheelock], Reflections Moral and Political on Great Britain and the Colonies (London, 1770), *p. 48. Franklin's copy in the Jefferson Collection of the Library of Congress.*

also stressed "the invention and acquisition of new and useful utensils and instruments" and concluded that "invention and improvement are prolific. . . . The present progress is rapid." However, he immediately added: "I see a little absurdity in what I have just written, but it is to a friend, who will wink and let it pass."[34]

There remains, then, a wide gulf between this qualified view of human progress and the exuberant joy over the progress of man's rational and moral faculties so perfectly expressed in the lines of a good friend of Franklin's, the British nonconformist clergyman and philosopher, Joseph Priestley:

> Whatever was the beginning of this world, the end will be glorious and paradisiacal beyond what our imaginations can now conceive. Extravagant as some people may suppose these views to be, I think I could show them to be fairly suggested by the true theory of human nature and to arise from the natural course of human affairs.[35]

Franklin himself was well aware of this gulf. He distinguished sharply between man's intellectual progress and the steadily increasing power of man over matter, on the one hand, and the permanency of moral imperfection, on the other. He wrote to Priestly in 1782:

> I should rejoice much, if I could once more recover the Leisure to search with you into the works of Nature; I mean the *inanimate*, not the *animate* or moral part of them, the more I discover'd of the former, the more I admir'd them; the more I know of the latter, the more I am disgusted with them. Men I find to be a Sort

of Beings very badly constructed, as they are generally more easily provok'd than reconcil'd, more disposed to do Mischief to each other than to make Reparation, much more easily deceiv'd than undeceiv'd, and having more Pride and even Pleasure in killing than in begetting one another.

He had begun to doubt, he continued, whether "the Species were really worth producing or preserving. . . . I know, you have no such Doubts because, in your zeal for their welfare, you are taking a great deal of pains to save their Souls. Perhaps, as you grow older, you may look upon this as a hopeless Project."[36]

One is struck by the remarkable constancy of Franklin's views on human nature. In 1787 he tried to dissuade the author of a work on natural religion from publishing it. In this famous letter, we may find the quintessence of Franklin's concept of human nature. There is little of the trust in human reason which is so generally supposed to be a mark of his moral teachings:

> You yourself may find it easy to live a virtuous Life, without the Assistance afforded by Religion; you having a clear perception of the Advantages of Virtue, and the Disadvantages of Vice, and possessing a Strength of Resolution sufficient to enable you to resist common Temptations. But think how great a Proportion of Mankind consists of weak and ignorant Men and Women, and of inexperienc'd, and inconsiderate Youth of both Sexes, who have need of the Motives of Religion to restrain them from Vice, and support their Virtue, and retain them in the Practice of it till it becomes *habitual*, which is the Great Point for its Security. . . . If men are so wicked as we now see them *with religion*, what would they be *if without it?*[37]

[34] *Writings, Vol. 9, p. 651. See also Vol. 9, pp. 489, 530; Vol. 1, p. 226.*

[35] *Quoted by Bury,* The Idea of Progress (*cited in note 4*), *pp. 221–22.*

[36] *Writings, Vol. 8, pp. 451–52.*

[37] *Writings, Vol. 9, pp. 521–22. See also Vol. 2, pp. 203, 393, and Vol. 9, pp. 600–1.*

One is reminded of Gibbon's approval of conditions in the Rome of the Antonines, where all religions were considered equally false by the wise, equally true by the people, and equally useful by the magistrates.

III. The Belief in "Reason"

Reason as a temper in the conduct of human affairs counted much with Franklin, as we shall see later. However, reason as a faculty of the human mind, stronger than our desires or passions, counted far less. Often Franklin candidly and smilingly referred to the weakness of reason. In his *Autobiography*, he tells us of his struggle "between principle and inclination" when, on his first voyage to Philadelphia, his vegetarian principles came into conflict with his love of eating fish. Remembering that greater fish ate the smaller ones, he did not see any reason why he should not eat fish: "So convenient a thing it is to be a *reasonable creature*, since it enables one to find or make a reason for every thing one has a mind to do."[38]

Reason as a guide to human happiness was recognized by Franklin only to a limited degree.

> Our Reason would still be of more Use to us, if it could enable us to *prevent* the Evils it can hardly enable us to *bear.*—But in that it is so deficient, and in other things so often misleads us, that I have sometimes been almost tempted to wish we had been furnished with a good sensible Instinct instead of it.[39]

Trial and error appeared to him more useful to this end than abstract reasoning. "We are, I think, in the right Road of Improvement, for we are making Experiments. I do not oppose all that

seem wrong, for the Multitude are more effectually set right by Experience, than kept from going wrong by Reasoning with them." Another time he put it even more bluntly: "What assurance of the *Future* can be better founded than that which is built on Experience of the *Past?*"[40] His scepticism about the efficacy of "reason" also appears in his opinion that "happiness in this life rather depends on internals than externals; and that, besides the natural effects of wisdom and virtue, vice and folly, there is such a thing as a happy or an unhappy constitution."[41]

There remains one problem with regard to Franklin's rather modest view of the power of human reason in moral matters: his serenity—some might call it complacency—in spite of his awareness of the disorder and imperfection of human life. Sometimes, it is true, he was uneasy:

> I rather suspect, from certain circumstances, that though the general government of the universe is well administered, our particular little affairs are perhaps below notice, and left to take the chance of human prudence or imprudence, as either may happen to be uppermost. It is, however, an uncomfortable thought, and I leave it.[42]

---

[38] *Writings, Vol. 1, p. 267. See also Vol. 5, p. 225, and Vol. 9, p. 512.*

[39] The Letters of Benjamin Franklin & Jane Mecom, *ed. Carl Van Doren (Princeton, 1950), p. 112.*

[40] *Writings, Vol. 9, p. 489, and Vol. 4, p. 250. On another occasion Franklin acknowledged the weakness of reason by the use of a pungent folk saying: "An Answer now occurs to me, for that Question of Robinson Crusoe's Man Friday, which I once thought unanswerable,* Why God no kill the Devil? *It is to be found in the Scottish Proverb, 'Ye'd do little for God an the Dell' were dead.' " To John Whitehurst, New York, June 27, 1763. Unpub. letter in the Mason-Franklin Collection of the Yale University Library. Cf. also Vol. 3, pp. 16–17, Vol. 4, p. 120, and Vol. 6, p. 424.*

[41] *Writings, Vol. 3, p. 457. See also Vol. 9, p. 548.*

[42] *Rev. L. Tyerman, Life of the Rev. George White-field, 2 vols. (London, 1876), Vol. 2, pp. 540–41, quoted in Benjamin Franklin, Representative Selections (cited in note 3), p. cxxxvi.*

But on another occasion Franklin felt obliged to quiet the anxieties of his sister, who had been upset by his remark that men "are devils to one another":

> I meant no more by saying Mankind were Devils to one another, than that being in general superior to the Malice of the other Creatures, they were not so much tormented by them as by themselves. Upon the whole I am much disposed to like the World as I find it, & to doubt my own Judgment as to what would mend it. I see so much Wisdom in what I understand of its Creation and Government, that I suspect equal Wisdom may be in what I do not understand: And thence have perhaps as much Trust in God as the most pious Christian.[43]

Indeed, Franklin's pessimism does not contain that quality of the tragic sense of life which inevitably presents itself wherever a recognition of the discrepancy between man's actual depravity and the loftiness of his aspirations exists.

We suggest a threefold explanation for this phenomenon: first of all, as we have pointed out, the complex of ideas associated with the concept of the "Great Chain of Being," predominant at the time of Franklin's youth, worked in favor of bridging this gulf by lowering the goals of human endeavor. Secondly, the success story of his own life taught him that certain valuable things in human life can be achieved. Thirdly, we cannot help thinking that Franklin himself was endowed with that "happy constitution" which he deemed a requisite for true happiness in this life.

IV. The Passion of Pride

Having discovered that Franklin acknowledged the imperfection of human reason and consequently the existence and importance of the passions to a greater degree than one might have supposed, let us specify in greater detail his insight into the nature of the two outstanding passions of social life, the desire for wealth and the desire for power—avarice and ambition. "That I may avoid Avarice and Ambition . . . —Help me, O Father," was Franklin's prayer in the "Articles of Belief" of 1728.[44]

The universal fame of Poor Richard and the description of Franklin's own "way to wealth" in his *Autobiography* (Franklin's account of his life ends with his arrival in London in 1757 for the first of his three great public missions in Europe) have led many people to see in Franklin only the ingenious businessman pursuing thrift for thrift's sake and money for money's sake. Nothing could be further from the truth than this conception. To be sure, he recognized the existence and the nature of avarice in unequivocal terms: "The Love of Money is not a Thing of certain Measure, so as that it may be easily filled and satisfied. Avarice is infinite; and where there is not good Oeconomy, no Salary, however large, will prevent Necessity."[45] He denied, however, that desire for more wealth actuated his work. His early retirement from business (1748) to devote himself to the higher things of life—chiefly to public service and scientific research—seems to prove this point.

Franklin considered wealth essentially as means to an end. He knew that it was not easy "for an empty sack to stand upright." He looked upon his fortune as an essential factor in his not having succumbed to corruption.[46] In a famous and often quoted letter to his mother, Franklin said that at the end of his life he "would rather have it said,

[43] The Letters of Benjamin Franklin & Jane Mecom (*cited in note 39*), *pp. 124, 125–26.* See also Writings, *Vol. 2, p. 61; Vol. 4, p. 388; Vol. 9, p. 247.*

[44] Writings, *Vol. 2, p. 99.*

[45] Writings, *Vol. 5, p. 325.*

[46] The Letters of Benjamin Franklin & Jane Mecom (*cited in note 39*), *p. 123.*

He lived usefully than *He died Rich*." At about the same time (two years after his retirement) he wrote to his printer friend William Strahan in England: "London citizens, they say, are ambitious of what they call *dying worth* a great sum. The very notion seems to me absurd."[47]

On the other hand, the motive of power and prestige found much earlier recognition in Franklin's writings; he even confessed candidly that he himself was not free from this desire and from the feeling of being superior to his fellowmen. At the age of sixteen, in his first secret contributions to his brother's *New-England Courant* (he wrote under the pseudonym Mrs. Dogood), he gave a satisfactory definition of what we nowadays would call lust for power, and what was in the eighteenth century called Pride:

> Among the many reigning Vices of the Town which may at any Time come under my Consideration and Reprehension, there is none which I am more inclin'd to expose than that of *Pride*. It is acknowledged by all to be a Vice the most hateful to God and Man. Even those who nourish it themselves, hate to see it in others. The proud Man aspires after Nothing less than an unlimited Superiority over his Fellow-Creatures.[48]

As Arthur O. Lovejoy has pointed out, the idea of Pride was frequently contemplated during the earlier half of the eighteenth century.[49] There are two different, though not unrelated, conceptions

of Pride. First of all, it means "the most powerful and pervasive of all passions," which manifests itself in two forms: self-esteem and desire for the admiration of others. The second conception is closely connected with the idea of the Scale of Being; it means the generic Pride of man as such, the sin against the laws of order, of gradation, the revolt of man against the station which has been allotted to him by the Creator.

These different conceptions of Pride are indeed inseparable. In Franklin's own writings, the accent is on the first rather than on the second meaning. This topic runs through his work like a red thread. In 1729, at the age of 23, he wrote that "almost every Man has a strong natural Desire of being valu'd and esteem'd by the rest of his Species."[50] Observations in a letter written in 1751 testify to his keen psychological insight:

> What you mention concerning the love of praise is indeed very true; it reigns more or less in every heart, though we are generally hypocrites, in that respect, and pretend to disregard praise.... Being forbid to praise themselves, they learn instead of it to censure others; which is only a roundabout way of praising themselves.... This fondness for ourselves, rather than malevolence to others, I take to be the general source of censure....[51]

Quite revealing with regard to our discussion is Franklin's well-known account of his project of an "Art of Virtue." His list of virtues to be practiced contained at first only twelve: "But a Quaker friend having kindly informed me that I was generally thought proud ... I added *Humility* to my list. ... I cannot boast of much success in acquiring the *reality* of this virtue, but I had a good deal with regard to the *appearance* of it."[52] His

[47] Writings, *Vol. 3, pp. 5, 6. Cf. Benjamin Rush to John Adams: "The Doctor was a rigid economist, but he was in every stage of his life charitable, hospitable, and generous." August 19, 1811, in* Letters of Benjamin Rush (*cited in note 10*), Vol. 2, p. 1093.

[48] Writings, *Vol. 2, pp. 18-19.*

[49] Lovejoy, " 'Pride' in Eighteenth Century Thought," (*cited in note 26*), p. 62–68.

[50] Writings, *Vol. 2, p. 108.*
[51] Writings, *Vol. 3, pp. 54–55.*
[52] Writings, *Vol. 1, p. 337.*

account of his rise in Pennsylvania's public life and politics reflects his joy and pride about his career. In 1737 he was appointed Postmaster of Philadelphia and Justice of the Peace; in 1744 he established the American Philosophical Society; in 1748 he was chosen a member of the Council of Philadelphia; in 1749 he was appointed Provincial Grandmaster of the Colonial Masons; in 1750 he was appointed one of the commissioners to treat with the Indians in Carlisle; and in 1751 he became a member of the Assembly of Pennsylvania. He was particularly pleased with this last appointment, and he admitted candidly that his ambition was "flatter'd by all these promotions; it certainly was; for, considering my low beginning, they were great things to me."[53]

There is no change of emphasis with respect to Pride during his long life. The old man of 78 denounces the evil of Pride with no less fervor, though with more self-knowledge, than the boy of 16:

> In reality, there is, perhaps, no one of our natural passions so hard to subdue as *pride*. Disguise it, struggle with it, beat it down, stifle it, mortify it as much as one pleases, it is still alive, and will every now and then peep out and show itself; you will see it, perhaps, often in this history; for even if I could conceive that I had compleatly overcome it, I should probably be proud of my humility.[54]

Furthermore, the experience of English political life which he acquired during his two protracted stays in England (from 1757 to 1762, and from 1765 to 1775) made an indelible impression on his mind. The corruption and venality in English politics and the disastrous blunders of English politicians which Franklin traced back to this cause[55] probably were the main reasons why he advocated at the Federal Convention of 1787 what he himself said some might regard as a "Utopian Idea": the abolition of salaries for the chief executive. The reason he gave for advocating such a step has hitherto not been appreciated as being of crucial importance for an understanding of his political thought:

> There are two Passions which have a powerful Influence in the Affairs of Men. These are *Ambition* and *Avarice;* the Love of Power and the Love of Money. Separately, each of these has great Force in prompting Men to Action; but when united in View of the same Object, they have in many minds the most violent Effects. Place before the Eyes of such Men a Post of *Honour*, that shall at the same time be a Place of *Profit*, and they will move Heaven and Earth to obtain it.[56]

It has never been pointed out that this scheme of what might be called the "separation of passions" had been ripening in Franklin's mind for several years. The first expression of it is to be found early in 1783.[57] In 1784 he mentioned it several times, and it is in these statements that we find one of the few allusions to the concept of checks and balances in Franklin's thought. He recommended: "Make every place of *honour* a place of *burthen*. By that means the effect of one of the passions above-mentioned would be taken away

---

[53] Writings, *Vol. 1, p. 374. For Franklin's acknowledgment of his own political ambition, see* Writings, *Vol. 5, pp. 148, 206, 357; Vol. 9, pp. 488, 621.*

[54] Autobiography (*end of the part written in Passy, France, 1784*), Writings, *Vol. 1, p. 339.*

[55] Writings, *Vol. 10, p. 62. See also Vol. 5, pp. 100, 112, 117, 133. See also* Benjamin Franklin's Letters to the Press, 1758–1775, *ed. Verner W. Crane (Chapel Hill, 1950), pp. 59, 164, 232.*

[56] Writings, *Vol. 9, p. 591.*

[57] Writings, *Vol. 9, p. 23.*

and something would be added to counteract the other."[58]

V. The Nature of Politics

Franklin's frequent praise of the general welfare did not blind him to the fact that most other people had a much narrower vision than his own. "Men will always be powerfully influenced in their Opinions and Actions by what appears to be their particular Interest," he wrote in his first tract on political economy, at the age of twenty-three.[59] Fortunately, one of the very few memoranda and notes dealing with the studies and discussions of young Franklin which have come to our knowledge directly concerns this problem. Franklin himself, in his *Autobiography*, gives us the text of "*Observations* on my reading history, in Library, May 19th, 1731" which, in his words, had been "accidentally preserv'd":

> That the great affairs of the world, the wars, revolutions, etc., are carried on and affected by parties.
> That the view of these parties is their present general interest, or what they take to be such.
> That the different views of these different parties occasion all confusion.
> That while a party is carrying on a general design, each man has his particular private interest in view.
> That as soon as a party has gain'd its general point, each member becomes intent upon his particular interest; which, thwarting others, breaks that party into divisions, and occasions more confusion.
> That few in public affairs act from a mere view of the good of their country, whatever they may

pretend; and, tho' their actings bring real good to their country, yet men primarily considered that their own and their country's interest was united, and did not act from a principle of benevolence.
> That fewer still, in public affairs, act with a view for the good of mankind. . . . [60]

These lines do not mirror Shaftesbury's benevolent altruism; Franklin's contention that men act primarily from their own interest "and...not...from a principle of benevolence," "tho' their actings bring real good to their country," strongly suggests the general theme of Mandeville's work: "Private vices, public benefits."

Many decades after the foregoing observations, the contrast between Franklin's views on politics and those of the enlightened rationalism of contemporary France is clearly expressed in a discussion with the French physiocrat Dupont de Nemours. Dupont had suggested that the Federal Convention be delayed until the separate constitutions of the member states were corrected—according to physiocratic principles, of course. Franklin mildly observed that "we must not expect that a new government may be formed, as a game of chess may be played." He stressed that in the game of politics there were so many players with so many strong and various prejudices, "and their particular interests, independent of the general, seeming so opposite," that "the play is more like *tric-trac* with a box of dice."[61] In public, and when he was propagandizing for America in Europe, Franklin played down the evils of party strife: after the end of the War of Independence he conceded somewhat apologetically that "it is true, in some of the States there are Parties and

[58] Writings, *Vol. 9, p. 170.* See also ibid., *pp. 172 and 260.*
[59] Writings, *Vol. 2, p. 139.*
[60] Writings, *Vol. 1, pp. 339–40. Cf. also Vol. 2, p. 196, and Vol. 4, p. 322.*
[61] Writings, *Vol. 9, p. 659; see also p. 241.*

Discords." He contended now that parties "are the common lot of Humanity," and that they exist wherever there is liberty; they even, perhaps, help to preserve it. "By the Collision of different Sentiments, Sparks of Truth are struck out, and Political Light is obtained."[62]

In private, Franklin did not conceal his suspicion that "unity out of discord" was not as easily achieved as his just quoted method of obtaining "political light" might suggest. But he certainly did not believe that passions and prejudices always, or even usually, overrule enlightened self-interest. He held that "there is a vast variety of good and ill Events, that are in some degree the Effects of Prudence or the want of it."[63] He believed that "reasonable sensible Men, can always make a reasonable scheme appear such to other reasonable Men, if they take Pains, and have Time and Opportunity for it. . . ." However, this dictum is severely limited by the conclusion: ". . . unless from some Circumstance their Honesty and Good Intentions are suspected."[64] That Franklin thought those circumstances to exist frequently, we learn from a famous message to George Washington, written in France in 1780. He told Washington how much the latter would enjoy his reputation in France, "pure and free from those little Shades that the Jealousy and Envy of a Man's Countrymen and Cotemporaries are ever endeavouring to cast over living Merit."[65]

Although Franklin himself talked so much about "Common Interests," he could be impatient when others built their arguments on this point. He observed that "it is an Insult on common sense to affect an Appearance of Generosity in a Matter of obvious Interest."[66] This belief in self-interest as a moving force of politics appears with rare clarity in marginal notes in a pamphlet whose author argued that "if the Interests of Great Britain evidently raise and fall with those of the Colonies, then the Parliament of Great Britain will have the same regard for the Colonists as for her own People." Franklin retorted:

All this Argument of the Interest of Britain and the Colonies being the *same* is fallacious and unsatisfactory. Partners in Trade have a *common* Interest, which is the same, the Flourishing of the Partnership Business: But they may moreover have each a *separate* Interest; and in pursuit of that *separate* Interest, one of them may endeavour to impose on the other, may cheat him in the Accounts, may draw to himself more than his Share of the Profits, may put upon the other more than an equal Share of the Burthen. Their having a common Interest is no Security against such Injustice. . . . [67]

VI. Democracy

It is fair to ask how Franklin's views on the above matters square with his avowal of radically democratic notions after 1775. In view of the foregoing, Franklin would not, it seems, agree with the underlying assumptions of Jeffersonian democracy, stated by Jefferson himself: "Nature hath implanted in our breasts a love of others, a sense of duty to them, a moral instinct, in short, which prompts us irresistibly to feel and to succor their

[62] Writings, *Vol. 10, pp. 120–21. See also Vol. 4, p. 35.*

[63] Writings, *Vol. 7, p. 358.*

[64] Writings, *Vol. 3, pp. 41–42.*

[65] Writings, *Vol. 8, p. 28. Cf. the expression of the same idea 36 years earlier in* Writings, *Vol. 2, p. 242.*

[66] Benjamin Franklin's Letters to the Press (*cited in note 55*), p. 183.

[67] *Marginal comments in* Good Humour, or, A Way with the Colonies (*London, 1766*), pp. 26–27. *Franklin's copy is in the library of the Historical Society of Pennsylvania, Philadelphia. This comment is reprinted in* A Collection of the Familiar Letters and Miscellaneous Papers of Benjamin Franklin, *ed. Jared Sparks (Boston, 1833), p. 229.*

distresses. . . ." It was also Jefferson who believed "that man was a rational animal, endowed by nature with rights, and with an innate sense of justice."[68] On this faith in the rationality and goodness of man, the theory of Jeffersonian democracy has been erected. Vernon L. Parrington said of Franklin that "he was a forerunner of Jefferson, like him firm in the conviction that government was good in the measure that it remained close to the people."[69] Charles A. Beard, discussing the members of the Federal Convention, tells us that Benjamin Franklin "seems to have entertained a more hopeful view of democracy than any other member of that famous group."[70] All this must seem rather strange in view of the none too optimistic conception of human nature which we have found in Franklin. His radically democratic views after 1775—before that time his outlook seemed essentially conservative—baffled contemporary observers as it has later students.

There is, as a matter of fact, plenty of evidence of Franklin's sincere devotion to monarchy during the greater part of his life. It was the most natural thing for him to assure his friend, the famous Methodist preacher George Whitefield, that a settlement of colonies on the Ohio would be blessed with success "if we undertook it with sincere Regard to . . . the Service of our gracious King, and (which is the same thing) the Publick Good."[71] Franklin loved to contrast the corruption of Parliament and the virtues of George III. To an American friend, he said that he could "scarcely conceive a King of better Dispositions, of more exemplary virtues, or more truly desirous of promoting the Welfare of all his Subjects."[72]

Another "conservative" aspect of Franklin which cannot be glossed over lightly is his acceptance of the Puritan and mercantilistic attitude towards the economic problems of the working class. Throughout his life he was critical of the English Poor Laws. He deplored "the proneness of human nature to a life of ease, of freedom from care and labour," and he considered that laws which *compel the rich to maintain the poor*" might possibly be "fighting against the order of God and Nature, which perhaps has appointed want and misery as the proper punishments for, and cautions against, as well as necessary consequences of, idleness and extravagance."[73] This was written in 1753. But as late as 1789, long after he had come out for the political equality of the poor and for a radical theory of property, he still confirmed to an English correspondent that "I have long been of your opinion, that your legal provision for the poor is a very great evil, operating as it does to the encouragement of idleness."[74]

[68] *Jefferson to Thomas Law, June 13, 1814, and to Judge William Johnson, June 12, 1823, quoted by Adrienne Koch,* The Philosophy of Thomas Jefferson (*New York, 1943*), *pp. 19, 139.*

[69] *Vernon L. Parrington,* The Main Currents of American Thought, *3 vols. (New York, 1930), Vol. 1, pp. 176–77.*

[70] *Charles A. Beard,* An Economic Interpretation of the Constitution (*New York, 1913*), *p. 197.*

[71] Writings, *Vol. 3, p. 339. See also Vol. 2, pp. 377–78; Vol. 4, pp. 94, 213.*

[72] Writings, *Vol. 5, p. 204. See also Vol. 5, p. 261. Another sign of Franklin's anti-radical attitude during his stay in England is his disgust with the Wilkes case. See* Writings, *Vol. 5, pp. 121, 133, 134, and 150. Also* Letters and Papers of Benjamin Franklin and Richard Jackson, 1753–1785, *ed. Carl Van Doren (Philadelphia, 1947), p. 139.*

[73] Letters and Papers of Benjamin Franklin and Richard Jackson, *op. cit., pp. 34, 35.*

[74] Writings, *Vol. 10, p. 64. See for an elaboration of his arguments "On the Labouring Poor,"* Writings, *Vol. 5, pp. 122–27, and "On the Price of Corn, and Management of the Poor,"* Writings, *Vol. 5, pp. 534–39.*

Franklin's endorsement of democracy is most emphatically revealed in his advocacy of a unicameral legislature for the Commonwealth of Pennsylvania, as well as for the federal government. The issue of unicameral versus bicameral legislative bodies—an issue much discussed in the latter decades of the eighteenth century—reflected faithfully, as a rule, the clash of views of two different theories of human nature and of politics. The bicameral system was based on the principle of checks and balances; a pessimistic view of human nature naturally would try to forestall the abuse of power in a single and all-powerful assembly. On the other hand, most of those who trusted in the faculties of human reason did not see the necessity for a second chamber to check and harass the activities of a body of reasonable men.

In the case of Franklin, however, this correspondence of political convictions with views on human nature is lacking. He was the president of the Pennsylvania Convention of 1776 which—almost uniquely among the American states—set up a unicameral system. This, of course, filled many of the French *philosophes* with great joy. Franklin, they supposed, had secured a triumph of enlightened principles in the new world. Condorcet, in his "Éloge de Franklin," had this to say:

Franklin's voice alone decided this last provision. He thought that as enlightenment would naturally make rapid progress, above all in a country to which the revolution had given a new system, one ought to encourage the devices of perfecting legislation, and not to surround them with extrinsic obstacles. . . . The opinion contrary to his stands for that discouraging philosophy which considers error and corruption as the habitual state of societies and the development of virtue and reason as a kind of miracle which one must not expect to

make enduring. It was high time that a philosophy both nobler and truer should direct the destiny of mankind, and Franklin was worthy to give the first example of it.[75]

As a matter of fact, it has since been shown that Franklin, who at the time of the Pennsylvania Convention also served in the Continental Congress, played a minor role in the adoption of the unicameral system. The unicameral legislature was rooted in the historical structure of Pennsylvania's proprietary government.[76] This, however, is irrelevant from our point of view, since Franklin endorsed and defended the unicameral system in his "Queries and Remarks respecting Alterations in the Constitution of Pennsylvania," written in November, 1789.[77]

In the opposition to checks and balances and a second chamber, Franklin's most famous companion was Thomas Paine, author of *The Age of Reason*. This similarity of views between Franklin and one of the most vocal spokesmen of the creed of reason and the perfectibility of man perhaps contributes to the misinterpretation of Franklin's position among the eighteenth-century philosophers. Paine's arguments against the system of checks and balances and for a single house were characteristic of the later Enlightenment:

Freedom is the associate of innocence, not the companion of suspicion. She only requires to be cherished, not to be caged, and to be beloved is, to her, to be protected. Her residence is in the undis-

[75] Oeuvres de Condorcet (*cited in note 1*), *Vol. 3, pp. 401–2.*

[76] *See J. Paul Selsam*, The Pennsylvania Constitution of 1776 (*Philadelphia, 1926*), *and Charles M. Andrews*, The Colonial Period of American History, 4 vols. (*New Haven, 1934–38*), *Vol. 3, p. 320.*

[77] Writings, *Vol. 10, pp. 54–60.*

tinguished multitude of rich and poor, and a partisan to neither is the patroness of all.[78]

This argument, of course, presupposes the rationality and goodness of human nature. We might perhaps agree with Paine that "no man was a better judge of human nature than Franklin,"[79] but Paine certainly did not have Franklin's conception of human nature.

The reasons for Franklin's almost radical attitude in 1776 and 1787 appear in his own writings. One thing seems certain: belief in the goodness and the wisdom of the people is *not* at the root of his democratic faith. This idea is quite foreign to Franklin. Discussing the Albany Plan of Union in 1754, he thought that "it is very possible, that this general government might be as well and faithfully administered without the people, as with them."[80] Nor did he fundamentally change his view in the last years of his life. "Popular favour is very precarious, being sometimes *lost* as well as *gained* by good actions." In 1788, he wrote publicly that "popular Opposition to a public Measure is no Proof of its Impropriety."[81] What a strange democrat it was who told the Federal Convention that "there is a natural Inclination in Mankind to kingly Government."[82] The most plausible and popular reason for belief in democracy, then, is eliminated.

On the other hand, Franklin did not believe in the intrinsic goodness of the wealthy or the wisdom of the powerful; he had no liking for aristocratic government, be it by an aristocracy of wealth or an aristocracy of birth. He was scornful of the House of Lords and thought "Hereditary Professors of Mathematicks" preferable to hereditary legislators because they could do less mischief.[83]

It is noteworthy that in the whole of Franklin's work only one reference to Montesquieu can be found; and that concerns his ideas on criminal law. Separation of powers, the role of the aristocracy in a healthy society—these are doctrines which never took possession of Franklin's mind.

The antithesis between Adams, under the influence of Harrington, and Franklin, chiefly influenced by his own experience, is remarkably complete. Adams wrote:

> It must be remembered that the rich are *people* as well as the poor; that they have rights as well as others; they have as clear and as *sacred* a right to their large property as others have to theirs which is smaller; that oppression to them is as possible and wicked as to others. . . . [84]

Franklin mounts a formidable counterattack:

> And why should the upper House, chosen by a Minority, have equal Power with the lower chosen by a majority? Is it supposed that Wisdom is the necessary concomitant of Riches . . . and why is Property to be represented at all? . . . The

[78] "*A Serious Address to the People of Pennsylvania on the Present Situation of their Affairs*" (*Dec., 1778*), in The Complete Writings of Thomas Paine, ed. Philip S. Foner, 2 vols. (New York, 1945), Vol. 2, p. 284.

[79] "Constitutional Reform" (1805), ibid., pp. 998–99.

[80] Writings, Vol. 3, p. 231. See also p. 309.

[81] Writings, Vol. 9, pp. 564, 702. In 1788, Franklin repeatedly said that there was at present the "danger of too little obedience in the governed," although in general the opposite evil of "giving too much power to our governors" was more dreaded. Writings, Vol. 9, p. 638; and Vol. 10, p. 7.

[82] Writings, Vol. 9, p. 593.

[83] Writings, Vol. 6, pp. 370–71. For other attacks on the principle of hereditary honors and privileges, in connection with the Order of the Cincinnati, see Writings, Vol. 9, pp. 162, 336.

[84] Quoted by Zoltán Haraszti, John Adams and the Prophets of Progress (Cambridge, Mass., 1952), p. 36.

Combinations of Civil Society are not like those of a Set of Merchants, who club their Property in different Proportions for Building and Freighting a Ship, and may therefore have some Right to Vote in the Disposition of the Voyage in a greater or less Degree according to their respective Contributions; but the important ends of Civil Society, and the personal Securities of Life and Liberty, these remain the same in every member of the Society; and the poorest continues to have an equal Claim to them with the most opulent. . . . [85]

It is this strong objection against the attempt to use—openly or covertly—a second chamber as a tool of class rule which seems to underlie Franklin's disapproval of the bicameral system. Franklin, it should be pointed out, was aware of the necessity and inevitability of poises and counterpoises. This is shown by his attempt, referred to above, to create a sort of balance of passions, checking avarice with ambition. There exist some, though quite rare, allusions to a balance of power concept in his utterances on imperial and international relations. The most pointed and direct reference to the idea of checks and balances, however, may be found in an unpublished letter to a well-known figure of Pennsylvania politics, Joseph Galloway, in 1767. Franklin discussed and welcomed a new Circuit Bill for the judges of Pennsylvania. He suggested and encouraged an increase in the salaries to be granted by the Assembly for the judges to offset the nominating and recalling powers of the Proprietor: "From you they should therefore receive a Salary equal in Influence upon their Minds, to be held during your Pleasure. For where the Beam *is moveable*, it is only by equal Weights in opposite scales that it can possibly be kept even."[86]

Consequently, the arguments of Thomas Paine or the French *philosophes*, which derive their validity from assumptions about the goodness or rationality of human nature, do not hold in the case of Franklin. In a brilliant recent essay it has been suggested that "despite the European flavor of a Jefferson or a Franklin, the Americans refused to join in the great Enlightenment enterprise of shattering the Christian concept of sin, replacing it with an unlimited humanism, and then emerging with an early enterprise as glittering as the heavenly one that had been destroyed."[87] As far as Franklin is concerned, however, the alternatives of Calvinist pessimism and the "unlimited humanism" of the European Enlightenment do not really clarify the essential quality of his political thought. His thought is rooted in a climate of opinion which combined the rejection of the doctrine of original sin with a rather modest view of human nature.

It seems, then, that the desire for equality, rather than any rationalistic concepts, offers the clue to an adequate understanding of those elements in Franklin's political thought which at first sight appear inconsistent with his not too cheerful view of human goodness. His striving for equality also suggests a solution to the thorny problem of reconciling his democratic views after

[85] *"Queries and Remarks . . . ," Writings, Vol. 10, pp. 58–61. For Franklin's disagreement with the bicameral system of the United States Constitution, see* Writings, *Vol. 9, pp. 645, 674. The paradox of Franklin's attitude is thrown into relief if one considers that even Jefferson, in his* Notes on Virginia, *raised his voice against the dangers of an "elective despotism," and exalted "those benefits" which a "proper complication of principles" would produce. The Works of Thomas Jefferson, ed. Paul Leicester Ford (New York and London, 1904–5), Vol. 4, p. 19.*

[86] *April 14, 1767, in the William L. Clements Library, Ann Arbor, Michigan.*

[87] *Louis Hartz, "American Political Thought and the American Revolution," this* Review, *Vol. 46, pp. 321–42, at p. 324 (June, 1952).*

he had decided for American independence with his faithful loyalty to the Crown before that date. The American interest obliged him to fight against Parliament—an aristocratic body in those days—while remaining loyal to the King; in recognizing the King's sovereignty while denying the Parliament's rights over the Colonies, Franklin by necessity was driven into a position which—historically speaking—seemed to contradict his Whig principles. The complaining Americans spoke, as Lord North rightly said, the "language of Toryism."[88] During the decade before 1775 Franklin fought for the equal rights of England and the Colonies under the Crown. But his desire for equality went deeper than that. In his "Some good Whig Principles," while conceding that the government of Great Britain ought to be lodged "in the hands of King, Lords of Parliament, and Representatives of *the whole body* of the freemen of this realm," he took care to affirm that *"every man* of the commonalty (excepting infants, insane persons, and criminals) is, of common right, and by the laws of God, *a freeman"* and that "the poor man has an *equal* right, but *more* need, to have representatives in the legislature than the rich one."[89] It has not been widely known that Franklin, in a conversation with Benjamin Vaughan, his friend and at the same time emissary of the British Prime Minister Lord Shelburne during the peace negotiations of 1782, has confirmed this view. Vaughan reported to Shelburne that "Dr. Franklin's opinions about *parliaments* are, that people should not be rejected as electors because they are at *present* ignorant"; Franklin thought that "a statesman should meliorate his people," and Vaughan supposed that Franklin "would put this, among other reasons for extending the

privilege of election, that it *would* meliorate them." It was Franklin's opinion, Vaughan thought, "that the lower people are as we see them, because oppressed; & then their situation in point of manners, becomes the reason for oppressing them."[90] The fact is that Franklin's overriding concern for equality foreshadows the attacks of the socialism of later generations on the absolute sanctity of private property:

All the Property that is necessary to a Man, for the Conservation of the Individual and the Propagation of the Species, is his natural Right, which none can justly deprive him of: But all Property superfluous to such purposes is the Property of the Publik, who, by their Laws, have created it, and who may therefore by other Laws dispose of it, whenever the Welfare of the Publick shall demand such Disposition.[91]

Franklin's previously quoted speech in the Federal Convention provides us with an essential insight: he expressed belief in "a natural Inclination in Mankind to kingly Government." His reasons are revealing: "It sometimes relieves them from Aristocratic Domination. They had rather one Tyrant than 500. It gives more of the Appearance of Equality among Citizens; and that they like."[92] Equality, then, is not incompatible with monarchy.

From all this a significant conclusion may be drawn. It is an oversimplification to speak of Franklin's "conservatism" before 1775 and of his

[88] *Quoted by G. H. Guttridge,* English Whiggism and the American Revolution *(Berkeley, 1942), p. 62.*

[89] Writings, *Vol. 10, p. 130.*

[90] *Benjamin Vaughan to Lord Shelburne, November 24, 1782. Benjamin Vaughan Papers in the American Philosophical Society, Philadelphia. Photostat in the Benjamin Vaughan Collection in the William L. Clements Library, Ann Arbor, Michigan.*

[91] Writings, *Vol. 9, p. 138 (written in 1783). See also Vol. 10, p. 59.*

[92] Writings, *Vol. 9, p. 539.*

"radicalism" after 1775. Professor MacIver illustrates the conservative character of the first stage of American political thought preceding the appeal to natural rights by reference to Franklin, who, in spite of his later attacks on the Order of the Cincinnati, "nevertheless clung to the principle of a hereditary, though constitutional monarchy, until the tide of revolution rendered it untenable."[93] The term "conservative" does not do justice to the possibility of paying faithful allegiance to a monarchy and still disliking aristocracies of heredity or wealth. Because of his innate desire for equality, as well as his defense of the American cause against the encroachments of Parliament, Franklin found it much easier to be a monarchist. Monarchy, rather than aristocracy, was compatible with those elements of his thought which after 1775 made him a democrat.

Another of the factors which, while not incompatible with monarchical feelings, contributed greatly to Franklin's acceptance of democracy, is the belief which he shared with Hume that power, in the last analysis, is founded on opinion. "I wish some good Angel would forever whisper in the Ears of your great Men, that Dominion is founded in Opinion, and that if you would preserve your Authority among us, you must preserve the Opinion we us'd to have of your Justice."[94] He thought that "Government must depend for it's Efficiency either on Force or Opinion." Force, however, is not as efficient as Opinion: "Alexander and Caesar...received more faithful service, and performed greater actions, by means of the love their soldiers bore them, than they could

possibly have done, if, instead of being beloved and respected, they had been hated and feared by those they commanded." Efficiency, then, became an argument for democracy. "Popular elections have their inconvenience in some cases; but in establishing new forms of government, we cannot always obtain what we may think the best; for the prejudices of those concerned, if they cannot be removed, must be in some degree complied with."[95]

It has rarely been noticed how detached Franklin, the greatest champion of democracy in the Federal Convention, was from the problem of the best government. His speech at the conclusion of the deliberations of the Constitutional Convention may give us a clue to the perplexing problem of why he gave comparatively little attention to the theoretical questions of political philosophy and devoted almost all his time to the solution of concrete issues. He stated his disagreement with several points of the Constitution, nevertheless urging general allegiance and loyalty to its principles. Asking his colleagues to doubt a little their feeling of infallibility, Franklin summed up the experience of his life: "I think a general Government necessary for us, and there is no *form* of government but what may be a blessing to the people, if well administered."[96] Perhaps in speaking these words he was thinking of one of the favorite writers of his younger days, Alexander Pope:

> For Forms of Government let fools contest;
> Whate'er is best administer'd is best.[97]

[93] R. M. MacIver, "European Doctrines and the Constitution," in The Constitution Reconsidered (*cited in note 25*), p. 55.

[94] Letters and Papers of Benjamin Franklin and Richard Jackson (*cited in note 72*), p. 145 (*written in 1764*). See also Writings, Vol. 6, p. 129; Vol. 9, p. 608.

[95] Benjamin Franklin's Letters to the Press (*cited in note 55*), p. 193; Writings, Vol. 2, p. 56; Vol. 3. p. 228. See also Vol. 3, 231; Vol. 5, p. 79.

[96] Writings, Vol. 9, p. 607.

[97] Pope, "Essay on Man," Epistle 3, Selected Works (*cited in note 17*), p. 124.

VII. The Duality of Franklin's Political Thought

There are two outstanding and sometimes contradictory factors in Franklin's political thought. On the one hand, we find an acute comprehension of the power factor in human nature, and, consequently, in politics. On the other hand, Franklin always during his long life revolted in the name of equality against the imperfections of the existing order. He himself stated the basic antithesis of his political thought: Power versus Equality.

Fortunately, Franklin's notes on the problem at hand have been preserved; they are to be found in his marginal comments to Allen Ramsay's pamphlet, *Thoughts on the Origin and Nature of Government*, which presents the straight view of power politics. Franklin rebelled against the rationalization and justification of the power factor. "The natural weakness of man in a solitary State," Ramsey proclaimed, "prompts him to fly for protection to whoever is able to afford it, that is to some one more powerful, than himself; while the more powerful standing equally in need of his service, readily receives it in return for the protection he gives." Franklin's answer is unequivocal: *"May not Equals unite with Equals for common Purposes?"*[98]

In the last analysis, Franklin looked upon government as the trustee of the people. He had stated this Whig principle in his very first publication as a sixteen-year-old boy[99] and he never deviated from it. So in opposition to Ramsay's doctrine, according to which the governed have no right of control whatsoever, once they have agreed to submit themselves to the sovereign, Franklin declared the accountability of the rulers:

> If I appoint a Representative for the express purpose of doing a business for me that is for *my Service* and that of others, & to consider what I am to pay as my Proportion of the Expense necessary for accomplishing that Business, I am then tax'd by my own Consent.—A Number of Persons unite to form a Company for Trade, Expences are necessary, Directors are chosen to do the Business & proportion those Expences. They are paid a Reasonable Consideration for their Trouble. Here is nothing of weak & Strong. Protection on one hand, & Service on the other. The Directors are the Servants, not the Masters; their Duty is prescrib'd, the Powers they have is from the members & returns to them. The Directors are also accountable.[100]

Franklin refused to recognize that power alone could create right. When Ramsay declared that according to nature's laws every man "in Society shall rank himself amongst the Ruling or the Ruled, . . . all Equality and Independence being by the Law of Nature strictly forbidden . . . ," Franklin rejoined indignantly, "I do not find this Strange Law among those of Nature. I doubt it is forged. . . ." He summarized Ramsay's doctrine as meaning that "He that is strongest may do what he pleases with those that are weaker," and commented angrily: "A most Equitable Law of Nature indeed."[101]

On the other hand, Franklin's grasp of the realities of power inevitably involved him in moral and logical ambiguities of political decision. At times he expressed the tragic conflict of ethics and politics. Characteristic of the peculiar contra-

---

[98] [*Allen Ramsay*], Thoughts on the Origin and Nature of Government (*London, 1769*), *p. 10. Franklin's copy in the Jefferson Collection of the Library of Congress. (My italics.)*

[99] "*Dogood Papers*," Writings, *Vol. 2, p. 26. Cf.* Benjamin Franklin's Letters to the Press (*cited in note 55*), *p. 140.*

[100] *Marginal notes to Ramsay, op. cit., pp. 33–34.*
[101] Ibid., *pp. 12, 13.*

diction within his political thought was this statement three years before the Declaration of Independence on England's prospects in the Anglo-American conflict: "*Power* does not infer *Right;* and, as the *Right* is nothing, and the *Power* (by our Increase) continually diminishing, the one will soon be as insignificant as the *other.*"[102] In this instance, obviously, he was trying to make the best of both worlds. But there were times when he was only too well aware of the conflict of these two worlds. In a passage which seems to have escaped the notice of most students of his political thought, Franklin observed that "*moral and political Rights sometimes differ, and sometimes are both subdu'd by Might.*"[103]

The measured terms of Franklin's political thinking present a striking contrast to the optimism and rationalism which we usually associate with the Age of Enlightenment. Franklin's insight into the passions of pride and power prevented him from applying the expectation of man's scientific and intellectual progress to the realm of moral matters. To be sure, he would not deny

the influence of scientific insights upon politics, and he thought that a great deal of good would result from introducing the enlightened doctrines of free trade and physiocracy into international politics. But Franklin, unlike many of his friends in France, was never inclined to consider these and other ideas as panaceas. The mutual adjustment of interests would always remain the chief remedy of political evils. It was in this domain that reason, as a temper in the conduct of human affairs, made its greatest contribution to his political thought. Moderation and equity, so he had been taught by his experience (rather than by abstract reasoning) were true political wisdom. His belief that the rulers ought to be accountable, together with his more pragmatic conviction that force alone, in the long run, could not solve the great problems of politics, brought forth his declaration of faith that "Government is not establish'd merely by *Power;* there must be maintain'd a general Opinion of its *Wisdom* and *Justice* to make it firm and durable."[104]

102 Writings, *Vol. 6, p. 87.*
103 Writings, *Vol. 8, p. 304. (My italics.)*

104 Benjamin Franklin's Autobiographical Writings, *ed. Carl Van Doren (New York, 1945), pp. 184–85. Cf.* Writings, *Vol. 4, p. 269; Vol. 7, p. 390.*

THE REVOLUTIONARY CHARACTER
OF THE AMERICAN REVOLUTION

*William H. Nelson**

For so great an event, the American Revolution is downright elusive. Nothing seems certain about it: what it was about, how and why it happened, when or perhaps even whether it happened.[1] Lest one suppose this inconclusiveness to result merely from the confusion of historians, consider these two familiar quotations from such clear-headed men of the Revolution as John Adams and Benjamin Rush: "The Revolution," Adams wrote Thomas Jefferson, "was in the Minds of the People, and this was effected, from 1760 to 1775, in the course of fifteen Years before a drop of blood was drawn at Lexington."[2] "The American war

is over," Rush wrote in 1787, "but this is far from being the case with the American Revolution. On the contrary, nothing but the first act of the great drama is closed."[3]

One can, of course, by putting these statements in context, easily see that their authors were not in disagreement, but were only considering different features of the Revolution. Looking back on it long afterward, Adams found the heart of the Revolution in the alienation of American feeling toward Britain and the British connection. Rush,

[1] Note the subheading under which Robert R. Palmer discusses this question: "The Revolution: Was There Any?" in The Age of the Democratic Revolution: A Political History of Europe and America, 1760–1800 (2 vols., Princeton, N. J., 1959, 1964), I, 185.

[2] The Adams-Jefferson Letters, ed. Lester J. Cappon (2 vols., Chapel Hill, N. C., 1959), II, 455; see also Adams' letter to Hezekiah Niles in The Selected Writings of John and John Quincy Adams, ed. Adrienne Koch and William Peden (New York, 1946), 203–204.

[3] Hezekiah Niles, Principles and Acts of the Revolution in America . . . (Baltimore, 1822), 402.

*WILLIAM H. NELSON (1923–   ) is a Professor of History at the University of Toronto. His publications include American Tory (1961) and Theory and Practice in American Politics (1961). Reprinted by permission of the author and the American Historical Review, Vol. 70, No. 4 (July, 1965), 998–1014.

on the other hand, was concerned with the necessity for a new national government, a need shortly to be met by the adoption of the Constitution, and, further, with the need to educate a republican citizenry: "It remains," he continued, "yet to establish and perfect our new forms of government; and to prepare the principles, morals, and manners of our citizens, for these forms of government."[4] Leaving aside, for the moment, some further implications of both Adams' and Rush's words, it is enough here to note, not that they differed about the Revolution, for their views were complementary, but that they could so easily and so early use the *term* "American Revolution" to cover so wide a span of time and purpose.

During the course of the nineteenth century, it is true, one interpretation of the Revolution came to be widely accepted in the United States. (One wonders whether it does not still lie, barely below the surface, in most American minds.) This is the interpretation usually associated with George Bancroft's great national history, though for much of the nineteenth century it was a view shared by most Americans and, indeed, by English Whigs as well (George Otto Trevelyan made a respectable contribution to it). In its simplest form this interpretation found the main issue of the Revolution in American independence from Great Britain—independence made necessary by the tyranny of George III, his ministers, and Parliament, and made glorious by the steadfast zeal for liberty of General Washington and the Continental Congress. In this view the Constitution was the natural and proper sequel to the Revolution; its adoption was simply the establishment of American independence on a rational republican foundation.

As has often been shown, it was around the turn of this century, with the end of American

isolation and innocence, that this established and complacent view of the Revolution was overthrown by a number of young historians whose work was to dominate scholarship in the field until after the Second World War. These historians seem now generally to be put into two or three groups: There was the imperial school, whose members did so much to free American colonial history from parochialism by regarding it as part of the history of the whole Britishs Empire. These men, among others, Charles M. Andrews, Herbert L. Osgood, George Louis Beer, Robert L. Schuyler, and Lawrence H. Gipson, produced a splendid monument to American scholarship and an impressive body of British imperial and American colonial history. But they seemed (Andrews perhaps less than the others) deliberately to avoid daeling with the central questions of American history in their period, that is, with the developmant of autonomous American institutions in a society that was not wholly colonial. Inevitably, of course, from the imperial historians' point of view, the Revolution has to be seen primarily as a failure of British policy, as a breakdown of the old Empire, and not as the means by which an American republic established itself.

There was always an academic and Anglo-American air about the imperial historians; their great contemporary, Charles Beard, on the other hand, seems purely American and has an air of the market place about him. Beard and those of his contemporaries who approached eighteenth-century America in a similar spirit, among them, John Franklin Jameson, Arthur Schlesinger, Sr., and Vernon L. Parrington, had, in one sense, the same concern as the imperial historians: to emancipate American history from its former insularity and smugness. But for these scholars the means of emancipation lay in plunging into the turbulent sea of economic determinants and class conflict.

[4] Ibid.

For Beard, the struggle to ratify the Constitution became a clear example of class struggle, the Constitution itself the embodiment of counterrevolution. And the Declaration of Independence—which to its author and his contemporaries was simply that—became for Beard a manifesto to American democrats and populists of his own day.

Whether Carl Becker should be regarded as a member of the Jameson-Beard group or not is open to question.[5] His own way of bringing American history into step with the great events of eighteenth-century Europe was not only to use the concept of class struggle, but to apply the standards of the Enlightenment, and even the dynamics of the French Revolution, to the American Revolution. A generation ago this attempt seemed exciting; now, increasingly, like much of Beard's work, it seems just unhistorical. Indeed, it is really rather sad that the great effort, not only of Becker and Beard but of nearly a whole generation of gifted historians, to bring American history into the mainstream of Western history now seems labored and contrived. As a recent critic has rather cruelly put it, it is as if these historians "felt they must at least repeat in ink and print what in other countries had been written with blood."[6]

Within recent years the outlines of a new interpretation of the Revolution have begun to appear. In some respects, as has been frequently observed, the new view of the Revolution much more nearly resembles Bancroft's than it does Beard's or Becker's. It is nationalist and particularist; it emphasizes the unique character, not only of the Revolution, but of American political and social life before and after it. The main issue of the Revolution has become once again, not, in Becker's phrase, "who should rule at home," but "home rule"—independence from Britain. The character of the Revolution appears again, not exactly as Bancroft saw it, but in a rather more subdued light as the sober affirmation of their rights by a mature and rational people. And the Constitution has become once again the logical fulfillment and necessary completion of the Revolution.[7]

No doubt the tendency to view the Revolution in such terms is a part of the more general effort

[5] *Daniel J. Boorstin makes a distinction between Becker's and Beard's interpretations of the Revolution; he points out that Becker's primary concern was to place the ideas of the American Revolution within a larger structure of revolutionary theory, while Beard's main interest was the role of the Revolution in the development of world capitalism. (Daniel J. Boorstin. The Genius of American Politics [Chicago, 1953], 80.)*

[6] *Hannah Arendt*, On Revolution (New York, 1963), 95.

[7] *Some of those working in this period who, while disagreeing with each other on many points, would probably subscribe to a substantial part of the new nationalist interpretation of the Revolution, for which they, collectively, are mainly responsible, are Bernard Bailyn, Daniel J. Boorstin, Robert E. Brown, Louis Hartz, Cecelia Kenyon, Forrest McDonald, Edmund S. Morgan, and Clinton Rossiter. There are, to be sure, some dissenters: Merrill Jensen, while critical of much of the point of view of Beard and Becker, shares their interest in class conflict in the Revolution; Lawrence H. Gipson has continued to carry on masterfully in the tradition of the imperial school; Robert R. Palmer sees the Revolution as only one aspect of a revolutionary transformation of the European world. Useful surveys of recent work on the Revolution may be found in Richard B. Morris, "Class Struggle and the American Revolution,"* William and Mary Quarterly, *XIX (Jan., 1962), 3–29; Peter Marshall, "Radicals, Conservatives, and the American Revolution,"* Past and Present, *XXIII (Nov., 1962), 44–56; and Wesley Frank Craven, "The Revolutionary Era,"* in The Reconstruction of American History, *ed. John Higham (New York, 1962), 46–63. Edmund S. Morgan made one of the first attempts to suggest a new approach to the study of the Revolution in his article, "The American Revolution: Revisions in Need of Revising,"* William and Mary Quarterly, *XIV (Jan., 1957), 3–15.*

of historians these days to trace a conservative "consensus" through American history. At the same time, there are within the new view of the Revolution a considerable diversity of points of view and some sharply varying emphases. In its scholarship, the new historiography of the revolutionary period is more precise than that of earlier generations, but much more limited in scope; it has still more an appearance of criticism and correction than of new assertion. Its strength, however, is in its having freed the study of the period from the doctrinaire assumptions of Beard's and Becker's generation. As far as it has emerged, the new view seems sensible, and, were it not for one or two considerations, one might assume we were on the way to understanding the Revolution.

A trace of unease arises, however, simply from recalling the habit that successive generations have had of viewing the Revolution in terms of their own needs and concerns. If, a generation ago, the social consequences of the American Revolution could be seriously discussed in terms that now obviously are far more appropriate to the French or Russian Revolutions, how are we to be certain that, a generation hence, our own insistence on the continuity and conservatism of the revolutionary period may not seem equally perverse? If Beard could mistake a founding father for an early twentieth-century capitalist, how can we be certain not to confuse General Washington with General Eisenhower? Living ourselves in an age of pitiless change, may we not have developed an excessive yearning for historic continuities? And, preoccupied as we are with defending our institutions, may we not mistake ancestral attackers for defenders, too? One recent student of the Revolution concludes that the "goal of the rebellious colonists was simply to consolidate, then expand by cautious stages, the large measure of liberty and prosperity that was already part of their way of life." He then goes on to observe that "our goal

seems to be exactly the same."[8] Might not this happy coincidence be less cause for comfort than for suspicion?

Another, and perhaps more serious, though even less tangible source of doubt about the Revolution as it is now regarded is that it is all, somehow, much too cold blooded and rational, even for an Age of Reason. Beard may have been wrong about *class* struggle in America, but he was right about *struggle*, about conflict as a fact in human society. The preachers of consensus have now nearly eliminated conflict from the revolutionary period (except, of course, for the almost irrelevant antipolice action against Britain). The Revolution has become "a prudential decision taken by men of principle";[9] "a revolution to preserve a social order rather than to change it";[10] an "orderly transference of allegiance from one set of magistrates to a slightly different set."[11]

One must face the possibility that this may all be true, that eighteenth-century Americans were really so judicious, so self-righteous, so inhumanly cool and deliberate. After all, Hannah Arendt, with a warm European despair, has written that the American was "the only revolution in which compassion played no role in the motivation of the actors."[12] One can have passion, however, even without compassion. And it is difficult to

[8] Clinton Rossiter, "*The Shaping of the American Tradition*," ibid., *XI* (*Oct., 1954*), 533.

[9] *Boorstin*, Genius of American Politics, *95.*

[10] *Robert E. Brown*, Middle-Class Democracy and the Revolution in Massachusetts, 1691–1780 (*Ithaca, N. Y., 1955*), 401.

[11] *Richard Buel, Jr.*, "*Democracy and the American Revolution*," William and Mary Quarterly, *XXI (Apr., 1964), 180. On the other hand, some recent writers on the Revolution, while regarding it as a nationalist movement, have, nevertheless, affirmed its revolutionary nature: Cecelia Kenyon and Bernard Bailyn, for example.*

[12] *Arendt*, On Revolution, *65.*

believe that the first of the great modern revolutions was so much like a Grant Wood painting or a scene from Thornton Wilder's *Our Town*. Its victims did not regard it so, if their testimony has any value: "The rage of civil discord," wrote the gentle Crèvecœur, "hath advanced among us with an astonishing rapidity. Every opinion is changed; . . . the son is armed against the father, the brother against the brother, family against family."[13] And that stalwart Tory, Jonathan Sewell, wrote: "Every thing I see is laughable, cursable, and damnable; my pew in the church is converted into a pork tub; my house into a den of rebels, thieves & lice; my farm in possession of the very worst of all God's creation; my few debts all gone to the devil with my debtors. . . . All this is *right*, says Doctor Pangloss, & this is the best of all possible worlds."[14]

In reading much of the current literature on the Revolution, one has sometimes the feeling that there is nothing missing from it except the Revolution itself. American society before, during, and after the Revolution has become so marvelously "seamless."[15] It is quite true, of course, that it is no longer possible to regard with much awe some of the social and institutional changes of the revolutionary period, which, a generation ago, were taken seriously. They now seem to have been slight in effect, like the abolition of entail and primogeniture, or not clearly a part of the Revolution, like many of the changes in property holding of the time.[16] Even those political changes that must be

regarded as revolutionary—the separation from Britain and the establishment of a republican form of government under written constitutions, federal and state—involved no complete break with the past. Indeed, American historians have, in general, not yet sufficiently acknowledged the debt of the new United States to colonial and British institutions and practices. Not only was the political theory underlying both the Revolution and the Constitution mainly English, but most of the new republican institutions of the United States were, in various ways, derived from British and colonial precedent.

This is obvious in the case, for example, of the two houses of Congress; it is less obvious but no less certain in the concept of executive power to be found in the presidency—a concept surely derived not only from the remembered role of the royal governors but also from that Whig idea of the proper powers of the king embodied in the settlement of 1688.[17] Even the new federal relationship among the states was familiar, in a rough way, from the virtually federal relationship that had prevailed among the colonies and between them and the imperial government in an earlier time.

To admit, or even to emphasize, such continuities as these does not, however, in any way diminish the importance and intensity of the Revolution as an American experience. Even if it were to be shown, beyond doubt, that there were no measurable institutional changes as a result of

[13] *M. G. J. (Hector St. John) de Crèvecœur*, Sketches of Eighteenth Century America, *ed. Henri L. Bourdin et al. (New Haven, Conn., 1925), 178–79.*

[14] *"Letters of Jonathan Sewell,"* Proceedings of the Massachusetts Historical Society, *2d Ser., X (Jan., 1896), 414.*

[15] *See Boorstin*, Genius of American Politics, *esp. Chap. 1.*

[16] *Richard B. Morris has observed that all the legal, educational, and religious reforms of the revolutionary period cannot be automatically ascribed to the Revolution; if they are, he suggests, then Woodrow Wilson could be charged with going to war in order to emancipate women. (Morris, "Class Struggle and the American Revolution," 26.)*

[17] *See Andrew C. McLaughlin,* The Foundations of American Constitutionalism *(New York, 1932).*

the Revolution, its significance would remain. Allowing for the fact that not much really is known about revolutions, about their origin, course, or effects, it still seems that the subject of revolution is often approached in an oddly mechanical way. If a man has a moving or harrowing experience, an experience of terror, anger, or exultation, from which he emerges without visible physical effect, his pulse beat and blood pressure restored to what they had been before his experience, it does not therefore follow that his experience was mild, slight, or without consequence. Societies, too, can experience traumata that leave no visible scar.

The change in sentiment that John Adams wrote about, the "Revolution . . . in the Minds of the People," may have taken, as Adams thought it did, fifteen years before 1775 to become articulate. It was, no doubt, a change made possible by 150 years of American experience resting on traditions of English dissent. But in its consciousness, in its self-realization, this revolution was sudden. "It is no Little Blessing of God," Cotton Mather had observed in 1700, "that we are a part of the *English Nation*."[18] Sixty years later Jonathan Mayhew, who in a few more years would become a most embittered Anglophobe, could still write: "We Britishers are still farther distinguished and favoured of God. . . ."[19] Even in the summer of 1775, after the War of Independence had begun, Joseph Hewes of North Carolina could write: "We are loyal subjects to our present most gracious Sovereign."[20] Yet within a few months

John Adams would write that he "mortally hated the Words 'Province' 'Colonies' and Mother Country."[21] And within a few more months both Adams and Hewes would sign the Declaration of Independence.[22] "For *God's* sake let there be a full Revolution," Joseph Hawley of Massachusetts wrote in the spring of 1776; ". . . Independency, and a well planned Continental Government, will save us."[23]

The quotations from Adams and from Rush at the beginning of this paper agreed on one point: the war had not much to do with the Revolution. Except for writers on the war itself, most recent historians of the Revolution seem to have taken the same view. Yet the war was a memorable American experience, an experience of danger and defeat, of all the acrid and bitter feelings raised by rebellion and civil conflict, of final and absolute victory. It was the war that made the British enemies rather than mere antagonists; it was the war that cut the Tories out of American society and set up a new sovereignty; it was the war that compelled Americans to regard themselves and to deal with foreigners as a new people, as Americans rather than as British colonials. It was during the course of the war that the "ancient rights of Englishmen" gave birth finally to the "rights of men" and to that "Novus Ordo Seclorum" that, for a time, caught the imagination of Europe. Perhaps there were more subtle and fundamental

---

[18] *Quoted in Clinton Rossiter,* Seedtime of the Republic: The Origin of the American Tradition of Political Liberty (*New York, 1953*), 6.

[19] *Quoted in Max Savelle, "Nationalism and Other Loyalties in the American Revolution,"* American Historical Review, *LXVII (July, 1962), 903.*

[20] American Archives: Consisting of a Collection of

Authentick Records, State Papers, Debates and Letters . . . , ed. Peter Force (*9 vols., Washington, D. C., 1837–53*), 4th Ser., II, 1757.

[21] Diary and Autobiography of John Adams, *ed. L. H. Butterfield (4 vols., Cambridge, Mass., 1961), III, 357.*

[22] *Hewes, it is true, supported the Declaration somewhat reluctantly. (See* Letters of Members of the Continental Congress, *ed. Edmund C. Burnett [8 vols., Washington, D. C., 1921–36], I, 537.)*

[23] American Archives, *ed. Force, 4th Ser., V, 1169.*

changes in American life during the war; a student of colonial religion has written of Massachusetts that, "During the fighting years a shift of center had been taking place in the common life, and by 1780 it had come to pass. The state, not the church, was now in sharp focus."[24] Whatever the role of the war in the fulfillment of the Revolution, it is worth noting that, a generation later, when Americans felt a desperate need to restore their self-esteem, to redeem their national honor, and to reaffirm the Revolution, they chose as their means of redemption a war with Britain.

If the Revolution was no more than "a prudential decision taken by men of principle," a revolution "to preserve a social order rather than to change it," one would not expect it to have dramatic consequences. If, on the other hand, it was a real revolution, with its own secret life, its own law, its autonomous power to change men's minds and turn their will, then one would expect it to leave a mark on the world and on generations to come. Here, however, in searching for the effects of the Revolution, we must be careful to distinguish consequence from sequence. By stretching causality, not beyond the limits of reason, but beyond the bounds of common sense, most of what has happened in the world since 1780 may be seen to be in consequence of the American Revolution: the Russian Revolution, to take one example, by direct descent through the French

Revolution. To judge the significance of the American Revolution in such grand, vague, all-encompassing terms as these would be, however, to indulge in that elastic logic which allowed one of the great American historians of our time to justify the lawless greed of the robber barons of American industry in the nineteenth century by the capacity of the United States to defeat Hitler and oppose Communism in the twentieth century.

There is, to be sure, one area of grand concern and vast significance in relation to which the American Revolution stands in some sort of relevant proximity: the historic complex out of which have come democracy and freedom as we now know them in the Western world. Even if the American revolutionists did not fight for democracy, they contributed to its coming simply because their individualistic concepts of government by consent and republican equality led irresistibly in a democratic direction. Similarly, while their revolt against Britain had, inherently, not a great deal in common with those scores of colonial revolts to follow, it became a beacon for them. It was not long after the Declaration of Independence before natives in the Comoro Islands would revolt against their Arab masters, saying, "America is free. Could not we be?"[25] However irrelevant some Americans may find this proposition, it is still, after two hundred years, a powerful and corrosive solvent of inequalities in the world.

Not least among the delicate imponderables that cluster around the American Revolution is its influence on Europe and, most directly, on the French Revolution. It is certain that enlightened men in Europe saw the American Revolution as representing the principles of the Enlightenment itself applied to a living society. It is certain also

---

[24] *Ola E. Winslow*, Meetinghouse Hill, 1630–1783(*New York, 1952*), *296. Savelle has emphasized the role of the war as a catalyst for American nationalism. (Savelle, "Nationalism and Other Loyalties," 918.) John Alden maintains that "The military triumph of the patriots and their allies led not only to independence but also to the firm establishment of republican government in the United States." (John Alden,* The American Revolution, 1775–1783 [*New York, 1954*], *265; see also Don Higginbotham, "American Historians and the Military History of the American Revolution,"* American Historical Review, *LXX* [*Oct., 1964*], *18–34.*)

[25] *Quoted in Palmer*, Age of the Democratic Revolution, *I, 258.*

that in France in the 1780's if not elsewhere, the American Revolution was closely studied. Alas, it is even more certain that "America was a screen on which Europe projected its own visions,"[26] and that America, as Europeans saw it, sometimes achieved, as it still does on occasion, wonderful unreality. Consider, for example, the Arcadian imaginings of that Frenchman who reported that a constitutional convention in Virginia had assembled, for the serenity of its deliberations, "in a peaceful wood, removed from the sight of the people, in an enclosure prepared by nature with banks of grass."[27]

For their part, the men of the Revolution had an ambivalent attitude toward Europe: they were both anxiously concerned for the good opinion of foreigners, and ultimately pessimistic about their regeneration. They never doubted that their revolution should stand as a model and example to the world, and they took measurable pride in the spread of its principles. In his old age, Jefferson wrote Adams with satisfaction that "the flames kindled on the 4th. of July 1776. have spread over too much of the globe to be extinguished by the feeble engines of despotism."[28] But Jefferson would surely also have agreed with Gouverneur Morris when, early in the French Revolution, he wrote contemptuously of the French that, "They want an American constitution without realizing they have no Americans to uphold it."[29] And

Jefferson made no argument when Adams wrote him that "The Europeans are all deeply tainted with prejudices both Ecclesiastical, and Temporal which they can never get rid of."[30]

In considering the shimmering distortions in Europe's view of America and America's view of Europe, it almost seems as if they saw each other, not across, but through the sea. The difficulty of separating what is real from what is unreal in the apparent interactions of Europe and America is formidable under the most favorable conditions. In the case of the American and French Revolutions, their very closeness in time, in spirit, in details of nomenclature and organization makes such an untangling nearly impossible. They stand in a fraternal relationship, though presumably it is of some significance that the American Revolution came first. The real paradox of the American Revolution is that what is least universal and least European about it—its impact on American society and American institutions—is hardly more tangible than its influence on the world.

At first sight, there seems to be a good argument for the current view that the consequences of the Revolution for America, ultimate as well as immediate, had a "conservative" character.[31] An appearance of conservatism arises partly from the Revolution's comparative mildness as a social

---

[26] Ibid., *253.*

[27] *Quoted ibid., 254. For an account of the influence of the American Revolution on the French, see, in addition to Palmer, Louis Gottschalk, "The Place of the American Revolution in the Causal Pattern of the French Revolution,"* in Publications of the American Friends of Lafayette (*No. 2, 1948*), *reprinted in* The Making of Modern Europe, *ed. Herman Ausubel (2 vols., New York, 1951),* I, *494–510.*

[28] Adams-Jefferson Letters, *ed. Cappon, II, 575.*

[29] *Quoted in Louis Hartz, "American Political Thought*

and the American Revolution," *American Political Science Review, XLVI (June, 1952), 323. Hartz comments here on the comparative indifference of Americans to Europe's enthusiasm for the Revolution.*

[30] Adams-Jefferson Letters, *ed. Cappon, II, 607.*

[31] *The best discussion of the confusing political terminology used to discuss the Revolution, as well as a powerful argument for its radical nature, may be found in Cecelia M. Kenyon's article, "Republicanism and Radicalism in the American Revolution: An Old-Fashioned Interpretation,"* William and Mary Quarterly, *XIX (Apr., 1962), 153–82.*

upheaval,[32] but perhaps even more from the successful embodiment of its main achievement in the Constitution: the establishment of an independent and stable American republic. Since the Constitution can no longer be regarded as a counterrevolution, but has, nevertheless, proved extremely resistant to radical change, it necessarily casts back on the Revolution itself a soft and mellow light of rational finality.

Underlying its "conservatism" is the obvious fact that the Revolution did not have to do, or have to try to do, in America all that the subsequent revolutions of the Old World had to attempt; that confining and elaborate system of legal inequalities and privileges in the old corporate society of Europe did not exist in America except in the most sketchy and rudimentary form and did not, therefore, have to be dismantled.[33] Even monarchy was much more nominal than

real in America. John Adams may have been arguing too literally when he wrote with customary impatience: "Kings We never had among Us, Nobles We never had. Nothing hereditary ever existed in the Country: Nor will the Country require or admit of any such Thing."[34] But the substance of his claim is clearly true.

The character of the Revolution as a confirmation of existing American social and political realities can easily tempt one to conclude that, so far at least as America itself is concerned, what is most important about the Revolution is what preceded rather than what followed it.[35] How did America come to be a place where the assertions of the Revolution could be so convincingly and finally stated? To pursue this line of inquiry is undoubtedly a worth-while enterprise, but to deny radical consequences to the Revolution because what it asserted rose naturally out of its society is to judge historic process too much in terms of origins. As it was produced, so did the Revolution produce. Like any historic event taken roughly out of a continuum for examination, the Revolution may be regarded as effect or cause, as an end or a beginning. Regarded as a beginning, what did the Revolution produce in America?

Here it is important to observe the sharply two-sided nature of the Revolution: it was both affirmation and denial, and its positive and negative qualities were indissolubly bound to each

[32] *Palmer* (Age of the Democratic Revolution, *I, 188–90) states that there were some sixty thousand American loyalist émigrés, representing a rate nearly five times that of the French Revolution; from this he concludes that the American Revolution was a greater social upheaval than is usually thought. The difficulty here, of course, is not only that it is hard sometimes to tell the difference between genuine and spurious loyalist refugees, but also that it was comparatively easy for the loyalists, by moving to one of the remaining provinces of British North America, to remain in an English-speaking, North American environment under the old flag; French dissenters from the French Revolution had no such option, and so the relative rates of emigration are not really comparable. [See my* The American Tory (*Oxford, Eng., 1961).]*

[33] *See Louis Hartz*, The Liberal Tradition in America: An Interpretation of American Political Thought since the Revolution (*New York, 1955); support for the pre-revolutionary liberalism of Massachusetts and Virginia society may be found in* Brown, Middle-Class Democracy, *and in* id. *and B. Katherine Brown*, Virginia, 1705–1786: Democracy or Aristocracy? (*East Lansing, Mich., 1964).*

[34] Diary and Autobiography of John Adams, *ed.* Butterfield, *III, 356.*

[35] *Perhaps the most unequivocal definition of the Revolution as such a confirmation is Bailyn's: "This completion, this rationalization, this symbolization, this lifting into consciousness and endowing with high moral purpose inchoate, confused elements of social and political change—this was the American Revolution." [Bernard Bailyn, "Political Experience and Enlightenment Ideas in Eighteenth-Century America,"* American Historical Review, *LXVII (Jan., 1962), 351.]*

other. To consider, as American historians have often done, the positive consequences of the Revolution without observing also its negative effects is to overlook a process of primary importance in American history. For the founding of the United States rested on the repudiation of a political connection with Britain and of an old British-American heritage. More abstractly, America's new republican institutions rested on a repudiation of monarchy and of that organic and familial social order for which monarchy stood. From the day of its birth, the United States has been accustomed to linking a silent "no" to an audible "yes" when approaching any fundamental question of political theory. May not this necessity, arising from the nature of the break with Britain, have contributed significantly to the American habit, so often deplored abroad, of seeing political issues in black and white, as "pairs of opposites"? May it not also have given a narrow and doctrinaire cast to American political thought when it touched upon such matters as monarchy and the status of colonies, or perhaps even on the more basic question of the claims of state authority over the individual?[36]

Even the modest institutional changes of the Revolution have a certain symbolic importance that is usually overlooked. Thus, to consider in a different light Jameson's discredited little list of social consequences of the Revolution: the laws concerning entail and primogeniture may have been easily and habitually evaded, but their very

existence was a reminder of a concept of land-ownership that was not absolute and not individualistic—that would soon seem "un-American." Similarly such feeble enclaves of legal privilege as the Penn family's exemption from taxes, or such faint traces of official aristocracy as were to be found in the old Governors' Councils carried little weight in themselves, but, in a society so uniform, so level, so "equal," they were reminders—some American Tories thought them useful reminders—of the more complicated and various society of Europe. The rickety establishment of the Church of England in the South and in lower New York was also a reminder, distasteful but perhaps educative, of an organic view of society alien to what was already becoming the secular orthodoxy of America. And while the expulsion of the loyalists did not deprive the new United States of social pretense, of oligarchy, or of gentility real or false, it did deprive America of a point of view, of a set of political convictions, from which, in the next century, most of the conservative as well as a part of the socialist thought of Europe was to be derived.[37]

The loss of a whole body of imperial regulation and of the rather ramshackle machinery of British administration that had enforced it—royal governors, vice-admiralty courts, customs officers, Indian agents, and all—may have been easily enough made up by the creation of a new administration more efficient in most respects than the old. George III himself, in a practical way, may have been more than adequately replaced by George Washington. But independence did firmly close the gates to one avenue of previously conceivable American development: Whatever experiments, fruitful or not, America and Britain might have made with the frail threads of their political con-

---

[36] *Cecelia Kenyon has ascribed "an element of rigidity in American political thinking" to the attachment Americans developed for republican institutions as a result of the Revolution; she also thinks the "ideological habit" thus acquired has been extended to more recent, rigid doctrinal positions in regard, for example, to socialism, imperialism, and colonialism. (Kenyon, "Republicanism and Radicalism in the American Revolution," 167.)*

[37] *Nelson,* American Tory, *170–90; see also Bailyn, "Political Experience and Enlightenment Ideas,"* 348–50.

nection were no longer possible after 1783. Whatever traditions of unbroken continuity with its European past America might have wanted to cultivate were, after the Revolution, no longer available. Whatever reservations America might have wanted to hold about its own dominant tendencies were disallowed. Jonathan Boucher liked to complain about the Enlightenment's lack of "caution and reverence" in dealing with the mysteries of social organization, and claimed, in his Tory fashion, that man had ultimately to *"live by faith and not by sight."*[38] After 1783 Americans would have to live by sight, or pretend to do so.

It should be clear that America suffered some real loss by the violence, abruptness, and, in a political sense, completeness of the break with Britain. Precisely because Americans did not in 1783 cease to be historically English, to speak English, to live by what had once been English law and English political theories, to follow English practices in local government and English habits of political compromise, precisely for these reasons, the severance of close political ties with Britain represented, in certain respects, an impoverishment for America. For America, in developing, reaffirming, and extending its independence, generation by generation, has increasingly widened the gulf across which political conversation with Britain must be held. And England, it should be remembered, though it too may have suffered some impoverishment by the severance of bonds with America, did not cease to be a vital and rich society, in its capacity for self-examination and change often more radical, more profound, more various than America. Indeed, Britain in 1783 was on the very eve of an age of political change far more comprehensive

and intense than anything the American Revolution contemplated.

Beyond the institutional and ideological deprivation that the break with Britain represented for America lie the psychological consequences, as yet largely unexamined, of this estrangement. Is it not tempting to detect in the stridency of American self-justification for the Revolution a trace of guilt? May there not be a hint of longing for things lost, however inconsiderable, in the very ferocity of that Anglophobia which used to form so regular a part of American political ritual? Perhaps it is not too farfetched to see the effects of some subtle deprivation in characteristic American attitudes toward the symbols of traditional and nonrevolutionary societies, especially in that curious and awkward mixture of awe, incomprehension, and amusement with which Americans have always regarded the trappings of monarchy, particularly British monarchy.

All in all, since Americans did not become wholly new men in 1776 or 1783, since they were long to remain, in many respects, Englishmen, the Revolution could not help but make them poorer Englishmen by increasing their alienation and remoteness from the main centers of English life. As men, Americans may have grown more cosmopolitan in consequence of the Revolution, but, as Englishmen, they grew more provincial. This is, no doubt, why Americans have not liked, since the eighteenth century, to think of themselves as English, and also why they were for so long at such pains to defend their isolation as the product of deliberate and philosophical choice.

To suggest that guilt and deprivation are among the effects, for Americans, of the Revolution seems worth while, if only because the possibility of such consequences is so rarely admitted into discussion. It would be foolish, however, to see these as primary in the heritage of the Revolution. America is, and was at the end of the eighteenth century,

[38] *Jonathan Boucher*, Reminiscences of an American Loyalist, 1738–1789, *ed. Jonathan Bouchier (Boston and New York, 1925)*, 46–47.

far more than an estranged English colony. The Revolution was genuinely two-sided: it meant alienation, but it also meant liberation. The American colonies had, perhaps since their founding, dissented in varying degree from the established social, ecclesiastical, and governmental arrangements in England. Now, suddenly, they were able, through the Revolution, to transform mere dissent into a new system, positive and ultimately lawful. Such a transformation of protest into affirmation is, at least in a narrow sense, what a revolution is.[39] Through the Revolution and the Constitution that was its culmination, Americans articulated a remarkable ideology, one that, without much revision, has given law and freedom, tenaciously if sometimes precariously balanced, to a continent.

The heart and center of this ideology is political individualism: individual man—*his* life, liberty, and pursuit of happiness—became the central concern of the whole political order. This represented a radical change of focus, away from a concept of state that Americans had probably never believed in, toward the individual whose life was already so vitally apparent in America. Such change of focus brought with it a train of logical consequences; the first of these was the necessary repudiation of monarchy in favor of a republic. This was necessary, not because monarchy was hostile to liberty, for it was not; and

not because it was incompatible with democracy, for it was not; nor was democracy an aim of the Revolution. The repudiation of monarchy was necessary because monarchy, as much as an established church, stood for a social order repugnant to individualism. Monarchy stood for a hierarchial order mysteriously linking present to past, irrationally claiming a greater total than the sum of its parts, and demanding service and obedience, not for the sake of self-interest, individual or even collective, but for the life and perpetuation of society itself. None of this had ever made much sense in American terms, and John Adams may well have been right when he wrote, years before the Revolution, that the settlers of the American colonies, "had an utter contempt of all that dark ribaldry of hereditary, indefeasible right," and ". . . knew that government was a plain, simple, intelligible thing, founded in nature and reason, and quite comprehensible by common sense."[40]

Monarchy disposed of, the other distinctive features of the revolutionary settlement followed logically: a written constitution was not only practically essential in setting up a republican government; it was, in the rational clarity of its text, further argument against all forms of "dark ribaldry" in government. A federal structure of government not only reflected the preexisting separation and autonomy of the old colonies, but also, by fragmenting the authority of the state, offered further security to the individual, as did the carefully devised system of checks and balances among the branches of government. The principle of judicial review (implicit rather than explicit in the Constitution) was not only familiar from prerevolutionary experience in appealing to higher authority in England, but, once again, kept the

---

[39] *Palmer defines a revolution as an "unlawful change in the conditions of lawfulness." (Palmer,* Age of the Democratic Revolution, *I, 198.) Such a definition cannot, of course, suggest the dynamic conflict inherent in the process of revolution. Gottschalk has described this process compactly in dialectical terms, the revolution, in his view, being a synthesis resulting from the conflict between an enfeebled old regime and aggressive discontent, and occurring "not so much because antithesis is irresistible as because thesis has collapsed." (See Gottschalk, "Place of the French Revolution," 501, 508–509.)*

[40] *"A Dissertation on the Canon and Feudal Law,"* in The Works of John Adams, *ed. Charles Francis Adams (10 vols., Boston, 1856), III, 454.*

practice of government within reach of individual reason.

And so, using old and familiar materials of construction, America went beyond British experience to build a new structure, simply proportioned, severe, but human in scale. It was an audacious and radical achievement, carried out so deliberately and independently: the establishment of a republic in a world of monarchies; the establishment of a federal system of government in a world of unitary states; the construction of governments, general and local, under plainly written constitutions, in a world ruled by fiat and custom; above all, the successful "reduction to practice" of the principle of government by consent of the governed—heretofore a mere theory of the Enlightenment.

It is perfectly true, of course, that all of this embodied pre-existing American leanings and preferences (it would be surprising if it did not). American individualism was a fact before the Revolution, but the Revolution made it an established and orthodox fact.[41] Until the Revolution, as has been pointed out, it was quite possible to believe that America's characteristic lines of development had been "*away from*, not *toward*, something."[42] Indeed, this was exactly what the leading American Tories and their English friends had believed. It was the Revolution and its successful confirmation in the Constitution that installed America's political predispositions behind solid

walls which could not easily be attacked, and, as a matter of fact, still stand four-square.

The architecture of the revolutionary settlement is the Revolution's most visible achievement. Its importance could hardly be overstated, for it was the means by which the ambitions, the interests, the energies liberated by the Revolution were to be successfully contained and reconciled, as well as preserved. Even so, its architecture is only one of the Revolution's manifestations, perhaps not even the most important. The Revolution was, above all else, an intense, painful, joyful, youthful American experience. It was an experience, by no means common to all societies, young or old, of estrangement and danger, of bitter family strife sometimes requiring principle to be put ahead of natural affection; it was also an experience of awesome new opportunity, of limitless horizons suddenly opened up. Contemplating the future of his new country, an American of the Revolution could say with Cortes' captain, "I stood looking at it and thought that never in the world would there be discovered other lands such as these."[43] Not merely a sense of discovery, but more, a sense of possession permeates the writings of the Revolution; it was as if now each man could say, for the first time, that the land was *his*.

And if Americans lost an old family, they gained a new: "The distinctions between Virginians, Pennsylvanians, New Yorkers, and New Englanders, are no more," said Patrick Henry, too soon but not untruly; "I am not a Virginian, but an American."[44] This new sense of nationhood was the child, not the parent of the Revolution, and, to this day, American patriotism retains some of the character of the Revolution: it is still austere

[41] Kenyon, *"Republicanism and Radicalism,"* 174. *Concerning American individualism, it is important to remember that it was, and perhaps still is, radical primarily in its claims against traditional state authority; it did not challenge non-governmental authority—that of the family, or the informal authority of the community, or the authority of a disestablished church; it did not even challenge revolutionary state authority, based, as it appeared to be, on reason.*

[42] Bailyn, *"Political Experience and Enlightenment Ideas,"* 350.

[43] *Quoted in John Bartlet Brebner,* The Explorers of North America, 1492–1806 (*New York, 1933*), 40.

[44] *Quoted in R. D. Meade,* Patrick Henry. Patriot in the Making (*Philadelphia and New York, 1957*), 325.

and self-conscious; it possesses a confessional and creedal quality, and withal a surprising verve and exuberance.

Perhaps it is just because so much of the spirit of the Revolution survives that the exact margins of its influence are so hard to delineate. For survive it surely does, sometimes with more than a trace of revolutionary zeal. There may be a hint of an explanation for the Revolution's vitality and longevity in those familiar words of John Adams and Benjamin Rush: "The Revolution was in the Minds of the People," wrote Adams; "It remains," said Rush, ". . . to prepare the principles, morals, and manners of our citizens, for these forms of government." It was not only that the founding fathers built solidly, but it was that they plainly understood, and have, in some way, never allowed their descendants to forget, that a revolutionary society lives by its principles and by their deliberate propagation, generation to generation.

Whatever its ultimate origin, the doctrinal tradition in American politics comes from the Revolution. It is a prickly tradition—rigid, moralistic, and self-righteous sometimes, yet with an ultimate respect for the rules of reason and a saving capacity for self-criticism. The world might often wish that America did not feel compelled to live by principle, and compelled, moreover, to discuss its principles in interminable and often crude public debate. The world might wish fervently that America did not flatly expect the world to live, now or some day, by American principles. But it is fortunate that the principles are as good as they are. At any rate, they and the compulsion to live and judge by them come straight from the Revolution.

PHILOSOPHER-STATESMEN
OF THE REPUBLIC

*Adrienne Koch**

The founding fathers were men of remarkably broad interests with an uncanny aptitude for political analysis and for the adaptation of theories to practice. There are some who describe this phenomenon as no more than the heritage of humanism which the American enlightenment merely re-embodied. Certainly the statesmen who shaped the Republic in its first form were confronting essentially the same issues as those formulated by the Renaissance humanists: the attempt to reconcile speculative thinking on the nature of man with the immediate task of creating a new political and social order. They differed from More, Erasmus, and their fellows in that these modern humanists were under more pressure to apply their theories to the urgent task at hand. But there is something breath-taking about the re-embodiment of broad humanist principles in a struggling and relatively unsophisticated people, beset on every side by the problems of living. The "fathers" therefore deserve either spontaneous admiration or informed respect, whether we study their ideas and actions as we find them, or trace their intellectual heritage to another age.

Of the first statesmen of the Republic, four—Jefferson, Madison, John Adams, and Hamilton—trained their sights higher than did any others. Addressing themselves to more than practical considerations, they seemed to be genuinely inspired by the historical uniqueness of the experience open to them, to launch a new civilization on a large scale. In final outcome, they proved equal to the challenge of planning republican government, and they could only have become so because they tried to understand not only the buried sources of power, but the moral objectives

*ADRIENNE KOCH (1912–   ) is a Professor of History at the University of Maryland. Her publications include The Philosophy of Thomas Jefferson (1943), Power, Morals and the Founding Fathers (1962), and The Age of the American Enlightenment (1965). Reprinted by permission of the author and The Sewanee Review, Vol. 55, No. 3 (July, 1947), 384–386, 392–405. Copyright by the University of the South.

161

of good government. In a sense they were, as Hamilton once contemptuously declared, "speculative" thinkers and "empirics." Even Hamilton himself belonged to the company he criticized, for he, with the others, assessed what he already found in existence as social habit and political tradition; he built upon that which was already "given"; and recommended, according to his lights, the best direction of change.

Jefferson, the greatest of them all, was conspicuously devoted to the theory and practice of good government. Further, he was actively critical of his own *methods* of establishing political judgments, and he was intellectually prepared to examine the logical, philosophical, scientific, or sentimental elements in his views of society. He learned to style himself an "ideologist," by which term he meant to identify himself with his friends, the French philosophers, who had founded a school of thought known as "Ideology" in the Napoleonic period. Hamilton, Madison, and Adams as well as Jefferson contributed characteristic ways of thought, individual tempers of belief which were to be important not only in the era of the Republic but for America thenceforth. The principles of the four philosopher-statesmen taken together almost define the range of our national ideology—our objectives, our character as a people, our economic and social patterns, our "Americanism."

The challenge of creating a new form of government gave rise to an atmosphere of intellectual adventure, in which the Platonic vision of the philosopher-king could for one brief period take on American reality. "Until philosophers take to government, or those who now govern become philosophers," Plato had boldly written, "so that government and philosophy unite, there will be no end to the miseries of states." In the timeless analogy of the cave in the *Republic*, the philosophers who struggle to free themselves from the chains of ignorance and superstition make their way to the light outside. They see the truth. Loving its clarity, they would bask in its light. But the thought of the chained multitude below gives them no rest, and they understand, as Platonic seekers of truth must, that they can not fail to carry glimmerings of light to the poorer minds who inhabit the cave.

The four great philosopher-statesmen of the American "Enlightenment" conform admirably to the Platonic pattern. They grope in authentic Platonic fashion for the true principles of social order, accepting the responsibility of administering the affairs of their less far-sighted fellow men; yet they reject the Platonic ideal as an explicit inspiration. They are willing to exemplify it if they must; but justify it, direct from its ancient source, never. Plato, even for Jefferson who had the most developed philosophic predilections of the group, was too full of metaphysical flights and trances to prove sympathetic to the common-sense orientation of the new nation. In any event the double drive of philosophy and leadership, thought and action, vision and its fortifying concrete detail is heeded by Jefferson, Madison, Adams, and even Hamilton. From the time of Franklin to the present this double drive has dictated a double destiny for the American nation and a dualistic orientation for its literature. In the great period of American political literature, both forces were present without fatal conflict, and lend a peculiar divided charm and predictive importance to this body of writing.

II

In its literary guise, the issue faced by the philosopher-statesmen was the reconciliation of potent ideas with traditions of style formalized by eighteenth-century English writers and imitated by our early writers of fiction, essay, and poetry.

The methods of *belles lettres* were inadequate to the urgent demand for clear and effective expression. These public-minded men wrote their state-papers, their reports, their tracts, and their letters with some care for the form as well as the content of what they wrote, but they subordinated the formal demands of art to the immediate need for communication. John Adams, who was himself a tyro in the "literary" essay, had made it all too plain: "substance" was to take precedence over "elegance." He had written: ". . . the simplest style, the most mathematical precision of words and ideas, is best adapted to discover truth and to convey it to others, in reasoning on this subject [politics]." That Adams himself, who once boasted that he had never had "time" to compress his written pieces nor to prune them of repetitions, did not always live up to the severe criterion of clarity and communicability he invoked, in no way affects the importance of the ideal. Amusingly enough, some of Adams' most notorious departures from this standard produced his best prose, the nervous and animated passages so eloquent of Adams' erratic brilliance. Jefferson and Madison never quite forsook the rounded and urbane prose line which by now seems characteristic of the Virginia political dynasty with the notable exception of George Washington, who strove, not always successfully, to restrict himself to a "plain stile." Yet even the Virginians never hesitated to put communication and content above consideration of style or form. Madison, ever judicious and temperate, best conformed to the utilitarian ideal. In criticizing a political pamphlet, he commented that it would have been "much improved by softer words and harder arguments," and he found the style attractive that had "the artless neatness always pleasing to the purest tastes." Hamilton, in the calculated fixity of his desire to convince, to silence the opposition by a brilliant show of fire before an enemy gun could

shoot, does not hesitate to employ rhetorical ornament and insistent, obvious rhythm. Although he too agreed that "our communications should be calm, reasoning, serious, showing steady resolution more than feeling, having force in the idea rather than in the expression," he often lapsed into purple passages whose melodramatic tones are as trying as they are insincere.

Throughout, the unorthodoxy of this political literature is a consequence of the fact that these statesmen were primarily devoted to the issues and principles growing out of a serious national undertaking. The motivation of interest seems to have been so compelling that communications tended to become direct colloquial exchanges, discussions of ideas, selfless presentation of the "argument" without stopping for artifice or formal discipline. For this reason it is a great pity that the most often quoted political "classics" have tended to come from the public documents and official papers of the nation's archives, rather than from the enormous correspondence which more truly characterizes this age of statesmen. This correspondence, in fact, should be the mainstay of our knowledge of the political thought and of the social continuum of the early Republic. In a sense, its excellence may be regarded as the nation's unearned reward for having once lived in an age with inadequate media of communication. It is hardly an exaggeration to say that there is no Jefferson, no Adams, and no Madison without the body of letters they left. For an understanding of Hamilton and Madison, notes for their speeches in the Constitutional Convention and elsewhere must be added to the justly famous papers they separately contributed to *The Federalist* (1787–88).

All the statesmen had been trained in Congress or had read deeply in the law. None in the country knew better than they the amount of power that could be borrowed from the logical ordering of material, the legal-rhetorical habit of defining terms. A truly impressive endurance also marks the longer writings of Jefferson and his colleagues, as they patiently investigate detailed charges and sternly cleave to the political issues under discussion. Their writing is suffused with a kind of lofty passion born of the consciousness of the cosmic importance of the "infant nation" with which they identified themselves so intimately. What a terrible disaster it would be, they seem to say, if the "ark" as Madison put it, "bearing as we have flattered ourselves the happiness of our country & the hope of the world," should be shipwrecked. It is not surprising that an earnestness of moral tone is the keynote of this literature which in general is neither original in metaphor nor polished in style.

On occasions, the utilitarian limitations upon expression are conceived of as a *moral* question, intimately related to the simple and severe needs of republican society. Jefferson, gentle lover of the fine arts, was keenly aware that America, unlike Europe, was not yet ready for the highest and most cultivated art-forms. His travel journals through Italy and France conscientiously record technical improvements in agriculture and contain long passages on how to make wines and cheese. This attitude is at war, all during Jefferson's varied European sojourn, with such projects as the adaptation of Palladio's Villa Rotunda to his plan for the second Monticello and his general enthusiasm for the ancients in literary form and moral leadership, and to the highest expression of what was then "modern" music, painting, "beauty" in general. John Adams, prone to state reasons for his actions, epitomized the stage of American literary and artistic needs by declaring: "It is not indeed the fine arts which our country requires; the useful, the mechanic arts are those which we have occasion for in a young country as yet simple and not far advanced in luxury, although perhaps much too far for her age and

character. . . . The science of government is my duty to study, more than all other sciences. . . . I must study politics and war, that my sons may have liberty to study mathematics and philosophy, geography, natural history and naval architecture, navigation, commerce, and agriculture, in order to give their children a right to study painting, poetry, music, architecture, statuary, tapestry, and porcelain."

Jefferson had clearly announced that in "a republic nation, whose citizens are to be led by reason and persuasion, and not by force, the art of reasoning becomes of first importance," and had recommended the speeches of Livy, Sallust, and Tacitus as "preeminent specimens of logic, taste and that sententious brevity which, using not a word to spare, leaves not a moment for inattention to the hearer." Amplification, he thought, was the "vice of modern oratory," and he avoided speech-making when he could. But it was Jefferson who developed that flowing and "felicitous" line for which all America came to know him— the rhythmic yet thoughtful line that moves unchecked in our most famous public *Declaration*, in our early official papers and documents, and in that remarkable corpus of Jefferson letters with which no subsequent political correspondence can compete.

Madison we have remarked as the advocate of the tightened composition of logical demonstration. He felt that the "only effectual precaution against fruitless and endless discussion" was the definition of our political terms. Hamilton nursed a notorious and constitutional fear that republican government would not weather the storm; but in his *Federalist* essays, when he was promoting the cause of the new constitution, he shared the general excitement over political innovation. "The people of this country, by their conduct and example" he wrote, "will decide the important question, whether societies of men are really capable or not of establishing good government from reflection and choice, or whether they are forever destined to depend for their political constitutions on accident and force." Adams, paternal watchdog of his beloved New England, had further called attention to the specific virtues found in the self-government local to his region. These virtues he kept in mind from his early directives on government in his influential letters, "Thoughts on Government" (1776), to half a century later when he wrote his last review of the revised constitution of Massachusetts. Madison added to his theoretical contribution a practical demonstration of superior journalism in the unique service he performed by reporting the Constitutional Convention. Demonstrating selfless honesty, patience, and comprehension, Madison early set a high standard for American political reporting. Thus, in different ways, the statesmen of the American Republic demonstrated their sense of a supreme political mission, and it was this dominant aim of constructing a government compatible with freedom which gave unity to their writing— not in the sense of formal arrangement or style, but in the homogeneous conviction which flowed from their dedication to political ends.

The very issue of English versus American idiom adds the final touch to the thesis that there was a separate quality in American political writing as early as the formative years of the new Republic. The British critics who mocked American writing for forsaking "purity" of standard English form and style were met with singular equanimity. Jefferson, for example, whose use of the word "belittle" in *Notes on Virginia* (1784) had been the occasion for reproof by the *Edinburgh Review*, was unperturbed. Languages, he explained had always grown by innovation. They fattened on flexible adaptation and change. Who would expect a vast *new* American nation, with its very different regions, to bind itself in an iron cask of

ready-made English speech and prose? No, "neology" must clearly replace purism, since the price of purism was stagnation. "Had the preposterous idea of fixing the language been adopted by our Saxon ancestors, of Peirce Plowman, of Chaucer, of Spenser, the progress of ideas must have stopped with that of the language . . . what do we not owe to Shakespeare for the enrichment of the language, by his free and magical creation of words?" To be sure, "uncouth words will sometimes be offered; but the public will judge them, and receive or reject, as sense or sound shall suggest."

No matter how often the debates in Congress, or the individual statesmen in writing, might call upon the eloquent models of antiquity; no matter how much the balanced sentence of the English essayists, Addison and Steele, or the English political theorists of the Seventeenth and Eighteenth Centuries might be copied—a sense of the American scene in all its heady potentialities was so strong in the minds of these architects of the Republic that they could scarcely avoid giving direct expression to nascent American culture. In the authentic idiom of American thought and speech the statesmen of the greatest experimental democracy in history put pen to paper.

III

The ideology of American democracy began its career with a set of political principles termed "Republican." Although John Adams was quick to warn of the shifting meanings of the term "republic," it became a fixed pole of political reference in American political theory, directly contraposing that other pole, Monarchy, against which the Revolution had been waged. Adams himself believed in republican doctrine and, like the other political leaders of his day, made standard references to the ancient republics as the historical alternative to monarchy and to feudal hierarchic society. Almost everyone in early America agreed on the minimal connotation of the term, either explicitly or by implication. Like late eighteenth-century philosophers elsewhere, they understood that a republic was a government which derived its power from the people "originally," referred back to the people for an ultimate court of appeal in "crucial" questions transcending the ordinary affairs of legislation, and exercised its granted powers through representatives chosen by a majority of the voting citizens. In theory, at least, these voting citizens were further supposed to represent the "will of the people," and while they confided specific powers to their representatives, it was understood that a republic was essentially a government of laws rather than of men.

Were one to try to locate the maximum adherence to this republican ideal, one could project an imaginary political line with the left terminal point designating "maximum faith" and the right terminal point "minimum faith." We should then have to place Jefferson at the left and Hamilton at the right. John Adams accordingly must occupy the middle ground, to the left of Hamilton and the right of Jefferson; but he is also to the right of Madison, who is closer to Jefferson on most fundamental political matters—although it is important to note that Madison is sometimes closer to Hamilton in economic questions than is either Adams or Jefferson.

Had Jefferson written no more than the initial draft of the *Declaration of Independence* he would probably have earned his place on the radical left of our American political line. The achievement of the *Declaration*, if it proves nothing else, certainly established its author's title to the greatest pen in the patriotic cause. Certain contemporaries, either through faulty judgment or through jealousy of Jefferson's ability to fashion a line of fundamental

national policy that could sing itself into the country's ears, challenged the author on the score of "originality." Madison was incensed for he knew that it was absurd to cavil thus. "The object," he protested, "was to assert not to discover truths, and to make them the basis of the Revolutionary Act. The merit of the Draught could only consist in a lucid communication of human Rights, a condensed enumeration of the reasons for such an exercise of them, and in a style and tone appropriate to the great occasion, and to the spirit of the American people." But if the content of the *Declaration* is not enough to establish Jefferson in his pre-eminence on the left, there is the *Notes on the State of Virginia* (1784), the first American book to become an accidental "expatriate," published in England and France in pirated versions before it reached print in the country of its origin. This series of informal essays ranges far and wide over disputed questions in philosophy, science, politics, and morals, and is the natural discourse of a born humanistic rationalist. Proud of his friend's prowess as a thinker, Madison once observed that Jefferson was "greatly eminent for the comprehensiveness and fertility of his genius, for the vast extent and rich variety of his acquirements; and particularly distinguished by the philosophic impress left on every subject which he touched." And then as if the *Notes* had come to mind, Madison hastened to add: "Nor was he less distinguished from an early and uniform devotion to the cause of liberty, and systematic preference of a form of Government squared in the strictest degree to the equal rights of man."

Indeed, although Madison had been a friend, follower, and co-worker of Jefferson's for many years when he wrote this tribute, it is notable that in all the advancing and receding waves of historical interpretation the residual significance of Jefferson's contribution to the American tradition has grown rather than diminished. Of American presidents, this statesman of the "Enlightenment" most closely approximates the Platonic philosopher-king. No other incumbent of the presidency, and no other of the liberal philosophic spirits of his age—many-sided men like Franklin, Benjamin Rush, and Thomas Cooper—could match Jefferson's happy union of learning, independence, and competent judgment in diverse fields such as social morality, government, education, natural science, agriculture, and the arts. What Washington began to do for the American personality by example and by the sheer weight of personal decency and leadership, Jefferson moulded into an intellectualized ideal of social order. The entire development of American affairs, as the definition of our national ideology, is consequently more indebted to Jefferson than it is to any other single man.

This is not to say that Jefferson was an illustration of that *cliché*, the crusader of eighteenth-century enlightenment who preached the gross "goodness" of man and the inevitable rational progress of society. Jefferson, who never wearied of reading history—he knew excellently the classical and the best of modern historians—had come to recognize the hazards of evil in human as in social affairs. He had so acute an awareness of the consequences of entrenching evil men in public positions that he concluded no society would be safe without an informed, alert citizenry participating actively in government. Devoted to human possibilities of growth, he out-distanced the faith of the other philosopher-statesmen— although Madison and Adams both had their areas of hope and solid, if less generous, funds of good-will. Another way of viewing the difference between Jefferson and all others is to recognize his philosophy of education for what it was—a conscious "ideological" program to create right-thinking, tolerant citizens whose management of local affairs would be but a neighborly orientation

for their wise judgment and activity in the affairs of the Union. It was a program fitted to practical needs and political responsibilities, and yet attuned to the highest cultivation of the arts, the sciences, and *belles lettres*.

If it was Jefferson who recommended the fullest participation in political control, just as he sustained the greatest confidence in the educability of the American people, it was Hamilton who had most concern for government as a *force*, who saw little to worry about in its suppressive intrusions upon local or personal "rights." It must be understood that the whole of the political "line" ranging from Jefferson to Madison to Adams and to Hamilton operated within *realistic* limits. Each statesman feared different contingencies, each phrased his hopes in typical or unique terms, each seized upon symbols of approbation or aversion sympathetic to his own personality and to the range of his ideational life. One might almost conclude: *therefore*, the republic was made possible —through the very variety and divergence of the founders' visions, ideas, and wishes.

Hamilton, for instance, saw very clearly the vast economic potentialities of America if the government would ally itself on the side of those who possessed large fortunes and legislate in the direction of the expansion of financial and commercial activities. In the "people" Hamilton bought virtually no stock. He thought they might listen to a debate and repeat with fair accuracy another man's line of argument, but they were by and large susceptible to the flatteries and the manipulations of natural politicians. Indeed, when left to his own selfish and irrational devices, the "great beast" might actually retard the productive energy of the nation, rather than build it up.

It was some time after Hamilton's memorable project of the *Federalist* (1787–88)—that lucid exposition of constitutional republican government, not always consistent in its internal logic, but always impressive in its powerful defense of the need for national unity—that he began to voice his gloomiest thoughts about the survival of the republican experiment in self-government. "It is yet to be determined by experience whether it be consistent with that stability and order in government which are essential to public strength and private security and happiness" he wrote in 1792, having already tasted the strength of Jefferson's principled opposition. He seemed eager to give voice to his fear that republicanism might not "justify itself by its fruits." His progress tory-wise away from what he had called "the fair fabric of republicanism . . modelled and decorated by the hand of federalism" was complete. In this short-sightedness Hamilton showed himself less of a philosopher and less of a statesman than one would desire. Were it not for the towering importance of certain of his administrative and governmental principles, Hamilton's temperament and the transparency of his self-interest would hardly qualify him as a philosopher-statesman. But there is great penetration in his theory that the extension of national prerogative is indispensable for achieving internal uniformity and efficiency in a genuinely "central" government. And there is undeniable truth in his perception that this is the first essential of defense against foreign powers. Another realistic principle of capitalist development appreciated by Hamilton early in the nation's life was that it was a direct obligation of the government to foster the development of the productive resources and activities of the nation—by whatever combination of interests might prove effective. The first of these principles figures in Hamilton's masterful *First Report on the Public Credit* (1790), when he unhesitatingly decides that "If the voice of humanity pleads more loudly in favor of some [classes of creditors] than of others, the voice of policy, no less than of justice, pleads in favor of all." The second principle is the

key argument of Hamilton's classical treatise on protectionism, the *Report on Manufactures* (1791).

By a peculiar concentration of interest, Hamilton attained a definiteness in the body of his belief which sounds surprisingly modern in tone. Read today, his justification of strong efficient government comes close to a native American defense of totalitarian political management. But clever though his analysis was, it did not succeed in reconciling the two inseparable demands of prospering republicanism: national power, exercised to the full by an unimpeded, energetic central administration, and mature responsibility vested in the people of a free society.

The conservatism and legalism of John Adams and Madison explain almost as much about the success of the American republic as they do about the absence of these names from most of the emotional appraisals of the early American tradition. Adams was a testy man, given to incalculable fits of temper that could shake his soul and harden his behavior to the utmost expression of stubbornness. Madison was naturally prudent, neither commanding in person nor captivating in his imaginative vistas. He did not permit himself the occasional exaggerations of the genius which he himself detected in Jefferson, while Adams, unlike Hamilton, *never* lost sight of his high duty to guard the national interest and subordinate his own political welfare to the paramount needs of the American republic. Adams was therefore saved from the extravagancies of Hamiltonian ambition. Since the "mean," in politics, is not golden, not, at any rate, in the "memory of the race," both Adams, the unorthodox federalist, and Madison, the conservative republican, paid the political price of hewing to the Aristotelian middle. Without Adams, the preservation of the dignified ideal of lawful, responsible government and a great example of Bolingbroke's ideal

"Patriot King" who comes to guard like an "angel" the destiny and the long-range interests of his country might not have been realized. Without Madison, the amelioration of factional (including "class") strife would not so early have been made a governmental objective, nor would the allocation of sovereign power in the federal and in state contexts have found so subtle an expositor.

The surety of republican foundations, one might say, depended upon the Jeffersonian "left," with its key insights that the preservation of individual freedom and the moral development of cooperative society were the ultimate objectives of free society. It depended upon the Hamiltonian "right" with its knowledge that governments need effective organization and the power which comes from having the substantial productive and financial forces in the nation solidly united behind the administration. The stability of the Republic and its true course depended much upon the labors of Madison, with his realistic conviction that the main purpose of a government is the protection of the many and diverse economic interests into which every country is divided—and with his belief that this protection can be accomplished through a limited, federal republic capable of preventing the monopolistic dictation of one faction or combine over the people of the nation. The experienced conclusion of the elder Adams, that republicanism would not dispel disparities of wealth and station and the aristocracies which there entail, was a grave note of warning. When Adams added that the chief function of wise governors would be to protect the separate but "balanced" powers delegated to them, by compact with the people, in order to prevent tyranny, chaos, or the anarchy of the impassioned mob, he further safeguarded the Republic from what the ancients had been pleased to characterize as the "inevitable" degeneration of the good society.

The main task of republican government, in the long view of John Adams, appeared to be the prevention of excessive power in the hands of any one group. Believing that "vice and folly are so interwoven in all human affairs that they could not, possibly, be wholly separated from them without tearing and rending the whole system of human nature and state," Adams had to put his trust in the rare statesmanlike leaders who would possess wisdom to formulate just laws, and discipline to abide by them. Adams thought the network of checks and balances would defeat the ambitious and power-hungry few who might design to capture government for their private ends, and would ensure fair representation of the interests of every region in the nation, thereby allowing the propertied and "responsible" citizens who were the mainstay of each region a voice in governmental affairs. By these devices, he thought he could make the most of fallible human nature. A republic, devoted to the interests of the people and operating through their own representatives, should be the outcome of these precautionary mechanisms. Adams accordingly thought his own republicanism as firm as that of anyone, including the leader of the Republican party, his good friend and occasional enemy, Thomas Jefferson, who, in Adams' opinion, differed from himself only in that he was for "liberty and straight hair. I thought curled hair was as republican as straight."

Madison's starting point was less psychological and more sociological. It began with the observed differences in group interests, differences which he took to calling "factions." Factions for Madison were special-interest groups arising out of the fundamental conflict present in every society between those who are rich and maintain their riches, and those who are poor and struggle to relieve their condition. "All civilized societies are divided into different interests and factions" he wrote in the interesting year of 1787, "as they happen to be creditors or debtors—rich or poor—husbandmen, merchants or manufacturers—members of different religious sects—followers of different political leaders—inhabitants of different districts—owners of different kinds of property, etc." The advantage of modern republicanism over other governments Madison expected to find in its ability to impede the full force of factional combinations, preventing them from controlling the state, and from usurping the rights of one or more minorities. Madison as a Virginian feared the added danger that the majority (the North) might suppress the rights of the minority (the South), contending in a letter to Jefferson that "Where the real power in a government lies, there is the danger of oppression. In our Governments the real power lies in the majority of the Community, and the invasion of private rights is chiefly to be apprehended, not from acts of Government contrary to the sense of its constituents, but from acts in which the Government is the mere instrument of the major number of the constituents." Madison thus called to the attention of all men the inflexible requirement that democracies protect the civil rights of minorities from the real or reported "will" of the majority.

Madison and Adams made more of property rights than Jefferson did, but neither of them deserted the democratic theories of natural rights, popular sovereignty, limited government, anti-monarchism and anti-aristocracy. Nor did the two conservatives ever approach Hamilton's justification of plutocracy. Both Adams and Madison inclined to the ideal of a republic which was economically agrarian at base, but supplemented by mercantile and manufacturing interests. Madison perhaps a little more than Adams realized the vital role of credit and of government-financed expansion of the country's natural resources and communications—the role which John Adams' son, John Quincy Adams, was to develop fully

in his program of "Internal Improvement." Theoretically, therefore, it was Hamilton, of doubtful birth, who thought most exclusively of the moneyed interests of the country, partly because he saw in them the source of national strength, while Jefferson, graceful and learned "landed esquire," cared most deeply about the widespread independent well-being of the "people," farmers and laborers included. Adams and Madison, each aristocratic in taste in the typical styles of Massachusetts and Virginia, but far from dazzling in the family fortunes to which they were born, were actively promoting a scheme of society favorable to widespread middle-class prosperity and power.

IV

The ethical theories of these men were influential factors upon the political and economic views they maintained. Save for the four philosopher-statesmen of the Republic, the American character might never have been given more than haphazard or perfunctory significance. Jefferson, Madison, and John Adams all understood the importance of character for those who would be leaders in a republic, and Hamilton sometimes did and sometimes paid only lip-service to the ideal. Jefferson and Madison and Adams advocated that "the purest and noblest characters" (Madison's phrase) should serve as the people's representatives, since they alone would do so from the "proper motives." Because these men dedicated themselves to the cause of their country before they consulted their immediate personal needs, the inceptive principles of the American republic betoken seekers of truth and wisdom, and good citizens in the Roman sense, rather than mere men of office.

Jefferson, perceiving that government was necessary for the release of man's fullest potentialities, liked to speak of it as of secondary or instrumental value—a habit which was later perversely construed to mean that government was "evil." The range of realistic political choice for Jefferson lay entirely between repressive government and republicanism, and he identified the essence of republicanism as "action by the citizens in person in affairs within their reach and competence, and in all others by representatives, chosen immediately, and removable by themselves. . . ." For this reason, a republic was the "only form of government that is not eternally at open or secret war with the rights of mankind." To achieve republican freedom, citizens must pay a price, the wakefulness of "eternal vigilance," and, therefore, a citizenry trained in the principles of government, an *educated* citizenry, is the indispensable support of freedom.

Thus, subtly and indirectly, a moral climate had been postulated for the America in which republicanism was to be tried. Benevolence and moral sense, self-created will rather than coercive force, are the dynamic daily agents in free society as well as the purely *theoretical* factors of its ethics. "Natural" moralism is opposed to the reputed "natural" rule of force, which Jefferson saw as the breeder of authoritarian society, whether of "kings, hereditary nobles, and priests" or, in the language of our own day, of leaders, demagogues, and commissars. Jefferson's agrarianism, so often made the catch-word for his variety of democracy, is in reality a by-product of an almost sentimental preference for the simplicity of classical republicanism joined to the supposed purity of "primitive" Christianity. Yet when Jefferson realized that the evolution of his nation demanded the self-sufficiency and expansion of her manufacture and trade—when he perceived that free society would be jeopardized if it were unable to defend itself on the high seas—he protested that "he . . . who is now against domestic manufacture, must be for reducing us either to dependence . . .

or to be clothed in skins, and to live like wild beasts in dens and caverns. I am not one of these; experience has taught me that manufactures are now as necessary to our independence as to our comfort. . . ." Despite this, Jefferson's instinctive trust reposed in the fair and free interchange of nation with nation, as in citizen with citizen—which is to say that he was a man of peace, conceiving productive society basically as a peaceful society, an earnest judgment in which he was fully joined by James Madison.

Economically and politically, to Hamilton's expert eye the softer fringe of social morality was not a subject for enthusiasm nor even for *belief*. "The seeds of war are sown thickly in the human breast," Hamilton had written, and the rivalry that precipitated wars, in his view, stemmed partly from "the temper of societies," and partly from the human disposition to "prefer partial to general interest." Coming to terms with self-interested reality was accordingly Hamilton's basic preoccupation, whether that "reality" meant strong armies and navies for defense against foreign powers, or a strong system of national credit. In an ultimate separation of himself from his idealistic associates, whom he termed "political empirics," Hamilton in an important unfinished paper called "Defence of the Funding System" (1795), identified the "true" politician as one who "takes human nature (and human society its aggregate) as he finds it, a compound of good and ill qualities, of good and ill tendencies, endued with powers and actuated by passions and propensities which blend enjoyment with suffering and make the causes of welfare the causes of misfortune." Afraid to warp this fundamental human complex by urging a happiness not suited to it, the true politician supposedly aims at the social measures designed to "make men happy according to their natural bent, which multiply the sources of individual enjoyment and increase national resources and strength." The great objective of the statesman should thus be to find the cement for compounding diverse elements of a state into a "rock" of national strength.

Governments would not need to be afraid to take power, Hamilton believed, could they strip themselves of false attitudes of modesty. In the logic of economic stability and national expansion, of credit and appropriations and "sound policy" versus the misguided pleadings of "common humanity," Hamilton saw an unanswerable imperative: to wit, that the "sacred" right of property must be defended by the laws and by the constitutions of the land and that even the non-propertied groups in the community should protect property rights lest the general principles of public order" be subverted.

John Adams, the self-styled "John Yankee" who could not bear to kowtow to "John Bull"—nor for that matter to any foreign power—seems more at home in Jefferson's and Madison's company than he is with Hamilton, the "boss" of his own party. Without Adams, the democratic precedent of the New England meeting-hall, the training green, and the system of self-support for local schools, churches, and cultural institutions might have spoken only with muffled voice in the American tradition. The political "virtues" of Massachusetts even Jefferson commended, pointing to that state as the best exponent of the theme that knowledge is power. In Adams' championship of New England, there is a nucleus of national pride useful and perhaps necessary to a rising nation. To this Adams personally added the dignified appeal that however much republican government consisted of equal laws justly administered, it further required consistent benevolence and encouragement for the arts and sciences. Almost a humanist, but never quite freed of a Puritan sense of guilt and sin, Adams privately reveled in

the classics just as Jefferson did. The late correspondence which flourished between Adams and Jefferson as the two aged statesmen with great *éclat* enacted the roles of sages in retirement is a phenomenon of tireless learning and peppery jest, joined in a correspondence the like of which is not known elsewhere in the annals of American statesmen.

V

Such were the philosopher-kings of the American "Enlightenment." However often they may have erred—in description, in prognosis, in emphasis, and sometimes in behavior as statesmen—they seem to have possessed that rare wisdom about human and political affairs which never quite exhausts its power to suggest. On occasions, it restores its own original vitality and suffices to sanction an important change in national or international policy. We know that in the curious reversals of history, the truths of an age are likely to suffer sea-change. As Lincoln pointed out, the maxim "all men are created equal," once thought a self-evident truth, is termed a "self-evident lie," once we have "grown fat, and lost all dread of being slaves ourselves." So it may be with the far-ranging insights and veridical principles of the philosopher-statesmen of the Republic. Since the advent of the Jacksonian age—a "calamitous" presidency in Madison's prediction—the objectives of tempered democracy have been often ignored or ingeniously misinterpreted. As the letters and state papers of the Republican era again come under review, it is apparent that democratic ideology can still benefit by its own articulate original. The foundation of our national literature is present here, as well in the practical literature of ideas as in the imitative experiments of the deliberately "literary" work of the day.

Albert Pinkham Ryder "The Temple of the Mind"   Albright-Knox Art Gallery, Buffalo, New York

PART 4

THE TRANSCENDENTALISTS

Introduction

Transcendentalism, the radical extension of Romanticism, was one of the most exciting intellectual movements of the nineteenth century. Originating with the idealism of the German philosopher Immanuel Kant and English writers such as Samuel Taylor Coleridge and Thomas Carlyle, Transcendentalism flourished in the United States. Among its American spokesmen were Ralph Waldo Emerson, Henry David Thoreau, Bronson Alcott, and Theodore Parker. Opposed to the characteristics of an increasingly materialistic society, they emphasized intuitive contemplation, individuality, diversity, and nature.

The historical evolution of Transcendentalism from its Puritan origins to the mid-nineteenth century is analyzed by Perry Miller. He notes the tremendous influence of Europe on American Transcendentalists but places far more significance on the Puritan past. Miller maintains that the Puritan nature hungered for an inward communication and a divine symbolism of nature. The tradition of emotionalism temporarily gave way to the prevailing rationalism of the nineteenth century.

The ideas of Theodore Parker (1810–1860) are the subject of historian Henry Steele Commager.

Parker was a liberal Unitarian minister whose ideas were illustrative of the glaring contradictions in Transcendentalist thought. He was a dualist who espoused transcendental principles known through intuition, while he sought to prove intuitive principles through historical evidence. His was a strong voice and he spoke not only to his Boston congregation but to all New England.

Unlike Commager who is sympathetic with the Transcendentalists, Lawrence C. Porter is critical. He argues that the failure of Transcendentalism was inherent in its philosophy. It encouraged self-confidence, but it formulated no system, created little cooperation, and was above the heads of most people. These weaknesses prevented Transcendentalism from becoming a significant part of the American intellectual tradition.

Frederic I. Carpenter surveys the genteel tradition in the United States. He insists that the Transcendentalists were not a part of that impressive tradition. They were instead offsprings of the radical wing of Puritanism which worshipped an "unknown God" and refused to accept American morality. The Transcendentalists were rejected by the conservative society of the nineteenth century.

JONATHAN EDWARDS TO EMERSON

Perry Miller*

Ralph Waldo Emerson believed that every man has an inward and immediate access to that Being for whom he found the word "God" inadequate and whom he preferred to designate as the "Over-Soul." He believed that this Over-Soul, this dread universal essence, which is beauty, love, wisdom, and power all in one, is present in nature and throughout nature. Consequently Emerson, and the young Transcendentalists of New England with him, could look with complacence upon certain prospects which our less transcendental generation beholds with misgiving:

> If the red slayer think he slays,
> Or if the slain think he is slain,
> They know not well the subtle ways
> I keep, and pass, and turn again.

Life was exciting in Massachusetts of the 1830's and '40's: abolitionists were mobbed, and for a time Mr. Emerson was a dangerous radical; Dr. Webster committed an ingenious murder; but by and large, young men were not called upon to confront possible slaughter unless they elected to travel the Oregon Trail, and the only scholar who did that was definitely not a Transcendentalist. Thus it seems today that Emerson ran no great risk in asserting that should he ever be bayoneted he would fall by his own hand disguised in another uniform, that because all men participate in the Over-Soul those who shoot and those who are shot prove to be identical, that in the realm of the transcendental there is nothing to choose between eating and being eaten.

It is hardly surprising that the present generation, those who may be called upon to serve not merely as doubters and the doubt but also as slayers and slain, greet the serene pronouncements of Brahma with cries of dissent. Professors somewhat nervously explain to unsympathetic under-

*PERRY MILLER (1905–1963) was Professor of American Literature at Harvard University. His publications include Orthodoxy in Massachusetts (1933), The New England Mind (1939), and Errand Into the Wilderness (1956). Reprinted by permission of the New England Quarterly, Vol. 13, No. 4 (December, 1940), 589–617.

graduates that of course these theories are not the real Emerson, much less the real Thoreau. They were importations, not native American growths. They came from Germany, through Coleridge, they were extracted from imperfect translations of the Hindoo Scriptures, misunderstood and extravagantly embraced by Yankees who ought to have known better—and who fortunately in some moments did know better, for whenever Emerson and Parker and Thoreau looked upon the mill towns or the conflict of classes they could perceive a few realities through the haze of their Transcendentalism. They were but Transcendental north-northwest; when the wind was southerly they knew the difference between Beacon Hill and South Boston. I suppose that many who now read Emerson, and surely all who endeavor to read Bronson Alcott, are put off by the "philosophy." The doctrines of the Over-Soul, Correspondence, and Compensation seem nowadays to add up to shallow optimism and insufferable smugness. Contemporary criticism reflects this distaste, and would lead us to prize these men, if at all, for their incidental remarks, their shrewd observations upon society, art, manners, or the weather, while we put aside their premises and their conclusions, the ideas to which they devoted their principal energies, as notions too utterly fantastic to be any longer taken seriously.

Fortunately, no one is compelled to take them seriously. We are not required to persuade ourselves the next time we venture into the woods that we may become, as Emerson said we might, transparent eyeballs, and that thereupon all disagreeable appearances—"swine, spiders, snakes, pests, madhouses, prisons, enemies"—shall vanish and be no more seen.[1] These afflictions have not proved temporary or illusory to many, or the

compensations always obvious. But whether such ideas are or are not intelligible to us, there remains the question of whence they came. Where did Emerson, Alcott, Thoreau, and Margaret Fuller find this pantheism which they preached in varying degrees, which the Harvard faculty and most Boston businessmen found both disconcerting and contemptible? Was New England's Transcendentalism wholly Germanic or Hindoo in origin? Is there any sense, even though a loose one, in which we can say that this particular blossom in the flowering of New England had its roots in the soil? Was it foolishly transplanted from some desert where it had better been left to blush unseen? Emerson becomes most vivid to us when he is inscribing his pungent remarks upon the depression of 1837, and Thoreau in his grim comments upon the American *Blitzkrieg* against Mexico. But our age has a tendency, when dealing with figures of the past, to amputate whatever we find irrelevant from what the past itself considered the body of its teaching. Certain fragments may be kept alive in the critical test tubes of the Great Tradition, while the rest is shoveled off to potter's field. The question of how much in the Transcendental philosophy emerged out of the American background, of how much of it was not appropriated from foreign sources, is a question that concerns the entire American tradition, with which and in which we still must work. Although the metaphysic of the Over-Soul, of Self-Reliance, and of Compensation is not one to which we can easily subscribe, yet if the particular formulations achieved by Emerson and Thoreau, Parker and Ripley, were restatements of a native disposition rather than amateur versions of *The Critique of Pure Reason*, then we who must also reformulate our traditions may find their philosophy meaningful, if not for what it held, at least for whence they got it.

Among the tenets of Transcendentalism is one which today excites the minimum of our sym-

---

[1] *Emerson,* Works, *Centenary Edition (Boston, 1904), I, 10 and 76.*

pathy, which declared truth to be forever and everywhere one and the same, and all ideas to be one idea, all religions the same religion, all poets singers of the same music of the same spheres, chanting eternally the recurrent theme. We have become certain, on the contrary, that ideas are born in time and place, that they spring from specific environments, that they express the force of societies and classes, that they are generated by power relations. We are impatient with an undiscriminating eclecticism which merges the *Bhagvad-gita*, Robert Herrick, Saadi, Swedenborg, Plotinus, and Confucius into one monotonous iteration. Emerson found a positive pleasure—which he called "the most modern joy"—in extracting all *time* from the verses of Chaucer, Marvell, and Dryden, and so concluded that one nature wrote all the good books and one nature could read them. The bad books, one infers, were written by fragmentary individuals temporarily out of touch with the Over-Soul, and are bad because they do partake of their age and nation. "There is such equality and identity both of judgment and point of view in the narrative that it is plainly the work of one all-seeing, all-hearing gentleman."[2] We have labored to restore the historical time to Chaucer and Dryden; we do not find it at all plain that they were mouthpieces of one all-seeing agency, and we are sure that if there is any such universal agent he certainly is not a gentleman. We are exasperated with Emerson's tedious habit of seeing everything *sub specie aeternitatis*. When we find him writing in 1872, just before his mind and memory began that retreat into the Over-Soul which makes his last years so pathetic, that while in our day we have witnessed great revolutions in religion we do not therefore lose faith "in the eternal pillars which we so differently name, but cannot choose but see

their identity in all healthy souls," we are ready to agree heartily with Walt Whitman, who growled that Emerson showed no signs of adapting himself to new times, but had "about the same attitude as twenty-five or thirty years ago," and that he himself was "utterly tired of these scholarly things."[3] We may become even more tired of scholarly things when we find that from the very beginning Emerson conceived the movement which we call Transcendentalism as one more expression of the benign gentleman who previously had spoken in the persons of Socrates and Zoroaster, Mohammed and Buddha, Shakespeare and St. Paul. He does not assist our quest for native origins, indeed for any origins which we are prepared to credit, when he says in 1842, in the Boston Masonic Temple, that Transcendentalism is a "Saturnalia of Faith," an age-old way of thinking which, falling upon Roman times, made Stoic philosophers; falling on despotic times, made Catos and Brutuses; on Popish times, made Protestants; "on prelatical times, made Puritans and Quakers; and falling on Unitarian and commercial times, makes the peculiar shades of Idealism which we know."[4] Were we to take him at his word, and agree that he himself was a Stoic revisiting the glimpses of the moon, and that Henry Thoreau was Cato *redivivus*, we might then decide that both of them could fetch the shades of their idealism from ancient Rome or, if they wished, from Timbuctoo, and that they would bear at best only an incidental relation to the American scene. We might conclude with the luckless San Francisco journalist, assigned the task of reporting an Emerson lecture, who wrote, "All left the church feeling that an elegant tribute had been paid to the Creative genius of the First

---

2 Works, *III, 232.*

3 The Letters of Ralph Waldo Emerson, *edited by Ralph L. Rusk (New York, 1939), VI, 192–193.*
4 Works, *I, 339.*

Cause," but we should not perceive that any compliments had been paid to the intellectual history of New England.

But to take Emerson literally is often hazardous. We may allow him his Stoics, his Catos and Brutuses, for rhetorical embellishment. He is coming closer home, however, when he comes to Puritans, Quakers, and Unitarian and commercial times. Whether he intended it or not, this particular sequence constitutes in little an intellectual and social history of New England: first Puritans and Quakers, then Unitarians and commercial times, and now Transcendentalists! Emerson contended that when poets spoke out of the transcendental Reason, which knows the eternal correspondence of things, rather than out of the short-sighted Understanding—which dwells slavishly in the present, the expedient, and the customary, and thinks in terms of history, economics, and institutions—they builded better than they knew. When they were ravished by the imagination, which makes every dull fact an emblem of the spirit, and were not held earthbound by the fancy, which knows only the surfaces of things, they brought their creations from no vain or shallow thought. Yet he did not intend ever to dispense with the understanding and the fancy, to forget the customary and the institutional—as witness his constant concern with "manners." He would not raise the siege of his hen-coop to march away to a pretended siege of Babylon; though he was not conspicuously successful with a shovel in his garden, he was never, like Elizabeth Peabody, so entirely subjective as to walk straight into a tree because "I saw it, but I did not realize it." Could it be, therefore, that while his reason was dreaming among the Upanishads, and his imagination reveling with Swedenborg, his understanding perceived that on the plain of material causation the Transcendentalism of New England had some connection with New England experience, and

that his fancy, which remained at home with the customary and with history, guided this choice of words? Did these lower faculties contrive, by that cunning which distinguishes them from reason and imagination, in the very moment when Transcendentalism was being proclaimed a Saturnalia of faith, that there should appear a cryptic suggestion that it betokened less an oriental ecstasy and more a natural reaction of some descendants of Puritans and Quakers to Unitarian and commercial times?

I have called Emerson mystical and pantheistical. These are difficult adjectives; we might conveniently begin with Webster's Dictionary, which declares mysticism to be the doctrine that the ultimate nature of reality or of the divine essence may be known by an immediate insight. The connotations of pantheism are infinite, but in general a pantheist holds that the universe itself is God, or that God is the combined forces and laws manifested in the existing universe, that God is, in short, both the slayer and the slain. Emerson and the others might qualify their doctrine, but when Professor Andrews Norton read that in the woods "I become a transparent eyeball; I am nothing, I see all; the currents of the Universal Being circulate through me; I am part or particle of God," in his forthright fashion he could not help perceiving that this was both mysticism and pantheism, and so attacking it as "the latest form of infidelity."

Could we go back to the Puritans whom Emerson adduced as his predecessors, and ask the Emersons and Ripleys, not to mention the Winthrops, Cottons, and Mathers, of the seventeenth century whether the eyeball passage was infidelity, there would be no doubt about the answer. They too might call it the "latest" form of infidelity, for in the first years of New England Winthrop and Cotton had very bitter experience with a similar doctrine. Our wonder is that they did not have more. To our minds, no longer at home in the fine distinctions of theology, it might seem that from the Calvinist doctrine of regeneration, from the theory that a regenerate soul receives an influx of divine spirit, and is joined to God by a direct infusion of His grace, we might deduce the possibility of receiving all instruction immediately from the in-dwelling spirit, through an inward communication which is essentially mystical. Such was exactly the deduction of Mistress Anne Hutchinson, for which she was expelled into Rhode Island. It was exactly the conclusion of the Quakers, who added that every man was naturally susceptible to this inward communication, that he did not need a special and supernatural dispensation. Quakers also were cast into Rhode Island or, if they refused to stay there, hanged on Boston Common. Emerson, descendant of Puritans, found the descendants of Quakers "a sublime class of speculators," and wrote in 1835 that they had been the most explicit teachers "of the highest article to which human faith soars [,] the strict union of the willing soul to God & so the soul's access at all times to a verdict upon every question which the opinion of all mankind cannot shake & which the opinion of all mankind cannot confirm."[5] But his ancestors had held that while the soul does indeed have an access to God, it receives from the spirit no verdict upon any question, only a dutiful disposition to accept the verdict confirmed by Scripture, by authority, and by logic. As Roger Clap remarked, both Anne Hutchinson and the Quakers "would talk of the Spirit, and of revelations by the Spirit without the Word, . . . of the Light within them, rejecting the holy Scripture";[6] and the Puritan minister declared that the errors of the Antinomians, "like strong

wine, make men's judgments reel and stagger, who are drunken therwith."[7] The more one studies the history of Puritan New England, the more astonished he becomes at the amount of reeling and staggering there was in it.

These seventeenth-century "infidels" were more interested in enlarging the soul's access to God from within than in exploring the possibilities of an access from without, from nature. But if we, in our interrogation of the shades of Puritans, were to ask them whether there exists a spirit that rolls through all things and propels all things, whose dwelling is the light of setting suns, and the round ocean, and the mind of man, a spirit from whom we should learn to be disturbed by the joy of elevated thoughts, the Puritans would feel at once that we needed looking after. They would concede that the visible universe is the handiwork of God, that He governs it and is present in the flight of every sparrow, the fall of every stone, the rising and setting of suns, in the tempests of the round ocean. "Who set those candles, those torches of heaven, on the table? Who hung out those lanterns in heaven to enlighten a dark world?" asked the preacher, informing his flock that although we do not see God in nature, yet in it His finger is constantly evident.[8] The textbook of theology used at Harvard told New England students that every creature would return into nothing if God did not uphold it— "the very cessation of Divine conservation, would without any other operation presently reduce every Creature into nothing."[9] In regard of His essence, said Thomas Hooker, God is in all places alike, He is in all creatures and beyond them,

[5] Letters, I, 433.

[6] *Alexander Young*, Chronicles of the First Planters (Boston, 1846), 360.

[7] *Thomas Shepard*, Works, *edited by John A. Albro* (Boston, 1853), III, 94.

[8] *Thomas Shepard*, Works, I, 10.

[9] *William Ames*, The Marrow of Sacred Divinity (London, 1643), 42.

"hee is excluded *out* of no place, included *in* no place."[10] But it did not follow that the universe, though created by God and sustained by His continuous presence, was God Himself. We were not to go to nature and, by surrendering to the stream of natural forces, derive from it our elevated thoughts. We were not to become nothing and let the currents of Universal Being circulate through us. Whatever difficulties were involved in explaining that the universe is the work of God but that we do not meet God face to face in the universe, Puritan theologians knew that the distinction must be maintained, lest excitable Yankees reel and stagger with another error which they would pretend was an elevated thought. The difficulties of explanation were so great that the preachers often avoided the issue, declaring "this is but a curious question: therefore I will leave it," or remarking that the Lord fills both heaven and earth, yet He is not in the world as the soul is in the body, "but in an incomprehensible manner, which we cannot expresse to you."[11] Thomas Shepard in Cambridge tried to be more explicit: the Godhead, he said, is common to everything and every man, even to the most wicked man, "nay, to the vilest creature in the world." The same power that made a blade of grass made also the angels, but grass and angels are not the same substance, and so the spirit of God which is in the setting sun and the round ocean is not the same manifestation which He puts forth as a special and "super"-natural grace in the regenerate soul. "There comes another spirit upon us, which common men have not."[12] This other spirit teaches us, not elevated thoughts, but how to submit our corrupt thoughts to the rule of Scripture, to the law and the Gospel as expounded at Harvard College and by Harvard graduates.

The reason for Puritan opposition to these ideas is not far to seek. The Renaissance mind—which was still a Medieval mind—remembered that for fifteen hundred years Christian thinkers had striven to conceive of the relation of God to the world in such a fashion that the transcendence of God should not be called in question, that while God was presented as the creator and governor of the world, He would always be something other than the world itself. Both mysticism and pantheism, in whatever form, identified Him with nature, made Him over in the image of man, interpreted Him in the terms either of human intuitions or of human perceptions, made Him one with the forces of psychology or of matter. The Renaissance produced a number of eccentrics who broached these dangerous ideas—Giordano Bruno, for instance, who was burned at the stake by a sentence which Catholics and Calvinists alike found just. The Puritans carried to New England the historic convictions of Christian orthodoxy, and in America found an added incentive for maintaining them intact. Puritanism was not merely a religious creed and a theology, it was also a program for society. We go to New England, said John Winthrop, to establish a due form of government, both civil and ecclesiastical, under the rule of law and Scripture.[13] It was to be a medieval society of status, with every man in his place and a place for every man; it was to be no utopia of rugged individualists and transcendental free-thinkers. But if Anne Hutchinson was correct, and if men could hear the voice of God within themselves, or if they could go into the woods

---

[10] *Thomas Hooker,* Heavens Treasury Opened (*London, 1645*), *20–21.*

[11] *John Preston,* Life Eternall (*London, 1631*), *Part II, 45 and 148.*

[12] *Shepard,* Works, *I, 168; II, 212–213.*

[13] Winthrop Papers, *Massachusetts Historical Society, II (1931), 293.*

and feel the currents of Universal Being circulate through them—in either event they would pay little heed to governors and ministers. The New England tradition commenced with a clear understanding that both mysticism and pantheism were heretical, and also with a frank admission that such ideas were dangerous to society, that men who imbibed noxious errors from an inner voice or from the presence of God in the natural landscape would reel and stagger through the streets of Boston and disturb the civil peace.

Yet from the works of the most orthodox of Calvinists we can perceive that the Puritans had good cause to be apprehensive lest mystical or pantheistical conclusions arise out of their premises. Anne Hutchinson and the Quakers commenced as Calvinists; from the idea of regeneration they drew, with what seemed to them impeccable logic, the idea that God imparted His teaching directly to the individual spirit. With equal ease others could deduce from the doctrines of divine creation and providence the idea that God was immanent in nature. The point might be put thus: there was in Puritanism a piety, a religious passion, the sense of an inward communication and of the divine symbolism of nature. One side of the Puritan nature hungered for these excitements; certain of its appetites desired these satisfactions and therefore found delight and ecstasy in the doctrines of regeneration and providence. But in Puritanism there was also another side, an ideal of social conformity, of law and order, of regulation and control. At the core of the theology there was an indestructible element which was mystical, and a feeling for the universe which was almost pantheistic; but there was also a social code demanding obedience to external law, a code to which good people voluntarily conformed and to which bad people should be made to conform. It aimed at propriety and decency, the virtues of middle-class respectability,

self-control, thrift, and dignity, at a discipline of the emotions. It demanded, as Winthrop informed the citizens of Massachusetts Bay in 1645, that men forbear to exercise the liberty they had by nature, the freedom to do anything they chose, and having entered into society thereafter, devote themselves to doing only that which the authorities defined as intrinsically "good, just and honest."[14] The New England tradition contained a dual heritage, the heritage of the troubled spirit and the heritage of worldly caution and social conservatism. It gave with one hand what it took away with the other: it taught men that God is present to their intuitions and in the beauty and terror of nature, but it disciplined them into subjecting their intuitions to the wisdom of society and their impressions of nature to the standards of decorum.

In the eighteenth century, certain sections of New England, or certain persons, grew wealthy. It can hardly be a coincidence that among those who were acquiring the rewards of industry and commerce there should be progressively developed the second part of the heritage, the tradition of reason and criticism, and that among them the tradition of emotion and ecstasy should dwindle. Even though a few of the clergy, like Jonathan Mayhew and Lemuel Briant, were moving faster than their congregations, yet in Boston and Salem, the centers of shipping and banking, ministers preached rationality rather than dogma, the Newtonian universe and the sensational psychology rather than providence and innate depravity. The back country, the Connecticut Valley, burst into flame with the Great Awakening of the 1740's; but the massive Charles Chauncy, minister at the First Church, the successor of John Cotton, declared that "the passionate dis-

---

14 *Winthrop,* Journal, *edited by J. K. Hosmer (New York, 1908), II, 239.*

covery" of divine love is not a good evidence of election. "The surest and most substantial Proof is, *Obedience to the Commandments of God*, and the *stronger* the Love, the more uniform, steady and pleasant will be this *Obedience*." Religion is of the understanding as well as of the affections, and when the emotions are stressed at the expense of reason, "it can't be but People should run into Disorders."[15] In his ponderous way, Chauncy was here indulging in Yankee understatement. During the Awakening the people of the back country ran into more than disorders; they gave the most extravagant exhibition of staggering and reeling that New England had yet beheld. Chauncy was aroused, not merely because he disapproved of displays of emotion, but because the whole society seemed in danger when persons who made a high pretense to religion displayed it in their conduct "as something wild and fanciful." On the contrary, he stoutly insisted, true religion is sober and well-behaved; as it is taught in the Bible, "it approves itself to the Understanding and Conscience, . . . and is in the best Manner calculated to promote the Good of Mankind."[16] The transformation of this segment of Puritanism from a piety to an ethic, from a religious faith to a social code, was here completed, although an explicit break with the formal theology was yet to come.

Charles Chauncy had already split the Puritan heritage. Emerson tells that Chauncy, going into his pulpit for the Thursday lecture (people at that time came all the way from Salem to hear him), was informed that a little boy had fallen into Frog Pond and drowned. Requested to improve the occasion,

the doctor was much distressed, and in his prayer he hesitated, he tried to make soft approaches, he prayed for Harvard College, he prayed for the schools, he implored the Divine Being "to-to-to bless to them all the boy that was this morning drowned in Frog Pond."[17]

But Jonathan Edwards felt an ardency of soul which he knew not how to express, a desire "to lie in the dust, and to be full of Christ alone; to love him with a holy and pure love; to trust in him; to live upon him; to serve and follow him; and to be perfectly sanctified and made pure, with a divine and heavenly purity."[18] To one who conceived the highest function of religion to be the promotion of the good of mankind, Jonathan Edwards stood guilty of fomenting disorders. Chauncy blamed Edwards for inciting the populace, and was pleased when the congregation at Northampton, refusing to measure up to the standards of sanctification demanded by Edwards, banished him into the wilderness of Stockbridge. Edwards, though he was distressed over the disorders of the Awakening, would never grant that a concern for the good of mankind should take precedence over the desire to be perfectly sanctified and made pure. In his exile at Stockbridge he wrote the great tracts which have secured his fame for all time, the magnificent studies of the freedom of the will, of the nature of true virtue, of the purpose of God in creating the universe, in which Chauncy and Harvard College were refuted; in which, though still in the language of logic and systematic theology, the other half of the Puritan heritage—the sense of God's overwhelming presence in the soul and in nature—once more found perfect expression.

Though the treatises on the will and on virtue are the more impressive performances, for our

[15] *Charles Chauncy*, Seasonable Thoughts on the State of Religion (*Boston, 1743; hereinafter* Seasonable Thoughts), *26 and 422.*

[16] Seasonable Thoughts, *406.*

[17] Works, *VIII, 127.*

[18] *Edwards*, Works (*New York, 1844*), *I, 25.*

purposes the eloquent *Dissertation Concerning the End for which God Created the World* is the more relevant, if only because when he came to this question Edwards was forced to reply specifically to the scientific rationalism toward which Chauncy and Harvard College were tending. He had, therefore, to make even more explicit than did the earlier divines the doctrines which verged upon both mysticism and pantheism, the doctrines of inward communication and of the divine in nature. It was not enough for Edwards to say, as John Cotton had done, that God created the world out of nothing to show His glory; rationalists in Boston could reply that God's glory was manifested in the orderly machine of Newtonian physics, and that a man glorified God in such a world by going about his rational business, real-estate, the triangular trade, or the manufacture of rum out of smuggled molasses. God did not create the world, said Edwards, merely to exhibit His glory; He did not create it out of nothing simply to show that He could: He who is Himself the source of all being, the substance of all life, created the world out of Himself by a diffusion of Himself into time and space. He made the world, not by sitting outside and above it, by modeling it as a child models sand, but by an extension of Himself, by taking upon Himself the forms of stones and trees and of man. He created without any ulterior object in view, neither for His glory nor for His power, but for the pure joy of self-expression, as an artist creates beauty for the love of beauty. God does not need a world or the worship of man; He is perfect in Himself. If He bothers to create, it is out of the fullness of His own nature, the overflowing virtue that is in Him. Edwards did not use my simile of the artist; his way of saying it was, "The disposition to communicate himself, or diffuse his own fulness, which we must conceive of as being originally in God as a perfection of his nature, was what moved

him to create the world,"[19] but we may still employ the simile because Edwards invested his God with the sublime egotism of a very great artist. God created by the laws of His own nature, with no thought of doing good for anybody or for mankind, with no didactic purpose, for no other reason but the joy of creativeness. "It is a regard to himself that disposes him to diffuse and communicate himself. It is such a delight in his own internal fulness and glory, that disposes him to an abundant effusion and emanation of that glory."[20]

Edwards was much too skilled in the historic problems of theology to lose sight of the distinction between God and the world or to fuse them into one substance, to blur the all-important doctrine of the divine transcendence. He forced into his system every safeguard against identifying the inward experience of the saint with the Deity Himself, or of God with nature. Nevertheless, assuming, as we have some right to assume, that what subsequent generations find to be a hidden or potential implication in a thought is a part of that thought, we may venture to feel that Edwards was particularly careful to hold in check the mystical and pantheistical tendencies of his teaching because he himself was so apt to become a mystic and a pantheist. The imagery in which a great thinker expresses his sense of things is often more revealing than his explicit contentions, and Edwards betrays the nature of his insight when he uses as the symbol of God's relation to the world the metaphor that has perennially been invoked by mystics, the metaphor of light and of the sun:

And [it] is fitly compared to an effulgence or emanation of light from a luminary, by which this glory of God is abundantly represented in Scripture. Light is the external expression, exhi-

19 *Edwards*, Works, *II, 206.*
20 *Edwards*, Works, *II, 215.*

bition and manifestation of the excellency of the luminary, of the sun for instance: it is the abundant, extensive emanation and communication of the fulness of the sun to innumerable beings that partake of it. It is by this that the sun itself is seen, and his glory beheld, and all other things are discovered; it is by a participation of this communication from the sun, that surrounding objects receive all their lustre, beauty and brightness. It is by this that all nature is quickened and receives life, comfort, and joy.[21]

Here is the respect that makes Edwards great among theologians, and here in fact he strained theology to the breaking point. Holding himself by brute will power within the forms of ancient Calvinism, he filled those forms with a new and throbbing spirit. Beneath the dogmas of the old theology he discovered a different cosmos from that of the seventeenth century, a dynamic world, filled with the presence of God, quickened with divine life, pervaded with joy and ecstasy. With this insight he turned to combat the rationalism of Boston, to argue that man cannot live by Newtonian schemes and mathematical calculations, but only by surrender to the will of God, by reflecting back the beauty of God as a jewel gives back the light of the sun. But another result of Edwards's doctrine, one which he would denounce to the nethermost circle of Hell but which is implicit in the texture, if not in the logic, of his thought, could very easily be what we have called mysticism or pantheism, or both. If God is diffused through nature, and the substance of man is the substance of God, then it may follow that man is divine, that nature is the garment of the Over-Soul, that man must be self-reliant, and that when he goes into the woods the currents of Being will indeed circulate through him. All that prevented this deduction was the orthodox theology, sup-

posedly derived from the Word of God, which taught that God and nature are not one, that man is corrupt and his self-reliance is reliance on evil. But take away the theology, remove this overlying stone of dogma from the well-springs of Puritan conviction, and both nature and man become divine.

We know that Edwards failed to revitalize Calvinism. He tried to fill the old bottles with new wine, yet none but himself could savor the vintage. His disciples, Bellamy and Hopkins, continued filling the bottles, but the wine soured. Meanwhile, in the circles where Chauncy had begun to reeducate the New England taste, there developed, by a very gradual process, a rejection of the Westminster Confession, indeed of all theology, and at last emerged the Unitarian Church. Unitarianism was entirely different wine from any that had ever been pressed from the grapes of Calvinism, and in entirely new bottles, which the merchants of Boston found much to their liking. It was a pure, white, dry claret that went well with dinners served by the Harvard Corporation, but it was mild and was guaranteed not to send them home reeling and staggering. As William Ellery Channing declared, to contemplate the horrors of New England's ancestral creed is "a consideration singularly fitted to teach us tolerant views of error, and to enjoin caution and sobriety."[22]

In Unitarianism one half of the New England tradition—that which inculcated caution and sobriety—definitely cast off all allegiance to the other. The ideal of decorum, of law and self-control, was institutionalized. Though Unitarianism was "liberal" in theology, it was generally conservative in its social thinking and in its metaphysics. Even Channing, who strove always to avoid controversy and to appear "mild and ami-

21 *Edwards*, Works, II, 254.

22 *Channing*, Works, (Boston, 1880), 5.

able," was still more of an enthusiast than those he supplied with ideas, as was proved when almost alone among Unitarian divines he spoke out against slavery. He frequently found himself thwarted by the suavity of Unitarian breeding. In his effort to establish a literary society in Boston, he repaired, as Emerson tells the story, to the home of Dr. John Collins Warren, where

> he found a well-chosen assembly of gentlemen variously distinguished; there was mutual greeting and introduction, and they were chatting agreeably on indifferent matters and drawing gently towards their great expectation, when a side-door opened, the whole company streamed in to an oyster supper, crowned by excellent wines; and so ended the first attempt to establish aesthetic society in Boston.[23]

But if the strain in the New England tradition which flowered so agreeably in the home of Dr. Warren, the quality that made for reason and breeding and good suppers, found itself happily divorced from enthusiasm and perfectly enshrined in the liberal profession of Unitarianism, what of the other strain? What of the mysticism, the hunger of the soul, the sense of divine emanation in man and in nature, which had been so important an element in the Puritan character? Had it died out of New England? Was it to live, if at all, forever caged and confined in the prison-house of Calvinism? Could it be asserted only by another Edwards in another treatise on the will and a new dissertation on the end for which God created the universe? Andover Seminary was, of course, turning out treatises and dissertations, and there were many New Englanders outside of Boston who were still untouched by Unitarianism. But for those who had been "liberated" by Channing

and Norton, who could no longer express their desires in the language of a creed that had been shown to be outworn, Calvinism was dead. Unitarianism rolled away the heavy stone of dogma that had sealed up the mystical springs in the New England character; as far as most Unitarians were concerned, the stone could now be lifted with safety, because to them the code of caution and sobriety, nourished on oyster suppers, would serve quite as well as the old doctrines of original sin and divine transcendence to prevent mankind from reeling and staggering in freedom. But for those in whom the old springs were still living, the removal of the theological stopper might mean a welling up and an overflowing of long suppressed desires. And if these desires could no longer be satisfied in theology, toward what objects would they now be turned? If they could no longer be expressed in the language of supernatural regeneration and divine sovereignty, in what language were they to be described?

The answer was not long forthcoming. If the inherent mysticism, the ingrained pantheism, of certain Yankees could not be stated in the old terms, it could be couched in the new terms of transcendental idealism, of Platonism, of Swedenborg, of "Tintern Abbey" and the *Bhagavad-gita*, in the eclectic and polyglot speech of the Over-Soul, in "Brahma," in "Self-Reliance," in *Nature*. The children of Puritans could no longer say that the visible fabric of nature was quickened and made joyful by a diffusion of the fullness of God, but they could recapture the Edwardean vision by saying, "Nature can only be conceived as existing to a universal and not to a particular end; to a universe of ends, and not to one,—a work of *ecstasy*, to be represented by a circular movement, as intention might be signified by a straight line of definite length."[24] But in this case the circular

---

23 *Emerson*, Works, *X, 340–341.*

24 Works, *I, 201.*

conception enjoyed one great advantage—so it seemed at the time—that it had not possessed for Edwards: the new generation of ecstatics had learned from Channing and Norton, from the prophets of intention and the straight line of definite length, that men did not need to grovel in the dust. They did not have to throw themselves on the ground, as did Edwards, with a sense of their own unworthiness; they could say without trepidation that no concept of the understanding, no utilitarian consideration for the good of mankind, could account for any man's existence, that there was no further reason than "*so it was to be.*" Overtones of the seventeenth century become distinctly audible when Emerson declares, "The *royal* reason, the Grace of God, seems the only description of our multiform but ever identical fact," and the force of his heredity is manifest when he must go on to say, having mentioned the grace of God, "There is the incoming or the receding of God," and as Edwards also would have said, "we can show neither how nor why." In the face of this awful and arbitrary power, the Puritan had been forced to conclude that man was empty and insignificant, and account for its recedings on the hypothesis of innate depravity. Emerson does not deny that such reflections are in order; when we view the fact of the inexplicable recedings "from the platform of action," when we see men left high and dry without the grace of God, we see "Self-accusation, remorse, and the didactic morals of self-denial and strife with sin"; but our enlightenment, our liberation from the sterile dogmas of Calvinism, enables us also to view the fact from "the platform of intellection," and in this view "there is nothing for us but praise and wonder."[25] The ecstasy and the vision which Calvinists knew only in the moment of vocation, the passing of which left them agonizingly aware

25 Works, *I, 204.*

of depravity and sin, could become the permanent joy of those who had put aside the conception of depravity, and the moments between could be filled no longer with self-accusation but with praise and wonder. Unitarianism had stripped off the dogmas, and Emerson was free to celebrate purely and simply the presence of God in the soul and in nature, the pure metaphysical essence of the New England tradition. If he could no longer publish it as orthodoxy, he could speak it fearlessly as the very latest form of infidelity.

At this point there might legitimately be raised a question whether my argument is anything more than obscurantism. Do words like "New England tradition" and "Puritan heritage" mean anything concrete and tangible? Do they "explain" anything? Do habits of thought persist in a society as acquired characteristics, and by what mysterious alchemy are they transmitted in the blood stream? I am as guilty as Emerson himself if I treat ideas as a self-contained rhetoric, forgetting that they are, as we are now discovering, weapons, the weapons of classes and interests, a masquerade of power relations.

Yet Emerson, transcendental though he was, could see in his own ideas a certain relation to society. In his imagination Transcendentalism was a Saturnalia of faith, but in his fancy it was a reaction against Unitarianism and in his understanding a revulsion against commercialism. We can improve his hint by remarking the obvious connection between the growth of rationalism in New England and the history of eighteenth-century capitalism. Once the Unitarian apologists had renounced the Westminster Confession, they attacked Calvinism not merely as irrational, but as a species of pantheism, and in their eyes this charge was sufficient condemnation in itself. Calvinism, said Channing, robs the mind of self-determining force and makes men passive recipients of the universal force:

It is a striking fact that the philosophy which teaches that matter is an inert substance, and that God is the force which pervades it, has led men to question whether any such thing as matter exists. . . . Without a free power in man, he is nothing. The divine agent within him is every thing, Man acts only in show. He is a phenomenal existence, under which the One Infinite Power is manifested; and is this much better than Pantheism?[26]

One does not have to be too prone to economic interpretation in order to perceive that there was a connection between the Unitarian insistence that matter is substance and not shadow, that men are self-determining agents and not passive recipients of Infinite Power, and the practical interests of the society in which Unitarianism flourished. Pantheism was not a marketable commodity on State Street, and merchants could most successfully conduct their business if they were not required to lie in the dust and desire to be full of the divine agent within.

Hence the words "New England tradition" and "Puritan heritage" can be shown to have some concrete meaning when applied to the gradual evolution of Unitarianism out of the seventeenth-century background; there is a continuity both social and intellectual. But what of the young men and young women, many of them born and reared in circles in which, Channing said, "Society is going forward in intelligence and charity," who in their very adolescence instinctively turned their intelligence and even their charity against this liberalism, and sought instead the strange and uncharitable gods of Transcendentalism? Why should Emerson and Margaret Fuller, almost from their first reflective moments, have cried out for a philosophy which would reassure them that matter is the shadow and spirit the substance, that man acts by an influx of power

—why should they deliberately return to the bondage from which Channing had delivered them? Even before he entered the divinity school Emerson was looking askance at Unitarianism, writing in his twentieth year to his Southern friend, John Boynton Hill, that for all the flood of genius and knowledge being poured out from Boston pulpits, the light of Christianity was lost: "An exemplary Christian of today, and even a Minister, is content to be just such a man as was a good Roman in the days of Cicero." Andrews Norton would not have been distressed over this observation, but young Emerson was. "Presbyterianism & Calvinism at the South," he wrote, "at least make Christianity a more real & tangible system and give it some novelties which were worth unfolding to the ignorance of men." Thus much, but no more, he could say for "orthodoxy": "When I have been to Cambridge & studied Divinity, I will tell you whether I can make out for myself any better system than Luther or Calvin, or the *liberal besoms* of modern days."[27] The *Divinity School Address* was forecast in these youthful lines, and Emerson the man declared what the boy had divined when he ridiculed the "pale negations" of Unitarianism, called it an "icehouse," and spoke of "the corpse-cold Unitarianism of Harvard College and Brattle Street." Margaret Fuller thrilled to the epistle of John read from a Unitarian pulpit: "Every one that loveth is born of God, and knoweth God," but she shuddered as the preacher straightway rose up "to deny mysteries, to deny second birth, to deny influx, and to renounce the sovereign gift of insight, for the sake of what he deemed a 'rational' exercise of will." This Unitarianism, she argued in her journal, has had its place, but the time has now come for reinterpreting old dogmas: "For one I would now preach the Holy Ghost as zealously as they have been preaching Man, and faith in-

26 *Channing*, Works, 4.

27 Letters, *I, 128.*

stead of the understanding, and mysticism instead &c—."28 And there, characteristically enough, she remarks, "But why go on?"

A complete answer to the question of motives is probably not possible as yet. Why Waldo and Margaret in the 1820's and '30's should instinctively have revolted against a creed that had at last been perfected as the ideology of their own group, of respectable, prosperous, middle-class Boston and Cambridge—why these youngsters, who by all the laws of economic determinism ought to have been the white-headed children of Unitarianism, elected to become Transcendental black sheep, cannot be decided until we know more about the period than has been told in *The Flowering of New England* and more about the nature of social change in general. The personal matter is obviously of crucial importance. The characters of the Transcendentalists account for their having become Transcendental; still two facts of a more historical nature seem to me worth considering in the effort to answer our question.

The emergence of Unitarianism out of Calvinism was a very gradual, almost an imperceptible, process. One can hardly say at what point rationalists in eastern Massachusetts ceased to be Calvinists, for they were forced to organize into a separate church only after the development of their thought was completed. Consequently, although young men and women in Boston might be, like Waldo and Margaret, the children of rationalists, all about them the society still bore the impress of Calvinism: the theological break had come, but not the cultural. In a thousand ways the forms of society were still those determined by the ancient orthodoxy, piously observed by persons who no longer believed in the creed.29 We do not need to posit some magical transmission of Puritanism from the seventeenth to the nineteenth century in order to account for the fact that these children of

Unitarians felt emotionally starved and spiritually undernourished. In 1859 James Cabot sent Emerson *The Life of Trust*, a crude narrative by one George Muller of his personal conversations with the Lord, which Cabot expected Emerson to enjoy as another instance of man's communion with the Over-Soul, which probably seemed to Cabot no more crackbrained than many of the books Emerson admired. Emerson returned the volume, accompanied by a vigorous rebuke to Cabot for occupying himself with such trash:

I sometimes think that you & your coevals missed much that I & mine found: for Calvinism was still robust & effective on life & character in all the people who surrounded my childhood, & gave a deep religious tinge to manners & conversation. I doubt the race is now extinct, & certainly no sentiment has taken its place on the new generation,—none as pervasive & controlling. But they were a high tragic school, & found much of their own belief in the grander traits of the Greek mythology,—Nemesis, the Fates, & the Eumenides, and, I am sure, would have raised an eyebrow at this pistareen Providence of . . . George Muller.30

At least two members of the high tragic school Emerson knew intimately and has sympathetically described for us—his stepgrandfather, the Reverend Ezra Ripley, and his aunt, Mary Moody Emerson. Miss Emerson put the essence of the

28 *Margaret Fuller*, Memoirs (*Boston, 1884*), II, 84–85.

29 Cf. *Emerson's meditation while still minister of the Second Church, persuading himself to observe the Fast Day not for what it had originally signified but "as a connecting link by which the posterity are bound to the fathers" (Journals, II, 371); in a later lecture he confesses that he saw "with some pain the disuse of rites so charged with humanity and aspiration," yet speaks of the process of discarding the old "offices" as not yet fully completed: men and women "find some violence, some cramping of their freedom of thought, in the constant recurrence of the form" (Works, X, 107).*

30 Letters, V, 145.

Puritan aesthetic into one short sentence: "How insipid is fiction to a mind touched with immortal views!" Speaking as a Calvinist, she anticipated Max Weber's discovery that the Protestant ethic fathered the spirit of capitalism, in the pungent observation, "I respect in a rich man the order of Providence." Emerson said that her journal "marks the precise time when the power of the old creed yielded to the influence of modern science and humanity"; still in her the old creed never so far yielded its power to the influence of modern humanity but that she could declare, with a finality granted only to those who have grasped the doctrine of divine sovereignty, "I was never patient with the faults of the good."[31] When Thomas Cholmondeley once suggested to Emerson that many of his ideas were similar to those of Calvinism, Emerson broke in with irritation, "I see you are speaking of something which had a meaning once, but is now grown obsolete. Those words formerly stood for something, and the world got good from them, but not now."[32] The old creed would no longer serve, but there had been power in it, a power conspicuously absent from the pale negations of Unitarianism. At this distance in time, we forget that Emerson was in a position fully to appreciate what the obsolete words had formerly stood for, and we are betrayed by the novelty of his vocabulary, which seems to have no relation to the jargon of Calvinism, into overlooking a fact of which he was always aware—the great debt owed by his generation "to that old religion which, in the childhood of most of us, still dwelt like a sabbath morning in the country of New England, teaching priva-

tion, self-denial and sorrow!"[33] The retarded tempo of the change in New England, extending through the eighteenth into the nineteenth century, makes comprehensible why young Unitarians had enough contact with the past to receive from it a religious standard by which to condemn the pallid and unexciting liberalism of Unitarianism.[34]

Finally, we do well to remember that what we call the Transcendental movement was not an isolated phenomenon in nineteenth-century New England. As Professor Whicher has remarked, "Liberal ideas came slowly to the Connecticut Valley."[35] They came slowly also to Andover Theological Seminary. But slowly they came, and again undermined Calvinist orthodoxies as they had undermined orthodoxy in eighteenth-century Boston; and again they liberated a succession of New Englanders from the Westminster Confession, but they did not convert them into rationalists and Unitarians. Like Emerson, when other New Englanders were brought to ask themselves, "And what is to replace for us the piety of that race?" they preferred to bask "in the great morning which rises forever out of the eastern sea" rather than to rest content with mere liberation. "I stand here to say, Let us worship the mighty and

[31] Emerson, Works, X, 399 and 411; Letters, II, 395; James Elliott Cabot, A Memoir of Ralph Waldo Emerson (Boston, 1887), I, 37.

[32] F. B. Sanborn and William T. Harris, A. Bronson Alcott (Boston, 1893), 486.

[33] Works, I, 220; cf. his letter to Aunt Mary after the death of Ezra Ripley, September 21, 1841: "Great, grim, earnest men! I belong by natural affinity to other thoughts & schools than yours but my affection hovers respectfully about your retiring footprints, your unpainted churches, strict platforms & sad offices, the iron gray deacon and the wearisome prayer rich with the diction of ages" (Letters, II, 451).

[34] Cf. "There was in the last century a serious habitual reference to the spiritual world, running through diaries, letters and conversation—yes, and into wills and legal instruments also, compared with which our liberation looks a little foppish and dapper" (Works, X, 203–204).

[35] George Frisbie Whicher, This Was a Poet (New York, 1939), 189.

transcendent Soul"—but not the good of mankind![36] Over and again the rational attack upon Calvinism served only to release energies which then sought for new forms of expression in directions entirely opposite to rationalism. Some, like Sylvester Judd, revolted against the Calvinism of the Connecticut Valley, went into Unitarianism, and then came under the spell of Emerson's Transcendentalist tuition. Others, late in the century, sought out new heresies, not those of Transcendentalism, but interesting parallels and analogues. Out of Andover came Harriet Beecher Stowe, lovingly but firmly underlining the emotional restrictions of Calvinism in *The Minister's Wooing* and *Old-town Folks*, while she herself left the grim faith at last for the ritualism of the Church of England. Out of Andover also came Elizabeth Stuart Phelps in feverish revolt against the hard logic of her father and grandfather, preaching instead the emotionalism of *Gates Ajar*. In Connecticut, Horace Bushnell, reacting against the dry intellectualism of Nathaniel Taylor's Calvinism just as Margaret Fuller had reacted a decade earlier against the dry rationalism of Norton's Unitarianism, read Coleridge with an avidity equal to hers and Emerson's, and by 1849 found the answer to his religious quest, as he himself said, "after all his thought and study, not as something reasoned out, but as an inspiration—a revelation from the mind of God himself." He published the revelation in a book, the very title of which tells the whole story, *Nature and the Supernatural Together Constituting One System of God*, wherein was preached anew the immanence of God in nature: "God is the spiritual reality of which nature is the manifestation." With this publication the latest—and yet the oldest—form of New England infidelity stalked in the citadel of orthodoxy, and Calvinism itself was, as it were,

transcendentalized. At Amherst, Emily Dickinson's mental climate, in the Gilded Age, was still Emerson's; the break-up of Calvinism came later there than in Boston, but when it had come, the poems of Emily Dickinson were filled with "Emersonian echoes," echoes which Professor Whicher wisely declines to point out because, as he says, resemblances in Emerson, Thoreau, Parker, and Emily Dickinson are not evidences of borrowings one from another, but their common response to the spirit of the time, even though the spirit reached Emily Dickinson a little later in time than it did Emerson and Thoreau. "Their work," he says, "was in various ways a fulfillment of the finer energies of a Puritanism that was discarding the husks of dogma."[37] From the time of Edwards to that of Emerson, the husks of Puritanism were being discarded, but the energies of many puritans were not yet diverted—they could not be diverted—from a passionate search of the soul and of nature, from the quest to which Calvinism had devoted them. These New Englanders—a few here and there—turned aside from the doctrines of sin and predestination, and thereupon sought with renewed fervor for the accents of the Holy Ghost in their own hearts and in woods and mountains. But now that the restraining hand of theology was withdrawn, there was nothing to prevent them, as there had been everything to prevent Edwards, from identifying their intuitions with the voice of God, or from fusing God and nature into the one substance of the transcendental imagination. Mystics were no longer inhibited by dogma. They were free to carry on the ancient New England propensity for reeling and staggering with new opinions. They could give themselves over, unrestrainedly, to becoming transparent eyeballs and debauchees of dew.

---

[36] *Emerson*, Works, I, 221.

[37] *Whicher*, This Was a Poet. *199.*

THE DILEMMA OF THEODORE PARKER

Henry Steele Commager*

Theodore Parker was, for a brief span of years, one of the most distinguished men in American public life. From his pulpit in the Music Hall, Boston, he addressed a congregation—the famous twenty-eighth—of over seven thousand, but his real parish was the entire north. He was the self-appointed conscience to the nation, but never a still, small voice. Sumner, Chase, and Hale he advised, encouraged, and scolded; Webster, Choate, and Douglas he lashed with scorpions. Wherever he went in his ceaseless travelling men and women thronged to hear him pass in review the great moral questions of the day, and from the Penobscot to the Mississippi his short, stocky, ungainly figure with the great Socrates-like head, prematurely bald, was a familiar, though not always a welcome one. Only Greeley and Beecher exceeded him in popular fame, and he disdained the eccentricity of the one and avoided the pomp-ousness of the other. Emerson counted him one of the four great men of his generation, and the gallant Samuel Gridley Howe named him "the foremost man of this continent";[1] he himself confessed with unnecessary frequency to the distinction of being the best-hated man in the country. His was the most liberal and humane voice in the American church, and thousands, revolting from an oppressive Calvinism, heard him gladly. He was the leader in that movement which has come to be known as the socialization of Christianity, and he grappled with the problems of society, with labor and poverty, crime and vice, with a realism strikingly modern. His scholarship was monumental; Thomas Wentworth Higginson, who knew every one, called him "the most vari-

[1] *Samuel Gridley Howe*, Letters and Journals (*Boston, 1909*), *II, 463.*

HENRY STEELE COMMAGER (1902–) is a Professor of History at Amherst College. His publications include Theodore Parker (*1936*), The American Mind (*1950*), *and* The Era of Reform, 1830–1860 (*1960*). *Reprinted by permission of the author and the* New England Quarterly, *Vol. 6, No. 2 (June, 1933), 257–277.*

ously learned of living Americans,"[2] while Wendell Phillips remembered that the lordly *Tribune* when it would not publish even his speeches "bent low before the most thorough scholarship of New England."[3] He was, with Garrison and Phillips, the most active and ardent of the anti-slavery agitators; like these, he excited passion and furnished social statistics, but his peculiar contribution was to throw over the movement a well-knit mantle of transcendental philosophy.

On the church, on society, and on the state he impressed his powerful intellect, but it was a progressive church, a fluid society, and a state about to be revolutionized, and in the heat of the Civil War his impression disappeared as in melted wax. His personality remains, vivid, robust, and gallant, but his actual contributions suffer from two limitations paralyzing to historical immortality. On their practical side they were so largely in the spirit of the times that they have been incorporated into the body of American life and thought; the contributions of learning, when they are successful, are necessarily suicidal. On their philosophical side they present a division, a duality, that crippled their contemporary effectiveness and insured their subsequent rejection. It is this philosophical dilemma that I wish to examine more particularly, a dilemma peculiarly interesting because it was the dilemma implicit in transcendentalism generally.

Transcendentalism is the philosophy which holds that ultimate and absolute truths are to be apprehended by the mind rather than through the senses, that these truths transcend experimental proof, and are *a priori*. It asserts that all things are first an idea in the mind, are known intuitively

and absolutely, are not susceptible to nor affected by sensational experience, nor subject to any authority but a subjective one. Santayana calls it a systematic subjectivism,[4] but the emphasis upon system is misleading. Few philosophies, not excepting pragmatism, have been so informal, so unsystematized. Transcendentalism in its American character, was indeed rather an attitude of mind than a logical dogma: it was by its own logic utterly individualistic and unorganized. It was, on its negative side, a revolt from the sensationalism of Locke and Hume and Priestley; on its positive side a re-affirmation of the ultimate authority and dignity of the human spirit. Though its philosophic origins were distinctly German and it was carried to America through English literary channels, it was peculiarly American: it had, indeed, in its political character, made its appearance at the time of the American Revolution, for the doctrines of natural law, liberty, equality, democracy, are necessarily transcendental.

But what was an attitude of mind in Emerson and Thoreau, and an emotion in Bronson Alcott and Walt Whitman, became with Theodore Parker an organized intellectual method. The most succinct statement of transcendentalism is to be found in Parker's essay by that name, delivered in 1855[5]: it is as clear-cut and definite as Emerson's essay on transcendentalism is vague and irrelevant, but Santayana insists that it is the peculiar glory of Emerson that he refrained from confining his philosophy in the frame of a system.[6] What Parker condensed in the essay on transcendentalism he expanded in the learned *Discourse of Matters Pertaining to Religion*, and it was implicit in all of

[2] *Thomas Wentworth Higginson*, Contemporaries (Boston, 1899), 38.

[3] *Wendell Phillips*, Speeches, Lectures and Letters, *Second Series (Boston, 1891), 426.*

[4] *George Santayana, "The Genteel Tradition in American Philosophy":* Winds of Doctrine (*New York, 1926), 194.*

[5] Transcendentalism. A Lecture by Theodore Parker (*Boston, 1876*), Free Religious Tracts, *No. 4.*

[6] *Santayana,* Winds of Doctrine, *197.*

his voluminous writing. No American transcendentalist elaborated his idealism in more detail, embroidered it with richer scholarship, formulated it with greater precision, applied it more widely or more vigorously. Having discovered and established a system of intuitive truths, Parker rigorously reviewed not only sensational philosophy but orthodox religion, conventional society, and organized government. With relentless logic he reduced complex problems of church and state and society to first principles and judged them by his absolute and transcendental standards. Was it a stubborn Calvinism that exercised its ancient tyranny over the minds of men? That Calvinism was a result of a false philosophy of man, a sensational philosophy that accepted the authority of the written word or of the authenticated miracle instead of the intuitive authority of the individual spirit. Did hunkerism rear its evil head in the land and demand obedience to man-made laws? That demand was based on the wicked fallacy that there is no higher law, no absolute right. Did man exploit his fellow-men, did wealth accumulate and men decay? It was because a sensational philosophy had distorted values, impaired the dignity of the human spirit and enhanced the significance of material things. Did slave-owners plead the justification of the Bible or of history, or the complex and difficult character of the problem? The apology was based on a denial of absolute right, absolute justice, it took refuge in historical precedents and justified itself by an appeal to experience rather than to *a priori* truth.

But it was to the problem of religion that Parker first and most rigorously applied his idealistic philosophy, it was as a religious reformer that he became nationally known, and it was as the foremost representative of the higher criticism that he made his chief contributions to scholarship. His intuition assured him that man was instinctively religious, and instinctively reverenced

a God, that mankind might attain to divinity, and that there was an after life. It affirmed for him the infinite perfection of God and the adequacy of man for all his functions.[7] These grand truths, it must be repeated, were "laid in human nature, there spontaneously given by the great primal instincts of mankind." Their application to the religion, the theology, the church, of the 1830's, first in the *Levi Blodgett Letter* (1840), then in the explosive *Discourse of the Transient and the Permanent in Christianity* (1841), and finally in the elaborate *Discourse of Religion* (1842), created a furor which reverberated through the length of the land The character of these successive pronouncements is illuminating: Parker began with criticism, advanced to an announcement of general principles, and then developed these principles by an exhaustive argument from facts of necessity and facts of demonstration. The remaining eighteen years of Parker's life were given over to the elaboration of these philosophical principles, their application to a wide variety of social problems, and their substantiation by factual proof. This was a natural development: how utterly illogical it was in its methods and its results, and to what inconsistencies it led, will appear upon closer examination.

It is unnecessary to remark that Parker was not the first in this conflict between orthodox Unitarianism and transcendentalism. The historical-minded will recall Channing's "Baltimore Discourse" of 1819 as the opening skirmish[8]; the scholarly will remember Furness's "Remarks on

---

[7] For a concise statement of Parker's religious philosophy, see "Letter from Santa Cruz called Theodore Parker's Experience as a Minister," in the appendix to John Weiss, Life and Correspondence of Theodore Parker (New York, 1864), II, 470 ff.

[8] "Unitarian Christianity: A Discourse at the Ordination of the Rev. Jared Sparks": Works of William E. Channing, D.D. (Boston, 1841), III, 59.

the Four Gospels," of 1836. Whatever the importance of these, and of the writings of Walker, and Noyes, and Kneeland,[9] it was, of course, with Emerson's "Divinity School Address" that the battle was joined. And the conflict once precipitated, it raged with ever-increasing intensity all along the line of philosophy, theology, and society. Heady with the wine of new ideas, militant theologians rushed out into the arena of public affairs, into the market-place, the legislative chambers, the school-rooms, and even the home, challenging institutions, defying custom, and demanding reform. Emerson has described it, not without malice, in his *New England Reformers*; his explanation of the new critical spirit in *Man the Reformer* is more illuminating:

> We are [he wrote] to revise the whole of our social structure, the state, the school, religion, marriage, trade, science, and explore their foundations in our own nature; we are to see that the world not only fitted the former men, but fits us, and to clear ourselves of every usage which has not its roots in our own mind. What is a man born for but to be a Reformer, a Remaker of what man has made, a renouncer of lies; a restorer of truth and good, imitating that great Nature which embosoms us all, and which sleeps no moment on an old past, but every hour repairs herself, yielding us every morning a new day, and with every pulsation a new life? . . . The power which is at once spring and regulator in all efforts of reform is the conviction that there is an infinite worthiness in man, which will appear at the call of worth, and that all particular reforms are the removing of some impediment.[10]

What a ferment was there in New England of the thirties and the forties! The atmosphere was charged with new ideas, filled with the din of new names. German idealism, Hellenism, the French enlightenment, Swedenborgian, mysticism, Oriental pantheism, clamored for naturalization, for translation into the American vernacular. Never was the American scholar so thoroughly American, so indigenous, so conscious of the homely phrase, of the native application; never was he so cosmopolitan, so catholic, so sensitive to the thought and the literature of other nations and other times. It was a motley but magnificent crew that came sailing into Boston harbor in the eighteen-thirties, bringing a precious cargo: Kant and Goethe, Herder and Hegel, Schelling and Schiller, Strauss and Schleiermacher, Vatke and De Wette, Baur and Ewald, Jacobi and Fichte, from German ports; Cousin and Fourier, Jouffrey, Constant, and Comte, from France; Coleridge and Carlyle, from England and Scotland. "The wharves," wrote John Weiss, "were littered with the spoils of a century. . . . We all rushed in and helped ourselves."[11] We can picture the throng of omnivorous transcendentalists hurrying down to the docks: the energetic Ripley and the aggressive Margaret Fuller, fickle Brownson and timid Convers Francis, Olympian Emerson and keen-eyed Thoreau, the poetic Dwight, rebellious young Frothingham, awkward George Bancroft, gallant Sam Howe, charming William Henry Channing and lovable, dreamy Bronson Alcott. But the self-appointed chairman of the reception committee was Theodore Parker.

Even as a student in the Divinity School he had astonished his contemporaries by the breadth of his learning and the catholicity of his interests. He was satisfied with nothing less than omniscience: he wished to master all languages, to read

---

[9] *On the early stages of the Unitarian controversy, see especially William C. Gannett,* Ezra Stiles Gannett. A Memoir by his Son *(Boston, 1875), chapter VII.*

[10] *Ralph Waldo Emerson,* Nature, Addresses and Lectures *(Boston, 1892), 236–237.*

[11] *Weiss,* Theodore Parker, *I, 161.*

all books, to be familiar with all thought. His energy was colossal, his industry indefatigable, his memory fabulous. He hurled himself on knowledge with tigerish ferocity; he belabored his opponents, Lowell says, "with the whole tree of knowledge torn up by the roots." He undertook to familiarize his countrymen with the progress of theological studies in Germany, and to establish here the scientific and historical study of theology. He introduced Strauss, advertised the Tübingen school of Ewald and Baur, reviewed Oldhausen and Dorner, and prepared a translation of De Wette's *Introduction to the Old Testament* that was a monument of labor and a marvel of erudition.[12] It can scarcely be doubted that the *Discourse of Religion* of 1842—published when the author was scarcely thirty years of age—was the most learned contribution to theological scholarship of this period, not excepting even the mighty Norton's *Evidences of the Genuineness of the Gospels*. He planned a "History of the Reformation," he collected material for a "History of Religious Thought since the Reformation," he projected an enormous work on the "Historical Development of Religion."[13] His energy was equalled only by his ambition, and they were both surpassed by his knowledge. The ever-delightful Thomas Wentworth Higginson tells us that a projected series of volumes on various aspects of religious history and philosophy was abandoned because nothing was proposed but that Parker had already accumulated material for just such a volume.[14] The latest

scholarly books would be noticed in the *Christian Examiner*, or perhaps in the *Dial*, or the *Massachusetts Quarterly*—that *Dial* with a beard—which Parker edited single-handed[15]; and every incoming ship brought the treasures of European bookshops to create the richest private library in Boston.[16]

It was, indeed, his scholarship that betrayed him. Not content with asserting truths of intuition, he spent himself in substantiating them by facts of demonstration. His love of learning was an appetite, it came to be a passion, it may have grown into a vice. His learning was the most massive, perhaps, in all America—more varied than thorough, if you will, more ambitious than profound —it was acquired not in the uninterrupted leisure of the study but in a lifetime tragically brief, crowded with the duties of an enormous parish, hot with the insistent duties of anti-slavery work. His information was as encyclopædic as it was exact: he could fling a thundering bibliography at the scholarly Professor Francis in response to a cry for aid[17]; he could cite the very page of an obscure monograph on Salic Law when Sumner turned to him in desperation; he was the one man, so the classicist, John King of Salem, records, with whom it was possible to discuss intelligently a disputed reading in a Greek play.[18] He took Buckle severely to task for bibliographical omissions in

[12] A Critical and Historical Introduction to the Canonical Scriptures of the Old Testament. From the German of De Wette. *Translated and Enlarged by Theodore Parker (Boston, 1843).*

[13] *Some 270 pages in manuscript contain all that Parker left of this ambitious plan. Fragments are printed in Weiss,* Theodore Parker, *II, 49 ff.*

[14] *Higginson,* Contemporaries, *41.*

[15] *The* Massachusetts Quarterly Review *was published from 1847 to 1850. R. W. Emerson, J. E. Cabot, and Parker composed the original board of editors. Cabot himself is authority for the statement that Parker was actually sole editor:* Memoir of Ralph Waldo Emerson *(Boston, 1887), 498.*

[16] *Parker's library, now housed in the Boston Public Library, contained some 16,000 volumes. For a detailed description, see T. W. Higginson, "Report on the Parker Library":* Annual Report Boston Public Library *(Boston, 1883), 19 ff.*

[17] *See, for example, the letters to Francis in Weiss,* Theodore Parker, *I, 358, 360, 361.*

[18] *Higginson,* Contemporaries, *43–45.*

the *History of Civilization*, corrected Hildreth in detail, and administered to Prescott the most severe scholarly lacing that that historian was to receive.[19] His knowledge of legal institutions and history excited the admiration of the learned Sumner (who was not given to admiring others), and when indicted for violation of the fugitive slave law, he prepared for his own defence a masterly treatise on the history of English and American law.[20] His appetite for languages was insatiable: Greek, Latin, Hebrew, French, German, Italian, and Spanish he acquired in student days; Syriac, Arabic, Coptic, Bohemian, Russian, Icelandic, Danish, Finnish, Lithuanian (and a score more) came later; at the end, he was wrestling with native African dialects. He confessed a curious interest in the occult sciences, collected an imposing library on folk-lore and balladry, admitted a passion for geography. His knowledge of science was more superficial, but he dared to jeer at Agassiz, anticipated the doctrine of evolution,[21] participated in geological expeditions, had an astonishing familiarity with the flora and fauna of New England, brought geological specimens to Thoreau, and read avidly the transactions of German and French scientific societies. "His mind," remarks Weiss, "was like the republican idea itself; it could afford to be hospitable but could not afford to be exclusive."

It is clear that Parker was fascinated by knowledge for its own sake; it is possible that he came, quite unconsciously, to make a fetish of facts. He read, to borrow a neat phrase from Santayana, not transcendentally, but historically, not to find out what he himself felt but to discover what others had felt.[22] His friend John Dwight warned him of this danger. "Don't you often," he wrote, "turn aside from your own reflections from the fear of losing what another has said or written on the subject? Have you not too much of a mania for all printed things,—as if books were more than the symbols of that truth to which the student aspires? You write, you read, you talk, you think in a hurry for fear of not getting all."[23] There speaks the transcendentalist, and he speaks as if to the most stubborn sensationalist. But Parker would not be warned: his vice grew on him with the passing years—his respect for facts, his use of the historical and the inductive method.

He had begun by announcing *a priori* truths which might be clarified by reference to some facts of demonstration; he ended by burying his intuitive argument under a veritable avalanche of facts. It was a shift in method, and a gradual one, but here method and emphasis were everything. It was a substitution, or at least a confusion, of means and end that the transcendentalist, of all philosophers, could not afford to make. The method was increasingly the method of science; the emphasis was increasingly on the authenticating facts. And though Parker professed scorn for the formal and deliberate application of the scientific method to philosophy, he confessed nevertheless the ultimate admiration for that method—imitation. He was, indeed, naive enough to believe that if he only stated his conclusions

[19] *The essay on Buckle is in the* Collected Works of Theodore Parker . . . (*Frances Power Cobbe, Ed., London, 1863–1865*), XI; *the essay on Hildreth and the two essays on Prescott are to be found in* X.

[20] The Trial of Theodore Parker . . . with the Defence, *by Theodore Parker (Boston, 1855).*

[21] *See the* "Sermon on Christian Advancement," "Sermon on Natural Religion," "Sermon to Progressive Friends," *No. 3, the* Five Sermons on the Testimony of Matter and Mind to the Existence of God. *In his scientific views and his attitude toward Agassiz, Parker was influenced by his close friend, the Swiss geologist, Desor.*

[22] *Santayana,* Winds of Doctrine, *192.*

[23] *John White Chadwick,* Theodore Parker, Preacher and Reformer (*Boston, 1900*), *154.*

first instead of last he had preserved the idealistic philosophy, and the picture of this ardent transcendentalist systematically ransacking the facts of history with the tools of science in order to prove his intuitive truths is not without its comic character. Three examples will suffice: one from the realm of theological scholarship, one from the field of political reform, and one from the struggle against slavery.

Few of Parker's essays were more learned, more incisive, than the lengthy review of Dorner's *Entwicklungsgeschichte der Lehre von der Person Christi*, which appeared in the *Dial* in 1842. Here Parker scored the low state of theological studies in America and England and ridiculed the preconceptions and superstitions with which the subject was commonly approached. In theology, he charges:

> Common Sense rarely shows his honest face; Reason seldom comes. It is a land shadowy with the wings of Ignorance, Superstition, Bigotry, Fanaticism, the brood of clawed and beaked and hungry Chaos and most ancient Night. . . . In science we ask first What are the facts of observation whence we shall start? . . . The first work is to find the facts, then their law and meaning.[24]

If theology is to be rescued from its shameful state, he continued, it must be approached historically and scientifically: we must create a science of theology comparable to the science of geology, or of medicine. And even as he was penning this essay, he was confiding to his friend, Francis:

> All study of theology must be abandoned, or it must be studied in a method and with a thoroughness and to an extent which bears some resemblance to the state of other sciences. Theology is

contemptible at present in comparison with astronomy, geology, or even the pretended science of phrenology.[25]

Yet, in the same essay in which these laudable sentiments appear, Parker turned aside to denounce the application of sensationalism to religion and philosophy and to charge as inevitable results materialism, selfishness, scepticism, and atheism.

> No skill of the artist [he thundered], no excellence of heart, can counteract the defects of the *Novum Organum* when applied to morals, metaphysics or theology. . . . We are not surprised that no one, following Bacon's scheme, has ever succeeded in driving materialism, selfishness and scepticism from the field of philosophy, morals and religion. The answer to these systems must come from men who adopt a different method.[26]

It would be difficult to find a clearer example of trying to have philosophical cake and eat it too.

Let us look next to the tremendous sermons on the Mexican War.[27] Parker's attitude toward that conflict was that of most of his transcendentalist friends, but he found occasion to express it more frequently and more publicly, perhaps, than any other. In the sermons on the war he takes the position of a Christian moralist. "War," he asserts, "is an utter violation of Christianity. If war be right, then Christianity is wrong, false, a lie. But if Christianity be true, if reason, conscience, the religious sense, the highest faculties of man, are to be trusted, then war is the wrong, the falsehood, the lie." The precepts of brotherhood, of

24 Works (*Cobbe, Ed.*), IX, 214–215.

25 *Weiss*, Theodore Parker, *I, 186*.

26 Works (*Cobbe, Ed.*), IX, 220–221.

27 Discourses of Politics (Works, *IV*), *"A Sermon of War," June 7, 1846; "Speech Delivered at the Anti-War Meeting," February 4, 1847; "Sermon of the Mexican War," June 25, 1848.*

peace and of love are not only those of Christianity, but are "the dictates of man's nature, only developed and active; a part of God's universal revelation; His law writ on the soul of man true after all experience and true before all experience."[28] This is lofty ground; it is distinctly transcendental ground. These truths are intuitive truths—true "before all experience." If this is truth, it is absolute truth; if it is true before all experience, the lessons of experience are irrelevant and impertinent. Yet read further in the great "Sermon of War" of 1846, and what do we find? Parker is authenticating these *a priori* truths by facts of demonstration. Here are pages and pages of bewildering statistics—the cost of war in money, in hours of labor, in misapplied energy, in social demoralization, in lives. Here are figures on the effect of the war on the fisheries of Massachusetts, on the annual expenditures for docks, arsenals, forts, on the daily cost of subsistence for a soldier. Here we can read comparisons between the appropriations for military purposes and for public education, appropriations to West Point and to the colleges of New England. Here are appeals to the lessons of history, to the cost in money and lives of past wars, to the experience of other nations. It is all most effective, but, like "the flowers that bloom in the spring," it has nothing to do with the thing of absolute truth. The appeal from the deductive to the inductive seems safe enough, but suppose it could be demonstrated that war actually developed the economic energies of a people, increased wealth, regenerated society? Would the transcendentalist be forced from his high ground? If intuitive truth transcends experience, what is the value of an appeal to experience; if *a priori* truth is not susceptible to factual proof, what is to be gained by citing statistics?

It was to the struggle against slavery that

Parker devoted the energy and eloquence of the last decade of his life, and it is as a radical abolitionist that he is, perhaps, best remembered. His attitude toward the institution was grounded in his philosophy. Slavery, he insisted, was an absolute wrong, an evil, a sin, a crime against humanity, a violation of nature. Its maintenance was possible only by dependence on a false philosophy of life—the sensational one. Historian though he was, Parker deliberately closed his eyes to the historical evolution of the institution; sociologist though he was, he refused to recognize its complex social character. Like Garrison, he held that slavery must fall, regardless of consequences. "There is something in man," he wrote, "which scoffs at expediency, which will do right, justice, truth, though Hell itself should gape and bid him hold his peace; the morality which *anticipates* history loves the right for itself."[29] Granting the *a priori* premises, the conclusions followed logically enough. But for all his ardent transcendentalism Parker was not content to rest his case on absolute right. On the contrary, his two volumes of *Discourses of Slavery*[30] read like Helper's *Impending Crisis*. The discourses reek with statistics, they spill over with historical references. Here are comparisons of land values, population growth, school attendance, crime, newspaper circulation, commercial activities: all that body of unanalyzed data which (even in hands more skilful than Parker's) lends itself readily to misinterpretation. Government reports, historical documents, papers and journals, all hurried their tribute to this tran-

28 *"Sermon of War"*; Works (*Cobbe, Ed.*), *IV, 4.*

29 Transcendentalism, a Lecture.

30 Works (*Cobbe, Ed.*), *V* and *VI. See especially "A Letter to the People of the United States touching the Matter of Slavery"; "An Address on the Condition of America," May 12, 1854; "Some Thoughts on the Progress of America and the Influence of Her Diverse Institutions," May 31, 1854; "The Present Crisis in American Affairs," May 7, 1856.*

scendental statistician, all went to prove a principle by its very nature not susceptible to proof.

This, precisely, was the dilemma of Theodore Parker. His love of learning, his intellectual acquisitiveness, his respect for facts, proved his undoing. He never abandoned his original intuitional philosophy, but every new accumulation of proof represented a vote of no confidence. He remained to the end as transcendental as Whitman, and as experimental as Spencer, as intuitive as Jefferson, and as sensational as Franklin. He maintained the complete and unique validity of facts of consciousness and then proved them by facts of demonstration. He elaborated the absolute and submitted first principles to laboratory tests. Others noted this dualism, but it was so instinctive with Parker that he was never aware of it. He jumped to and fro between the deductive and the inductive, the *a priori* and the *a posteriori*, with an acrobatic agility. "Transcendentalism," he wrote, "has a work to do to show that physics, politics, ethics, religion, rest on facts of necessity and have their witness and confirmation in facts of observation."[31] But as John Dewey points out, "the claim to formulate *a priori* the legislative constitution of the universe is by its nature a claim that may lead to elaborate dialectic developments. But it is also one that removes these very conclusions from subjection to experimental test, for by definition, these results make no difference."[32]

The most persistent and most glaring example of Parker's philosophic dualism was his habit of judging the tree by its fruit, judging men, institutions, philosophies, by their results. Sensationalism was rejected because it resulted in hunkerism, orthodox Calvinism because it brought fear and unhappiness, slavery because it led to poverty and degeneration. Actually, Parker was interested in results rather than in first principles. Thus he subjected his whole philosophy to the vicissitudes of fortune, to the vagaries of human chance. But this was the measuring-rod of sensationalism, of pragmatism, even. "Our great difference," wrote William James in contrasting the philosophy of the scholastic spirit with that of the pragmatist:

> Our great difference lies in the way we face. . . . The strength of his system lies in the principles, the origin, the *terminus a quo* of his thought; for us the strength is in the outcome, the upshot, the *terminus ad quem*. Not where it comes from but where it leads to is to decide.

Parker's mind was not metaphysical. He was naturally a man of action rather than a contemplative philosopher. It is illuminating to remember that he reserved his greatest admiration for Benjamin Franklin rather than for Jefferson. He was the Luther rather than the Melanchthon of the new religious reformation. Vigor, breadth, energy, simplicity, ruggedness, homeliness, enthusiasm characterized his thought rather than depth, subtlety, refinement, or serenity.[33] Philosophical problems he was inclined to overwhelm with learning rather than to penetrate with understanding. Nice metaphysical points he ignored or muddled. He accumulated facts more readily than he matured ideas, and he seldom probed ideas to their depths. His interpretation of the crucial problem of evil, for example, was both puerile and undignified—puerile because, as Josiah Royce points out, it justifies evil as necessary to avoid other greater but unexplained evils; undignified because, as Ludwig Lewisohn observes, its doctrine of compensation robs life of its tragic significance.

This confusion of intuition and experience was

[31] Transcendentalism, a Lecture.

[32] *John Dewey*, The Influence of Darwinism Upon Philosophy (*New York, 1910*), 17.

[33] *Chadwick, Parker's ablest biographer, brings this out clearly. See his* Theodore Parker, *VII and XIV*, passim.

not so much a personal idiosyncracy as a social characteristic. Parker's dualism was to an extent the dualism of that entire group of ardent New England reformers who would recreate society in the name of first principles, who glorified individualism in Fourierist phalanxes; perhaps it was implicit in the conflict between the possibilities of a New World environment and Old World institutions. Those fathers whose wisdom Parker loved to celebrate had justified a Declaration of Independence on intuitive principles and established a new form of government on experimental precepts, and indeed a large part of American history may be interpreted as an attempt to vindicate by facts of demonstration the transcendental ideas of democracy and equality and liberty. Not until half a century after Parker did pragmatism resolve the apparent paradox by announcing that transcendental ideals might and should be progressively realized by experience—by the "Will to Believe," and in our own day Professor Thomas Vernor Smith has applied the instrumentalist philosophy specifically to this problem and in his *American Philosophy of Equality*[34] discovered that the ultimate justification of the ideal of equality is precisely its functional value.

When Parker was a young man, just installed in his West Roxbury parish, he went one day to visit the already venerable Dr. Channing. They discussed conscience. "I asked him," Parker recorded in his journal, "if conscience were not an *infallible* guide. He seemed to doubt it, but is going to think of the question. To me it seems that conscience will always decide right, if the case is fairly put and old habits have not obscured the vision."[35] Conscience—and the clear vision, that was it; the triumph of the right when the mind is educated and all the facts are in. Over twenty years later he was in Rome, fighting a hopeless fight against consumption. See him as he trudges patiently down three flights of stairs out into the cold drizzle of a February day. Darwin's *Principles of Selection in Natural History* had just come to hand, and he had been writing his friend, George Ripley, reaffirming his intuitive faith in God and immortality. He is hurrying off now to a bookstall: he has heard that an obscure book by a Dutchman, Nieuwendt, on the existence of God, can be found there, and he has been hunting for it for years. Death stalks him as he hastens through the gathering dusk of the late afternoon, but his eye is alight with excitement, and his brain is burning with enthusiasm, and the tenderest of smiles turns up the corners of his mouth as he thinks of old George Ripley back there in New York, and remembers Brook Farm days.

[34] *Thomas Vernor Smith*, American Philosophy of Equality (*Chicago, 1927*). *See also his* Democratic Way of Life (*Chicago, 1926*).

[35] *Weiss*, Theodore Parker, *I, 108–109.*

TRANSCENDENTALISM: A SELF-PORTRAIT

Lawrence C. Porter*

Transcendentalism, like most movements, has various images. Its official, public pronouncements (in essays and lectures) supply one; its enemies' attacks another; its friends' defenses still another. These images—or a synthesis of them—are familiar to those who read in the history of the movement. But it is another image that this paper will examine, a more inferential one, developed from non-public comments found in the Transcendentalists' more private statements. Here, in letters and journals, we find them discussing their personal relationships, defining their positions, working out their ethics, reacting to their world—all of this away from the world's scrutiny. Here we may expect to find a less guarded self-image than that presented to the largely hostile world of their time. And, although it may not differ significantly from the commonly held view of Transcendentalism, it may add another dimension to it.[1]

First of all, what view did the Transcendentalists have of themselves as individuals? Can we safely oversimplify, as we often do, and think of a "movement" as composed of interlocking units? To do so with the Transcendentalists would be almost ludicrously wrong. For, although there was a general flow of mutual respect and good will among them, they were not hesitant to express distaste for or disappointment in each other's character and actions. Some antagonism resulted from personal polarities, some grew out of differences of opinion. Often relationships ran hot and cold.

Amos Bronson Alcott's reactions to Emerson, for example, shifted quickly. In April, 1837, he

[1] *Unless otherwise noted, all persons mentioned in this paper will be considered members—either at the center or at the periphery—of the Transcendental movement. Almost all of the writings cited fall between 1836 and 1847.*

LAWRENCE C. PORTER (1925–   ) is Associate Professor of Experimental and General Education at Antioch College. Reprinted by permission of the author and the New England Quarterly, *Vol. 35, No. 1 (March, 1962), 27–47.*

wrote that Emerson was a friend, from whom it was "gratifying to receive . . . words and sentiments of approval and confidence."[2] But only a month later he wrote that Emerson held himself "somewhat too proudly," that he was "an eye more than a heart. . . ."[3] At about the same time, Alcott himself was drawing criticism, for Margaret Fuller wrote F. H. Hedge about a rumor that had reached her: "Why is it that I hear you are writing a piece to 'cut up' Mr. Alcott? I do not believe you are going to cut up Mr. Alcott. There are plenty of fish in the net created solely for markets, etc.;—no need to try your knife on a dolphin like him."[4] A year later Alcott was catechized by the

Reverend George Ripley, who asked him for his "theory of God," and, upon hearing it, likened it to "the doctrines of atheism,"[5] or so Alcott tells us in his journal. In 1839, Alcott wrote of the "polarity" between Jones Very and Orestes Brownson: "It was comic to behold them. They tried to speak, but Very was unintelligible to the proud Philistine."[6]

Margaret Fuller's relations with others in the group were often strained. The letters between her and Emerson contain some almost poignant attempts at friendship. He, for example, wrote that he would gladly have talked with her where they might have "more reverently" spoken of things "than in a cold room at abrupt & stolen moments." He talks of their "wide sights," and ends with what might be construed as an appeal, couched in Transcendental phraseology: "Let us float along through the great heavens a while longer and whenever we come to a point whence our observations agree, the time when they did not will seem but a moment."[7] Later we receive a more-than-usually-intimate glimpse of Emerson, when Miss Fuller writes him:

> I have not felt separated from you yet.—It is not yet time for me to have my dwelling near you. I get, after a while, even *intoxicated* with your mind, and do not live enough in my self. Now don't screw up your lip to an ungracious pettiness, but hear the words of frank affection as they deserve 'mentis cordis.'[8]

[2] *Odell Shepard, editor,* The Journals of Bronson Alcott *(Boston, 1938), 87. Hereafter cited as* AJ.

[3] *AJ, 91. The inconsistency of Alcott's attitude toward Emerson is typical of the shifts found in the Transcendentalists' opinions of each other. In May, 1846, Alcott wrote in his journal, "Emerson, Miss Fuller, Thoreau, and myself, are the only persons who treat things in the new spirit, each working the same mine of Being."—p. 180. He apparently was not bothered by—or had forgotten—a journal entry for the previous January: ". . . the idealism of his [Emerson's] mind, debasing the primitive ascendency of the moral sentiment, leaves him without basis for upholding the verity of Being."—p. 172. Emerson also changed opinions. In 1840 he told Margaret Fuller that there seemed always to be a fence between him and F. H. Hedge, but two years later he thought of Hedge as a man "well mixed & so intellectual: In this country a nonpareil."—Quoted in Perry Miller, editor,* The Transcendentalists *(Cambridge, 1950), 67. It was after Hedge that the Transcendental group—also known as "The Symposium" and "The Transcendental Club"—was sometimes called "Hedge's Club." This group first met on Sept. 19, 1836. (Perry Miller,* The Transcendentalists, *106, gives the date as September 16.)*

[4] *Thomas W. Higginson,* Margaret Fuller Ossoli *(Boston, 1889), 78. Mason Wade (in* The Writings of Margaret Fuller, *1941), carries the letter as far as "There are plenty of fish in the . . ." and then notes "page missing."—p. 547.*

[5] *AJ, 101. Interestingly enough, it was this "atheistic" man who noted in his journal (Jan., 1846) that Emerson was "unable to escape wholly his taint of unbelief. . . ."—p. 172.*

[6] *AJ, 130.*

[7] *Ralph L. Rusk, editor,* The Letters of Ralph Waldo Emerson *(New York, 1939), II, 349. Hereafter cited as* EL.

[8] *Wade,* Writings . . . , *564.*

Margaret Fuller often showed this wistful self-doubt over her relations with others. To W. E. Channing, Jr., she wrote, "You may not like or enjoy meeting me. . . ."[9] But she is also capable of what could be called a bland ungraciousness, as when she writes Thoreau, regarding his doubts over her adverse judgment of an essay he had submitted to the *Dial:* "It is true [she writes] . . . that essays not to be compared with this have found their way into the Dial. But then these were more unassuming in their tone, and have an air of quiet good breeding which induces us to permit their presence."[10]

Perhaps naturally enough, almost every Transcendentalist at one time or another grew impatient with Alcott. Emerson, for example, noted in his journal that Alcott "dissatisfies everybody and disgusts many. When the conversation is ended, all is over."[11] And Lidian Emerson preserved a tart discussion for us when she added a postscript to Thoreau's letter to her absent husband (February 20, 1843). She described a discussion—between Thoreau, Alcott, and Charles Lane—in which the subject was "love of nature." Thoreau said that neither Lane nor Alcott was capable of judging the issue, since both were deficient in the quality under discussion. Alcott replied, wrote Lidian, that he and Lane only

seemed so to Thoreau, because they "went beyond the mere material objects and were filled with spiritual love and perception (as Mr. Thoreau was not). . . ."[12] Some years later, in a letter to Emerson (December 29, 1847), Thoreau referred to Alcott's "creaking and sneaking Connecticut philosophy."[13] And Emerson, some months after the Thoreau-Lane-Alcott "discussion," almost completes the circle with a journal entry deprecating Thoreau's rhetorical trickery:

> . . . it consists in substituting for the obvious word and thought its diametrical antagonist. He praises wild mountains and winter forests for their domestic air; snow and ice for their warmth; . . . and the wilderness for resembling Rome and Paris.[14]

Of course, personal tensions existed outside this foursome. James Freeman Clarke, for example, wrote Margaret Fuller that he, W. H. Channing, and Emerson had talked "on high matters—Evil, etc.," adding that "with Mr. Emerson it is hard for me to talk on such subjects. We seem to run on two parallel lines, and never meet."[15]

Nor were things always smooth with the group as a whole. The first meeting of their "Symposium" inspired hopeful journal entries, but it was not long before a mild disenchantment set in. After the first meeting in 1836 Emerson wrote (in a September 20th journal entry) that the conversation had "inspired hope,"[16] but only eight

[9] *Wade*, Writings . . . , *562.*

[10] *Walter Harding and Carl Bode, editors,* The Correspondence of Henry David Thoreau (*New York, 1958*), *42.*

[11] *E. W. Emerson and W. E. Forbes, editors,* The Journals of Ralph Waldo Emerson (*New York, 1909–1914*), *VI, 173. Hereafter cited as EJ. Apparently Alcott's part in the conversation was not always a success either. Emerson reports that in a discussion, Theodore Parker "wound himself around Alcott like an anaconda: you could hear poor Alcott's bones crunch."—Quoted in Henry S. Commager,* Theodore Parker (*Boston, 1947*), *284.*

[12] *Harding and Bode, 91–92. There is a certain charm to the delicacy that leads her to parenthesize the* coup de grâce.

[13] *Harding and Bode, 200.*

[14] *EJ, VI, 440.*

[15] *John W. Thomas, editor,* The Letters of James Freeman Clarke to Margaret Fuller (*Hamburg, Germany, 1957*), *142.*

[16] *EJ, IV, 86.*

months later he wrote of the divisiveness of men and of the difficulties of conversing, even with those "who most fully accord in life and doctrine with ourselves."[17] Following the second meeting, Alcott's journal records that Emerson had given the group "many good things, as usual," in a discussion that was "lively, well sustained, and interesting."[18] But less than a year later (August, 1837) Emerson's melancholy report is that he grew drowsy in the company of Alcott and Hedge;[19] and, less than a year after this (May, 1838), he reports:

> I was at Medford the other day at a meeting of Hedge's Club. I was unlucky in going after several nights of vigils, and heard as though I heard not, and among gifted men I had not one thought or inspiration. . . . I . . . read today with wicked pleasure the saying ascribed to Kant, that "detestable was the society of mere literary men." It must be tasted sparingly to keep its gusto. . . .[20]

Emerson's reactions to the Brook Farm and Fruitlands ventures disappointed some of his associates. But he could not be interested in Brook Farm, because "it was not the cave of persecution which is the palace of spiritual power, but only a room in the Astor House hired for the Transcendentalists."[21] He refers to Alcott and his cohorts at Fruitlands as "the divine lotus-eaters."[22] Even the *Dial*, that "Bible" of the Transcendentalists, was not beyond his criticism. As we shall see later, he complained of its impracticality, and in 1841 he wrote his aunt, Mary Moody Emerson, that the then-current number interested him so little that he had "not yet succeeded in reading it. . . ."[23]

A great deal of cavilling and dissension, one might say, and this is true. But to say no more than this is to miss what is known to be an essential element of Transcendentalism, as its adherents saw it—composed of free spirits who thought for themselves, who put themselves under no man's domination for long.[24] It is important to note that this is no latter-day view, but one held by the men under discussion. C. P. Cranch summarizes it well in a letter to his father, writing that "union in sympathy differs from union in belief," and adding that he would prefer the name "New School" to Transcendentalism, because

---

17 EJ, *IV, 239.*

18 AJ, *79.*

19 EJ, *IV, 278–279. Emerson continued, "In able conversation we have glimpses of the Universe, perceptions of the soul's omnipotence, but not much to record." That some of the meetings were less spiritual is suggested by a letter written by C. P. Cranch to his sister in the winter of 1839–1840: "We have transcendental and aesthetic gatherings at a great rate—and they make me sing at them all. I have worn my Tyrolese yodlers almost to the bones."—Quoted in F. DeWolfe Miller, Christopher Pearse Cranch and His Caricatures of New England Transcendentalism (Cambridge, 1951), 12.*

20 EJ, *IV, 456–457. Emerson's opinions on the Symposium fluctuated greatly. The cited journal entry is reinforced by one made some three weeks earlier: "Even the disciples of the new unnamed or misnamed Transcendentalism that now is, vain of the same, do already dogmatize and rail at such as hold it not, and cannot see the worth of the antagonism also."*

—EJ, *IV, 434. Two years later, however, he wrote Margaret Fuller: ". . . our round table is not, I fancy, in imminent peril of party & bigotry, & we shall bruise each the other's whims by the collision."—EL, II, 322–323.*

21 EJ, *V, 473.*

22 EJ, *VI, 386.*

23 EL, *II, 389.*

24 *The Emerson-Thoreau association is a well-known case in point. It began warmly, with Thoreau as a "disciple," but ended soon, apparently because Thoreau, like most of the Transcendentalists, could not long rest comfortably in any man's shadow.*

"this could comprehend all free seekers after truth, however their opinions differ."[25]

We see here a group held together not by any easy personal rapport, but by the most tenuous and at the same time the most powerful of adhesives—ideas. But about any given idea men may have different opinions, if the framework within which they operate allows them to, or, indeed, encourages them to. It was to this kind of framework that the Transcendentalists paid homage, and to those who ridiculed their heterogeneity they would all probably have responded, as did Cranch, that Transcendentalism's glory was that it was *many*-headed.

Transcendentalism's enemies often compounded charges of heterogeneity with accusations of vagueness, pointing out that even its own adherents could not define it.[26] The two faults—if indeed they *are* faults—go logically together, for it follows that a group as assorted as the Transcendentalists were could scarcely function under hard-and-fast definition. What they required, and what they insisted upon, was freedom to think new thoughts and examine old ones; "definition," may be merely another name for "formula," "creed," "rule," or "dogma"—and these were things to be reacted against, not sought for.

It is perhaps because of this that there is, sometimes, a casualness—one could almost say a breeziness—in the Transcendentalists' handling of this issue, as though a precise definition were beside the point. In 1840, for example, Emerson wrote his mother (from Providence) that people had "a great appetite to know" what "this dread Transcendentalism" was. "In vain," he continues, "I disclaim all knowledge of that sect of Lidian's . . . ."[27] Less than a month later Margaret Fuller reported that things were going well, "but doubtless people will be disappointed, for they seem to be looking for the Gospel of Transcendentalism."[28] What seems significant is that neither suggests that this hunger for definition should be fed. It is almost the case of "if you have to ask for a definition, then you wouldn't be able to understand one if we gave it to you."

Nonetheless, we find that in both their private writings and in their public statements the Transcendentalists did "define"—or, perhaps more accurately, discuss—their position. Emerson wrote, after the first Symposium meeting. "Transcendentalism means, says our accomplished Mrs. B.,

[25] *Leonora Cranch Scott*, The Life and Letters of Christopher Pearse Cranch (*Boston, 1917*), *51. Of course, all of this corresponds to what the Transcendentalists made clear in their public pronouncements. Clarke and Cranch, in "R. W. Emerson and the New School" (1838), disclaimed any unanimity in the movement and replied to a critic that he had "failed in his definition . . . because he sought it in their [the Transcendentalists'] opinions and manners, rather than in their principles and spirit."—Quoted in P. Miller, The Transcendentalists, 203. Orestes Brownson, briefly a member of the group, wrote, "They differ widely in their opinions, and agree in little except in their common opposition to the old school. . . . No single term can describe them."—"Two Articles . . ." (1840), P. Miller, The Transcendentalists, 242. Cranch, responding to criticism of the diversity within the movement, wrote (in "Transcendentalism," 1841), "As if the 'New School,' as it is termed, could be a sect, with a fixed creed before it: as if it were not its glory that it is many-headed. . . ." P. Miller, The Transcendentalists, 300.*
[26] *Hawthorne's attack, in "The Celestial Railroad," is possibly the best known of the type: "He is a German by birth, and is called Giant Transcendentalist; but as to his form, his features, his substance, and his nature generally, it*

is the chief peculiarity of this huge miscreant that neither he for himself, nor anybody for him, has ever been able to describe him."
[27] EL, II, 266.
[28] *R. W. Emerson, J. F. Clarke, and W. H. Channing, Memoirs of Margaret Fuller Ossoli (Boston, 1852), II, Chapter 6, "Jamaica Plain," by W. H. Channing, 25–26.*

with a wave of her hand, *a little beyond*."[29] Cranch seemed to shelter himself in the movement's vague center, assuring his worried father (July, 1840) that Transcendentalism had always struck him "as a cold, barren system of Idealism . . . ." But then, with many protestations of ignorance,[30] he doubled back and gave an enthusiastic appraisal, which comes close to being a definition:

> . . . somehow the name "Transcendentalist" has become a nickname here for all who have broken away from the material philosophy of Locke, and the old theology of many of the early Unitarians, and who yearn for something more satisfying to the soul. It has almost become a synonym for one who, in whatever way, preaches the spirit rather than the letter. . . . It is convenient to have a name which may cover all those who contend for perfect freedom, who look for progress in philosophy and theology, and who sympathize with each other in the hope that the future will not always be as the past. The name "Transcendentalist" seems to be thus fixed upon all who profess to be on the movement side. . . .[31]

And the quest for a consistent definition is not aided by a tendency at all-inclusiveness that seems to be in conflict with Cranch's statement. Emerson, for example, asks, ". . . is there a Christian, or a civilian, a lawyer, a naturalist, or a physician so bold as not to rely at last on Transcendental truths?"[32] This kind of omnibus claim has been made by spokesmen for many movements.

We must also take into account the fact that Emerson sometimes made statements contrary to his own beliefs, possibly because he sometimes spoke in pique, for the sake of confounding an opponent rather than in the interests of accuracy. Thus he told one questioner, looking for a definition, that "he might simply omit what in his own mind he added from the tradition, and the rest would be Transcendentalism."[33] This is a strong statement of the movement's thrust away from tradition and toward individual freedom, and Emerson was aware of the dangers of anarchy implicit in such a position. Only three weeks earlier, he had criticized the Brook Farm people on this very issue. The Farm, he wrote,

> . . . contains several bold and consistent philosophers, both men and women, who carry out the theory, odiously enough, inasmuch as this centripetence of theirs is balanced by no centrifugence; this wish to obey impulse is guarded by no old, old Intellect—or that which knows metes and bounds.[34]

Finally, a newspaper story records that Alcott addressed a meeting, explaining his Transcendental doctrines "as far as could be done (for he ad-

29 EJ, *IV, 114.*

30 *Including such qualifying clauses as "So far . . . as I do know anything about it," "which is what I suppose to be the Transcendental philosophy," and "from the very slight idea I have of it. . . ."*

31 *Scott, 50–51. The emphasis on "the movement side" is similar to a definition quoted by Emerson: "A young man named Rodman, answered an inquiry by saying 'It [Transcendentalism] was a nickname which those who stayed behind, gave to those who went ahead.' "—EL, II, 266.*

32 *EJ, VI, 109. This statement is an echo of one made three months earlier in the* Dial. *In "Prophesy—Transcendentalism—Progress," J. A. Saxton wrote that Transcendentalism "is, in reality, the philosophy of common life, and of common experience. . . . It is the practical philosophy of belief and conduct. Every man is a transcendentalist, and all true faith, the motives of all just action, are transcendental."—Vol. II, No. 1, 87. The point here is not that Emerson's statement is indebted to Saxton, but that both of them reflect a feeling common to the group.*

33 EJ, *VI, 380.*

34 EJ, *VI, 374.*

mitted that they could not be explained by words). . . ."[35]

Transcendentalism's enemies ridiculed it for this inability to define its position,[36] but a more

objective appraisal would suggest that, as previously suggested, a clear and compelling definition would alter the nature of the movement. A strong "letter" can kill the "spirit;" a distinct position can lead to a distinct responsibility to conform: and it should be clear at this point that the Transcendentalists could not submerge their personalities in any highly formalized position.[37] This cloudiness of definition, then, at the same time that it suggests a certain weakness within the movement, is not inconsistent with the view it took of itself as able to accommodate that individualism which it so strongly advocated for all men.

This casualness of relationship and indifference to systematization is reflected in Alcott's description of Hedge's Club as "a company of earnest persons enjoying conversation on high themes and having much in common."[38] We may assume that these "high themes" often included issues central to the Transcendentalists—among these the immanence of God, the dominance of intuition over reason, the ability of man to perfect himself without divine aid, and the correspondence

---

[35] *F. B. Sanborn and W. T. Harris*, A. Bronson Alcott: His Life and Philosophy (*Boston, 1893*), *I, 327. Not all of his colleagues would agree, of course, and some of them did attempt to explain their position "by words"; but even in his own circle, Alcott's reputation was not that of a logician. For example, when Emerson received (for the* Dial) *Alcott's "Orphic Sayings," he wrote to Margaret Fuller that they were better than he had feared they would be, and, though they labored "with his inveterate faults," they would "pass for just and great" if she made sure to put Alcott's name over them.—EL, II, 291–292. To be certain she understood, he wrote again two weeks later: "Give them his name & those who know him will have his voice in their ear whilst they read, & the sayings will have a majestical sound."—EL, II, 294. Clearly, in Emerson's view, they had more sound than sense.*

Later in his life (in the 1870's), when Alcott was chairman of a discussion which began to get out of hand, he declared that he wished the disputants could find a higher footing on which they could agree. When they said that they did not know what he meant, he "subsided into his seat," muttering, "Well, I don't know as I know what I mean myself. . . . I am a mystic, you know."—Quoted in Henry A. Pochman, New England Transcendentalism and St. Louis Hegelianism (*Philadelphia, 1948), 52.*

[36] *This is not to suggest that no definitions were ever publicly attempted. In his lecture, "The Transcendentalist," Emerson wrote that "What is popularly called Transcendentalism among us, is Idealism; Idealism as it appears in 1842."—In* Miscellanies; Embracing Nature, Addresses, and Lectures (*Boston, 1866), 319. Further on he writes that Transcendentalism is "the Saturnalia or excess of Faith. . . ."—p. 328. Neither of these statements defines Transcendentalism clearly, nor is it probable—in the light of earlier quotations—that Emerson thought it either desirable or possible to do so. His statement in the* Dial *that "the more liberal thought of intelligent persons acquires a new name in each period or community; and in ours . . . has been designated as Transcendentalism" (Vol. II, No. III, 382), serves only*

the familiar purpose of appropriating to Emerson's position some words that have virtuous connotations. It does little to separate Transcendentalism from other movements of the time, many of which would probably have been pleased to exist under the same high-sounding phraseology.

[37] *An important part of their self-image is this willingness to entertain all views. After the Symposium's first meeting, Emerson wrote, "The role suggested for the club was this, that no man should be admitted whose presence excluded any one topic."—EJ, IV, 87. In the light of this statement Hedge's statement that "Brownson met with us once or twice, but became unbearable and was not afterward invited" suggests not intolerance on the part of the group so much as a feeling that Brownson's presence inhibited free discussion. Quoted in Arthur M. Schlesinger, Jr.,* Orestes A. Brownson: A Pilgrim's Progress (*Boston, 1939), 46.*

[38] *Odell Shepard,* Pedlar's Progress: the Life of Bronson Alcott (*Boston, 1937), 246.*

between the natural and the moral universe—but was it only their mutual interest in such ideas that held them together, or was there something else—something that will tell us more about their image of themselves?

Certainly they had in common what almost every new group receives—and often profits from—pressure from without, a pressure which sometimes holds together a group which might otherwise fly apart.[39] They were well aware of their radical position, and their reactions to attack ranged from Theodore Parker's almost cheerful comment that he was preaching "Transcendentalism, the grand heresy,"[40] to Alcott's soberer, "A day of controversy is coming over our heads. . . . Persecutions fierce and unrelenting are to be waged against us. Our tempers are to be tried."[41] But Alcott's prophecy, however grim, was not made out of fear, for although the Transcendentalists saw themselves as besieged by the parties of tradition, reaction, and vested interest, they doubted neither the rightness of their stand nor the inevitability of their victory. Their utterances, both public and private, show a view of themselves as invincible, a belief that at times takes the form of an almost serene self-confidence, but often is openly militant.

If an ability to satirize one's own position is indicative of confidence, then J. F. Clarke and C. P. Cranch epitomized this with their caricatures of Transcendental statements—especially some of Emerson's.[42] These were not merely furtive gestures of frivolity, for Clarke wrote the great man about the sketches—"not of the gravest character"—saying, "I should like to show them to you, for I think you would like them." It was Clarke's belief, the letter to Emerson continues, that since "the gravest things have also a comic side, it is very well . . . to detect it if one has the faculty."[43]

But the confidence also displays itself to outsiders. Alcott, for example, met a businessman who commiserated with him (without being asked to, and condescendingly, the report suggests) over the recent closing of his school. Alcott wanted no mealy-mouthed sympathy, and though his reply began almost plaintively, it ended with ringing confidence:

A man . . . who swims with the stream, shall indeed do well; but if, for conscience' sake, he turn and breast it, implying that it sets the wrong way, he is deemed fool-hardy; and if he duck under and disappear, it is just retribution, and best of all means of amendment. Yet see! he rises again in his time, lord of the wave, whose current he has turned in his own direction.[44]

Emerson could be even more sanguine. He

[39] It could be argued that Transcendentalism ceased to operate as a coherent movement—insofar as it ever did—when its ideas became "respectable," eliminating the outside pressure which held it together.

[40] Commager, 71.

[41] Pedlar's Progress, 224.

[42] For example, Cranch drew a thin human figure, surmounted by a giant eyeball, and wrote under it, "I become a transparent eyeball. . . ." This and other of his caricatures are shown in F. D. Miller's book (see note 19, p. 31). Sanborn and Harris note that "these caricatures were exhibited by Cranch with great glee to Theodore Parker . . . , to George Ripley, . . . and, no doubt, to Emerson himself, . . . but it is doubtful if anyone would have ventured to show them to Alcott at that period—so serious and superior was he."—II, 359n. It should be kept in mind that Cranch was satirizing the movement, not ridiculing it: ". . . the first things I did in that way were really for the private amusement of Clarke and myself and a few other Emersonians. . . . I always took pains to repudiate any Philistine idea that anything like ridicule was here attempted."—Quoted in F. D. Miller, p. 37.

[43] EL, II, 190.

[44] Sanborn and Harris, I, 319–320.

wrote Carlyle, ". . . if I live my neighbors must look for a great many more shocks, and perhaps harder to bear,"[45] and assured Hedge that "the present Church rattles ominously. It must vanish presently; & we shall have a real one. . . ."[46] He wrote enthusiastically to W. E. Channing, Jr., that "next Spring or Summer . . . we are to have a new Journal of better promise than any we have had or have in America. . . ."[47] And while this journal was in preparation, he warned its editor, Margaret Fuller, that some of her phrasing was too defensive: "Don't cry before you are hurt," he wrote the redoubtable Margaret.[48]

Theodore Parker's self-assurance evidences itself in a whimsical ridiculing of Transcendentalism's opponents. To a fellow clergyman he wrote (and it must be quoted at length to retain its flavor),

> Bowen has written a piece in the *Examiner* . . . on what think you? Why, on Emerson's "Nature." Pelion on Ossa is bad, Jew upon Bacon, but Bowen upon "Nature" caps the climax. He has given transcendentalism "sich a lick" that it is almost dead. Kant, Fichte, and Schelling appeared to me in a vision in the night, and deplored their sad estate. "Transcendentalism is clean gone," said Kant. "Verdammt," said Fichte. "What shall we do?" exclaimed Schelling. They could not be appeased.[49]

It was the same man, however, speaking more earnestly, who said, "I will go eastward and west-ward, and northward and southward, and make the land *ring*."[50]

It is apparent that in part the Transcendental confidence was inspired by their image of themselves as bringers of a new message, by a messianic self-portrait. As noted earlier, Cranch had written that Transcendentalism was composed of those who were "on the movement side," and members of the group used the word *prophet* freely. Alcott thought that men "should fight against their own age," that "whatever of honorable name they shall obtain, of lasting good which they shall effect for their race, is to be achieved by overcoming the evils of their time."[51] Emerson was constantly prodding the *Dial* in the direction of "newness." He wrote Margaret Fuller, for example, that a manuscript by Elizabeth Peabody had "great merits, but the topics Abraham Isaac Jacob & Esau [*sic*] . . . were a little too venerable for our slight modern purpose."[52] At about the same time he wrote her that he thought an Alcott paper was important to their journal because the forthcoming issue seemed to contain little else that might not appear in any other journal. "We have better things," he wrote, "but not in a new spirit."[53] The same note is sounded in a letter to Hedge almost two years later, written as the editorship was being transferred from Miss Fuller to Emerson: "It [the *Dial*] wants mainly

---

45 *Sanborn and Harris, I, 285.*

46 EL, *II, 219.*

47 EL, *II, 253.*

48 EL, *II, 286.* "*Simply say, 'We do not think alike' &c but leave out this canny bit of American caution,*" *he advised.*

49 *Commager, 64. This quotation, and others like it, makes one wonder how Perry Miller can write* (The Transcendentalists, *179*) *that among the Transcendentalists only Cranch "had a feeling for frivolity."*

50 *To Parker's frivolity and fire we may add a calm serenity. As Andrews Norton attacked Emerson's "Divinity School Address," Parker calmly wrote, "It is thought that chaos is coming back; the world is coming to an end. Some seem to think the Christianity which has stood some storms will not be able to weather this gale; and that truth, after all my Lord see that the sun still shines, the rain rains, and the dogs bark, and I have great doubts whether Emerson will overthrow Christianity this time."—Quoted in Commager, p. 68.*

51 AJ, *84.*

52 EL, *II, 350.*

53 EL, *II, 313.*

& only, some devotion on the part of its conductor to it, that it may not be the herbarium that it is of dried flowers, but the vehicle of some living & advancing mind."[54]

Related to this sense of a new mission was the need for action, a word with which not all of the Transcendentalists were comfortable. Many of them wanted to act, knew that they should, but could not. And so, characteristically, each saw action in his own way. Sometimes it was to be direct, as in the courageous parts played by Parker and Alcott in the fugitive slave demonstrations in 1854. Sometimes it was more sedentary—sermons, lectures, conversations, essays.[55] But at other times it was passive and withdrawn, as in Jones Very's quietism,[56] or in Alcott and Thoreau choosing prison rather than pay taxes, or Thoreau withdrawing to the woods "to transact some private business."

Perhaps because of the different guises which action wore, perhaps because of an exalted self-image of themselves as prophets of a new order, many of the Transcendentalists agonized over what they thought to be their own inaction or that of others. In 1838, Emerson wanted to ask

"these Reformers, Democrats, New Churches and Transcendentalists, Where is your Poetry, your Science, your Art? Why slumbers the Creative Hand?"[57] Later (August, 1839) he wrote Margaret Fuller that he wished Alcott "would work a small farm for his bread and dictate his gospel thence."[58] And one can sense Thoreau's impatience as he wrote Emerson (in 1847), "Mr. Alcott seems to have sat down for the winter. He has got Plato and other books to read. . . . If he would only stand upright and toe the line!"[59] But, as mentioned above, action can assume many forms, and Alcott himself, though unaware of these criticisms, disagreed with them. "I am no scholar," he wrote in his journal. "My might is not in my pen. . . . My organ is action. . . ."[60] In fact, Alcott turns the attack upon Emerson, who does not act, who lives only "to see and to write," whereas Alcott "must think," and set his thoughts "in the drapery of action. . . ."[61]

These comments, while suggesting disagreement over the nature of action and concern over the difficulties of taking it, in no way conceal its importance for the Transcendentalists. Each of them, if he were not a man of action, thought of himself as one—or longed to be one. Emerson, for example, in a letter to Caroline Sturgis, mentioned the security of their lives, the lack of doubt. Then he cited the early martyrs, who had died for their beliefs[62]—classic examples, we might

54 EL, *III, 36. Note also the first words in the* Dial: *"We invite the attention of our countrymen to a new design." However, in "The Transcendentalist" he wrote, "The first thing we have to say respecting what are called* new *views here in New England, at the present time, is, that they are not new, but the very oldest of thoughts cast into the mould of these new times."—*Miscellanies, *319. Here also we may recall his criticism of the Brook Farm people, who were too obedient to impulse, unguarded by "old, old Intellect. . . ."

55 *This is less true of the energetic Parker. Emerson wrote, "T. P. has beautiful fangs and the whole amphitheatre delights to see him worry and tear his victim."—Quoted in Commager, p. 84. The "anaconda" which had crushed "poor Alcott" now uses its fangs.*

56 *In "The Hand and Foot" Very begins:*
  The hand and foot that stir not, they shall find
  Sooner than all the rightful place to go . . .

57 *EJ, IV, 484.*
58 *EL, II, 216.*
59 *Quoted in Harold Clarke Goddard,* Studies in New England Transcendentalism *(New York, 1908), 159.*
60 *AJ, 128.*
61 *Pedlar's Progress, 227.*
62 *A little over a year later he wrote, in "The Transcendentalist," "The Martyrs were sawn asunder, or hung alive on meat-hooks. Cannot we screw our courage to patience and truth, and without complaint, or even with good-humour, await our turn of action in the Infinite Counsels?"—Miscellanies, 341.*

say, of a kind of "passive action" which Emerson found attractive. He continued:

> When I see how false our life is, how oppressive our politics, that there is no form of a redeeming man appearing in the whole population, & myself & my friends so inactive & acquiescent . . . that our protest & the action of our character is quite insignificant, heroism seems our dream & our insight a delusion. I am daily getting ashamed of my life.[63]

But despite this momentary disappointment, he was able to see that the movement *was* taking part in the affairs of the day. In one journal entry he noted (with evident relish) that "the view taken of Transcendentalism in State Street is that it threatens to invalidate contracts,"[64] and in another, "Machinery and Transcendentalism agree well. Stage-Coach and Railroad are bursting the old legislation like green withes."[65]

The *Dial*, too, was to play an active role in the life of the times. On the grounds that "the times demand of us all a more earnest aim," Emerson wished it "to contain the best advice on the topics of Government, Temperance, Abolition, Trade, and Domestic Life," and not be "a mere literary journal."[66] This journal entry was echoed a few days later in a letter to Margaret Fuller, in which he suggested that they "might court some of the good fanatics and publish chapters on every head in the whole Art of Living."[67] Some months later he again wrote, hopefully, "I should for once in our too spiritual magazine write

something that by courtesy might be called practical."[68]

Finally, a journal entry by the youthful Thoreau (February, 1838) urges action, and ends on the familiar messianic note:

> It is wholesome advice,—"to be a man amongst folks." Go into society if you will, or if you are unwilling, and take a human interest in its affairs. . . . Armed with a manly sincerity, you shall not be trifled with, but drive this business of life. It matters not how many men are to be addressed,—rebuked,—provided one man rebuke them.[69]

Systemlessness of program, strong self-confidence, a messianic desire for action—all these acted to separate the Transcendentalists from the common man, whom many of them saw as timid, indifferent, passive. As is common with reformers, the Transcendentalists saw themselves as dwelling above the crowd, and their oft-repeated cries for action frequently came to nothing because of this.[70] Emerson, who on the one hand wanted the *Dial* to be practical, on the other wanted it to have nothing to do with "the drowsy public,"[71] and to one *Dial* contributor he wrote that an article appearing in "that modest mendicant magazine" would be "a very harmless rehearsal to a very small private audience. . . ."[72] "The poor old

[63] EL, *II, 347.*
[64] EJ, *VI, 82.*
[65] EJ, *VI, 397.*
[66] EJ, *V, 447.*
[67] EL, *II, 322.*

[68] EL, *II, 381.*
[69] *Bradford Torrey and Francis H. Allen, editors,* The Journal of Henry D. Thoreau *(Boston, 1949), I, 27–28.*
[70] *There was, of course, a reform wing—with Orestes Brownson as one of its leaders—which looked with misgivings at Emerson. Nonetheless, one has the feeling that the Transcendentalists saw themselves waging war against Unitarianism far over the heads of the men on the street.*
[71] EL, *II, 285.*
[72] EL, *III, 198–199. On taking over the editorship of the* Dial *(in 1842), Emerson found that it had fewer than 300 subscribers.*

public," he wrote Margaret Fuller, "stand just where they always did,—garrulous orthodox conservative [sic] whilst you say nothing; silent the instant you speak; and perfectly & universally convertible the moment the right word comes."[73] Those knowing Margaret's imperiousness can be certain that she shared these views, and we are not surprised to find her describing the typical Unitarian congregation as "that crowd of upturned faces with their look of unintelligent complacency."[74] And at least one minister believed that his safety lay not in his parishioners' courage, but in their ignorance. Theodore Parker, whose congregation stood by him as the other Unitarian ministers sought to oust him, wrote, "I preach abundant heresies, and they all go down, for the listeners do not know how heretical they are. I preach the worst of all things, Transcendentalism."[75]

This thrust toward exclusiveness, coupled in this case with a high degree of sensitivity to criticism, led Alcott to find a kind of solace in Emerson's loss of favor following his address at the Divinity School. For, reasoned Alcott, this would mean that Emerson's lectures "will . . . be honored by the absence of coxcombs. Bigots will hold him as a profane person. Only . . . fair, noble, free souls will appear."[76]

Like many of his associates, Emerson had mixed

feelings regarding this gulf between them and the public, feelings that doubtless were interwoven with his ambivalence toward action. He seemed to believe that things must be accomplished by all men working together, yet his own personality drove him from easy communion, even with his close associates. In "The Transcendentalist," which seems an apology for or justification of "passive action," he argued at length that withdrawal has a logic of its own. Nevertheless, he wrote,

> The good, the illuminated, sit apart from the rest, censuring their dulness and vices, as if they thought that, by sitting very grand in their chairs, the very brokers, attorneys, and congressmen would see the error of their ways, and flock to them. But the good and wise must learn to act, and carry salvation to the combatants and demagogues in the dusty arena below.[77]

A self-image may be inferred from these last lines, which posit two levels of existence: in "the dusty arena below" are the "combatants and demagogues"; above (as potential bringers of salvation), and—Emerson implies—not engaged, are the Transcendentalists.[78]

To these more-or-less indirect causes for separation between the Transcendentalists and the world at large we may add a direct cause (one suggested in part by the first section of this paper), which

[73] EL, II, 271. Rusk alludes to a newspaper review of Emerson's lecture, "Politics," in which Emerson is supposed to have implied "that the common people were an unintelligent brute force. . . ."—EL, II, 266n.
[74] P. Miller, The Transcendentalists, 8.
[75] Commager, 71.
[76] AJ, 103. Two months later (Dec. 1838) he feels that his prophecy has been borne out: "The audience was choice. The truly worthy of the metropolis were present. Fashion was not there. Timid conservativism was not there. Bigotry did not show her face. . . . The free, the bold, the seeking, docile, were there. . . ." AJ., 107.

[77] Miscellanies, 328.
[78] Here, again, we must except the reform wing. In 1838, for example, Brownson wrote that "the masses are . . . not so dependent on us, the enlightened few, as we sometimes think them." In fact, he added, "philosophy is not needed by the masses: but they who separate themselves from the masses, and who believe that the masses are entirely dependent on them for truth and virtue, need it, in order to bring them back, and bind them again to universal Humanity."—"Francis Bowen," in P. Miller, The Transcendentalists, 185.

intensified any tendency toward aloofness. This was the Transcendentalists' reverence for the human spirit and the emphasis which this threw onto the need for individualism and self-reliance. Emerson's "Self-Reliance" is an extended statement of this interest, as is *Walden*. And neither Emerson nor Thoreau had much use for reform insofar as it implied that *they* should reform *others* (though they might "carry salvation" to them). Thoreau, who in 1838 had looked for one man to rebuke mankind, by 1840 is moving toward *Walden*:

> How shall I help myself? By withdrawing into the garret, and associating with spiders and mice, determining to meet myself face to face sooner or later. . . . The most positive life that history notices has been a constant retiring out of life, a wiping one's hands of it, seeing how mean it is, and having nothing to do with it.[79]

And Alcott asked, in his journal, why a man needed a state to maintain and protect him. "Self-helping is the best economy," he added.[80]

The self-image that emerges from the private writings of the Transcendentalists is in keeping, I believe, with the image created by their public statements. We see a group of men and women, each dedicated to a combination of ideas, but each retaining his own individuality, each interpreting and utilizing these ideas as his own conscience and

intelligence demand. Much of their time was spent defending their position. To the charge that they were heretics they would reply that they were indeed, but that they took their places in a long line of heretics, each of whom had ultimately triumphed—as they would themselves—to mankind's benefit. To the charge that they took too much action, they would reply that the times required it; that they took too little action, that one must first put his own house in order. To the charge that they were overly optimistic, they would reply that confidence in the rightness of their position gave them no other choice; that they seemed too pessimistic, especially about each other, that one whose ideals are high is often disappointed.

It is an exalted self-image—a messianic one. They saw themselves as the forerunners of a better day. "There is no such thing as a Transcendental party," Emerson wrote; "there is no pure Transcendentalist; . . . we know of none but prophets and heralds of such a philosophy."[81] It was of such a one that Margaret Fuller wrote in 1830, six years before the formal beginnings of the movement, and it seems fitting to close this essay with the Transcendental image in its most ideal form:

> *May 4th, 1830.*—I have greatly wished to see among us such a person of genius as the nineteenth century can afford—*i.e.*, one who has tasted in the morning of existence the extremes of good and ill, both imaginative and real. I had imagined a person endowed by nature with that acute sense of Beauty (*i.e.*, Harmony or Truth) and that vast capacity of desire, which give soul to love and ambition. I had wished this person might grow up to manhood alone (but not alone in crowds); I would have placed him in a situation so retired, so obscure, that he would quietly, but

79 *Torrey and Allen, I, 132–133.*

80 AJ, *189. Here is a good example of the distinction between the world's image of a man and his own. The story of Alcott's dependence upon his hard-working and practical wife is well known to those who have read of the Fruitlands experiment or who know anything about Alcott's life. His later years were made comfortable not by "self-helping," but by the financial success and generosity of his daughter, Louisa May Alcott.*

81 "*The Transcendentalist," 327–328.*

without bitter sense of isolation, stand apart from all surrounding him. I would have had him go on steadily, feeding his mind with congenial love, hopefully confident that if he only nourished his existence into perfect life, Fate would, at fitting season, furnish an atmosphere and orbit meet for his breathing and exercise. I wished he might adore, not fever for, the bright phantoms of his mind's creation, and believe them but the shadows of external things to be met with hereafter. After this steady intellectual growth had brought his powers to manhood, so far as the ideal can do it, I wished this being might be launched into the world of realities, his heart glowing with the ardor of an immortal toward perfection, his eyes searching everywhere to behold it; I wished he might collect into one burning point those withering, palsying convictions, which, in the ordinary routine of things, so gradually pervade the soul, that he might suffer, in brief space, agonies of disappointment commensurate with his unpreparedness and confidence. And I thought, thus thrown back on the representing pictorial resources I supposed him originally to possess, with such material, and the need he must feel of using it, such a man would suddenly dilate into a form of Pride, Power, and Glory,—a centre, round which asking, aimless hearts might rally,—a man fitted to act as interpreter to the one tale of many-languaged eyes![82]

[82] *P. Miller*, The Transcendentalists, *333.*

THE GENTEEL TRADITION:
A RE-INTERPRETATION

Frederic I. Carpenter*

Some thirty years ago, George Santayana first named and described "The Genteel Tradition."[1] Since then many men have repeated his words:

> America is not simply a young country with an old mentality: it is a country with two mentalities, one a survival of the beliefs and standards of the fathers, the other an expression of the instincts, practices and discoveries of the younger generations. . . . The one is all aggressive enterprise; the other is all genteel tradition.[2]

The persistent popularity of his description suggests that it is essentially true. But the partisan violence which it has engendered suggests that its meaning is confused. Santayana described truly the general conflict between aristocratic tradition and democratic practice in American life and thought. But he misunderstood the historic origins of this conflict, and he misinterpreted its modern manifestations. During the last generation, the terms of the dualism have become clearer.

In naming the genteel tradition, Santayana fathered two major confusions. First, he identified this tradition with Puritanism,* and traced the genteel mentality to Calvinistic theology. This accentuated the confusion in general usage between "puritanism" as a state of mind, and Puri-

---

[1] George Santayana, "The Genteel Tradition in American Philosophy," in Winds of Doctrine (New York, 1912; hereinafter, "The Genteel Tradition"), 186–215.

[2] "The Genteel Tradition," 187–188.

*Throughout this essay, as uniformly in the New England Quarterly, Puritanism, the historical, religious, and political movement, is distinguished by capitalization from puritanism, a temperament prevalent throughout Anglo-Saxon history [Editor's Note].

---

*FREDERIC I. CARPENTER (1903–   ) is a Research Associate in English at the University of California. His publications include Emerson Handbook (1953), American Literature and the Dream (1958), and Robinson Jeffers (1962). Reprinted by permission of the author and the New England Quarterly, Vol. 15, No. 3 (September, 1942), 427–443.

216

tanism as a historical movement. Second, Santayana denied that the ideal opposite of the genteel tradition was really a "mentality" at all. "Instincts practices, and discoveries," he called it, and added that "in all the higher things of the mind—in religion, in literature, in the moral emotions—it is the hereditary spirit that prevails."[3] Specifically he charged that Walt Whitman possessed nothing more than "sensations,"[4] and that William James possessed no consistent philosophy.[5] Identifying the genteel tradition with Puritan theology, he also denied that popular democracy had any clear ideal basis.

These two opinions may be disproved. The genteel tradition which Santayana named was something less—and something more—than Puritanism in America. Historically, it derived only from the conservative half of the Puritan religion. And beyond Puritanism, it derived from the traditionally aristocratic culture of the Central and Southern States, as well.[6] It may be defined broadly as the traditionalist mentality in America, as that has been influenced by Puritan morality and aristocratic culture.

Historically, the genteel tradition sprang from Puritanism, but only from one half of that religion. For the Puritanism of early New England

had included a liberal, and even radical, element. The most conservative theocrat recognized that "the unknown God" did not always follow the customs of traditional morality. "Moral living" was good, but "divine grace" was infinitely better. The stern realism that recognized this unpalatable truth, and the intense "piety"[7] which positively gloried in it, gave greatness to the old faith. But the narrow traditionalism and intolerant moralism which we often call puritan, resulted in its later decadence.

In opposition to the genteel tradition, this radical element of the earlier Puritanism developed into the Transcendentalism of later New England: the Transcendental idealists worshiped the unknown God with intense piety. Although Santayana called them genteel, these transcendentalists were neither traditional nor moralistic. Emerson prophesied a new America, and Whitman continued his prophecy. Even the later pragmatists stemmed from this root.[8] The worst confusion of American thought is that which seeks to divorce the idealism of the early Puritans and the Transcendentalists from the idealism of the later democrats and pragmatists. Not only Santayana but many popular critics have furthered this interpretation. Yet Emerson did more than any other single writer to discredit the genteel tradition of orthodox morality: in him Transcendentalism became "the philosophy of democracy,"[9] and the arch enemy of conservatism. It stemmed from Puritan piety,

[3] *"The Genteel Tradition,"* 188.

[4] *In* Interpretations in Poetry and Religion (*New York, 1900*), *180. See also H. A. Myers,"Whitman's Conception of the Spiritual Democracy,"* American Literature, *VI* (November, 1934), *241; and F. I. Carpenter, "Walt Whitman's Eidolon,"* College English, *III (March, 1942), 534–545.*

[5] *In* Character and Opinion in the United States (*New York, 1920*), *64–97.*

[6] *If this essay emphasizes the Puritanism of New England to the partial exclusion of the culture of the Central and Southern States, it is partly because the Puritanism of New England was more articulate than the religious culture of other regions, and partly because Santayana so emphasized it.*

[7] *See Joseph Haroutunian,* Piety versus Moralism (*New York, 1932*); *and Perry Miller,* The New England Mind (*New York, 1939; hereinafter, "Miller."*)

[8] *See F. I. Carpenter, "William James and Emerson,"* American Literature, *XI (March, 1939), 39–57; and "Charles Sanders Peirce: Pragmatic Transcendentalist,"* New England Quarterly, *XIV (March, 1941), 34–48.*

[9] *John Dewey, "Emerson: the Philosopher of Democracy,"* in Characters and Events (*New York, 1929*), *69–77.*

but repudiated the authoritarian moralism of the past.

Neither the intense piety of the old Puritanism, nor the enthusiasm of the later Transcendental idealists was traditional, or "genteel." But from this point of view, the anti-transcendental morality of Hawthorne *was*; and the tragic vision of Melville also described the futility of the transcendental ideal. In *The Scarlet Letter* Hawthorne recognized a certain heroism in self-reliance, but emphasized its greater evil. And in *Moby Dick*, Melville described the heroism of Ahab, but also his fanatical delusion. In their later novels, both authors denounced the libertarian heresy and returned to traditional orthodoxy: although they borrowed the new techniques to describe the liberal emotions, their moral philosophy remained traditional. Therefore they illustrate the genteel tradition at its best, recognizing the beauty and the heroism of the Transcendental ideal but denouncing its romantic extravagances.

Through three centuries of American life, this genteel tradition has developed and changed. From the early Puritans to the new humanists, its champions have denounced as utopian all dreams of a new world. But from the early Puritans to the modern pragmatists, the democratic dreamers have opposed, or "transcended" this tradition.

Like most Americans, the early Puritans really worshiped two Gods: they worshiped an absolute and unknown God, whose will was secret and whose face was hidden;[10] but also they worshiped the God of revelation or tradition, whose will was declared in the Bible, and whose face was turned toward man. Between the great "I Am" of piety and the revealed "I Ought" of morality, they admitted no discrepancy, in theory. The few sought the grace of the hidden God, while the

many obeyed literally the laws laid down. The Bible, and after the Bible, literature, revealed this God to the populace.

The narrow puritanism against which the modern mind has revolted is that traditional half of historic Puritanism which deduced inflexible moral law from Biblical revelation. What we call the genteel tradition has elevated past precept into omnipotence, and conversely, has minimized the difficult truth which Calvin taught: that divine grace may supersede traditional precept. Looking back, the modern historian can see that "the space between the revealed will and the secret will . . . was the portal through which ran the highway of intellectual development."[11] But although the greater Puritans gloried in the unknown God and kept the portal open, their gentler descendants institutionalized revelation and sought to close the gate.

Moralistic "Puritanism" and secular "humanism," therefore, both sought to interpret and to apply God's will as revealed in the Bible and the classics. They disagreed only in the supreme authority which Puritanism granted to the Bible. They agreed that "the Revival of *Letters* . . . prepared the World for the Reformation of *Religion*."[12] They both appealed to logic and human reason to interpret the Bible and the classics. They both applied their interpretations primarily to the fields of morality and human conduct. And they agreed that art (in its broadest sense) was all-important: "Perhaps we have laid bare the innermost essence of the Puritan mind when we find that its highest philosophical reach was a systematic delineation of the liberal arts."[13] The arts direct conduct, and therefore man should imitate art. "Nature is inchoate art; art is nature consum-

---

10 *See Miller, 20.*

11 *Miller, 21.*
12 *Miller, 97.*
13 *Miller, 161.*

mated."[14] The nature of God may never be understood, but the Book of man may be.

This all-too-human half of Puritanism reached its nadir in eighteenth-century New England when the old piety became mere complacency, and the old morality, ritual:

> Our churches turn genteel:
> Our parsons grow trim and trig,
> With wealth, wine and wig
> And their heads are covered with meal.[15]

Of the old religion, only the moral and churchly forms remained. But these forms were, and always had been, important: the new "gentility" was no "reversal" of the Puritan philosophy, as has been asserted,[16] but rather a distortion of it, through exaggeration of the formal element. The old revelation had merely become absolutely systematized.

This moralistic puritanism, on the other hand, reached its most mature development in the proverbial wisdom of Benjamin Franklin. Wholly "emancipated" from the old Puritan piety, Franklin reasserted the Puritan morality in its simplest terms: "Revelation had indeed no weight with me, as such; but I entertained an opinion, that, though certain actions might not be bad, *because* they were forbidden by it . . . ; yet probably these actions might be forbidden *because* they were bad for us."[17] Having freed himself, that is, from the dead hand of the past, he nevertheless returned to the past for wisdom.

This was valid. Tradition is good. As Stuart

Sherman has pointed out,[18] "tradition" also includes the tradition of revolt, of progress, and of change. It is good, therefore, as long as it includes all the wisdom of the past, and not merely the prudential part. But when tradition excludes novelty and freedom, it becomes genteel. It denies the unknown God in the name of the God of Moses.

Franklin himself escaped this narrow traditionalism by virtue of his broad tolerance, his instinctive democracy, and his scientific spirit. But his wisdom remained partial. He emphasized the traditional morality so exclusively that he seemed to deny the religious idealism. In his phrase, "health, wealth, and wisdom" became the ideal ends of life. And this fairly translated one-half of the Puritan gospel. But the other half—"the Covenant of Grace" and the practice of piety—he omitted. The intense devotion to the unknown God which motivated Jonathan Edwards would have to wait for the advent of Transcendentalism. Then the religious ideals of "God, freedom, and immortality" would compete anew with the moralistic ideals of "health, wealth, and wisdom" for the devotion of the descendants of the Puritans. Then the mind of America would revolt against the too-narrow Puritan morality with a violence fathered by the almost forgotten Puritan piety.

Considered politically, of course, Transcendentalism was not necessarily a liberal philosophy. It might result either in revolt or in reaction, for "God, freedom, and immortality" were not partisan ideals. The thought of Kant, developing through Hegel, resulted eventually in a justification of the totalitarian state. Only in America did the alliance of Transcendentalism with the anti-slavery movement and with Western democracy produce complete liberalism.

[14] *Miller, 166.*

[15] *Quoted in Herbert Schneider*, The Puritan Mind (*New York, 1930*), 90.

[16] *See Schneider*, The Puritan Mind, 97.

[17] The Autobiography *in* The Complete Works of Benjamin Franklin, *edited by John Bigelow (New York, 1887–1888), I, 139.*

[18] *S. P. Sherman, "Tradition," in* Americans (*New York, 1924), 13–27.*

But considered intellectually, Transcendentalism was liberalism itself. It was "the newness." It was the revolt of the younger generation against the forces of conservative tradition. It was the deification of the undiscovered. It was the worship of the unknown God.

Therefore Transcendentalism stood opposed to all forms of traditionalism. As Santayana recognized, it "embodied, in a radical form, the spirit of Protestantism as distinguished from its inherited doctrines; it was autonomous, undismayed, calmly revolutionary."[19] But this historic Transcendentalism had no new system to offer, specifically, in place of the old. Therefore it often resulted in "the dilemma of the liberated." By reaction, it sometimes caused a blind return to tradition. "Similarly in Italy, during the Renaissance, the Catholic tradition could not be banished from the intellect, since there was nothing articulate to take its place."[20] Therefore Santayana considered Transcendentalism a failure. And modern American humanists have sought to escape this frustration by a return to tradition—to religion—to authority—even to Catholicism.[21]

It is true that the negative or anti-authoritarian element of Transcendentalism gave grounds for this negative, or anti-liberal, reaction against it. If the old idealism had resulted only in emptiness and denial, the reaction of the traditional humanists would have been wholly justified. But even the hostile Santayana recognized that Walt Whitman had developed an inarticulate democracy in place of the old moralism, and that William James had developed a more articulate pragmatism. These developments were positive and progressive. But the reactions of nineteenth-century

traditionalists against "the newness" were more obvious.

By far the greatest of the latter-day puritans were two who escaped the smugness of gentility through their intense sympathy with the followers of the unknown God. Having been tempted, like Faust, with the desire for freedom, they did not imagine all apostates from traditional morality to be absolute sinners—rather they described them as the dupes of a romantic idealism. In *The Scarlet Letter* Hawthorne recognized the integrity of his transcendental heroine, even though he condemned her. And in *Moby Dick* Melville realized the magnificence of Ahab, even while describing the inevitable destruction of his romantic ideal. Although these two writers went beyond the genteel tradition to pay homage to the unknown God, they returned to tradition, arguing that men should follow a known god rather than seek a fancied perfection.

Perhaps Hawthorne was the most typical, as well as one of the greatest, writers of the genteel tradition. Born in puritan Salem, in an atmosphere of genteel poverty, he learned to revere as well as to hate his heritage. If he accepted for himself the curse of Maule, which he described in *The House of the Seven Gables*, he did not accept it blindly. In *The Scarlet Letter* he followed in imagination the alternative of individual freedom to its end, and concluded that, like Dimmesdale, it was not for him. In *The Blithedale Romance* he rejected the alternative of social liberalism. And finally, in *The Marble Faun*, his imagination sought refuge in Rome, the source of all orthodox tradition. Through the character of Hilda, who worshiped at the shrine of the Virgin Mary and became "almost a Catholic," he prophesied the return of modern Americans such as T. S. Eliot to the Catholic faith. But Hawthorne remained true to his own tradition, and ended his days in ancestral New England. Rejecting the two living religions

19 *"The Genteel Tradition,"* 196.
20 *"The Genteel Tradition,"* 201.
21 See Yvor Winters, Maule's Curse (*Norfolk, Connecticut, 1938*).

of militant liberalism and of Roman Catholicism, he resigned himself, without hope, to his own puritan traditionalism.

Less genteel and less puritan than Hawthorne, Melville followed a less familiar path to the same end. Where Hawthorne experimented with freedom at Brook Farm and in imagination, Melville actually pursued this ideal over the seven seas. But in *Mardi* he concluded that ideal freedom was empty, and in *Pierre* that it was immoral. In *Clarel* he recorded his pilgrimage to the traditional Holy Land. And in *Billy Budd* he reaffirmed the justice of the established morality, even when it condemned a righteous man to death. With the sad eyes of a reformed romantic, he accepted as inevitable the defeat of human freedom. And like Hawthorne, he too resigned himself to fate.

Thus Transcendental liberty caused reaction: to escape the apparent emptiness following the new revolt from tradition, Hawthorne returned to the Puritan past and Melville to the stern old morality. Hawthorne even suggested that the vacuum might be filled by the Roman Catholic faith. But meanwhile other descendants of the Puritans sought to fill it instead with the rich culture of a humanistic past. If the religion of liberty seemed empty, if the religion of Puritanism was outmoded, and the religion of Rome alien, there remained the religion of human culture. This was more credible than Calvinism, and more universal than Catholicism. The immense popularity of the writings of Longfellow and Lowell bears witness to the genuine spiritual need which their gentility satisfied. If the narrow Puritan humanism had failed, the broad classical humanism might succeed.

To be exact, Puritan humanism now expanded to become classical humanism; the religion of the Bible became the religion of Books. Lowell felt this continuity when he prophesied, with characteristically heavy humor, that "the broad fore-

heads and the long heads will win the day at last . . . , and it will be enough if we feel as keenly as our Puritan founders did that those organs of empire may be broadened and lengthened by culture."[22] Although it is significant that he described culture as a means to empire, it is even more significant that he traced it to the Puritan past and that he made it a continuing means to salvation: "It will be enough."

As a religion, genteel humanism had two aspects, the first moralistic, the second pious (in the more modern sense of the word). The first found expression in Longfellow's famous "Psalm of Life," and second in his "The Day is Done." Although the first bore a certain resemblance to the Transcendental faith, it preached a morality not of self-reliance but of dutiful acceptance: "With a heart for any fate . . . Learn to labor and to wait." And the second preached the religion of culture, that literature has power to make life acceptable:

> . . . songs have power to quiet
> The restless pulse of care
> And come like the benediction
> That follows after prayer.

But the purpose of both poems was religious, like the purpose of Puritan humanism. Either poetry inspires, like a psalm, or else it consoles, like a prayer. To take the place of the Puritan faith which had faded, Longfellow substituted a more humanistic piety.

For this reason, perhaps, Longfellow was greater than Lowell: where the critic merely preached the culture of the classical past, the poet made it live. He filled the spiritual emptiness which the Transcendental revolt from tradition had caused. He

[22] From "*New England Two Centuries Ago*," Among My Books (*Boston, 1871*), 244.

invoked the gods of Olympus and of Valhalla to reinforce the old Puritan God. And in a twilight realm of poetry, his fabulous heroes kept the faith. Lowell was to make clear the implications of that faith.

Like Hawthorne and Melville, Lowell had shared in the Transcendental dream. His essay on Thoreau describes this enthusiasm from the mature perspective of *My Study Windows*. There was something good in it, of course: "the Puritanism that cannot die" had produced Emerson. But there was more that was bad in it; Thoreau reflected its selfishness, its moral emptiness, and its morbid escape to nature.

Instead of this naturalism with its worship of newness, Lowell sought to substitute the solid wisdom of the human past: "What a sense of security in an old book that Time has criticised for us!" From the confusion of modern thought, he turned to the "sane and balanced" writers before Rousseau. More liberal than his follower, Irving Babbitt, he agreed that Rousseau "is as consistent as a man who admits new ideas can ever be." But his conclusion is clear: what is new cannot be consistent, and what is traditional is good. "Democracy" is good, he said, because "properly understood, it is a conservative force." And America, the child of Great Britain, is "a democracy with conservative instincts." To strengthen this hereditary conservatism the genteel descendant of the Puritans preached a religion of humanistic culture: *Among My Books*.

Following Lowell, a host of minor gentlemen refined the old tradition still further. Thomas Bailey Aldrich, E. C. Stedman, E. P. Whipple, and Charles Eliot Norton became so exclusively "genteel," indeed, that they hardly remained human. Were it not for their far-reaching influence—first, on the thought of the new humanists, and secondly, on popular taste—they might now be forgotten. But they helped carry the old ideas to their logical conclusions.

While this gentility was developing, the meaning of words was changing, and narrowing. For instance, "puritanism" was slowly coming to mean an exclusive, moral traditionalism. And "humanism" was coming to mean an equally exclusive cultural traditionalism. The content of "puritanism" and of "humanism" was being divided in half. Reacting against the Transcendental enthusiasm, gentility was supplanting the old gods with half-gods; soon, only the cultured would be human.

The exclusive aspect of this "new humanism" found its clearest expression in the first book of Irving Babbitt, in which the young author specifically avowed his debt to the gentle Charles Eliot Norton. In *Literature and the American College*, Babbitt outlined all his major ideas. The Renaissance humanists, he said, had taken for their motto Terence's "*humani nihil a me alienum puto*," and had embraced everything human. But they had missed true (*i.e.*, classical) humanism because they had denied "the idea of selection," which Aristotle had first established. "Very few of the early humanists were really humane . . . Rabelais, for instance, is neither decorous or select."[23] So the new humanist emphasized selection rather than humanity—classical culture rather than human sympathy. Rejecting the indecorous elements of the broadly humanistic past, he sought to establish a strict cultural tradition, just as the latter-day puritans had rejected the unknown God to establish a strict moral tradition.

As Santayana was to point out, this was really not humanism at all, but supernaturalism.[24] It was

[23] Literature and the American College (*Boston, 1908*), *20.*

[24] The Genteel Tradition at Bay (*New York, 1931*), *28.*

the degradation of one half of humanity and the deification of the other half, an attempt "to sacrifice ruthlessly one set of passions merely in order to intensify another set." That the virtuous set of passions were called "human," and were even denied the name of "passions" made little difference. Essentially this new humanism sought to reinforce a passionate conservatism by an appeal to the quasi-religious authority of classical literature. It made cultural absolutism the cloak for moral absolutism. "The new humanism" was really the old Puritan moralism in new clothes.

The virtue of this new humanism was that it recaptured some of the religious enthusiasm and logical rigor of the old Puritan theology. Unlike the urbane Lowell and the genteel Norton, Babbitt fought for his convictions against all comers, using all the weapons of the intellect. Let an opponent once admit his premises, and his conclusions were inescapable. The only way to conquer him (besides ignoring him, as many critics did) was to attack his first principles (as Santayana did). His logic was powerful.

The weakness of Babbitt's "humanism" was partly the narrowness of his moral principles, but even more the rigidity with which he applied them to literature. If his moral philosophy was authoritarian, it was nevertheless based upon a classical tradition. But his literary applications of this moral philosophy were wholly negative: he damned every important modern writer since Rousseau. Where others had been content to describe the failure of the romantic enthusiasm, he sought utterly to eradicate it. Where Hawthorne, Melville, and even Lowell, had sympathized while they condemned, Babbitt denied all human value to Romance. He insisted not only that literature should inculcate strict morality, but also that it should refrain from treating the romantic passions with sympathy. *Moby Dick* seemed to him bad

because the character of Ahab lacked all self-restraint, or "decorum": that it described the self-destruction of the monomaniac hero was not enough.

Clearly, this narrow "humanism" implied "puritanism," and even a genteel censorship: it would not merely condemn all unrestrained emotion in literature but would wholly exclude it. Against this narrowness, therefore, other "humanists" objected. Paul Elmer More sought to apply Babbitt's standards with greater tolerance, although with less precision. Yvor Winters showed how even the romantic heroism of Melville's Ahab and of Hawthorne's Hester implied a traditional morality. And a recent humanist has suggested that, although Babbitt's ethical or moral criticism was usually excellent, his literary criticism was merely negative.[25]

Thus the genteel tradition which began as Puritan moralism, has returned to orthodox morality as the source of all judgment and the end of all argument. It has rejected, therefore, the Puritan piety which admitted the omnipotence of a hidden God. It has rejected the Transcendental enthusiasm which sought to discover the hidden God, even in defiance of established morality. It has rejected the naturalistic science which has called all revealed truth into question. It has rejected even that part of the humanistic tradition which gloried in the natural instincts of man. Although it has recognized the strength, and even the beauty, of the human instinct of liberty and desire for newness, it has opposed this liberalism in the name of morality and of law.

If the genteel tradition is narrow, illiberal, and opposed to everything modern, why is it so strong? Santayana prophesied its death, but lived

[25] *Wylie Sypher, "Irving Babbitt," in the* New England Quarterly (*March, 1941*), *XIV*, 64.

to describe its renaissance. A Marxian critic has attacked it as "fantastic," but has approved T. S. Eliot's statement that only this tradition and Marxian socialism offer living faiths to modern man.[26] In American universities, even in the untraditional West, the tradition continues to flourish. And it continues to govern popular taste, as evidenced by the best-seller lists and by the frequent outbursts of "moral" censorship by elected authorities. The genteel tradition is not dead, nor is it dying.

The reason for this vitality is suggested by the words of a hostile critic: "In the plainest, least evasive of words, gentility is conservatism. It is the moral and social orthodoxy of the bourgeois who has, so to speak, been 'refined.' "[27] But if the genteel tradition is conservatism, a fair majority of Americans are genteel; a recent poll of public opinion showed that fifty-three per cent of all American citizens consider themselves "conservative," rather than "liberal." And if the genteel tradition is "bourgeois," a majority of Americans believe that they belong to the middle class. Finally, most middle-class Americans still desire to become "refined," as well: the old cultural ideal remains popular in our political democracy.

Actually, the genteel tradition has developed from historic American beginnings, and remains widely popular today. But beyond these clear facts, the tradition also includes permanent values. It reaffirms the truth of those humanistic ideals which were preliminary, and therefore remain necessary, even to the naturalistic philosophy of a scientific age. And it reaffirms the eternal necessity of ideals, or "standards" of some sort, to every age: it challenges democratic naturalism to define its own new standards.

The old Puritan and humanistic virtues of hard work, discipline, moderation, and the rest (which Franklin formulated and which Irving Babbitt reaffirmed) can never be discarded. Emerson and Whitman did not deny them, but rather relegated them to the realm of unconscious habit, and then went on to emphasize that imagination, invention, and artistic creation are greater virtues than these. But in the process of revolt from the extreme discipline of the old morality, Transcendental self-reliance and equalitarian democracy often neglected, and often still neglect, the preliminary needs of discipline and routine. The old Puritans and the new humanists have wisely emphasized the evil consequences of this neglect.

The genteel tradition has recently found imaginative embodiment in the character of Henry Pulham, Esquire, hero of John Marquand's novel. As the personnel director of a New York advertising firm says of him: "There is something basic there."[28] Among the "idea-men" and high-pressure salesmen of the modern metropolis, this genteel and conscientious routineer remains indispensable. And the solid strength of his character emphasizes the unstable weakness of his associates'.

But when this typical Henry Pulham, Esquire, returns to his ancestral Boston to fill the niche which his father has occupied in the mahogany offices of a securities investment firm, he becomes merely genteel. He cuts himself off from the struggle of modern life to take refuge in a decadent security. He denies the potentialities of growth which have always lain dormant in his character, until what was "basic" becomes merely solid. The fundamentals of human morality which he has embodied become fundamentalism. And in him, "the great tradition" of American life for-

---

[26] *Bernard Smith,* Forces in American Criticism (*New York, 1939*), *384.*

[27] Forces in American Criticism, *40.*

[28] *John P. Marquand,* H. M. Pulham, Esquire (*Boston, 1941*), *131.*

gets the principle of growth and change, and becomes merely "the genteel tradition."

To summarize: this genteel tradition of American humanism has become reactionary only when it has divorced itself from the forces of change and renewal; just as the old Puritan moralism became decadent only when divorced from the old Puritan piety. When gentlemen have sought to impose a rigidly classical culture upon a growing, democratic society; when conservatives have sought to impede the processes of democratic change; when "puritans" have denied the possibility of a more liberal morality than the old, and when "humanists" have taken refuge from the unknown God of high religion and of science in the revealed literature of the past—then the great tradition has become decadent and partial. Too often has this been so. But when the old tradition has married the new idealism and merged itself in the larger life of the country, it has contributed "something basic" and indispensable, and has ceased to be "genteel."

Albert Bierstadt "View from the Wind River Mountains, Wyoming"   M. and M. Karolik Collection, Museum of Fine Arts, Boston

PART 5

THE AMERICAN WEST

Introduction

Students of American intellectual history have always been fascinated by the lure and mystique of the West. As the population grew along the Atlantic seaboard during the seventeenth century, many colonists began moving westward, unaware that they were starting a movement that would endure for more than three hundred years. Most intellectual historians prefer Puritanism and the Enlightenment to the frontier. But the frontier West has had an immeasurable impact on the development of the national mind, and it deserves evaluation.

Loren Baritz examines the idea of the West from ancient times to the late nineteenth century. The idea of the West certainly was not unique in the American experience. He believes that since the days of the Egyptians people have viewed the West as a utopian paradise, a place of happiness and justice. The Puritans, who came to the New World to create a city of God, Christianized the idea of the West. This idea was later secularized to justify the building of an empire.

The "Turner thesis" was first presented at the annual convention of the American Historical Association in 1893. The ideas set forth at that meeting by Frederick Jackson Turner are still subject to debate whenever professional historians congregate. Turner stated that "the existence of an area of free land, its continuous recession, and the advance of American settlement westward, explain American development."

Frederick Jackson Turner did not have the last word. Henry Nash Smith criticizes him for the contradictory concepts of nature and civilization that he used to explain the American past. According to Smith, Turner's thesis left America without a source of renewal for democracy as the amount of free land diminished, and it tended to encourage later historians to avoid the problems of industrialism, urbanism, technology, and diplomacy. Smith believes Turner did a disservice to the American people.

The article by Ray Allen Billington presents a more moderate analysis of Turner and the influence of the West. Billington, like most contemporary historians of the West, views his position as a "healthy reaction" to Turner, his thesis, and his critics. He argues that the West was far more complex than Turner imagined, and that the frontier alone does not explain the uniqueness of America. Nevertheless, he insists that among the factors that influenced the nation "none has bulked larger than the operation of the frontier process."

THE IDEA OF THE WEST

*Loren Baritz**

> There lies your way, due west.
> Then westward-hoe . . . .
>
> *Twelfth Night*

Once upon a time, dragons lived in the west, and sirens whose sea voices gave men to the sea, and monsters who preyed on fools, and to the west was darkness and danger and death. In its wisdom the sun daily searched the western sky in its flight from the east. At that point where the sun crossed the horizon, there was a happy other-world hidden from men, and toward that place earthly glory and power tended. Perhaps the creatures who defended this place could be slain, perhaps men could turn deaf ears to the sea voices, perhaps the storms could be weathered and the darkness pierced. Then the promise of the west would be known as men tasted the fruits of their yearnings and hopes, as the brave fools who sailed in ignorance became wise in their victory. If men were brave enough, strong enough, and perhaps good enough, they would be able to climb the

LOREN BARITZ (1928–   ) is a Professor of History at the State University of New York at Albany. His publications include Servants of Power (*1960*), City on a Hill (*1964*), *and* Sources of the American Mind (*2 vols., 1966*). *Reprinted by permission of the author and the* American Historical Review, *Vol. 66, No. 3 (April, 1961), 618–640.*

mountains or cross the seas or placate or vanquish the creatures that stood just east of Elysium. And, once there, the condition of men would be profoundly altered, for there nature's bounty was endless, happiness was certain, and death was banished forever.

As a whole, this composite west was not the usual inspiration of any single man; the shadings of the idea would lighten and darken in time and place. But one of these strands seems virtually constant in the human story: a yearning for a land of laughter, of peace, and of life eternal. The location of this land, whether Elysium, Eden, or the Isle of Fair Women, engaged the attention of poets and sailors, and frequently it was located to the west of the man who wondered where it was. Another important strand revolved around the concept of the destiny of nations, the notion that the secular sword must be taken by a nation to the west. From Troy to Greece, Rome, and England, "westward the course of empire takes its way." Sometimes eternity, happiness, and millennial themes were woven into one conception of the west; sometimes the imperial theme stood alone. At other times different arrangements and combinations were needed to serve the purposes of those who utilized some idea of the west, a west that might be either a place, a direction, an idea, or all three at once.

Where do the gods live, where do they most bless the earth, where is God's garden, or where does His spirit still walk? "From Menelaus to Columbus and beyond, it was thought that there was a magic otherworld hidden somewhere on earth, and all men had to do was find it."

Homer's description of a happy land, because it was vague as to location, created a problem for those who came later. On his authority it could be assumed that the Elysian Plain existed. Where was it? After capturing the ever-changing Proteus, Menelaus asked this herdsman of Neptune to foretell his destiny. Proteus replied that Menelaus was not ordained to die, that the gods would take him "to the Elysian plain and the world's end, where is Rhadamanthus of the fair hair, where life is easiest for men." And then came a picture of Elysium: "No snow is there, nor yet great storm, nor any rain; but always ocean sendeth forth the breeze of the shrill West to blow cool on men. . . ."[1] As a son of Zeus, and not because of particular human qualities, Menelaus would be translated to Elysium. Could mere mortals go, could they get there themselves, and just where was this world's end on which the west wind blew? Resting on this fair plain, one may recall the song of the west as sung by those who dreamed and sailed after the fortunate Menelaus, those who followed in his wake, in the salt spray of a distant sea.

Hesiod helped somewhat. When Zeus created the fourth race of men, "a god-like race of hero-men," those who fought at Thebes and Troy, the god gave them "a living and an abode apart from men, and made them dwell at the ends of the earth. And they lived untouched by sorrow in the islands of the blessed along the shore of deep swirling Ocean. . . ." The land was still god-given and was still at the end of the earth, but it was now an island, on the shore of the ocean, probably to the west, where "the Hesperian nymphs . . . guard the beautiful golden apples."[2] This was an ocean, however, that made men quake; "when they looked out upon the empty

---

[1] The Odyssey, *Bk. IV, tr. Samuel H. Butcher and Andrew Lang (New York, n.d.), 62; cf. Hendrik Wagenvoort,* Studies in Roman Literature, Culture and Religion *(Leiden, 1956), 282.*

[2] Works and Days, *156–69,* The Homeric Hymns and Homerica, *tr. Hugh G. Evelyn-White (London, 1943), 13, 15;* Theogony, *215–16, tr. N. O. Brown (New York, 1953), 59, n. 14.*

and spectral Atlantic,"[3] the otherworld seemed beyond man's reach.

Increasingly now, this remote happy land was speculated about and used by the Greeks. They might use Elysium in a didactic fashion, as a land whose perfection was the measure of the evils of their own society, or as a counterpoise to their conception of Hades,[4] or simply as a genuine place without immediate relevance. Plato, for instance, described the glories of ancient Athens in her war against the kings of Atlantis, of a whole lost world west of the Pillars of Hercules, an island "larger than Libya [Africa] and Asia together" long since sunk beneath the seas, leaving only shallow water that made navigation in the western ocean impossible.[5] Pindar, whose didacticism took the form of making the nature of this life a condition of entrance to Elysium, saw the westward Pillars "as far-famed witnesses of the furthest limit of voyaging."[6] The general belief, as in Euripides,[7] was that this usually western land of flowers was reserved for descendants or favorites of the gods,[8]

where even blood guilt might be washed away.[9] For those who would search for this land, Aristotle had cheering information: "the earth is spherical and . . . its periphery is not large. . . . For this reason those who imagine that the region around the Pillars of Hercules joins on to the regions of India, and that in this way the ocean is one, are not . . . suggesting anything utterly incredible." Only the sea, he said, "prevents the earth from being inhabited all round."[10]

The west was thought to hide this land of happiness and also to be "the natural goal of man's last journey." Both happiness and death, in ancient thought, formed the dialectic of the west, which the Egyptian legend of Isis implied.[11] The west was the region of death, whose personification was often headless, that is, lifeless, or who wore an ostrich feather on top of her head, or in place of a head. As a hieroglyph an ostrich feather signified both "west" and "justice," and in time Isis became also the goddess of justice. Thus both death and justice lived in the west. As justice, Isis was present when Osiris judged the dead, and she, in fact, introduced "the dead to Osiris and to their second life."[12] Thus it turned out that Isis of the west (death) was the goddess of the second life, and the region of one death was the region of

[3] *Clark B. Firestone*, The Coasts of Illusion (*New York, 1924*), 267.

[4] *Alfred Nutt in Kuno Meyer and Alfred Nutt*, The Voyage of Bran (*2 vols., London, 1895*), I, 279; *Martin P. Nilsson*, Geschichte der griechischen Religion (*2 vols., Munich, 1941*), I, 302–03, 447–48.

[5] Timaeus, *24E–25D*, Critias, *108E–109, tr. R. G. Bury* (*London, 1929*), 41–43, 265–67.

[6] Olympian Ode *III, 43–45*, Nemean Ode *III, 20–25*, Isthmian Ode *IV, 10–15*, The Odes of Pindar, *tr. Sir John Sandys* (*London, 1925*), 39, 337, 461.

[7] Hippolytus, *tr. A. S. Way, in* An Anthology of Greek Drama, *ed. C. A. Robinson, Jr.* (*New York, 1949*), 205.

[8] *There is no attempt here at comprehensiveness. Other Greeks placed Elysium elsewhere, e.g., Aristophanes*, The Frogs, *73–176. William S. Fox*, Greek and Roman Mythology, *Vol. I of* The Mythology of All Races, *ed. L. H. Gray* (*12 vols., Boston, 1916–28*), 147: "*The Greeks naturally thought of this land as lying in the distant west,*

some even identifying it with the islands of the Phaiakians, or again with Leuke . . . at the western end of the Euxine." *Cf. Howard R. Patch*, The Other World (*Cambridge, Mass., 1950*), 26.

[9] *Robert Graves*, The Greek Myths (*2 vols., New York, 1957*), II, 35.

[10] *Aristotle*, On the Heavens, *II, 14, 298a, tr. W. K. C. Guthrie* (*London, 1939*), 253; *Aristotle*, Meteorologica, *II, 5, 28–29, tr. E. W. Webster* (*Oxford, Eng., 1923*); *cf. Vivien de Saint-Martin*, Histoire de la géographie (*Paris, 1873*), 112–24.

[11] *Max Cary and E. W. Warmington*, The Ancient Explorers (*New York, 1929*), 202–03.

[12] *W. Max Muller*, Egyptian Mythology, *in* Mythology, *ed. Gray, XII, 99–100*.

new life. And so it may be true that "sunrise inspired the first prayers," but "sunset was the other time when again the whole frame of man would tremble." The dawn was promise, and dusk a mystery. Perhaps the life of man was reflected in the sun's own travels, so that the west became the region of death.[13] For those people who had a concept of a second life the west, as death, necessarily signified the life which comes from death.

The idea of the imperial west came from imperial Rome, and this was a west which presumably rested on fact. Poets could sing of this west too, but, unlike the west of Elysium, this west was proved by history, that is, by the historical myths of the poets of the imperial west. Moving Aeneas from Troy to Italy, "an antique land, well warded, possessed of a rich soil," Virgil set the direction for Rome[14] and clearly expressed the imperial theme of the west.

The Islands of the Blest were thought to be westward from Rome, in a specific place, discoverable by unaided mortals. Horace emphasized not empire but the west of the hidden happy land:

See, see before us the distant glow
Through the thin dawn-mists of the West
Rich sunlit plains and hilltops gemmed with snow,
The Islands of the Blest![15]

By the first century B.C. the Elysian Plain of Homer had been located. Plutarch had Sertorius meet some sailors in Spain who had just returned from a voyage to two distant Atlantic islands.

These are called the Islands of the Blest; rain falls there seldom, and in moderate showers, but for the most part they have gentle breezes, bringing along with them soft dews, which render the soil not only rich for ploughing and planting, but so abundantly fruitful that it produces spontaneously an abundance of delicate fruits, sufficient to feed the inhabitants, who may here enjoy all things without trouble or labour . . . so that the firm belief prevails, even among the barbarians, that this is the seat of the blessed, and that these are the Elysian Fields celebrated by Homer.[16]

The ocean goes only west from Troy, and the journey to Elysium for any Mediterranean voyager by now was westward.[17] Rome knew of the globe, guessed about the existence of a westward continent, and speculated about circumnavigation. Seneca's prophecy was unequivocal:

The times will arrive later on . . . in which the ocean will remove the impediments which now retard human affairs, and a new earth will be opened up to mankind, and the votaries of Tiphys will discover fresh worlds, and the present Thule will not be the Ultima Thule in future worlds.[18]

Seventh- or eight-century Ireland produced a pagan tale of lasting importance in the evolution of the idea of the west. There is a place in the

[13] *Firestone*, Coasts of Illusion, *205, quoting Max Muller.*
[14] Aeneid, *I, 531, tr. C. D. Lewis (New York, 1952), 25.*
[15] Epode 16, *tr. C. J. Kraemer, Jr. (New York, 1936), 119.*

[16] The Lives of the Noble Grecians and Romans, *tr. John Dryden, rev. A. H. Clough (New York, n.d.), 681–83.*
[17] *Patch*, Other World, *20.*
[18] *Pliny*, Naturalis Historiae, *II, 167; Strabo*, Geography, *citing Eratosthenes: "if the immensity of the Atlantic Sea did not prevent, we could sail from Iberia to India along one and the same parallel . . . ," I, 4, 6, and I, 1, 8, tr. Horace L. Jones (8 vols., London, 1917–32), I, 17, 241; Seneca*, Medea, *376–80, tr. Watson Bradshaw (London, 1902), 428–29; cf. Seneca*, Quaestiones Naturales, *I, preface, 11; James Oliver Thomson*, History of Ancient Geography *(Cambridge, Eng., 1948), 163–67; Francisco Lopez de Gómara, "Other Notable Thynges as Tovchynge the Indies," in Richard Eden*, The First Three English Books on America, *ed. Edward Arber (Birmingham, Eng., 1885), 337.*

west, sang the lady of the silver wood in her invitation to Bran to come to the Isle of Fair Women, whose land is

> Without grief, without sorrow, without death,
> Without any sickness, without debility. . . .
> There will come happiness with health
> To the land against which laughter peals. . . .

Following her call, Bran was told, in one of the earliest *imrama*, of a place where

> There are thrice fifty distant isles
> In the ocean to the west of us;
> Larger than Erin twice
> Is each of them, or thrice.

This timeless otherworld of sensual and sensuous delights could be reached only by mortals who were invited by the inhabitants. Manannan, the guardian of the islands, would not molest those whose invitation was in good order.[19]

Among the contributions of Christianity to the Roman world was the popularization of the idea that Horace and others were wrong about the west. "And Jehovah God planted a garden eastward in Eden. . . ."[20] The eastward Eden, as the westward Elysium, was characterized by abundance and ease, where the sweat of one's brow was unnecessary for the sustenance of life: "Thou wast in Eden, the Garden of God; every precious stone was thy covering, the sardius, the topaz, and the diamond, the beryl, the onyx, and the jasper, the sapphire, the emerald, and the carbuncle, and gold. . . ."[21] By the twelfth century the Christian idea of an eastward paradise had assumed rather definite form, even though St. Augustine had said that the westward course of empire had

divine sanction, but that the concept of a terrestrial paradise was simply allegorical, and even though the pagan tale of Bran remained substantially unchanged in Christian Ireland.[22] In the east also were the fearful people of Gog and Magog who had been barricaded by Alexander but who, just before judgment, would break out and eat all who stood in their way.[23] In some way, by high mountains, impassable seas, or perhaps a wall of fire, Eden was cut off from the rest of the world.[24]

Of the many ideas, tales, and myths concerning the location of the earthly paradise, the land of Bran and the *imrama* produced the most important. The traditions of the Celtic *imrama* were, in the tales of the voyages of St. Brendan, wrapped in properly Christian cloth. It is not now possible to piece together the original version of the voyage of St. Brendan, whose exploits were told in virtually every European tongue, and which became one of the most widespread tales of adventure in the western sea in Christendom,[25] with a remarkably similar counterpart even in Japan.[26]

A Celtic version of Brendan's motive in sailing

---

19 *Meyer and Nutt*, Bran, *I, 3–4, 6, 12, 142–43.*

20 *Genesis 2:8.*

21 *Ezekiel 28:13.*

22 *St. Augustine*, City of God, *V, 13, XVIII, 2; Meyer and Nutt*, Bran, *I, 149–50; Howard R. Patch, "Some Elements in Mediaeval Descriptions of the Otherworld,"* Publications of the Modern Language Association, *XXXIII (No. 1, 1918), 604, n. 6; cf., however, John K. Wright,* The Geographical Lore of the Time of the Crusades *(New York, 1925), 262.*

23 *Andrew R. Anderson*, Alexander's Gate, Gog and Magog, and the Inclosed Nations *(Cambridge, Mass., 1932), passim.*

24 *Patch*, Other World, *148; George H. T. Kimble,* Geography in the Middle Ages *(London, 1938), 24–25, 185.*

25 *Meyer and Nutt*, Bran, *I, 161; Joseph Dunn, "The Brendan Problem,"* Catholic Historical Review, *VI (Jan., 1921), 415, 445.*

26 *Edwin S. Hartland*, The Science of Fairy Tales *(London, 1891), 194–95.*

was appropriately fantastic. A mysterious flower from the promised land appeared to the twelve apostles of Ireland, all of whom wanted to set out in search of that land. The lot fell to the aged Brendan of Birr, the oldest saint of Ireland. It was decided that Brendan the younger should go, whereupon he and 158 companions set out in one boat.[27] Other versions told how St. Brendan wanted to find a place of peace, remote from the envy and jealousy of men, a place "over the wave-voice of the strong-maned sea, and over the storm of the green-sided waves and over the mouth of the marvelous, awful; bitter ocean. . . ." Wherever Brendan was when the dawn of Easter showed, some huge sea creature would surface so that the saint and his crew could worship on its back. Before he succeeded, according to the Irish version, the saint had sought the promised land for seven years. An attempted amalgam of Christian spiritualism and the sensuality of the earlier *imrama* produced the *Tír Tairngire*, "the Land of Promise," desired by Brendan.[28]

The persistent attempts to derive geography from scripture resulted in countless confusions,[29] from which of course paganism had been free. But the halting progress of geographical knowledge toward the level of Aristotle, Eratosthenes, and Seneca eased the tension between the pagan west and the Biblical, and more precisely, Christian east. When, for example, Dante, who probably knew and made use of the *Navigatio Sancti Brendani*,[30] was amazed at seeing the sun shining on his left as Virgil led him up the island mountain of Eden, Virgil explained:

> Consider Zion: picture how it lies
> On earth directly opposite this mount,
> So that they share together one horizon
> In different hemispheres.[31]

From Jerusalem therefore the way to Eden became irrelevant, except in terms of convenience. If one considers the opposite side of the earth as east (and it is quite as sensible to think of it as west), still one may get there by moving west. On a round earth, place has more cosmic significance than direction, but direction and route remain the first problem for those in search of Eden. Thus toward the end of the thirteenth century an ill-fated Genoese expedition under the Vivaldi brothers was sent out to find the east by sailing west.[32] The roundness of the earth was the knowledge by which Christendom began to revive the pagan idea of the west, though the east lingered as a place while the west, for the Catholic nations, became mere direction.

For some, the proof of the meaningfulness of the west lay not in theology or legend, but in what was supposed to be history. What Virgil did for Italy, Geoffrey of Monmouth tried to do for England in the twelfth century by elaborating the Virgilian imperial theme of the west, virtually ignoring the legendary and millennial wests, and applying it to England. Claiming to have discovered a lost British book that chronicled the history of the British kings, Geoffrey in fact

---

[27] *Carolus Plummer*, Vitae Sanctorum Hiberniae (*2 vols., Oxford, Eng., 1910), I, xli; Dunn, "Brendan Problem," 424.*

[28] Ibid., *424–25, 430, 444.*

[29] *For example, St. Augustine*, City of God, XVI, 9; *Kimble*, Geography in the Middle Ages, *37, 163–64.*

[30] *C. H. Grandgent, "Cato and Elijah," Publications of the Modern Language Association, XVII (No. 1, 1902), 82–83.*

[31] *Dante*, Purgatorio, *Canto IV, 68–71, tr. Lawrence G. White (New York, 1948), 71.*

[32] *William H. Babcock*, Legendary Islands of the Atlantic (*New York, 1922), 8; Edgar Prestage, "The Search for the Sea Route to India," in* Travel and Travellers of the Middle Ages, *ed. Arthur P. Newton (London, 1926), 203.*

drew from the history of the sixth-century monk, Gildas, the *Nennius*, and Bede (eighth century), as well as the Roman historians, Welsh chroniclers, popular folk tales, and his own active imagination.[33] Empire moves westward from Troy, and England, said Geoffrey, is west of Rome.

After Aeneas killed Turnus in Italy, according to Geoffrey, Aeneas became king of Italy and married Lavinia, daughter of Latinus. A grandson of Aeneas married a niece of Lavinia who soon became or already was pregnant. Wizards prophesied that the child would be a boy, would kill his parents, and after much travel, would be highly exalted. The mother, giving birth to Brutus, died. When the boy was fifteen, he killed his father in a hunting accident. Brutus' kinfolk drove him from Italy. He sought refuge in Greece, where he joined the descendants of Helenus, son of Priam, who had been taken in bondage to Greece by Achilles' son. These seven thousand captive Trojans were thus of the same ancestry as Brutus himself, and because of his strength and wisdom he became their duke. In the war of liberation which he led, the Greek King was captured and by torture was compelled to supply the Trojans with 324 ships and provisions, as well as his daughter for the "scion of the house of Priam and Anchises."

Setting sail, Brutus discovered a deserted island on which was a temple of Diana. Asking the goddess where he was destined to dwell, repeating his question nine times, walking around the altar four times, Brutus fell asleep. Then Diana spoke:

Brute,—past the realms of Gaul, beneath the
  sunset
Lieth an Island, girt about by ocean,
Guarded by ocean—erst the haunt of giants,
Desert of late, and meet for this thy people.
Seek it! For there is thine abode for ever.
There by thy sons again shall Troy be builded;
There of thy blood shall Kings be born, hereafter
Sovran in every land the wide world over.[34]

Brutus returned to his ships and set "full sail for the West" in search of the site of New Troy, a search that took him past the Pillars of Hercules where he saw the coaxing sirens. After fighting in Aquitaine, Brutus, about 1100 B.C., finally landed at the island called Albion, which, in honor of himself, he called Britain, and the city he built on the Thames he called New Troy.[35]

The reputation of Geoffrey is the subject of much controversy, though most of the experts seem to agree that the "*Historia Regum Britanniae* is one of the most influential books ever written, certainly one of the most influential in the middle ages."[36] It is clear that his history was believed, and used by Henry VII and James I.[37] The impact

[33] *Discussion of Geoffrey's sources is voluminous; see, e.g.,* Acton Griscom, The Historia Regum Britanniae of Geoffrey of Monmouth (*London, 1929), 99 ff., 163–65, 195;* Six Old English Chronicles, *ed. J. A. Giles (London, 1848), 92, 387–88;* Ernest Jones, Geoffrey of Monmouth, 1640–1800 (*Berkeley, Calif., 1944), 376–77;* Rachel Bromwich, "*The Character of the Early Welsh Tradition," in* H. M. Chadwick *et al.*, Studies in Early British History (*Cambridge, Eng., 1954), 128.*

[34] *Edmond Faral*, La légende arthurienne (*3 vols., Paris, 1929), II, 80, shows that the oracular verses are taken at least in part from Bks. I and VII of the* Aeneid.

[35] *Geoffrey of Monmouth*, Histories of the Kings of Britain, *tr. Sebastian Evans (New York, 1911), 3–23. For a discussion of the presumed Trojan origins of other European nations, see Denys Hay*, Europe: The Emergence of an Idea (*Edinburgh, 1957), 48–49, 108–109.*

[36] *J. S. P. Tatlock*, The Legendary History of Britain (*Berkeley, Calif., 1950), 3; cf. Griscom*, Historia, *6, 166;* Jones, Geoffrey, *357–77; George Gordon, "The Trojans in Britain," Essays and Studies by Members of the English Association (32 vols., Oxford, Eng., 1910–47), IX, 9–30;* A. E. Parsons, "The Trojan Legend in England," *Modern Language Review*, XXIV (*July, 1929), 253.*

[37] "*Basilikon Doron," in* The Political Works of James I, *ed. C. H. McIlwain (Cambridge, Mass., 1918), 37;* Parsons, "Trojan Legend," *398, 401–407.*

on literature of Geoffrey's stories of Kings Lear and Arthur is too vast to catalogue here.[38] But by 1700 the reputation of Geoffrey began to suffer as the Enlightenment mood grew increasingly unhappy with "monkish fictions,"[39] though the twentieth century seems to be kinder.[40] Regardless, however, of Geoffrey's many trials, he contributed in a popular and powerful way to the idea that empire drifts to the west, "beneath the sunset," and that England, because of her westwardness, was destined for empire. As Brutus had traveled, so must empire; where Brutus stopped his journey, so must empire. John of Gaunt, with his dying breath, showed to what extent Shakespeare accepted Geoffrey's conception of England, the ancient seat of kings.[41]

The excitement over Columbus' success inevitably led to a more intense and general interest in the west, but still, as everyone knows, the west for the admiral was a way to get to the east. The west as west, as place as well as direction, had not yet been rescued from antique ruins. It was still eclipsed by the glare of the Christian east. Slowly, however, the west was once more to become a place, to assume a glitter of its own, and in fact to be Christianized.

Now in the age of the discoveries, the earlier myths, ideas, and attitudes about the west were to play an important role in providing at least some of the explorers and early settlers with a framework useful in understanding, explaining, and justifying their activities. It is perhaps too much to say that the myth of St. Brendan's voyage, for instance, "drove forth adventurers into the Western Sea, and was one of the contributory causes of the discovery of the New World,"[42] but it was clear that the search for Eden, Antillia, Brasil, a new Canaan, El Dorado, the Amazons, Ophir, the Country of Cinnamon, the Enchanted City of the Caesars, the Sepulchres of Zenu, the Seven Cities of Cibola, Quivira, or simply a fountain of eternal youth was the purpose of some of the explorers and early settlers.[43]

The special significance of the St. Brendan stories is illustrated by the fact that a number of the early cartographers located the saint's islands on the maps used by some of the explorers. Brendan thus moved easily from myth to ostensible fact, and the wonderful *Tír Tairngire* he had found, now, if the map makers were right, could be found again. On the Hereford map of about 1275, approximately where the Canaries belong, the saint's islands made their debut as "Fortunate Insulae sex sunt Insulae Sct Brandani." In 1339 Angelinus Dulcert located Brendan's islands in the Madeiras, as did the Pizigani brothers in 1367, and Battista Beccario in 1426 and 1435. Others in the fifteenth century located the islands elsewhere, though on the controversial map which Paolo Toscanelli may have made for Columbus they are resting in their accustomed place southwest of the Canaries. By the sixteenth century the islands had floated up to the North Atlantic, so that by

---

[38] *See, e.g., Gordon, "Trojans," Essays and Studies, 23.*

[39] *Jones, Geoffrey, 376–78.*

[40] *"I should like to see the Fables of the Britons restored to their place in the first chapter of our histories." Gordon, "Trojans," Essays and Studies, 25.*

[41] *Shakespeare, King Richard II, II, i.*

[42] *Meyer and Nutt, Bran, I, 161.*

[43] *Richard Hennig, "Atlantische Fabelinseln und Entdeckung Amerikas," Historische Zeitschrift, CLIII (Mar., 1936), 494–95; A. P. Newton, "Travellers' Tales of Wonder and Imagination," in Travel, ed. Newton, 162–67; Patch, Other World, 173; Leonardo Olschki, "Ponce de León's Fountain of Youth," Hispanic American Historical Review, XXI (Aug., 1941), 372; Firestone, Coasts of Illusion, 312–33; Kimble, Geography in the Middle Ages, 92; J. L. Phelan, The Millennial Kingdom of the Franciscans in the New World (Berkeley, Calif., 1956), 67–70. Brendan's voyage and some other myths associated with the discovery of America have been popularized in Life, XLVII (Aug. 31, 1959), 55–67.*

1608 they were between Ireland and America.[44] For at least four hundred years, then, Brendan's *Tír Tairngire* was discussed in literature and located on some of the best maps of the period. So powerfully did Brendan assert himself that in the Treaty of Evora (1519), for example, Emmanuel of Portugal specifically relinquished his claim to the saint's islands. At different times expeditions were sent in search of them; always, however, when the sailors got close, a storm or a mist would cloud their view. Search parties were set afloat in 1526, 1570, 1604, 1633, and in 1721 when "two holy friars as apostolical chaplains" were sent along as special assistants.[45]

Columbus' son believed that among his father's motives in sailing was the desire to search for these perverse islands "of which so many marvels are told."[46] Later, on his first voyage, the admiral himself referred to a western isle which, according to information he had, was "Antillia y San Borondon."[47] Some must have believed that Columbus was motivated "to seek out the Antipodes, and the rich *Cipango* of Marco Polo, because he had read in Plato's *Timaeus* an argument respecting the great island of Atlantis, and of a hidden land larger than Asia and Africa," since an Italian traveler to the New World repeated the story, though he declared it to be "fabulous."[48] The admiral did cite the authority of Aristotle, Pliny, and Seneca for some of his notions of geography,[49] and his son thought such authority "did more than all else to convince the Admiral that his idea was sound."[50] That Columbus was in search of the garden planted eastward in Eden is well known. He had learned from one of his masters, Pierre d'Ailly, of Taprobane, an island which "lies in the east where the Indian Ocean begins," and which "is full of pearls and precious stones." The people, wrote d'Ailly, "are powerful in body beyond all measurements; with red hair, blue eyes and harsh voices. . . . With them life is prolonged beyond human infirmity, so that one who dies a centenarian comes to his end immaturely." To get to this eastern isle, according to d'Ailly, was not impossible since, agreeing with Aristotle and Seneca, "the water [of the ocean] runs down from one pole toward the other into the body of the sea and spreads out between the confines of Spain and the beginning of India, of no great width. . . ."[51] Columbus agreed that the garden in the east must be approached from the west.[52]

Because of their relevance, some of the details of the admiral's own thought are worth repeating. On a calm summer day of 1498 he recorded in his journal a conclusion made up of his no-

---

[44] Hennig, "*Atlantische Fabelinseln*," 469–70, 485; Babcock, Legendary Islands, 38–39, 42–48; Dunn, "Brendan Problem," 459–61; cf., however, Henry Vignaud, The Columbian Tradition on the Discovery of America and of the Part Played therein by the Astronomer Toscanelli (*Oxford, Eng., 1920*), 39–41.

[45] Dunn, "Brendan Problem," 463–64.

[46] The Life of the Admiral Christopher Columbus by His Son Ferdinand, tr. *Benjamin Keen (New Brunswick, N. J., 1959)*, 25; cf. Hennig, "Atlantische Fabelinseln," 465.

[47] Jueves, 9 de Agosto 1492, Martín Fernández de Navarrete, Colección de los viajes y descubrimientos (2d ed., 5 vols., Madrid, 1858), I, 157–59.

[48] Girolamo Benzoni, History of the New World, tr. W. H. Smyth (London, 1857), 15–16.

[49] Navarrete, Colección, I, 409–10; Edward G. Bourne, Essays in Historical Criticism (New York, 1901), 221.

[50] Life of the Admiral, 17–19.

[51] Pierre d'Ailly, Imago Mundi, tr. Edwin F. Keever (Wilmington, N. C., 1948), Chaps. XIV, XLII, XLIX; cf. Roger Bacon, Opus Majus, IV, tr. R. B. Burke (2 vols., Philadelphia, 1928), I, 312–13.

[52] Kimble, Geography in the Middle Ages, 42; Bourne, Essays, 221, n. 3; Louis Salembier, Pierre d'Ailly et la découverte de l'Amérique (Paris, 1912); cf. Sebastian Munster, Of the Newe India (1543), in Eden, First Three English Books, 22.

tions of geography and his belief in the reality of the garden. He had become convinced that he had just found, not an island, but a continent, on which Eden was located "because all men say that it's at the end of the Orient, and that's where we are." What he believed about the geography of Eden seemed to coincide with his observations of the land, including the alleged discovery of the river that became four. The admiral, however, was not one to rely only on observation. Because of his puzzlement over the fact that elevations of Polaris varied on the same latitude, he concluded that the earth "is not round . . . but [is] of the form of a pear, which is very round except where the stalk grows . . . ; or like a round ball, upon one part of which is a prominence like a woman's nipple, this protrusion being the highest and nearest the sky." On the nipple of this breast, the point of earth closest to heaven, would be found the desired garden, "where," he said, "I believe in my soul that the earthly paradise is situated. . . ." Unfortunately we do not know how the sovereigns reacted to this contribution to knowledge. Others like Gerónimo de Mendieta, Bartolomé de Las Casas, and Amerigo Vespucci while more skeptical than Columbus, agreed that somewhere on the shores of the Caribbean the seat of the terrestrial paradise would be found.[53]

For those like Columbus,[54] to whom the east was a place while the west was mere direction, the New World could not assume independent importance. For this mentality, long active, the New World was an obstacle to westward progress toward the east. The search for a southwest or northwest passage occupied men's attention for over four hundred years. One of the earliest was Hernán Cortés who, in his third letter to Charles V, had made more precise the lure of the eastern ocean that lay to the west: "Most of all do I exult in the tidings lately brought me of the Great Ocean; for in it . . . are scattered innumerable isles teeming with gold and pearls, abounding in precious stones, as well as in spices, and where . . . many wonderful secrets and admirable things may be discovered."[55] As more exact knowledge of the Atlantic was gathered, that ocean was demythologized by the Catholic nations, while the South Sea, or Pacific, was invested with all the romance earlier lavished on the Atlantic. While the Atlantic continued to excite some, others who turned west to face east sought that elusive passage that would bring the wealth of Cipango and the ease of Eden within the reach of sail.

In his conception of Eden, Columbus also referred to a fountain that was the source of the four principal rivers of the world.[56] Nowhere in the Bible is this fountain mentioned, and again Columbus was showing that the distinctions be-

---

53 Select Letters of Christopher Columbus, *tr. R. H. Major* (London, 1847), 130, 136–37; Samuel Eliot Morison, Admiral of the Ocean Sea (*Boston, 1942*), 556–58; Phelan, Millennial Kingdom, *66; cf. Babcock*, Legendary Islands, *188; George E. Nunn*, The Geographical Conceptions of Columbus (*New York, 1924*), 31–90; Edmundo O'Gorman, La invención de América (*México, D.F., 1958*), 29–76, 119–20. *A recent newspaper article announced that* "Satellite Confirms Earth is Like Pear," *New York* Herald Tribune, *European ed., June 22, 1960, 1.*

54 *Cf. Vignaud*, Columbian Tradition, *47:* ". . . *the object of the enterprise was not to reach the East by way of the West, but to carry out the contract made with their Catholic Majesties for the discovery of an island the existence of which Columbus declared that he knew, an island which is not named, but which in all likelihood was Antilia."*

55 The Fifth Letter of Hernan Cortes to the Emperor Charles V, *tr. Don Pascual de Gayangos* (London, 1868), *viii, 151–52; E. G. R. Taylor*, Tudor Geography (*London, 1930*), 97–99, 130; Howard Mumford Jones, *"The Colonial Impulse,"* Proceedings of the American Philosophical Society, *XC (May, 1946), 145.*

56 Select Letters of Columbus, *135.*

tween theology, legend, and fact were blurred in his mind. But he was a creature of time, and his conceptions, with the possible exception of the cosmic breast, were common property of men of some education. This fountain of paradise belonged, along with Brendan's islands, to a literary tradition, one whose impact was even greater on Juan Ponce de León.[57]

The fountain of youth seems to have first appeared in the forged twelfth-century *Letter of Prester John*, in which a lush land, richer, more Christian, and more powerful than all of Europe was described, along with the magical water which, in one version, was said to be "full of the grace of the holy goost.and who so we in this same water wasshed his body he shall become yonge of.xxx.yere." The fountain, according to other editions of the *Letter*, was to be found on an island, at the eastern edge of the world.[58] As the cartographers began to dot the Atlantic with many islands heavy with Edenic association, it was an easy step for one engaged in the real business of exploration to assume that on one of these islands the magic fountain might be found, and the farther west (east) the better. Thus Ponce's party searched for the fountain on Bimini Isle in an archipelago supposedly at the easternmost rim of Asia. Columbus had said nothing of the rejuvenating qualities of his fountain, but in 1514 Peter Martyr, the first historian of the New World and a messenger of the Renaissance from Italy to Spain, wrote that to the west "is an island . . . [which] is celebrated for a spring whose waters

restore youth to old men." Martyr himself rejected the story because it violated his theology, but reported that the story of Ponce's exploits had made "such an impression that the entire populace, and even people superior by birth and influence, accepted it as a proven fact."[59] In the patent of 1514, Ponce was authorized to colonize the tantalizing Bimini, whose name was to continue to awaken "Dreams of youth, with youth that perished."[60]

The imagination of the age was ablaze with the marvels to be found to the west. Columbus and Ponce were not unique. Virtually nothing was too much to imagine in the place where God had planted His garden. There was agreement not only about the reality of the garden, but its general equatorial location. A man of God who had accompanied Sir Francis Drake described their voyage into the area:

> being now entered into torrida Zona that is the burning Zone we found the vaine guesses & imagined conjectures to be vntrue & false concerning the same & the surmised opinion of the antient & great philosophers to be contrary to appearance & experience. & indeed to Reason: for wheras Aristotill Pithagoras Thales & many others both Greekes and Latins haue taught that Torrida Zona was not habitable . . . we proued the same to bee altogeather false & the same Zone to be the Earthly paradise in the world both at sea & lande

57 Olschki, *"Ponce de León,"* 380.

58 Ibid., *365, 370–72, 380; Patch, "Mediaeval Descriptions," 619–23; Wright,* Geographical Lore, *285; E. D. Ross, "Prester John and the Empire of Ethiopia," in* Travel, *ed. Newton, 176; Eden,* First Three English Books, *xxxiv, 339; Richard Hennig,* Wo lag das Paradies? *(Berlin, 1950), 226–37.*

59 *Peter Martyr d'Anghiera,* De Orbe Novo, *tr. F. A. MacNutt (2 vols., New York, 1912), I, 274; cf. Gómara in* Eden, First Three English Books, *345; O'Gorman,* La invención de América, *37–38, 111, n. 34–35, 115, n. 49. The concern with the fabulous, and its impact on the Spanish, is discussed in Irving A. Leonard,* Books of the Brave *(Cambridge, Mass., 1949), 11 ff.*

60 *Heinrich Heine, "Bimini," tr. Margaret Armour,* Works, *gen. tr. C. G. Leland (16 vols., New York, 1906), XII, 188.*

yea the increase of things & the Excellency of all Gods creatures in that Zone is 7 degrees aboue all other parts in the Earth. . . .[61]

Contact with the Indians of South America probably introduced the exploring white men to at least some of the myths of the various tribes. Some of these myths may have helped to re-inforce the idea of the west in the minds of the Europeans, as the Indians repeatedly told the white men that what they were looking for could be found further west. One of these tribes, the Guarayú, migrated from Paraguay in the fifteenth and sixteenth centuries to raid the Inca Empire, settling finally in the vicinity of the cordillera, where they were encountered by Jesuits in the sixteenth century and by Spaniards exploring Bolivia in the seventeenth. The eschatology of this tribe is a good example of the west of eternity:

> Soon after burial, the soul starts a long dangerous journey to the land of Tamoi, which is located in the west. The soul is ferried across a river on the back of a caiman, jumps on a tree trunk . . . , passes by the Grandfather of the worms. . . . Before reaching the abode of Tamoi, the soul must en-dure the ordeal of being tickled by a monkey without laughing, must walk past a magic tree without heeding the voices issuing from it, and must look at colored grasses without being blinded by them. After all of these ordeals, the soul is received by Tamoi, who washes it and re-stores its youth and good looks.

Another tribe living in the same general area was the Yuracare, who did not make contact with the invading Europeans until the seventeenth cen-tury, but whose creation and judgment myth suggested again that eternity was to be found in the west:

> Tiri [the son of the first parents of the world, and creator of most of the world] decided to retire [after his creations] to the end of the world. In order to know its extent, he sent a bird to the four directions of the horizon. On the fourth trip, from the west, the bird returned with beauti-ful new plumage. Tiri went to the west, where he lives with his people who, upon reaching old age, rejuvenate.[62]

Because most of the Elizabethans thought of the west imperially, as a place as well as a direc-tion, they could dismiss much of the fabulous which was accepted by those in search of Eden. But the Elizabethans made their own contribution

---

[61] *Francis Fletcher*, The First Part of the Second Voyage about the World Attempted Continued and Happily Accomplished . . . by Mr. Francis Drake, *in Sir Francis Drake*, The World Encompassed (*London, 1926*), 102; *cf. Munster in Eden,* First Three English Books, 41.

[62] *Alfred Métraux, "Tribes of Eastern Bolivia,"* United States Bureau of American Ethnology, Handbook of South American Indians, *ed. J. H. Seward (3 vols., Washington, D. C., 1948), III, 430, 437; Métraux, "Tribes of the Eastern Slopes of the Bolivian Andes," ibid., 485, 503. Other South American tribes, especially the dominant Gua-rani, looked for salvation in the east; Métraux argued that this was inspired by contact with Christianity. "The Gua-rani," ibid., 69, 93–94; Hartley B. Alexander,* Latin Amer-ican Mythology, *in* Mythology, *ed. Gray, XI, 240, 315. Marshallese folklore also invests the god in the west with the power to create life: William H. Davenport, "Marshallese Folklore Types,"* Journal of American Folklore, *LXVI (July–Sept., 1953), 221–22. In Hawaiian mythology, the god of the east represents masculine reproductive power; the god of the west, Hina, "is the expression of female fecundity and the power of growth and production." Martha Beckwith,* Hawaiian Mythology *(New Haven, Conn., 1940), 12–13, cf. 79. Several of the Indian tribes of North America similarly had their gods live in the west. Stith Thompson,* Tales of the North American Indians *(Cambridge, Mass., 1929), 274, n. 11; cr. Pascual de Andagoya,* Pedrarias Davila in the Provinces of Tierra Firme or Castilla del Oro, *tr. C. R. Markham (London, 1865), 14–15, 67.*

to the idea of the west. As early as about 1519, an English versifier of the imperial west, and brother-in-law of Thomas More, found it intolerable that England had missed the chance at the wealth of the southern New World. And it was the fault of Englishmen without vision, without a grasp of the imperial west, the fault of Englishmen

> Which wold take no paine to saile farther
> Than their owne lyst and pleasure.

Because the early explorers had put person above nation, England, in the age before her navy and her God had defeated the Armada, could only dream of what might have been:

> O what thynge a had be than
> Yf that they that be englyshe men
> Myght haue ben the furst of all
> That there shulde haue take possessyon
> And made furst buyldynge and habytacion
> A memory perpetuall
> And also what an honorable thynge
> Both to the realme and to the kynge
> To haue had his domynyon extendynge
> There into so farre a grounde.[63]

Regret was to become exultation when it was realized that it was not yet too late even though Pope Alexander VI had already divided the undiscovered world between Spain and Portugal, that even the Englishman could sail for his king.

The sea itself, as Columbus had earlier suggested,[64] presumably moved from "east to west

continually." One result of Sir Martin Frobisher's voyages was the conclusion that ". . . water being an inferior element, must needes be governed after the superior Heaven, and so to follow the course of *Primum mobile* from east to weast."[65] For Henry Hudson, still seeking the east by way of the west, in search of the Northwest Passage, the west wind was, he wrote in 1607, "the meane of our deliverance," an uncommon wind sent specially by God.[66] The conspiracy of sea and wind led this generation westward, whether for the greater glory of England, or the pay of Holland, whether to explore or settle this new land, or to find a waterway through the New World.

Of Elizabethan thought none perhaps is as illustrative as Sir Walter Raleigh's, whose wife rightly feared her husband's destiny in the west and secretly asked a friend to "rather draw Sir Walter towards the East, than help him forward toward the sunset. . . ."[67] In his *History of the World*, Raleigh denied Geoffrey's tale of the Trojan origin of Britain, though he knew that "the British language hath remained among us above 2000 years. . . ."[68] Rejecting Geoffrey's Brutus, he retained Geoffrey's idea of imperial England. He could not treat the "mighty, rich, and beautiful

[63] *Eden*, First Three English Books, *xx–xxi, cf. 6;* A. L. Rowse, The Elizabethans and America *(London, 1959), 3.*

[64] *"I hold it for certain, that the waters of the sea move from east to west with the sky. . . ."* Select Letters of Columbus, *138.*

[65] *George Best*, The Three Voyages of Martin Frobisher *(London, 1867), 244. It was on the voyage of 1578 that the* Busse *of Bridgewater reported the discovery of perhaps the last of the fabulous islands of the Atlantic. Named in honor of the ship which "sayled three dayes alongst the coast," Busse Island was vainly sought by others, including, for example, Henry Hudson in 1609, who "could not find it."* Ibid., *280;* Henry Hudson the Navigator, *ed. G. M. Asher (London, 1860), 49.*

[66] Ibid. *19; cf.* "Voyage of John de Verazzano along the Coast of North America," *tr. J. G. Cogswell, ibid., 224.*

[67] *Willard M. Wallace*, Sir Walter Raleigh *(Princeton, N. J., 1959), 110.*

[68] *Sir Walter Raleigh*, History of the World *(11th ed., 2 vols., London, 1736), I, 81, 260.*

empire of *Guiana*, and . . . that great and golden city which the Spaniards call El Dorado," with exactly equal skepticism, but even here his eye for the practical rather than the romantic seldom failed. "*Guiana* is a country that hath yet her maidenhead, never sacked, turned, nor wrought. . . ."[69] Thus, for Raleigh, the lands to the west were divested of magic and invested with the main chance. Here were undreamed of riches, unlimited fertility, and the mine which imperial England should exploit in the interest of both her glory and her power. The preacher-geographer, Richard Hakluyt, who influenced and was influenced by Raleigh, similarly took the business approach to exploration, hardly troubling himself with the romance of the west. He was concerned with the use of the material abundance of the west for the strengthening of England, with the state of the economy at home, and with the fact that Spain had power and riches he thought England should have.[70]

Unable to divorce theology and religion from ideas about exploration, the Catholic nations could make little use of the essentially secular west of empire. But the west for these Elizabethans was primarily a device utilized to maintain and strengthen the view of England held by Geoffrey and Shakespeare. In demythologizing the west they hoped to remythologize England as the most recent and—hopefully—final repository of empire. The lands to the west of the civilized west should be squeezed dry of the juices healthful to "this earth of majesty." Because civilization is anterior to empire, the primitive west, so long as it remained primitive, was no threat to the Renaissance

mythology of England. Occupying the westernmost reaches of civilization, England could wear the cloak of Troy with grace; to the west of the European west could be found the raw stuff necessary to reinforce and beautify that cloak.[71]

Another of these Englishmen was the vicarious traveler and the intellectual heir of Hakluyt, Parson Samuel Purchas, whose work was devoured by James I and lingered on to inspire later English poets.[72] Because of his commitment to Geoffrey's notion that empire had moved to England, where it would stay, Purchas rejected the other ideas of the west, the wests of happiness and eternity. He rejected Plato's Atlantis, Plutarch's report of voyages, and asserted that the Roman Island of the Blest was simply one of the Canaries or some other quite normal island. Purchas dismissed Columbus' notion that he had been close to the Ophir of King Solomon, though Purchas was convinced of the existence of Ophir in India (where it had been located by some cartographers[73]). Purchas, however, began to suggest what was eventually to become the English con-

[69] Id.; The Discovery of Guiana (*New York, 1910*), *313, 391*.

[70] *Richard Hakluyt*, A Discourse on Western Planting, ed. Charles Deane (*Cambridge, Mass., 1877*), passim; *cf. Jones, "Colonial Impulse," 139–46.*

[71] *Wallace*, Raleigh, *36–37, 58, 109–10, 119, 298; Ernest A. Strathmann*, Sir Walter Raleigh (*New York, 1951*), *251–52; Richard Hakluyt*, Divers Voyages Touching the Discovery of America, ed. *J. W. Jones* (*London, 1850*), *xvi; E. G. R. Taylor*, Late Tudor and Early Stuart Geography (*London, 1934*), *4; Rowse*, Elizabethans and America, *16, 31–32, 191; cf. Best*, Three Voyages of Frobisher, *5–7; Robert G. Cleland, "Westward the Course of Empire,"* Huntington Library Quarterly, *VII (Aug., 1944), 4–6, suggests that the westward urge was peculiarly Anglo-Saxon, and that their westward expansion began with the fifth-century invasion, and "the conquest of North America by English-speaking peoples is merely the Anglo-Saxon occupation of Britain transferred to another and much vaster theater."*

[72] *Taylor*, Late Tudor and Early Stuart Geography, *56.*

[73] *Wright*, Geographical Lore, *275; Hennig*, Wo lag das Paradies? *69–71.*

tribution to the idea of the west. Medieval romances and legendary islands made little impression on his thinking, but theology grew in stature. "I speak," he said, "not in Poeticall fiction, or Hyperbolicall phrase, but Christian sincerity." For the sake of Christendom, God had withheld the knowledge necessary to navigation from "the Persian, the Mogoll, the Abassine, the Chinois, the Tartarian, the Turke." Probably remembering Malachi 4:2, he concluded that "thus hath God given opportunitie by Navigation into all parts, that in the Sun-set and Evening of the World, the Sunne of righteousnesse might arise out of our West to Illuminate the East. . . ."[74] While this sun rose in the west, the world would be at its evening and the kingdom of the apocalypse would be near. Turning from the concept of a lost golden age or Eden, Purchas looked forward to the time when the city of God would exist on earth, the earth of the western New World. The millennium would see Christ walking from the west.

It remained for Edward Hayes, Sir Humphrey Gilbert's rear admiral, to complete the Anglicization of the idea of the west. Arguing that England had a good claim to America, north of Florida, by virtue of John Cabot's discoveries, Hayes adduced also God's consent to English ambitions. Christianization of the heathen was noble work, and the French and Spanish agreed. France and Spain, however, would ensnarl the witless Indian in the net of Rome, so that only England could truly serve God's purpose. It would be folly for the Catholic nations to attempt to impede the progress of England, for her victory was as inevitable as the fact that true religion moved from east to west:

God's word and religion . . . from the beginning hath moved from the east towards, and at last unto, the west, where it is like to end, unless the same begin again where it did in the east, which were to expect a like world again. But we are assured of the contrary by the prophecy of *Christ*, whereby we gather that after His word preached throughout the world shall be the end.[75]

There could not be a new beginning for, agreeing with Purchas, Hayes's thinking moved forward to the apocalypse, not backward to Eden. In his eschatology, the creation of English America was the final step necessary to the millennium.[76] When the word of Christ had been heard everywhere, the day of doom would follow. After America, judgment.

With the settlers in English America several strands of the idea of the west were pulled together. Some still searched for Eden or Ophir; more thought with Raleigh and Hakluyt that the west meant economic opportunity for themselves and for England. But the Puritans of Massachusetts Bay occupied what they believed was God's country, that western land where, they said, His word would be obeyed. In no other nation on earth did God walk. These Puritans were merely following the Lord's instructions when they sailed, not merely westward, but *to* the west, from England:

[74] *Samuel Purchas*, Purchas His Pilgrimes (*London, 1625*), *in* Hakluytus Posthumus (*20 vols., Glasgow, 1905–1907*), *I, 52–53, 66–67, 74, 87, 164, 173, 207, 251; Taylor*, Late Tudor and Early Stuart Geography, *114–15; cf. Hay*, Europe, *120–22.*

[75] *Edward Hayes*, Sir Humphrey Gilbert's Voyage to Newfoundland (*New York, 1910*), *274–75.*

[76] *Cotton Mather*, Magnalia Christi Americana (*2 vols., Hartford, Conn., 1820*), *I, 302. See also Charles L. Sanford, "An American* Pilgrim's Progress," American Quarterly, *VI (Winter, 1954), 298–302; Sidney Lee, "The Call of the West," Scribner's Magazine, XLI (June, 1907), 677–79; Michael Kraus, "America and the Utopian Ideal in the Eighteenth Century," Mississippi Valley Historical Review, XXII (Mar., 1936), 487–504.*

It is true, that from the first planting of Religion among men, it hath always held a constant way from East to West, and hath, in that Line, proceeded so farre, that it hath extended to the uttermost Westerne bounds of the formerly knowne world. . . . And they conceive withall, that our Saviours Prophecie, *Matth. 24.27.* points out such a progresse of the Gospell. It is true, that the comparison there used taken from the Lightning, aymes at the sudden dispersing of the knowledge of Christ by the Apostles ministery: but whereas wee know, the Lightning shines from divers parts of the heaven, shewing it selfe indifferently, sometimes in the West, sometimes in the North, or South; why doth our Saviour . . . choose to name the Lightning that shines out of the East into the West, unlesse it be to expresse not only the sudden shining out of the Gospell; but withall the way, and passage, by which it proceeds from one end of the world to the other, that is, from East to West?[77]

It was not merely the true Word that must move westward. Of all the world's nations, wrote Samuel Sewall in 1713, America was best suited for the "Government of Christ" precisely because it was "*the Beginning of the* East, *and the End of the West,*" for which reason, he supposed, Columbus had pronounced the continent "*Alpha* and *Omega.*" It was the last new world because it was at the western extremity, and "if the *Last ADAM* did give Order for the engraving of his own Name upon this *last Earth:* 'twill draw with it great Consequences; even such as will, in time, bring the poor *Americans* out of their Graves, and make them live." Because of its western and therefore holy location the new nation was destined, by the inevitable course of affairs, for a future bathed in divine glory: "May it not with more, or equal

strength be argued, *New-Jerusalem* is not the same with *Jerusalem:* but as *Jerusalem* was to the westward of *Babylon;* so *New-Jerusalem* must be to the westward of *Rome;* to avoid disturbance in the Order of these Mysteries."[78] The city of God had had many capitals, and as each failed, the new emerged to the west. Now, at the last western point, the new capital was established and because there was no west left, it was man's last chance. Mankind's prayer for salvation thus depended upon the success of the most western and most holy commonwealth.[79]

It was the most inclusive mind of colonial America whose conception of the cosmic significance of the New World was partly determined by the idea that God faced west. Jonathan Edwards, synthesizing the earlier ideas of Purchas, Hayes, and John White, wrote that:

> when the Sun of Righteousness, the Sun of the new heavens and new earth, comes to rise . . . , the sun shall *rise in the west,* contrary to the course of this world, or the course of things in the old heavens and earth. . . . The Sun of Righteousness has long been going down from east to west; and probably when the time comes of the church's deliverance from her enemies . . . the light will rise in the west, until it shines through the world like the sun in its meridian brightness.[80]

Rising out of New England the real sun and the sun of righteousness would light and warm the saints throughout the world. Through the past, nature had been preparing for this great reversal,

[77] *John White,* The Planters Plea (*London, 1630*), *reprinted in* Tracts and Other Papers, *ed. Peter Force (4 vols., Washington, D. C., 1838–46), II, 7.*

[78] *Samuel Sewall,* Phaenomena quaedam Apocalyptica ad Aspectum Novi Orbis Configurata (*Boston, 1713*), *2–3, 31.*

[79] *Samuel Stillman,* An Oration Delivered July 4th, 1789 (*Boston, 1789*), *29.*

[80] *Jonathan Edwards,* Thoughts on the Revival of Religion in New England, 1740 (*New York, n.d.*), *196–97.*

which would signify the greater reversal in man's depraved nature. It can be suggested that the usual course of the sun was itself an aberration, marking man's own fall from grace. Both nature and human nature would be corrected when God led men far enough to the west.

Thus, as the west once more became a place, as it had been for Horace and Bran, and a direction, as it had been for Virgil and Columbus, America, in the minds of the Puritans, became the best and last refuge for Christ. Standing on what was thought of as the westernmost part of the round earth, it was inevitable, according to this Puritan mentality, that it should be so. All that was necessary now was to revive the still older idea of the course of empire, couple it with the course of Christ, and America would have her ideology of might and right. As seventeenth-century Americans had Christianized the idea of the west by relating it to the kingdom of God, eighteenth-century Americans secularized it by recalling the west of empire.

The imperial idea of the west became one basis of the hope that America would one day be great in power. Before the middle of the eighteenth century, Bishop George Berkeley, employing the same kind of argument that Virgil and Geoffrey had used, applied the imperial west to America:

> Westward the course of empire takes its way;
> The four first Acts already past,
> A fifth shall close the Drama with the Day;
> Time's noblest offspring is the last.[81]

Joel Barlow, the poet of republican virtue, who also identified the apocalypse and America, agreed by writing:

> Earth's blood-stain'd empires, with their Guide the Sun
> From Orient climes their gradual progress run;
> And circling far, reach every western shore,
> 'Til earth-born empires rise and fall no more.[82]

Just past mid-century, Nathaniel Ames, of almanac fame, took a less political view: "the Progress of Humane Literature (like the Sun) is from the East to the West; thus has it travelled thro' *Asia* and *Europe*, and now is arrived at the Eastern Shore of *America* . . . ," and Benjamin Franklin agreed.[83] By 1775, John Witherspoon, preaching at Princeton, could combine every one of these ideas when he articulated what was to become the usual

are borne with . . . complexion white as our nation, but their mothers in their infancy make a bath of Wallnut leaves . . . and such things as will staine their skinne for ever, wherein they dip and washe them to make them tawny. . . ." Thomas Morton, New English Canaan (*n.p.*, 1632), 16–18, 24, 39–40; *cf. Sidney Lee, "The Call of the West,"* Scribner's Magazine, *XLII (Sept., 1907), 313.*

[82] *Leon Howard,* The Connecticut Wits (*Chicago, 1943), 136; cf. Philip Freneau,* Poems, *ed. F. L. Pattee (8 vols., Princeton, N. J., 1902–1907), I, 82. The idea also continued to inspire English poets, e.g., Percy B. Shelley, "Hellas,"* Works, *ed. H. B. Forman (8 vols., London, 1876–80), III, 50; William Blake, "America,"* The Poems and Prophecies of William Blake, *ed. Max Plowman (London, n.d.), 64; David V. Erdman,* Blake (*Princeton, N. J., 1954), 353.*

[83] *Sam Briggs,* The Essays, Humor, and Poems of Nathaniel Ames (*Cleveland, 1891), 285–86; Benjamin Franklin,* Writings, *ed. A. H. Smyth (10 vols., New York, 1905–1907), IV, 194; cf. Thomas Paine,* Life and Works, *ed. W. M. Van der Weyde (9 vols., New Rochelle, N. Y., 1925), VI, 236; John Adams,* Works, *ed. C. F. Adams (10 vols., Boston, 1855–56), IX, 597, 599–600.*

[81] *George Berkeley,* Works, *ed. A. C. Fraser (3 vols., Oxford, Eng., 1871), III, 232. One curious use of Geoffrey's tale of Brutus was made by the incorrigible Thomas Morton of Merrymount in 1629; he argued "that the originall of the Natives of New England may be well conjectured to be from the scattered Trojans, after such time as Brutus departed from Latium." Because these Indians were Trojans it was necessary for Morton to explain the color of their skin: "Their infants*

American formula—"some have observed that true religion, and in her train, dominion, riches, literature, and art, have taken their course in a slow and gradual manner, from East to West, since the earth was settled after the flood: and from thence forebode the future glory of America."[84] The secular and sacred ideas of the west were thus brought back together, where they stayed throughout the nineteenth century in the United States, appearing in most marked fashion in the concept of manifest destiny. Remembering Seneca's prophecy, Edward Everett said that with the United States it had finally come true.[85]

Appropriately enough, it was Henry David Thoreau who personified the American mythology of the west. The west meant freedom: "Eastward I go only by force; but westward I go free." It was the way of the race: "I must walk toward Oregon, and not toward Europe. And that way the nation is moving, and I may say that mankind progresses from east to west." To the east lay history, while westward was the apocalypse, the future, and "adventure." That he involuntarily consented "in his pettiest walk with the general movement of the race," indicated to him that the west excited deep in his consciousness an irresistible urge: "Every sunset which I witness inspires me with the desire to go to a West as distant and as fair as that into which the sun goes down." Feeling this he could understand "the foundation of all those fables" of the west from the report of Atlantis to his own day. But, as an American, his song of the west was tied to the nation; only in America did the west exist, else "why was America discovered?" Clearly, to give men their chance, the last the race would have, to be born again, and to give the nation its chance too. "To Americans," he said, "I hardly need to say,—'Westward the star of empire takes its way.'"[86] In his own person, Thoreau, as American,[87] combined the west of happiness and eternity, the west of millennium, and that of empire, the west of direction, and the west of place. He could not do more.

As the continent began to fill up, the American West, like Brendan's islands, seemed to disappear as one got closer. From Thomas Jefferson through Frederick Jackson Turner, the American West faded from the Atlantic shore. An American artist saw the problem: "Few people even know the true definition of the term 'West'; and where is its location?—phantom-like it flies before us as we travel. . . ."[88] But before the hopeful west flew from America, it had meant salvation for the nation and identity for those who partook of its magic.

For so long then did men turn westward with

[84] *Rutherford E. Delmage, "The American Idea of Progress,"* Proceedings of the American Philosophical Society, XCI (Oct., 1947), 310; *cf. Andrew Burnaby,* Travels through the Middle Settlements in North America, ed. John Pinkerton (London, 1812), 750; L'Abbé F. Galiani. Correspondence, ed. C. C. Levy (2 vols., Paris, 1889), II, 553; John Galt, The Life, Studies, and Works of Benjamin West (London, 1820), 114–17.

[85] *"There are no more continents to be reached; Atlantis hath arisen from the ocean . . . ; there are no more retreats beyond the sea, no more discoveries, no more hopes." Edward Everett,* Orations and Speeches on Various Occasions (7th ed., 3 vols., Boston, 1865), I, 42.

[86] *Henry David Thoreau,* Excursions (*Riverside ed., 11 vols., Boston, 1894–95*), IX, 266–73.

[87] *Wyndham Lewis,* America and Cosmic Man (*New York, 1949*), 26–27. Suggestions about the application of a more or less undifferentiated west are in John M. Anderson, The Individual and the New World (State College, Pa., 1955), 15–38; Arthur K. Moore, The Frontier Mind (Lexington, Ky., 1957), 1–24; Sanford, "An American," 297–302.

[88] *George Catlin,* Letters and Notes on the Manners, Customs, and Conditions of the North American Indians (*Philadelphia, 1859*), 110.

their cravings and aspirations. And beyond the golden gate of the western world the east began, so that the New World, and finally the United States, was thought of by some as the last refuge for man and God, that western world where woe and wail would be no more. A later poet, himself in this tradition, believed that America had been

> Foreseen in the vision of sages,
> Foretold when martyrs bled,
> She was born of the longing of ages. . . .[89]

The list of sages was long, stretching at least from Horace to Horace Greeley. In this way men made of Columbia the last of the many gems of the ocean, an apocalyptical land where men could hope to plant their seed and live happily ever after.

[89] *Bayard Taylor,* The National Ode *(Boston, 1877), 39, delivered July 4, 1876. See also Richard Watson Gilder, "The White City," in* Poems of American History, *ed. Burton E. Stevenson (Boston, 1908), 602; William Faulkner,* Mosquitoes *(New York, 1953), 27.*

THE SIGNIFICANCE OF THE FRONTIER IN AMERICAN HISTORY

*Frederick Jackson Turner** *

In a recent bulletin of the Superintendent of the Census for 1890 appear these significant words: "Up to and including 1880 the country had a frontier of settlement, but at present the unsettled area has been so broken into by isolated bodies of settlement that there can hardly be said to be a frontier line. In the discussion of its extent, its westward movement, etc., it can not, therefore,

*FREDERICK JACKSON TURNER (1861–1932) was a Professor of American History at the University of Wisconsin and Harvard University. His publications include The Rise of the New West *(1906),* The Frontier in American History *(1920), and* The Significance of Sections in American History *(1932). From* The Frontier in American History *by Frederick Jackson Turner. Copyright 1920 by Frederick Jackson Turner. Copyright 1948 by Caroline M. S. Turner. Reprinted by permission of Holt, Rinehart and Winston, Inc.*

any longer have a place in the census reports." This brief official statement marks the closing of a great historic movement. Up to our own day American history has been in a large degree the history of the colonization of the Great West. The existence of an area of free land, its continuous recession, and the advance of American settlement westward, explain American development.

Behind institutions, behind constitutional forms and modifications, lie the vital forces that call these organs into life and shape them to meet changing conditions. The peculiarity of American institutions is, the fact that they have been compelled to adapt themselves to the changes of an expanding people—to the changes involved in crossing a continent, in winning a wilderness, and in developing at each area of this progress out of the primitive economic and political conditions of the frontier into the complexity of city life. Said Calhoun in 1817, "We are great, and rapidly—I was about to say fearfully—growing!"[1] So saying, he touched the distinguishing feature of American life. All peoples show development; the germ theory of politics has been sufficiently emphasized. In the case of most nations, however, the development has occurred in a limited area; and if the nation has expanded, it has met other growing peoples whom it has conquered. But in the case of the United States we have a different phenomenon. Limiting our attention to the Atlantic coast, we have the familiar phenomenon of the evolution of institutions in a limited area, such as the rise of representative government; the differentiation of simple colonial governments into complex organs; the progress from primitive industrial society, without division of labor, up to manufacturing civilization. But we have in addition to this a recurrence of the process of evolution in each western area reached in the process of expansion.

[1] *Abridgment of Debates of Congress, v., p. 706.*

Thus American development has exhibited not merely advance along a single line, but a return to primitive conditions on a continually advancing frontier line, and a new development for that area. American social development has been continually beginning over again on the frontier. This perennial rebirth, this fluidity of American life, this expansion westward with its new opportunities, its continuous touch with the simplicity of primitive society, furnish the forces dominating American character. The true point of view in the history of this nation is not the Atlantic coast, it is the great West. Even the slavery struggle, which is made so exclusive an object of attention by writers like Prof. von Holst, occupies its important place in American history because of its relation to westward expansion.

In this advance, the frontier is the outer edge of the wave—the meeting point between savagery and civilization. Much has been written about the frontier from the point of view of border warfare and the chase, but as a field for the serious study of the economist and the historian it has been neglected.

The American frontier is sharply distinguished from the European frontier—a fortified boundary line running through dense populations. The most significant thing about the American frontier is, that it lies at the hither edge of free land. In the census reports it is treated as the margin of that settlement which has a density of two or more to the square mile. The term is an elastic one, and for our purposes does not need sharp definition. We shall consider the whole frontier belt, including the Indian country and the outer margin of the "settled area" of the census reports. This paper will make no attempt to treat the subject exhaustively; its aim is simply to call attention to the frontier as a fertile field for investigation, and to suggest some of the problems which arise in connection with it.

In the settlement of America we have to observe how European life entered the continent, and how America modified and developed that life and reacted on Europe. Our early history is the study of European germs developing in an American environment. Too exclusive attention has been paid by institutional students to the Germanic origins, too little to the American factors. The frontier is the line of most rapid and effective Americanization. The wilderness masters the colonist. It finds him a European in dress, industries, tools, modes of travel, and thought. It takes him from the railroad car and puts him in the birch canoe. It strips off the garments of civilization and arrays him in the hunting shirt and the moccasin. It puts him in the log cabin of the Cherokee and Iroquois and runs an Indian palisade around him. Before long he has gone to planting Indian corn and plowing with a sharp stick; he shouts the war cry and takes the scalp in orthodox Indian fashion. In short, at the frontier the environment is at first too strong for the man. He must accept the conditions which it furnishes, or perish, and so he fits himself into the Indian clearings and follows the Indian trails. Little by little he transforms the wilderness, but the outcome is not the old Europe, not simply the development of Germanic germs, any more than the first phenomenon was a case of reversion to the Germanic mark. The fact is, that here is a new product that is American. At first, the frontier was the Atlantic coast. It was the frontier of Europe in a very real sense. Moving westward, the frontier became more and more American. As successive terminal moraines result from successive glaciations, so each frontier leaves its traces behind it, and when it becomes a settled area the region still partakes of the frontier characteristics. Thus the advance of the frontier has meant a steady movement away from the influence of Europe, a steady growth of independence on American lines. And to study this advance, the men who grew up under these conditions, and the political, economic, and social results of it, is to study the really American part of our history.

In the course of the seventeenth century the frontier was advanced up the Atlantic river courses, just beyond the "fall line," and the tidewater region became the settled area. In the first half of the eighteenth century another advance occurred. Traders followed the Delaware and Shawnese Indians to the Ohio as early as the end of the first quarter of the century.[2] Gov. Spotswood, of Virginia, made an expedition in 1714 across the Blue Ridge. The end of the first quarter of the century saw the advance of the Scotch-Irish and the Palatine Germans up the Shenandoah Valley into the western part of Virginia, and along the Piedmont region of the Carolinas.[3] The Germans in New York pushed the frontier of settlement up the Mohawk to German Flats.[4] In Pennsylvania the town of Bedford indicates the line of settlement. Settlements had begun on New River, a branch of the Kanawha, and on the sources of the Yadkin and French Broad.[5] The King attempted to arrest the advance by his proclamation of 1763,[6] forbidding settlements beyond the sources of the rivers flowing into the Atlantic; but in vain. In the period of the Revolution the frontier crossed the

[2] *Bancroft* (1860 ed.), III, pp. 344, 345, citing Logan MSS.; [Mitchell] *Contest in America*, etc. (1752), p. 237.

[3] *Kercheval, History of the Valley; Bernheim, German Settlements in the Carolinas; Winsor, Narrative and Critical History of America*, V, p. 304; *Colonial Records of North Carolina*, IV, p. xx; *Weston, Documents Connected with the History of South Carolina*, p. 82; *Ellis and Evans, History of Lancaster County, Pa.*, chs. iii, xxvi.

[4] *Parkman, Pontiac*, II; *Griffis, Sir William Johnson*, p. 6; *Simms's Frontiersmen of New York*.

[5] *Monette, Mississippi Valley*, I, p. 311.

[6] *Wis. Hist. Cols.*, xi, p. 50; *Hinsdale, Old Northwest*, p. 121; *Burke, "Oration on Conciliation," Works* (1872 ed.), I, p. 473.

Alleghanies into Kentucky and Tennessee, and the upper waters of the Ohio were settled.[7] When the first census was taken in 1790, the continuous settled area was bounded by a line which ran near the coast of Maine, and included New England except a portion of Vermont and New Hampshire, New York along the Hudson and up the Mohawk about Schenectady, eastern and southern Pennsylvania, Virginia well across the Shenandoah Valley, and the Carolinas and eastern Georgia.[8] Beyond this region of continuous settlement were the small settled areas of Kentucky and Tennessee, and the Ohio, with the mountains intervening between them and the Atlantic area, thus giving a new and important character to the frontier. The isolation of the region increased its peculiarly American tendencies, and the need of transportation facilities to connect it with the East called out important schemes of internal improvement, which will be noted farther on. The "West," as a self-conscious section, began to evolve.

From decade to decade distinct advances of the frontier occurred. By the census of 1820[9] the settled area included Ohio, southern Indiana and Illinois, southeastern Missouri, and about one-half of Louisiana. This settled area had surrounded Indian areas, and the management of these tribes became an object of political concern. The frontier region of the time lay along the Great Lakes, where Astor's American Fur Company operated in the Indian trade,[10] and beyond the Mississippi, where Indian traders extended their activity even to the Rocky Mountains; Florida also furnished frontier conditions. The Mississippi River region was the scene of typical frontier settlements.[11]

The rising steam navigation[12] on western waters, the opening of the Erie Canal, and the westward extension of cotton[13] culture added five frontier states to the Union in this period. Grund, writing in 1836, declares: "It appears then that

7 Roosevelt, *Winning of the West*, and citations there given; *Cutler's Life of Cutler*.

8 *Scribner's Statistical Atlas*, xxxviii, pl. 13; MacMaster, *Hist. of People of U. S.*, I, pp. 4, 60, 61; Imlay and Filson, *Western Territory of America* (London, 1793); Rochefoucault-Liancourt, *Travels Through the United States of North America* (London, 1799); Michaux's "Journal," in *Proceedings American Philosophical Society*, XXVI, No. 129; Forman, *Narrative of a Journey Down the Ohio and Mississippi in 1780–90* (Cincinnati, 1888); Bartram, *Travels Through North Carolina, etc.* (London, 1792); Pope, *Tour Through the Southern and Western Territories, etc.* (Richmond, 1792); Weld, *Travels Through the States of North America* (London, 1799); Baily, *Journal of a Tour in the Unsettled States of North America, 1796–97* (London, 1856); *Pennsylvania Magazine of History*, July, 1886; Winsor, *Narrative and Critical History of America*, VII, pp. 491, 492, citations.

9 *Scribner's Statistical Atlas*, xxxix.

10 Turner, *Character and Influence of the Indian Trade in Wisconsin* (Johns Hopkins University Studies, Series IX), pp. 61 ff.

11 Monette, *History of the Mississippi Valley*, II; Flint, *Travels and Residence in Mississippi*; Flint, *Geography and History of the Western States*; *Abridgment of Debates of Congress*, VII, pp. 397, 398, 404; Holmes, *Account of the U. S.*; Kingdom, *America and the British Colonies* (London, 1820); Grund, *Americans*, II, chs. i, iii, vi (although writing in 1836, he treats of conditions that grew out of western advance from the era of 1820 to that time); Peck, *Guide for Emigrants* (Boston, 1831); Darby, *Emigrants' Guide to Western and Southwestern States and Territories*; Dana, *Geographical Sketches in the Western Country*; Kinzie, *Waubun*; Keating, *Narrative of Long's Expedition*; Schoolcraft, *Discovery of the Sources of the Mississippi River*, *Travels in the Central Portions of the Mississippi Valley, and Lead Mines of the Missouri*; Andreas, *History of Illinois*, I, 86–99; Hurlbut, *Chicago Antiquities*; McKenney, *Tour to the Lakes*; Thomas, *Travels through the Western Country, etc.* (Auburn, N. Y., 1819).

12 Darby, *Emigrants' Guide*, pp. 272 ff.; Benton, *Abridgment of Debates*, VII, p. 397.

13 *De Bow's Review*, IV, p. 254; XVII, p. 428.

the universal disposition of Americans to emigrate to the western wilderness, in order to enlarge their dominion over inanimate nature, is the actual result of an expansive power which is inherent in them, and which by continually agitating all classes of society is constantly throwing a large portion of the whole population on the extreme confines of the State, in order to gain space for its development. Hardly is a new State or Territory formed before the same principle manifests itself again and gives rise to a further emigration; and so is it destined to go on until a physical barrier must finally obstruct its progress."[14]

In the middle of this century the line indicated by the present eastern boundary of Indian Territory, Nebraska, and Kansas marked the frontier of the Indian country.[15] Minnesota and Wisconsin still exhibited frontier conditions,[16] but the dis-

tinctive frontier of the period is found in California where the gold discoveries had sent a sudden tide of adventurous miners, and in Oregon, and the settlements in Utah.[17] As the frontier had leaped over the Alleghanies, so now it skipped the Great Plains and the Rocky Mountains; and in the same way that the advance of the frontiersmen beyond the Alleghanies had caused the rise of important questions of transportation and internal improvement, so now the settlers beyond the Rocky Mountains needed means of communication with the East, and in the furnishing of these arose the settlement of the Great Plains and the development of still another kind of frontier life. Railroads, fostered by land grants, sent an increasing tide of immigrants into the far West. The United States Army fought a series of Indian wars in Minnesota, Dakota, and the Indian Territory.

By 1880 the settled area had been pushed into northern Michigan, Wisconsin, and Minnesota, along Dakota rivers, and in the Black Hills region, and was ascending the rivers of Kansas and Nebraska. The development of mines in Colorado had drawn isolated frontier settlements into that region, and Montana and Idaho were receiving settlers. The frontier was found in these mining camps and the ranches of the Great Plains. The superintendent of the census for 1890 reports, as previously stated, that the settlements of the West lie so scattered over the region that there can no longer be said to be a frontier line.

In these successive frontiers we find natural boundary lines which have served to mark and to affect the characteristics of the frontiers, namely: The "fall line"; the Alleghany Mountains; the Mississippi; the Missouri, where its direction approximates north and south; the line of the arid lands, approximately the ninety-ninth meridian; and the Rocky Mountains. The fall line marked

14 *Grund, Americans, II, p. 8.*

15 *Peck, New Guide to the West (Cincinnati, 1848), ch. IV; Parkman, Oregon Trail; Hall, The West (Cincinnati, 1848); Pierce, Incidents of Western Travel; Murray, Travels in North America; Lloyd, Steamboat Directory (Cincinnati, 1856); "Forty Days in a Western Hotel" (Chicago), in Putnam's Magazine, December, 1894; Mackay, The Western World, II, ch. II, III; Meeker, Life in the West; Bogen, German in America (Boston, 1851); Olmstead, Texas Journey; Greeley, Recollections of a Busy Life; Schouler, History of the United States, V, 261–267; Peyton, Over the Alleghanies and Across the Prairies (London, 1870); Loughborough, The Pacific Telegraph and Railway (St. Louis, 1849); Whitney, Project for a Railroad to the Pacific (New York, 1849); Peyton, Suggestions on Railroad Communication with the Pacific, and the Trade of China and the Indian Islands; Benton, Highway to the Pacific (a speech delivered in the U. S. Senate, December 16, 1850).*

16 *A writer in The Home Missionary (1850), p. 239, reporting Wisconsin conditions, explains: "Think of this, people of the enlightened East. What an example, to come from the very frontiers of civilization!" But one of the missionaries writes: "In a few years Wisconsin will no longer be considered as the West, or as an outpost of civilization, any more than western New York, or the Western Reserve."*

17 *Bancroft (H. H.), History of California, History of Oregon, and Popular Tribunals; Shinn, Mining Camps.*

the frontier of the seventeenth century; the Alleghanies that of the eighteenth; the Mississippi that of the first quarter of the nineteenth; the Missouri that of the middle of this century (omitting the California movement); and the belt of the Rocky Mountains and the arid tract, the present frontier. Each was won by a series of Indian wars.

At the Atlantic frontier one can study the germs of processes repeated at each successive frontier. We have the complex European life sharply precipitated by the wilderness into the simplicity of primitive conditions. The first frontier had to meet its Indian question, its question of the disposition of the public domain, of the means of intercourse with older settlements, of the extension of political organization, of religious and educational activity. And the settlement of these and similar questions for one frontier served as a guide for the next. The American student needs not to go to the "prim little townships of Sleswick" for illustrations of the law of continuity and development. For example, he may study the origin of our land policies in the colonial land policy: he may see how the system grew by adapting the statutes to the customs of the successive frontiers.[18] He may see how the mining experience in the lead regions of Wisconsin, Illinois, and Iowa was applied to the mining laws of the Rockies,[19] and how our Indian policy has been a series of experimentations on successive frontiers. Each tier of new States has found in the older ones material for its constitutions.[20] Each frontier has made similar contributions to American character, as will be discussed farther on.

[18] *See the suggestive paper by Prof. Jesse Macy. The Institutional Beginnings of a Western State.*

[19] *Shinn, Mining Camps.*

[20] *Compare Thorpe, in Annals American Academy of Political and Social Science, September, 1891; Bryce, American Commonwealth (1888), II, p. 689.*

But with all these similarities there are essential differences, due to the place element and the time element. It is evident that the farming frontier of the Mississippi Valley presents different conditions from the mining frontier of the Rocky Mountains. The frontier reached by the Pacific Railroad, surveyed into rectangles, guarded by the United States Army, and recruited by the daily immigrant ship, moves forward at a swifter pace and in a different way than the frontier reached by the birch canoe or the pack horse. The geologist traces patiently the shores of ancient seas, maps their areas, and compares the older and the newer. It would be a work worth the historian's labors to mark these various frontiers and in detail compare one with another. Not only would there result a more adequate conception of American development and characteristics, but invaluable additions would be made to the history of society.

Loria,[21] the Italian economist, has urged the study of colonial life as an aid in understanding the stages of European development, affirming that colonial settlement is for economic science what the mountain is for geology, bringing to light primitive stratifications. "America," he says, "has the key to the historical enigma which Europe has sought for centuries in vain, and the land which has no history reveals luminously the course of universal history." There is much truth in this. The United States lies like a huge page in the history of society. Line by line as we read this continental page from west to east we find the record of social evolution. It begins with the Indian and the hunter; it goes on to tell of the disintegration of savagery by the entrance of the trader, the pathfinder of civilization; we read the annals of the pastoral stage in ranch life; the exploitation of the soil by the raising of unrotated crops of corn and wheat in sparsely settled farming

[21] *Loria, Analisi della Proprieta Capitalista, II., p. 15.*

communities; the intensive culture of the denser farm settlement; and finally the manufacturing organization with city and factory system.[22] This page is familiar to the student of census statistics, but how little of it has been used by our historians. Particularly in eastern States this page is a palimpsest. What is now a manufacturing State was in an earlier decade an area of intensive farming. Earlier yet it had been a wheat area, and still earlier the "range" had attracted the cattle-herder. Thus Wisconsin, now developing manufacture, is a State with varied agricultural interests. But earlier it was given over to almost exclusive grain-raising, like North Dakota at the present time.

Each of these areas has had an influence in our economic and political history; the evolution of each into a higher stage has worked political transformations. But what constitutional historian has made any adequate attempt to interpret political facts by the light of these social areas and changes?[23]

The Atlantic frontier was compounded of fisherman, fur-trader, miner, cattle-raiser, and farmer. Excepting the fisherman, each type of industry was on the march toward the West, impelled by an irresistible attraction. Each passed in successive waves across the continent. Stand at Cumberland Gap and watch the procession of civilization, marching single file—the buffalo following the trail to the salt springs, the Indian, the fur-trader and hunter, the cattle-raiser, the pioneer farmer—

and the frontier has passed by. Stand at South Pass in the Rockies a century later and see the same procession with wider intervals between. The unequal rate of advance compels us to distinguish the frontier into the trader's frontier, the rancher's frontier, or the miner's frontier, and the farmer's frontier. When the mines and the cow pens were still near the fall line the traders' pack trains were tinkling across the Alleghanies, and the French on the Great Lakes were fortifying their posts, alarmed by the British trader's birch canoe. When the trappers scaled the Rockies, the farmer was still near the mouth of the Missouri.

Why was it that the Indian trader passed so rapidly across the continent? What effects followed from the trader's frontier? The trade was coeval with American discovery. The Norsemen, Vespuccius, Verrazani, Hudson, John Smith, all trafficked for furs. The Plymouth pilgrims settled in Indian cornfields, and their first return cargo was of beaver and lumber. The records of the various New England colonies show how steadily exploration was carried into the wilderness by this trade. What is true for New England is, as would be expected, even plainer for the rest of the colonies. All along the coast from Maine to Georgia the Indian trade opened up the river courses. Steadily the trader passed westward, utilizing the older lines of French trade. The Ohio, the Great Lakes, the Mississippi, the Missouri, and the Platte, the lines of western advance, were ascended by traders. They found the passes in the Rocky Mountains and guided Lewis and Clarke,[24] Frémont, and Bidwell. The explanation of the rapidity of this advance is connected with the effects of the trader on the Indian. The trading post left the unarmed tribes at the mercy of those that had purchased fire-arms—a truth which the Iroquois

[22] *Compare Observations on the North American Land Company, London, 1796, pp. xv, 144; Logan, History of Upper South Carolina, I, pp. 149–151; Turner, Character and Influence of Indian Trade in Wisconsin, p. 18; Peck, New Guide for Emigrants (Boston, 1837), ch. iv; Compendium Eleventh Census, I, p. xl.*

[23] *See pages 220, 221, 223, post, for illustrations of the political accompaniments of changed industrial conditions.*

[24] *But Lewis and Clarke were the first to explore the route from the Missouri to the Columbia.*

Indians wrote in blood, and so the remote and unvisited tribes gave eager welcome to the trader. "The savages," wrote La Salle, "take better care of us French than of their own children; from us only can they get guns and goods." This accounts for the trader's power and the rapidity of his advance. Thus the disintegrating forces of civilization entered the wilderness. Every river valley and Indian trail became a fissure in Indian society, and so that society became honeycombed. Long before the pioneer farmer appeared on the scene, primitive Indian life had passed away. The farmers met Indians armed with guns. The trading frontier, while steadily undermining Indian power by making the tribes ultimately dependent on the whites, yet, through its sale of guns, gave to the Indians increased power of resistance to the farming frontier. French colonization was dominated by its trading frontier; English colonization by its farming frontier. There was an antagonism between the two frontiers as between the two nations. Said Duquesne to the Iroquois, "Are you ignorant of the difference between the king of England and the king of France? Go see the forts that our king has established and you will see that you can still hunt under their very walls. They have been placed for your advantage in places which you frequent. The English, on the contrary, are no sooner in possession of a place than the game is driven away. The forest falls before them as they advance, and the soil is laid bare so that you can scarce find the wherewithal to erect a shelter for the night."

And yet, in spite of this opposition of the interests of the trader and the farmer, the Indian trade pioneered the way for civilization. The buffalo trail became the Indian trail, and this because the trader's "trace"; the trails widened into roads, and the roads into turnpikes, and these in turn were transformed into railroads. The same origin can be shown for the railroads of the South, the far

West, and the Dominion of Canada.[25] The trading posts reached by these trails were on the sites of Indian villages which had been placed in positions suggested by nature; and these trading posts, situated so as to command the water systems of the country, have grown into such cities as Albany, Pittsburgh, Detroit, Chicago, St. Louis, Council Bluffs, and Kansas City. Thus civilization in America has followed the arteries made by geology, pouring an ever richer tide through them, until at last the slender paths of aboriginal intercourse have been broadened and interwoven into the complex mazes of modern commercial lines; the wilderness has been interpenetrated by lines of civilization growing ever more numerous. It is like the steady growth of a complex nervous system for the originally simple, inert continent. If one would understand why we are to-day one nation, rather than a collecting of isolated states, he must study this economic and social consolidation of the country. In this progress from savage conditions lie topics for the evolutionist.[26]

The effect of the Indian frontier as a consolidating agent in our history is important. From the close of the seventeenth century various intercolonial congresses have been called to treat with Indians and establish common measures of defense. Particularism was strongest in colonies with no Indian frontier. This frontier stretched along the western border like a cord of union. The Indian was a common danger, demanding united action. Most celebrated of these conferences was the Albany congress of 1754, called to treat with the

[25] *Narrative and Critical History of America, VIII, p. 10; Sparks' Washington Works, IX, pp. 303, 327; Logan, History of Upper South Carolina, I; McDonald, Life of Kenton, p. 72; Cong. Record, XXIII, p. 57.*

[26] *On the effect of the fur trade in opening the routes of migration, see the author's Character and Influence of the Indian Trade in Wisconsin.*

Six Nations, and to consider plans of union. Even a cursory reading of the plan proposed by the congress reveals the importance of the frontier. The powers of the general council and the officers were, chiefly, the determination of peace and war with the Indians, the regulation of Indian trade, the purchase of Indian lands, and the creation and government of new settlements as a security against the Indians. It is evident that the unifying tendencies of the Revolutionary period were facilitated by the previous cooperation in the regulation of the frontier. In this connection may be mentioned the importance of the frontier, from that day to this, as a military training school, keeping alive the power of resistance to aggression, and developing the stalwart and rugged qualities of the frontiersman.

It would not be possible in the limits of this paper to trace the other frontiers across the continent. Travelers of the eighteenth century found the "cowpens" among the canebrakes and peavine pastures of the South, and the "cow drivers" took their droves to Charleston, Philadelphia, and New York.[27] Travelers at the close of the War of 1812 met droves of more than a thousand cattle and swine from the interior of Ohio going to Pennsylvania to fatten for the Philadelphia market.[28] The ranges of the Great Plains, with ranch and cowboy and nomadic life, are things of yesterday and of to-day. The experience of the Carolina cowpens guided the ranchers of Texas. One element favoring the rapid extension of the rancher's frontier is the fact that in a remote country lacking transportation facilities the product must be in small bulk, or must be able to transport itself, and the cattle raiser could easily drive his product to market. The effect of these great ranches on the

subsequent agrarian history of the localities in which they existed should be studied.

The maps of the census reports show an uneven advance of the farmer's frontier, with tongues of settlement pushed forward and with indentations of wilderness. In part this is due to Indian resistance, in part to the location of river valleys and passes, in part to the unequal force of the centers of frontier attraction. Among the important centers of attraction may be mentioned the following: fertile and favorably situated soils, salt springs, mines, and army posts.

The frontier army post, serving to protect the settlers from the Indians, has also acted as a wedge to open the Indian country, and has been a nucleus for settlement.[29] In this connection mention should also be made of the Government military and exploring expeditions in determining the lines of settlement. But all the more important expeditions were greatly indebted to the earliest pathmakers, the Indian guides, the traders and trappers, and the French voyageurs, who were inevitable parts of governmental expeditions from the days of Lewis and Clarke.[30] Each expedition was an epitome of the previous factors in western advance.

In an interesting monograph, Victor Hehn[31] has traced the effect of salt upon early European development, and has pointed out how it affected the lines of settlement and the form of administration. A similar study might be made for the salt springs of the United States. The early settlers were tied to the coast by the need of salt, without which they could not preserve their meats or live in comfort. Writing in 1752, Bishop Spangenburg says of a colony for which he was seeking lands in North Carolina, "They will require salt & other

---

[27] *Lodge, English Colonies, p. 152 and citations; Logan, Hist. of Upper South Carolina, I, p. 151.*

[28] *Flint, Recollections, p. 9.*

[29] *See Monette, Mississippi Valley, I, p. 344.*

[30] *Coues', Lewis and Clarke's Expedition, I, pp. 2, 253–259; Benton, in Cong. Record, XXIII, p. 57.*

[31] *Hohn, Das Salz (Berlin, 1873).*

necessaries which they can neither manufacture nor raise. Either they must go to Charleston, which is 300 miles distant * * * Or else they must go to Boling's Point in Vᵃ on a branch of the James & is also 300 miles from here * * * Or else they must go down the Roanoke—I know not how many miles—where salt is brought up from the Cape Fear."³² This may serve as a typical illustration. An annual pilgrimage to the coast for salt thus became essential. Taking flocks or furs and ginseng root, the early settlers sent their pack trains after seeding time each year to the coast.³³ This proved to be an important educational influence, since it was almost the only way in which the pioneer learned what was going on in the East. But when discovery was made of the salt springs of the Kanawha, and the Holston, and Kentucky, and central New York, the West began to be freed from dependence on the coast. It was in part the effect of finding these salt springs that enabled settlements to cross the mountains.

From the time the mountains rose between the pioneer and the seaboard, a new order of Americanism arose. The West and the East began to get out of touch of each other. The settlements from the sea to the mountains kept connection with the rear and had a certain solidarity. But the over-mountain men grew more and more independent. The East took a narrow view of American advance, and nearly lost these men. Kentucky and Tennessee history bears abundant witness to the truth of this statement. The East began to try to hedge and limit westward expansion. Though Webster could declare that there were no Alleghanies in his politics, yet in politics in general they were a very solid factor.

³² *Col. Records of N. C., V, p. 3.*
³³ *Findley, History of the Insurrection in the Four Western Counties of Pennsylvania in the Year 1794 (Philadelphia, 1796), p. 35.*

The exploitation of the beasts took hunter and trader to the west, the exploitation of the grasses took the rancher west, and the exploitation of the virgin soil of the river valleys and prairies attracted the farmer. Good soils have been the most continuous attraction to the farmer's frontier. The land hunger of the Virginians drew them down the rivers into Carolina, in early colonial days; the search for soils took the Massachusetts men to Pennsylvania and to New York. As the eastern lands were taken up migration flowed across them to the west. Daniel Boone, the great backwoodsman, who combined the occupations of hunter, trader, cattle-raiser, farmer, and surveyor—learning, probably from the traders, of the fertility of the lands on the upper Yadkin, where the traders were wont to rest as they took their way to the Indians, left his Pennsylvania home with his father, and passed down the Great Valley road to that stream. Learning from a trader whose posts were on the Red River in Kentucky of its game and rich pastures, he pioneered the way for the farmers to that region. Thence he passed to the frontier of Missouri, where his settlement was long a landmark on the frontier. Here again he helped to open the way for civilization, finding salt licks, and trails, and land. His son was among the earliest trappers in the passes of the Rocky Mountains, and his party are said to have been the first to camp on the present site of Denver. His grandson, Col. A. J. Boone, of Colorado, was a power among the Indians of the Rocky Mountains, and was appointed an agent by the Government. Kit Carson's mother was a Boone.³⁴ Thus this family epitomizes the backwoodsman's advance across the continent.

The farmer's advance came in a distinct series of waves. In Peck's New Guide to the West, pub-

³⁴ *Hale, Daniel Boone (pamphlet).*

lished in Boston in 1837, occurs this suggestive passage:

> Generally, in all the western settlements, three classes, like the waves of the ocean, have rolled one after the other. First comes the pioneer, who depends for the subsistence of his family chiefly upon the natural growth of vegetation, called the "range," and the proceeds of hunting. His implements of agriculture are rude, chiefly of his own make, and his efforts directed mainly to a crop of corn and a "truck patch." The last is a rude garden for growing cabbage, beans, corn for roasting ears, cucumbers, and potatoes. A log cabin, and, occasionally, a stable and corn-crib, and a field of a dozen acres, the timber girdled or "deadened," and fenced, are enough for his occupancy. It is quite immaterial whether he ever becomes the owner of the soil. He is the occupant for the time being, pays no rent, and feels as independent as the "lord of the manor." With a horse, cow, and one or two breeders of swine, he strikes into the woods with his family, and becomes the founder of a new county, or perhaps state. He builds his cabin, gathers around him a few other families of similar tastes and habits, and occupies till the range is somewhat subdued, and hunting a little precarious, or, which is more frequently the case, till the neighbors crowd around, roads, bridges, and fields annoy him, and he lacks elbow room. The preemption law enables him to dispose of his cabin and cornfield to the next class of emigrants; and, to employ his own figures, he "breaks for the high timber," "clears out for the New Purchase," or migrates to Arkansas or Texas, to work the same process over.
>
> The next class of emigrants purchase the lands, add field to field, clear out the roads, throw rough bridges over the streams, put up hewn log houses with glass windows and brick or stone chimneys, occasionally plant orchards, build mills, schoolhouses, court-houses, etc., and exhibit the picture and forms of plain, frugal, civilized life.
>
> Another wave rolls on. The men of capital and enterprise come. The settler is ready to sell out and take the advantage of the rise in property, push farther into the interior and become, himself, a man of capital and enterprise in turn. The small village rises to a spacious town or city; substantial edifices of brick, extensive fields, orchards, gardens, colleges, and churches are seen. Broadcloths, silks, leghorns, crapes, and all the refinements, luxuries, elegancies, frivolities, and fashions are in vogue. Thus wave after wave is rolling westward; the real Eldorado is still farther on.
>
> A portion of the two first classes remain stationary amidst the general movement, improve their habits and condition, and rise in the scale of society.
>
> The writer has traveled much amongst the first class, the real pioneers. He has lived many years in connection with the second grade; and now the third wave is sweeping over large districts of Indiana, Illinois, and Missouri. Migration has become almost a habit in the West. Hundreds of men can be found, not over 50 years of age, who have settled for the fourth, fifth, or sixth time on a new spot. To sell out and remove only a few hundred miles makes up a portion of the variety of backwoods life and manners.[35]

Omitting those of the pioneer farmers who move from the love of adventure, the advance of the more steady farmer is easy to understand. Obviously the immigrant was attracted by the cheap lands of the frontier, and even the native farmer felt their influence strongly. Year by year the farmers who lived on soil whose returns were diminished by unrotated crops were offered the

[35] Compare Baily, *Tour in the Unsettled Parts of North America* (London, 1856), pp. 217–219, *where a similar analysis is made for 1796. See also Collot,* Journey in North America *(Paris, 1826), p. 109;* Observations on the North American Land Company *(London, 1796), pp. XV, 144;* Logan, History of Upper South Carolina.

virgin soil of the frontier at nominal prices. Their growing families demanded more lands, and these were dear. The competition of the unexhausted, cheap, and easily tilled prairie lands compelled the farmer either to go west and continue the exhaustion of the soil on a new frontier, or to adopt intensive culture. Thus the census of 1890 shows, in the Northwest, many counties in which there is an absolute or a relative decrease of population. These States have been sending farmers to advance the frontier on the plains, and have themselves begun to turn to intensive farming and to manufacture. A decade before this, Ohio had shown the same transition stage. Thus the demand for land and the love of wilderness freedom drew the frontier ever onward.

Having now roughly outlined the various kinds of frontiers, and their modes of advance, chiefly from the point of view of the frontier itself, we may next inquire what were the influences on the East and on the Old World. A rapid enumeration of some of the more noteworthy effects is all that I have time for.

First, we note that the frontier promoted the formation of a composite nationality for the American people. The coast was preponderantly English, but the later tides of continental immigration flowed across to the free lands. This was the case from the early colonial days. The Scotch Irish and the Palatine Germans, or "Pennsylvania Dutch," furnished the dominant element in the stock of the colonial frontier. With these peoples were also the freed indented servants, or redemptioners, who at the expiration of their time of service passed to the frontier. Governor Spotswood of Virginia writes in 1717, "The inhabitants of our frontiers are composed generally of such as have been transported hither as servants, and, being out of their time, settle themselves where land is to be taken up and that will produce the necessarys of life with little labour."[36] Very generally these

redemptioners were of non-English stock. In the crucible of the frontier the immigrants were Americanized, liberated, and fused into a mixed race, English in neither nationality nor characteristics. The process has gone on from the early days to our own. Burke and other writers in the middle of the eighteenth century believed that Pennsylvania[37] was "threatened with the danger of being wholly foreign in language, manners, and perhaps even inclinations." The German and Scotch-Irish elements in the frontier of the South were only less great. In the middle of the present century the German element in Wisconsin was already so considerable that leading publicists looked to the creation of a German state out of the commonwealth by concentrating their colonization.[38] Such examples teach us to beware of misinterpreting the fact that there is a common English speech in America into a belief that the stock is also English.

In another way the advance of the frontier decreased our dependence on England. The coast, particularly of the South, lacked diversified industries, and was dependent on England for the bulk of its supplies. In the South there was even a dependence on the Northern colonies for articles of food. Governor Glenn, of South Carolina, writes in the middle of the eighteenth century: "Our trade with New York and Philadelphia was of this sort, draining us of all the little money and bills we could gather from other places for their bread, flour, beer, hams, bacon, and other things of their produce, all which, except beer, our new townships begin to supply us with, which are

36 "*Spottswood Papers,*" in *Collections of Virginia Historical Society,* I, II.

37 [*Burke*], *European Settlements, etc.* (1765 ed.), II, p. 200.

38 *Everest,* in *Wisconsin Historical Collections,* XII, pp. 7 ff.

settled with very industrious and thriving Germans. This no doubt diminishes the number of shipping and the appearance of our trade, but it is far from being a detriment to us."[39] Before long the frontier created a demand for merchants. As it retreated from the coast it became less and less possible for England to bring her supplies directly to the consumer's wharfs, and carry away staple crops, and staple crops began to give way to diversified agriculture for a time. The effect of this phase of the frontier action upon the northern section is perceived when we realize how the advance of the frontier aroused seaboard cities like Boston, New York, and Baltimore, to engage in rivalry for what Washington called "the extensive and valuable trade of a rising empire."

The legislation which most developed the powers of the National Government, and played the largest part in its activity, was conditioned on the frontier. Writers have discussed the subjects of tariff, land, and internal improvement, as subsidiary to the slavery question. But when American history comes to be rightly viewed it will be seen that the slavery question is an incident. In the period from the end of the first half of the present century to the close of the civil war slavery rose to primary, but far from exclusive, importance. But this does not justify Dr. von Holst (to take an example) in treating our constitutional history in its formative period down to 1828 in a single volume, giving six volumes chiefly to the history of slavery from 1828 to 1861, under the title "Constitutional History of the United States." The growth of nationalism and the evolution of American political institutions were dependent on the advance of the frontier. Even so recent a writer as Rhodes, in his "History of the United States Since the Compromise of 1850," has treated the legislation called out by the western advance as incidental to the slavery struggle.

This is a wrong perspective. The pioneer needed the goods of the coast, and so the grand series of internal improvement and railroad legislation began, with potent nationalizing effects. Over internal improvements occurred great debates, in which grave constitutional questions were discussed. Sectional groupings appear in the votes, profoundly significant for the historian. Loose construction increased as the nation marched westward.[40] But the West was not content with bringing the farm to the factory. Under the lead of Clay—"Harry of the West"—protective tariffs were passed, with the cry of bringing the factory to the farm. The disposition of the public lands was a third important subject of national legislation influenced by the frontier.

The public domain has been a force of profound importance in the nationalization and development of the Government. The effects of the struggle of the landed and the landless States, and of the ordinance of 1787, need no discussion.[41] Administratively the frontier called out some of the highest and most vitalizing activities of the General Government. The purchase of Louisiana was perhaps the constitutional turning point in the history of the Republic, inasmuch as it afforded both a new area for national legislation and the occasion of the downfall of the policy of strict construction. But the purchase of Louisiana was called out by frontier needs and demands. As frontier States accrued to the Union the national power grew. In a speech on the dedication of the

[40] *See, for example, the speech of Clay, in the House of Representatives, January 30, 1824.*

[41] *See the admirable monograph by Prof. H. B. Adams, Maryland's Influence on the Land Cessions; and also President Welling, in Papers American Historical Association, III, p. 411.*

[39] *Weston, Documents connected with History of South Carolina, p. 61.*

Calhoun monument Mr. Lamar explained: "In 1789 the States were the creators of the Federal Government; in 1861 the Federal Government was the creator of a large majority of the States."

When we consider the public domain from the point of view of the sale and disposal of the public lands we are again brought face to face with the frontier. The policy of the United States in dealing with its lands is in sharp contrast with the European system of scientific administration. Efforts to make this domain a source of revenue, and to withhold it from emigrants in order that settlement might be compact, were in vain. The jealousy and the fears of the East were powerless in the face of the demands of the frontiersmen. John Quincy Adams was obliged to confess: "My own system of administration, which was to make the national domain the inexhaustible fund for progressive and unceasing internal improvement, has failed." The reason is obvious; a system of administration was not what the West demanded; it wanted land. Adams states the situation as follows: "The slaveholders of the South have bought the cooperation of the western country by the bribe of the western lands, abandoning to the new Western States their own proportion of the public property and aiding them in the design of grasping all the lands into their own hands. Thomas H. Benton was the author of this system, which he brought forward as a substitute for the American system of Mr. Clay, and to supplant him as the leading statesman of the West. Mr. Clay, by his tariff compromise with Mr. Calhoun, abandoned his own American system. At the same time he brought forward a plan for distributing among all the States of the Union the proceeds of the sales of the public lands. His bill for that purpose passed both Houses of Congress, but was vetoed by President Jackson, who, in his annual message of December, 1832, formally recommended that all public lands should be gratuitously given away to

individual adventurers and to the States in which the lands are situated.[42]

"No subject," said Henry Clay, "which has presented itself to the present, or perhaps any preceding, Congress, is of greater magnitude than that of the public lands." When we consider the far-reaching effects of the Government's land policy upon political, economic, and social aspects of American life, we are disposed to agree with him. But this legislation was framed under frontier influences, and under the lead of Western statesmen like Benton and Jackson. Said Senator Scott of Indiana in 1841: "I consider the pre-emption law merely declaratory of the custom or common law of the settlers.

It is safe to say that the legislation with regard to land, tariff, and internal improvements—the American system of the nationalizing Whig party—was conditioned on frontier ideas and needs. But it was not merely in legislative action that the frontier worked against the sectionalism of the coast. The economic and social characteristics of the frontier worked against sectionalism. The men of the frontier had closer resemblances to the Middle region than to either of the other sections. Pennsylvania had been the seed-plot of frontier emigration, and, although she passed on her settlers along the Great Valley into the west of Virginia and the Carolinas, yet the industrial society of these Southern frontiersmen was always more like that of the Middle region than like that of the tide-water portion of the South, which later came to spread its industrial type throughout the South.

The Middle region, entered by New York harbor, was an open door to all Europe. The tide-water part of the South represented typical Englishmen, modified by a warm climate and servile labor, and living in baronial fashion on great

[42] *Adams Memoirs, IX, pp. 247, 248.*

plantations; New England stood for a special English movement—Puritanism. The Middle region was less English than the other sections. It had a wide mixture of nationalities, a varied society, the mixed town and county system of local government, a varied economic life, many religious sects. In short, it was a region mediating between New England and the South, and the East and the West. It represented that composite nationality which the contemporary United States exhibits, that juxtaposition of non-English groups, occupying a valley or a little settlement, and presenting reflections of the map of Europe in their variety. It was democratic and non-sectional, if not national; "easy, tolerant, and contented"; rooted strongly in material prosperity. It was typical of the modern United States. It was least sectional, not only because it lay between North and South, but also because with no barriers to shut out its frontiers from its settled region, and with a system of connecting waterways, the Middle region mediated between East and West as well as between North and South. Thus it became the typically American region. Even the New Englander, who was shut out from the frontier by the Middle region, tarrying in New York or Pennsylvania on his westward march, lost the acuteness of his sectionalism on the way.[43]

The spread of cotton culture into the interior of the South finally broke down the contrast between the "tide-water" region and the rest of the State, and based Southern interests on slavery. Before this process revealed its results the western portion of the South, which was akin to Pennsylvania in stock, society, and industry, showed tendencies to fall away from the faith of the fathers into internal improvement legislation and nationalism. In the Virginia convention of 1829–'30, called to revise the constitution, Mr. Leigh, of Chesterfield, one of the tide-water counties, declared:

> One of the main causes of discontent which led to this convention, that which had the strongest influence in overcoming our veneration for the work of our fathers, which taught us to condemn the sentiments of Henry and Mason and Pendleton, which weaned us from our reverence for the constituted authorities of the State, was an overweening passion for internal improvement. I say this with perfect knowledge, for it has been avowed to me by gentlemen from the West over and over again. And let me tell the gentleman from Albemarle (Mr. Gordon) that it has been another principal object of those who set this ball of revolution in motion, to overturn the doctrine of State rights, of which Virginia has been the very pillar, and to remove the barrier she has interposed to the interference of the Federal Government in that same work of internal improvement, by so reorganizing the legislature that Virginia, too, may be hitched to the Federal car.

It was this nationalizing tendency of the West that transformed the democracy of Jefferson into the national republicanism of Monroe and the democracy of Andrew Jackson. The West of the war of 1812, the West of Clay, and Benton, and Harrison, and Andrew Jackson, shut off by the Middle States and the mountains from the coast sections, had a solidarity of its own with national tendencies.[44] On the tide of the Father of Waters, North and South met and mingled into a nation. Interstate migration went steadily on—a process of cross-fertilization of ideas and institutions. The fierce struggle of the sections over slavery on the western frontier does not diminish the truth of this statement; it proves the truth of it. Slavery was a sectional trait that would not down, but in

---

[43] *Author's article in The Ægis (Madison, Wis.), November 4, 1892.*

[44] *Compare Roosevelt, Thomas Benton, Chap. i.*

the West it could not remain sectional. It was the greatest of frontiersmen who declared: "I believe this Government can not endure permanently half slave and half free. It will become all of one thing or all of the other." Nothing works for nationalism like intercourse within the nation. Mobility of population is death to localism, and the western frontier worked irresistibly in unsettling population. The effects reached back from the frontier and affected profoundly the Atlantic coast and even the Old World.

But the most important effect of the frontier has been in the promotion of democracy here and in Europe. As has been indicated, the frontier is productive of individualism. Complex society is precipitated by the wilderness into a kind of primitive organization based on the family. The tendency is anti-social. It produces antipathy to control, and particularly to any direct control. The tax-gatherer is viewed as a representative of oppression. Prof. Osgood, in an able article,[45] has pointed out that the frontier conditions prevalent in the colonies are important factors in the explanation of the American Revolution, where individual liberty was sometimes confused with absence of all effective government. The same conditions aid in explaining the difficulty of instituting a strong government in the period of the confederacy. The frontier individualism has from the beginning promoted democracy.

The frontier States that came into the Union in the first quarter of a century of its existence came in with democratic suffrage provisions, and had reactive effects of the highest importance upon the older States whose peoples were being attracted there. An extension of the franchise became essential. It was *western* New York that forced an extension of suffrage in the constitu-

tional convention of that State in 1821; and it was *western* Virginia that compelled the tide-water region to put a more liberal suffrage provision in the constitution framed in 1830, and to give to the frontier region a more nearly proportionate representation with the tide-water aristocracy. The rise of democracy as an effective force in the nation came in with western preponderance under Jackson and William Henry Harrison, and it meant the triumph of the frontier—with all of its good and with all of its evil elements.[46] An interesting illustration of the tone of frontier democracy in 1830 comes from the same debates in the Virginia convention already referred to. A representative from western Virginia declared:

But, sir, it is not the increase of population in the West which this gentleman ought to fear. It is the energy which the mountain breeze and western habits impart to those emigrants. They are regenerated, politically I mean, sir. They soon become *working politicians;* and the difference, sir, between a *talking* and a *working* politician is immense. The Old Dominion has long been celebrated for producing great orators; the ablest metaphysicians in policy; men that can split hairs in all abstruse questions of political economy. But at home, or when they return from Congress, they have Negroes to fan them asleep. But a Pennsylvania, a New York, an Ohio, and a western Virginia statesman, though far inferior in logic, metaphysics, and rhetoric to an old Virginia statesman, has this advantage, that when he returns home he takes off his coat and takes hold of the plow. This gives him bone and muscle, sir, and preserves his republican principles pure and uncontaminated.

So long as free land exists, the opportunity for a competency exists, and economic power secures political power. But the democracy born of free

---

[45] *Political Science Quarterly, II, p. 457. Compare Sumner, Alexander Hamilton, Chaps. ii–vii.*

[46] *Compare Wilson, Division and Reunion, pp. 15, 24.*

land, strong in selfishness and individualism, intolerant of administrative experience and education, and pressing individual liberty beyond its proper bounds, has its dangers as well as its benefits. Individualism in America has allowed a laxity in regard to governmental affairs which has rendered possible the spoils system and all the manifest evils that follow from the lack of a highly developed civic spirit. In this connection may be noted also the influence of frontier conditions in permitting lax business honor, inflated paper currency and wild-cat banking. The colonial and revolutionary frontier was the region whence emanated many of the worst forms of an evil currency.[47] The West in the war of 1812 repeated the phenomenon on the frontier of that day, while the speculation and wild-cat banking of the period of the crisis of 1837 occurred on the new frontier belt of the next tier of States. Thus each one of the periods of lax financial integrity coincides with periods when a new set of frontier communities had arisen, and coincides in area with these successive frontiers, for the most part. The recent Populist agitation is a case in point. Many a State that now declines any connection with the tenets of the Populists, itself adhered to such ideas in an earlier stage of the development of the State. A primitive society can hardly be expected to show the intelligent appreciation of the complexity of business interests in a developed society. The continual recurrence of these areas of paper-money agitation is another evidence that the frontier can be isolated and studied as a factor in American history of the highest importance.[48]

The East has always feared the result of an unregulated advance of the frontier, and has tried to check and guide it. The English authorities would have checked settlement at the headwaters of the Atlantic tributaries and allowed the "savages to enjoy their deserts in quiet lest the peltry trade should decrease." This called out Burke's splendid protest:

If you stopped your grants, what would be the consequence? The people would occupy without grants. They have already so occupied in many places. You can not station garrisons in every part of these deserts. If you drive the people from one place, they will carry on their annual tillage and remove with their flocks and herds to another. Many of the people in the back settlements are already little attached to particular situations. Already they have topped the Appalachian mountains. From thence they behold before them an immense plain, one vast, rich, level meadow; a square of five hundred miles. Over this they would wander without a possibility of restraint; they would change their manners with their habits of life; would soon forget a government by which they were disowned; would become hordes of English Tartars; and, pouring down upon your unfortified frontiers a fierce and irresistible cavalry, become masters of your governors, and your councelors, your collectors and comptrollers, and of all the slaves that adhered to them. Such would, and in no long time must, be the effect of attempting to forbid as a crime and to suppress as an evil the command and blessing of Providence, "Increase and multiply." Such

---

[47] *On the relation of frontier conditions to Revolutionary taxation, see Sumner, Alexander Hamilton, Chaps. iii.*

[48] *I have refrained from dwelling on the lawless characteristics of the frontier, because they are sufficiently well known. The gambler and desperado, the regulators of the Carolinas and the vigilantes of California, are types of that line of scum that the waves of advancing civilization bore before them, and* of the growth of spontaneous organs of authority where legal authority was absent. Compare Barrows, United States of Yesterday and To-morrow; Shinn, Mining Camps; and Bancroft, Popular Tribunals. The humor, bravery, and rude strength, as well as the vices of the frontier in its worst aspect, have left traces on American character, language, and literature, not soon to be effaced.*

would be the happy result of an endeavor to keep as a lair of wild beasts that earth which God, by an express charter, has given to the children of men.

But the English Government was not alone in its desire to limit the advance of the frontier and guide its destinies. Tide-water Virginia[49] and South Carolina[50] gerrymandered those colonies to insure the dominance of the coast in their legislatures. Washington desired to settle a State at a time in the Northwest; Jefferson would reserve from settlement the territory of his Louisiana purchase north of the thirty-second parallel, in order to offer it to the Indians in exchange for their settlements east of the Mississippi. "When we shall be full on this side," he writes, "we may lay off a range of States on the western bank from the head to the mouth, and so range after range, advancing compactly as we multiply." Madison went so far as to argue to the French minister that the United States had no interest in seeing population extend itself on the right bank of the Mississippi, but should rather fear it. When the Oregon question was under debate, in 1824, Smyth, of Virginia, would draw an unchangeable line for the limits of the United States at the outer limit of two tiers of States beyond the Mississippi, complaining that the seaboard States were being drained of the flower of their population by the bringing of too much land into market. Even Thomas Benton, the man of widest views of the destiny of the West, at this stage of his career declared that along the ridge of the Rocky mountains "the western limits of the Republic should be drawn, and the statue of the fabled god Terminus should be raised upon its highest peak, never to be thrown down."[51]

But the attempts to limit the boundaries, to restrict land sales and settlement, and to deprive the West of its share of political power were all in vain. Steadily the frontier of settlement advanced and carried with it individualism, democracy, and nationalism, and powerfully affected the East and the Old World.

The most effective efforts of the East to regulate the frontier came through its educational and religious activity, exerted by interstate migration and by organized societies. Speaking in 1835, Dr. Lyman Beecher declared: "It is equally plain that the religious and political destiny of our nation is to be decided in the West," and he pointed out that the population of the West "is assembled from all the States of the Union and from all the nations of Europe, and is rushing in like the waters of the flood, demanding for its moral preservation the immediate and universal action of those institutions which discipline the mind and arm the conscience and the heart. And so various are the opinions and habits, and so recent and imperfect is the acquaintance, and so sparse are the settlements of the West, that no homogeneous public sentiment can be formed to legislate immediately into being the requisite institutions. And yet they are all needed immediately in their utmost perfection and power. A nation is being 'born in a day.' * * * But what will become of the West if her prosperity rushes up to such a majesty of power, while those great institutions linger which are necessary to form the mind and the conscience and the heart of that vast world. It must not be permitted. * * * Let no man at the East quiet himself and dream of liberty, whatever may become of the West. * * * Her destiny is our destiny."[52]

---

49 *Debates in the Constitutional Convention, 1829–1830.*
50 [*McCrady*] *Eminent and Representative Men of the Carolinas, I, p. 43; Calhoun's Works, I, pp. 401–406.*

51 *Speech in the Senate, March 1, 1825; Register of Debates, I, 721.*
52 *Plea for the West (Cincinnati, 1835), pp. 11 ff.*

With the appeal to the conscience of New England, he adds appeals to her fears lest other religious sects anticipate her own. The New England preacher and school-teacher left their mark on the West. The dread of Western emancipation from New England's political and economic control was parallel by her fears lest the West cut loose from her religion. Commenting in 1850 on reports that settlement was rapidly extending northward in Wisconsin, the editor of the Home Missionary writes: "We scarcely know whether to rejoice or mourn over this extension of our settlements. While we sympathize in whatever tends to increase the physical resources and prosperity of our country, we can not forget that with all these dispersions into remote and still remoter corners of the land the supply of the means of grace is becoming relatively less and less." Acting in accordance with such ideas, home missions were established and Western colleges were erected. As seaboard cities like Philadelphia, New York, and Baltimore strove for the mastery of Western trade, so the various denominations strove for the possession of the West. Thus an intellectual stream from New England sources fertilized the West. Other sections sent their missionaries; but the real struggle was between sects. The contest for power and the expansive tendency furnished to the various sects by the existence of a moving frontier must have had important results on the character of religious organization in the United States. The multiplication of rival churches in the little frontier towns had deep and lasting social effects. The religious aspects of the frontier make a chapter in our history which needs study.

From the conditions of frontier life came intellectual traits of profound importance. The works of travelers along each frontier from colonial days onward describe certain common traits, and these traits have, while softening down, still persisted as survivals in the place of their origin, even when a higher social organization succeeded. The result is that to the frontier the American intellect owes its striking characteristics. That coarseness and strength combined with acuteness and inquisitiveness; that practical, inventive turn of mind, quick to find expedients; that masterful grasp of material things, lacking in the artistic but powerful to effect great ends; that restless, nervous energy;[53] that dominant individualism, working for good and for evil, and withal that buoyancy and exuberance which comes with freedom—these are traits of the frontier, or traits called out elsewhere because of the existence of the frontier. Since the days when the fleet of Columbus sailed into the waters of the New World, America has been another name for opportunity, and the people of the United States have taken their tone from the incessant expansion which has not only been open but has even been forced upon them. He would be a rash prophet who should assert that the expansive character of American life has now entirely ceased. Movement has been its dominant fact, and, unless this training has no effect upon a people, the American energy will continually demand a wider field for its exercise. But never again will such gifts of free land offer themselves. For a moment, at the frontier, the bonds of custom are broken and unrestraint is triumphant. There is not *tabula rasa*. The stubborn American environment is there with its imperious summons to

[53] *Colonial travelers agree in remarking on the phlegmatic characteristics of the colonists. It has frequently been asked how such a people could have developed that strained nervous energy now characteristic of them. Compare Sumner, Alexander Hamilton, p. 98, and Adams's History of the United States, I, p. 60; IX, pp. 240, 241. The transition appears to become marked at the close of the war of 1812, a period when interest centered upon the development of the West, and the West was noted for restless energy. Grund, Americans, II, ch. i.*

accept its conditions; the inherited ways of doing things are also there; and yet, in spite of environment, and in spite of custom, each frontier did indeed furnish a new field of opportunity, a gate of escape from the bondage of the past; and freshness, and confidence, and scorn of older society, impatience of its restraints and its ideas, and indifference to its lessons, have accompanied the frontier. What the Mediterranean Sea was to the Greeks, breaking the bond of custom, offering new experiences, calling out new institutions and activities, that, and more, the ever retreating frontier has been to the United States directly, and to the nations of Europe more remotely. And now, four centuries from the discovery of America, at the end of a hundred years of life under the Constitution, the frontier has gone, and with its going has closed the first period of American history.

THE FRONTIER HYPOTHESIS AND THE MYTH OF THE WEST

*Henry Nash Smith**

By far the most influential piece of writing about the West produced during the nineteenth century was the essay on "The Significance of the Frontier in American History" read by Frederick Jackson Turner before the American Historical Association at Chicago in 1893. The "frontier hypothesis" which he advanced on that occasion revolutionized American historiography and eventually made itself felt in economics and sociology, in literary criticism, and even in politics.

Turner's central contention was that "the existence of an area of free land, its continuous re-

HENRY NASH SMITH (1906–   ) is a Professor of English at the University of California. His publications include Virgin Land: the American West as Symbol and Myth *(1950),* Mark Twain: A Collection of Critical Essays *(1963), and* Mark Twain's Fable of Progress *(1964). Reprinted by permission of the author and the* American Quarterly, *Vol. 2, No. 1 (Spring, 1950), 3–11. Published by the University of Pennsylvania. Copyright, 1950, Trustees of the University of Pennsylvania.*

cession, and the advance of American settlement westward explain American development." This proposition does not sound novel now because it has been worked into the very fabric of our conception of our history, but in 1893 it was a polemic directed against the two dominant schools of historians: the group interpreting American history in terms of the slavery controversy, led by Hermann Eduard von Holst; and the group headed by Turner's former teacher, Herbert B. Adams of Johns Hopkins, who explained American institutions as the outgrowth of English, or rather ancient Teutonic, germs planted in the New World. Turner maintained that the West, not the proslavery South or the antislavery North, was the most important among American sections, and that the novel attitudes and institutions produced by the frontier, especially through its encouragement of democracy, had been more significant than the imported European heritage in shaping American society.

Whatever the merits or demerits of the frontier hypothesis in explaining actual events, the hypothesis itself developed out of a mythical conception of the West as the Garden of the World that had slowly taken form through many decades as an imaginative interpretation of the westward movement. The emphasis of this myth on agricultural settlement places it clearly within the stream of agrarian theory that flows from eighteenth-century England and France through Jefferson to the men who elaborated the ideal of a society of yeoman farmers in the Northwest from which Turner sprang. Turner's immersion in this stream of intellectual influence had an unfortunate effect in committing him to certain archaic assumptions which hampered his approach to social problems of his own day. But one must not forget that the tradition was richer than these assumptions, and that it conferred on him the authority of one who speaks from the distilled experience of

his people. If the myth of the garden embodied certain erroneous judgments made by westerners concerning the economic forces that had come to dominate American life in the course of the nineteenth century, it was still true to their experience in the large, because it expressed beliefs and aspirations as well as statistics. This is not the only kind of historical truth, but it is a kind historians need never find contemptible.

Turner's most important debt to his intellectual tradition is the ideas of savagery and civilization that he uses to define his central factor, the frontier. His frontier is explicitly "the meeting point between savagery and civilization." For him as for his predecessors, the outer limit of agricultural settlement is the boundary of civilization, and in his thought as in that of so many earlier interpreters we must therefore begin by distinguishing two Wests, one beyond and one within this all-important line.

From the standpoint of economic theory the wilderness beyond the frontier, the realm of savagery, is a constantly receding area of free land. Mr. Fulmer Mood has demonstrated that Turner derived this technical expression from a treatise on economics by Francis A. Walker, used as a text by one of his teachers at Johns Hopkins, Richard T. Ely. In Walker's analysis Turner found warrant for his belief that free land had operated as a safety valve for the East and even for Europe by offering every man an opportunity to acquire a farm and become an independent member of society. Free land thus tended to relieve poverty outside the West, and on the frontier itself it fostered economic equality. Both these tendencies made for an increase of democracy. Earlier writers from the time of Franklin had noted that the West offered freedom and subsistence to all, but Turner restated the idea in a more positive form suggested by his conviction that democracy, the rise of the common man, was one of the great movements of modern history.

In an oration delivered in 1883 when he was still an undergraduate he had declared: "Over all the world we hear mankind proclaiming its existence, demanding its rights. Kings begin to be but names, and the sons of genius, springing from the people, grasp the real sceptres. The reign of aristocracy is passing; that of humanity begins." Although *humanity* is a broad term, for Turner it referred specifically to farmers. He conceived of democracy as a trait of agricultural communities. In systems of land tenure, he felt, lay the key to the democratic upsurge that had reached a climax in the nineteenth century. This is the theoretical background of the proposition in the 1893 essay that "democracy [is] born of free land," as well as of the celebrated pronouncement made twenty years later: "American democracy was born of no theorist's dream; it was not carried in the Susan Constant to Virginia, nor in the Mayflower to Plymouth. It came stark and strong and full of life out of the American forest, and it gained new strength each time it touched a new frontier."

But while economic theory still underlies this later statement, the change of terminology has introduced new and rich overtones. We have been transferred from the plane of the economist's abstractions to a plane of metaphor, and even of myth—for the American forest has become almost an enchanted wood, and the image of Antaeus has been invoked to suggest the power of the western earth. Such intimations reach beyond logical theory. They remind us that the wilderness beyond the limits of civilization was not only an area of free land; it was also nature. The idea of nature suggested to Turner a poetic account of free land as a rebirth, a regeneration, a rejuvenation of man and society constantly recurring where civilization came into contact with the wilderness along the frontier.

Rebirth and regeneration are categories of myth rather than of economic analysis, but ordinarily Turner kept his metaphors under control and used them to illustrate and vivify his logical propositions rather than as a structural principle or a means of cognition; that is, he used them rhetorically not poetically. The nonpoetic use of a vivid metaphor is illustrated in a speech he delivered in 1896:

> Americans had a safety valve for social danger, a bank account on which they might continually draw to meet losses. This was the vast unoccupied domain that stretched from the borders of the settled area to the Pacific Ocean. . . . No grave social problem could exist while the wilderness at the edge of civilizations [*sic*] opened wide its portals to all who were oppressed, to all who with strong arms and stout heart desired to hew out a home and a career for themselves. Here was an opportunity for social development continually to begin over again, wherever society gave signs of breaking into classes. Here was a magic fountain of youth in which America continually bathed and was rejuvenated.

The figure of the magic fountain is merely a rhetorical ornament at the end of a paragraph having a rational structure and subject to criticism according to recognized canons. But sometimes, especially when the conception of nature as the source of occult powers is most vividly present, Turner's metaphors threaten to become themselves a means of cognition and to supplant discursive reasoning. This seems to happen, for example, in an essay he wrote for the *Atlantic* in 1903. After quoting a clearly animistic passage from Lowell's Harvard Commemoration Ode on how nature had shaped Lincoln of untainted clay from the unexhausted West, "New birth of our new soil, the first American," Turner builds an elaborate figurative structure:

Into this vast shaggy continent of ours poured the first feeble tide of European settlement. European men, institutions, and ideas were lodged in the American wilderness, and this great American West took them to her bosom, taught them a new way of looking upon the destiny of the common man, trained them in adaptation to the conditions of the New World, to the creation of new institutions to meet new needs; and ever as society on her eastern border grew to resemble the Old World in its social forms and its industry, ever, as it began to lose faith in the ideal of democracy, she opened new provinces, and dowered new democracies in her most distant domains with her material treasures and with the ennobling influence that the fierce love of freedom, the strength that came from hewing out a home, making a school and a church, and creating a higher future for his family, furnished to the pioneer.

It would be difficult to maintain that all these metaphors are merely ornamental. Is it wholly meaningless, for example, that the West, the region close to nature, is feminine, while the East, with its remoteness from nature and its propensity for aping Europe, is neuter?

In the passage just quoted, a beneficent power emanating from nature is shown creating an agrarian utopia in the West. The myth of the garden is constructed before our eyes. Turner is asserting as fact a state of affairs that on other occasions he recognized as merely an ideal to be striven for. Earlier in the same essay, for example, he had summarized Jefferson's "platform of political principles" and his "conception that democracy should have an agricultural basis." The "should" easily becomes "did"; Jefferson's agrarian ideal proves to be virtually identical with the frontier democracy that Turner believed he had discovered in the West. To imagine an ideal

so vividly that it comes to seem actual is to follow the specific procedure of poetry.

The other member of the pair of ideas which defined the frontier for Turner was that of civilization. If the idea of nature in the West provided him with a rich and not always manageable store of metaphorical coloring, his use of the idea of civilization had the equally important consequence of committing him to the theory that all societies, including those of successive Wests, develop through the same series of progressively higher stages.

Turner's acceptance of this theory involved him in the difficulties that it had created for earlier observers of frontier society, such as Timothy Flint. For the theory of social stages was basically at odds with the conception of the western farmer as a yeoman surrounded by utopian splendor. Instead it implied that the western farmer was a coarse and unrefined representative of a primitive stage of social evolution. Turner's adoption of these two contradictory theories makes it difficult for him to manage the question of whether frontier character and society, and frontier influence on the rest of the country, have been good or bad. As long as he is dealing with the origins of democracy in the West he evidently considers frontier influence good. A man who refers to "the familiar struggle of West against East, of democracy against privileged classes" leaves no doubt concerning his own allegiance. This attitude was in fact inevitable as long as one maintained the doctrine that frontier society was shaped by the influence of free land, for free land was nature, and nature in this system of ideas is unqualifiedly benign. Indeed, it is itself the norm of value. There is no way to conceive possible bad effects flowing from the impact of nature on man and society.

But when Turner invokes the concept of civilization, the situation becomes more complex. His basic conviction was that the highest social values were to be found in the relatively primitive society just within the agricultural frontier. Yet the theory of social stages placed the highest values at the other end of the process, in urban industrial society, amid the manufacturing development and city life which Jefferson and later agrarian theorists had considered dangerous to social purity. Turner wavered between the two views. For one thing, he strongly disapproved of the western love of currency inflation, which he considered a consequence of the primitive state of frontier society. "The colonial and Revolutionary frontier," he asserted in the 1893 essay, "was the region whence emanated many of the worst forms of an evil currency," and he pointed out that each of the periods of lax financial integrity in American history had coincided with the rise of a new set of frontier communities. The Populist agitation for free coinage of silver was a case in point.

Many a state that now declines any connection with the tenets of the Populists [he wrote] itself adhered to such ideas in an earlier stage of the development of the state. A primitive society can hardly be expected to show the intelligent appreciation of the complexity of business interests in a developed society.

In his revision of the essay in 1899 Turner noted with satisfaction that Wisconsin had borne out his principles:

Wisconsin, to take an illustration, in the days when it lacked varied agriculture and complex industrial life, was a stronghold of the granger and greenback movements; but it has undergone an industrial transformation, and in the last presidential contest Mr. Bryan carried but one county in the state.

Here the evolution of society from agrarian simplicity toward greater complexity is assumed to bring about improvement.

Yet if Turner could affirm progress and civilization in this one respect, the general course of social evolution in the United States created a grave theoretical dilemma for him. He had based his highest value, democracy, on free land. But the westward advance of civilization across the continent had caused free land to disappear. What then was to become of democracy? The difficulty was the greater because in associating democracy with free land he had inevitably linked it also with the idea of nature as a source of spiritual values. All the overtones of his conception of democracy were therefore tinged with cultural primitivism and tended to clash with the idea of civilization. But Turner had accepted the idea of civilization as a general description of the society that had been expanding across the continent, and with the final disappearance of free land this idea was the only remaining principle with which he could undertake the analysis of contemporary American society.

Since democracy for him was related to the idea of nature and seemed to have no logical relation to civilization, the conclusion implied by his system was that post-frontier American society contained no force tending toward democracy. Yet he was compelled somehow to find a basis for democracy in the civilization he observed about him in the United States. His determined effort in this direction showed that his mind and his standards of social ethics were subtler and broader than the conceptual system within which the frontier hypothesis had been developed, but he was the prisoner of the assumptions he had taken over from the agrarian tradition. He turned to the rather unconvincing idea that the midwestern state universities might be able to save democracy by producing trained leaders, and later he placed science beside education as another force to which men might turn for aid in their modern perplexity. But these suggestions were not really satisfying to him, and he fell back at last on the faith he had confided to his commonplace book as an undergraduate—a faith neither in nature nor in civilization but simply in man, in the common people. In 1924, after reviewing the most urgent of the world's problems, Turner declared with eloquence and dignity:

> I prefer to believe that man is greater than the dangers that menace him; that education and science are powerful forces to change these tendencies and to produce a rational solution of the problems of life on the shrinking planet. I place my trust in the mind of man seeking solutions by intellectual toil rather than by drift and by habit, bold to find new ways of adjustment, and strong in the leadership that spreads new ideas among the common people of the world; committed to peace on earth, and ready to use the means of preserving it.

This statement is an admission that the notion of democracy born of free land, colored as it is by primitivism, is not an adequate instrument for dealing with a world dominated by industry, urbanization, and international conflicts. The first World War had shaken Turner's agrarian code of values as it destroyed so many other intellectual constructions of the nineteenth century. He continued to struggle with the grievous problems of the modern world, but his original theoretical weapons were no longer useful.

Turner's predicament illustrates what has happened to the tradition within which he worked. From the time of Franklin down to the end of the frontier period almost a century and a half later, the West had been a constant reminder of the importance of agriculture in American society.

It had nourished an agrarian philosophy and an agrarian myth that purported to set forth the character and destinies of the nation. The philosophy and the myth affirmed an admirable set of values, but they ceased very early to be useful in interpreting American society as a whole because they offered no intellectual apparatus for taking account of the industrial revolution. A system which revolved about a half-mystical conception of nature and held up as an ideal a rudimentary type of agriculture was powerless to confront issues arising from the advance of technology. Agrarian theory encouraged men to ignore the industrial revolution altogether, or to regard it as an unfortunate and anomalus violation of the natural order of things.

In the restricted but important sphere of historical scholarship, for example, the agrarian emphasis of the frontier hypothesis has tended to divert attention from the problems created by industrialization for a half century during which the United States has become the most powerful industrial nation in the world. An even more significant consequence of the agrarian tradition has been its effect on politics. The covert distrust of the city and of everything connected with industry that is implicit in the myth of the garden has impeded cooperation between farmers and factory workers in more than one crisis of our history, from the time of Jefferson to the present.

The agrarian tradition has also made it difficult for Americans to think of themselves as members of a world community because it has affirmed that the destiny of this country leads her away from Europe toward the agricultural interior of the continent. This tendency is quite evident in Turner. Although he devoted much attention to the diplomatic issues arising out of westward expansion, the frontier hypothesis implied that it would be a last misfortune for American society to maintain close connections with Europe. The frontier which produced Andrew Jackson, wrote Turner with approval in 1903, was "free from the influence of European ideas and institutions. The men of the 'Western World' turned their backs upon the Atlantic Ocean, and with a grim energy and self-reliance began to build up a society free from the dominance of ancient forms." It was only later, when he was trying to find a theoretical basis for democracy outside the frontier, that Turner criticized the American attitude of "contemptuous indifference" to the social legislation of European countries.

But if interpretation of the West in terms of the idea of nature tended to cut the region off from the urban East and from Europe, the opposed idea of civilization had even greater disadvantages. It not only imposed on westerners the stigma of social, ethical, and cultural inferiority, but prevented any recognition that the American adventure of settling the continent had brought about an irruption of novelty into history. For the theory of civilization implied that America in general, and the West a fortiori, were meaningless except in so far as they managed to reproduce the achievements of Europe. The capital difficulty of the American agrarian tradition is that it accepted the paired but contradictory ideas of nature and civilization as a general principle of historical and social interpretation. A new intellectual system was requisite before the West could be adequately dealt with in literature or its social development fully understood.

HOW THE FRONTIER SHAPED
THE AMERICAN CHARACTER

Ray Allen Billington*

Since the dawn days of historical writing in the United States, historians have labored mightily, and usually in vain, to answer the famous question posed by Hector St. John de Crèvecœur in the eighteenth century: "What then is the American, this new man?" Was that composite figure actually a "new man" with unique traits that distinguished him from his Old World ancestors? Or was he merely a transplanted European? The most widely accepted—and bitterly disputed—answer was advanced by a young Wisconsin historian named Frederick Jackson Turner in 1893. The American was a new man, he held, who owed his distinctive characteristics and institutions to the unusual New World environment—characterized by the availability of free land and an ever-receding frontier— in which his civilization had grown to maturity. This environmental theory, accepted for a genera-tion after its enunciation, has been vigorously attacked and vehemently defended during the past two decades. How has it fared in this battle of words? Is it still a valid key to the meaning of American history?

Turner's own background provides a clue to the answer. Born in Portage, Wisconsin, in 1861 of pioneer parents from upper New York state, he was reared in a land fringed by the interminable forest and still stamped with the mark of youth. There he mingled with pioneers who had trapped beaver or hunted Indians or cleared the virgin wilderness: from them he learned something of the free and easy democratic values prevailing among those who judged men by their own ac-complishments rather than those of their ancestors. At the University of Wisconsin Turner's faith in cultural democracy was deepened, while his intel-

*RAY ALLEN BILLINGTON (1903–   ) is a Senior Research Associate at the Huntington Library. His publications include The Protestant Crusade, 1800–1860 (1952), The Far Western Fron-tier, 1830–1860 (1956), and America's Frontier Heritage (1966). © Copyright 1958 by American Heritage Publishing Co., Inc. (AMERICAN HERITAGE, April, 1958). Reprinted by permission.

lectual vistas were widened through contact with teachers who led him into that wonderland of adventure where scientific techniques were being applied to social problems, where Darwin's evolutionary hypothesis was awakening scholars to the continuity of progress, and where searchers after truth were beginning to realize the multiplicity of forces responsible for human behavior. The young student showed how well he had learned these lessons in his master's essay on "The Character and Influence of the Fur Trade in Wisconsin"; he emphasized the evolution of institutions from simple to complex forms.

From Wisconsin Turner journeyed to Johns Hopkins University, as did many eager young scholars of that day, only to meet stubborn opposition for the historical theories already taking shape in his mind. His principal professor, Herbert Baxter Adams, viewed mankind's development in evolutionary terms, but held that environment had no place in the equation; American institutions could be understood only as outgrowths of European "germs" that had originated among Teutonic tribes in the forests of medieval Germany. To Turner this explanation was unsatisfactory. The "germ theory" explained the similarities between Europe and America, but what of the many differences? This problem was still much in his mind when he returned to the University of Wisconsin as an instructor in 1889. In two remarkable papers prepared during the next few years he set forth his answer. The first, "The Significance of History," reiterated his belief in what historians call "multiple causation"; to understand man's complex nature, he insisted, one needed not only a knowledge of past politics, but a familiarity with social, economic, and cultural forces as well. The second, "Problems in American History," attempted to isolate those forces most influential in explaining the unique features of American development. Among these Turner

believed that the most important was the need for institutions to "adapt themselves to the changes of a remarkably developing, expanding people."

This was the theory that was expanded into a full-blown historical hypothesis in the famous essay on "The Significance of the Frontier in American History," read at a conference of historians held in connection with the World Fair in Chicago in 1893. The differences between European and American civilization, Turner stated in that monumental work, were in part the product of the distinctive environment of the New World. The most unusual features of that environment were "the existence of an area of free land, its continuous recession, and the advance of American settlement westward." This free land served as a magnet to draw men westward, attracted by the hope of economic gain or adventure. They came as Europeans or easterners, but they soon realized that the wilderness environment was ill-adapted to the habits, institutions, and cultural baggage of the stratified societies they had left behind. Complex political institutions were unnecessary in a tiny frontier outpost; traditional economic practices were useless in an isolated community geared to an economy of self-sufficiency; rigid social customs were outmoded in a land where prestige depended on skill with the axe or rifle rather than on hereditary glories; cultural pursuits were unessential in a land where so many material tasks awaited doing. Hence in each pioneer settlement there occurred a rapid reversion to the primitive. What little government was necessary was provided by simple associations of settlers; each man looked after his family without reliance on his fellows; social hierarchies disintegrated, and cultural progress came to a halt. As the newcomers moved backward along the scale of civilization, the habits and customs of their traditional cultures were forgotten.

Gradually, however, newcomers drifted in, and

as the man-land ratio increased, the community began a slow climb back toward civilization. Governmental controls were tightened and extended, economic specialization began, social stratification set in, and cultural activities quickened. But the new society that eventually emerged differed from the old from which it had sprung. The abandonment of cultural baggage during the migrations, the borrowings from the many cultures represented in each pioneer settlement, the deviations natural in separate evolutions, and the impact of the environment all played their parts in creating a unique social organism similar to but differing from those in the East. An "Americanization" of men and their institutions had taken place.

Turner believed that many of the characteristics associated with the American people were traceable to their experience, during the three centuries required to settle the continent, of constantly "beginning over again." Their mobility, their optimism, their inventiveness and willingness to accept innovation, their materialism, their exploitive wastefulness—these were frontier traits: for the pioneer, accustomed to repeated moves as he drifted westward, viewed the world through rose-colored glasses as he dreamed of a better future, experimented constantly as he adapted artifacts and customs to his peculiar environment, scorned culture as a deterrent to the practical tasks that bulked so large in his life, and squandered seemingly inexhaustible natural resources with abandon. Turner also ascribed America's distinctive brand of individualism, with its dislike of governmental interference in economic functions, to the experience of pioneers who wanted no hindrance from society as they exploited nature's riches. Similarly, he traced the exaggerated nationalism of the United States to its roots among frontiersmen who looked to the national government for land, transportation outlets, and protection against the Indians. And he believed that America's faith in democracy had stemmed from a pioneering experience in which the leveling influence of poverty and the uniqueness of local problems encouraged majority self-rule. He pointed out that these characteristics, prominent among frontiersmen, had persisted long after the frontier itself was no more.

This was Turner's famous "frontier hypothesis." For a generation after its enunciation its persuasive logic won uncritical acceptance among historians, but beginning in the late 1920's, and increasingly after Turner's death in 1932, an avalanche of criticism steadily mounted. His theories, critics said, were contradictory, his generalizations unsupported, his assumptions inadequately based: what empirical proof could he advance, they asked, to prove that the frontier experience was responsible for American individualism, mobility, or wastefulness? He was damned as a romanticist for his claim that democracy sprang from the forest environment of the United States and as an isolationist for failing to recognize the continuing impact of Europe on America. As the "bait-Turner" vogue gained popularity among younger scholars of the 1930's, with their international, semi-Marxian views of history, the criticisms of the frontier theory became as irrational as the earlier support rendered it by overenthusiastic advocates.

During the past decade, however, a healthy reaction has slowly and unspectacularly gained momentum. Today's scholars, gradually realizing that Turner was advancing a hypothesis rather than proving a theory, have shown a healthy tendency to abandon fruitless haggling over the meaning of his phrases and to concentrate instead on testing his assumptions. They have directed their efforts primarily toward re-examining his hypothesis in the light of criticisms directed against it and applying it to frontier areas beyond the borders of the United States. Their findings have modified many of the views expressed by Turner but have gone far toward proving that the frontier hypothesis remains one essential tool—albeit not the only one—for interpreting American history.

That Turner was guilty of oversimplifying both the nature and the causes of the migration process was certainly true. He pictured settlers as moving westward in an orderly procession—fur trappers, cattlemen, miners, pioneer farmers, and equipped farmers—with each group playing its part in the transmutation of a wilderness into a civilization. Free land was the magnet that lured them onward, he believed, and this operated most effectively in periods of depression, when the displaced workers of the East sought a refuge from economic storms amidst nature's abundance in the West. "The wilderness ever opened the gate of escape to the poor, the discontented and oppressed," Turner wrote at one time. "If social conditions tended to crystallize in the east, beyond the Alleghenies there was freedom."

No one of these assumptions can be substantiated in the simplified form in which Turner stated it. His vision of an "orderly procession of civilization, marching single file westward" failed to account for deviations that were almost as important as the norm; as essential to the conquest of the forest as trappers or farmers were soldiers, mill-operators, distillers, artisans, storekeepers, merchants, lawyers, editors, speculators, and town dwellers. All played their role, and all contributed to a complex frontier social order that bore little resemblance to the primitive societies Turner pictured. This was especially the case with the early town builders. The hamlets that sprang up adjacent to each pioneer settlement were products of the environment as truly as were the cattlemen or Indian fighters; each evolved economic functions geared to the needs of the primitive area surrounding it, and, in the tight public controls

maintained over such essential functions as grist-milling or retail selling, each mirrored the frontiersmen's community-oriented views. In these villages, too, the equalitarian influence of the West was reflected in thoroughly democratic governments, with popularly elected councils supreme and the mayor reduced to a mere figurehead.

The pioneers who marched westward in this disorganized procession were not attracted by the magnet of "free land," for Turner's assumption that before 1862 the public domain was open to all who could pay $1.25 an acre, or that acreage was free after the Homestead Act was passed in that year, has been completely disproved. Turner failed to recognize the presence in the procession to the frontier of that omnipresent profit-seeker, the speculator. Jobbers were always ahead of farmers in the advance westward, buying up likely town sites or appropriating the best farm lands, where the soil was good and transportation outlets available. When the settler arrived his choice was between paying the speculator's price or accepting an inferior site. Even the Homestead Act failed to lessen speculative activity. Capitalizing on generous government grants to railroads and state educational institutions (which did not want to be bothered with sales to individuals), or buying bonus script from soldiers, or securing Indian lands as the reservations were contracted, or seizing on faulty features of congressional acts for the disposal of swampland and timberland, jobbers managed to engross most of the Far West's arable acreage. As a result, for every newcomer who obtained a homestead from the government, six or seven purchased farms from speculators.

Those who made these purchases were not, as Turner believed, displaced eastern workers fleeing periodic industrial depressions. Few city-dwelling artisans had the skills or inclination, and almost none the capital, to escape to the frontier. Land prices of $1.25 an acre may seem low today, but they were prohibitive for laborers earning only a dollar a day. Moreover, needed farm machinery, animals, and housing added about $1,000 to the cost of starting a farm in the 1850's, while the cheapest travel rate from New York to St. Louis was about $13 a person. Because these sums were always beyond the reach of factory workers (in bad times they deterred migration even from the rural East), the frontier never served as a "safety valve" for laborers in the sense that Turner employed the term. Instead, the American frontiers were pushed westward largely by younger sons from adjacent farm areas who migrated in periods of prosperity. While these generalizations apply to the pre–Civil War era that was Turner's principal interest, they are even more applicable to the late nineteenth century. During that period the major population shifts were from country to city rather than vice versa; for every worker who left the factory to move to the farm, twenty persons moved from farm to factory. If a safety valve did exist at that time, it was a rural safety valve, drawing off surplus farm labor and thus lessening agrarian discontent during the Granger and Populist eras.

Admitting that the procession to the frontier was more complex than Turner realized, that good lands were seldom free, and that a safety valve never operated to drain the dispossessed and the malcontented from industrial centers, does this mean that his conclusions concerning the migration process have been completely discredited? The opposite is emphatically true. A more divergent group than Turner realized felt the frontier's impact, but that does not minimize the extent of the impact. Too, while lands in the West were almost never free, they were relatively cheaper than those in Europe or the East, and this differential did serve as an attracting force. Nor

can pages of statistics disprove the fact that, at least until the Civil War, the frontier served as an indirect safety valve by attracting displaced eastern farmers who would otherwise have moved into industrial cities; thousands who left New England or New York for the Old Northwest in the 1830's and 1840's, when the "rural decay" of the Northeast was beginning, would have sought factory jobs had no western outlet existed.

The effect of their exodus is made clear by comparing the political philosophies of the United States with those of another frontier country, Australia. There, lands lying beyond the coastal mountains were closed to pioneers by the aridity of the soil and by great sheep ranchers who were first on the scene. Australia, as a result, developed an urban civilization and an industrialized population relatively sooner than did the United States; and it had labor unions, labor-dominated governments, and political philosophies that would be viewed as radical in America. Without the safety valve of its own West, feeble though it may have been, such a course might have been followed in the United States.

Frederick Jackson Turner's conclusions concerning the influence of the frontier on Americans have also been questioned, debated, and modified since he advanced his hypothesis, but they have not been seriously altered. This is true even of one of his statements that has been more vigorously disputed than any other: "American democracy was born of no theorist's dream; it was not carried in the *Susan Constant* to Virginia, nor in the *Mayflower* to Plymouth. It came out of the American forest, and it gained a new strength each time it touched a new frontier." When he penned those oft-quoted words, Turner wrote as a propagandist against the "germ theory" school of history; in a less emotional and more thoughtful moment, he ascribed America's democratic institutions not to "imitation, or simple borrowing," but to "the evolution and adaptation of organs in response to changed environment." Even this moderate theory has aroused critical venom. Democracy, according to anti-Turnerians, was well advanced in Europe and *was* transported to America on the *Susan Constant* and the *Mayflower;* within this country democratic practices have multiplied most rapidly as a result of eastern lower-class pressures and have only been imitated in the West. If, critics ask, some mystical forest influence was responsible for such practices as manhood suffrage, increased authority for legislatures at the expense of executives, equitable legislative representation, and women's political rights, why did they not evolve in frontier areas outside the United States—in Russia, Latin America, and Canada, for example—exactly as they did here?

The answer, of course, is that democratic theory and institutions were imported from England, but that the frontier environment tended to make them, in practice, even more democratic. Two conditions common in pioneer communities made this inevitable. One was the wide diffusion of land ownership; this created an independent outlook and led to a demand for political participation on the part of those who had a stake in society. The other was the common social and economic level and the absence, characteristic of all primitive communities, of any prior leadership structure. The lack of any national or external controls made self-rule a hard necessity, and the frontiersmen, with their experience in community co-operation at cabin-raisings, logrollings, corn-huskings, and road or school building, accepted simple democratic practices as natural and inevitable. These practices, originating on the grass roots level, were expanded and extended in the recurring process of government-building that marked the westward movement of civilization. Each new territory that was organized—there were 31 in all—required a frame of government; this was drafted

by relatively poor recent arrivals or by a minority of upper-class leaders, all of whom were committed to democratic ideals through their frontier community experiences. The result was a constant democratization of institutions and practices as constitution-makers adopted the most liberal features of older frames of government with which they were familiar.

This was true even in frontier lands outside the United States, for wherever there were frontiers, existing practices were modified in the direction of greater equality and a wider popular participation in governmental affairs. The results were never identical, of course, for both the environment and the nature of the imported institutions varied too greatly from country to country. In Russia, for instance, even though it promised no democracy comparable to that of the United States, the eastward-moving Siberian frontier, the haven of some seven million peasants during the nineteenth and early twentieth centuries, was notable for its lack of guilds, authoritarian churches, and all-powerful nobility. An autocratic official visiting there in 1910 was alarmed by the "enormous, rudely democratic country" evolving under the influence of the small homesteads that were the normal living units; he feared that czarism and European Russia would soon be "throttled" by the egalitarian currents developing on the frontier.

That the frontier accentuated the spirit of nationalism and individualism in the United States, as Turner maintained, was also true. Every page of the country's history, from the War of 1812 through the era of Manifest Destiny to today's bitter conflicts with Russia, demonstrates that the American attitude toward the world has been far more nationalistic than that of non-frontier countries and that this attitude has been strongest in the newest regions. Similarly, the pioneering experience converted settlers into individualists, although through a somewhat different process than Turner envisaged. His emphasis on a desire for freedom as a primary force luring men westward and his belief that pioneers developed an attitude of self-sufficiency in their lone battle against nature have been questioned, and with justice. Hoped-for gain was the magnet that attracted most migrants to the cheaper lands of the West, while once there they lived in units where co-operative enterprise—for protection against the Indians, for cabin-raising, law enforcement, and the like—was more essential than in the better established towns of the East. Yet the fact remains that the abundant resources and the greater social mobility of frontier areas did instill into frontiersmen a uniquely American form of individualism. Even though they may be sheeplike in following the decrees of social arbiters or fashion dictators, Americans today, like their pioneer ancestors, dislike governmental interference in their affairs. "Rugged individualism" did not originate on the frontier any more than democracy or nationalism did, but each concept was deepened and sharpened by frontier conditions.

His opponents have also cast doubt on Turner's assertion that American inventiveness and willingness to adopt innovations are traits inherited from pioneer ancestors who constantly devised new techniques and artifacts to cope with an unfamiliar environment. The critics insist that each mechanical improvement needed for the conquest of the frontier, from plows to barbed-wire fencing, originated in the East; when frontiersmen faced such an incomprehensible task as conquering the Great Plains they proved so tradition-bound that their advance halted until eastern inventors provided them with the tools needed to subdue grasslands. Unassailable as this argument may be, it ignores the fact that the recurring demand for implements and methods needed in the frontier advance did put a premium on inventiveness by

Americans, whether they lived in the East or West. That even today they are less bound by tradition than other peoples is due in part to their pioneer heritage.

The anti-intellectualism and materialism which are national traits can also be traced to the frontier experience. There was little in pioneer life to attract the timid, the cultivated, or the aesthetically sensitive. In the boisterous western borderlands, book learning and intellectual speculation were suspect among those dedicated to the material tasks necessary to subdue a continent. Americans today reflect their background in placing the "intellectual" well below the "practical businessman" in their scale of heroes. Yet the frontiersman, as Turner recognized, was an idealist as well as a materialist. He admired material objects not only as symbols of advancing civilization but as the substance of his hopes for a better future. Given economic success he would be able to afford the aesthetic and intellectual pursuits that he felt were his due, even though he was not quite able to appreciate them. This spirit inspired the cultural activities—literary societies, debating clubs, "thespian groups," libraries, schools, camp meetings—that thrived in the most primitive western communities. It also helped nurture in the pioneers an infinite faith in the future. The belief in progress, both material and intellectual, that is part of modern America's creed was strengthened by the frontier experience.

Frederick Jackson Turner, then, was not far wrong when he maintained that frontiersmen did develop unique traits and that these, perpetuated, form the principal distinguishing characteristics of the American people today. To a degree unknown among Europeans, Americans do display a restless energy, a versatility, a practical ingenuity, an earthy practicality. They do squander their natural resources with an abandon unknown elsewhere; they have developed a mobility both social and physical that marks them as a people apart. In few other lands is the democratic ideal worshiped so intensely, or nationalism carried to such extremes of isolationism or international arrogance. Rarely do other peoples display such indifference toward intellectualism or aesthetic values; seldom in comparable cultural areas do they cling so tenaciously to the shibboleth of rugged individualism. Nor do residents of nonfrontier lands experience to the same degree the heady optimism, the rosy faith in the future, the belief in the inevitability of progress that form part of the American creed. These are pioneer traits, and they have become a part of the national heritage.

Yet if the frontier wrought such a transformation within the United States, why did it not have a similar effect on other countries with frontiers? If the pioneering experience was responsible for our democracy and nationalism and individualism, why have the peoples of Africa, Latin America, Canada, and Russia failed to develop identical characteristics? The answer is obvious: in few nations of the world has the sort of frontier that Turner described existed. For he saw the frontier not as a borderland between unsettled and settled lands, but as an accessible area in which a low man-land ratio and abundant natural resources provided an unusual opportunity for the individual to better himself. Where autocratic governments controlled population movements, where resources were lacking, or where conditions prohibited ordinary individuals from exploiting nature's virgin riches, a frontier in the Turnerian sense could not be said to exist.

The areas of the world that have been occupied since the beginning of the age of discovery contain remarkably few frontiers of the American kind. In Africa the few Europeans were so outnumbered by relatively uncivilized native inhabitants that the need for protection transcended any impulses toward democracy or individualism. In Latin America the rugged terrain and steaming jungles restricted areas exploitable by individuals to the Brazilian plains and the Argentine pampas; these did attract frontiersmen, although in Argentina the prior occupation of most good lands by government-favored cattle growers kept small farmers out until railroads penetrated the region. In Canada the path westward was blocked by the Laurentian Shield, a tangled mass of hills and sterile, brush-choked soil covering the country north and west of the St. Lawrence Valley. When railroads finally penetrated this barrier in the late nineteenth century, they carried pioneers directly from the East to the prairie provinces of the West; the newcomers, with no prior pioneering experience, simply adapted to their new situation the eastern institutions with which they were familiar. Among the frontier nations of the world only Russia provided a physical environment comparable to that of the United States, and there the pioneers were too accustomed to rigid feudal and monarchic controls to respond as Americans did.

Further proof that the westward expansion of the United States has been a powerful formative force has been provided by the problems facing the nation in the present century. During the past fifty years the American people have been adjusting their lives and institutions to existence in a frontierless land, for while the superintendent of the census was decidedly premature when he announced in 1890 that the country's "unsettled area has been so broken into by isolated bodies of settlement that there can hardly be said to be a frontier line" remaining, the era of cheap land was rapidly drawing to a close. In attempting to adjust the country to its new, expansionless future, statesmen have frequently called upon the frontier hypothesis to justify everything from rugged individualism to the welfare state, and from isolationism to world domination.

Political opinion has divided sharply on the necessity of altering the nation's governmental philosophy and techniques in response to the changed environment. Some statesmen and scholars have rebelled against what they call Turner's "Space Concept of History," with all that it implies concerning the lack of opportunity for the individual in an expansionless land. They insist that modern technology has created a whole host of new "frontiers"—of intensive farming, electronics, mechanics, manufacturing, nuclear fission, and the like—which offer such diverse outlets to individual talents that governmental interference in the nation's economic activities is unjustified. On the other hand, equally competent spokesmen argue that these newer "frontiers" offer little opportunity to the individual—as distinguished from the corporation or the capitalist—and hence cannot duplicate the function of the frontier of free land. The government, they insist, must provide the people with the security and opportunity that vanished when escape to the West became impossible. This school's most eloquent spokesman, Franklin D. Roosevelt, declared: "Our last frontier has long since been reached. . . . Equality of opportunity as we have known it no longer exists. . . . Our task now is not the discovery or exploitation of natural resources or necessarily producing more goods. It is the sober, less dramatic business of administering resources and plants already in hand, of seeking to reestablish foreign markets for our surplus production, of meeting the problem of under-consumption, of adjusting production to consumption, of distributing wealth and products more equitably, of adapting existing economic organizations to

the service of the people. The day of enlightened administration has come." To Roosevelt, and to thousands like him, the passing of the frontier created a new era in history which demanded a new philosophy of government.

Diplomats have also found in the frontier hypothesis justification for many of their moves, from imperialist expansion to the restriction of immigration. Harking back to Turner's statement that the perennial rebirth of society was necessary to keep alive the democratic spirit, expansionists have argued through the twentieth century for an extension of American power and territories. During the Spanish-American War imperialists preached such a doctrine, adding the argument that Spain's lands were needed to provide a population outlet for a people who could no longer escape to their own frontier. Idealists such as Woodrow Wilson could agree with materialists like J. P. Morgan that the extension of American authority abroad, either through territorial acquisitions or economic penetration, would be good for both business and democracy. In a later generation Franklin D. Roosevelt favored a similar expansion of the American democratic ideal as a necessary prelude to the better world that he hoped would emerge from World War II. His successor, Harry Truman, envisaged his "Truman Doctrine" as a device to extend and defend the frontiers of democracy throughout the globe. While popular belief in the superiority of America's political institutions was far older than Turner, that belief rested partly on the frontier experience of the United States.

These practical applications of the frontier hypothesis, as well as its demonstrated influence on the nation's development, suggest that its critics have been unable to destroy the theory's effectiveness as a key to understanding American history. The recurring rebirth of society in the United States over a period of three hundred years did endow the people with characteristics and institutions that distinguish them from the inhabitants of other nations. It is obviously untrue that the frontier experience alone accounts for the unique features of American civilization; that civilization can be understood only as the product of the interplay of the Old World heritage and New World conditions. But among those conditions none has bulked larger than the operation of the frontier process.

Unknown Artist "A City of Fantasy"   Garbisch Collection, National Gallery of Art, Washington, D.C.

PART 6

THE IDEA OF PROGRESS

Introduction

The idea of progress has been a central theme in American intellectual history. It originated in the enlightened thought of the eighteenth-century philosophers, became a dominant factor during the nineteenth century, and persisted into the contemporary era. Because of the spacious frontier, the fluid social structure, and the optimistic nature of the people, the cult of progress flowered in America more than in Europe. It is a topic of great concern to students of the American intellectual tradition.

Rush Welter introduces the idea of progress and illustrates the distinctions between the European and American ways of viewing this idea. Europeans see progress as a sharp upturn in human affairs, while Americans consider it a gradual forward motion. The author describes the idea of progress in America as a conservative belief which has served as a safeguard to democracy.

Stow Persons reviews the cyclical theory of history during the eighteenth century and its relationship to the idea of progress. He emphasizes the different views of history held by the revivalists, their opponents, and the generation of the American Revolution. Unlike Welter, who

sees the idea of progress as conservative, Persons argues that it was a rallying point for reformers who hoped to improve society and perfect the world. The idea of progress became the basis for expressing discontent.

Clarke A. Chambers examines the idea of progress during the twentieth century. Since World War I, Americans have suffered one serious setback after another. The disillusionment following the failure of Versailles, the Great Crash of 1929, and World War II threatened to destroy the belief in progress. Yet, by mid-century, there was still evidence of progress. Science, technology, freedom, and "faith in the judgment and conscience of the people . . . constituted the hard irreducible core at the heart of the belief in progress."

The article by Georg G. Iggers reviews the evolution of the idea of progress in America from the Enlightenment to the twentieth century. The goals of progress—education, health, welfare, and individual dignity—have not been significantly altered. He believes that now, more than ever before, the idea of progress is part of our public policy.

THE IDEA OF PROGRESS IN AMERICA

Rush Welter*

In an able survey of American opinion in the Middle Period, Arthur Ekirch has discussed a multiplicity of ways in which the idea of progress characterized our political and social thought between 1815 and 1860.[1] His analysis clearly shows that both "conservatives" and "liberals" subscribed to the doctrine of a systematic and presumably perpetual improvement of the human estate, and that well before 1860 the main outlines of a belief which had originated in Europe were translated into American terms, to enter upon a period of faithful service in the American people's characteristic ideology.

It is the purpose of this essay to put the idea into a different context and perspective from that which he used, to analyze its historic significance from a novel and in some senses highly speculative point of view. Such an analysis owes its very existence to Mr. Ekirch's work, which has been of real service to intellectual historians in tracing out the many appearances of so significant an idea in its American setting, and what is suggested here is the result rather of revising some of his categories than of challenging his conclusions. The primary basis of such an approach is a comparison of the American with the European idea of progress as described by J. B. Bury and other writers, on the hypothesis that the differences in formula between the two versions of the idea reflected and even shaped corresponding differences between the two areas of the Atlantic civilization, Europe and America.

Bury found that there were a number of logical prerequisites for a doctrinaire theory of progress, which European civilization did not provide

[1] The Idea of Progress in America, 1815–1860 (*New York, 1944*).

*RUSH WELTER (1923–   ) is a Professor of the History of American Civilization at Bennington College. His publications include Popular Education and Democratic Thought in America (1962) and "The History of Ideas in America: An Essay in Redefinition" (1965). Reprinted by permission of the author and the Journal of the History of Ideas, Vol. 16, No. 3 (June, 1955), 401–415.

until modern times.[2] First to appear was a monistic and synthetic view of history, as opposed to that cyclical view which had characterized late Greek and Roman thought; this was provided by the Hebraic and Christian assumption of a long-range meaning and direction in historic change. Second of these prerequisites to appear was a willingness after the first flush of Renaissance classicism to turn to natural facts rather than ancient classics for an understanding of the contemporary world; in time such a willingness would imply that the present world was quite as important as the past, and might even have progressed beyond it in knowledge. A third factor, also a function of the Renaissance, was secularization of thought, which would ultimately enable men to break free of the Christian view of history so far as it tended to deprecate progress in this world in favor of that to be achieved by transition to another. Coupled with it was a growing belief in the immutable laws of nature, which by definition excluded the arbitrary workings of a divine Providence from the course of historic development, and thus made progress if it existed at all implicit in history itself.

Almost needless to say these basic cultural attitudes did not of themselves insure the birth of a concept of systematic and constant progress. In the first place the idea in its early appearances was only incidental to some other doctrine or purpose. It seemed necessary to argue only that progress was *possible*, for instance, in order to take the side of the Moderns in the Battle of the Books of the seventeenth century. Furthermore, during the course of this controversy the doctrine appeared simply as a commentary on the state of human knowledge, and until knowledge was related in some direct way to social patterns the implications of its progress would remain limited. Lastly, of course, there was the simple fact of intellectual inertia. In the absence of the idea, or of a major conceptual application for it, it was not so obvious a deduction or invention as it was in later retrospect, and those who acknowledged its several components did not necessarily synthesize them. Thus, among the thinkers who brought the doctrine to the verge of explicit statement, Bodin continued to think in providential terms, Descartes ignored the links of the present with the past which might have led him to postulate progress as well as reason, and even Francis Bacon—otherwise most congenial to the progressive frame of mind as it was to be—established his New Atlantis distant in space but not in time from England, a fact which Bury thinks implies his kinship with the precursors of the doctrine rather than with its adherents.

How important the geographical location of utopia was may be seen by a comparison of Bacon's with those of a number of later French reformers, who brought the idea of progress into the strategic rôle it was to have for many decades, and which indeed it was never entirely to lose. First among them was the Abbé de Saint-Pierre, a reformer cast more or less in the utilitarian mold, who proposed the creation in France of a Political Academy which would institute a deliberate and constantly developing progress, not only in knowledge but in the whole of society. Even Saint-Pierre pales beside still later French thinkers, who in any event probably had more influence than he. Turgot grappled with the historic setting for progress, insisting dogmatically that even where progress had not been apparent it had been working, thus justifying a belief in its continued efficacy, while the Encyclopedists placed human

[2] *J. B. Bury*, The Idea of Progress: An Inquiry into Its Origin and Growth (*London, 1920*). *Carl Becker*, The Heavenly City of the Eighteenth Century Philosophers (*New Haven, 1932*) *and Kingsley Martin*, French Liberal Thought in the Eighteenth Century (*Boston, 1929*), *chapter 11, have suggestive comments on the European version.*

perfectibility and the general doctrine of progress in the balance against what they held to be ancient and unnatural institutions in the Europe of their own day. They thus gave it a potency which merely descriptive statement could never lend to it. As finally it matured it was a revolutionary dogma, revolutionary not in the specific political techniques for which it called so much as in the point of view it implied toward existing societies. The answer to social problems of all kinds was implicitly the eradication (by whatever means) of the society from which they had sprung, the substitution of another almost entirely different from it.

This is crucially important. On this view progress would amount to a sharp step *upward* and not merely an easy movement forward in human affairs. It required as well as promised a distinct break with the past and with institutions inherited from the past. To all intents and purposes its doctrinaires had secularized Christian millennarianism and introduced its theological assurance and inclusiveness into the diagnosis of contemporary affairs.[3] And although they optimistically assumed that the increase of rational knowledge would magically achieve the necessary social innovations, when the French thinkers had thus related the Enlightenment directly to social problems it seriously threatened to be a kind of social dynamite for so long as men continued to experience an accretion of knowledge. Hence a generation after the Encyclopedists Condorcet, first of the post-1789 theorists of progress, made the history of the progress of knowledge identical with the his-

tory of progress, and discussed in all seriousness the new era—the Tenth Epoch—into which mankind now moved; even the fact that he was a victim of revolutionary persecution did not dim the luster of his vision. And years later August Comte, living after the era of disenchantment with revolution which Condorcet did not survive, continued nevertheless to find a fundamentally revolutionary hope in much the same nexus of belief, in the theory of separate and identifiable stages of human progress. (The problem was to achieve an adequate science of society paralleling the discoveries of the less complex sciences to implement it.) For despite its disappointments, the French Revolution had not so much destroyed the idea of progress as modified enthusiasm for it. As the utopianism of even "scientific" socialism clearly shows, the millennial idea remained part of the heritage of European political thought long after the Revolution had betrayed but mixedly progressive tendencies.

By contrast, most American thinkers virtually eschewed the radical millennarian formulation of the European idea of progress from the time of its first introduction into their thinking. As an almost infinite number of Fourth of July orations testify, as the pages of such vehicles of popular thought as the *Democratic Review* clearly indicate, as the multitudinous citations of Mr. Ekirch's study show, the American idea of progress in the Middle Period was one intrinsically satisfied with most things as they were.[4] Americans believed that progress was to be sought in a continued unfolding of the bene-

---

3 *It will be noted that even the back-to-nature utopias which abounded in this period had much the same implication despite the supposed retrogression they urged. This is one of the conclusions suggested by Lois Whitney's* Primitivism and the Idea of Progress *(Baltimore, 1934).*

4 *Here and elsewhere the author assumes a knowledge of Ekirch's* Idea of Progress in America *which makes extensive documentation unnecessary. He also has made considerable use of the Harvard College Library's collection of Fourth of July orations, which he wishes to take this opportunity to acknowledge.*

fits which the inhabitants of the United States increasingly became sure were unique in their continent. Progress, that is, would be a continuation of the present. To use the distinction already drawn, it would have forward movement but not upward; it would be horizontal, not vertical.[5]

In part, this distinct reading of the idea of progress may be attributed to the fact that Americans had been nurtured in English rather than Continental traditions of thought. As R. S. Crane has shown, the English doctrine of progress was from its very beginnings very largely the product of a conservative Anglican attempt to disarm modernizing tendencies in religion and social thought by making progress unfold directly and almost imperceptibly from the present.[6] Yet Americans

were not Anglican in either their religious or their social orientation, except perhaps for declining heirs of the Federalist tradition who were long convinced (and often on the *classical* analogy of cycles) that American "progress" could lead only downward. In any event Americans' adoption of the idea in the Middle Period must be explained in terms of its functional validity for their situation rather than in terms of their national origin.

Granting, then, that Americans inherited the necessary ingredients of the doctrine as much from England as from the Continent, it is nonetheless not difficult to see that the American experience itself had much to do with molding the doctrine in a conservative form. The geography, the social structure, presumably even the origins of the inhabitants of the new country all conspired to the same result. Geographically the existence of a "frontier," or at least of areas of accessible land, indicated that the way to achieve bliss was to move directly to it and take advantage of it. Whether or not the frontier was "real" in an economic sense, it was unmistakably real for a number of individuals. Moreover the existence of a basically prosperous middle-class social order undoubtedly encouraged the growing belief that the improvement of human affairs would best be achieved by protection of individuals in their accustomed autonomous ways of making a living —their progress would be within the framework of the existing social order.

On the other hand the fact that Americans were, or were descended from, recent immigrants may well have suggested a similar conclusion to them. If progress in European terms implied a shattering of ancient social bonds, a step upward basically revolutionary in character, the mere fact of having crossed the ocean satisfied this requirement, yet satisfied it without making necessary any signif-

[5] *In this respect the thought of Thomas Jefferson deserves a separate acknowledgment, for Jefferson was something of an ideologue and professional revolutionary. Thanks to an innate curiosity he was able to sympathize with a more genuine radicalism than most of his countrymen could tolerate, and quite characteristically he projected the rewriting of American constitutions every nineteen years to accord with the mathematical and biological requirements of the theory of the social compact. Yet it is not wholly irrelevant that his project appeared not in a state paper but in a private letter, nor is it evading the issue entirely to suggest that Jefferson where he was most progress-minded was least American. Furthermore it is important to remember that in addition to being an amateur of philosophical ideas Jefferson had an extremely practical side, and that his construction of the principle of progress held no very great terrors except for those who did not trouble themselves to understand him. In consequence he succeeded in keeping a mass American following where Thomas Paine—world-citizen, doctrinaire, and genuine revolutionary—could not even find a comfortable refuge in the nation to which he too had helped give birth.*

[6] R. S. Crane, *"Anglican Apologetics and the Idea of Progress, 1609–1745,"* Modern Philology, XXXI (February and May, 1934), 273–306 and 349–382.

icant changes in American society. The very progress of which European thinkers spoke was already a part of the American past.[7]

The United States, that is to say, both *had* progressed and *was* progress; the almost universal experience of its inhabitants testified to the fact. The ambiguous way in which orators handled the fact of the American Revolution in the retrospect of the Middle Period provides a further insight into the peculiar outlines of the American idea of progress as simultaneously past accomplishment and present practice. As has been fairly well established ever since Edmund Burke insisted that the American Revolution was a conservative rebellion, the American more than any other similar political upheaval was a defense of the revolutionaries in their previous habits of political and social existence. At the time, and in terms of the categories of the idea of progress, it was perhaps a step forward but hardly a step upward. Even such radicalism as appeared in the course of it was for the most part a kind of accidental consequence of the violence entailed by the defense of traditional freedom. In the end the American Revolution called for independence, but for a national independence and not an independence of the American past, and the Fourth of July orators frequently pointed to this fact as a vindication of the conservative wisdom of their great ancestors.[8]

Yet often in the same breath these orators proclaimed to the world that the Americans of the revolutionary period had undertaken a progressive step in political affairs, in declaring their independence and establishing an "experiment" in social and political liberty. Here we can see their need to understand themselves in all their national uniqueness, their emergent patriotism, operating to create and to shape their doctrine of progress. In their backward glance their Revolution began to seem a radical step upward, a step which fits the dogmatic pattern of progress. The very fact they were actually so conservative probably exaggerated the impact on their thinking of their ancestors' apparent departure from tradition—their apparent progress in politics—and thus strengthened their own tendency to refer conservatively to their recent past while identifying the simple perpetuation of its institutions with what the Europeans termed "progress."

Ideas and their interrelationships are fascinating in themselves, but they have a further historic significance: ideas have consequences. While they inevitably reflect the circumstances which surround their birth, they also tend in the course of time to have ramifications which exceed the apparent categories and limitations of their origins, as witness Europe's practical experience with the revolutionary applications of the idea of progress.

Given that the Americans believed in progress—or rather (in the light of the European interpretation of the idea) believed that they believed in progress—it seems plausible that a distinctly American reading of the idea helped to differentiate the whole complex of American thought and behavior from that of Europe. This is not simply, then, a matter of describing two different concepts as "characteristic" of two different sub-

---

[7] *Following Charles Beard, Ekirch points out most of these sources for the idea of progress, but does not concern himself with the ramifications of the facts. Beard himself, as both recorder of the doctrine and doctrinaire himself, testifies to the same conservative interpretation of progress throughout his writings on the subject. See in particular his introduction to the American edition of Bury,* The Idea of Progress *(New York, 1932), xxxi ff.*

[8] *A significant modern interpretation of the American Revolution which supports this general view is Louis Hartz's "American Political Thought and the American Revolution,"*

American Political Science Review, *XLVI* (June, 1952), *321–342.*

cultures in Western civilization; the idea itself, *and* the difference, were functionally important to Americans. It is, at any rate, a legitimate undertaking to suggest tentatively and quite speculatively that there were significant ways in which the American idea worked itself out in practice, which may be measured by interpreting Americans' thought and behavior in terms of the unique elements in their idea of progress.

In a sense the success of such an enterprise depends on accepting its premises on faith, yet it may properly be urged that much the same thing is true of (say) the economic interpretation which has often been used to "explain" American history. The proof of economic motivation almost invariably takes on a *post-hoc-propter-hoc* quality, in which all that is truly demonstrated is the original assumptions of the writer. At the very least, as Mr. Ekirch's work shows, most Americans of the Middle Period had an articulate belief in the idea on which our speculation is to be based.[9] It must also be admitted that there is sometimes extreme difficulty in saying decisively whether the American idea of progress was chiefly a motivating force in American life or more nearly a passive reflection of its historic tendencies. But if it is looked upon rather as a habit of mind this difficulty begins to disappear; a habit of mind is cause as well as consequence, and may truly be said to have shaped thought and action as well as followed from them.

With these preliminaries stated let us consider

how the idea may have worked. Taking first the period covered by Mr. Ekirch's study, it has already been suggested that in the political sphere a sense of past progress, as well as of present progress defined as continuing well-being, helped despite the potential implications of progress to guide American thinking into a conservative mode. One apparent consequence of their idea of progress was the Americans' belief in a "higher law," which Ralph Gabriel has so brilliantly described in *The Course of American Democratic Thought*.[10] By its very nature the higher law, with all of its traditional overtones, seemingly would have demanded of contemporary Americans a radically progress-minded orientation. Yet in the thought of the period it was in fact a conservative doctrine; it was a mode of self-identification which reflected a sense of possession rather than of yearning. This is the more significant in view of that religiosity which marked the Middle Period. Usually the Christian—even the Anglicized Christian—is more conscious of human inadequacies than this view implies. But it remained almost alone for the frankly millennarian sects to draw the traditionally obvious conclusion from the implied aspiration of a higher law. The reason for this, it seems clear, was that (like its secular counterpart the Constitution) higher law signified to many Americans something already substantially achieved, and in almost millennial terms. It could not very well have existed in the terms it did without some such sense of things. Nor is it without significance that, as Mr. Gabriel's essay shows, the higher-law concept was in fact essentially political in spite of its religious symbolism. For Americans the most that needed to be done in order to progress toward it was to find a way to extend the benefits of an existing perfection to as

[9] *By way of further establishing some of the terms of the inquiry it may be noted that if the idea of progress was a class doctrine (of the middle class), that class was dominant in America, and apparently its idea was relatively widely spread. If there was in the people at large no articulate "idea" but only a general attitude, this makes contentions based on its existence more difficult to prove, but hardly less relevant if demonstrated to some degree of satisfaction.*

[10] *Ralph H. Gabriel*, The Course of American Democratic Thought (*New York, 1940*), *ch. 2.*

large a part of the population as possible, and this was very largely a political enterprise.[11]

There were differences of opinion among Americans as to the most desirable means for reaching this goal, and it may well be that like Anglican clergymen in England Whigs in the United States were not above manipulating the dogma of progress for partisan purposes. But such differences in its application obscure far more important patterns of likeness. One of the most puzzling facts for the scholar who approaches the age of Andrew Jackson as a quasi-revolutionary one is a constant reference in the writings of ostensible revolutionaries to the restoration of the Constitution and of the Declaration of Independence as major political goals—this, be it remembered, in an age and among men who explicitly believed in "progress." While occasionally a European visitor like Fanny Wright cut nearer to the heart of the matter and made progress a question of fundamental change in the social and economic structure through determined political action, for native Americans the problem was quite clearly the purification of existing institutions.[12] How else understand such a man as George Bancroft, an avowed intellectual leader of the more radical Democrats, whose *History of the United States* nonetheless made the accomplishment of American independence tantamount to the achievement of the Last Epoch? It seems an inescapable conclusion that a vivid conception of progress as simply an extension of benefits already obtained lay behind even "radical" political agitation in the 1820's and 1830's. American radicals wanted not change in the revolutionary European sense but at the most a minor adjustment of the existing political machinery, and this despite the fact that some of them urged against the "aristocrats" all of the crimes with which European radicals were wont to accuse their oppressors. In view, moreover, of their devotion to the terminology of class struggle it is surprising at first glance to find them thinking that political egalitarianism supplemented only by such simple devices as universal public education will make established forms of government take on new life. It is the more surprising when one considers the historic European estimate of the causal connections between the spread of knowledge and the accomplishment of progress. But education, conceived by the Americans of the Middle Period as a great engine against "despotism," was intended only to preserve the present structure of government and society, albeit with some minor changes.[13]

---

[11] *Although debate on the extension of slavery into the territories invoked a superficially more stringent interpretation of higher law—one which controverted even the Constitution—it was both an unrepresentative application and a misleading one. Slavery was the single social problem that ultimately necessitated disrupting the continuity of American history. And meanwhile William H. Seward's appeal to a higher law challenged slavery in the territories but not in the existing states.*

[12] *It is not merely chauvinistic to point out in this context that a disproportionate number of the utopian experiments for which the period is now famous were of European origin or design.*

[13] *To some extent American political and social ideas were radical when compared with those of many Europeans, but this does not mean that they were radical within the American context. The discrepancy in the definition of what is radical is in this sense a reflection of the extent to which the United States had genuinely "progressed" beyond Europe.*

The discrepancy also has been a source of confusion among American historians concerning the significance of our apparently radical movements. On the one hand too many historians with European connotations in mind have imposed foreign categories uncritically on American political thought. On the other hand the existence of a distinctly American attitude toward progress has on occasion given political agitators a peculiar kind of immunity. Some of them have been able to use the categories of class war in their exhortations simply because there was in objective fact no danger that the exhortations would be taken literally or have practical revolutionary effects.

The configurations of thought peculiar to American progress also influenced this same generation (and often the same individuals) in their orientation to political change in the outside world. Although they agreed that the spread of knowledge in Europe was progressively redeeming the people from centuries of tyranny, the very educational conception of political action that Americans were in the process of establishing suggested that foreign progress must take place in an orderly fashion. Despite their own rhetoric of a revolutionary past, Americans did not hesitate in deprecating if not actually repudiating those Europeans who sought to imitate the example of 1776 in their own way. Witness the declining popularity of Kossuth on his visit in the 1850's; at first a hero to the liberal democracy of the United States, he soon found that he lost their interest when he ceased merely to glorify their principles by his presence and instead sought direct support for his. Indeed Kossuth excited the American democrats only because he held a mirror up to them; the Americans had by now developed a disconcerting habit of seeing others as they saw themselves. Not only were European aspirants to progress expected by Americans to avoid the pitfalls which revolution has historically meant, but the image of a progressed European world which Americans projected was remarkably similar to the United States of their own experience. Because Americans understood neither Europe nor the necessities of progress in European terms they expected Europeans to arrive at precisely the same destination *they* had. Kossuth was more welcome as refugee than as revolutionary.

Nor did this manner of thought restrict itself to interpretations of European politics. The American idea of progress quite apparently had a crucial significance in that whole feeling for a continental "Manifest Destiny" which Albert K. Weinberg has so exhaustively analyzed.[14] Certainly it was appealed to in exhortations on the subject, and it has the advantage of helping to explain the total sentiment in subtler ideological and psychological terms than the clearly inadequate categories of pure greed or Southern pro-slavery expansionism. It obviously underlay the categories of destiny which Mr. Weinberg identifies as beliefs in "the destined use of the soil" by American farmers rather than by barbaric Indians, and in "the extension of the area of freedom" in which pioneer Americans might pursue their individualistic economic goals. As his work demonstrates, this pair of concepts at first had reference only to areas already incorporated into the territorial United States, but under the impact of the diplomatic crisis over Texas and subsequently the war with Mexico they were easily transferred to the larger sphere of as-yet unacquired territories. Moreover, he might have added that to many Americans in the late 1840's and 1850's it began to seem plausible that outsiders might really achieve progress only by analogy with the method immigrants to America had used; for best results they should somehow be absorbed into the American system territorially or at least ideologically and institutionally. With this at the back of their minds Americans could overcome their remaining scruples about imperialism as effectively in 1848 as they would in 1898.

They did not, of course, always have a concrete choice to make, and filibusterers tended to discredit even beneficent imperialism, but the war with Mexico is an epitome of the imperial democratic mentality, and illustrates the multiple workings of the American idea of progress. One of the major sources of belligerent friction between the United States and Mexico is commonly agreed to have been the repugnant anarchy which followed Mexico's declaration of her independence.

14 *Albert K. Weinberg*, Manifest Destiny: A Study of Nationalist Expansionism in American History (*Baltimore, 1935*), *chapters 2–7.*

Considered as a revolutionary power the United States was singularly intolerant of the inevitable difficulties of her revolutionary neighbor. But considered as a people not only consciously progressed but also intolerant of genuine revolution because they did not understand its necessities, the Americans make sense. Progress in other lands must conform to the placid American precedent or be rejected, and the result must also be compatible. The trouble with the Mexicans was their inability to apply American knowhow—easily accessible in the periods of Fourth of July orations—and drift forward. Hence the Americans were willing both to chastise them, and temporarily at least to absorb part or all of their territory under a self-imposed "mission of regeneration," as Mr. Weinberg calls it. That they did not occupy all of Mexico was, as his study indicates, a matter less of ideology than of political accident.

There was a more nearly open-ended doctrine of progress in American thought than these ambivalent political dogmas suggest. During this same period Americans came to uphold a generalized conception of individual progress as the basis and definition of social. However it is of primary importance that this socio-economic conception of progress is inherently conservative; it was implicit in this view, which the Whigs adopted but by no means monopolized, that progress in America would take care of itself. Certain characteristic intellectual traits of the Americans presumably derived much of their strength from the progressive point of view understood in these terms.

One of the most widespread was the evil-man theory of social problems, which has been so congenial to American thinking at least since Jackson entered the White House. If progress in the corporate and institutional sense has been achieved, yet does not in fact progressively benefit its inhabitants, there can by definition be nothing systematically wrong, and the logical inference is to attribute such evil to evil men's interposition between progress and individuals. Of course this was a large part of the Jacksonian animus toward the "aristocrats," but it long survived the success of specifically Jacksonian reforms, and like the American conception of the nature of foreign political problems continues to assert itself in every domestic crisis.

Otherwise complacency was the outcome of both kinds of progress, that achieved in the past and that demonstrated in the present. To this influence may in large part be attributed the patterns of intellectual inquiry of the Middle Period, which have been the despair of historians trying to find profound philosophical and intellectual developments outside the handful of Transcendentalists and displaced Calvinists who dissented from so much of the culture around them. Hawthorne, satirizing in *The Celestial Railroad* the easy assumption that basic moral problems are taken care of and that life consists of a mechanized pilgrimage; Melville, insisting on probing to the point of agony the age's conveniently innocuous romantic clichés, are in their dissent a measure of the impact of the idea of progress on the ordinary American's mind. The fact is that there *was* no philosophical inquiry outside of that undertaken by these dissenters, and of course the dissenters were not understood. For the most part they could be ignored; but it was one of the further characteristics of American complacency that they might also be adapted to the purposes of the Americans, as Emerson's basically terrifying individualism was to the purposes of exploitive capitalism. Thus the idea of progress shaped American thought in precisely that fashion which would make few intellectual demands of the thinkers.

Besides a philosophical complacency there were other traits to which the absence of a deeper grasp of progress and the dominance of its counterfeit gave encouragement. Does it not seem that the "tyranny of the majority," the uniformity enforced by public opinion which Alexis de Tocqueville described and lamented, was the outgrowth not so much of social conditions themselves as of the habits of thought to which social conditions taken as evidence of progress had given rise? Were the Americans not convinced by their knowledge of past achievements and by their comfortable circumstances that progress was already defined, and hence sure that deviation from the consensus of opinion and behavior could not be anything but wilful and immoral?[15] In any event this was the nation to which educated and thoughtful Europeans came to study the meaning of a democratic experiment, but even on its best behavior it did not seem to know what mattered most. On the classic European view, the conflict of opinions produces truth; in the light of the idea of progress truth will be constantly accruing new meanings. But in the United States neither conflict nor innovation was deemed necessary. Indeed all that was necessary, according to a commonly held view, was the education of all children in the accepted truths of their parents. So simple a proposition did this sometimes seem that some advocates of a democratic education believed teachers might be hired in rotation from the body politic, on an analogy with the rotation in office which was then considered to be adequate to the slight demands made by public office.

A complacency which on the popular level took the form of a tyranny of the majority—this was the chief defect of the American democrats,

which Tocqueville mistakenly imputed to their political and social institutions *per se*. Indirectly of course his view had some merit; democracy *was* a step "upward" with respect to Europe and thus to some extent was responsible for the Americans' opinions, but he did not understand all the ways in which they had arrived at them. Apart from these two central characteristics of the Americans' culture there were others which may be better explained in terms of their concept of progress than by reference solely to American democracy or to any other single cultural circumstance; most important among them is the Americans' view of evil. Mention has already been made of the evil-man theory in politics. It had a more general cultural corollary in attitudes toward the evil in mankind, a concept which on first glance seems to refute any description of complacency. Yet of their relationship to this evil it is apparent that many Americans of the Middle Period conceived of their religious obligation as chiefly one of *eradicating* it by eliminating individual malpractices like intemperance—practices which might be measured and dealt with in concrete and secular terms, the terms of social progress rather than theology. This was the attitude which flourished in the innumerable movements for humanitarian reform into which American Christianity of the period entered. In its underlying self-assurance, in its implied belief in individual efficacy in the face of all problems, this was the apotheosis of American progressive culture.

Nothing that has been said significantly restricts the patterns and effects of the American idea of progress to the period before the Civil War. As the natural perseverance of traits of character might suggest, both the social and the political orientation of Americans remained substantially unchanged after 1865. To bring this discussion more nearly up to date mention need be made only of the nexus of thought of Social Darwinism,

15 *Consider in this light Frederick Jackson Turner's dictum (in "Contributions of the West to American Democracy,"* The Frontier in American History [*New York, 1920*], *chap. 9) that American democracy and American individualism have been the product not of theoretical statement but of practices stemming from economic and social forces.*

a theory which in the hands of Herbert Spencer was both uncompromising and a little ridiculous, but which many Americans were able to accept lock, stock, and barrel. To them the doctrine of achieving progress by maintaining the status quo inviolate was not a palpable idiocy but a self-evident statement of American practice in the past, and following already well-established patterns of thinking it ramified into every department of their lives. Their complacency, their humanitarianism, their sense of a Manifest Destiny, their prescriptions for foreign progress, their individualism all found themselves renewed and strengthened by this shoddy doctrine from which even the best of their thinkers did not entirely escape.

Yet it was the strategic weakness of the American promise of progress that it required results. Occasionally movements of social protest arose in the lower ranks of society to challenge the happy complacency of the progressed. On the other hand the protestants were at the same time Americans themselves, and their reform movements in the postwar period indulged like the Jacksonian movement before them in recriminations against the handful of evil men (in this case trust and railroad magnates) who blocked progress—and promptly disbanded when a momentary business recovery was achieved. The protests were easily disarmed not simply by periods of prosperity but also by virtue of their own fundamental weakness in social analysis, which assumed each time that in the United States a general prosperity was the norm; they could not conceive of their situation in any other terms than those of present emergency. Even the era of the muckrakers which succeeded that of primarily agrarian protest did not challenge very deeply the premises and configurations of progress in its American guise. Muckraking begot progressivism in its several forms, but a

conscious "progressivism" meant little more than restraining evil men through extending democratic practices, even though some of its outstanding intellectual leaders attempted briefly to recast American social thinking. It is certainly not an accident that the leading Progressive politician, he of the Big Stick, not only repudiated and thus gave a name to the muckrakers, but also explicitly and articulately asserted his conservatism at the instant he proposed his seemingly most drastic reforms.

It remained to Franklin D. Roosevelt among our political spokesmen to suggest that more fundamental reforms were necessary than had yet been proposed. To him as to his generation the American economy suddenly seemed basically sick. Yet even in this crisis of American belief what was most significant was not that the idea of progress was reinterpreted so much as that the American sense of progress began to falter as a result of the failure of the economy. What the ultimate ideological outcome of a recognition of its failure might have been we have so far been spared, mainly by the economic revival which recurrent wars have brought, and secondarily by the renewed sense of our superiority which emergence from a provincial isolation has fostered. The patterns of belief apparently remain unchanged, and we still think to solve grave international problems by "exporting" our indigenous democracy. Even so we have not entirely escaped. There is an unmistakable search in American intellectual circles for a new kind of cosmic belief which can replace the idea of progress and simultaneously assimilate the feeling that fundamental changes are in the offing. It follows naturally from the limited conception of progress we have held that this search for a new pattern of self-identification is a work of despair, not hope.

THE CYCLICAL THEORY OF HISTORY IN EIGHTEENTH CENTURY AMERICA[1]

Stow Persons[*]

A concise statement of the cyclical view of history was set forth by Bolingbroke in *The Patriot King* of 1738, as follows:

> Absolute stability is not to be expected in anything human; for that which exists immutably exists alone necessarily, and this attribute of the Supreme Being can neither belong to man, nor to the works of man. The best instituted governments, like the best constituted animal bodies, carry in them the seeds of their destruction: and though they grow and improve for a time, they will soon tend visibly to their dissolution. Every hour they live is an hour the less that they have to live. All that can be done therefore to prolong the duration of a good government, is to draw it back, on every favorable occasion, to the *first good principles* on which it was founded. When these occasions happen often, and are well improved, such governments are prosperous and durable. When they happen seldom, or are ill improved, these political bodies live in pain or in langour, and die soon.[2]

My purpose is to indicate the general currency of such a cyclical theory of history in late eighteenth century America, and to explore its relationship to the idea of progress, which has generally been regarded as the characteristic outlook on history

[1] *An earlier version of this paper was presented at the Newberry Library Conference on American Studies, October 13, 1951.*

[2] *Henry Saint-John Bolinbroke,* Letters on the Spirit of Patriotism: on the Idea of a Patriot King: and on the State of Parties, at the Accession of King George the First (*New ed., London: Cadell, 1783*), p. 128.

STOW PERSONS (1913–   ) is a Professor of History at the University of Iowa. His publications include Free Religion, An American Faith (*1947*), Evolutionary Thought in America (*co-author, 1950*), *and* American Minds: A History of Ideas (*1958*). *Reprinted by permission of the author and the* American Quarterly, *Vol. 6, No. 2 (Summer, 1954), 147–163. Published by The University of Pennsylvania. Copyright, 1954, Trustees of the University of Pennsylvania.*

of enlightened thinkers, both in Europe and in America.

As an epoch in the history of thought the American Enlightenment may be taken to have commenced with the reaction to the great religious revival of the 1740's and to have ended with the War of 1812. The function of the revival was to precipitate issues and crystallize parties. Conflicts of interest helped to sharpen objectives and straighten the lines of thought. The Great Awakening presented the first common intellectual issues for Anglo-Americans widely scattered along the continental seaboard, and from it radiate the intellectual traditions that are properly to be called American rather than provincial. Three distinct theories of history were to be found in the thought of the time, with one of which, the cyclical theory, I am particularly concerned.

The investigation involves an approach to the mind of the Enlightenment in America that may seem heretical on at least two counts. On the one hand, it was a complex of ideas which stemmed from the interests of a particular group. We should not be misled by the cosmopolitan content of enlightened thought—its emphasis upon natural law, reason, universal benevolence, and the rights of man. Here was perhaps the first instance of those ambiguous relationships between interest and profession which have given the history of our national ideology its elusive character. To force enthusiastic believers in immediate revelation and special providences to recognize the primacy of natural law and submit to the rule of reason was at the outset precisely the point at issue. On the other hand, by emphasizing the utility of enlightened ideas as weapons in the hands of a class of men in America, I am also risking the charge of ignoring the fact that these ideas were current throughout most of Western civilization in the eighteenth century, with the implication that their analysis in the purely local

context must be inadequate. While there is much truth in this, I would nevertheless suggest that the relationship between enlightened thinkers in Europe and in America is one of descent from a common parentage, the English latitudinarians of the previous century, and that the differences between the eighteenth century offspring are to be understood in part at least as the consequence of local controversies. In short, the mind of the American Enlightenment was not a mass mind, but the creed of a party, several of whose doctrines are fully understood only as planks in a party platform.

The first of the three conceptions of history was that of the revivalists of the Great Awakening. It was a frankly supernaturalist interpretation of history as the unfolding revelation of divine purpose. Human history was conceived to be, in Jonathan Edwards' phrase, the work of redemption, a work which would be completed with the second coming of Christ and the establishment of his millennial kingdom. Many were convinced that the wholesale conversions accomplished by the revival entailed that purification of spirit and morals presumably characteristic of the "latter day" foretold by the prophets. Edwards himself believed that the new world had been reserved for recent discovery and the conversion of the heathen aborigines, in order that a seat might be prepared for the imminent establishment of Christ's kingdom.[3] Night after night expectant revivalists "flew as doves to their windows" to witness the coming of the Lord in clouds of glory.

The relevance of this quaint excitement to our exploration of the moderate and empirical temper of the enlightened mind was suggested twenty years ago by Carl Becker in his study of the

[3] *Jonathan Edwards*, A History of the Work of Redemption (*3rd. Amer. ed., Worcester: Thomas, 1792*), *pp. 280–81, 310–11.*

French *philosophes.* The idea of progress, Becker observed, is to be understood as a secularization of the millennialist interpretation of history. The conception of the progress of the human race from the earliest primitive horde postulated by Condorcet to its estimable condition in the eighteenth century with its infinitely enticing prospects for the future, is nothing but the pious Christian's account of the work of redemption, with somewhat different characters and emphases, to be sure, but with essentially the same form of plot. Becker's thesis has been employed in a similar analysis of the origins of the idea of progress in America by Professor Rutherford Delmage,[4] who has assembled some interesting evidence tracing the transformation of the one view into the other. One may well be reluctant, however, to accept an historical connection established in terms of the similarity of idea-form alone, when in other crucial respects the millennial expectation and the idea of progress represent such sharply contrasting interests and temperaments. The cyclical theory seems to have performed a mediating function in accommodating these theories of history to each other.

A central issue in the controversies arising out of the Great Awakening concerned the method of God's governance of the world. Did he intervene by means of special providences and direct inspiration for the guidance of men of the historical process, or was he content to achieve his ends through those "general and steady laws" known to men through Scripture, experience, and the observation of nature? The revivalists held the former view and their opponents the latter. The millennial expectation was the culminating affirmation of men prepared to commit human

history to a transcendent purpose which would in the end give history its meaning. The millennial hope itself, however, could not become a major issue in the conflict because either party insisted upon its Protestant orthodoxy, and all acknowledged the testimony of Scripture that Christ would ultimately return to judge the quick and the dead.[5] The work of the anti-revivalists was less to reject the millennial hope than to reformulate the issues in such a way that the expectation of the second coming would eventually become a radically different concept.

The intellectual spokesmen for the opponents of the revival were the Anglican Alexander Garden, John Thomson the Presbyterian, and Charles Chauncy the Congregationalist.[6] In the controversial tracts of these men, published between 1740 and 1743, and aimed at Whitefield, Tennent, Edwards, and their followers, one finds dressed in religious garb several of the characteristic ideas and attitudes more commonly associated with the secular thinkers of the following generation. As the expression of a group conscious of its interests and of the identity of its foe enlightened ideas in America find their source here.

Fear of the social chaos anticipated in the revivalists' attack upon the privileged position of the established churches was the prime consideration which motivated the counter-attack of the

[4] *Rutherford E. Delmage, "The American Idea of Progress, 1750–1800,"* Proceedings of the American Philosophical Society, XCI (1947), pp. 307–14.

[5] *Charles Chauncy,* Seasonable Thoughts on the State of Religion in New England (*Boston: Eliot, 1743*), *pp. 370–73.*
[6] *Alexander Garden,* Regeneration, and the Testimony of the Spirit (*Charlestown: Timothy, 1740*); Six Letters to the Rev. Mr. George Whitefield (*2nd ed., Boston: Fleet, 1740*). *John Thomson,* The Doctrine of Convictions Set in a Clear Light (*Philadelphia: Bradford, 1741*); The Government of the Church of Christ (*Philadelphia: Bradford, 1741*). *Charles Chauncy,* Enthusiasm Describ'd and Caution'd Against (*Boston, 1742*); Seasonable Thoughts.

anti-revivalists. All of their doctrinal argument points to this conclusion. Its essence was expressed in Chauncy's dictum that in the work of conversion the divine spirit operates upon the reason, bringing about a change in the temper of mind, and disciplining the unruly passions in accordance with the new and clearer insight into the nature of divine truth.[7] The consequence was to submerge the operation of divine grace within the human process of striving measured in moral terms, to be detected in conduct. By the use of reason and Scripture men were to discover and do God's will, confident that God would not withhold his grace from the truly penitent. This of course implied a merciful and benevolent deity.[8] The evidence of regeneration was not to be found in subjective impressions, ecstatic impulses, or "heightened affections," but in an enrichment of Christian graces, the chief of which was love. Nothing illustrates more clearly the social affiliations of the anti-revivalists than their enumeration of the qualities of the gracious Christian convert. According to Chauncy, believers should display "a spiritual *Likeness* to the LORD JESUS CHRIST, in *Faith;* in *Purity;* in *Lowliness* and *Humility;* in *Love* to GOD, and our *Neighbors;* in *Patience*, *Meekness*, and *Gentleness;* in *Contempt* of the *World*, Contentedness with their Condition, Resignation to God; and in a Word, a *Zeal* to *honor him*, and *do all the good they can* in the World."[9] The worst that could be said of enthusiasts was that they were "Porters, Cobblers, Barbers, etc. . . . ignorant and impudent wretches," whose restiveness under the disciplined religious leadership of an educated clergy caused

them to abandon their proper stations and flock to the revivalists. As the *Boston Evening-Post* observed: "It is one of the main Disorders and Infelicities of the present Age, that many of the *meanest Rank*, and of *Inferior Capacities*, are puffed up with a Pride that is become almost past dealing with. Some of the most contemptible Creatures among us yet think themselves sufficient to direct *Statesmen*, dictate to *Legislators*, and teach *Doctors* and *Divines*."[10]

The function of reason as the monitor of the moral law is understood in this context. As Chauncy put it, "One of the most *essential* Things necessary in the *new-forming* Men, is the reduction of their *Passions* to a proper Regimen, i.e., the Government of a *sanctified Understanding*. . . . The plain Truth is, an *enlightened Mind*, and not *raised Affections*, ought always to be the Guide of those who call themselves Men."[11] Enlightened thinkers commenced by glorifying reason as a disciplinary agency, and only gradually did the course of events suggest its use as a revolutionary solvent.

I have emphasized the circumstances under which the constellation of enlightened ideas was composed because they underline the originally conservative character of the movement. The theory of history which began to emerge from this line of thought I propose to designate the theory of organic cycles. Opponents of the revival acknowledged the biblical authority upon which the millennial hope rested, but they rejected as an enthusiastic delusion the expectation that the revival itself heralded the second coming. Direct inspiration in either of its forms, as subjective

---

7 *Chauncy*, Seasonable Thoughts, *pp. 108–19.*

8 *Stephen Williams to Eleazer Wheelock, July 18, 1740. Wheelock MSS.* Boston Evening-Post, *April 19, 1742.*

9 *Chauncy*, Enthusiasm Describ'd, *pp. 8–14. Cf. Thomson,* Doctrine of Convictions, *pp. 21–25.*

10 Boston Evening-Post, *April 5, 1742. For similar allusions to the class character of the revival see the issues of September 29, October 6, 1740; February 8, 22, 1742; January 24, 1743.*

11 *Chauncy*, Seasonable Thoughts, *pp. 324–27.*

impression or as overt historical event, was decisively repudiated, and with it the possibility or relevance of interpreting history as the special revelation of God's will.[12] For the opponents of the revival a pertinent interpretation of history must concern itself with the issues deemed of paramount importance, namely, the reasoned and moderate disciplining of the mind and appetites consistently with what had been vouchsafed men to know of the intentions of deity and of their obligations to their fellows.

The new view of history which came into vogue among conservative thinkers in the years following the revival found the source of historical dynamics in the operation of the universal moral law, the effect of which upon history was an endless cyclical movement analogous to the life cycle of the individual organism. Societies and nations rise and fall in endless sequence according as they observe or disregard those universal moral laws ordained of God and graven upon men's consciences for their governance and happiness. Suggestions of the cyclical theme were to be found both in the writers of classical antiquity, especially the historians and moralists, and more recently in the popular English literature of the early eighteenth century. It was subsequently to become a familiar theme in romantic thought. Both John Adams and Jefferson were familiar with the *Patriot King*, where they would have found the passage quoted at the opening of this paper. It is also perhaps pertinent to call attention to the prevalence in contemporary thought of two ideas easily related to the cyclical theme. One was the physiographic notion of primitive corruption and aged refinement, as popularized in the natural histories of Buffon and Raynal. The other was the historical idea of the westward transit of culture. In any event, the universal relevance of

the cyclical theory appealed mightily to an age coming to pride itself upon its cosmopolitanism and to view with increasing embarrassment the sectarian limitations of the Christian pretensions. It was held by men many of whom had no immediate interest in the party battles of the revival, but who were at least united with the anti-revivalists in opposition to the emotionalism and democratic inclinations of the religious enthusiasts. The cyclical theory of history was to become for a brief period one of the distinctive historical conceptions of the dominant social group in America.

The following passage from a sermon of the Rev. David Tappan, Hollis Professor of Divinity at Harvard College, preached in 1798, will serve to illustrate the cyclical view in its most literal form.

Experience proves that political bodies, like the animal economy, have their periods of infancy, youth, maturity, decay, and dissolution. In the early stages of their existence their members are usually industrious and frugal, simple in their manners, just and kind in their intercourse, active and hardy, united and brave. Their feeble, exposed, and necessitous condition in some sort forces upon them this conduct and these habits. The practice of these virtues gradually nourishes them to a state of manly vigor. They became mature and flourishing in wealth and population, in arts and arms, in almost every kind of national prosperity. But when they have reached a certain point of greatness, their taste and manners begin to be infected. Their prosperity inflates and debauches their minds. It betrays them into pride and avarice, luxury and dissipation, idleness and sensuality, and too often into practical and scornful impiety. These, with other kindred vices, hasten their downfall and ruin. [History shows that] virtue is the soul of republican freedom; that luxury tends to extinguish both sound morality and piety; and that the loss of these renders men

[12] Ibid., *pp. 183–84, 370–73.*

incapable of estimating and relishing, of preserving or even bearing the blessings of equal liberty.[13]

The special function of the clerical adherents to the cyclical view was to relate it to the divine government of the world. The moral law establishes an irrevocable connection between virtue and happiness on the one hand, and between vice and misery on the other. "The benevolent Ruler of the universe delights in the happiness of his subjects," and while his judgments are for their transgressions, they are also for their instruction.[14] In this most rational and equably governed of worlds sin does not always provoke speedy and sufficient retribution, for if it did there would be no scope for that testing and development of individual character which is necessary to prepare men for the future state.

The actual measures, therefore, of the divine government towards communities and particular persons appear full of wisdom and beauty. While the former receive such a recompense of their conduct, as gives a general, though incomplete display of the governing justice of God; the latter have sufficient advantages and motives to prepare for and confidently expect the ultimate triumph of virtue in the unmixed and endless happiness of

its friends, and the final destruction of its obdurate enemies.[15]

Thus it appears that history is virtue teaching by example; and the decline and fall of empires represents a divine judgment upon the corruption of men.

Perhaps because it performed a didactic function in the exhortations of the clergy, we find more explicit expression of the cyclical theme in their writings. But it was widely presupposed by lay thinkers as well, at least before the French Revolution. John Adams, for instance, held it for more than half a century. As early as 1755, he attributed the rise and fall of nations to "some minute and unsuspected cause," a cause which, judging by his reflections upon the fall of Rome, the rise of America, and other great historical events, he assumed to be invariably moral in character.[16] Sixty-four years later he was still harping upon the same theme, challenging Jefferson to cite a single illustration of a nation once corrupted that had been able to cleanse itself and restore political liberty. "Will you tell me," he asked, "how to prevent riches from becoming the effects of temperance and industry? Will you tell me how to prevent riches from producing luxury? Will you tell me how to prevent luxury from producing effeminacy, intoxication, extravagance, vice and folly?"[17] This plaintive cry reminds us of John Wesley's inexorable cycle of piety, virtue, riches, and corruption before which the great evangelical for all his zeal for souls stood helpless. In fact, the thoroughly moralistic char-

[13] *David Tappan*, A Discourse, Delivered to the Religious Society in Brattle-Street, Boston . . . on April 5, 1798 (*Boston: Hall, 1798*), pp. 18–19. *For similar views of clerics, see Charles Backus*, A Sermon, Preached in Long-Meadow, at the Public Fast, April 17, 1788 (*Springfield: Weld and Thomas, 1788*), p. 9; *Thomas Barnard*, A Sermon, Delivered on the Day of National Thanksgiving, February 19, 1795 (*Salem: Cushing, 1795*), pp. 21–22; *Samuel Stanhope Smith*, The Divine Goodness to the United States of America. A Discourse . . . February 19, 1795 (*Philadelphia: W. Young, 1795*), pp. 20–21.

[14] *Joseph Lathrop*, National Happiness, Illustrated in a Sermon, Delivered at West-Springfield, on February 19, 1795 (*Springfield: Hooker and Stebbins, 1795*), p. 13.

[15] *Tappan*, Discourse, April 5, 1798, *pp. 24–25*.

[16] *Adams to Nathan Webb, October 12, 1755*. Works (*C. F. Adams, ed.*), I, 23.

[17] *Paul Wilstach, ed.*, Correspondence of John Adams and Thomas Jefferson (*Indianapolis: Bobbs-Merrill, 1925*), *pp. 169–70 (December 18, 1819)*.

acter of enlightened social theory is so striking that it is remarkable that in an age as remote from this concern as is our own it has been so seldom commented upon.

If the cyclical view of history was as widely entertained as I have assumed, we are provided with a possible explanation of why it was that the enlightened mind in America did not express itself in any more important measure in the historiographical form. In the final analysis history can only reiterate its great theme; the same yesterday, today, and forever. There was nothing to be learned from it that could not be found in one's personal experience, or in the life of one's own time. In his treatise devoted specifically to the philosophy of history, the *Discourses on Davila*, John Adams tells us that the "key . . . to the rise and fall of empires" is found in the universal operation of the human passion for distinction, in its various forms of emulation, ambition, jealousy, envy and vanity.[18] This was the psychological source and motivation of those dynamic cycles which constitute the course of history. It appears to have been assumed that the connection ordained of God between nature, personality, and history was so tight as to deprive history of that range of possibilities which alone is capable of endowing it with more than passing interest. "Such is our unalterable moral constitution," wrote Adams, "that an internal inclination to do wrong is criminal; and a wicked thought stains the mind with guilt, and makes it tingle with pain." Hence of necessity history unfolds the perennial struggle between "the cause of liberty, truth, virtue, and humanity," on the one hand, and slavery, ignorance, misery, and despotism on the other; virtue prevailing during the great days of Roman culture, darkness and misery from the fourth to the fourteenth century. Once we have

grasped the principle further study will merely substantiate the thesis.[19]

Jefferson also conceived of history as a series of cyclical fluctuations within a larger static framework, at least until his last years. Like Adams he also found the source of historical change to reside in the moral nature. Reflecting upon the revolutionary experiences of his own state, he expressed the opinion in the *Notes on Virginia* that when a state of public virtue prevails it is high time to erect safeguards for the protection of liberty, since "the spirit of the times may alter, will alter," and corrupt men will arise to persecute their fellows.[20] Anticipating Lord Acton's dictum that power corrupts, he appealed to history for proof that even the best governments are eventually perverted into tyrannies by those entrusted with power. To forestall this sad fate in Virginia he drafted the celebrated Bill for the More General Diffusion of Knowledge (1778), the preamble of which expresses the conviction that education aids the citizen in recognizing "ambition" and thus defeating its aims.[21] It was, in other words, the constant uniformities or repetitions of history, not its unique occurrences, that impressed Jefferson as being of value.[22] He was still of the same opinion many years later when he wrote to Adams that "in fact, the terms of whig and tory belong to natural as well as civil history. They denote the temper and constitution of mind of different individuals."[23] Such a point of view was well adapted to nurture a distinguished political science

---

[18] *Adams*, Works, *VI, 239, 232–34.*

[19] Ibid., *IV* (Novanglus and Massachusettensis), *44, 17–18.*

[20] *Adrienne Koch and William Peden, eds.,* The Life and Selected Writings of Thomas Jefferson (*New York: Modern Library, 1944), p. 277.*

[21] *Jefferson,* Papers (*Boyd, ed.*), *II, 526–27.*

[22] *Koch and Peden, p. 265.*

[23] *Wilstach, p. 59.*

—as indeed it did—but it was not conducive to a fruitful investigation of history.

It would not do, however, to leave the reader with the impression that the cyclical conception of history was merely a convenient device whereby enlightened thinkers were enabled to concentrate their attention elsewhere. It had an integral part in the conception which the age entertained of itself, and its projection into the future suggested an attitude towards human and social possibilities that was one of the most distinctive features of the enlightened mind. Those who employed the cyclical idea were uniformly agreed that the America of their day belonged in the youthful stage of growth approaching maturity. The Rev. Thomas Barnard of Salem, for instance, comparing the prospects of the new United States with those of older European countries which had nothing to look forward to except "decline and mortification, according to the course of human affairs," remarked upon the opportunities for growth and progress which lay before her. "I should prefer youth and early manhood, ever employed, lively, and full of hope, to complete manhood and old age, when we every day become less active, and less pleased. I should prefer the present period of our nation, for my life, to the more perfect state to which it will gradually advance."[24] Sometimes the cyclical idea is employed in the appraisal of specific issues, as when President Samuel Stanhope Smith of the College of New Jersey warns the country against involvement in the French revolutionary wars on the ground that peace is especially important to a "young and growing country not yet enervated by luxury, nor sunk into effeminacy and sloth. These vices indeed sometimes require the purifying flame of war to purge them off; and the state emerges from its fires regenerated, as it were, and

new created."[25] Or it is used to justify the spirit and form of political institutions in America, as when the Rev. Samuel Williams opined that "on all accounts, a *free and equal government* is best suited to our infant and rising state."[26]

The self-consciousness with which the Enlightened age identified itself was in part at least the consequence of a theory of history which presupposed a series of epochs alternating in character. General Washington's letter to the state governors at the end of the Revolution is characteristic of this spirit. "The foundation of our empire," he wrote, "was not laid in the gloomy age of ignorance and superstition; but at an epocha when the rights of mankind were better understood and more clearly defined, than at any former period."[27] Similar sentiments are frequently encountered, and if taken out of the cyclical context may be misunderstood to indicate a belief in unlimited progress. Actually, most enlightened thinkers had a keen sense of the precariousness of the felicity which they enjoyed, of the moral and social conditions which would make its continuation possible, and of the ultimate likelihood of its dissipation. The cyclical conception of history was the crystallization of their hopes and fears. By reading back into their thought ideas which more commonly belong to their descendants we may seriously misunderstand their point of view.

The function of the cyclical idea can perhaps be most briefly and effectively illustrated from the field of thought in which the enlightened mind achieved its supreme expression, political theory. The conservative, defensive character of that

24 *Barnard*, Sermon, February 19, 1795, *pp. 21–22.*

25 *Smith*, Divine Goodness, *pp. 20–21.*

26 *Samuel Williams*, A Discourse on the Love of Our Country; Delivered on a Day of Thanksgiving, December 15, 1774 (*Salem: S. & E. Hall, 1775*), *p. 18.*

27 *Washington*, Writings (*Ford ed.*), X, 256.

theory is now pretty generally recognized. Liberty, the supreme good, could be achieved only if men exercised those moral virtues enjoined by the anti-revivalists, the practical fruit of which was the accumulation of property. The economic basis of enlightened political theory is aptly illustrated in the famous syllogism of President John Augustine Smith of William and Mary college, an ardent Jeffersonian Republican: since ninety-nine per cent of all legislation relates to property; and since it is the essence of republicanism that laws should emanate from those upon whom they bear; then restriction of the franchise to men of property is good republicanism. But property was more than an arbitrary qualification for political participation; it was an index of the moral health of the community. Unfortunately, property as we have seen was presumed to entail its own peculiar corruptions, the avoidance of which constituted a major preoccupation of political theorists. Jefferson pinned his faith to agriculture, writing to Madison in 1787 that Americans could be expected to preserve their liberties "as long as we remain virtuous, and I think we shall be so, as long as agriculture is our principal object, which will be the case, while there remain vacant lands in any part of America. When we get piled upon one another in large cities, as in Europe, we shall become corrupt as in Europe, and go to eating one another, as they do there."[28] These rural loyalties of the republican political theorists are not to be understood entirely in economic or regional terms, but perhaps primarily in moral terms. Even Benjamin Franklin, incorrigible cosmopolite, shared this sentimental agrarianism. The American counterpart of the European myth of the noble savage, living under the full light of nature, and uncorrupted by the vices of urban life, was of course the freehold farmer, whose virtuous life was the one sure foundation of national felicity.

Sound social and political institutions were, however, but temporary bulwarks against the inexorable processes of nature and history. The cyclical theory was perfectly compatible with the anticipated transformation of sturdy farmers into a landless proletariat, and with the degeneration of republican liberty into democratic license and ultimately to the tyranny of dictatorship. In his old age, John Adams looked back upon the eighteenth century and pronounced it to be, on the whole, the century "most honorable to human nature;" but he had no inclination to assume that the nineteenth century would be even more so. "My duties in my little infinitesimal circle," he wrote, "I can understand and feel. The duties of a son, a brother, a father, a neighbor, a citizen, I can see and feel, but I trust the ruler with his skies."[29]

In view of the typical emphasis upon moral conditions as the agents of cyclical change one might well question the appropriateness or significance of the use of the organic analogy. But I think the association is worth preserving in our descriptive terminology if only because it serves to illustrate the intimate connection between nature and value, which was perhaps the most distinctive feature of enlightened thought. The transmutation of natural law into natural right was the neatest trick of the age, and although we in our time can understand it with difficulty and may even suspect fraud, we cannot fail to admire the assurance and virtuosity with which the trick was performed. The inexorable rise and fall of nations might well be ordained of God after the pattern of the life cycle of organisms, but from the creature's point of view the Deity in his beneficent wisdom has provided that our own

---

[28] *Jefferson*, Writings (*1903 ed.*), VI, 392–93.

[29] *Adams to Jefferson, November 13, 1815; September 15, 1813. Wilstach, pp. 118, 86.*

vices and virtues, wisdom and folly, shall register a proximate if not immediate effect upon the course of human events. This we can understand, and we trust the ruler with his skies.

The third conception of history to be found in the thought of eighteenth century America was embodied in the idea of progress. I shall not attempt to document the rise of this idea in America, but will merely indicate what I understand to be its impact upon the revolutionary generation. To put it bluntly: the notion of progress was repugnant to the characteristic convictions and temper of the class of men who in the generation prior to the Revolution had synthesized enlightened ideas in America. But at the same time it held a fatal fascination for them. Much of their practical experience recommended its validity. With diminishing reluctance they accommodated themselves to the idea, and in the end those of them who lived long enough, like Adams and Jefferson, embraced it heartily. But in so doing they signed, as it were, articles of intellectual abdication, and the enlightened mind thus became something else.

From a genetic point of view the idea of progress as it appeared in America was the offspring of a union of the millennial hope with the moralism of the cyclical view of history. The womb in which the progeny was nurtured was the excitement of the revolutionary struggle. The respects in which the Revolution involved a domestic class struggle have been familiar to students of American history for a generation, and it is possible that the competition between these attitudes towards history might be fruitfully related to the social class struggle. In any event, certain modifications in either theory of history looking towards a rapprochement may be indicated.

As contemplated by the revivalists of the seventeen-forties, the imminent coming of the Lord represented the divine will imposed upon history. It was that not-so-far-off divine event towards which the whole creation moved; and the events of the revival, including the saving or hardening of sinners, were to be understood as but reflex actions of that mighty upheaval. But as revival enthusiasm within the Reformed churches rapidly ebbed after 1745 its proponents were placed on the defensive by a changing mood and by the extravagances of fanatics. Leading evangelicals now realized that their millennial expectations had been at best premature, and that if the hope were to be kept alive it must not disregard historical possibilities. The survival of the millennial vision was made possible, among the more intellectually respectable of the clergy at least, by measuring progress towards the final event in moral terms.[30]

To illustrate this significant tendency, again in its most literal form, I have chosen a sermon of the Rev. Ebenezer Baldwin of Danbury, Connecticut, preached in 1775 on the eve of hostilities with Britain. Baldwin looked hopefully beyond the dark days immediately ahead to a glorious future. He anticipated that the colonies were to be the "foundation of a great and mighty Empire; the largest the World ever saw, to be founded on such Principles of Liberty and Freedom, both civil and religious, as never before took place in the World; which shall be the principal Seat of that glorious Kingdom, which Christ shall erect upon Earth in the latter Days." When Baldwin delivered his sermon to the printer he appended a long footnote in amplification of this prediction in which he observed that the American population, then numbering some three million souls, was doubling every twenty-five years. This rate of increase could be expected to continue for about a century, with a somewhat lesser rate of

---

30 *See the sermon by Samuel Langdon,* Joy and Gratitude to God for the Long Life of a Good King, and the Conquest of Quebec. A Sermon Preached . . . November 10, 1759 (*Portsmouth: Fowle, 1760*).

increase for a second century, at the end of which time (i. e. 1975) a unified North American empire would contain a population of some 192 millions, a curiously accurate prediction. Because this late twentieth century empire would be the product of natural growth rather than of conquest its original principles of civil and religious liberty would have survived intact. Baldwin then reminded his readers of the common Christian conviction that Christ would establish his millennial kingdom on earth before the end of the world, and that calculations based on the prophecies in Daniel and Revelation fixed the date of the second advent at about 2000 A.D., when America would be at the height of its glory, and Europe sunk beneath tyranny, corruption, and luxury. Christ's kingdom must of course be established upon a system of civil liberty; it could not be compatible with despotism or tyranny. Since by the end of the twentieth century it would be highly improbable that liberty would prevail anywhere but in America was it "chimerical to suppose America will largely share in the Happiness of this glorious Day, and that the present Scenes are remotely preparing the Way for it?"[31] The significant features of this revised form of millennial hope are first the deferment of the great event to the remote future; but more important, the estimation of conditions under which its consummation would occur in moral terms. One could now measure the advance of mankind towards the millennium in terms of the state of civil and religious liberty.

Essentially similar sentiments were expressed a few months later in more succinct and secular terms in the greatest of revolutionary tracts, Tom Paine's *Common Sense*. "We [Americans]," cried Paine, "have it in our power to begin the world over again. A situation, similar to the present, hath not happened since the days of Noah until now. The birth day of a new world is at hand."[32] Whether Baldwin or Paine entertained the more extravagant hopes we are not required to determine. Our attention is directed to the lengthened historical perspective in which thinkers were beginning to frame their judgments. The life cycle of empires, or the "Revolution of Ages," in the phrase of the pre-revolutionary historian William Douglass, gave way to *the* revolution which marks off all history since Noah, or to the cumulative effect of specified factors pointing towards the millennium in 2000 A.D.

The "poet of the Revolution," Philip Freneau, in a Princeton commencement poem of 1771, paid his respects to the intellectual conventions of the age with an even more comprehensive synthesis. He succeeded in combining the ideas of the cyclical rise and fall of states, the westward passage of empire from Asia across Europe to the new world, and the final establishment of the millennial kingdom in America.[33]

Passages from the correspondence of Adams and Jefferson, chiefly during the second decade of the nineteenth century, both illustrate the weakening of the cyclical theory, and suggest the character of the new point of view. In their discussion of the sources of political power, Adams was inclined to stress such Machiavellian forces as selfishness, physical or psychological energy, or economic power. Jefferson, on the other hand, influenced perhaps in his later years by the French thinkers, pointed out that certain innovations of an apparently permanent character were rendering

31 *Ebenezer Baldwin*, The Duty of Rejoicing under Calamities and Afflictions (*New York: Hugh Gaine, 1776*), *pp. 38–40 and note.*

32 *Thomas Paine*, Writings (*Conway ed.*), I, *118–19.*

33 "*The Rising Glory of America*," in F. L. Pattee, ed., The Poems of Philip Freneau (*3 vols. Princeton: University Library, 1902*), I, *49–84.*

Adams' analysis obsolete. The invention of gun powder had deprived the physically strong of their primordial advantage. In the United States at least, where labor was properly rewarded, economic power was more widely distributed than ever before, with consequent equalization of political power. Even in Europe, which was lagging behind America in these respects, a sensible change was occurring. "Science," Jefferson reported, "has liberated the ideas of those who read and reflect, and the American example has kindled feelings of right in the people. An insurrection has consequently begun, of science, talents, and courage, against rank and birth, which have fallen into contempt. . . . Science is progressive, and talents and enterprise on the alert."[34] In similar vein, he was now prepared to redefine republicanism as the conviction of those who believe in the "improvability of the condition of man, and who have acted on that behalf, in opposition to those who consider man as a beast of burden made to be rode by him who has genius enough to get a bridle into his mouth."[35] We readily recognize these ideas—the cumulative character of technology, the liberating power of science, the kindling of feelings of right, and the improvement of the condition of mankind—to be authentic features of the new faith in human progress.

Franklin was perhaps the first American to use these doctrines in such a way as to suggest a unilinear conception of history. The invention of printing, the accumulation and dissemination of knowledge, and the consequent strengthening of the spirit of liberty were coming to be regarded as unique occurrences which could not be properly evaluated within a pattern of cyclical repetition. We find these views frequently recurring in Franklin's correspondence during the 1780's.[36] In later years, the aged Jefferson agreed with Adams' favorable judgment of the eighteenth century, but he pointed out that the operation of those characteristics which rendered it notable could be traced back at least as far as the fifteenth century.[37] The age of enlightenment was not therefore to be regarded as a cyclical episode, but as a phase of a secular trend extending far back in history, and one which would conceivably project indefinitely into the future.

It is worth noting that in these early expressions of the idea of progress the moral element is strongly emphasized, and that there is nothing of the note of complacent inevitability which Ekirch, in his study of the use of the idea after 1815, finds to be one of its most prominent features. I am inclined to suspect that the enlightened theory of divine benevolence, with its associated conviction that this is the best of all possible worlds, was itself paradoxically the strongest barrier against the idea of human progress. The idea of progress was to be the fighting faith of men with a mission to perform, whether to feed the hungry, convert the heathen, or accumulate one's pile. It connoted a certain discontent with the prevailing state of affairs. Its inevitability in the minds of its nineteenth-century disciples was no more incompatible with energetic effort than were the similar features of inevitability in Puritan or Marxist thinking. But such a temper of mind was largely alien to the American Enlightenment, and certain changes had to occur before the new point of view could recommend itself with any force.

We can see one such change occurring in the

34 *Wilstach, pp. 93–94.*

35 *Jefferson to Joel Barlow, January 24, 1810.* Writings (Ford ed.), IX, 269.

36 *Writings (Smyth ed.), IX, 102, 657; X, 66–67. I am obliged to Professor Delmage for these references,* op cit., *note 4 above.*

37 *Wilstach, pp. 119–20.*

increasing discontent of John Adams towards the end of his life with the hedonic calculus which was a characteristic feature of the thought of his generation. The preponderance of pleasure over pain, he concluded, is not in itself sufficient to make life endurable, even for the most fortunate. Only from the hope of a future heavenly life free from pain could he draw the strength to face the ills of earthly existence. "Without the supposition of a future state," he remarked, "mankind and this globe appear to me the most sublime and beautiful bubble and bauble that imagination can conceive."[38] For Adams the future state had become what it has been to most Christian Americans ever since: an otherworldly heaven eternally removed from earth to which souls repair after death, and where the ultimate balance of pleasure over pain is assured by divine benevolence. The "heaven" of modern Christianity thus came to the rescue of a faltering hedonism, which was not quite sure after all whether the balance of earthly pleasure over pain was worth the candle.

But what had all of this to do with attitudes towards history? It simply indicated that for at least one representative of the age the idea that the creation was infinitely good and that evil or pain had a sufficient function in displaying that goodness was no longer convincing. Human experience, individually and collectively, was both incomplete and imperfect, and while for personal fulfillment one looked to heaven beyond the grave, for social fulfillment one anticipated the steady advance of morals and intellect. These matters were rather elaborately developed in the famous deistic tract, *Reason the Only Oracle of Man* (1784), traditionally ascribed to Ethan Allen. But to find the argument in the last letters of John Adams, who in earlier life had been such a staunch representative of enlightened modes of thought, suggests the pervasiveness of the new point of view. Christians, Jews, Mohammedans, and Hindoos, Adams observed, all share a similar hope for a future state analogous to the Christian millennium. But "you and I," he wrote to Jefferson in 1821, "hope for splendid improvements in human society, and vast amelioration in the condition of mankind. Our faith may be supposed by more rational arguments than any of the former. I own I am very sanguine in the belief of them, as I hope and believe you are."[39]

When he had earlier employed the cyclical view of history Adams would hardly have called it a "faith." His emotions had not then been attached to a future which would right current evils, which was incidentally one reason why his interest in history had revealed such a different quality from that found in nineteenth century romantics who searched the past for confirmation of their faith in the future.

Thus the reaction to the millennialism of enthusiastic revivalists was a theory of cyclical fluctuation within a static historical continuum. The dynamic element within the cycle was the moral factor. But the implicit conservatism of this view, and the countervailing weight of American experience, seriously limited its utility in the revolutionary environment of the seventeen-seventies and eighties. The new synthesis which began to emerge after the revolution, the idea of progress, drew from millennialism its sense of the irreversible secular trend of the historical process, and from the moralism of the cyclical theory the assumption that the role of the individual in history is a purposive and creative one.

38 *Wilstach, pp. 136–37.*

39 *Wilstach, pp. 176–77.*

THE BELIEF IN PROGRESS IN TWENTIETH-CENTURY AMERICA

Clarke A. Chambers*

Celebrating the great American success story, Henry Luce, prophet of "The American Century," recently proclaimed: "The business of America is to progress; and Progress is the business of America. We are a nation forever on the march."[1] Here summarized is a tenet of the American creed to which the American people, for generations, have committed themselves: the belief that America's mission was to lead the world in the unfolding of an ever finer tomorrow, that the direction of history, in America at least, was onward and upward. That the reaffirmation of this faith came in the midst of what others have known as an "Age of Anxiety" was remarkable;

remarkable that is if one chooses not to recognize the tremendous force that the belief in progress has exerted throughout the whole sweep of the American past. That such a reaffirmation appears fatuous optimism to many other observers of the contemporary American scene may warrant still another survey of the idea of progress and an analysis of what that belief has meant for twentieth century America.

The belief, in the classic words of J. B. Bury, that "civilization has moved, is moving, and will move in a desirable direction," was, as so many scholars have pointed out, a product of the modern era of Western history.[2] As a way of looking at

---

[1] Henry Luce, "The Promised Land," New Republic, 131:23 (Dec. 6, 1954), 19. His article was first delivered as an address upon the occasion of the fortieth anniversary of the New Republic.

[2] J. B. Bury, The Idea of Progress (London, 1920), 2. In addition to Bury's classic historical analysis of the idea of progress, excellent analyses may also be found in: John Baillie, The Belief in Progress (New York, 1951); Charles A.

---

*CLARKE A. CHAMBERS (1921–   ) is a Professor of History at the University of Minnesota. His publications include California Farm Organizations (1952), Seedtime of Reform (1963), and The New Deal at Home and Abroad (1964). Reprinted by permission of the author and the Journal of the History of Ideas, Vol. 19, No. 2 (April, 1958), 197–224.

the course of human events, it demanded the rejection of traditional authority, for to believe in progress was to insist that far better ways of life were still to be discovered, and that truth was in a continual process of revelation. It required, moreover, a scientific view of the universe as responsive to uniform, immutable laws, laws that men of intelligence and good will could discover and then use for the creation of ever better ways of life on earth. Upon these postulates, elaborated by seventeenth- and eighteenth-century scientists and philosophers, later champions of progress—Turgot, Condorcet, Comte, Marx—came to declare that through an understanding of the laws of society, men could establish direction over the course of history and could thus mold the

future to fulfill their own needs and desires.[3]

Most of these disciples of progress, however, were not yet prepared to assert that the forward advance of man was inevitable. Even such an optimistic partisan of progress as Condorcet insisted that the realization of such potentials was contingent upon man's freedom to think and to act. Only if man were released from the burdens of ignorance, superstition, and tyranny, only if outmoded institutions were broken and abandoned, could the progress of the human spirit be assured.

In what the champions of progress considered as the wonderful century that stretched from Waterloo to Sarajevo, the belief in the contingent possibility of progress was transformed into a belief in the inevitability of progress. Here operative were not only the internal logic of the idea itself but also the historical conditions of the nineteenth century that permitted Western civilization to embark upon exuberant adventures in the full confidence that progress was "not an accident, but a necessity," and that it was "certain that man must become perfect."[4] It was a century of peace,

Beard, Introduction to J. B. Bury, The Idea of Progress (*New York, 1932), ix–xl; Charles A. Beard, ed.,* A Century of Progress (*New York, 1933); Carl L. Becker, "Progress,"* in Encyclopedia of Social Sciences, *XII (1949), 495–99; Carl L. Becker,* Progress and Power (*New York, 1949), Arthur A. Ekirch,* The Idea of Progress in America, 1815–1860 (*New York, 1944); Sidney B. Fay, "The Idea of Progress,"* American Historical Review, *LII:2 (Jan., 1947), 231–46; Morris Ginsberg,* The Idea of Progress: A Reevaluation (*London, 1953), Reinhold Niebuhr,* Faith and History: A Comparison of Christian and Modern Views of History (*New York, 1949); Stow Persons, ed.,* Evolutionary Thought in America (*New Haven, 1950); Frederick J. Teggart, ed.,* The Idea of Progress: A Collection of Readings (*Berkeley, 1949), see especially the introductory essay by George H. Hildebrand. I am also indebted to the analyses and evaluations of the belief in progress made in a series of lectures delivered at the University of Minnesota during the Spring of 1956 on the theme: "Progress: Real or Imaginary." Participating in the program were Professors Michael Scriven, Maurice B. Visscher, Ralph Rapson, Mulford Q. Sibley, E. Adamson Hoebel, Allen Tate, and the writer. I am indebted to Professor Leo Marx, who organized and moderated the sessions, for many important leads and suggestions.*

[3] *Particularly valuable for an understanding of the relationship of the rise of modern science to the idea of progress are: Vannevar Bush, "Science and Progress?"* American Scientist, *43:2 (April, 1955), 241–58; and Edgar Zilsel, "The Genesis of the Concept of Scientific Progress," this* Journal, *VI:3 (June, 1945), 325–49.*

[4] *Herbert Spencer quoted in Fay,* American Historical Review, *LII:2, 237. Carl Becker commented that to nineteenth-century Europeans "progress was indeed not so much a theory to be defended as a fact to be observed. In that prosperous, coal-smudged age it seemed hardly necessary for man to take thought in order to add a cubit to his stature: a cubit would obviously be added to his stature whether he took thought or not. Men had only to go about their private affairs, and something not themselves would do whatever else was necessary."* Progress and Power, *2–3.*

broken only by short, limited wars that seemed to prove that victorious nationalism was an indication of advancing civilization. It was a century marked by substantial economic expansion, in which it seemed that the machine, man's servant, would assure higher standards of living for all. It was a century during which the Western world advanced steadily toward the realization of all those humanitarian and equalitarian goals against which real progress could be measured.

In America, especially, conditions favored an absolute faith in and a nearly universal, popular acceptance of progress as the rule of life.[5] The whole history of the American nation seemed to suggest an unbroken continuity of betterment. America came into existence after Western feudal institutions had lost their vigor; and those vestiges of the old Europe that were transplanted across the ocean failed to take root in the virgin soil of the new world. America, unlike Europe, never had to turn against its own past in order to progress, it had only to extend and perfect lines of development that were present from the beginning.[6] The American continent, moreover, was

blessed with natural resources awaiting exploitation. Material plenty, product of science and technology, meant rising spirals of prosperity and of national power. Here, in the triumph of industrial capitalism, was progress that could be measured, in miles of railroad built, in tons of steel forged, in billions of dollars accumulated. Machines—"engines of democracy"—became symbols of America's advance.[7] And when America celebrated, in the depths of a great depression, a "Century of Progress," science and technology and the machine were the dominant symbols chosen to represent a nation's progress.[8]

In a land and in an age in which individual

---

[5] *In addition to the works cited above in footnote number 2, especially the Ekirch monograph, see Boyd C. Shafer, "The American Heritage of Hope, 1865–1940," Mississippi Valley Historical Review, XXXVII:3 (Dec., 1950), 427–50. Readers of this article will recognize my indebtedness to Professor Shafer at many points. See also Hugo A. Meier, "Technology and Democracy, 1800–1860," ibid., XLIII:4 (March, 1957), 618–40. The idea of progress, in its American forms, is a recurring theme in Ralph Henry Gabriel, The Course of American Democratic Thought (New York, 1940¹, 1956²), and in Merle Curti, The Growth of American Thought (New York, 1943).*

[6] *Rush Welter, "The Idea of Progress in America," this Journal, XVI:3 (June, 1955), 401–15. This article applies Daniel Boorstin's thesis of the continuity of American history to an analysis of the American belief in progress. Welter suggests that whereas the European belief in progress was*

necessarily "revolutionary" because the achievement of progress depended upon the rejection of the past, in America the idea was a "conservative" one because Americans sought to realize rather than reverse the innate tendencies of their own history.

[7] *Roger Burlingame, Engines of Democracy: Inventions and Society in America (New York, 1940). See James J. Hill, Highways of Progress (New York, 1910). Here the building of a network of national rail transportation is featured as both fact and symbol of a nation's progress. Andrew Carnegie had drawn on the same source of inspiration when he cried: "The old nations of the earth creep on at a snail's pace, the Republic thunders past with the rush of the express." Triumphant Democracy; or Fifty Years' March of the Republic (New York, 1886), 1. The relationship of machine technology to the 19th-century American belief in progress is explored in Leo Marx, "The Machine in the Garden," The New England Quarterly, XXIX:1 (March, 1956), 27–41.*

[8] *Lowell Tozer, "A Century of Progress, 1833–1933, Technology's Triumph over Man," American Quarterly, IV:1 (Spring, 1952), 78–81. Tozer suggests that whereas technology had been originally conceived as man's servant, by 1933 technology appeared as man's master. He quotes the theme of the Chicago World's Fair Official Guide Book: "SCIENCE FINDS—INDUSTRY APPLIES—MAN CONFORMS." One is reminded of Henry Thoreau's warning, issued a century earlier: "We do not ride on the railroad: it rides upon us."*

opportunity was maximized, in which everyone could "get along" and nearly everyone could "get ahead" or, at the least, "keep up," popular faith in the reality of progress was understandably exuberant. The American mission to lead the world in the paths of progress seemed to be justified by the good works of nineteenth-century America. No wonder that Professor E. E. Channing, setting out to tell the American story, professed to see "in the annals of the past the story of living forces, always struggling onward and upward toward that which is better and higher in human conception."[9] To Americans, all things were possible. Even those who saw the evils that had been insinuated into American society by the machine, the factory, and the city were confident that reform could right what was wrong.[10]

America, and the Western world generally, did not require a theory of biological evolution to persuade them of the soaring flight of life; but the writings of Darwin, and of his followers, who argued the creed of social evolution by analogy from the biological world, gave a fillip to man's faith in progress in the latter decades of the nineteenth century.[11] Life, it was taught, all life, had evolved from simple to complex forms; man, descended from lower orders of life, had ascended. "So far from degrading Humanity," wrote the American historian John Fiske, "the Darwinian theory shows us distinctly for the first time how the creation and the perfecting of Man is the goal toward which Nature's work has all the while been tending."[12] Just as the species had evolved upward, just as man had learned to manipulate the universe through science for his own comfort and security, so had civilization evolved toward "spiritual ends" through the innate tendencies of the human heart toward altruism, brotherhood and peace. "The future is lighted for us with the radiant colours of hope," he rejoiced. "Strife and sorrow shall disappear. Peace and love shall reign supreme."

Clearly, however, men, although agreed upon the indisputable fact of progress, were not agreed upon the nature of the methods of social evolution. To some the logic of progress was teleological: man was drawn inevitably upward toward ultimate perfection. To others progress depended on the discovery of and obedience to the natural laws of the physical, social, and moral universe. To spokesmen for industrial capitalism, progress was to come through unfettered competition, through the free exploitation of resources both natural and human, and through the preservation of the sanctity of property. To still others, who in America rejoiced in the label of "progressivism," social advance depended upon the "application of intelligence to the construction of

9 *E. E. Channing*, The Planting of a Nation in the New World, 1000–1660 (*New York, 1905*), *vi*.

10 *As one Social Gospel leader, Samuel Z. Batten, wrote early in the twentieth century: "Man is called in the providence of God to build on earth the city of God. There are no necessary evils. There are no insoluble problems. Whatever is wrong cannot be eternal, and whatever is right cannot be impossible." Quoted by John C. Bennett in Samuel Cavert, ed.*, The Church Through Half a Century (*New York, 1936*), *117.*

11 *The literature on "Social Darwinism" is very extensive. Of special relevance to this essay are: Richard Hofstadter,* Social Darwinism in American Thought, 1860–1915 (*Philadelphia, 1945*); *Persons,* Evolutionary Thought in America.

12 *This quotation and those that follow may be found in John Fiske,* The Destiny of Man Viewed in the Light of His Origin (*Boston, 1884*), *25, 118. In a series of lectures, first delivered in 1879, and published under the title,* American Political Ideas: Viewed from the Standpoint of Universal History (*New York, 1884*), *Fiske had suggested these same related themes of evolution and progress.*

proper social devices," and the deliberate manipulation of society through the "instrumentality" of government, guided by a humane concern for the promotion of the general welfare.[13]

Here were scholars, politicians, editors, men of the cloth, men of affairs, who came to dominate thought and action during the early years of the twentieth century. They believed in the sufficiency of democracy because they believed in man, in his capacity for rational behavior, in his "contriving and constructive intelligence."[14] Rejecting the notion that progress would come with the release of man's competitive instincts, they posited instead a faith in man's natural instinct for cooperation and love. They believed, moreover, in the efficacy of man's will. Men were not passive instruments of either divine will or natural processes; they were, potentially at least, masters of their own fate if only they would take thought, apply the methods of science to man and society, and strive purposefully for reform. Through such methods, wrote the youthful Walter Lippmann just before the first World War, man could come to assert "mastery" over the "drift" of life. All men need do, he wrote, was deal deliberately with life, "devise its social organizations, alter its tools, formulate its method, educate and control it. In endless ways we put intention where custom has reigned. We break up routines, make decisions, choose our ends, select means."[15] Thus, but always contingent upon man's will to use his social intelligence, was progress assured. Man, if he would, had history in his grasp.

The belief in progress, like other religions, was syncretic: it picked up all manner of attitudes through the generations, adding scraps and bits along the way and sloughing off others. Although their rhetoric often borrowed from Darwinism and pragmatism, progressives more often stood upon old-fashioned postulates.[16] It became the goal of many reformers, moved by the Social Gospel, to transform "life on earth into the harmony of the heavens."[17] To the eighteenth-century belief in man's rationality and goodness, and in the existence of an all-encompassing moral order, was added a nineteenth-century romantic belief in the soundness and benevolence of man's emotions, and a Transcendental faith in his infinite perfectibility.

One can see in the thought of William Allen White the way in which progressivism drew upon diverse concepts and incorporated them into one

[13] *The words were those of John Dewey, "Progress,"* International Journal of Ethics *(April, 1916), reprinted in* Character and Events, *Vol. II (New York, 1929), 826. In this essay Dewey, who had such a large influence on the thought of "progressivism," warned that if real progress were to be achieved men would have to awaken from their "dream of automatic uninterrupted progress" (p. 823). Progress was contingent upon man's will to harness history and steer it toward the goal of better institutional arrangements, through the devices of what he called "constructive social engineering" (p. 827). These phrases and these concepts were to crop up constantly in the thought of many twentieth-century believers in progress.*

[14] Ibid., *827.*

[15] *Walter Lippmann,* Drift and Mastery; an Attempt to Diagnose the Current Unrest *(New York, 1914), 266–67.*

[16] *David Noble has returned to this hypothesis in several significant essays: "The Paradox of Progressive Thought,"* American Quarterly, *V:3 (Fall, 1953), 201–12; "The Religion of Progress in America, 1890–1914,"* Social Research, *XXII:4 (Winter, 1955), 417–40; "Simon Patten: Relativist,"* Antioch Review, *XIV:3 (Sept., 1954), 333–44; "Veblen and Progress: The American Climate of Opinion,"* Ethics, *LXV:4 (July, 1955), 271–85. See also Cushing Strout, "The Twentieth Century Enlightenment,"* American Political Science Review, *XLIX:2 (June, 1955), 321–39.*

[17] *Walter Rauschenbush,* Christianity and the Social Crisis *(New York, 1907), 65.*

conglomerate system. Delivering a Phi Beta Kappa address at Columbia University in 1908, he traced "A Theory of Spiritual Progress."[18] Science, he noted, was just beginning to push back the veil of mystery that obscured the truths of life; but science could vouchsafe, at least, that life had direction, and that "determinate and purposeful change" was the rule of modern society. If life were "outward bound, but to an unknown port," the more proximate goal, towards which civilization assuredly was advancing, was the enlargement of man's sensibilities and knowledge. Awareness of human suffering, kindness, concern for the welfare of one's brothers, these qualities were ever more coming to dominate over the baser passions of the human race. Through inventions, life was made easier for all men; through social justice, the fruits of technology were more equitably distributed; and as life moved forward, "in the way of the Lord," mercy and charity conquered over cruelty. In the modern era, biological and material evolution could advance into the spiritual realm. Looking about at the moral advances of the modern age,[19] man could not but conclude that "Progress to some upward ideal of living among men is the surest fact of history."

White decried the fancy that men of wealth could lead the nation in the paths of true progress. Like the Hebrew prophets of old, he cried that the rich "get things and things oppress them. Things curse them. Things corrupt their children. . . . Things make men cowards and cheats, and bind them to unholy tasks." Rather, the nation was exalted by the leadership of the humble

and the unselfish who alone could direct the people's course in the paths of righteousness. The unselfish would lead, and the nation would follow, because man's nature demanded progress: "The divine spark is in every soul. In a crisis the meanest man may become a hero. . . . This holy spirit is in every heart. . . . It is the fundamental claim men have upon one another as brothers. . . . Over and over the spark is planted in untold billions of hearts as the ages pass; and slowly as our sensibilities widen, our customs change. So comes progress, and the fire grows larger in our common lives."

Here in one great peroration were so many of the varied strands that had been woven into the fabric of the belief in progress during the nineteenth century; science and technology, Darwinism, romantic humanitarianism, Christian moralism, and Transcendental idealism. This vision of progress drew but slightly from the pragmatic rebellion of that era.

Progressives, then, were exuberantly confident of the future, and they invested their enthusiasms with the faith that men of good will would act with good will toward man. But other voices were heard in the land. The Irish bartender and philosopher, Mr. Dooley, wryly noted: "I sometimes wondher whether prog-gress is anny more thin a kind . . . of merry-go-round. We get up on a speckled wooden horse an' th' mechanical pianny plays a chune an' away we go, hollerin'. We think we're thravellin' like th' divvle, but th' man that doesn't care about merry-go-rounds knows that we will come back where we were. We get out dizzy an' sick an' lay on th' grass an' gasp: 'Where am I? Is this the meelinyum?' An' he says: 'No, 'tis Arrchey Road.' "[20]

And then the war came, striking down the

[18] *William Allen White*, A Theory of Spiritual Progress (*Emporia, Kansas, 1910*).

[19] *Specifically noted were: the growth toward universal education and universal suffrage, the establishment of direct democracy, old-age pensions, workmen's compensation, profit-sharing, institutional churches, parks and playgrounds.*

[20] *Elmer Ellis, ed.*, Mr. Dooley at His Best (*New York, 1938*), 32.

dreams of a secular millennium.[21] In Europe, and even in America, men set out to inventory what remained. Disenchantment and disillusion set in; disillusion exactly because these same men had believed so firmly in eternal progress and in the regeneration of the human race. War, and its attendant evils, persuaded many that if knowledge were power, men would not necessarily manipulate power virtuously. Indeed, the very same advances in technology that had promised enlarged vistas for civilization could also become instruments of retrogression. A young journalist, writing in the postwar era, summed up his generation's disillusionment: "after the colossal follies of the twentieth century, what sensitive and thoughtful person can believe in the natural goodness of man?" In full flight from the "Age of Rousseau," he wrote, Americans had become critical "of the democratic ideal, of humanitarian gospels, of romantic enthusiasms of all kinds." The suspicion is, he despaired, "that man, far from being virtuous when undisciplined by a civilized culture, is selfish, irrational and unwittingly absurd."[22]

Frederic C. Howe, an old-line progressive embittered by war and the collapse of the reform movement, confessed his own disenchantment.[23]

The attack upon civil liberties, product of wartime intolerance, had been led by members of Wilson's New Freedom administration. Liberal critics had been hounded into silence, and with the return of "normalcy" the crusade against the "orgy of commercialism" had collapsed. Wilson had betrayed international idealism, and a new mood of corruption and reaction prevailed. "Facts were of little value; morality did not guide man. In America, as in Europe, there was conquest, plunder." His earlier belief that an enlightened middle class, "aroused from indifference, from money-making, from party loyalty and coming out into the clear light of reason," had given way before the revival of economic self-seeking. "I now began to see that men were not concerned over the truth," he concluded. "It did not interest them when economic interests were at stake."

Howe, The Confessions of a Reformer (*New York, 1925*), *196, 318. In his disillusionment with the efficacy of middle-class reform, Howe, like many other pre-war progressives, turned to the laboring masses of America for leadership, but with little of the verve that had moved his earlier enthusiasms. See also: William Allen White, Introduction to Fremont Older,* My Own Story (*New York, 1926), ix–xiii, cited by George Mowry,* The California Progressives (*Berkeley, 1951), 301. Oswald G. Villard later confessed: "I have often been accused of yielding to misguided enthusiasms for public men and believing that in this one or in that one a political saviour was at hand, and I must plead guilty to the charge— until Woodrow Wilson and Ramsey MacDonald cured me of that habit."* Fighting Years: Memoirs of a Liberal Editor (*New York, 1939), 183. Also see, Elmer Davis, "Good Old 1913, Reminiscences of a Golden Age,"* Forum, *85:5 (May, 1931), 266–71. Don Marquis, satirizing the earlier optimism of progressivism, gave the human race three million years to achieve "The Almost Perfect State," and proposed the axiom: "The chief obstacle to the progress of the human race is the human race."* The Almost Perfect State (*New York, 1927), 167.*

[21] *Lewis Mumford, writing at a time when the second world war had broken the uneasy truce, looked back upon the hopes that Western civilization had entertained, even during the years of war themselves: "we expected that at the end of that fierce and rancorous conflict . . . the beat of angels' wings would at once be heard in the sky and concord and brotherly love would immediately settle over the earth. That lack of realism was fatal to us, that too-virtuous idealism, that too-exacting purity, is even now taking its toll in cynical inertia."* Faith for Living (New York, 1940), 222.

[22] *Frank Snowden Hopkins, "After Religion, What?" in William H. Cordell, ed.,* Molders of American Thought, 1933–1934 (New York, 1934), 222–23.

[23] *The quotations that follow may be found in Frederic C.*

The first world war undoubtedly marked a great turning point in the belief in progress. It again accustomed man to violence, made him callous to humane values and to human suffering. A crude amoralism was fostered by what Harold Stearns, one of that generation that thought of itself as "lost," called the "cynicism and brutality and meaninglessness" of war.[24] Progressives had

thought, with Wilson, that war could be waged against the institution of war, only to discover in the post-1920 world it had been foolish to dream that men could "pluck liberal flowers from the wastelands of violence and unreason."[25]

It was not war alone, however, that conjured up the spectre of degeneration and even catastrophe. The disenchantment ran deeper into the essentials of modern life. War, it appeared to many mourners, was but a symptom of the cancerous diseases that ate at the vitals of modern civilization.[26] The mechanization and urbanization of society, so it was said, stunted man's creative urges, stultified his initiative, deprived him of his wholeness, and uprooted him. Not harmony and altruism, but cacophony and divisiveness were the rules of life. Cultural aridity, oppressive standardization, levelling mediocrity, the corruption of art and taste were the products of a technically progressive society. Lost in the infinite complexities and distractions of modern life were the sense

---

[24] *Harold Stearns,* America Now *(New York, 1938), 162. For other expressions of disillusionment in inter-war America see, for example:* Carl Becker, "Liberalism—a Way Station," in Everyman His Own Historian *(New York, 1935), 91–100;* John Dos Passos, The Ground We Stand On *(New York, 1941), 5–6;* Irwin Edman, Adam, the Baby, and the Man from Mars *(Cambridge, 1929),* The Contemporary and His Soul *(New York, 1931), and* Candle in the Dark *(New York, 1939); Michael Straight, "The Ghost at the Banquet,"* New Republic, *131:21 (Nov. 22, 1954), 11–16. For historical comments see:* John Chamberlain, Farewell to Reform; Being a History of the Rise, Life, and Decay of the Progressive Mind in America *(New York, 1932); Arthur A. Ekirch, Jr., "Parrington and the Decline of American Liberalism,"* American Quarterly, *III:4 (Winter, 1951), 295–308; Eric Goldman,* Rendezvous with Destiny: A History of Modern American Reform *(New York, 1952), Chapters XII–XIII; Richard Hofstadter,* The Age of Reform: from Bryan to F.D.R. *(New York, 1955), Chapter VII; Sidney Kaplan, "Social Engineers as Saviors: Effects of World War I on Some American Liberals,"* this *Journal, XVII:3 (June, 1956), 347–69; Edgar Kemler,* The Deflation of American Ideals; An Ethical Guide for New Dealers *(Washington, D. C., 1941); Phil L. Snyder, "Carl L. Becker and the Great War; A Crisis for a Human Intelligence,"* Western Political Quarterly, *IX:1 (March, 1956), 1–10; Merle Curti, "Human Nature in American Thought: Retreat from Reason in the Age of Science,"* Political Science Quarterly, *LXVIII:4 (Dec., 1953), 492–510; Henry F. May, "Shifting Perspectives in the 1920's,"* Mississippi *Valley Historical Review, XLIII:3 (Dec., 1956), 405–27; A. M. Schlesinger, Jr.,* The Crisis of the Old Order *(Boston, 1957), Chapters II, VI, XVII, XVIII.*

[25] *Harold Stearns,* The Street I Know *(New York, 1935), 162.*

[26] *The summary discussion that follows draws from the writings of such representative critics as: James Truslow Adams,* Our Business Civilization *(New York, 1929); Irving Babbitt,* Democracy and Leadership *(Boston, 1924); Robert C. Binkley, "The Twentieth Century Looks at Human Nature,"* Virginia Quarterly Review, *X:3 (July, 1934), 336–50; Ralph Borsodi,* This Ugly Civilization *(New York, 1929); Waldo Frank,* The Re-discovery of America *(New York, 1929); Erich Fromm,* Escape from Freedom *(New York, 1941); Karen Horney,* The Neurotic Personality of Our Time *(New York, 1937); Joseph Wood Krutch,* The Modern Temper: A Study and a Confession *(New York, 1929); Walter Lippmann,* A Preface to Morals *(New York, 1929); Lewis Mumford,* Faith for Living *(New York, 1940); P. A. Sorokin,* The Crisis of Our Age *(New York, 1941); Twelve Southerners,* I'll Take My Stand: The South and the Agrarian Tradition *(New York, 1930).*

of belonging and the sense of community, lost were all the moral sanctions and disciplines of personal restraint. The individual was engulfed by the increasing corporateness and collectivization that marked all areas of life. The machine, that "undreamed of reservoir of power," had been harnessed to the dollar, wrote John Dewey, rather than to the "liberation and enrichment of human life."[27] Technical and industrial progress had led to the "supremacy of mechanism over organism, and organization over spontaneity."[28] Lewis Mumford, decrying the impoverishment of the internal life, described the crisis in civilization: "External order: internal chaos. External progress: internal regression. External rationalism: internal irrationality."[29]

Even more central to the attack upon the belief that civilization was bound to move forward was the charge that history had gotten out of control, that man had surrendered his capacity for the intelligent and deliberate ordering of life to forces quite beyond his control. Walter Lippmann, who had once celebrated man's capacity to assert mastery over life, now resigned himself to man's abdication of the exercise of significant decision. The people "are managed, if they are managed at all," he wrote, "at distant centers, from behind the scenes, by unnamed powers." The private

citizen, he concluded, "does not know for certain what is going on, or who is doing it, or where he is being carried. . . . He lives in a world in which he cannot see, does not understand, and is unable to direct."[30]

Above all, men came to doubt that progress could be the law of life when the new sciences of psychology and society described human nature in terms of behaviorism and determinism. The portrait of man as essentially rational and innately good gave way to a sketch of man as a creature of passion and subconscious impulses over which he had little, if any, control, and of which he was, in all probability, ignorant. On the other hand, it was fancied that man was totally dominated by his external environment. Man appeared now as a creature rather than a creator, victim rather than hero, a passive bit of nature rather than an active participant in the drama of destiny. If one accepted these new concepts of the nature of human nature, one was bound to question the validity of earlier theories of democracy which proposed that a citizenry was competent to decide and govern itself. Now it appeared that the citizen could gain neither the capacity to understand the issues of politics nor the competence to exert a sustained direction over program and policy. The American voter, pictured by a leading political behaviorist, was: "chock-full of passions and prejudices, easily affected by personalities and

---

[27] *John Dewey*, Individualism: Old and New (*New York, 1930*), 96.

[28] *Yale Brozen, "The Value of Technological Change,"* Ethics, LXII:4 (*July, 1952*), 256. *Brozen's essay presents an incisive analysis of the relationship of technology to the belief in progress. It summarizes and evaluates the various criticisms made of technological progress by G. J. Burch, Roger Burlingame, J. G. Crowther, A. P. Herman, W. F. Ogburn, Ortega y Gasset, E. Pendell, Karl Polanyi, and Ferdynand Zweig.*

[29] *Lewis Mumford*, Art and Technics (*New York, 1952*), 10.

[30] *Walter Lippmann*, The Phantom Public (*New York, 1925*), 13–14. *Heinz Eulau has analyzed the trend of Lippmann's thought during these years in "Mover and Shaker, Walter Lippmann as a Young Man,"* Antioch Review, XI:3 (*Sept., 1951*), 291–312; *"Man Against Himself: Walter Lippmann's Years of Doubt,"* American Quarterly, IV:4 (*Winter, 1952*), 291–304; *"Wilsonian Idealist: Walter Lippmann Goes to War,"* Antioch Review, XIV:1 (*March, 1954*), 87–108.

propaganda, swayed by the popular currents and winds, susceptible to clap-trap and humbug."[31]

Edward Sapir, noted linguist and anthropologist writing in the 1920's, pointed out that the apparent advances in civilization constituted spurious progress when measured against the criterion of a "harmonious, balanced, self-satisfactory" culture.[32] Suggesting that much of modern civilization was "spiritually meaningless," marked by "a sense of frustration, of misdirected or unsympathetic effort," he noted that modern industry, beyond harnessing machines to man's use, harnessed man to the machine. In such a world the individual suffered from "spiritual disharmony," from a "fragmentary existence." "Part of the time we are dray horses; the rest of the time we are listless consumers of goods which have received no least impress of our personality." True culture, measured by the "spiritual primacy of the individual soul," he concluded, may decay while the technical apparatus of civilization continues to progress. So ran the indictments of the old-fashioned, simplistic belief in progress. How deeply the ordinary citizen was moved by the disaffection of the intellectuals, it is difficult to determine.

Then came the Great Depression and the eclipse of the popular belief that American capitalism guaranteed the material advance, at the very least, of society. Although the Great Depression shook the confidence of Americans in the seemingly irreversible upward trend of economic development, faith in the possibilities of progress was partially revived under the buoyant leadership of Franklin D. Roosevelt. Having assured the nation that it had nothing to fear but fear itself, Roosevelt proceeded to enact a program for relief, recovery, and reconstruction; and although the New Deal achieved only partial success toward these goals, a mood of confidence was restored—confidence, as the President said, that even in the "darkest moments" of crisis men could master their destiny, and "improve their material and spiritual status through the instrumentality of the democratic form of government."[33] Particular problems were attacked by specific programs. Science and technology were mobilized through the agency of government for the well-being of the entire community. The participation of all individuals and groups, at every level of decision-making, guaranteed that planning would be democratic, vital, and effective.[34]

Novel as the methods of reform occasionally were, the ultimate objectives for which the New Deal strove were shamelessly old-fashioned; and much of the political effectiveness of the New Deal arose out of Roosevelt's ability to give new content and life to the hallowed traditions of American liberalism. Again and again he returned

[31] *Frank R. Kent,* Political Behavior *(New York, 1928), 23. Also see, by the same author:* The Great Game of Politics *(New York, 1923); and Walter Lippmann,* Public Opinion *(New York, 1922). The influence of H. L. Mencken upon political attitudes, especially of the younger generation, during the 1920's should be recalled at this point.*

[32] *Edward Sapir, "Culture, Genuine and Spurious,"* American Journal of Sociology, *XXIX:4 (Jan., 1924), 401–29, reprinted in* Selected Writings of Edward Sapir in Language, Culture, and Personality *(Berkeley, 1949), 308–31.*

[33] *Fireside Chat, April 28, 1935, in* The Public Papers and Addresses of Franklin D. Roosevelt, *IV, 140.*

[34] *David Lilienthal spoke for these views in* TVA: Democracy on the March *(New York, 1944). These themes also ran through the writings of Henry A. Wallace:* Democracy Reborn *(New York, 1944);* New Frontiers *(New York, 1934);* Sixty Million Jobs *(New York, 1945);* Technology, Corporations, and the General Welfare *(New York, 1937);* Whose Constitution: An Inquiry into the General Welfare *(New York, 1936).*

to those principles that other generations had held as essential to a belief in progress: the capacity of man to uncover the natural harmony of society and through understanding to reach that neighborly accord which was the mark of a democratic society; the equal and original goodness of all men in the spiritual democracy of creation; the sufficiency of the individual and group will to win orderly advance toward the goals of full opportunity, security, social justice, and a life more abundant for all men. The final truth of these axioms made possible "infinite progress in the improvement of human life," so long as democracy prevailed.[35] "Among men of good will," Roosevelt proclaimed, "science and democracy together offer an ever-richer life and ever-larger satisfaction to the individual. With this change in our moral climate and our rediscovered ability to improve our economic order, we have set our feet upon the road of enduring progress."[36]

Elsewhere in the Western world, however, there was less cause for confidence. The rise of the coercive states in Italy, Germany, and Russia disturbed such optimism that had survived the first great war. Then came a second world war, more terrible than the first. Guernica, Buchenwald, Lidice, the Siberian camps could hardly serve as symbols of advance. The mushroom clouds over Hiroshima and Nagasaki suggested that science, far from guaranteeing progress, was morally ambivalent; and at least one observer, Norman Cousins, raised the query of modern

man's obsolescence.[37] The disintegration of the victorious coalition of the United Nations, the cold war with all its attendant anxieties, the race for weapons of massive destruction, Korea—all gave men cause to wonder about the direction that history was taking. In the United States, the experience of national frustration gave rise to suspicions of disloyalty and treason. Many wondered if America were not about to surrender its peculiar insulation from the stream of history.

Back in 1912, Frederick Lynch, soon to become executive secretary of the Carnegie-endowed Church Peace Union, had confidently asserted: "It looks as though this were going to be an age of treaties rather than an age of wars, the century of reason rather than the century of force."[38] As late as 1923 Professor E. P. Cheyney, in his presidential address before the American Historical Association, was willing to proclaim the certainty of an historical "law of moral progress."[39] But Joseph Wood Krutch, who had in 1929 suggested that "The Modern Temper" made untenable a belief in progress, had concluded by mid-century that "man's ingenuity has outrun his intelligence," and that "we are believers in catastrophe rather than evolution."[40] Many others agreed. Arthur M. Schlesinger, Jr., liberal historian and adviser to liberal politicians, spoke of the "inadequacy of man to most of the problems which confront him," and concluded: "I think that if there is anything the twentieth century knows, it is that the more

[35] *The Third Inaugural Address, Jan. 20, 1941, ibid., X, 4.*

[36] *The Second Inaugural Address, Jan. 20, 1937, ibid., VI, 3. Henry Wallace added to this belief that "new frontiers" of human existence were to be won by "continuous social inventions" the honored belief that progress in a democratic society was made possible by the existence of a "spark of divine spirit" in the heart of every man. New Frontiers, 276, 277.*

[37] *Norman Cousins,* Modern Man is Obsolete (*New York, 1945*).

[38] *Quoted in Robert E. Osgood,* Ideals and Self-Interest in American Foreign Relations; the Great Transformation of the Twentieth Century (*Chicago, 1953*), *92.*

[39] *Edward P. Cheyney,* "Law in History," American Historical Review, *XXIX:2 (Jan., 1924), 244–5.*

[40] *Joseph Wood Krutch,* The Measure of Man; On Freedom, Human Values, Survival and the Modern Temper (*Indianapolis, 1954*), *17, 25.*

knowledge people have of more manipulations, the more that knowledge is used for evil purposes."[41]

In such an atmosphere it was natural that American theological neo-orthodoxy, a revival led most notably by Reinhold Niebuhr, should stress again the emergence of human evil not out of imperfect institutions and a deficient environment, but rather out of man's inclinations to assert his radical freedom for selfish ends and out of the tendency of all power to corrupt even the highest and most worthy of ideals.[42] Denying that progress was the necessary direction of history, neo-orthodoxy insisted that every advance in life was precarious, that every particular interest and position was partial and relative, that there were no final resolutions of man's problems on earth, and that a sentimental and uncritical devotion to the creed of progress was bound ultimately to lead to disillusion and despair for it rested upon false assumptions regarding the nature of man. If knowledge were power, knowledge was not necessarily virtue; in this regard Bacon had the better of Socrates. Here the confession of St. Paul was relevant: "The good that I would do, I do not; and the evil that I would not, that I do."[43] The twentieth century should have taught men what other generations had known, wrote Niebuhr in 1940: "History does not move forward without catastrophe, happiness is not guaranteed by the multiplication of physical comforts, social harmony is not easily created by more intelligence, and human nature is not as good or as harmless as had been supposed."[44]

The neo-orthodox movement proposed that to insist upon man's limitations, his capacity for error, the corruption of his will by pride and self-interest was not to deny his potentialities and his responsibilities to seek the reform of specific evils in society, even if there were no final assurance that a reformed environment would lead to a regeneration of humanity. Man stood under the commandment of love and under the ultimate

[41] *Remarks of Arthur M. Schlesinger, Jr. in a forum recorded in the* American Scholar, *XX:3 (Summer, 1951), 356, 347. Another historian, H. Stuart Hughes, traced out the implications of "terror" and "the new barbarism" for older faiths in the "excellence of man and his capacity for progress."* An Essay for Our Times *(New York, 1950), 108.*

[42] *Reinhold Niebuhr's list of publications is a long one. The following works may be considered indispensable:* The Children of Light and the Children of Darkness *(New York, 1944);* Christian Realism and Political Problems *(New York, 1953);* Christianity and Power Politics *(New York, 1940);* Faith and History; Moral Man and Immoral Society *(New York, 1932);* The Nature and Destiny of Man: A Christian Interpretation *(New York, 1941, 1943), 2 vols. Also see the writings of the following men who— although they cannot be properly considered as "neo-orthodox" in every regard—certainly represent the broad movement toward orthodoxy in contemporary Protestant theology: John C. Bennett, Joseph Haroutunian, H. Richard Niebuhr, James A. Pike, Henry Van Dusen. For comments about and criticisms of "neo-orthodoxy," see: Edward John Carnell,* The Theology of Reinhold Niebuhr *(Grand Rapids, 1950); Francis W. Coker, "Some Present-Day Critics of Liberalism,"* American Political Science Review, *XLVII:1 (March, 1953), especially 12–25; John H. Hallo-well,* Main Currents in Modern Political Thought *(New York, 1950), 651–95; Walter M. Horton, "The New Orthodoxy,"* American Scholar, *VII:1 (Winter, 1938), 3–11; Charles W. Kegley and Robert W. Bretall, eds.,* Reinhold Niebuhr: His Religious, Social and Political Thought *(New York, 1956); Holtan P. Odegard,* Sin and Science: Reinhold Niebuhr as Political Theologian *(Yellow Springs, Ohio, 1956).*

[43] *Used by Reinhold Niebuhr, "Christ vs. Socrates; a Remonstrance for Christmas,"* Saturday Review, *XXXVII:51 (Dec. 18, 1954), 7.*

[44] *Reinhold Niebuhr,* Christianity and Power Politics, *188.*

judgment of God. A more just society was possible, if progress itself were not inevitable.

How widely this critique of the belief in progress was felt cannot easily be judged. There is evidence, however, that many had taken it to heart. The mood was reflected, for example, by Adlai Stevenson in his "Call to Greatness."[45] In this series of lectures, delivered at Harvard University in 1954, Stevenson warned against the ingrained American habit of seeking total solutions through panaceas. The world itself was tough, and the love of men for the good not as absolute as Americans had easily assumed. American traits of "impatience, arrogance, and our faith in quick solutions" were likely, in modern circumstances, to lead to irresponsibility of na-

tional action. "As long as this habit of mind persists—and it is fundamentally an un-Christian attitude, ignoring the pervasiveness of evil and loaded with arrogance and pride—we shall never be able to face our problems realistically. Our first job, it seems to be, is to school ourselves in cold-eyed humility; to recognize that our wisdom is imperfect, and that our capacities are limited." He urged upon his audience the "conscious acceptance of Christian humility" as a necessary temper for national greatness. Even the most "innocent" of nations, it would seem, was liable to the common tendency of the race toward the corruption of ideals by the cardinal sin of pride.

Many of the attacks that neo-orthodoxy made upon the "heretical" creed of progress were paralleled by the admonitions of those intellectuals who, in recent years, have been labelled as the "neo-conservatives."[46] A motley lot, differing in doctrine from the flexible to the dogmatic, in tone from the relaxed to the strident, they shared a firm conviction of the invalidity and insufficiency of the belief in progress. American civilization had fallen short of greatness, they believed, because it

[45] *The quotations that follow are from Adlai Stevenson,* Call to Greatness (*New York, 1954*), *96, 97. These essays were originally delivered as the Godkin Lectures at Harvard University, March 1954. Here Adlai Stevenson was speaking as a political philosopher; when he offered a philosophy for politics, as he did during the campaign of 1952, the rhetoric was more traditionally optimistic. Another liberal, Professor Schlesinger, Jr., reflected the influence of neo-orthodoxy, and particularly the influence of his friend and fellow-worker in the Americans for Democratic Action, Reinhold Niebuhr. Seeking to describe the "vital center" of democratic belief, Schlesinger wrote in 1949: "The degeneration of the Soviet Union taught us a useful lesson, however. It broke the bubble of the false optimism of the nineteenth century. Official liberalism had long been almost inextricably identified with a picture of man as perfectible, as endowed with sufficient wisdom and selflessness to endure power and to use it infallibly for the general good. The Soviet experience, on top of the rise of fascism, reminded my generation rather forcibly that man was, indeed, imperfect, and that the corruptions of power could unleash great evil in the world. We discovered a new dimension of experience—the dimension of anxiety, guilt and corruption. (Or it may well be, as Reinhold Niebuhr has brilliantly suggested, that we were simply rediscovering ancient truths which we should never have forgotten.)"* The Vital Center (*Boston, 1949*), *viii–ix.*

[46] *Representative works include: Carl J. Friedrich,* The Democratic Process (*New London, Conn., 1948*), *and* The New Belief in the Common Man (*Boston, 1948*); *John Hallowell,* Main Currents in Modern Political Thought, *and* The Moral Foundations of Democracy (*Chicago, 1954*); *August Heckscher,* A Pattern of Politics (*New York, 1947*); *Russell Kirk,* The Conservative Mind, from Burke to Santayana (*Chicago, 1953*); *John U. Nef,* War and Human Progress; an Essay on the Rise of Industrial Civilization (*Cambridge, Mass., 1950*); *Clinton Rossiter,* Conservatism in America (*New York, 1955*); *Peter Viereck,* Conservatism Revisited; the Revolt against Revolt, 1815–1949 (*New York, 1949*), *and* Shame and Glory of the Intellectuals; Babbitt, Jr., vs. the Rediscovery of Values (*Boston, 1953*); *Francis G. Wilson,* The Case for Conservatism (*Seattle, 1951*), *and "Human Nature and Politics,"* Journal of Politics, *VIII:4 (Nov., 1946), 478–98.*

had been too fervently committed to the romantic notion that man, being rational and good, could and would channel history along an ascending path of virtue. A civilization, they said, was a product of long and painful experience through time and liable to perversion at any juncture. Central to their argument at every point was the belief "that evil arises from the nature of man, not from a lack of more science, or more education, however laudable these things may be."[47] It is no purpose of this essay to analyze the roots and consequences of this revival among intellectuals, but to note merely that it was consistent with the new conservative mood of the post-World War II era, and that it necessarily entailed an explicit rejection of the belief in the beneficence of change.[48]

Whatever the influence of neo-orthodoxy and neo-conservatism upon popular attitudes, there is little doubt that the actual historical experience of this generation did little to support faith in progress. That there was confusion and turmoil, doubt, uncertainty and insecurity no sensitive person wished to deny. Political regimentation, social disorganization, intellectual bewilderment were all part of the new climate, if not its whole truth. "Technology, while adding daily to our physical ease, throws daily another loop of fine wire around our souls," wrote Adlai Stevenson. "It contributes largely to our mobility, which we must not confuse with freedom."[49] The "massiveness" of modern life, he continued—"mass population, mass education, mass communications— yes, and mass manipulation"—threatened to undermine and corrode the foundations of human dignity. We are more in danger of "becoming robots than slaves."[50] There was a great deal to fear beyond fear itself, for always there was the chance that some untoward and unforeseen act would trigger the hydrogen bomb. As Vannevar Bush, scientist and educator, concluded at mid-century: "the first World War shook our optimism, the depression shook it further, and the second World War nearly destroyed it. Now, though we may still hope that our race will go forward in progress, we are confronted with facts

[47] *Francis Graham Wilson, "The Scholar and the Inarticulate Premise,"* Western Political Quarterly, *II:3 (Sept., 1949), 320.*

[48] *Analyses and criticisms of the "neo-conservative" revival may be found in: Daniel Aaron, "Conservatism, Old and New,"* American Quarterly, *VI:2 (Summer, 1954), 99–110; Stuart Gerry Brown, "Democracy, the New Conservatism, and the Liberal Tradition in America,"* Ethics, *LXV:4 (July, 1955), 1–8; Francis W. Coker, "Some Present-Day Critics of Liberalism," loc. cit. (fn. 42, above), 1–27; Bernard Crick, "The Strange Quest for an American Conservatism,"* Review of Politics, *XVII:3 (July, 1955), 359–76; Raymond English, "Conservatism: The Forbidden Faith,"* American Scholar, *XXI:4 (Autumn, 1952), 393– 412; Heinz Eulau, "Liberals versus Conservatives,"* Antioch Review, *XI:4 (Dec., 1951), 397–403; Franklyn S. Haman, "A New Look at the New Conservatism,"* Bulletin of the A.A.U.P., *41:3 (Autumn, 1955), 444–53; Chadwick Hall, "America's Conservative Revolution,"* Antioch Review, *XV:2 (June, 1955), 204–16; Ralph L. Ketcham, "The Revival of Tradition and Conservatism in America,"* Bulletin of the A.A.U.P., *41:3 (Autumn, 1955), 425–43; Gordon K. Lewis, "The Metaphysics of Conservatism,"* Western Political Quarterly, *VI:4 (Dec., 1953), 728–41; C. Wright Mills, "The Conservative Mood,"* Dissent, *I:1*

(Winter, 1954), 22–31; Robert A. Nisbet, "Conservatism and Sociology," American Journal of Sociology, *LVIII:2 (Sept., 1952), 167–75; Arthur M. Schlesinger, Jr., "The New Conservatism in America: a Liberal Comment,"* Confluence: An International Forum, *II:4 (Dec., 1953), 61– 71; Arthur M. Schlesinger, Jr., "The New Conservatism: Politics of Nostalgia,"* Reporter, *XII:12 (June 16, 1955), 9–12; Lawrence Sears, "Liberals and Conservatives,"* Antioch Review, *XIII:3 (Sept., 1953), 361–70.*

[49] *Adlai Stevenson, "My Faith in Democratic Capitalism,"* Fortune, *LI:10 (Oct., 1955), 156.*

[50] *Adlai Stevenson,* What I Think *(New York, 1956), 8.*

that take all the former exuberance out of our hope, reducing it almost to a wish of despair."[51] Professor Edward Arlington Ross, once a harbinger of progressive dreams, put it still more bluntly: "After the horrors of Nazi concentration camps, the butcheries of the Jews, the treatment of civilians in occupied Russia, the easy optimism of a half century ago will be left to born ninnies and youths in their early 'teens."[52]

Yet we know that such doubts were not universally entertained; men who were neither born ninnies nor in their 'teens did continue in the traditional faith of progress. To them the modern era held forth promise that somehow civilization would survive and grow. The militant force of Fascism, Nazism, and Japanese imperialism had been overcome; and in a decade of uneasy armistice the world had not slipped over the precipice of nuclear war. Two total wars had been fought, they noted, without that sacrifice of democratic institutions, which many had feared. The principle that government must exercise responsibility for the general welfare of the community had been established without that consequent regimenta-

tion of which some had warned. The advance of the medical sciences contributed surcease from pain, healthier and longer life for millions, and partial relief from the pangs of mental derangement. Fantastic advances in modern technology had already raised the standards of living of millions so that they might lead decent and secure lives, while automation and atomic power promised even further progress within the foreseeable future. To many it seemed that if the ledger had not been balanced, no clear and simple conclusion of progress or retrogression was possible.[53]

It was understandable, then, that Henry Luce could still rejoice that "Progress is the business of America." Acknowledging the possibility of another war, he proclaimed in what was admittedly a "brief overstatement," that "we have almost solved all the internal problems which have been the traditionally proper subjects for political agitation and debate." An "American Age of Plenty" was in the making; abundance, widely shared, promised release from drudgery, increased leisure, and the opportunity to advance beyond the satisfaction of material needs toward the

51 *Vannevar Bush*, American Scientist, *43:2 (April, 1955), 243. About the same time Bernard Baruch stated: "When I was a younger man, I believed that progress was inevitable—that the world would be better tomorrow and better still the day after. The thunder of war, the stench of concentration camps, the mushroom cloud of the atomic bomb are, however, not conducive to optimism. All our tomorrows for years to come will be clouded over by the threat of a terrible holocaust. Yet my faith in the future, though somewhat shaken, is not destroyed. I still believe in it. If I sometimes doubt that man will achieve his moral potentialities, I never doubt he can. I still believe that with courage and intelligence we can make the future bright with fulfillment." A Philosophy for Our Time (New York, 1954), 10–11.*

52 *Edward Arlington Ross, "The Post-war Intellectual Climate,"* American Sociological Review, *X:5 (Oct., 1945), 650.*

53 *Granville Hicks, "Liberalism in the Fifties,"* American Scholar, *25:3 (Summer, 1956), 283–96, recites many of the real advances made over the past generation and defends "responsible and moderate" liberalism against its radical detractors. Frederick Lewis Allen,* The Big Change *(New York, 1952) is similarly optimistic. For less hopeful evaluations of contemporary American culture, see: Bernard Iddings Bell,* Crowd Culture; An Explanation of the American Way of Life *(New York, 1952); Arthur A. Ekirch, Jr.,* The Decline of American Liberalism *(New York, 1955); Joseph Wood Krutch et al.,* Is the Common Man Too Common? An Informal Survey of Our Cultural Resources and What We are Doing About Them *(Norman, Oklahoma, 1954); Rollo May,* The Meaning of Anxiety *(New York, 1950); Alan Valentine,* The Age of Conformity *(Chicago, 1954); James Wechsler,* The Age of Suspicion *(New York, 1953).*

realization of spiritual and moral values."[54] Machine technology guaranteed that the "monstrous offenses" of "plague, famines, mass hysteria, superstitions, fanaticisms" would be dispelled, gave assurance of a "decent life, a life of air and light and chosen food and education and recreation and length of years."[55] Drawing upon the inspiration of Lecomte du Nouy's *Human Destiny*, Luce returned to that theme which had done so much to fortify man in his will to believe; that evolution could not have happened by chance; that it had been a response to God's will. Then, somewhere along the long line of evolution, God had breathed freedom of will into a species, and it became man. Man was then on his own, free to work with Providence for the mission of spiritual evolution.

In America, man had learned the methods of progress: "the gospel of work ('free enterprise') and the social gospel ('humanitarianism'),'' science, voluntary cooperation, and organization (by which Luce meant not only the modern "responsible" corporation but all the intricate organizations of state of society). "The habit and spirit of voluntary cooperation form the ideal base for Organization. Today, to a degree never before known, man is Organized Man. . . . We have brought to birth that cooperative society . . . which Kropotkin foresaw in his answer to Darwin." The individual could, if he would, be the mutation that impelled mankind forward; but, at the same time, progress was a transcendent force. "For if, as we believe, the Spirit is at work in the race of man, then the work of the Spirit is done not only in the atom of the individual but also through the generations of men and in traditions and in treasured wisdom and in the moral law slowly apprehended and in the beloved community and in the Church."

If evidence were required of the syncretic nature of the religion of progress, it is certainly supplied here. Many others, captivated by the amazing increases in technological efficiency, joined in the hymn to progress. David Sarnoff, President of the Radio Corporation of America, took up the refrain in the first of a series of articles by notable Americans published by *Fortune* magazine in celebration of its twenty-fifth anniversary, on the theme of what the next twenty-five years held in store.[56] The marriage of human freedom and science had brought to America, "the classic land of technology . . . the largest freedom from destitution, ignorance, and disease, along with political rights and social improvements unique in history." Science was not, as some had claimed, "the natural enemy of the soul." Evil arose, not out of technology, but out of the failure of man to keep pace with accelerating changes in the economic sphere; but cultural lag could be overcome if man applied his intelligence to the resolution of social problems, just as man's mind had learned to control the physical universe. As long as American liberties, and particularly the freedom of the mind, were maintained and extended, 1980 promised to be an immeasurably richer age.

Writing in the same series, Robert Sherwood, endorsing President Eisenhower's admonition that "there is no longer any alternative to peace," warned that unless the world disarmed within the next twenty-five years it would, in all probability,

54   *Henry Luce*, New Republic, *131:23 (Dec. 6, 1954),* *19–21.*

55 *The quotations that follow are from Henry Luce, "A Speculation About A.D. 1980,"* Fortune, *LI:12 (Dec., 1955), 104–5, 214ff. Critical comments on the businessman's faith in progress may be found in Francis X. Sutton* et al., The American Business Creed (*Cambridge, Mass., 1956*), passim.

56 *The quotations that follow are from David Sarnoff, "The Fabulous Future,"* Fortune, *LI:1 (Jan., 1955), 82–83, 114ff.*

commit suicide.[57] This eventuality he refused to entertain. By 1980, he concluded, the "threat of a third world war will be a malodorous memory." Why? Because God had created man in His own image, and man's unique spirit had impelled him ever forward. "Thus believing, I find it inconceivable that man is about to destroy himself with the products of his own God-given genius."

Gilbert Burck elaborated upon the same themes.[58] A belief in progress was itself the essential ingredient for the achievement of real progress. This faith America had practiced. The American "genius for innovating, adapting, simplifying, and improving," the American willingness to experiment, the American system of free enterprise had all propelled the nation forward. The American character, "individualistic and competitive yet cooperative," ingenious, confident, practical, and ambitious had placed the nation in "the vanguard of that progress" which all other peoples now wished to emulate. No need to cry that the machine had demeaned life; quite the contrary, "the machine provided the only way . . . of making life decent and even of ennobling it."

These sentiments, far from being peculiar in mid-twentieth century, probably constituted a main stream of American aspiration. The best was yet to come. To Morris Ernst the ushering in of a Utopia of abundance would be possible if only men believed that progress was attainable and acted confidently upon that faith.[59] Science and technology would provide the environment in which potentialities of man for good would be released. He foresaw an age in which security and plenty would release all men from jealousy, envy, antagonism, and strife. New folkways of male-female comradeship would be evolved, children would be raised with neither complexes nor repressions, and the growth of premarital experience would make sexuality in marriage less inept. Abundance and leisure would permit Americans to transcend the present status of an "audience society" and enter a "fully participating culture."

---

[57] *Robert Sherwood, "'There Is No Alternative to Peace,'" Fortune, LI:7 (July, 1955), 84–85, 152ff.*

[58] *Gilbert Burck, "The American Genius for Productivity," Fortune, LI:7 (July, 1955), 86–87, 159ff. To the tenor of such views another critic took issue. Max Lerner, writing in 1947, commented upon the long love affair that Americans had carried on with the machine: "Yet the fact is that the faster and more powerful and yet more delicate the machine becomes, the narrower grows the margin for error, and the greater becomes the machine's destructive possibilities. That is the big fact we don't quite face about the machine in our time. We have learned, in a life of limited possibilities, to set limits for most things. We set no limits to the machine. We assume it will go on forever; that it will never end, never explode, never revolt; that we can go on indefinitely piling up new structures of machine risk on the same narrow base of human intelligence, human instinct, and human will."*

"The fact is that we cannot, and the sooner we face it, the healthier will our future be. We often laugh at the eighteenth and nineteenth centuries because they so uncritically accepted the doctrine of unending progress. Yet I doubt that we have cause to laugh. For to those centuries, the machine was a new and exciting thing; they saw it moving forward, and they thought that the inevitable march of the machine was a phase of the inevitable march of human progress. They were wrong. . . ."

Despite such reservations, however, Lerner concluded, in the tradition of pragmatic liberalism which trusted still in man's social intelligence: the only alternative available to man now "is to shift the emphasis from inventing the machines to running and controlling them, from mechanical invention to social invention." Max Lerner, "The Machine Explodes,"

PM (*Feb. 26, 1947*) *in* Actions and Passions: Notes on the Multiple Revolution of Our Time (*New York, 1949*), *19–20.*

[59] *Morris Ernst, Utopia, 1976 (New York, 1955), 3–13, 288–303. Some may be disturbed that Ernst's "Utopia, 1976," and Henry Luce's "Age of Plenty," 1980, are uncomfortably close to George Orwell's anti-Utopia, 1984.*

All this was possible, if men took heart, because man was inherently rational and good. "I abhor the dogma—man is inherently evil. I decry it. Man is potentially good and tender, limited only by prior environment. The new setting will invite and make possible the best—and the best is unbelievably heartening."

One can select similar evidence of continuing belief almost at random.[60] Charles Merriam, distinguished political scientist, placed his faith in man's proven capacity to control the world and society for his own finer purposes. Referring to the anxiety created by the atomic bomb, he countered Norman Cousins' fears: "To say that modern man is obsolete is an interesting literary phrase, but the precise opposite is true. Modern man is coming of age. . . . The mind is king, not the atom. We trapped the atom; we have mastered some secrets of its latent forces, not by accident, but by deliberate design, by organization and ingenuity."[61] Sidney B. Fay, American historian, while not as confident as John Fiske or E. E. Channing, or E. P. Cheyney before him, and while admitting that civilizations had displayed "oscilla-

tions of advance and retreat," concluded, in 1947: "Progress is not constant, automatic, and inevitable in accordance with cosmic laws, but it is possible and even probable as a result of man's conscious and purposeful efforts."[62] Ashley Montagu, anthropologist and philosopher, held that society was "infinitely perfectible," if only men realized the eternal truth that the way to social evolution was not through competition and strife, but through cooperation and love. All the evidence of modern biology and psychology indicated "that human beings are born good—'good' in the sense that there is no evil or hostility in them." "*Human nature*," he continued, "is good. It is our present *human nurture* that is bad." The acceptance and practice of a new theory of learning that would place emphasis upon "cooperation, on adaptive association, on love, on shared relationships," would hasten the day when all problems would be more capable of solution than ever before in the long history of humanity.[63]

Even Adlai Stevenson who, in addressing nonpolitical audiences, expressed his personal reservations about the adequacy of a belief in progress, was moved, on purely political occasions, to express more traditional and popular ideas. During the campaign of 1952, he exclaimed: "I do say to you soberly and sincerely that on the evidence of science, of technology, and of our own common sense, the United States at mid-century stands on the threshold of abundance for all, so great as to exceed the happiest dreams of the pioneers who opened the vast Western country. Unless we allow ourselves to be held back by fear, we shall

[60] *Walter Reuther, President of the United Automobile Workers, was on record to the effect that automation promised "almost unlimited opportunities for human betterment . . . if we can bring into moral balance man's great technical movement forward," and if America's economic system could be made "socially responsible." In Joseph O'Mahoney et al.,* The Challenge of Automation: Papers Delivered at the National Conference on Automation (*Washington, D.C., 1955*), 45–55. *Morris Llewellyn Cooke, engineer and public servant, expressed his faith that the wonders of modern technology could be used to "enhance the dignity and the freedom of the individual" if men adopted "with deep conviction the idea of possible and continuous progress." In Seymour E. Harris, ed.,* Saving American Capitalism: A Liberal Economic Program (*New York, 1948*), 109–10.

[61] *Charles E. Merriam, "Physics and Politics,"* American Political Science Review, *XL:3 (June, 1946), 445–46.*

[62] *Fay,* American Historical Review, *LII:2 (Jan., 1947), 246.*

[63] *M. F. Ashley Montagu,* The Direction of Human Development: Biological and Social Bases (*New York, 1955*), 289–309, 312. *Also see, by the same author:* Darwin, Competition and Cooperation (*New York, 1952*).

in God's good time realize the golden promise of our future."[64] If the presidential aspirant spoke from the heart of this occasion, it is significant of the continued force of the idea of progress upon the liberal mind; if he spoke rather what he felt might be politically expedient, what the American voter wished to be assured of, his optimism was even more significant for an evaluation of the persistence of this belief.[65]

[64] Major Campaign Speeches of Adlai E. Stevenson, 1952 (*New York, 1953*), *117. Also see Stevenson's speech accepting nomination for president on the Democratic ticket at Chicago, Aug. 17, 1956, in which he spoke of his vision of a "new America." It is instructive to compare and contrast the tone of these political speeches with the more conservative mood of his* Call to Greatness *and of the non-political essays in* What I Think.

[65] *For other affirmations of the belief in science and technology as the necessary, if not the sufficient, cause for progress, and of the belief in man's capacity to determine his own destiny see: Adolf A. Berle,* The Twentieth Century Capitalist Revolution (*New York, 1954*); *Lyman Bryson,* The Drive Toward Reason in the Service of a Free People (*New York, 1954*); *F. I. Cairns,* Progress Is Unorthodox (*Boston, 1950*); *Norman V. Carlisle and Frank B. Latham,* Miracles Ahead! Better Living in the Postwar World (*New York, 1944*). *In* Big Business: A New Era (*New York, 1952*), *204, David E. Lilienthal tells of his dream of "a world of great machines, with man in control, devising and making use of these inanimate creatures to build a new kind of independence, a new awareness of beauty, a new spirit of brotherliness." See also: David E. Lilienthal,* This I Do Believe (*New York, 1949*). *One may sample the continued belief in progress in almost any selection in Edward R. Murrow, ed.,* This I Believe: The Personal Philosophies of One Hundred Thoughtful Men and Women (*New York, 1952*), *and* This I Believe: II (*New York, 1954*). *Here are summarized all the old traditions of American liberalism: the goodness of man and his rationality, the ultimate freedom of his will, the inviolability of his person, the assurance of material and spiritual progress toward perfection. That*

The belief in progress has exhibited remarkable toughness in twentieth-century America. Despite the weight of historical evidence to the contrary, many Americans seemed determined still to believe in the necessary advance of society and culture. This faith traditionally rested upon certain axioms: the beneficence of Providence, the lawfulness of the world, the potential coherence and harmony of social organizations, the innate rationality and goodness of natural man, his capacity to compel the material world to serve his purpose through science and his ability to evolve ever-higher systems of law and government, morality and ethics through the exercise of social intelligence. But even in its most exuberant phase, the faith was a conditional one, contingent upon the preservation or creation of particular circumstances conducive to the realization of man's potentialities for infinite perfectibility. At various times different conditions were declared to be essential: machine technology, social mobility, free enterprise, the cooperation of men in voluntary associations, the willingness to experiment, the will to believe, and always, above all else, freedom of the mind.

The last two prerequisites were often linked together, for in the last analysis man's intelligence stood at nought unless he was determined to use his intelligence constructively for human advance, while his will was rudderless without the guidance that the free mind could apply. To believe that

these brief statements aimed at a broadly popular audience, were heavily sprinkled with old-fashioned clichés should surprise no one. As shallow and even fatuous as they may appear to critical listeners and readers, these affirmations ring with sincerity and conviction. The traditional faiths they express cannot be taken lightly. For a critique of these thumbnail philosophies see: William Phillips, "The Success of Faith; or Is It the Faith of Success?" Commentary, *XVII:3 (March, 1954), 272–75.*

progress was possible was to make that progress probable. Time and again, during the past decade of mounting crises, Americans were exhorted to believe.

From the academic world, where pessimism, such as it was, was perhaps the deepest, came the call "to recover confidence in social progress and in man's ability to adjust his difficulties through human intelligence."[66] Clark Kerr, Provost of the University of California in Berkeley, taking note that the evidence of the recent past did not exactly support a view of historical progress called upon educational leaders not to be "intimidated by history." The University, he said, was dedicated to freedom of investigation and the discovery of truth in order that men may "control their destiny" and "consciously direct human progress."[67] A spokesman for liberal elements of the business community put the same thought directly and bluntly: progress is not automatic, it depends upon "human will and human intelligence."[68] The same confidence in the efficacy of faith was uttered by Adlai Stevenson during the presidential campaign of 1952 when he proclaimed: "We can win the war against war because we must. Progress is what happens when inevitability yields to necessity. And it is an article of the democratic faith that progress is a basic law of life."[69]

Willing would make it so. President Eisenhower, then of Columbia University, hammered home the same point in March, 1950: "we must

not be discouraged by the inescapable slowness of world progress. However disappointing may be the lack of speed, every new evidence of advance brings immediate hope of a brighter tomorrow to millions; and peoples hopeful of their domestic future do not use war as a solution to their problems. Hope spurs humans everywhere to work harder, to endure more now that the future might be better; but despair is the climate of war and death. Even America, without American optimism, can accomplish nothing beyond the needs of each day."[70]

The will to believe, then, was one of the necessary ingredients to make possible that progress for which men yearned. The other prerequisite was freedom of the mind. Upon this last condition, advocates of progress would admit of no dispute, although they rejected the practice in the Soviet Union where men tyrannized over the mind and spirit of man while still professing a belief in the progress of humanity. Freedom of inquiry was the one undeniable postulate that the liberal mind cherished. Progress might not be inevitable but it was not even possible unless the mind were free, for as David Sarnoff emphasized: "if freedom is lost, if the dignity of man is destroyed, advances on the material plane will not be 'progress' but a foundation of a new savagery."[71]

Only in a pluralistic, open society were no limits set to the inquiring mind; only in a democratic society in which all men enjoyed continuous access to full and candid information was faith in the judgment and conscience and common sense of the people justified as a means to promote the

[66] William C. Carleton, "*Toward Man's Maturity*," Antioch Review, X:2 (*June, 1950*), 192.

[67] Clark Kerr, "*The University in a Progressive Society*," Pacific Spectator, VII:3 (*Summer, 1953*), 271, 268.

[68] Eric Johnston, America Unlimited (*New York, 1944*), 241.

[69] Adlai Stevenson, Radio Address on United Nations Day, Oct. 24, 1952, in Major Campaign Speeches, 276.

[70] Dwight D. Eisenhower, address at Columbia University, March 23, 1950, in Allan Taylor, ed., What Eisenhower Thinks (*New York, 1952*), 175.

[71] David Sarnoff, Fortune, LI:1 (*Jan., 1955*), 118.

progress of the nation, spiritually as materially.[72] This faith constituted the hard irreducible core at the heart of the belief in progress. All else was relatively peripheral and friable. In the end, faith in the possibility of progress, or even in its probability, had swung full circle back to the original formulations of Francis Bacon.

It was significant, therefore, that in mid-twentieth century another pure scientist, J. Robert Oppenheimer, should explore the domain of "The Open Mind." Science had wrought a revolution in what men conceived to be the nature of their world and of themselves; technology had accelerated the pace of social change. Atomic scientists had discovered that adequate as the Newtonian concept of an ordered and determinate universe was for most of the common problems of "statistical mechanics," at the heart of the universe, in the infinitely minute world of the atom, lay causal anomalies, unpredictability.[73] This view in itself was deeply disturbing to traditional systems of thought and action. "Short of

rare times of great disaster, civilizations have not known such rapid alteration in the conditions of their life, such rapid flowering of many varied sciences, such rapid changes in the ideas we have about the world and one another. . . . the ways that we learned in childhood are only very meagerly adequate to the issues that we must meet in maturity."[74] For those who participated in the creation of a new world view and a new world there was "terror as well as exaltation."[75] In particular, the creation of a new instrument of "massive terror" out of the free search of devoted scientists for truth made men "anxiously aware that the power to change is not always necessarily good." The use of science for the alleviation of "hunger and poverty and exploitation" depended now upon the need to eliminate organized violence among nations.[76]

Atomic physics could not be repealed; the methods of science could not be scrapped. "To assail the changes that have unmoored us from the past is futile, and in a deep sense, I think, it is wicked. We need to recognize the change and learn what resources we have." In a world of terrifying complexity one could strive only to render "partial order" out of "total chaos."[77] That much was possible for the very methods of free inquiry had vastly extended man's freedom and had given to society the instruments with which the ancient problems of humanity might be solved. Science and democracy flourished or foundered together; without the freedom to inquire, science and man could not progress.[78]

[72] *This is the main thesis of David Lilienthal, "Machines with and without Freedom,"* Saturday Review of Literature, *XXXII:32 (Aug. 6, 1949), 58, 60, 62.*

[73] *Oppenheimer went on to note that the atomic world "is not causal; there is no complete causal determination of the future on the basis of available knowledge of the present." In atomic physics, "predictions are in the form of assertions of probability and only rarely and specially in the form of certitudes." British Broadcasting Company,* Listener *(Dec. 10, 1953), 992. Professor Oppenheimer was quick to add, however, that it would be an error to misapply by analogy the "indeterminate character of atomic events" to support "that sense of freedom which characterizes man's behaviour in the face of decision and responsibility." Ibid. (Dec. 17, 1953), 1036. To this warning he added, however, an affirmation of man as both creature and creator: our life, he wrote, "is part free and part inevitable, is part creation and part discipline, is part acceptance and part effort." Neither one side nor the other can be maintained exclusively without "folly" and "death to the spirit." Ibid. (Dec. 24, 1953), 1075.*

[74] Ibid., *1076.*

[75] Ibid. *(Dec. 3, 1953), 941.*

[76] Ibid. *(Dec. 24, 1953), 1077.*

[77] *Address at Columbia University, Nov. 1954, in* The Open Mind *(New York, 1955), 141, 145.*

[78] *Address to winners of the Annual Westinghouse Science Talent Search, March 7, 1950, ibid., 113–14.*

Given such conditions, man's ways "point not merely to change, to decay, to alteration, but point with a hopeful note of improvement that our progress is inevitable."[79]

It was fitting that Professor Oppenheimer should commend to one of his audiences a letter of Thomas Jefferson:

> I am among those who think well of the human character generally. I consider man as formed for society, and endowed by nature with those dispositions which fit him for society. I believe also, with Condorcet, . . . that his mind is perfectible to a degree of which we cannot as yet form any conception. . . .
>
> . . . I join you therefore in branding as cowardly the idea that the human mind is incapable of further advances. This is precisely the doctrine which the present despots of the earth are inculcating; and applying especially to religion and politics; "that it is not probable that anything better will be discovered than what was known to our fathers." . . . But thank heaven the American mind is already too much opened, to listen to these impostures; and while the art of printing is left to us, science can never be retrograde; what is once acquired of real knowledge can never be lost. To preserve the freedom of the human mind then and freedom of the press, every spirit should be ready to devote itself to martyrdom; for as long as we may think as we will, and speak as we think, the condition of men will proceed in improvement. . . .[80]

The belief in progress had arisen during an age of faith in man's capacities for rational and effective action. Could it survive when many men could cling no longer to the Enlightenment's view of human nature? It had been elaborated at a time when science and machine technology appeared to promise material abundance and the increasing control of men over their environment. Could it survive when the acceleration of technological change threatened to engulf man and to alienate him from traditional systems of morality and value? It had grown in force during generations of relative peace and advancing democracy. Could it survive an era of war, social chaos and totalitarianism? The evidence would suggest that if widespread doubts were entertained throughout Western civilization, most Americans were still inclined to act upon the faith that the future held forth the promise of ever better things to come. America, at mid-century, was not yet prepared to reject as no longer relevant or viable the belief in progress, rooted as that faith was in the experience of generations. Continuity of thought and hope survived the discontinuities posed in an age of anxiety. "Progress" was still "the business of America." The nation, "forever on the march," was certain that it was advancing into a better land.

[79] *Address to the Association of Graduate Alumni, Princeton University, Jan. 1, 1953, ibid., 121.*

[80] Ibid., *111–12. In elaborating upon these sentiments, Professor Oppenheimer admitted: "In our contemporary expressions of hope that catastrophe can be averted and civilization yet be saved, that confidence has lost much of its robustness." Ibid., 113.*

THE IDEA OF PROGRESS:
A CRITICAL REASSESSMENT

Georg G. Iggers*

In the course of the nineteenth century a profound crisis in Western consciousness occurred,
perhaps the deepest since the emergence of the
great traditional value systems in Greece and
Palestine two and a half millenniums ago. The fundamental metaphysical assumption of the Western intellectual tradition, the certainty of the
ethical meaningfulness of the universe, collapsed.
The full realization of the "death of God," proclaimed by Heinrich Heine, Friedrich Nietzsche,
and others, suddenly took hold of Western
thought. Modern man confronted what Jean-Paul
Sartre has pictured as the logical consequence of
the atheistic position,[1] the recognition that he
lived in a world without objective value and
hence without objective meaning.

In a sense this ethical nihilism was the end product of a long process of secularization of life and
thought that had begun in the Middle Ages. The

scientific discoveries and formulations of the seventeenth century had ushered in a demythologiza-
tion of world views. The Enlightenment marked
the height of the belief in the applicability of empirical analysis to the problems of human behavior
as well as of ethics. Yet, in another way, the gulf
which separated the naturalistic world view of the
eighteenth-century Enlightenment from the modern denial of the existence of objective value was
much deeper than that which separated the demythologized world of the Enlightenment from
the religious world picture of the prescientific
age. Carl Becker has with justice noted that in a

---

[1] See Jean-Paul Sartre, Existentialism, tr. Bernard Frecht-
man (New York, 1947); see also Heinrich Heine, "Zur
Geschichte der Religion und Philosophie in Deutschland," in
Heinrich Heine's Gesammelte Werke, ed. Gustav Karpeles
(2d ed., 9 vols., Berlin, 1893), V, 94.

---

*GEORG G. IGGERS (1926–   ) is a Professor of History at the State University of New York at
Buffalo. His publications include The Cult of Authority (1958) and The German Conception of His-
tory (1968). Reprinted by permission of the author and the American Historical Review, Vol. 71, No. 1
(October, 1965) 1–17.

very basic way "the *Philosophes* were nearer the Middle Ages, less emancipated from the preconceptions of medieval Christian thought, than they quite realized or we have commonly supposed."[2] For in their belief that there was a basic moral structure inherent in the universe, the eighteenth-century advocates of natural law still stood in a line of thought that linked them with Isaiah, Aristotle, and Thomas Aquinas.

The relation between the doctrine of natural law and the idea of progress is a complex one. The belief in rational ethical values does not necessarily carry with it the belief in the perfectibility of man. Eighteenth-century rationalist thought was marked by strong undercurrents of pessimism.[3] The doctrine of natural law did not imply that men would act rationally, but merely that they had a rational choice. Voltaire saw in history the perennial struggle of reason and unreason. Nevertheless, without the belief in the existence of rational values, the idea of progress is meaningless. The idea of progress in its classical form was born in the confidence of the Enlightenment that through the systematic application of reason to society, rational conditions of human life could be created. Certain critics, such as Karl Löwith,[4] have therefore interpreted the idea of progress as a secularized form of the Judaeo-Christian conception of Providence. This is true only to the extent that the theorists of progress of the eighteenth and nineteenth centuries viewed history as a unilinear process toward a meaningful end. But not only did most theorists of progress see the ful-

fillment of this end in worldly terms, but, as in the case of Condorcet and John Stuart Mill (in sharp contrast to the Augustinian view), they emphasized the active role that men played in the historical process through the application of reason and science to society.

What constitutes reason and science, of course, underwent considerable development in the course of the seventeenth and eighteenth centuries. Ernst Cassirer has sharply contrasted pre- and post-Newtonian conceptions of philosophy and science. If most seventeenth-century thinkers still believed that an understanding of the rational structure of the universe, including the realm of values, was possible through an a priori deductive approach, the dominant note of the eighteenth century was a much humbler one. Reason was no longer looked upon as the "sum total of 'innate ideas' given prior to all experience which reveal the absolute essence of things,"[5] but was restricted to the world of phenomena. John Locke, Denis Diderot, or Voltaire no longer hopefully assumed that the fundamental problems of cosmic reality could be solved through human reason. All of this involved a conscious rejection of metaphysics. Nevertheless, no matter how vociferously eighteenth-century empiricists or nineteenth-century positivists repudiated metaphysics, their concepts of reason and science involved a thoroughly metaphysical assumption. Reason was not merely a methodological tool for reasoning or planning, but a normative concept and a guide to ultimate value. The universe was not an ethically indifferent world. Locke, Voltaire, Pierre Bayle, Jean Jacques Rousseau, Gotthold Lessing, and Immanuel Kant were all agreed that there was a rational ethics. From reason there followed axiomatically certain

---

[2] *Carl L. Becker*, The Heavenly City of the Eighteenth-Century Philosophers (*New Haven, Conn., 1932*), 29.

[3] See *Henry Vyverberg*, Historical Pessimism in the French Enlightenment (*Cambridge, Mass., 1958*).

[4] See *Karl Lowith*, Meaning in History: The Theological Implications of the Philosophy of History (*Chicago, 1949*).

[5] *Ernst Cassirer*, The Philosophy of the Enlightenment, tr. *F. C. A. Koelln and J. P. Pettegrove* (*Princeton, N. J., 1951*).

ethical conclusions, such as the rights and dignity of the individual or the categorical imperative. And although such eighteenth-century political thinkers as Frederick the Great and Benjamin Franklin might differ on the type of political institutions—absolutist, constitutional, or democratic—by which these ethical principles were best achieved, they generally agreed on what constituted a rational minimum ethics. Nor was this metaphysical element absent in the dominant nineteenth-century conceptions of science. For none of the important social philosophers in the positivistic tradition of the early or mid-nineteenth century was science a value-free method of inquiry as it was to become later for physical scientists like Albert Einstein or Max Planck or for cultural scientists like Max Weber. Science for Henri de Saint-Simon, Auguste Comte, John Stuart Mill, Henry Thomas Buckle, Karl Marx, Ludwig Büchner, Walter Bagehot, Herbert Spencer, or Hippolyte Taine was not merely a method, but also a system. Scientific inquiry would inevitably reveal the lawfulness of the universe and social science the lawfulness of society. For Pierre Proudhon, Condorcet, Comte, Marx, Mill, and Spencer, there was such a thing as a scientific or rational society. For most of these thinkers, the steady advance of the sciences became identical with the progress of society. And despite their great differences regarding the specific political and economic institutions reserved for the future, men as divergent as Condorcet, Marx, and Spencer were agreed on the general character of the normative, that is, scientific, society. For them the scientific study of society aimed at the discovery of general laws governing social movement and these general laws were formulated as laws of social progress. History was seen as movement toward a normative society. In their best-known form, the laws of social movement were formulated in Comte's "Law of the Three Stages," but

they appeared in similar forms in Turgot, Condorcet, Marx, Buckle, Spencer, and many other writers. More careful thinkers such as John Stuart Mill also recognized the tendency, but questioned whether at this point of empirical study one could speak of "laws of progress."[6] There was, however, general agreement regarding the steady accumulation of knowledge, and what was felt to be the progressive replacement of conjectural, that is, theological or metaphysical, notions by scientific ones. There was also broad agreement that this process was accompanied by the steady growth of industry and the transformation of a warlike society and its spirit into an industrial and pacific one. There was further consensus that the course of history reflected the steady decline of coercion in government and the increasing role of rule by consent. As nineteenth-century social thought in reaction to the French Revolution increasingly recognized the role of impersonal social and historical forces, less emphasis was placed on intellect as a moving force in historical change, and progress was seen to an increasing extent as the result of an inner logic of society. The belief in the basic harmony of science and values, nevertheless, remained. Marx and Friedrich Engels, who most vehemently asserted that their social theory was scientific and free of moral presuppositions, also most insistently declared that scientific analysis provided the key to the final, that is, the scientific, normative social state of man. How widely spread the belief in the scientific certainty of progress was even later in the nineteenth century was demonstrated by the *Grand Larousse du* XIXe *siècle*, which only a year after the national debacle of 1870–1871 noted

6 *John Stuart Mill*, A System of Logic, Ratiocinative and Inductive, Being a Connected View of the Principles of Evidence and the Methods of Scientific Investigation (*7th ed., 2 vols., London, 1868*), *II, 510.*

under the entry "Progress" that virtually all intelligent men now accepted the idea.

As attempts at a scientific explanation of social phenomena, the theories of progress stated as general laws of social development proved to be untenable. As scientific theories they required empirical validation. None of the great theories of progress of the nineteenth century were or could be thus validated. Despite their scientific terminology, they remained speculative systems.[7]

In the decline of the faith in progress, nevertheless, the scientific or logical critique of the idea was of relatively little importance. Serious philosophical examination of the idea of progress came largely only in the late nineteenth and the twentieth centuries, when the idea had already lost much of its respectability. More important was the critique of the conception of reason upon which the theories of progress had rested. This critique occurred in two stages. In its earlier form, to which we shall refer as "historism" for lack of a better term, the critics recognized the normative character of reason and the objective meaningfulness of the universe and of history, but insisted that reason in human matters was not universal and abstract but individual and concrete. In a later form, which Erich Kahler has called "historicism" to distinguish it from the earlier "historism,"[8] this critique led to ethical nihilism, to the position that there is no objective value in the universe or objective meaning in history, and that reason and science can therefore only tell us what *is*, even when they are describing value systems, but never what *ought to be*.[9]

Historism was the main competitor of the idea of progress in the early nineteenth century. The term, of course, needs definition. As we use the term here, perhaps somewhat arbitrarily because it has been given so many meanings,[10] it refers to an orientation rather than to a structured movement in German historical thought. Historism, as we use the term, signifies the position that history rather than nature is the key to truths and values. The nature of anything is contained in its history. Historism rejects the abstract concepts employed by philosophy and by the natural sciences as inadequate for rendering the concrete, living realities found within history. The theoretical foundations of historism are contained in the late eighteenth-century critique of natural law doctrine as found in Herder's early writings, especially in his *Also a Philosophy of History*. But on closer examination, the break between historism and the Enlightenment is not as profound as it first seems. Despite the insistence on the inadequacies of reason and the role of intuition, of *Verstehen* and *Anschauung*, in historical cognition, the main currents of historism were by no means antischolarly or even antiscientific. In a sense, the Enlightenment first made possible an objective, empirical approach to historical reality by freeing history from theology and thus making possible the study of history for its own sake. Historism indeed adopted the Enlightenment ideals of methodological correctness and tried to introduce the ideal of scientific objectivity into historical study. History as a scholarly discipline was born

---

[7] *For a discussion of the inadequacies of the idea of progress as a scientific explanation of social phenomena, see, e.g., Karl Popper,* The Poverty of Historicism (*London, 1957*).

[8] *Erich Kahler,* The Meaning of History (*New York, 1964*), 200.

[9] *Cf. Arnold Brecht,* Political Theory: The Foundations of Twentieth-Century Political Thought (*Princeton, N. J., 1959*).

[10] *Cf. Dwight E. Lee and Robert N. Beck, "The Meaning of 'Historicism,'"* American Historical Review, *LIX (Apr., 1954), 568–77; cf. also* The Philosophy of History in Our Time: An Anthology, *ed. Hans Meyerhoff (New York, 1959), 10–11.*

in large part under the impact of historism. But in another way, too, the historism of the early nineteenth century was still deeply rooted in the Enlightenment. It assumed that there was reason in history, either in the Hegelian sense that all history was the manifestation of reason, or in the sense of Johann Gottfried von Herder, Edmund Burke, or Leopold von Ranke, that behind the diversity of values and individualities, there rested a divine will. "What happens is visible only in part in the world of senses," Wilhelm von Humboldt commented. "Every human individuality is only the phenomenal manifestation of an idea." And the "goal of history can only be the realization of the idea that mankind is to represent."[11] Similarly Ranke perceived in the states something "real and spiritual at one and the same time [*real-geistig*]." States were not "passing conglomerations" but "spiritual substances, original creations of the human mind—I might say thoughts of God."[12]

In a very real sense this belief in the meaningfulness of the historical world led to an optimism that exceeded even that implied in the idea of progress. By seeing in the forces of history the will of God, historism tended to erase the dichotomy of what is and what ought to be. Every epoch was equally "immediate unto God."[13] Acting in terms of its great historical interests, the state for G. W. F. Hegel or Johann Gustav Droysen could not really sin.[14] "But seriously,"

Ranke had Friedrich, one of the characters in the "Dialogue on Politics," say, "you will be able to name few significant wars for which it could not be proved that genuine moral energy achieved the final victory."[15] The skepticism with which most natural law thinkers had regarded power was almost entirely lacking. The border line between historism and the idea of progress was often blurred. The affirmative historism of the nineteenth century did not involve as total a negation of the idea of progress as later writers have suggested;[16] it was rather the expression of confidence that all was basically well. The optimism of Droysen's *Historik*, Heinrich von Treitschke's *Deutsche Geschichte*, and even Friedrich Meinecke's *Weltbürgertum und Nationalstaat* was much more blatant than that of Ernest Renan's *L'Avenir de la science*, John Stuart Mill's *Essay on Liberty*, or Herbert Spencer's *The Man versus the State*.

The disenchantment with the optimism inherent in the idea of progress and in the earlier affirmative historism comes in stages, with the disillusionment following the French Revolution, the disappointments accompanying the Revolution of 1848, and the cultural malaise manifesting itself already very early in the nineteenth century in the consciousness of many writers such as Alexis de Tocqueville, John Stuart Mill, Sören Kierkegaard, and Aleksandr Herzen of the "crisis of modern civilization," a malaise that increased with the growth of a technological mass society. And although optimism remained dominant until the calamities of the First World War, and in

11 *Wilhelm von Humboldt*, Über die Aufgabe des Geschichtschreibers (*Berlin, 1822*), I, 17.

12 *Leopold von Ranke, "A Dialogue on Politics," in Theodore H. Von Laue*, Leopold Ranke: The Formative Years (*Princeton, N. J., 1950*), 169; *cf. Leopold von Ranke*, Sammtliche Werke (*2d and 3d ed., 54 vols., Leipzig, 1875–90*), IL/L, 329.

13 Id., Weltgeschichte (*9 vols., Leipzig, 1888–1902*), IX, Pt. II, 5.

14 *Cf. Johann Gustav Droysen*, Historik: Vorlesungen über Enzyklopädie und Methodologie der Geschichte, *ed. Rudolf Hübner (Munich, 1937*), 266.

15 *Ranke*, "Dialogue on Politics," 167.

16 *E.g., Helmuth Plessner, "Conditio Humana," in* Propyläen-Weltgeschichte (*10 vols., Frankfurt, 1960–*), I, 33–86.

America even later, the voices of cultural pessimism multiplied. The optimism of both the idea of progress and of historism was replaced by new orientations toward history. The cyclical theories of history have perhaps received more attention than they deserve in terms of their influence on modern thought or their value as scientifically defensible systems. Ernst von Lasaulx, Nikolai Danilevsky, Oswald Spengler, and Arnold Toynbee (in the first six volumes of the *Study of History*) have each in a brilliant work of synthesis developed a countersystem to the idea of progress. In place of a unilinear development, these writers have seen the history of man in terms of the rise and fall of separate cultures. Each civilization was viewed in "morphological" terms, as a self-contained unit governed by inherent laws of growth and decline. The humanistic values of science, industry, equality, liberty, and humaneness which the adherents of the classical idea of progress had seen as rational norms and as the end products of history were now viewed as doomed.[17] These morphological systems were presented as scientific laws—by Toynbee as the result of supposed empirical investigation—and as such suffered all the logical weaknesses of the idea of progress. They remained speculative systems, lacking empirical validation. Their serious contribution lay rather in their attempt to analyze the nature of modern civilization. They raised the important question—although this is a question that was asked by Tocqueville, Mill, Jakob, Burckhardt, Max Weber, and many others— whether the progress of civilization would not through the intellectualization and rationalization of life undermine the very values it had created.

Despite the pessimistic core of the cyclical theories, their denial of ultimate values, their insistence on the historicity of all cognition and all valuation, their rejection of the unity of human civilization, they nevertheless still affirmed the existence of structure and pattern, if not of meaning, in history. But even this became problematic in the course of the nineteenth century. The logical consequence of the secularization of thought was the collapse of the traditional theological and metaphysical concepts and the rise of the conception of nature as a purely impersonal, blind force devoid of purpose. The collapse of the belief in purpose in history did not follow directly upon the recognition that God is dead. Marx, Spencer, and Renan all viewed the world in naturalistic terms, and nevertheless failed to draw the ethical consequences of their atheistic or agnostic philosophical positions. The recognition that history had no structure or purpose and had only the meaning that men gave to it emerged only slowly in the nineteenth century, in Herzen, in Nietzsche, and in the epistemological debates of the German Neo-Kantians at the end of the nineteenth century. But even Wilhelm Dilthey and Wilhelm Windelband were confident that the varieties of *Weltanschauungen*, although rationally irreconcilable, reflected a fundamental cosmic unity. Heinrich Rickert stressed that the cultural sciences deal with values not as valid as such but as related to cultures, but even for him these values still appeared to possess reference to a transcendental ethics.[18] Only Max Weber among the Neo-Kantians drew the final conclusions of the historistic position: that values were cultural phenomena with no reference to ultimate value. All values were rooted in *Weltanschauungen*, and *Weltanschauungen* were in the final analysis irrational. Man was thus faced by the ethical irrationality of the world and the in-

[17] See Georg G. Iggers, "*The Idea of Progress in Recent Philosophies of History*," Journal of Modern History, XXX (Sept., 1958), 215–26.

[18] *Heinrich Rickert*, Die Grenzen der naturwissenschaftlichen Bergriffsbildung (*Tübingen, 1902*), 736–38.

soluble conflict of the systems of values.[19] With this recognition, German historical thought had passed from historism, the faith that history is the sole key to value and reason, to historicism, the recognition that all values are historical and that "historical is identical with relative."[20]

Modern historicism had many sources, of course. It was not merely or primarily the outcome of the methodological and epistemological discussions of a small circle of German Neo-Kantian philosophers and cultural scientists. Anthropology, sociology, Marxism, Darwinism, Freudianism, the study of comparative religion, the naturalistic attitudes that accompanied the increasing role science played in the course of the nineteenth century, all helped to undermine the belief in objective value. Under the emotional impact of the First World War and its aftermath, these realizations became a dominant strain in Western historical thought. Not only were all values viewed as historical, but history too was viewed now as "a tale told by an idiot" signifying nothing.[21]

The position that "history has no meaning"[22] is shared today by thinkers coming from very different intellectual positions. It is a key concept in the existentialism of Jean-Paul Sartre, in the Protestant crisis theology of Karl Barth and of Reinhold Niebuhr, and in the positivism of Karl Popper. It denies not only the objectivity of value but also the coherence of history and for the existentialist position, at least, even the objectivity of method. Theodor Lessing's assertion that "history, originating in desires and volitions, needs and intentions, is a realization of the 'dream visions' of the human race . . . meaning of history is solely meaning which I give myself, and historical evolution is a development from myself to myself,"[23] is essentially as acceptable to the existentialist position as it is to Popper. History confronts us with facts, but "facts as such have no meaning," Popper reminds us; "they gain it only through our decisions."[24] And while it would not be correct to say that history has no meaning in Martin Heidegger's *Existenzphilosophie*, history ceases to have "objective meaning" for him because "objective meaning" presupposes that history confronts man as an object. To Heidegger, man is "thrown" into an ethically absurd universe in which, driven by care (*Sorge*) and anguish (*Angst*), confronted by death, he is forced to define himself. Within the framework of the concrete possibilities of the situation, man is confronted by a heritage that contained not one history but the "possibility of various histories." The individual "created" his history not on the basis of the objective happenings of the past, but by his decisions directed toward the future. What

---

[19] *See Max Weber, " 'Objectivity' in Social Science and Social Policy" and "The Meaning of 'Ethical Neutrality' in Sociology and Economics,"* in The Methodology of the Social Sciences, *tr. Edward A. Shils and Henry A. Finch (Glencoe, Ill., 1949); see also Max Weber, "Science as a Vocation" and "Politics as a Vocation,"* in From Max Weber: Essays in Sociology, *tr. H. H. Gerth and C. Wright Mills (New York, 1946).*

[20] *Ernst Troeltsch,* Die Absolutheit des Christentums und die Religionsgeschichte *(Tübingen, 1902), 49.*

[21] *See Leo Strauss,* Natural Right and History *(Chicago, 1953), 18.*

[22] *Karl Popper,* The Open Society and Its Enemies *(2 vols., London, 1945), II, 264, 265. An exception to this position is found in Edward Hallett Carr,* What Is History? The George Macaulay Trevelyan Lectures Delivered in the University of Cambridge January–March 1961 *(New*

York, 1962), *an emphatic reassertion and redefinition of objectivity, meaning, and progress in history.*

[23] *Theodor Lessing,* Geschichte als Sinngebung des Sinnlosen *(2d ed., Munich, 1921), 10, quoted in Kahler,* Meaning of History, *19–20.*

[24] *Popper,* Open Society and Its Enemies, *II, 265.*

distinguishes Heidegger and such decisionist German thinkers of the 1920's as Ernst Jünger and Carl Schmitt[25] from Popper is that Heidegger, Jünger, and Schmitt opt against the humanistic and scholarly values of intellect, civilization, human welfare, and humaneness, and Popper opts for them, but Popper like Max Weber before him is aware of the element of faith in his decision.[26] Thus both for existentialist thought with its negative attitude toward intellect as well as for defenders of the scientific spirit such as Popper, history has no objective meaning. And with the death of meaning in history, the idea of progress is dead, too. Only in Communist countries does the idea of progress survive in an antiquated nineteenth-century form kept artificially alive by official policy.

The questions of value, meaning, and coherence in history are, nevertheless, not as easily disposed of as the literature leads us to believe. The basic assumption of the historicist position is, as José Ortega y Gasset has worded it, that "man has no nature but only history"[27] and that hence no rational ethics, no ethics based on human nature is possible. But is this really true?

Here is, of course, the heart of the difference between historism and historicism on the one hand and the doctrine of natural law on the other. Historism and historicism assume that all is flux; natural law assumes that in the midst of change there is an element of stability in the lawful structure of the universe.

It is, of course, a great step from conceptions of the lawfulness of physical nature to those of human nature. A large number of thinkers who denied the possibility of objective or universally valid judgments in the cultural sciences have accepted them in the natural sciences. Men such as Heinrich Rickert, Karl Mannheim, and Popper were willing to recognize in nature what they were unwilling to admit in history: objective coherence. If nature is coherent, then natural science is possible. Although every scientific theory is merely a system of symbols that only indirectly and inaccurately conceptualizes "reality," it nevertheless refers to an objective coherence. There is thus a norm in scientific research that we call truth even if we can never perfectly attain it. And connected with this norm is another norm closely related to it; this we may call methodological correctness. All this has a direct relevance to the idea of progress because these norms provide the criteria of progress in the sciences. Even in the age of historicism, few thinkers would agree with Oswald Spengler that all systems of science and mathematics have no truth values beyond the cultures to which they relate.[28] And even Spenglerians are forced to act as if they lived in a world governed by an objective physical order.

But not only is there coherence in the physical world; there also appears to be a degree of coherence in that area of history which we call the history of science. The historistic admonition that *individuum est ineffabile*, that it is the task of the historian not to judge, but merely to show *wie es eigentlich gewesen*, that every epoch is "immediate unto God" is clearly inadequate in the history of science. We are dealing not merely with the variety of scientific views but with theories of greater or lesser truth value. The existence of coherence in nature makes progress in scientific

[25] *See Christian Graf von Krockow*, Die Entscheidung: Eine Untersuchung über Ernst Jünger, Carl Schmitt, Martin Heidegger (*Stuttgart, 1958*).

[26] *Popper*, Open Society and Its Enemies, II, 265.

[27] *José Ortega y Gasset*, Obras Completas (*9 vols., Madrid, 1953–62*), VI, 41.

[28] *See Oswald Spengler*, The Decline of the West (*2 vols., New York, n.d.*), I, Chap. 11, *"The Meaning of Numbers."*

knowledge theoretically possible. It is, of course, impossible at this stage (or probably ever) to validate a law of progress in scientific knowledge such as Comte postulated, but we can observe more or less clearly definable trends. This does not exclude reversal. The heliocentric theory and the circulation of the blood, both known to Hellenistic science, had to be "rediscovered" in modern times. Nevertheless, the reality of objective coherence to an extent guides the direction of scientific inquiry. It makes it possible, moreover, to draw lines of development. It also means that the historian is not confronted by a multiplicity of equally meaningless facts, as Popper suggested, but by facts of greater or lesser significance. The selection of these facts in the writing of the history of science is no longer left entirely to the subjective decision of the historian.

What is true of the history of science is also true of the history of technology. But here we are not yet on very controversial ground. For much of historicist theory would admit the possibility of civilizational (scientific, technical, even organizational) progress, but not of cultural (spiritual or moral) progress. This, of course, involves the question whether there is a "human nature" and the even more difficult question whether there are generally applicable norms that derive from this human nature.

To an extent, of course, we shall probably all agree, despite Ortega y Gasset and Sartre's stand to the contrary, that there is a minimal common basis of human nature not only on a biological but also on a psychological level. In a sense existentialist philosophy which has insisted so forcefully that "there is no human nature"[29] has paradoxically itself traveled on the road back to the recognition of a common human nature, at least in its extreme preoccupation with the "human

condition" in which we all share. *Sorge, Dasein zum Tod, Angst, Nausée* are all states that are universally human rather than in Herder's words "national . . . and individual."[30] The practicing historian, no matter how committed to historistic principles, has never been able to escape the assumption of a constancy in human nature. For what was the critical method in history of which the nineteenth-century historians were so proud but the insistence on the recognition of the coherence of physical nature in the case of the criteria of external criticism and of human nature in relation to the principles of internal criticism. As W. H. Walsh suggested:

> It was generalizations about human nature which ultimately lay behind historical explanations . . . we could not even begin to understand [the past], unless we presupposed some propositions about human nature, unless we applied some notion of what is reasonable or normal in human behavior.[31]

Again, if we look at the history of institutions, we see certain lines of continuity. The Saint-Simonians formulated as a social law the ever-widening circle of association of man in the course of history from family to city, nation, church, and finally world state.[32] We can hardly speak of law, and even less of progress in a valuative sense, but we are nevertheless confronted by an observable trend, by what Kahler has called "the gradual expansion of existential scope," an "evolution,

[29] *Sartre*, Existentialism.

[30] *Johann Herder*, Auch eine Philosophie der Geschichte zur Bildung der Menschheit, *in* Sämmtliche Werke, *ed. Bernhard Suphan (33 vols., Berlin, 1877–1913), V, 505.*

[31] *W. H. Walsh*, An Introduction to Philosophy of History *(5th ed., London, 1958), 107. For a similar line of reasoning, see Carr*, What Is History? *122–23.*

[32] *See* The Doctrine of Saint-Simon: An Exposition. First Year, 1828–1829, *tr. Georg G. Iggers (Boston, 1958), 60–61.*

not to be confounded with progress, which has a moral or merely functional connotation—... from the tribe to city and city-state" to feudal principalities, territorial estates, dynastic and nation-states, popular nations "to civilizational and ideological power blocs, and finally to the technically, technologically prepared 'one world' which is humanly, psychologically, very far from organized realization, but which looms as the only alternative that science and technology have presented us to their opposite achievement, nuclear or biological annihilation."[33] Other trends are equally observable. Max Weber has spoken of a continuous process of intellectualization and rationalization of life since the beginnings of civilization in the ancient Near East.[34] In a similar vein, Kahler observes the steady "secularization, rationalization, scientification and technicalization" of human existence.[35]

These trends do not necessarily represent progress in so far as we mean by progress development toward more moral institutions and more moral man. They may constitute change rather than improvement, change which in the growing rationalization of life may actually be undermining the very values that the classical theorists of progress regarded as the criteria of progress. Moreover, we are admittedly confronted by the methodological problem of measuring these "trends."

We come closer to the problem of values when we deal with another set of trends that appear to be operating in modern society. Condorcet predicted the disappearance of slavery, the rise of literacy, the diminution of inequalities among the sexes, reforms of prison codes, and the decline of poverty. Again one can hardly deny that these trends have operated during the past 175 years, although it is difficult to measure them. We are, of course, dealing with trends over a relatively short span of time, which may conceivably be reversed either catastrophically through thermonuclear warfare or through the very contradictions within society that these social developments, considered beneficial by Condorcet, may have created. The future may correspond more closely to George Orwell's 1984 than to Edward Bellamy's Boston of the year 2000. Certainly we have in the course of the twentieth century approached Orwell's 1984 in many ways, but we have approximated Bellamy's Boston in even more ways.

In rereading the optimistic literature of the late eighteenth and of the nineteenth centuries we are impressed both by how right the prophets of those days were and by how wrong they were. Condorcet, Saint-Simon, Mill, and Spencer all underestimated the role of evil. "No one, whose opinion deserves a moment's consideration," Mill writes, "can doubt that most of the positive evils of the world are in themselves removable, and will, if human affairs continue to improve, be in the end reduced within narrow limits."[36] They overconfidently predicted the disappearance of war and tyranny. But they were right in many other ways. For, on the whole, the modern world has moved in the direction that the optimists of the Enlightenment and of the nineteenth century predicted. We need only reopen a book like Taine's *Notes on England* in the 1870's or the Quaker report on the condition of the colored population of Philadelphia in 1849 to be reminded how widespread and how severe was the spiritual and material degradation existing a century ago.

[33] *Kahler*, Meaning of History, *195–96.*
[34] *Weber, "Science as a Vocation."*
[35] *Kahler*, Meaning of History, *196.*

[36] *John Stuart Mill, "Utilitarianism," in* The Philosophy of John Stuart Mill, *ed. Marshall Cohen (New York, 1961), 339.*

Not that such degradation does not exist today even in the technologically more developed countries, but for the first time we can envisage the radical decline of disease, ignorance, and poverty throughout the entire world. Barring a world war, we may safely predict the continued increase in levels of health, education, and welfare throughout the world, at least in the foreseeable future.

Certainly we cannot formulate a law of progress in the sense in which Comte and Buckle sought such laws. The very complexity of human society makes it doubtful that quantitative formulations similar to those developed in the natural sciences will ever be of more than restricted use in the cultural sciences. There is no certainty that the trends we have described will not be reversed. Moreover, we may be accused of having chosen values by which to measure progress that have no basis in human nature as such, but are merely the products of a time or of our subjective decisions. Finally, it may be argued again that the very values of modern civilization that we have identified as progressive may lead to their own destruction.

This brings us back to the question of whether there are real norms by which historical change can be measured. The idea of progress, rooted in the doctrine of natural law, assumed that there were. It assumed that there was a human nature, that the end of human life was happiness, that the full achievement of happiness for man involved the full development of his rational as well as his physical potentialities,[37] and that the structure of human nature therefore gave the moral world a degree of rational coherence. The core of this ethics was summed up in the doctrine of natural rights, in the belief in the right of the individual to his person. This assumed that violation of these rights, as constituted by murder, slavery, or exploitation, represented objective wrongs. Neither Locke, nor Voltaire, nor Kant attempted to prove the existence of such rights by reason. They considered them to be self-evident truths, data known through direct ethical intuition, conditions of human consciousness.[38]

Was the Enlightenment belief in a rational ethics mere wishfulness, or did it possess a basis in reality? Is there below the pattern of diverse customs and manners a basic substratum of human values? Historism has denied this. Related to this problem is the question of whether there is such a thing as mental health. Are there criteria of mental normalcy, or is normalcy merely a statistical concept relative to a given culture? May we speak of a sane society, as Erich Fromm has? Was Nazi Germany merely a different or a sick society? Was Auschwitz merely an instrument of policy or of immorality? Is the murderer merely a man with a different morality or a morally sick man?

If there are norms of morality deriving from human nature, or even merely norms of mental health, then there exists the theoretical possibility of a normal society. We may then conceivably in the moral and social world be confronted by something resembling the progress in the sciences and technology, by a tendency to achieve greater rationality. We may then perhaps see in the great revolutionary movements of modern history the groping toward morally more rational institutions, even though there are reverses and we can discern no clear or predetermined pattern.

All of this must be said with extreme caution. We are not dealing with a movement that as yet (or perhaps ever) can be formulated as a general

[37] Ibid., *331.*

[38] *See Alfred Cobban,* The Crisis of Civilization *(London, 1941), 108–09.*

social law, as certain of the nineteenth-century advocates of the theory of progress had believed possible. We are dealing at most with certain observable trends about whose direction there can be disagreement. And even if we agree that society has moved toward greater intellectualization, equality, and wealth, we may question whether such a movement has been beneficial to man or whether, as cultural pessimists from Kierkegaard to Ortega y Gasset have suggested, it has merely emptied man of his spiritual substance and laid the foundations for the most systematic tyranny of man over man. How can we speak of progress in a moral sense in the age of totalitarianism and total war? The Final Solution, which in a sense symbolized the high point of the application of modern science and technology in the service of inhumanity, appears to spell the total absurdity of progress. Gerhard Ritter, Meinecke, and many others have suggested that the roots of the Nazi Revolution were to be found in the rationalistic and equalitarian beliefs of the French Revolution and in the breakdown of religious beliefs and traditional class structures. The growing concern with economic welfare, which Comte and Spencer had hailed, Ritter saw as a major contributing factor to modern barbarism. But was Nazism really a phenomenon of the "failure of modern mass democracy" as Ritter suggested?[39] Was it not in an important way the revolt of an atavistic political romanticism against the conditions of modern society in a country in which, Ritter and Meinecke notwithstanding, Enlightenment values and democratic institutions were underdeveloped,

in which the gap between modern realities and premodern attitudes and class structure was much greater than in most Western democratic countries?

It was the great failing of the prophets of progress that they underestimated the extent of man's destructiveness and irrationality. The failing of historism and of historicism has been in misunderstanding the role of rationality and morality in human behavior. We can accept the idea of progress today only with serious qualifications. Progress as yet is only a hypothesis and a very questionable one. The reality of human evil, as Reinhold Niebuhr has suggested, makes the attainment of any perfect social state impossible. The complexities of history, in which, as Löwith pointed out, conscious human action always has results other than those intended,[40] make calculated progress much more problematic than the great believers in social engineering of the last century had believed. As Popper has warned us, the idea of progress as a "belief in Inexorable Laws of Historical Destiny" has led to the sacrifice of countless men and women upon the altar of totalitarian fanaticism.[41] While progress seems to be invalidated as a universal idea, there is, nevertheless, a rational basis to the belief that within limited spheres man's actions can create more rational conditions. Despite the strong currents of cultural pessimism that have marked our age, the social policies of all nations have proceeded on the assumption that within limited, defined goals, planned progress is possible. And the goals of this progress, except where they have turned toward war and repression, have remained the classical values of the Enlightenment: the improvement

---

[39] See Gerhard Ritter, *"The Fault of Mass Democracy,"* in The Nazi Revolution: Germany's Guilt or Germany's Fate? ed. *John Snell (Boston, 1959), 76–84; cf. Friedrich Meinecke,* The German Catastrophe: Reflections and Recollections, *tr. Sidney B. Fay (Cambridge, Mass., 1950).*

[40] *Karl Lowith, "Die Dynamik der Geschichte und der Historismus,"* Eranos-Jahrbuch, *XXI (1952), 217–54.*

[41] See the dedication to Popper's Poverty of Historicism.

of education, health, welfare, and individual dignity. The programs of aid to underdeveloped countries have underlined to what extent modern civilization, despite its negative aspects, has been regarded in both the Western as well as the non-Western countries as a positive good, not only in a material, but also in a spiritual sense. Indeed, the twentieth century, which has seen the decline of the idea of progress as a respectable theory of history, has also witnessed the idea more firmly established as a working assumption of public policy than it ever was in the optimistic century that preceded it.[42]

In conclusion, we must frankly admit that the idea of progress is untenable as a scientific explanation of historical movement. The theory is not, however, without rational foundations and deserves much more serious re-examination than it has received in recent thought. And independent of its role as a cognitive theory regarding the nature of history, the idea of progress must also be viewed as an ethical hypothesis that assumes, rationally or on faith, the reality of positive values and the meaningfulness of ethical behavior.

[42] *Carr in* What Is History? *notes an "expansion of reason" (p. 190) in the twentieth century and optimistically interprets the increase in social and economic planning as "an advance in the application of reason to human affairs, an increased capacity in man to understand and master himself and his environment, which I should be prepared, if necessary, to call by the old-fashioned name of progress" (pp. 188–89).*

George Caleb Bingham "The Country Election"   City Art Museum, St. Louis

PART 7

THE MEANING OF DEMOCRACY

Introduction

Even though they are unable to define the term "democracy," Americans are certain that they live in a democratic society. Intellectual historians, like other Americans who are embarrassed by their failure to define the term adequately, view democracy as Winston Churchill viewed the Soviet Union—as "a riddle wrapped in a mystery inside an enigma." The following selections may or may not be helpful for the purposes of definition, but they do aid in understanding the meaning of democracy.

J. R. Pole examines the problem of democracy during the colonial era. He disagrees with historians who claim that the colonists enjoyed democracy merely because many adult males had the right to vote. Pole believes that the seeds of democracy were actually submerged by the desire to maintain hereditary rule. The existence of a fluid social structure and the absence of an entrenched aristocracy doomed this aspiration and obliged Americans to take a more active role in political life.

The article by Louis Hartz analyzes differences between the American and foreign concepts of democracy. He claims that Americans already

were free at the time of the Revolution; they fought not for freedom but for independence. Since there was no rigid class structure in America, it was not necessary to destroy a social order to construct a free society. Most American revolutionaries, unable to understand the differences between themselves and their European counterparts, were reluctant to support the activities of other revolutions.

Max Lerner examines the influence of the Judeo-Christian tradition on American democracy. The question of whether the "emerging nations" of the twentieth century can develop democratic traditions depends largely on the existence of this tradition. Although the American tradition is secular, it is buttressed by religious freedom. The habit of religious dissent in America has given democracy its vitality.

The essay by Fletcher M. Green presents American democracy as "an evolving and expanding" institution. The author traces the development of democracy through five specific cycles beginning during the colonial period. He insists that the cyclical growth of democracy will be a continuous phenomenon in the United States.

HISTORIANS AND THE PROBLEM OF EARLY AMERICAN DEMOCRACY

J. R. Pole*

The earliest national period of United States history combines two themes. It is a period of revolution and also of constitution making. Charter governments, whether royal or proprietary, give way to new governments which claim to derive the whole of their authority from the American electorate. The Americans, though working from experience, build for the future. This fact is of cardinal importance for any attempt to understand their work or the state of mind in which it was undertaken.

The claim of the new government raises a problem that was not solved by the mere exercise of effective, but revolutionary powers. Was their authority strictly compatible with the doctrine that governments derive their just powers from the consent of the governed? What was meant by "consent"? How was such consent obtained or certified?

The attempt to answer these questions leads the historian into a reconstruction of the character of these early institutions and an inquiry into the ideas by which they were governed. In the light of subsequent American development, it has led historians to address themselves to the problem of deciding whether or not these institutions were democratic. Whether or not we choose to adopt this particular definition, whether or not we regard it as a useful tool of analysis, the underlying problem is one that the historian cannot easily avoid. No history of the American Revolution and of constitution making could be written without discussion of the doctrines on which the Americans based their resistance, the question of what meaning these doctrines bore for the different American participants, and of the degree of participation, the attitude and purposes of different elements in American society.

*J. R. POLE (1922–   ) is a reader in American History and Government and a fellow of Churchill College. His publications include Political Representation in England and the Origins of the American Republic (1966), The Advance of Democracy (1967), and The Revolution in America (1969). Reprinted by permission of the author and the American Historical Review, Vol. 67, No. 3 (April, 1962), 626–646.

There is a problem of the relationship of ideas to institutions; there is a previous problem of the ideas themselves. I do not think that the broad and undifferentiated use of the term "democracy" helps either to describe the institutions or to explain the ideas. I do not even think that our analysis of these matters will be much affected by the use of this concept. But the thesis has been advanced[1] that the American colonies were already full-fledged democracies before the American Revolution began, from which it follows that the cardinal principle of the Revolution was a defense of democratic institutions against royal or parliamentary tyranny. It is a thesis that has the advantage of an attractive simplicity, and it is one that can be supported by a good deal of evidence, especially if that evidence is read without much relation to the context of eighteenth-century political ideas. It also has the merit of providing the occasion, and in order that the argument should not go by default, the necessity of a more searching inquiry into the realities.

To use the word "democracy" is to raise, but not I think to solve, a problem of definition. And it is not an easy one. There is so little agreement about what is meant by "democracy," and the discussion has such a strong tendency to slide noiselessly from what we *do* mean to what we *ought* to mean, that for purposes of definition it seems to be applicable only in the broadest sense. And this sense has the effect of limiting, rather than of advancing, our understanding of the past.

But I must certainly admit that if I did think the word "democracy" in fact did justice to the problem, then I would have to accept it despite the risks involved. More than this: we ought to have some agreement as to what meaning it can

be made to bear. It makes good sense in a purely comparative view to call the American colonies and early states democratic when contrasting them with the Prussia of Frederick II or the Habsburg Empire; they were in the same sense democratic compared with France or with England, with which they had so much in common. There might be less unintended irony in calling them part of the "free world" than in doing the same today with Spain, Formosa, or the Union of South Africa. In the broad strokes we use to differentiate between tyrannies and free states the term will serve as a starting point, but not as a conclusion. It is interesting, when one begins to look more closely at the structure of the complex societies of the eighteenth century, how rapidly these broad distinctions lose their value and cease to serve any analytical purpose. As R. R. Palmer has recently remarked, surveying the Western world before the French Revolution, "No one except a few disgruntled literary men supposed that he lived under a despotism."[2] When one considers how complex the machinery of administration, of justice, for the redress of grievances and, if any, of political representation must become in any ancient and intricately diversified society, it is easy to feel that the more democratic virtues of the American societies were related, more than anything else, to their relative simplicity and lack of economic and functional diversity. But a closer inspection, not only of the structure, but of the development, of colonial institutions reveals a tendency that puts the matter in another light; for these institutions were unmistakably molded in the shape of English institutions and were conforming themselves, both socially and politically, to the conventions of the period.

The alternative view, which I want to suggest,

[1] *Robert E. Brown*, Middle-Class Democracy and the Revolution in Massachusetts, 1691–1780 (*Ithaca, N. Y., 1955*), *esp. 401–408.*

[2] *R. R. Palmer*, The Age of the Democratic Revolution (*Princeton, N. J., 1959*), 51.

does not confine itself merely to rejecting the "democratic" interpretation by putting in its place a flat, antidemocratic account of the same set of institutions. What it does, I think, is to see the democratic elements in their proper perspective by adding a further dimension without which the rest is flat, incomplete, and, for all its turbulence, essentially lifeless. This is the dimension of what Cecelia Kenyon has called "institutional thought."[3]

To take this view, one has to free oneself from a tendency that has become very difficult to resist. I mean the strong, though wholly anachronistic, tendency to suppose that when people who were accustomed to ways and ideas which have largely disappeared into the past felt grievances against their government, they must necessarily have wanted to express their dissatisfaction by applying the remedies of modern democracy; and, again, that when their demands were satisfied, the aspirations thus fulfilled must have been modern, democratic aspirations.

The idea that the great mass of the common people might actually have given their consent to concepts of government that limited their own participation in ways completely at variance with the principles of modern democracy is one that lies completely outside the compass or comprehension of the "democratic" interpretation. That interpretation insists on the all-importance of certain democratic features of political life, backed by certain egalitarian features of social life having a strong influence on political institutions. What it misses is that these features belonged within a framework which—to polarize the issue at the risk of using another broad term—was known to the world as Whiggism. The institutions of representative government derived from the time when

the Whig concept of representative government was being worked out in England and, both by extension and by original experience, in the American colonies (and when the foundations were laid for the Whig interpretation of history). Even where democratic elements were strong and dominant, the animating ideas belonged to a whole Whig world of both politics and society. More than this, the colonial and early national period in which they played so important a part was pervaded by a belief in and a sense of the propriety of social order guided and strengthened by principles of dignity on the one hand and deference on the other. It was, to use the term coined by Walter Bagehot in his account of Victorian England, a deferential society.[4]

There is, of course, nothing very new about the theory that early American society was relatively egalitarian and that this situation was reflected in political institutions and conduct. It was a view that became fashionable in the days of George Bancroft. But it has been reformulated, with formidable documentation, in Robert E. Brown's work on Massachusetts and in his attack on Charles Beard.[5] To regain our perspective it seems necessary for a moment to go back to Beard.

Beard, as we know, distinguished in his study of the Constitution between two leading types of propertied interest, basically those of land and commerce. Commercial property was supposed to have been strongly represented in the Constitutional Convention, landed property outside. The

[4] *See also E. S. Griffith,* History of American City Government: Colonial Period (*New York, 1938*), 191; *Clifford K. Shipton, review of Brown,* Middle-Class Democracy, Political Science Quarterly, *LXXI (No. 2, 1956), 306–308.*

[5] *Robert E. Brown,* Charles Beard and the Constitution: A Critical Analysis of "An Economic Interpretation of the Constitution" (*Princeton, N. J., 1956*).

[3] *Cecelia M. Kenyon, "Men of Little Faith: The Anti-Federalists on the Nature of Representative Government,"* William and Mary Quarterly, *XII (Jan., 1955), 4.*

opposition in some of the state ratifying conventions was supposed to have arisen from the outraged interests of the landed classes.

Despite intense opposition in certain states, the Constitution was eventually ratified. But here Beard went further. He asserted that ratification was not a true expression of the will of the people. He based this argument on the prevalence of property qualifications for the suffrage, which meant that only a minority of freeholders and other owners of property could participate in the elections to the ratifying conventions, which in consequence were not truly representative. There are two elements in Beard's hypothesis, as Brown has pointed out.[6] On the one hand, Beard advances the alleged clash between the mercantile and landed interests, with the mercantile coming out on top because of the power conferred by its economic advantages; on the other, he implies the existence of a connection between the landed opposition to ratification and the supposedly disfranchised masses, whose silence so damagingly detracts from the authority of the Constitution. It is not my purpose to discuss the question as to whether Beard's argument has stood the test of recent scrutiny. Another aspect, which may be called that of the moral consequences of Beard's work, deserves more consideration than it has received.

The Philadelphia Convention was described by Thomas Jefferson as "an assembly of demi-gods," a judgment to which posterity murmured "Amen." There are, however, marked disadvantages about being descended from demi-gods; they not only lack a sense of humor, but they set an appallingly high standard. What a relief it must have been, after the first shock of Beard's iconoclasm had died down, to find that they were only human after all! Beard had questioned the Constitution

at two points. In the first place, by implying that it was the work of men motivated by private economic interests he made it possible to reconsider its wisdom and justice; but in the second place, when he denied that it had received the sanction of a genuine, popular ratification he made it possible—perhaps obligatory—to question the authority of the Constitution precisely because it did not owe its origin to the only recognized source of such authority in the whole science of government as understood in America: the consent of the governed.

To this problem, Brown's critique of Beard is directly relevant. He not only pursues Beard with a determination that recalls John Horace Round's pursuit of Edward Freeman, but in his work on Massachusetts, he makes a thorough and painstaking investigation of the institutions of that province, in which he reaches the conclusion that colonial Massachusetts was already so fully democratic that no case can be made for an interpretation of the American Revolution there in terms of an internal "class war." It is in this connection that Brown broadens his front to develop an attack on Carl Becker.[7] The Revolution was a war of secession, fought for the preservation of American democracy against the antidemocratic policy of the crown. Nothing more, and nothing less. The joint foundations of all this are the wide extent of the suffrage franchise and the wide distribution of middling quantities of property.

The consequences are obvious. If the states, and not only the states but the colonies, were ruled by the consent of the governed, then Beard's unenfranchised masses disappear, and the Constitution is restored to its high place not only in the affection of the American people, but in their scale of approbation.

American history has been written not merely

[6] Ibid., *50–51, 53–55, 180–181, 194.*

[7] *Brown,* Middle-Class Democracy, *Chap. IV.*

as the story of the people who went to, and lived in, America. It has been developed as the history of liberty. Innumerable books carry in their titles the message that colonial development was a progress toward liberty; since the Revolution, it has sometimes been possible to discern in accounts of American history a certain messianic quality, which some have felt to have been reflected periodically in American diplomacy. History written in this way frequently finds itself obliged to ask how a man, or a movement, stands in relation to the particular values for which American history is responsible. A recent study of Alexander Hamilton's place in the origins of political parties, for example, speaks of the need to determine Hamilton's "rightful place in our history."[8] It becomes important, not just to write a man's biography or to assess his contribution, but to place him correctly on the eternal curve upon which American political performances seem to be graded.

The writing of history thus becomes a matter, not only of finding out what actually happened, but of judging the past. It is a process that cuts both ways. For earlier generations of Americans were keenly—almost disconcertingly—aware of the example they were setting for their descendants. (There is a town meeting entry in Massachusetts, in 1766, which calls the attention of future generations to the sacrifices the townsmen were making for their liberties.[9]) They knew that they would be judged. They were not only building institutions, they were setting standards, for the future. This can become a nerve-racking business. As has been remarked in a different connection (by a writer in the *Times Literary Supplement*) the past and the present seem to watch each other warily as from opposite boxes at the opera, each suspecting the other of being about to commit a *faux pas*.[10]

The two great instruments of American nationhood were the Revolution, with its banner, the Declaration of Independence, and the Constitution. Baptism and confirmation. It would be hard to imagine a more important commitment, not only for the interpretation of the American experience, but one might almost say for the emotional stability of the interpreter, than to place his own values in their proper relation to these events, or if that cannot be done, then to place these events in their proper relation to his values.

Accordingly, historians have brought the problem of values firmly into their assessment of history. They ask, "How democratic was early American society?" And they do not hesitate to reply, if their findings tell them so, that it was not democratic enough. Or, which is still more confusing, that it was struggling forward toward a fuller ideal of democracy. Accounts of this period repeatedly explain that such features of government as property qualifications for the suffrage and political office were still regarded as necessary at that time. "Still." These people had the right instincts; they were coming on nicely; but, unlike ourselves, they had not yet arrived.

There thus develops a tendency to adopt a completely anachronistic note of apology for the in-

---

[8] *Joseph E. Charles*, "*Hamilton and Washington*," William and Mary Quarterly, XII (*Apr., 1955*), *226. A further example in connection with Hamilton, whose career provokes this kind of judgment, is found in the title of Louis M. Hacker's* Alexander Hamilton in the American Tradition (*New York, 1957*).

[9] *Lucius R. Paige*, A History of Cambridge, Massachusetts, 1630–1877 (*New York, 1883*), *137.*

[10] "*Imaginative Historians: Telling the News about the Past,*" Times Literary Supplement, Special Supplement on The American Imagination, *Nov. 6, 1959.*

sufficiency of democratic principles in early American institutions.[11]

I would like here to anticipate the objection that I am advocating that moral judgments should be taken out of historical writing. Neither do I deny that major developments can and ought to be traced to their minor origins. Moral judgments about the past are not necessarily anachronistic. It is not, I think, unhistorical to believe that some of the acts of treachery and cruelty or of violent aggression which comprise so great a proportion of recorded human activity were morally wrong, or even to maintain that they influenced the course of events for the worse. But when judgments of moral value are applied to complex social systems, they expose the judge to a peculiar danger of self-deception, perhaps even of self-incrimination. The historian must not only be careful, he must also be highly self-critical, when he embarks on assessments of the moral shortcomings of the past.

The reading of values into historical analysis is particularly liable to deception when the values of the present are themselves made the basis for the selection of materials, which are then judged in the light of the values in question. This may happen when the importance of different institutions or opinions is estimated on the basis of our own opinion of the rôle they ought to have played in their own time.

Without doubt there is a place for such judgments. There is a place for criticism of the Hanoverian House of Commons—rather a large place. But when we discuss that body our task is not

that of apologizing for the fact that the bright light of nineteenth-century democracy had not yet broken on such persons as Pitt or Burke or Shelburne or Fox. Our problem, as I understand it, is that of reconstructing the inner nature of political society in their age and of asking how far Parliament answered the needs of that society, and how far it did not. And that is a matter of what history was actually about, not what it ought to have been about. The historian has a responsibility to the past, but it is not that of deciding within what limits he can recommend it to the approbation of his readers.

The American Revolution was certainly a war for self-determination. But self-determination and democracy are not interchangeable terms, though they can be confused with a facility that has not been without its significance in American diplomacy. A society need not be democratic in order to achieve a high degree of internal unity when fighting for self-determination. Again, a measure of democracy, or a wider diffusion of political power, may well be brought about as an outcome of such a struggle. Such a development was in fact one of the most important consequences of the American Revolution.

It must be acknowledged that the sources of colonial history supply an impressive quantity of material that can be marshaled against my own views of this subject, though not enough as yet to weaken my conviction of the validity of historical evidence.

Much evidence of this sort comes from New England, and Massachusetts is rich in examples. In 1768 General Thomas Gage wrote to Viscount Hillsborough, "from what has been said, your lordship will conclude, that there is no government in Boston, there is in truth, very little at present, and the constitution of the province leans so much to democracy, that the governor has not

---

[11] *Even Brown does so. In pointing out how few men were disfranchised in Massachusetts, he significantly remarks, "We cannot condone the practice of excluding those few," though he rightly adds that it makes a tremendous difference whether they were 95 per cent or 5 per cent. Brown,* Middle-Class Democracy, *402.*

the power to remedy the disorders which happen in it."[12] The next year Sir Francis Bernard wrote to Viscount Barrington,

> . . . for these 4 years past so uniform a system for bringing all power into the hands of the people has been prosecuted without interruption and with such success that all fear, reverence, respect and awe which before formed a tolerable balance against the power of the people, are annihilated, and the artificial weights being removed, the royal scale mounts up and kicks the beam. . . . It would be better that Mass. Bay should be a complete republic like Connecticut than to remain with so few ingredients of royalty as shall be insufficient to maintain the real royal character.[13]

In 1766 Thomas Hutchinson reported: "In the town of Boston a plebeian party always has and I fear always will command and for some months past they have governed the province."[14] Describing elections in 1772, Hutchinson told Hillsborough, "By the constitution forty pounds sterl.—which they say may be in clothes household furniture or any sort of property is a qualification and even into that there is scarce ever any inquiry and anything with the appearance of a man is admitted without scrutiny."[15]

The franchise was certainly broad. Brown has shown that in many towns as many as 80 per cent of the adult male population, in some more than 90 per cent, were qualified by their property to vote in provincial elections.[16] Three towns appear in the nineties, three in the fifties, the rest in between. These findings tend to confirm and strengthen the impression that prevailed among contemporaries, that Massachusetts was a hotbed of "democratical" or "levelling" principles: the more so after the Boston junta got control of the General Court.

These expressions raise two issues, one of definition, the other of interpretation.

The point of definition first: when the indignant officers of government described these provinces as "democratical," they were of course not talking about representative government with universal suffrage. They shared not only with their correspondents, but in the last analysis even with their political opponents, the assumption that the constitutions of the colonies, like that of Britain, were made up of mixed elements; they were mixed constitutions, in which the commons were represented in the assembly or commons house. In each constitution there were different orders, and the justification, the *raison d'etre*, of such a constitution was that it gave security to each. When they said that the government was becoming "too democratical" or "leaned towards democracy" they meant that the popular element was too weighty for the proper balance of a mixed constitution. They used these expressions as terms of abuse. Not that that matters: we may be impressed by their indignation, but we are not obliged to share it. What is more important to the historian is that the leaders of these movements which took control of the assemblies were in general prepared to accept the same set of definitions.

This they demonstrated when they came to establish new constitutions. The theory of mixed government was maintained with as little adultera-

12 Correspondence of General Thomas Gage . . . , *ed. Clarence E. Carter (2 vols., New Haven, Conn., 1931, 1933), I, 205.*

13 *Quoted by R. V. Harlow,* History of Legislative Methods before 1825 (*New Haven, Conn., 1917), 39–40.*

14 *Brown,* Middle-Class Democracy, *57.*

15 Ibid., *291.*

16 Ibid., *50.*

tion as possible. The difference they had to face was that all the "orders" now drew their position in the government from some form of popular representation. Most of the new constitutions represented the adaptation of institutions which undeniably received their authority from the people, an authority conceived, if not in liberty, then certainly in a revolutionary situation, to the traditional and equally important theory of balanced government.

This does not dispose of the second point, that of interpretation. Suppose that, in this form of mixed government, the "democratical" arm actually gathers up a preponderance of political power. This, after all, was what happened in the Revolution and had been happening long before. Does this give us a democracy? It is a question of crucial importance and one to which one school of thought returns an uncritically affirmative answer. Much of the power and internal influence within each colony was indeed concentrated in its assembly. This concentration reflected, or rather represented, the distribution of power and influence in the colony in general. If the domestic distribution of power tends toward oligarchy rather than democracy—to use the language of the time—then the power of that oligarchy will be exercised in, and through, the assembly itself: just as in the House of Commons. A difference of degree, not of kind. And in fact this most significant aspect of the domestic situation in the colonies applied with hardly less force in leveling Boston than in high-toned Virginia.

In Virginia one feels that an immigrant from England would at once have been at home.[17] There were many instances of hotly contested elections, of treating and corruption, of sharp practice by sheriffs. It would not be difficult, however, to adduce evidence of democratic tendencies in Virginia elections. Especially in the spring elec-

tions of 1776 there were many signs that the freeholders were taking their choice seriously, and several distinguished gentlemen were either turned out of their seats or given a nasty fright. But it is an unmistakable feature of Virginia elections that although the freeholders participated often quite fully, the contests were almost invariably between members of the gentry. To seek election to the House of Burgesses was to stake a distinct claim to social rank. Virginia elections were of course conducted viva voce under the friendly supervision of the local magnates. The comparatively broad base of politics in Virginia makes it all the more instructive to look into the real concentration of political power. There were two main areas: the House of Burgesses and the county courts (not taking account of the council and governor).

Effective power in the House of Burgesses was concentrated in a few hands. The house began to use the committee system in the late seventeenth century and had brought it to a high efficiency well before the middle of the eighteenth.[18] The famous Virginia ruling families of this era always occupied a large share of the key positions, enough to ensure their own domination. Before the Revolution, of some hundred members who regularly attended the house, only about twenty took an active part in proceedings. Three families, the Robinsons, the Randolphs, and the Lees, provided most of the leaders. A very recent study shows that of 630 members between 1720 and

[17] *Charles S. Sydnor*, Gentlemen Freeholders (*Chapel Hill, N. C., 1952*); *David J. Mays*, Edmund Pendleton, 1721–1803 (*2 vols., Cambridge, Mass., 1952*); *J. R. Pole*, "*Representation and Authority in Virginia from the Revolution to Reform*," Journal of Southern History, *XXIV* (*Feb., 1958*), *16–50*.

[18] *Harlow*, Legislative Methods, *10–11*.

1776, only 110 belonged throughout the period to the "select few who dominated the proceedings of the house."[19]

These men, many of whom were linked by ties of family, had the characteristics of a strong social and political elite. They were large landowners and generally were substantial slaveowners. Some were merchants. A few, such as Edmund Pendleton, had arrived by intellectual ability and hard work combined with legal training. But Pendleton had the patronage of a great family. All those with ambition were land speculators. This gave them an interest in western development, an interest which no doubt extended to the policy of making western areas attractive to the prospective settler. Probably for this reason they wanted to extend the suffrage, which they twice tried to do in the 1760's by reducing the amount of uncleared land required as a qualification. The crown disallowed these acts, though on other grounds. This reform was completed in the first election law after the Revolution. Despite the famous reforms pressed through by Jefferson, no concessions were made on matters of fundamental importance. It is a striking tribute to the tremendous security of their hold on the country that in the new state constitution there was no provision for special qualifications for membership in the legislature. The qualifications of voters and of representatives for the time being remained as before. It is a silent piece of evidence, possibly, but one that speaks loudly of their eminent self-confidence.

Life in the counties was dominated by the county courts, which touched the interests of the common people far more closely than did the remote and occasional meetings of the legislature.

19 Jack P. Greene, *"Foundations of Political Power in the Virginia House of Burgesses, 1720–1766,"* William and Mary Quarterly, *XVI (Oct., 1959), 485–506; quotation from p. 485.*

The courts, which knew little of any doctrine of separation of powers, exercised all the main functions of both legislative and judicial administration. These included tax assessment, granting licenses, supervising highways, and authorizing constructions. They had nothing elective in their nature. Membership was by co-option. The courts made the important county nominations for confirmation by the governor. And the county courts were made up of the leading men of the county, representing at the local level the material of which the House of Burgesses was composed at the central. They seem on the whole to have worked well enough. And it is likely that if they had in fact been elected by the freeholders, their membership would have been about the same. Assuredly they were not tyrannical; equally certainly they were not democratic. They were a good example of what is usually meant by oligarchy.

What happened in the American Revolution in Virginia was that the policies of the British government clashed with the interests of this ambitious, proud, self-assured, and highly competent provincial government. In arguing its case, both to the British authorities and to its own people, this government appealed to the principles on which it claimed to be founded, which were philosophically the same and historically comparable to those of Parliament itself. For historical reasons, the Virginia Whigs were somewhat closer to the radical, or popular side, of the Whig spectrum. But in Virginia as in other provinces, it was the principles generally understood as Whig principles that were at stake, and it was these principles which were affirmed and re-established in the new set of domestic state constitutions.

From time to time, as the war went on, the upper classes felt tremors of alarm in which they revealed something of their relationship to the common people.

Thus John Augustine Washington, writing to Richard Henry Lee of the difficulties of getting the militia to obey a marching order, and the secret proceedings by which they bound themselves to stand by each other in refusing to leave the state, remarked: "I fear we have among us some designing dangerous characters who misrepresent to ignorant, uninformed people, the situation of our affairs and the nature of the contest, making them believe it is a war produced by the wantonness of the gentlemen, and that the poor are very little, if any interested."[20] Another of Lee's correspondents, on the need to arouse popular support, wrote: "The spark of liberty is not yet extinct among our people, and if properly fanned by the Gentlemen of Influence will, I make no doubt, burst out again into a flame."[21]

These hints, these references which illuminate the assumptions of political life, often reveal more than formal expositions of doctrine, or even the official records.

These "Gentlemen of Influence," the ruling class, were prepared to extend the suffrage when it suited their interest to do so in the 1760's, but refused to take the same step when it would have opened the question of political power, a generation later. The first demands for reform, in both suffrage and distribution of representation, began to appear about the turn of the century. And these demands were met with a prolonged and bitter resistance, leading only to reluctant and unsatisfactory concessions even in the famous constitutional convention of 1829–1830. The struggle was carried on until a more substantial extension of political rights was at last achieved in 1850. The forces that Virginia's political leadership so long and so determinedly held at bay can, I think,

without exaggeration, be called the forces of democracy.

It is a very familiar fact about the early state constitutions that they were generally conservative in character, in that they retained much of the principles and structure of the governments of the colonies. The colonies were already self-governing in the main, and this self-government was administered by representative institutions. When one's attention is confined to these institutions, it can soon become rather difficult to see in what respect they were not, in a common-sense use of the word, democratic. After all, they were accessible to the people, they received petitions and redressed grievances, they possessed the inestimable right of free speech, and in the battles they fought, they were often engaged, in the interest of the colonies, against royal governors.

All these features were not merely consistent with, they were the formative elements of, the great Whig tradition of Parliament since the Glorious Revolution and before. They were, like so many other things, derivable from Locke. With certain exceptions, such as the difficulty of the Regulator rising in North Carolina, it would be true that colonial assemblies lay closer to the people than did the British House of Commons. For one thing, there were far more representatives per head of population in the colonies than in Britain. Parliament had 1 member to every 14,300 persons, the colonies approximately 1 to every 1,200.[22] And this meant that legislative methods and principles were more likely to be familiar to the ordinary colonist. To put it in contemporary terms, the colonies, on the whole, had a great many more constituencies like Middlesex or Westminster, except that they were mostly country and not town constituencies. It might be

[20] Quoted in Pole, "Representation and Authority in Virginia," 28.
[21] Ibid., 28–29.

[22] Mary P. Clarke, Parliamentary Privilege in the American Colonies (*New Haven, Conn., 1943*), 268.

very close to the mark to press the analogy further and say that they had a great many constituencies that very much resembled Yorkshire—the Yorkshire of Sir George Savile, the Yorkshire of Christopher Wyvill.

What does seem striking about these in many ways highly representative colonial assemblies is, as I suggested earlier, the determination and sureness of touch with which they assumed the characteristics of Parliament. These were characteristics originally designed to secure the liberty of the people's representatives: free speech in debate, freedom of members from arrest or molestation, and freedom of the assembly from abuse by breach of privilege. But there were all too many occasions on which it must have seemed that these safeguards were designed to secure the assemblies against abuse, in the form of free speech and fair comment, by their own constituents.[23]

The colonial assemblies became extraordinarily sensitive to the question of privilege. Strictly from an institutional viewpoint, they were deliberately building on the tradition of Parliament. But institutional studies always seem to tempt the historian to arrive at his answer the short way, by examining structure, without asking questions about development.

Much research has recently been done on what Palmer calls the "constituted bodies"[24] which held a strong and growing position in the Western world in the eighteenth century. They were numerous and differed greatly, one from another, and from one century to another—first of all the variety of political or judicial bodies: diets, estates, assemblies, parlements; then the professional associations or guilds; as well as religious orders, and those of the nobilities of Europe.

There seems strong reason for holding that the colonial assemblies were behaving in close conformity with the other bodies of this general type. At their best they were closer to local interests, but no less characteristically, they displayed a remarkable diligence in the adoption of parliamentary abuses. They would send their messengers far into the outlying country to bring to the bar of the house some individual who was to be humbled for having committed a breach of privilege, which very often meant some private action affecting the dignity or even the property of the sitting member. Criticism of the assemblies, either verbal or written, was a risky business. The freedom of the colonial press was very largely at the mercy of the assembly's sense of its own dignity, so much so that a recent investigator doubts whether the famous Zenger case,[25] which is supposed to have done so much toward the establishment of freedom of the press in the colonies, really had any general significance or immediate consequences. The fact is that restrictions on free press comment on assembly actions were not the policy of the crown but the policy of the assemblies.

Expulsions from colonial assemblies were frequent. And in case a parallel with the action of the Commons in the Wilkes case were needed to round off the picture, we may remark that colonial assemblies repeatedly excluded members who had been lawfully elected by their constituents.[26]

There was another feature in which these assemblies showed their affinity with the outlook of their times. In spite of the amount of choice

[23] Ibid., *127.*
[24] *Palmer,* Democratic Revolution, *27–44.*

[25] *Leonard W. Levy, "Did the Zenger Case Really Matter? Freedom of the Press in Colonial New York,"* William and Mary Quarterly, *XVII (Jan., 1960), 35–50.*
[26] *Clarke,* Parliamentary Privilege, *194–196.*

open to the electors, there was a growing tendency for public office, both the elective and the appointive kinds, to become hereditary. It was of course very pronounced in Europe; it is surely no less significant when we see it at work in America. The same family names occur, from generation to generation, in similar positions. And this was no less true in New England than in Virginia or South Carolina or Maryland.

If this was democracy, it was a democracy that wore its cockade firmly pinned into its periwig.

One of the most interesting consequences of the revolutionary situation was that it demanded of political leaders a declaration of their principles. Thus we get the famous Virginia Bill of Rights, the work of George Mason; the Declaration of Rights attached to the 1780 constitution of Massachusetts; and the constitutions themselves, with all that they reveal or imply of political ideas; and in the case of Massachusetts we can go even further, for there survive also, in the archives of that state in Boston, the returns of the town meetings which debated that constitution and in many cases recorded their vote, clause by clause.

This constitution, in fact, was submitted to the ratification of what counted then as the whole people—all the adult males in the state. The constitutional convention had been elected on the same basis. The constitution which was framed on this impressive foundation of popular sovereignty was certainly not a democratic instrument. It was an articulate, indeed a refined expression, of the Whig view of government—of government-in-society—as applied to the existing conditions in Massachusetts, and as interpreted by John Adams.

The property qualifications for the suffrage were, in round figures, about what they had been under the charter. In practice they proved to have very little effect by way of restricting participation in elections. The introduction of decidedly

steeper qualifications for membership in the assembly meant that that body would be composed of the owners of the common, upward of one-hundred-acre family farm, and their mercantile equivalent. The pyramid narrowed again to the senate, and came to a point in the position of governor. These restrictions were new, but gave little offense to the general sense of political propriety; the suffrage qualifications were objected to in about one-fifth of the recorded town meeting debates.[27]

The house and senate represented different types of constituency, and the difference is one of the clues to institutional thought. The house represented the persons of the electorate living in corporate towns, which were entitled to representation according to a numerical scale of population; very small communities were excluded. The town remained the basic unit of representation. The senate, on the other hand, represented the property of the state arranged in districts corresponding to the counties; the number of members to which each county was entitled depended, not on population, but on the taxes it had paid into the state treasury. The result in distribution of representatives in the senate was not actually much different from the apportionment that would have been obtained by population,[28]

[27] *The constitution of 1780 is discussed in:* S. E. Morison, *"The Struggle over the Adoption of the Constitution of Massachusetts, 1780," Massachusetts Historical Society* Proceedings, *L (Boston, 1916–17), 353–412;* Robert J. Taylor, Western Massachusetts in the Revolution (*Providence, R. I., 1954); J. R. Pole, "Suffrage and Representation in Massachusetts: A Statistical Note," William and Mary Quarterly, XIV (Oct., 1957), 560–592. The town meeting records are in Volumes CCLXXVI and CCLXXVII in the Massachusetts Department of Archives, the State House, Boston.*

[28] *As noted by Palmer,* Democratic Revolution, *226.*

but the intention was there, and the plan conformed to the principles of political order by which the delegates were guided.[29]

New York, which established popular election of its governor, and North Carolina took the matter further by differentiating between the qualifications of voters for the senate and the house of representatives.

How then are we to explain the paradox of popular consent to a scheme of government which systematically excluded the common people from the more responsible positions of political power? The historian who wishes to adopt the word "democracy" as a definition must first satisfy himself that it can be applied to a carefully ordered hierarchy, under the aegis of which power and authority are related to a conscientiously designed scale of social and economic rank, both actual and prospective; if this test fails him, then he must ask himself whether he can call the system a democracy, on the ground that it was a form of government established with the consent of the governed. Those who wish to argue this line have the advantage of finding much serviceable material that can be adopted without the rigors, or the risks, of a historically-minded analysis. It is possible to concentrate all attention on those aspects of the system which we would now call democratic, to assert that these elements exerted a controlling influence and that all the rest was a sort of obsolescent window dressing. Such a view may not be particularly subtle, but on the other hand it is not absolute nonsense. It is, perhaps, the easiest view to arrive at through an extensive reading of local economic records in the light of a clear, but vastly simplified, interpretation of the political process; but it leaves unfulfilled the rather more complex task of perceiving the democratic elements in their proper place within a system conceived in another age, under a different inspiration.

In the Whig philosophy of government the basic principle, preceding representative institutions, is the compact. The people already owned their property by natural right, and they are supposed to have come into the compact quite voluntarily to secure protection both to their property and to their persons. For these purposes government was formed. What was done in Massachusetts seems to have been a solemn attempt to reenact the original compact in the new making of the state. It was even possible to deploy the theory of compact as an excuse for seizing other people's property: in 1782 the legislature of Virginia resolved that the estates of British subjects might be confiscated because they had not been parties to the original contract of the people of that state.[30] And the Virginia constitution had not even been submitted for popular ratification!

Massachusetts and New Hampshire, in fact, were the only states in which popular ratification was sought for the revolutionary constitution. In a society whose moral cohesion was supplied by the sense of deference and dignity, it was possible for the broad mass of the people to consent to a scheme of government in which their own share would be limited. Some of them of course expected to graduate to the higher levels; government was not controlled by inherited rank.

This factor—the expectation of advancement—is an important feature of the American expe-

[29] *It may be permissible to mention that Brown, in his study of this constitution, omits to note this provision for tax payment as the basis of county representation. In itself, this may seem a small clue, but the thread leads into another world of political ideas than that of modern democracy. Brown,* Middle-Class Democracy, *393.*

[30] *Edmund Randolph to James Madison, Richmond, Dec. 27, 1782, Madison Papers, Manuscript Division, Library of Congress.*

rience; it is one which is often used to excuse the injustice of exclusion from government by economic status. The *Address* that the Massachusetts convention delegates drew up in 1780 to expound the principles on which they had acted makes the point that most of those excluded by the suffrage qualification could expect to rise sufficiently in their own property to reach the level of voters. The exclusion of the artisan and laborer from the assembly was, however, more likely to prove permanent.

It would be a mistake to suppose that the body of citizens included in the electoral system at one level or another, or expecting to gain their inclusion, was really the whole body. There are always farm laborers, journeymen, migrant workers, and one may suspect that the numbers excluded by law were larger than the terms of the *Address* suggest. But even if we are disposed to accept the high level of popular participation in elections as being weighty enough to determine our definitions, it is surely wise to pause even over the legal disfranchisement of one man in every four or five, and in some towns one man in three.

This constitutional scheme was derived from a mixture of experience, theory, and intention. It is the intention for the future which seems to call for scrutiny when we attempt a satisfactory definition of these institutions.

In the first place there is the deliberate disfranchisement of the small, perhaps the unfortunate, minority; the fact that the number is small is not more significant than that the exclusion is deliberate. In the second place, there is the installation of orders of government corresponding to orders of society; the fact that the lines are imprecise and that the results are uncertain is again not more significant than that the scale is deliberate.

It was a rule of Whig ideology that participation in matters of government was the legitimate concern only of those who possessed what was commonly called "a stake in society." In concrete terms this stake in society was one's property, for the protection of which, government had been originally formed. As a means to that protection, he was entitled, under a government so formed, to a voice: to some form of representation.

But there is a further problem. To put it briefly, what is to happen if the expected general economic advancement does not take place? Accumulations of wealth were far from being unknown; what if the further accumulation of wealth and the advance of the economy were to leave an ever-increasing residue of the population outside the political limits set by these constitutions? It is unlikely that their framers were ignorant of such possibilities. The growth of Sheffield, Manchester, and Leeds was not unknown; London was not easy to overlook; the Americans had close ties with Liverpool and Bristol. The fact is that a future town proletariat would be specifically excluded by the arrangements that were being made.

The historian who insists that this system was a model of democracy may find that the advance of the economy, a tendency already affecting America in many ways, leaves him holding a very undemocratic-looking baby. In the Philadelphia Convention, James Madison bluntly predicted that in future times "the great majority" would be "not only without landed, but any other sort of, property"—a state in which they would either combine, to the peril of property and liberty, or become the tools of opulence and ambition, leading to "equal danger on the other side."[31] The objection became common when state constitutions were under reform. Opponents of suffrage extension in the constitutions of the 1820's, who included many of the recognized leaders of political

[31] Records of the Federal Convention, *ed. Max Farrand (4 vols., New Haven, Conn., 1927), II, 203–204.*

life, had a better right than their opponents to claim to be the legitimate heirs of the Whig constitution makers of the revolutionary era.

The constitution of the two legislative houses was based on the view that society was formed for the protection of persons and their property and that these two elements required separate protection and separate representation. This was one of the leading political commonplaces of the day. It is implied by Montesquieu; Jefferson accepts it in his *Notes on Virginia;* Madison held the view throughout his career; Hamilton treated it as a point of common agreement.[32] It is worth adding that it lay behind the original conception of the United States Senate in the form envisaged by the Virginia plan, a form which was subverted when the Senate became the representative chamber of the states. The whole subject was, of course, familiar to John Adams, who went on thinking about it long after he had drawn up a draft for the constitution of his state in 1780.

John Adams, as he himself anticipated, has been a much-misunderstood man. But it is important that we should get him right. No American was more loyal to Whig principles, and none was more deeply read in political ideas.

Adams is often said to have been an admirer of aristocracy and of monarchy. His admiration for the British constitution was easy to treat as an admission of unrepublican principles. But he really believed in the British constitution as it ought to have been, and he prudently averted his gaze from what it was in his own day. If Adams had lived in England in the 1780's, he would have been an associator in Wyvill's parliamentary reform movement, rather than a Foxite Whig.

Adams was profoundly impressed with the advantages enjoyed by birth, wealth, superior education, and natural merit, and the tendency for these advantages to become an inherited perquisite of the families that enjoyed them. He was equally clear about the corrupting influence of this sort of power. For this reason he wanted to segregate the aristocracy in an upper chamber, a process which he called "a kind of ostracism." The strong executive in which he believed was intended as a check not on the commons so much as on the aristocracy.

He developed this view of the function of the upper chamber in his *Defence of the Constitutions of the United States* (1786–1787). It is not wholly consistent with the view given in the *Address,*[33] attached to the draft Massachusetts constitution of 1780, in which the position taken was that persons and property require separate protection in different houses. This view is itself a reflection of more than one tradition. It reflects the traditional structure of the legislature—council and assembly, lords and commons; it reflects also the idea that the state is actually composed of different orders (a word of which John Adams was fond) and that these orders have in their own right specific interests which are entitled to specific recognition. They are entitled to it because it is the purpose of the state to secure and protect them: that in fact was why the state was supposed to have come into existence.

Adams once, in later years, wrote to Jefferson: "Your *aristoi* are the most difficult animals to manage in the whole theory and practice of

[32] *Charles de Secondat, Baron de Montesquieu,* Oeuvres complètes (*Paris, 1838*), De l'esprit des lois, *267; James Madison,* Writings, *ed. Gaillard Hunt (9 vols., New York, 1910), V, 287; Hamilton's speech in* Debates and Proceedings of Convention of New York, at Poughkeepsie 1788 (*Poughkeepsie, N. Y., 1905*), 26.

[33] *This, however, was the work of Samuel Adams. (William V. Wells,* The Life and Public Services of Samuel Adams [*3 vols., Boston, 1865*], III, 89–97.)

government. They will not suffer themselves to be governed."[34] Yet in spite of his intense distrust of them, I think his attitude was two sided. I find it difficult to read his account of the role played in society by the aristocracy without feeling that there was to him, as there is to many others, something peculiarly distinguished and attractive about these higher circles, elevated by nature and sustained by society above the ordinary run of men. And had he not, after all, sons for whom he had some hopes? Some hopes, perhaps, for the family of Adams?

Governor Bernard had lamented the disappearance from prerevolutionary Massachusetts of those balancing factors, "Fear, reverence, respect and awe." Disappearance at least toward the royal authority. They did not disappear so easily from domestic life. There is nothing which reveals these deferential attitudes more fully than in respect to birth and family, given on trust. Adams therefore tells us much, not only of himself but of his times, when he draws attention to inequality of birth:

> Let no man be surprised that this species of inequality is introduced here. Let the page in history be quoted, where any nation, ancient or modern, civilized or savage, is mentioned, among whom no difference was made, between the citizens, on account of their extraction. The truth is, that more influence is allowed to this advantage in free republics than in despotic governments, or would be allowed to it in simple monarchies, if severe laws had not been made from age to age to secure it. The children of illustrious families have generally greater advantages of education, and earlier opportunities to be acquainted with public characters, and informed of public affairs, than those of meaner ones, or even than those in middle life; and what is more than all, a habitual national veneration for their names, and the characters of their ancestors, described in history, or coming down by tradition, removes them farther from vulgar jealousy and popular envy, and secures them in some degree the favour, the affection, the respect of the public. Will any man pretend that the name of Andros, and that of Winthrop, are heard with the same sensations in any village of New England? Is not gratitude the sentiment that attends the latter? And disgust the feeling excited by the former? In the Massachusetts, then, there are persons descended from some of their ancient governors, counsellors, judges, whose fathers, grandfathers, and great-grandfathers, are mentioned in history with applause as benefactors to the country, while there are others who have no such advantage. May we go a step further,— Know thyself, is as useful a precept to nations as to men. Go into every village in New England, and you will find that the office of justice of the peace, and even the place of representative, which has ever depended only on the freest election of the people, have generally descended from generation to generation, in three or four families at most.[35]

Deference: it does not seem, in retrospect, a very secure cement to the union of social orders. Yet to those who live under its sway it can be almost irresistible.

It was beginning to weaken, no doubt, in Adams' own political lifetime. "The distinction of classes," Washington said to Brissot de Warville in 1788, "begins to disappear." But not easily, not all at once, not without a struggle.

It was this which collapsed in ruins in the upheaval of Jacksonian democracy. And that, perhaps, is why the election of so ambiguous a leader was accompanied by such an amazing uproar.

[34] *Quoted in Palmer*, Democratic Revolution, *273, n. 52.*

[35] *John Adams*, Defence of the Constitutions of the United States . . . *(3 vols., Philadelphia, 1797), I, 110–11.*

THE PERSPECTIVES OF 1776

*Louis Hartz**

When Tocqueville wrote that the "great advantage" of the American lay in the fact that he did not have "to endure a democratic revolution,"[1] he advanced what was surely one of his most fundamental insights into American life. However, while many of his observations have been remembered but not followed up, this one has scarcely even been remembered. Perhaps it is because, fearing revolution in the present, we like to think of it in the past, and we are reluctant to concede that its romance has been missing from our lives. Perhaps it is because the plain evidence of the American revolution of 1776, especially the evidence of its social impact that our newer historians have collected, has made

the comment of Tocqueville seem thoroughly enigmatic. But in the last analysis, of course, the question of its validity is a question of perspective. Tocqueville was writing with the great revolutions of Europe in mind, and from that point of view the outstanding thing about the American effort of 1776 was bound to be, not the freedom to which it led, but the established feudal structure it did not have to destroy. He was writing too, as no French liberal of the nineteenth century could fail to write, with the shattered hopes of the Enlightenment in mind. The American revolution had been one of the greatest of them all, a precedent constantly appealed to in 1793. In the age of Tocqueville there was ground enough for reconsidering the American image that the Jacobins had cherished.

Even in the glorious days of the eighteenth

---

[1] *Alexis de Tocqueville*, Democracy in America, *ed. F. Bowen (Boston, 1873), Vol. 2, p. 123.*

LOUIS HARTZ (1919–   ) is a Professor of Government at Harvard University. His publications include The Liberal Tradition in America *(1955) and* The Founding of New Societies *(1964). This selection is from* The Liberal Tradition in America © *1955, by Louis Hartz. Reprinted by permission of Harcourt, Brace & World, Inc. It also appeared in* American Political Science Review, *Vol. 46, No. 2 (June, 1952), 321–342.*

century, when America suddenly became the revolutionary symbol of Western liberalism, it had not been easy to hide the free society with which it started. As a matter of fact, the liberals of Europe had themselves romanticized its social freedom, which put them in a rather odd position; for if Raynal was right in 1772, how could Condorcet be right in 1776? If America was from the beginning a kind of idyllic state of nature, how could it suddenly become a brilliant example of social emancipation? Two consolations were being extracted from a situation which could at best yield only one. But the mood of the Americans themselves, as they watched the excitement of Condorcet seize the Old World, is also very revealing. They did not respond in kind. They did not try to shatter the social structure of Europe in order to usher in a tenth and final epoch in the history of man. Delighted as they were with the support that they received, they remained, with the exception of a few men like Paine and Barlow, curiously untouched by the crusading intensity we find in the French and the Russians at a later time. Warren G. Harding, arguing against the League of Nations, was able to point back at them and say, "Mark you, they were not reforming the world."[2] And James Fenimore Cooper, a keener mind than Harding, generalized their behavior into a comment about America that America is only now beginning to understand: "We are not a nation much addicted to the desire of proselytizing."[3]

There were, no doubt, several reasons for this. But clearly one of the most significant is the sense that the Americans had themselves of the liberal history out of which they came. In the midst of the Stamp Act struggle, young John Adams con-

gratulated his colonial ancestors for turning their backs on Europe's class-ridden corporate society, for rejecting the "canon and feudal law."[4] The pervasiveness of Adams's sentiment in American thought has often been discussed, but what is easily overlooked is the subtle way in which it corroded the spirit of the world crusader. For this was a pride of inheritance, not a pride of achievement; and instead of being a message of hope for Europe, it came close to being a damning indictment of it. It saturated the American sense of mission, not with a Christian universalism, but with a curiously Hebraic kind of separatism. The two themes fought one another in the cosmopolitan mind of Jefferson, dividing him between a love of Europe and fear of its "contamination"; but in the case of men like Adams and Gouverneur Morris, the second theme easily triumphed over the first. By the time the crusty Adams had gotten through talking to politicians abroad, he had buried the Enlightenment concept of an oppressed humanity so completely beneath the national concept of a New World that he was ready to predict a great and ultimate struggle between America's youth and Europe's decadence. As for Morris, our official ambassador to France in 1789, he simply inverted the task of the Comintern agent. Instead of urging the French on to duplicate the American experience, he badgered them by pointing out that they could never succeed in doing so. "They want an American constitution" he wrote contemptuously, "without realizing they have no Americans to uphold it."[5]

Thus the fact that the Americans did not have to endure a "democratic revolution" deeply con-

---

[2] Rededicating America (*Indianapolis, 1920*), p. 137.

[3] *In J. L. Blau (ed.)*, Social Theories of Jacksonian Democracy (*New York, 1947*), p. 58.

[4] *"Dissertation on the Canon and Feudal Law," in John Adams,* Works, *ed. C. F. Adams (Boston, 1856), Vol. iii, pp. 447–465.*

[5] *Quoted in D. Walther,* Gouverneur Morris (*New York and London, 1934*), p. 76.

ditioned their outlook on people elsewhere who did; and by helping to thwart the crusading spirit in them, it gave to the wild enthusiasms of Europe an appearance not only of analytic error but of unrequited love. Symbols of a world revolution, the Americans were not in truth world revolutionaries. There is no use complaining about the confusions implicit in this position, as Woodrow Wilson used to complain when he said that we had "no business" permitting the French to get the wrong impression about the American revolution. On both sides the reactions that arose were well-nigh inevitable. But one cannot help wondering about something else: the satisfying use to which our folklore has been able to put the incongruity of America's revolutionary rôle. For if the "contamination" that Jefferson feared, and that found its classic expression in Washington's Farewell Address, has been a part of the American myth, so has the "round the world" significance of the shots that were fired at Concord. We have been able to dream of ourselves as emancipators of the world at the very moment that we have withdrawn from it. We have been able to see ourselves as saviours at the very moment that we have been isolationists. Here, surely, is one of the great American luxuries that the twentieth century has destroyed.

When the Americans celebrated the uniqueness of their own society, they were on the track of a personal insight of the profoundest importance. For the nonfeudal world in which they lived shaped every aspect of their social thought: it gave them a frame of mind that cannot be found anywhere else in the eighteenth century, or in the wider history of modern revolutions.

One of the first things it did was to breed a set of revolutionary thinkers in America who were human beings like Otis and Adams rather than secular prophets like Robespierre and Lenin. Despite the European flavor of a Jefferson or a Frank-

lin, the Americans refused to join in the great Enlightenment enterprise of shattering the Christian concept of sin, replacing it with an unlimited humanism, and then emerging with an earthly paradise as glittering as the heavenly one that had been destroyed. The fact that the Americans did not share the crusading spirit of the French and the Russians, as we have seen, is already some sort of confirmation of this, for that spirit was directly related to the "civil religion" of Europe and is quite unthinkable without it. Nor is it hard to see why the liberal good fortune of the Americans should have been at work in the position they held. Europe's brilliant dream of an impending millennium, like the mirage of a thirst-ridden man, was inspired in large part by the agonies it experienced. When men have already inherited the freest society in the world, and are grateful for it, their thinking is bound to be of a solider type. America has been a sober nation, but it has also been a comfortable one, and the two points are by no means unrelated.

Sam Adams, for example, rejects the hope of changing human nature: in a mood of Calvinist gloom, he traces the tyranny of England back to "passions of Men" that are fixed and timeless.[6] But surely it would be unreasonable to congratulate him for this approach without observing that he implicitly confines those passions to the political sphere—the sphere of parliaments, ministers, and stampmasters—and thus leaves a social side to man which can be invoked to hold him in check. The problem was a different one for Rousseau and Marx, who started from the view that the corruption of man was complete, as wide as the culture in which he lived, with the result that revolutions became meaningless unless they were based on the hope of changing him. Here,

6 *Samuel Adams*, Writings, *ed. F. H. Cushing (New York, 1904–1908), Vol. ii, p. 164.*

obviously, is a place where the conclusions of political thought breathe a different spirit from the assumptions on which they rest. Behind the shining optimism of Europe, there are a set of anguished grievances; behind the sad resignation of America, a set of implicit satisfactions.

One of these satisfactions, moreover, was crucially important in developing the sober temper of the American revolutionary outlook. It was the high degree of religious diversity that prevailed in colonial life. This meant that the revolution would be led in part by fierce Dissenting ministers, and their leadership destroyed the chance for a conflict to arise between the worldly pessimism of Christianity and the worldly ambitions of revolutionary thought. In Europe, especially on the Continent, where reactionary church establishments had made the Christian concept of sin and salvation into an explicit pillar of the status quo, liberals were forced to develop a political religion, as Rousseau saw, if only in answer to it. The Americans not only avoided this compulsion; they came close, indeed, to reversing it. Here, above all in New England, the clergy was so militant that it was Tories like Daniel Leonard who were reduced to blasting it as a dangerous "political engine," a situation whose irony John Adams caught when he reminded Leonard that "in all ages and countries" the church is "disposed enough" to be on the side of conservatism.[7] Thus the American liberals, instead of being forced to pull the Christian heaven down to earth, were glad to let it remain where it was. They did not need to make a religion out of the revolution because religion was already revolutionary.

Consider the case of Rev. William Gordon of Roxbury. In 1774, when all of Boston was seething with resentment over the Port Bill, Gordon opened one of his sermons by reminding his congregation that there were "more important purposes than the fate of kingdoms" or the "civil rights of human nature," to wit, the emancipation of men from the "slavery of sin and Satan" and their preparation "for an eternal blessedness." But the Sons of Liberty did not rise up against him; they accepted his remarks as perfectly reasonable. For instead of trying to drug Bostonians with a religious opiate, Gordon proceeded to urge them to prepare for open war, delivering a blast against the British that the Tories later described as a plea for "sedition, rebellion, carnage, and blood."* When Christianity is so explosive, why should even the most ardent revolutionary complain if heaven is beyond his grasp?

Of course, the Gordons and the Mayhews of America were quite unaware that their work had this significance—the indirect significance of keeping political thought down to earth. If anything impressed them in their rôle as religious figures, it was undoubtedly the crusade they were carrying forward against the "popery" of the Anglican Tories—in other words, what mattered to them was not that they were helping America to avoid the eighteenth century, but that they were helping it to duplicate the seventeenth. However, their achievement on the first count was actually far more important than their achievement on the second. The revolutionary attack on Anglicanism, with its bogy of a Bishop coming to America and its hysterical interpretation of the Quebec Act of 1774, was half trumped up and half obsolete; but

[7] *John Adams*, Works, *Vol. iv, p. 55.*

* *J. Thornton (ed.), The Pulpit of the American Revolution (Boston, 1876), pp. 196–97. The point I am making here about America in contrast to Europe is much the same point that Halevy makes about England in contrast to the Continent. We must not, of course, confuse French and English thought on this score. But the role of nonconformity in discouraging the rise of political religions was actually more marked in America than it was in England.*

the alliance of Christian pessimism with liberal thought had a deep and lasting meaning. Indeed, the very failure of the Americans to become seventeenth-century prophets like the English Presbyterians enhances this point considerably. For when we add to it the fact that they did not become latter-day prophets like the Jacobins and the Marxists, they emerge, if we wish to rank them with the great revolutionaries of modern history, as in a curious sense the most secular of them all.

Perhaps it was this secular quality that Joel Barlow was trying to describe when he declared, in a Fourth of July oration in Boston in 1778, that the "peculiar glory" of the American revolution lay in the fact that "sober reason and reflection have done the work of enthusiasm and performed the miracles of Gods."[8] In any case, there was something fateful about it. For if the messianic spirit does not arise in the course of a country's national revolution, when is it ever going to arise? The post-revolutionary age, as the experience of England, France, and even in some sense Russia shows, is usually spent trying to recuperate from its effects. The fact that the Americans remained politically sober in 1776 was, in other words, a fairly good sign that they were going to remain that way during the modern age which followed; and if we except the religiosity of the Civil War, that is exactly what happened. There have been dreamers enough in American history, a whole procession of "millennial Christians," as George Fitzhugh used to call them; but the central course of our political thought has betrayed an unconquerable pragmatism.

Sir William Ashley, discussing the origins of the "American spirit," once remarked that "as feudalism was not transplanted to the New World, there was no need for the strong arm of a central power to destroy it."[9] This is a simple statement but, like many of Ashley's simple statements, it contains a neglected truth. For Americans usually assume that their attack on political power in 1776 was determined entirely by the issues of the revolution, when as a matter of fact it was precisely because of the things they were not revolting against that they were able to carry it through. The action of England inspired the American colonists with a hatred of centralized authority; but had that action been a transplanted American feudalism, rich in the chaos of ages, then they would surely have had to dream of centralizing authority themselves.

They would, in other words, have shared the familiar agony of European liberalism—hating power and loving it too. The liberals of Europe in the eighteenth century wanted, of course, to limit power; but confronted with the heritage of an ancient corporate society, they were forever devising sharp and sovereign instruments that might be used to put it down. Thus while the Americans were attacking Dr. Johnson's theory of sovereignty, one of the most popular liberal doctrines in Europe, cherished alike by Bentham and Voltaire, was the doctrine of the enlightened despot, a kind of political deism in which a single force would rationalize the social world. While the Americans were praising the "illustrious Montesquieu" for his idea of checks and balances, that worthy was under heavy attack in France itself because he compromised the unity of power on which so many liberals relied. Even the English Whigs, men who were by no means believers in monarchical absolutism, found it impossible to go along with their eager young friends across the Atlantic. When the Americans, closing

[8] *Quoted in H. Niles (ed.),* Principles and Acts of the Revolution in America (*New York, 1876), p. 56.*

[9] Surveys Historic and Economic (*London and New York, 1900), p. 406.*

their eyes to 1688, began to lay the axe to the concept of parliamentary sovereignty, most of the Whigs fled their company at once.

A philosopher, it is true, might look askance at the theory of power the Americans developed. It was not a model of lucid exposition. The trouble lay with their treatment of sovereignty. Instead of boldly rejecting the concept, as Franklin was once on the verge of doing when he said that it made him "quite sick," they accepted the concept and tried to qualify it out of existence. The result was a chaotic series of forays and retreats in which a sovereign Parliament was limited, first by the distinction between external and internal taxation, then by the distinction between revenue and regulation, and finally by the remarkable contention that colonial legislatures were as sovereign as Parliament was. But there is a limit to how much we can criticize the Americans for shifting their ground. They were obviously feeling their way; and they could hardly be expected to know at the time of the Stamp Act what their position would be at the time of the First Continental Congress. Moreover, if they clung to the concept of sovereignty, they battered it beyond belief, and no one would confuse their version of it with the one advanced by Turgot or even by Blackstone in Europe. The meekness of the American sovereign testifies to the beating he had received. Instead of putting up a fierce and embarrassing battle against the limits of natural law and the separation of powers, as he usually did in the theories of Europe, he accepted those limits with a vast docility.

If we look at what happened to America's famous idea of judicial control when the physiocrats advanced it in France, we will get an insight into this whole matter. Who studies now the theory of legal guardianship with which La Rivière tried to bind down his rational and absolute sovereign? Who indeed remembers it? American students of the judicial power rarely go to Cartesian France to discover a brother of James Otis—and the reason is evident enough. When the physiocrats appealed to the courts, they were caught at once in a vise of criticism: either they were attacked for reviving the feudal idea of the *parlements* or they were blasted as insincere because they had originally advanced a despot to deal with the feudal problem. They had to give the idea up.[10] But in America, where the social questions of France did not exist and the absolutism they engendered was quite unthinkable, the claim of Otis in the Writs of Assistance Case, that laws against reason and the Constitution were "void" and that the "Courts must pass them into disuse," met an entirely different fate.[11] It took root, was carried forward by a series of thinkers, and blossomed ultimately into one of the most remarkable institutions in modern politics.*

The question, again, was largely a question of the free society in which the Americans lived. Nor ought we to assume that its impact on their view of political power disappeared when war and domestic upheaval finally came. Of course, there was scattered talk of the need for a "dictator," as Jefferson angrily reported in 1782;[12] and

---

[10] *Cf. M. Einaudi*, The Physiocratic Doctrine of Judicial Control (*Cambridge, Mass., 1938*).

[11] *Quoted in John Adams*, Works, *Vol. ii, p. 522.*

* *If one is primarily concerned with judicial review one must relate this interpretation to the fact, stressed throughout this book, that the moral unanimity of a liberal society nourishes a legalistic frame of mind and an acquiescence in restraints on the part of the majority. See especially pp. 103–04. These points, of course, fit together. You could not have social agreement if you had an earlier society to destroy, and if you had such a society, you would need a sharpened view of sovereign power.*

[12] *Thomas Jefferson*, Writings, *ed. P. L. Ford (New York, 1892–99), Vol. 3, p. 231.*

until new assemblies appeared in most places, committees of public safety had authoritarian power. But none of this went deep enough to shape the philosophic mood of the nation. A hero is missing from the revolutionary literature of America. He is the legislator, the classical giant who almost invariably turns up at revolutionary moments to be given authority to lay the foundations of the free society. He is not missing because the Americans were unfamiliar with images of ancient history, or because they had not read the Harringtons or the Machiavellis and Rousseaus of the modern period. Harrington, as a matter of fact, was one of their favorite writers. The legislator is missing because, in truth, the Americans had no need for his services. Much as they liked Harrington's republicanism, they did not require a Cromwell, as Harrington thought he did, to erect the foundations for it. Those foundations had already been laid by history.

The issue of history itself is deeply involved here. On this score, inevitably, the fact that the revolutionaries of 1776 had inherited the freest society in the world shaped their thinking in an intricate way. It gave them, in the first place, an appearance of outright conservatism. We know, of course, that most liberals of the eighteenth century, from Bentham to Quesnay, were bitter opponents of history, posing a sharp antithesis between nature and tradition. And it is an equally familiar fact that their adversaries, including Burke and Blackstone, sought to break down this antithesis by identifying natural law with the slow evolution of the past. The militant Americans, confronted with these two positions, actually took the second. Until Jefferson raised the banner of independence, and even in many cases after that time, they based their claims on a philosophic synthesis of Anglo-American legal history and the reason of natural law. Blackstone, the very Blackstone whom Bentham so bitterly attacked

in the very year 1776, was a rock on which they relied.

The explanation is not hard to find. The past had been good to the Americans, and they knew it. Instead of inspiring them to the fury of Bentham and Voltaire, it often produced a mystical sense of Providential guidance akin to that of Maistre—as when Rev. Samuel West, surveying the growth of America's population, anticipated victory in the revolution because "we have been prospered in a most wonderful manner."[13] The troubles they had with England did not alter this outlook. Even these, as they pointed out again and again, were of recent origin, coming after more than a century of that "salutary neglect" which Burke defended so vigorously. And in a specific sense, of course, the record of English history in the seventeenth century and the record of colonial charters from the time of the Virginia settlement provided excellent ammunition for the battle they were waging in defense of colonial rights. A series of circumstances had conspired to saturate even the revolutionary position of the Americans with the quality of traditionalism—to give them, indeed, the appearance of outraged reactionaries. "This I call an innovation," thundered John Dickinson, in his attack on the Stamp Act, "a most dangerous innovation."[14]

Now here was a frame of mind that would surely have troubled many of the illuminated liberals in Europe, were it not for an ironic fact. America piled on top of this paradox another one of an opposite kind and thus, by misleading them twice as it were, gave them a deceptive sense of understanding.

Actually, the form of America's traditionalism was one thing, its content quite another. Colonial

---

[13] The Pulpit of the American Revolution, *p. 311.*
[14] *John Dickinson,* Writings, *ed. P. L. Ford (Philadelphia, 1895), p. 316.*

history had not been the slow and glacial record of development that Bonald and Maistre loved to talk about. On the contrary, since the first sailing of the *Mayflower*, it had been a story of new beginnings, daring enterprises, and explicitly stated principles—it breathed, in other words, the spirit of Bentham himself. The result was that the traditionalism of the Americans, like a pure freak of logic, often bore amazing marks of antihistorical rationalism. The clearest case of this undoubtedly is to be found in the revolutionary constitutions of 1776, which evoked, as Franklin reported, the "rapture" of European liberals everywhere. In America, of course, the concept of a written constitution, including many of the mechanical devices it embodied, was the end-product of a chain of historical experience that went back to the Mayflower Compact and the Plantation Covenants of the New England towns: it was the essence of political traditionalism.[15] But in Europe just the reverse was true. The concept was the darling of the rationalists—a symbol of the emancipated mind at work.

Thus Condorcet was untroubled. Instead of bemoaning the fact that the Americans were Blackstonian historicists, he proudly welcomed them into the fraternity of the illuminated. American constitutionalism, he said, "had not grown, but was planned"; it "took no force from the weight of centuries but was put together mechanically in a few years." When John Adams read this comment, he spouted two words on the margin of the page: "Fool! Fool!"[16] But surely the judgment was harsh. After all, when Burke clothes

himself in the garments of Sieyès, who can blame the loyal rationalist who fraternally grasps his hand? The reactionaries of Europe, moreover, were often no keener in their judgment. They made the same mistake in reverse. Maistre gloomily predicted that the American Constitution would not last because it was created out of the whole cloth of reason.

But how then are we to describe these baffling Americans? Were they rationalists or were they traditionalists? The truth is, they were neither, which is perhaps another way of saying that they were both. For the war between Burke and Bentham on the score of tradition, which made a great deal of sense in a society where men had lived in the shadow of feudal institutions, made comparatively little sense in a society where for years they had been creating new states, planning new settlements, and, as Jefferson said, literally building new lives. In such a society a strange dialectic was fated to appear, which would somehow unite the antagonistic components of the European mind; the past became a continuous future, and the God of the traditionalists sanctioned the very arrogance of the men who defied Him.

This shattering of the time categories of Europe, this Hegelian-like revolution in historic perspective, goes far to explain one of the enduring secrets of the American character: a capacity to combine rock-ribbed traditionalism with high inventiveness, ancestor worship with ardent optimism. Most critics have seized upon one or the other of these aspects of the American mind, finding it impossible to conceive how both can go together. That is why the insight of Gunnar Myrdal is a very distinguished one when he writes: "America is . . . conservative. . . . But the principles conserved are liberal and some, indeed, are radical."[17]

[15] *Cf. B. F. Wright, Jr., "The Early History of Written Constitutions in America,"* in Essays in History and Political Theory in Honor of Charles Howard McIlwain *(Cambridge, Mass., 1936), pp. 344 ff.*

[16] *Quoted in J. Shapiro,* Condorcet and the Rise of Liberalism *(New York, 1934), p. 223.*

[17] An American Dilemma *(New York, 1944), p. 7.*

Radicalism and conservatism have been twisted entirely out of shape by the liberal flow of American history.

What I have been doing here is fairly evident: I have been interpreting the social thought of the American revolution in terms of the social goals *it did not need to achieve.* Given the usual approach, this may seem like a perverse inversion of the reasonable course of things; but in a world where the "canon and feudal law" are missing, how else are we to understand the philosophy of a liberal revolution? The remarkable thing about the "spirit of 1776," as we have seen, is not that it sought emancipation but that it sought it in a sober temper; not that it opposed power but that it opposed it ruthlessly and continuously; not that it looked forward to the future but that it worshipped the past as well. Even these perspectives, however, are only part of the story, misleading in themselves. The "free air" of American life, as John Jay once happily put it, penetrated to deeper levels of the American mind, twisting it in strange ways, producing a set of results fundamental to everything else in American thought. The clue to these results lies in the following fact: the Americans, though models to all the world of the middle class way of life, lacked the passionate middle class consciousness which saturated the liberal thought of Europe.

There was nothing mysterious about this lack. It takes the contemptuous challenge of an aristocratic feudalism to elicit such a consciousness; and when Richard Price glorified the Americans because they were men of the "middle state," men who managed to escape being "savage" without becoming "refined,"[18] he explained implicitly why they themselves would never have it. Franklin, of course, was a great American bourgeois thinker; but it is a commonplace that he had a

wider vogue on this score in Paris and London than he did in Philadelphia; and indeed there is some question as to whether the Europeans did not worship him more because he seemed to exemplify Poor Richard than because he had created the philosophy by which Poor Richard lived. The Americans, a kind of national embodiment of the concept of the bourgeoisie, have, as Mr. Brinkmann points out,[19] rarely used that concept in their social thought, and this is an entirely natural state of affairs. Frustration produces the social passion, ease does not. A triumphant middle class, unassailed by the agonies that Beaumarchais described, can take itself for granted. This point, curiously enough, is practically never discussed, though the failure of the American working class to become class conscious has been a theme of endless interest. And yet the relationship between the two suggests itself at once. Marx himself used to say that the bourgeoisie was the great teacher of the proletariat.

There can, it is true, be quite an argument over whether the challenge of an American aristocracy did not in fact exist in the eighteenth century. One can point to the great estates of New York where the Patroons lived in something resembling feudal splendor. One can point to the society of the South where life was extraordinarily stratified, with slaves at the bottom and a set of genteel planters at the top. One can even point to the glittering social groups that gathered about the royal governors in the North. But after all of this has been said, the American "aristocracy" could not, as Tocqueville pointed out, inspire either the "love" or the "hatred" that surrounded the ancient titled aristocracies of Europe.[20] Indeed, in America it was actually the "aristocrats" who were frus-

[18] Observations on the Importance of the American Revolution (*London, 1785*), p. 69.

[19] Encyclopedia of Social Sciences (*New York, 1937*), *Vol. ii, p. 645. By the same logic, we have never had a "Liberal Party" in the United States.*

[20] Democracy in America, *Vol. i, p. 58.*

trated, not the members of the middle class, for they were forced almost everywhere, even in George Washington's Virginia, to rely for survival upon shrewd activity in the capitalist race. This compulsion produced a psychic split that has always tormented the American "aristocracy"; and even when wealth was taken for granted, there was still, especially in the North, the withering impact of a colonial "character" that Sombart himself once described as classically bourgeois.[21] In Massachusetts, Governor Hutchinson used to lament that a "gentleman" did not meet even with "common civility" from his inferiors.[22] Of course, the radicals of America blasted their betters as "aristocrats," but that this was actually a subtle compliment is betrayed in the quality of the blast itself. Who could confuse the anger of Daniel Shays with the bitterness of Francis Place even in the England of the nineteenth century?

Thus it happened that fundamental aspects of Europe's bourgeois code of political thought met an ironic fate in the most bourgeois country in the world. They were not so much rejected as they were ignored, treated indifferently, because the need for their passionate affirmation did not exist. Physiocratic economics is an important case in point. Where economic parasites are few, why should men embark on a passionate search for the productive laborer? Where guild restrictions are comparatively slight and continental tariffs unknown, why should they embrace the ruthless atomism of Turgot? America's attack on the English Acts of Trade was couched in terms of Locke, not in terms of Quesnay; and though Franklin and Jefferson were much taken by the "modern economics," they did not, here as in certain other places, voice the dominant pre-

occupation of American thought. It had often been said, of course, that the Americans were passionately laissez faire in their thinking, but this is to confuse either bourgeois ease with bourgeois frustration or a hatred of absolute power with the very economic atomism which, in physiocratic terms, was allied to it. Turgot himself saw that the Americans did not long to smash a feudal world into economic atoms any more than they longed for a unified sovereign to accomplish this feat. A lover of the Americans who, like most European liberals, could not quite imagine life outside the *ancien régime*, he complained bitterly on both counts. His complaint on the count of sovereignty is legendary, but his complaint on the count of laissez faire has, alas, been entirely forgotten. This is because John Adams replied to the one in his *Defence of the Constitutions* but did not mention the other. And yet it appears in the same place, in Turgot's famous letter to Richard Price: "*On suppose partout le droit de regler le commerce . . . tant on est loin d'avoir senti que la loi de la liberté entière de tout commerce est un corrollaire du droit de proprieté.*"[23]

The lament of Turgot reveals that America's indifference to the bourgeois fixations of Europe had in itself a positive meaning: the failure to develop a physiocratic conscience led to a quiet and pragmatic outlook on the question of business controls. This is the outlook that characterizes a whole mass of early economic legislation that American historians are now beginning to unearth in what should have been, reputedly, the most "laissez faire" country in the world.[24] But

[21] W. Sombart, Quintessence of Capitalism (*London, 1915*), p. 306.
[22] Quoted in V. Parrington, Main Currents in American Thought (*New York, 1927–30*), Vol. i, p. 200.
[23] *The letter, dated 1778, is printed in Price's* Observations, p. 95. For a general discussion of the problem, see O. and M. Handlin, Commonwealth: Massachusetts (*New York, 1947*), and L. Hartz, Economic Policy and Democratic Thought (*Cambridge, Mass., 1948*).
[24] *Some of the finest work on this subject is being done by Professor Carter Goodrich of Columbia. See his recent articles in the* Political Science Quarterly.

it is in connection with materialism and idealism, utilitarianism and natural law, that the inverted position of the Americans comes out most clearly. There was no Bentham, no Helvetius among the superlatively middle-class American thinkers. On the contrary, they stuck with Puritan passion to the dogma of natural law, as if an outright hedonism were far too crass for consideration. In a purely political sense this may be interesting, because the Americans, at least during the Stamp Act phase of their struggle, were fighting that corrupt system of parliamentary representation which in England Benthamism later rose to assail. But it is in terms of the wider significance of utility as an attack on feudal norms, as an effort to make of "business a noble life," as Crane Brinton has put it,[25] that America's indifference to it takes on its deepest meaning. Benjamin Franklins in fact, the Americans did not have to become Jeremy Benthams in theory. Unchallenged men of business, they did not have to equate morality with it. And this has been a lasting paradox in the history of American thought. The American tradition of natural law still flourishes after a century and a half of the most reckless material exploitation that the modern world has seen. A persistent idealism of mind, reflected in Emerson's remark that utilitarianism is a "stinking philosophy," has been one of the luxuries of a middle class that has never been forced to become class conscious.

But this is not all. If the position of the colonial Americans saved them from many of the class obsessions of Europe, it did something else as well: it inspired them with a peculiar sense of community that Europe had never known. For centuries Europe had lived by the spirit of solidarity that Aquinas, Boussuet, and Burke romanticized: an organic sense of structured differences, an essentially Platonic experience. Amid the "free air" of American life, something new appeared: men

began to be held together, not by the knowledge that they were different parts of a corporate whole, but by the knowledge that they were similar participants in a uniform way of life—by that "pleasing uniformity of decent competence" which Crèvecoeur loved so much.[26] The Americans themselves were not unaware of this. When Peter Thacher proudly announced that "simplicity of manners" was the mark of the revolutionary colonists,[27] what was he saying if not that the norms of a single class in Europe were enough to sustain virtually a whole society in America? Richard Hildreth, writing after the leveling impact of the Jacksonian revolution had made this point far more obvious, put his finger directly on it. He denounced feudal Europe, where "half a dozen different codes of morals," often in flagrant contradiction with one another, flourished "in the same community," and celebrated the fact that America was producing "one code, one moral standard, by which the actions of all are to be judged. . . ."[28] Hildreth knew that America was a marvellous mixture of many peoples and many religions, but he also knew that it was characterized by something more marvelous even than that: the power of the liberal norm to penetrate them all.

Now a sense of community based on a sense of uniformity is a deceptive thing. It looks individualistic, and in part it actually is. It cannot tolerate internal relationships of disparity, and hence can easily inspire the kind of advice that Professor Nettels once imagined a colonial farmer giving his son: "Remember that you are as good as any man—and also that you are no better."[29] But in another sense it is profoundly anti-individualistic,

[25] Encyclopedia of Social Sciences, *Vol. xv, p. 199.*

[26] *M. G. Jean de Crevecoeur,* Letters from an American Farmer (*London, 1926*), *p. 40.*

[27] *Quoted in* Principles and Acts of the Revolution in America, *citeᴅ above (n. 8), p. 46.*

[28] Theory of Politics (*New York, 1854*), *p. 262.*

[29] *C. Nettels,* Roots of American Civilization (*New York, 1938*), *p. 315.*

because the common standard is its very essence, and deviations from that standard inspire it with an irrational fright. The man who is as good as his neighbors is in a tough spot when he confronts all of his neighbors combined. Thus William Graham Sumner looked at the other side of Professor Nettels's colonial coin and did not like what he saw: "public opinion" was an "impervious mistress. . . . Mrs. Grundy held powerful sway and Gossip was her prime minister."[30]

Here we have the "tyranny of the majority" that Tocqueville later described in American life; here too we have the deeper paradox out of which it was destined to appear. Freedom in the fullest sense implies both variety and equality; but history, for reasons of its own, chose to separate these two principles, leaving the one with the old society of Burke and giving the other to the new society of Paine. America, as a kind of natural fulfillment of Paine, has been saddled throughout its history with the defect which this fulfillment involves, so that a country like England, in the very midst of its ramshackle class-ridden atmosphere, seems to contain an indefinable germ of liberty, a respect for the privacies of life, that America cannot duplicate. At the bottom of the American experience of freedom, not in antagonism to it but as a constituent element of it, there has always lain the inarticulate premise of conformity, which critics from the time of Cooper to the time of Lewis have sensed and furiously attacked. "Even what is best in America is compulsory," Santayana once wrote, "—the idealism, the zeal, the beautiful happy unison of its great moments."[31] Thus while millions of Europeans have fled to America to discover the freedom of Paine, there have been a few Americans, only a

few of course, who have fled to Europe to discover the freedom of Burke. The ironic flaw in American liberalism lies in the fact that we have never had a real conservative tradition.

One thing, we might suppose, would shatter the unprecedented sense of uniform values by which the colonial American was beginning to live: the revolution itself. But remarkably enough, even the revolution did not produce this result; John Adams did not confront Filmer as Locke did, or Maistre, as the followers of Rousseau did. He confronted the Englishmen of the eighteenth century; and most of these men, insofar as the imperial struggle went, themselves accepted the Lockian assumptions that Adams advanced. Nor did the American Tories, with the fantastic exception of Boucher, who stuck to his thesis that Filmer was still "unrefuted," confront him with a vision of life completely different from his own. Samuel Seabury and Joseph Galloway accepted the Lockian principles, even sympathized with the American case, insisting only that peaceful means be used to advance it. Among their opponents, indeed, there were few who would fundamentally deny the "self-evident" truths the Americans advanced in 1776. The liberals of Europe always had a problem on their hands, which they usually neglected, to be sure, of explaining how principles could be "self-evident" when there were obviously so many people who did not believe them. Circumstance nearly solved this problem for the Americans, giving them, as it were, a national exemption from Hume's attack on natural law—which may be one of the reasons why they almost invariably ignored it. When one's ultimate values are accepted wherever one turns, the absolute language of self-evidence comes easily enough.

This then is the mood of America's absolutism: the sober faith that its norms are self-evident. It is one of the most powerful absolutisms in the world, more powerful even than the messianic spirit of the continental liberals which, as we saw, the

---

[30] *Quoted in A. G. Keller (ed.),* The Challenge of Facts and Other Essays *(New Haven, 1914), p. 318.*

[31] *G. Santayana,* Character and Opinion in the United States *(New York, 1924), p. 210.*

Americans were able to reject. That spirit arose out of contact with an opposing way of life, and its very intensity betrayed an inescapable element of doubt. But the American absolutism, flowing from an honest experience with universality, lacked even the passion that doubt might give. It was so sure of itself that it hardly needed to become articulate, so secure that it could actually support a pragmatism which seemed on the surface to belie it. American pragmatism has always been deceptive because, glacierlike, it has rested on miles of submerged conviction, and the conformitarian ethos which that conviction generates has always been infuriating because it has refused to pay its critics the compliment of an argument. Here is where the joy of a Dewey meets the anguish of a Fenimore Cooper; for if the American deals with concrete cases because he never doubts his general principles, this is also the reason he is able to dismiss his critics with a fine and crushing ease. But this does not mean that America's general will always lives an easy life. It has its own violent moments—rare, to be sure, but violent enough. These are the familiar American moments of national fright and national hysteria when it suddenly rises to the surface with a vengeance, when civil liberties begin to collapse, and when Cooper is actually in danger of going to jail as a result of the Rousseauan tide. Anyone who watches it then can hardly fail to have a healthy respect for the dynamite which normally lies concealed beneath the free and easy atmosphere of the American liberal community.

When we study national variations in political theory, we are led to semantic considerations of a delicate kind, and it is to these, finally, that we must turn if we wish to get at the basic assumption of American thought. We have to consider the peculiar meaning that American life gave to the words of Locke.

There are two sides to the Lockian argument: a defense of the state that is implicit, and a limitation of the state that is explicit. The first is to be found in Locke's basic social norm, the concept of free individuals in a state of nature. This idea untangled men from the myriad associations of class, church, guild, and place, in terms of which feudal society defined their lives; and by doing so, it automatically gave to the state a much higher rank in relation to them than ever before. The state became the only association that might legitimately coerce them at all. That is why the liberals of France in the eighteenth century were able to substitute the concept of absolutism for Locke's conclusions of limited government and to believe that they were still his disciples in the deepest sense. When Locke came to America, however, a change appeared. Because the basic feudal oppressions of Europe had not taken root, the fundamental social norm of Locke ceased in large part to look like a norm and began, of all things, to look like a sober description of fact. The effect was significant enough. When the Americans moved from that concept to the contractual idea of organizing the state, they were not conscious of having already done anything to fortify the state, but were conscious only that they were about to limit it. One side of Locke became virtually the whole of him. Turgot ceased to be a modification of Locke, and became, as he was for John Adams, the destruction of his very essence.

It was a remarkable thing—this inversion of perspectives that made the social norms of Europe the factual premises of America. History was on a lark, out to tease men, not by shattering their dreams, but by fulfilling them with a sort of satiric accuracy. In America one not only found a society sufficiently fluid to give a touch of meaning to the individualist norms of Locke, but one also found letter-perfect replicas of the very images he used. There was a frontier that was a veritable state of nature. There were agreements, such as the Mayflower Compact, that were veritable social contracts. There were new communities springing up *in vacuis locis*, clear evidence that men were using their Lockean right of emigration, which Jefferson soberly appealed to as "universal" in his defense of colonial land claims in 1774. A purist could argue, of course, that even these phenomena were not enough to make a reality out of the presocial men that liberalism dreamt of in theory. But surely they came as close to doing so as anything history has ever seen. Locke and Rousseau themselves could not help lapsing into the empirical mood when they looked across the Atlantic. "Thus, in the beginning," Locke once wrote, "all the world was America. . . ."[32]

In such a setting, how could the tremendous, revolutionary social impact that liberalism had in Europe be preserved? The impact was not, of course, missing entirely; for the attack on the vestiges of corporate society in America that began in 1776, the disestablishment of the Anglican church, the abolition of quitrents and primogeniture, the breaking up of the Tory estates, tinged American liberalism with its own peculiar fire. Nor must we therefore assume that the Americans had wider political objectives than the Europeans, since even their new governmental forms were, as Becker once said, little more than the "colonial institutions with the Parliament and king left out."[33] But after these cautions have been taken, the central point is clear. In America the first half of Locke's argument was bound to become less a call to arms than a set of preliminary remarks essential to establishing a final conclusion: that the

power of the state must be limited. Observe how it is treated by the Americans in their great debate with England, even by original thinkers like Otis and Wilson. They do not lavish upon it the fascinated inquiry that we find in Rousseau or Priestley. They advance it mechanically, hurry through it, anxious to get on to what is really bothering them: the limits of the British Parliament, the power of taxation. In Europe the idea of social liberty is loaded with dynamite; but in America it becomes, to a remarkable degree, the working base from which argument begins.

Here, then, is the master assumption of American political thought, the assumption from which all of the American attitudes discussed in this essay flow: the reality of atomistic social freedom. It is instinctive to the American mind, as in a sense the concept of the polis was instinctive to Platonic Athens or the concept of the church to the mind of the middle ages. Catastrophes have not been able to destroy it, proletariats have refused to give it up, and even our Progressive tradition, in its agonized clinging to a Jeffersonian world, has helped to keep it alive. There has been only one major group of American thinkers who have dared to challenge it frontally: the Fitzhughs and Holmeses of the pre-Civil War South who, identifying slavery with feudalism, tried to follow the path of the European reaction and of Comte. But American life rode roughshod over them—for the "prejudice" of Burke in America was liberal and the positive reality of Locke in America transformed them into the very metaphysicians they assailed. They were soon forgotten, massive victims of the absolute temper of the American mind, shoved off the scene by Horatio Alger, who gave to the Lockian premise a brilliance that lasted until the crash of 1929. And even the crash did not really shatter it.

It might be appropriate to summarize with a single word, or even with a single sentence, the

[32] Second Treatise on Civil Government (*Oxford,* *1947*), p. 29.
[33] *C. L. Becker,* Freedom and Responsibility in the American Way of Life (*New York, 1945*), p. 16.

political outlook that this premise has produced. But where is the word and where is the sentence one might use? American political thought, as we have seen, is a veritable maze of polar contradictions, winding in and out of each other hopelessly: pragmatism and absolutism, historicism and rationalism, optimism and pessimism, materialism and idealism, individualism and conformism. But, after all, the human mind works by polar contradictions; and when we have evolved an interpretation of it which leads cleanly in a single direction, we may be sure that we have missed a lot. The task of the cultural analyst is not to discover simplicity, or even to discover unity, for simplicity and unity do not exist, but to drive a wedge of rationality through the pathetic indecisions of social thought. In the American case that wedge is not hard to find. It is not hidden in an obscure place. We find it in what the West as a whole has always recognized to be the distinctive element in American civilization: its social freedom, its social equality. And yet it is true, for all of our Jeffersonian nationalism, that the interpretation of American political thought has not been built around this idea. On the contrary, instead of interpreting the American revolution in terms of American freedom, we have interpreted it in terms of American oppression, and instead of studying the nineteenth century in terms of American equality, we have studied it in terms of a series of cosmic Beardian and Parringtonian struggles against class exploitation. We have missed what the rest of the world has seen and what we ourselves have seen whenever we have contrasted the New World with the Old. But this is a large issue which brings us not only to the Progressive historians but to the peculiar subjectivism of the American mind that they reflect, and it is beyond the scope of our discussion here.

The liberals of Europe in 1776 were obviously worshipping a very peculiar hero. If the average American had been suddenly thrust in their midst, he would have been embarrassed by the millennial enthusiasms that many of them had, would have found their talk of classes vastly overdone, and would have reacted to the Enlightenment synthesis of absolutism and liberty as if it were little short of dishonest doubletalk. Bred in a freer world, he had a different set of perspectives, was animated by a different set of passions, and looked forward to different goals. He was, as Crèvecoeur put it, a "new man" in Western politics.

But, someone will ask, where did the liberal heritage of the Americans come from in the first place? Didn't they have to create it? And if they did, were they not at one time or another in much the same position as the Europeans?

These questions drive us back to the ultimate nature of the American experience, and, so doing, confront us with a queer twist in the problem of revolution. No one can deny that conscious purpose went into the making of the colonial world, and that the men of the seventeenth century who fled to America from Europe were keenly aware of the oppressions of European life. But they were revolutionaries with a difference, and the fact of their fleeing is no minor fact: for it is one thing to stay at home and fight the "canon and feudal law," and it is another to leave it far behind.* It is

---

* *In a real sense physical flight is the American substitute for the European experience of social revolution. And this, of course, has persisted throughout our national history, although nothing in the subsequent pattern of flight, the "safety-valve" notwithstanding, has approximated in significance the original escape from Europe. It is interesting how romance has been thrown alike around the European liberals who stayed home to fight and the American liberals who fled their battle. There are two types of excitement here, that of changing familiar things and that of leaving them, which both involve a trip into the unknown. But though one may find a common element of adventure in flight and revolution, it is a profound mistake to confuse the perspectives they engender. They are miles apart—figuratively as well as literally.*

one thing to try to establish liberalism in the Old World, and it is another to establish it in the New. Revolution, to borrow the words of T. S. Eliot, means to murder and create, but the American experience has been projected strangely in the realm of creation alone. The destruction of forests and Indian tribes—heroic, bloody, legendary as it was—cannot be compared with the destruction of a social order to which one belongs oneself. The first experience is wholly external and, being external, can actually be completed; the second experience is an inner struggle as well as an outer struggle, like the slaying of a Freudian father, and goes on in a sense forever.* Moreover, even the matter of creation is not in the American case a simple one. The New World, as Lord Baltimore's ill-fated experiment with feudalism in the seventeenth century illustrates, did not merely offer the Americans a virgin ground for the building of a liberal system: it conspired itself to help that system along. The abundance of land in America, as well as the need for a lure to settlers, entered it so completely at every point, that Sumner was actually ready to say, "We have not made America, America has made us."[34]

* *Note the words of Goethe:*
> *Amerika, du hast es besser*
> *Als unser Kontinent, das Alte*
> *Hast keine verfallene Schloesser*
> *Und keine Basalte.*
> *Dich stoert nicht im Innern*
> *Zu lebendiger Zeit*
> *Unnuetzes Erinnern*
> *Und vergeblicher Streit.*

It is this business of destruction and creation which goes to the heart of the problem. For the point of departure of great revolutionary thought everywhere else in the world has been the effort to build a new society on the ruins of an old society, and this is an experience America has never had. We are reminded again of Tocqueville's statement: the Americans are "born equal."

That statement, especially in light of the strange relationship which the revolutionary Americans had with their admirers abroad, raises an obvious question. Can a people that is born free ever understand peoples elsewhere that have to become so? Can it ever lead them? Or to turn the issue around, can peoples struggling for a goal understand those who have inherited it? This is not a problem of antitheses such, for example, as we find in Locke and Filmer. It is a problem of different perspectives on the same ideal. But we must not for that reason assume that it is any less difficult of solution; it may in the end be more difficult, since antitheses define each other and hence can understand each other, but different perspectives on a single value may, ironically enough, lack this common ground of definition. Condorcet might make sense out of Burke's traditionalism, for it was the reverse of his own activism, but what could he say about Otis, who combined both concepts in a synthesis that neither had seen? America's experience of being born free has put it in a strange relationship to the rest of the world.

[34] The Challenge of Facts and Other Essays, *p. 304.*

CHRISTIAN CULTURE AND AMERICAN DEMOCRACY

Max Lerner*

Our generation has witnessed—like none before it—new manifestations of the totalitarian spirit in Russia, Eastern Europe and China, where there have been drastic social transformations under the banners of secular science without religion. This raises the issue whether complete secularism must lead to the idolatry of man-centered power. But we have also seen vast areas of Asia and Africa exposed anew to the task of democratic construction without strong roots in Christian thought and tradition. The question of whether India and Burma, Japan and Indonesia, the Arab states, the emerging polities of North Africa and Central Africa, can develop democratic institutions comparable to those of Western Europe and America, suggests a fresh look at the Christian strain in democracy.

It should be clear that the issue is not between religion and secularism, but between the Judaeo-Christian tradition and the absence of it. Strong claims have been made for what may be called an inner attraction between Christian doctrine and democratic life. This may be so. But to see whether it is, we must break up the Christian complex and discuss some of its constituent elements of doctrine.

Each of these elements seems to have serious ambiguities in its relation to democracy. Take, for example, the Christian allegory of the sacrificial death of Jesus. Northup has pointed out that this leaves as its psychic deposit a human willingness to make the ultimate sacrifice for a finite end. It has inspired much of the humanist idealism of the struggle for democracy, but it has also turned up in a strangely transmuted form in the dedicated

*MAX LERNER (1902–   ) is a Professor of American Civilization and World Politics at Brandeis University and a syndicated columnist for the New York Post. His publications include America as a Civilization (1957), The Unfinished Country (1959), and Education and Radical Humanism (1962). Reprinted by permission of the author and the American Quarterly, Vol. 6, No. 2 (Summer, 1954), 126–137. Published by the University of Pennsylvania. Copyright, 1954, Trustees of the University of Pennsylvania.

commitment of Communists to the finite ends of their political religion. Thus the same zeal which inspired the American settlers to endure the rigors of a wilderness in quest of freedom has also inspired the visionary folly of the atomic spies and led to the fanaticism of native American political adventurers.

A similar analysis may be made of the Christian doctrines of the soul and sin. Much has been made of the Christian emphasis on the individual, and rightly, since it is hard for men to resist the tyranny of absolute power unless they do so to save their personal souls in the sight of God. Thus the doctrine of the soul and of the equality of men before God have given a crucial impetus to those movements for freedom out of which Western democracy has been born.

But the doctrine of sin, while it has had a healthy effect in preventing that idolatry of the merely human which is the base of much of totalitarianism, can also lead to the annihilation of the personality. If you are obsessed with the gap between God's perfection and your own nothingness, it is hard to find scope for that human action which rests on man's sense of his own worth. Thus the habit of religious abnegation may clear the path for an equal political abnegation which makes men subjects of authority rather than citizens of a community, and renders them submissive to the highest powers in both the secular and the sacred realm. Similarly the doctrine of salvation, which is the correlative of the doctrine of sin, may pave the way for those short-cut movements of political adventurism which Toynbee has described as the coming of the "Saviour with a sword." It should be added however that the emphasis on humanism in Western societies, and therefore man's control of his own destiny, has been partly responsible for the Marxist movements which are a form of Toynbee's "Saviour with a book."

Thus there are polar strains within the Christian doctrine which have made it compatible with both anti-democratic movements and democratic ones. All seminal ideas are ambiguous, capable of being used in several political directions. A good deal depends not so much on the doctrine itself as on the pressures of the surrounding intellectual and social forces. Thus there is a difference within the Judaeo-Christian tradition between its Judaic and its more strictly Christian elements. Although the concept of sin will be found in the attacks of the Hebrew prophets on a collapsing society, Judaism has been less imbued with sin and salvation than has Christianity, whose central allegory has been the sacrificial divine death for human sin. The emphasis of the Jewish prophetic tradition has been rather in the direction of social justice, with a strong strain of messianic hope which has reenforced the minority situation of Jews.

Within Christianity itself there have, of course, been crucial differences in the institutional setting and impact of Catholicism and Protestantism. Catholic societies have tended to retain an authoritarian spirit which has resisted the inroads both of the free-market society and of democratic thought, although—as Reinhold Neibuhr has remarked—they have developed graces of the spirit absent elsewhere. The Protestant societies, on the other hand, have nurtured both the spirit of capitalism and that of democracy. While historically they used the power of the secular monarchy as a weapon in the struggle against clerical control, their central tenet of private judgment stretched from the religious to the political realm and corroded the kingship as well as other forms of magic.

The doctrine of dissent, so strong in the Protestant tradition, has been the base of the commitment to civil liberties, just as the belief in private judgment has also supported the political doctrine of the consent of the governed which is at the core of majority rule. Most of all, however, the generative idea of Protestantism has been the belief in the individual personality as the subject of its own growth and scope and not as an object for manipulation, whether by authority or magic. The political implications of this for the life of democratic societies scarcely need underlining.

There is a moot problem here which concerns pre-Christian Greek society and thought. One can trace the beginnings of the doctrine of individual worth among the Greek philosophers, as one can also find its social roots in the civic-mindedness of the Greek city-state. This does not mean, despite Toynbee's over-zealous pleading for such a view, that Christian thought was already half-grown in classical society. It is true that the concept of *agape*—or divine love—will be found in Plato before it emerges fully (in a very different form and context) in Tertullian, Clement and Saint Augustine; and one finds in Aristotle's *Ethics* the idea of love as the surrogate of law. But it is also true that while there is a sense of sin against the tribal gods in the Greek tragedies, one finds little trace in Plato of any sense of either sin or salvation. The Platonic soul is not the Hebraic or Christian battleground between the armies of good and evil but rather the realm of essence.

The sensible view would seem to be, since intellectual history is (for all its contradictions) a continuum and not a series of surprises and leaps, that there was a continuity between the Greek ethos and the Judaeo-Christian. Which is to say that classical society contained within itself the seeds from which Judaism and Christianity were born. Yet the flowering beliefs and institutions were greatly different in the two sets of societies. With all its foreshadowings of Christian doctrine, Platonism was actually the base on which much of later anti-democratic thought has been built. It favored sharp stratification and the doctrine of the elite, rather than the brotherhood of man; and it

sought to manipulate the individual's mind with myths for the purposes of the state. Yet, as witness the Athenians of the time of Pericles, the Greek city-state did have its own brand of democracy along with institutions of privilege and sharp inequality. In that brand the individual personality reached its height in the service of the *polis*. Which means that we must balance the two facts about Greek democracy; it was not Christian, however much we may wish to push Christian history back; but it had, in an important sense, a form of democracy of its own.

But if there was democracy before the Christian metaphysic developed, highly Christian cultures have also at times had strong elements of authoritarianism—as witness Franco's Spain, Salazar's Portugal, the dictatorships of Latin America, and the inter-war fascist states of central Europe, not to mention the Puritan theocracies of several of the American colonies. Similarly one notes that the successful Communist movements of our time came in strongly Christian countries of Russia and Eastern Europe, and that today the strongest Communist movements in Western Europe challenge the Catholic life-view as well as the governments of the Catholic countries of France and Italy.

It is true, as a recent editorial in *Life* put it, that "the political self-government of all depends on the moral self-government of each." But the "moral self-government of each" is a vague concept of ethical individualism. One finds it in Christian Protestantism and in Judaism; one finds it also in some Oriental religions and in the humanism of such creeds as Unitarianism and the Ethical Culture movement. In fact the strongest emphasis on the moral self-government of the individual is found where the emphasis on transcendental religion and its mysteries is weakest.

If we take American society as the type-form of modern democracy, it is notable that American life-goals are strongly secular and their daily strivings revolve not around God but around man. American history reveals a striking mixture of theocracy and secularism, of dogma with indifferentism. One finds a clue to this mixture by noting the difference of religious climate at each important stage of American history. The colonies were settled under the stress of religious revolt, in an age of creative religious feeling marked by the Calvinist doctrine of determinism; American freedom was won at the end of the eighteenth century in an age of deism and revolutionary free thinking; the major growth of American power took place during the century of scientific rationalism that followed the Jeffersonian Era; in the contemporary Atomic Age there has been a revival of religious feeling under the stress of social tensions and personal insecurity. This mixture of seventeenth century Calvinism, eighteenth century deism, nineteenth century scientific rationalism, and mid-twentieth century anxiety may help explain some of the contradictions in the relations between God and man in America.

The result has been an American religious tradition which is at once deeply individualist, anti-authoritarian, salvation-minded yet secular and rationalist in its life-goals, Bible-reading in its habits, with its emphasis on man's relation to his own conscience and therefore to his private religious judgment.

Several of the resulting ambiguities are worth noting. One is between the religious pessimism of the sin-and-salvation strain in American Christianity and the organic optimism of the American economic and political attitudes. The Hebrew prophets, as they lamented the disintegration of Biblical society, called on each Jew to ward off God's wrath from his people by cleansing himself of his own inner guilt; the Christian allegory added to the somberness of this conception. But there have been few occasions on which Americans

could believe with any conviction in an impending social collapse. The sense of sin and the sense of doom were therefore importations from the Old and New Testaments that somehow flowered in the American soil in spite of the worship of money and success—or perhaps exactly because of this worship, which required a compensating doctrine to ease the conscience.

This conflict between secular social goals and the religious conscience has colored both the religious and democratic experience of America. It underlay the agonized conscience of early New England, the preoccupation with God's way with man in good and evil which characterized American Fundamentalism, the fear-drenched frontier religion filled with liberal-minded terrors, the Social Gospel movement; and it will be found in the latter day movement of neo-Calvinist thought, with its Atomic Age setting of apocalyptic guilt and terror. For all its optimism and its cult of action and success, American culture has been overlaid with both a sense of agony and of evil.

America owes much of the effectiveness of its democracy, as well as much of its dynamism, to this strain in its religious experience. I am suggesting that the fiber necessary for democracy is not the product of any particular religious doctrine but of the lonely debate within the free conscience. Democracy is the polity of individual choices and of majority consent; it can be run effectively only where there is a habituation to hard choices. Those who are certain of the simplicity of revealed truth make the initial choice of submission and do not have to make any subsequent choices; they do not furnish a fertile soil for the democratic see. Those who expect miracles will not take the risks of dissent. Those who are sure of dogma given to them will not make the arduous effort of winning the slow and gradual victories of an always unfinished society. Finally, those who suffer no conflict within the arena of their own minds will not generate the dynamism which they need in order to transcend the conflict and resolve their conscience.

American democracy, in the sense that it is linked with private judgment and freedom of dissent, is thus also linked with the stir and turmoil of free religious choice. To be sure, the psychic toll of this conflict and dynamism is a heavy one. But the stakes have been great—nothing less than the creation and sustaining of an open society which is based on the judging and choosing individual caught on the battleground of his own mind.

In our era, the great dangers to American democracy are conformism of mind and standardization of character. The great counter-force to these tendencies is the tradition of American religious non-conformism.

This non-conformism in turn has a number of contradictory elements. It developed, as Arthur G. Parker has put it, in "a religiously inflexible New England, with its mores forged upon the anvil of Jeremiah by the sledge of Calvin." Something of the dark intensity of this religious commitment has persisted in America until our own day. One finds it in Hawthorne, Melville, and Poe, as also in Mark Twain and Henry James, Thomas Wolfe and Faulkner. As long as this strain persists, there can be little danger of a total flattening out of personality and a herd-mindedness of opinion.

Yet one of the striking facts about American history has been the linkage between the so-called "religion of the fathers" and what Mencken delighted to call the "Bible Belt" mentality—a narrow view of life and morals, a belief in the literal inspiration of the Bible, and a reactionary code of political belief. The passion of the Hot Gospel and the archaism of the hell-fire-and-damnation religion have been put to work as a counterforce to the inherent humanism of the Christian teachings. It has enabled a number of demagogues, especially in the rural Midwest and South, to clothe their racist and reactionary appeals with Biblical references. In the big cities the tradition of Charles G. Finney and Dwight L. Moody has been continued for better or worse, with modern publicity techniques, by Billy Sunday, Aimee MacPherson, and Billy Graham. They illustrate how broad is the gulf in American religion between the loudly committed and the deeply committed. Unlike Puritanism, which with all its excesses embodied an internalized religious conviction—the product of people who wrestled with God as Jacob had done—present-day evangelism is a form of religiosity externalized in a public spectacle. As such it is closely related to that strain in the American character which Riesman has called the "other-directed" character structure, and which is one of the principal ingredients of contemporary conformism.

It should be clear that I am not speaking here of liberalism and conservatism, whether in politics or religion, but of religion and democracy in their broadest sense. Let me cite the example of the Populist political movements in the South and Midwest, in which the stress on saving one's soul and preserving religious orthodoxy was linked with an anti-capitalist radicalism. The type-figures were William Jennings Bryan and Tom Watson. In them a crusading Populism was fused with a harsh Catonian moralism. The mixture is one that will be hard to find outside of America. The common element was the need for the salvation of the believer from the wickedness of the Cities of the Plain where both wealth and free-thinking accumulate. The anti-corporate strand was thus intertwined with the moralistic, and Bryan's famous Cross of Gold speech was linked in direct line with the crusade for Prohibition and the Scopes monkey trial. In its characteristic latter-day form this amalgam has lost its anti-corporate militancy, replaced by an anti-labor, anti-Negro, and anti-Jewish emphasis. Thus in these areas religious Fundamentalism has ended by associating minority groups with the promiscuous liberalism of urban intellectuals who are vaguely felt to be undermining the tribal traditions.

I take my second illustration from the relation of Christian ideals to the American business spirit. Modern Protestantism and the modern business spirit were, of course, born out of the same historical soil. The real problem came with the harshness of the acquisitive spirit. Confronted with this the churches faltered, and instead of challenging it they too often emulated the premises of business enterprise, investing business power with religious sanctions.

Yet having said this one must add to this phase of American church history the Social Gospel phase, which dedicated the churches to a militant rôle in economic and social reform. Some of the best energies of the denominations, including the Methodists, Presbyterians, and Baptists—the three sects which also had made the greatest headway on the frontier—were turned toward the new pathways of social action in the spirit of a Jesus who had given himself to the poor and been denounced as agitator and revolutionary. In this spirit some of the pastors have fought for racial equality and economic justice, and have explored settlement work, adult education, and psychiatric pastoral counseling. These activities have been attacked as a secularizing of religion. It is true that they have turned the main stream of religious energy away from the supernatural, from transcending the human to the serving of human needs. Such a humanist emphasis has in many instances become thin. Yet the Social Gospel movement has been not only a vital phase in American religious history but also in the history of the American democratic impulse.

But the crucial division in American religion is not between fundamentalists and modernists, or between liberals and neo-Calvinists. It is between active and passive belief, between those for whom religion is commitment, and those for whom it is lip-service or conformist respectability. The Social Gospel and the new existentialist religion have at least one trait in common—that of seeking to bring vitality once again to the religious commitment. Both feel the difficulty of the human situation and the unremitting arduousness of the struggle for belief. The enemies of both are smugness, apathy, an easy optimism, and a shortcut conformism. The introspective religion flourishes best where man feels isolated, struggling against the eidola of society. The early America, with its lonely frontier communities torn up from their European roots, furnished such a soil. But when American society came into the full swing of prosperity, and became itself a great artifact with numberless institutional relationships, the lonely meeting of man and God became more difficult.

Much the same can be said of prophetic religion. Prophecy is the product and sign of social failure, and in the American myths there is no room for failure. Even the mid-nineteenth century sects, which used to forecast the doom of the world at an appointed time, could not survive the ridicule of their contemporaries when the time of doom came and the end was not yet. The voice of ridicule was the voice of a culture built on boundless hope and optimism. Even the Fourierist and other Utopian settlements of the nineteenth century were the product of millennialism rather than of social despair. Everything in America has seemed to conspire against pessimistic and otherwordly religions. It is hard to talk of the mysteries of Nature where science exploits it, or of compassion in a culture that flees failure, or of humility in an imperial culture that makes an idol out of wealth and power. It is hard to see how a religion of poverty can strike continuing root in the richest civilization of the world, or a religion of denial in one of the most Byzantine.

How then account for the strong pulsation today toward a religion which is imbued with a sense of the corruption and weakness of human institutions, and which is once again ridden with pessimism? I suggest that the revival of this impulse comes in an age of anxiety and alienation, when Americans are disillusioned with the idea of automatic progress, when the cold war and atomic doom have become pressing anxieties, and when optimism, liberalism, and modernism have come under suspicion. But this new mood, while it has led some of the best elements in the churches toward new depths of religious feeling, also marks a crisis both in religion and democracy. It is part of the dilemma that history presents to both. The religion-creating capacity, as witness the great period in the Middle East at the time of the Roman Empire, depends on social failure and catastrophe, while the open society depends on prosperity and peace. To put it in another way, the creative soil for religion is social anxiety, which may be the product or the harbinger of democratic failure.

I do not believe that such a sense of failure is likely to thrive long in the American cultural setting. The cultural strains that have given America its power and greatness are those of dynamism rather than despair. It may be that we will go down in doom because the world will go down in doom, and largely because of our blindness in making world decisions. If so, it will be the end of both democracy and religion in America. Perhaps a new religion will some day grow out of this social catastrophe as the religions of the Orient grew out of the collapse of the Greek and Roman worlds. But short of such an apocalyptic vision the American future is likely to grow out of the American past, whose chief features have been social optimism, dynamism, and a continuing equilibrium between the conflicting groups and pulls of American society.

When we put the spirit of American history thus it offers a clue to the creativeness of the American religious experience. It has differed from the religion-creating genius which showed itself in Asia and the Middle East in a relatively short span of history. Its striking character has been the luxuriant growth of religious denominations splitting off from each other amoeba-wise. Pluralist in most other phases, the American culture is supremely pluralist in religion. Staying mainly within the broad frame of historic Christianity, Americans have explored new ways of life in new communities (from the Shakers to Father Divine) or proclaimed new particular insights (as with the Mormons, Christian Scientists, Jehovah's Witnesses) or fragmented a denomination into cults and sects, bringing it closer to someone's soul's desire. Nowhere else could James' *Varieties of Religious Experience* have been so congenial to the cultural temper.

The sects have been derided because they split what might have been religious unity and cast themselves out of the "Eden of infallibility." Yet to attack them for this is to ask America to be other than it is, not only in religion but in every other aspect. For the pluralism of the American churches is like the pluralism of America's regions, its diverse economic forms, its ethnic and immigrant stocks. It is closely linked, as Madison saw, with religious freedom. The competition of creeds has prevented Americans from erecting intolerance into a principle of government.

I wonder whether we have seen the full import of this for the relations between religion and democracy. As one phase of the open society, America has been an open religious society. Despite the multiplicity of faiths, speaking as with a confusion of tongues, there have been no religious wars or massacres. You will find in American history *few* of those blood-encrusted crimes which in world history have been committed in the name of the only true God and the only true religious way. No other civilization offers a parallel in this respect. There has been marked bitterness between Catholics and Protestants in the struggle for political power, and between the Jews and both of them in economic rivalries. But the principle of the open society, with its rapid class mobility, its religious intermarriage, its respect for the right of religious dissent, has proved a dissolvent force both for bigotries and hostilities. It has also, of course, dissolved much of the religious intensity which Americans brought over from Europe in the successive waves of immigration. But a religious intensity which depends on bigotry and the crushing of dissent may be intense, but it is not religiously creative.

A note may be in order here on the relation of religion and the economy. The historians of Protestant society have stressed the doctrine of vocation and its carry-over from religious to secular uses. Given the history of American democracy, one should add another aspect—the inner relation between religious pluralism and a pluralist economy. What both have in common is the process of decision-making through the exercise of private judgment. The free-market economy, as Karl Polany has shown in *The Great Transformation*, was alien to the ethic and psychology of mediaeval Europe. It carried in its wake some devastating social irresponsibilities for the human costs of industrialism.

But what we have not seen until recently is that the decentralized decisions involved in capitalism put the burden of decision-making on numberless individuals. True, the growth of monopoly has diminished the scope of this; but as Professor Galbraith has shown in his *American Capitalism*, in great measure it still applies. I do not say that every small businessman or corporate manager or highly skilled worker carries the moral burden of the decision-making well. In many instances he

does not. But I do say that a society in which he ceases ever to make the attempt is a society in which the habit of decision-making in moral and political terms becomes also constricted. It is a striking fact that the same societies which have maintained a decentralized choice in religion have tended to maintain it also in the economy and in politics.

To those who believe that the Christian metaphysics or the religious culture has made American democracy possible and held it together, I would enter a qualification. It is the dissenting pluralist tradition in religion, the Covenanting tradition (as Professor H. Richard Niebuhr has put it) rather than the religious orientation as such, which has been most strongly linked with American democracy. Religious dissent has carried over with it the tradition of political dissent. It has fostered the democratic idea mainly through the stress on the right of the individual to face and master his own solitariness in his own way. Thus Americans have managed to remain largely a believing people—without the compulsion of imposing their religious beliefs on others. Finally there has been a carry-over from the hard task of squaring one's religious beliefs with one's day-to-day personal life into the equally hard task of making economic and political choices and decisions.

I am tempted to speak of this in the past tense because there are signs that the tradition of dissent is being replaced by new habits of conformism. The walls are closing in on intellectual diversity and the competition of political ideas. If this continues, the walls will soon also close in on the competition of religious ideas. I do not believe that the roots of this lie, as some seem to think, in the secularizing forces of American society. Rather do they lie in the uprooting of Americans from the soil, from the sense of dignity of work, from the multitude of small business enterprises where they have to make their own decisions.

The phase of immigration history when the American experience was being continually renewed for millions of newcomers under the conditions of individualism, seems to be at an end. We are in an era of corporate and governmental bureaucracies, and of a drive toward conformism in every phase of the personality.

It is notable that one of the main centers of resistance against the new trend has been in the leadership of the Protestant churches, with their tradition of religious and political dissent; and that the attacks have come from men who do not seem to see that their pressure toward uniformity will in the end crush religious freedom itself. Just as the tradition of religious dissent has given our democracy vitality, so also has it been our democracy which has made possible the survival of religious freedom.

CYCLES OF AMERICAN DEMOCRACY

*Fletcher M. Green**

Democracy is a term with which the American people are so familiar that they rarely attempt to define it, and whenever they do so they find the undertaking a most difficult one. Leading authorities in philosophy and political science are unable to agree upon its meaning. James Bryce defined it as a "form of government in which the ruling power of a state is legally vested, not in any particular class or classes, but in the members of the community as a whole," that is, "a government in which the will of the majority of qualified citizens rule." Not so, says Walter Lippmann: "We must abandon the notion that the people govern. Instead we must adopt the theory that, by their

**FLETCHER M. GREEN* (1895–   ) *was the Kenan Professor of History at the University of North Carolina at Chapel Hill. His publications include* Constitutional Development in the South Atlantic States, 1776–1860 *(1930),* Southern Wealth and Northern Profits *(1965), and* Memorials of a Southern Planter *(1965). Reprinted by permission of the author and the* Mississippi Valley Historical Review, *Vol. 48, No. 1 (June, 1961), 3–23.*

occasional mobilizing as a majority, the people support or oppose the individuals who actually govern." Another authority, Robert M. MacIver, says that "Democracy is not a way of governing, whether by a majority or otherwise, but primarily a way of determining who shall govern and, broadly, to what ends." And Harold J. Laski has said that "No definition of democracy can adequately comprise the vast history which the concept connotes. To some it is a form of government, to others a way of social life."[1] We may conclude then that democracy has no precise meaning, that there can be no one correct definition. Democracy is a relative term, one that has various meanings among different peoples and for the same peoples at different stages of their political development. In this paper the term will be used, as generally accepted by historians, to mean a form of government in which the ultimate sovereign power is held by the people and exercised through a system of representation in which the representatives are chosen by a large electorate and are responsible to the electors.[2]

In America, democratic government has been an evolving and expanding institution. It has grown with the country. Its origins, of course, may be traced back beyond the American Revolution to our colonial heritage; yet the Revolution itself was a struggle for political democracy, for government by "the consent of the governed," and it is from the Revolutionary era that we can date the beginning of a series of cycles in the growth of American democracy. In the course of our history, from then until the present, four cycles are clearly discernible. The first was the era

of the Revolution and of our first constitutions, when the people assumed authority to establish the governments by which they were to be governed. During the second cycle, from the close of the eighteenth century to 1860, the several states, acting as agents for the people, were responsible for democratic advance, with the federal government playing an insignificant or minor role. Since 1860, however, the situation has been reversed. When federalism gave way to nationalism in the years after the Civil War, the United States government assumed the dominant role and has held it ever since, and the states have contributed less and less to democracy's advance. During the latter third of the nineteenth century the Congress exercised a controlling influence in shaping American democracy and the judiciary served as a check to slow down progress. During the early years of the twentieth century, as the fourth cycle began, the executive seemed destined to replace Congress as the leader, but since the 1930's the judiciary has been in the ascendancy.

The developments of the nineteenth and twentieth centuries have been the working out of principles first enunciated as the tenets of American democracy during the Revolutionary era. Our fundamental concepts and principles, based upon the philosophy of natural rights and popular sovereignty, found full and adequate expression in such Revolutionary documents as the Virginia Bill of Rights of June 12, 1776, the Declaration of Independence of July 4, 1776, and the Massachusetts Bill of Rights of 1780.[3] In Virginia it was declared that "All men are by nature equally free and independent, and have certain inherent rights,

[1] *Hillman M. Bishop and Samuel Hendel (eds.)*, Basic Issues of American Democracy: A Book of Readings (*New York, 1948*), 14–18.

[2] *See Carl Becker*, Modern Democracy (*New Haven, 1941*), 4–6.

[3] *The introduction to this paper draws on the author's* Constitutional Development in the South Atlantic States, 1776–1860 (*Chapel Hill, 1930*) and "Democracy in the Old South," Journal of Southern History (*Baton Rouge*), XII (*February, 1946*), 3–23.

of which . . . they cannot by any compact deprive or divest their posterity; namely, the enjoyment of life and liberty, with the means of acquiring and possessing property, and pursuing and obtaining happiness and safety." In the same spirit, and in that same summer of 1776, Congress proclaimed the self-evident "truths" that "all men are created equal, that they are endowed by their Creator with certain unalienable rights, that among these are life, liberty and the pursuit of happiness. That to secure these rights, governments are instituted among men, deriving their just powers from the consent of the governed." In Massachusetts, provisions of the bill of rights were clear and detailed: "The people . . . have the sole and exclusive right of governing themselves. . . . Government is instituted for the common good, for the protection, safety, prosperity, and happiness of the people and not for the profit, honor, or private interest of any one man, family, or class of men. . . . All elections ought to be free; and all the inhabitants of this commonwealth, having such qualifications as they shall establish by their frame of government, have an equal right to elect officers, and to be elected, for public employments."

These and similar expressions of democratic equalitarianism were familiar to the American people during the last quarter of the eighteenth century, but they were not fully incorporated into the framework of government, either state or federal. Two of the original states chose to continue under the colonial charters, and the new constitutions were far from radical experiments in democratic self-government. Only one original state constitution was submitted to the people for popular approval; the others were promulgated by the bodies that framed them. Five of the constitutions contained no provision for amendment or revision, and some had no separate bill of rights. Nor was the principle of religious freedom fully recognized. Even the Pennsylvania constitution,

generally conceded to have been most democratic of all, required each member of the legislature to take an oath that he believed "in one God, the creator and governor of the universe, the rewarder of the good and the punisher of the wicked," and to acknowledge that the Old and New Testament had been "given by Divine inspiration." Suffrage was limited to free white males by property qualifications ranging from tax payments to freeholds of 100 acres or £60 in value. High property qualifications for office-holding prevailed. Members of the legislatures were required to be possessed of freeholds of 250 to 500 acres, and governors of freeholds of 1,000 acres to property worth £5,000. Members of the legislatures and some local officials were elected by popular vote, but governors and other state officials were chosen by the legislature.

Among democratic tendencies found in the first constitutions was the conscious move toward liberalizing suffrage by shifting from the freehold to tax payments. Some forbade imprisonment for debt after the delivery of all property; some the entailment of estates. Some provided for the separation of church and state and for state support of education. Georgia, for instance, declared that "Schools shall be erected in each county and supported at the general expense of the state." Most important of all were the "inherent rights" enumerated in the bill of rights. That of Virginia, written by George Mason, was the first adopted, and it served as a model for those that followed. The most characteristic feature of the bills of rights was their reflection of eighteenth-century natural rights of philosophy. They spoke of founding government by "compact only," of "natural and unalienable right," and of men being "by nature equally free and independent." They declared that freemen could not be deprived of liberty except by the law of the land. Trial by jury was safeguarded. When prosecuted, freemen were to be presented with an indictment, were to have the right to counsel and evidence, could not be compelled to give evidence against themselves, and could be convicted only by a jury of their peers. Excessive bail and fines, cruel and unusual punishments, bills of attainder, general warrants, and ex post facto laws were forbidden, as were perpetuities, monopolies, hereditary honors, special privileges, titles of nobility, standing armies in time of peace, and the suspension of the writ of habeas corpus. They proclaimed the right of free exercise of religion, of freemen to bear arms, and the supremacy of the civil over military power. They guaranteed freedom of elections, speech, and press; and recognized the right of people to assemble, to petition for redress of grievances, to instruct their representatives, and to participate in legislation. Taxation without consent was forbidden. They declared that the purpose of government was to promote the welfare and happiness of the people, that all political power was vested in the people, and that a majority of the people had the right to alter, change, or abolish the government when it became subversive of the purposes for which it was established.

Shadowy and indistinct as some of these concepts may be, they were the foundation stones upon which the superstructure of American democracy was to be erected. And while political leaders, North and South, were, during the 1830's and 1840's, to condemn the political axioms of the natural rights philosophy as "glittering and sounding generalities."[4] They were proclaimed

---

[4] *It was Rufus Choate, United States senator from Massachusetts, who used this particular phrase. Samuel G. Brown,* Life of Rufus Choate *(Boston, 1870), 328. See also Carl Becker,* The Declaration of Independence: A Study in the History of Political Ideas *(Vintage Books edition, New York, 1958), 240, 244. Rhode Island included a bill of rights in her first constitution in 1842; Virginia incorporated her Bill of Rights of 1776 in her revised constitution of 1850; and Minnesota included one in her constitution of 1858.*

anew in the state constitutions of that period. And the philosophical concept that all men are born equal and are possessed of inherent and unalienable rights continues even in 1961 to inspire and justify American democracy.

The Articles of Confederation, ratified in 1781, had little direct bearing on the establishment and development of democracy in the United States. Little more than a league of sovereign states, the Confederation had no authority to act upon the individual citizen. In the same decade, Congress, in adopting the Northwest Ordinance of 1787, set up property qualifications for voting and officeholding higher than those in most of the states. The elector was required to possess a freehold of fifty acres, members of the legislature two hundred, the secretary, judges, and councillors five hundred, and the governor one thousand acres. The Ordinance contained a few provisions similar to those in the state bills of rights and provided for the encouragement and support of education. Unlike any of the original state constitutions the Ordinance, however, excluded slavery from the Territory.

The delegates who assembled in Philadelphia in 1787, feared the excesses of democracy they professed to see in the state constitutions. Although they failed to include a formal bill of rights, they did incorporate some of the provisions of the state bills of rights into the Constitution. It forbade Congress to suspend the writ of habeas corpus except in case of rebellion or invasion, to pass bills of attainder or ex post facto laws, or to confer titles of nobility. And it provided for jury trial except in impeachment cases. It left the qualifications of voters for members of the House of Representatives to be determined by the individual states. Critics of the Constitution forced the adoption of ten amendments in 1791 which guaranteed freedom of speech, press, and assembly, the right of petition, and trial by jury with counsel and witnesses, and forbade excessive bail, fines, cruel and unjust punishments. The Federal Constitution and government were somewhat less inclined toward democracy, equality, and individual rights than were the state governments. The first cycle in American democracy had come to an end.

To the extent that democracy depends upon constitutional guarantees of individual rights the United States had embraced democracy. But these guarantees had not been fully implemented, and the principles and ideas associated with popular government had not gained wide acceptance. To a numerous and influential upper class, popularly called aristocrats, the word democracy stood for leveling tendencies, radicalism, and mobocracy. They hoped and expected that the conservative interests would overcome the democratic trends. John Adams called upon the aristocrats to "Remember, democracy never lasts long. It soon wastes, exhausts and murders itself. There never was a democracy that did not commit suicide."[5] James Fenimore Cooper maintained that equality was "no where laid down as a governing principle of the institutions of the United States, neither the word, nor any inference that can be fairly deduced from its meaning, occurring in the constitution."[6]

The democrats realized that democracy could not stand still, that a static democracy like a static society was a dying one, and that to live democracy must constantly change and grow. As one of their number expressed it, "Nothing is clearer than that genuine democracy must ever be progressive."[7] And from the beginning American citizens, individually and in organized groups,

have constantly striven to broaden the base of democracy and to attain their full liberty and equal rights and opportunities. Progress has been made, not by revolutionary action, but through the orderly processes of governmental action. The evolution of democracy in the United States has been greatly influenced by the dual system of state and federal governments and by the separation of governmental powers between the three branches —legislative, executive, and judicial. At times the two governments and the three branches of each have worked at cross purposes; at others they have supported each other in efforts to broaden and develop democracy.

The second cycle, from 1790 to 1860, can best be studied in the state constitutions which "so reflect the changing conditions and varied interests of the United States, that a study of them affords a perfect mirror of American democracy." Lord Bryce found them "a mine of instruction for the natural history of democratic communities."[8] In the period before 1860 the rights, privileges, and immunities of the citizen were much more dependent upon the political institutions of the several states than they were upon those of the federal government. In fact during most of this period the United States seemed to ignore the individual, left to the states nearly all the functions that affected individual rights, and in at least one case (the Dorr Rebellion in Rhode Island) failed to intervene or support the citizens in their effort to carry through a democratic reorganization of their state government. When the citizen

5 *Morris L. Ernst*, The Ultimate Power (*Garden City, N. Y., 1937*), 70.

6 *James Fenimore Cooper*, The American Democrat, *with an Introduction by H. L. Mencken (New York, 1936*), 42.

7 Report of the Debates and Proceedings of the Convention for the Revision of the Constitution of Ohio (*2 vols., Columbus, 1851*), II, 551.

8 *James Q. Dealey*, Growth of American State Constitutions from 1776 to the End of the Year 1914 (*Boston, 1915*), 117; *James Bryce*, The American Commonwealth (*2nd ed., 2 vols., London, 1891*), I, 434.

voted for his representative in Congress he did so under suffrage qualifications established by his state. Federal relations with the individual were generally negative rather than positive. The First Amendment to the Constitution forbade Congress to enact a law respecting the establishment of religion but did not restrain a state from doing so. Hence up to 1835 the North Carolina constitution forbade Catholics to hold office; and as late as 1930 those New Jersey citizens who did not profess to a belief in God were denied the right of testifying in the state courts.[9]

The major goal of the democratic reformers of the first half of the nineteenth century was political equality. This they hoped to attain by the abolition of religious and property tests for voting and officeholding, the adoption of the written ballot, the popular election of all state and local officials, and the more equitable distribution of representation. These reforms were generally opposed by the wealthy, aristocratic, conservative classes and supported by the lower classes, or plain people. Many of the leaders for reform, however, came from the upper class. Generally speaking the Federalist and Whig parties opposed while the Jeffersonian Republican and Jacksonian Democratic parties supported reform, although there was considerable criss-crossing of individuals within the parties. Minor parties—the workingmen's and labor groups, for instance—were supporters of the democratic revolution.

Constitutional revision designed to promote democracy was a never-ending process. The thirteen original states had grown to thirty-four by 1860 and each of them held a convention, some two, three, or even four; several had periodic revisions by a council established for that purpose; and many of them added amendments through legislative action. In the later period all new

constitutions, as well as revisals and some amendments, were submitted to a popular referendum. In several cases the voters, disappointed with the extent of reforms offered, rejected the revision and forced another convention. The territories forced Congress to keep step with state democracy in constitution making. The Northwest Ordinance had established a freehold of fifty acres of land for voting but the Mississippi Territory protested this as undemocratic, and pre-emptioners were added to the list of voters in 1807. This did not satisfy the democrats and they demanded that all taxpayers be permitted to vote. Congress acquiesced and abandoned the freehold in 1811. All new states carved out of the public domain between 1830 and 1860 except one called a convention and drafted a constitution without waiting for Congress to pass an enabling act.

The older states generally followed orderly and legal processes in constitutional revision, but the people were not averse to taking power into their own hands in order to secure their rights. One or two examples will suffice. In North Carolina, after the legislature had refused to call a convention, the reformers called upon the whole people to join forces and "by an unanimity and promptness of action, break to pieces the trammels of aristocracy, and show to the enemy of republican equality that the sons of freemen will still be free."[10] They declared that "a convention will be assembled . . . [and] the constitution *will be* amended." But they did not get the convention for more than a decade. The Georgia democrats went a step farther. They issued a call for a convention that declared, "the people have an undoubted right, in their sovereign capacity, to alter or change the form of their government, whenever in their opinion it becomes too obnoxious or oppressive

[9] *Ernst*, The Ultimate Power, *195.*

[10] *Salisbury* Western North Carolinian, *July 17, 1821,* October 22, 1822.

to be borne."[11] The people elected delegates to meet in an extra-legal constitutional convention. Whereupon the legislature capitulated and called for a legal convention to assemble at the place and time specified in the people's call. In Rhode Island the action resulted in the well-known Dorr Rebellion. The reformers called a people's convention which adopted a constitution providing for white manhood suffrage to replace the freehold requirement of the old charter-constitution. Thomas W. Dorr was elected and inaugurated governor. Both he and the legally elected governor, Samuel W. King, appealed to President John Tyler, who made it clear that the federal government would intervene if necessary to guarantee a republican form of government for the state. Dorr's Rebellion was crushed, but a legally assembled convention extended the suffrage to adult male citizens who were possessed of real estate worth $134 or who paid a rental of $7.00 per annum, and to native-born male citizens who paid a tax of $1.00, or contributed $1.00 for the support of public schools.[12]

In spite of the bitter controversy over slavery and abolition from 1830 to 1860 there was little sentiment to include the Negro in the free suffrage group. In fact the pendulum swung in the other direction. Between 1790 and 1838 ten states, six slave and four free, which had permitted limited Negro suffrage abolished it. New York abolished Negro suffrage in 1807 but re-established it in 1821 for those who owned a freehold worth $250 clear of debt and on which they had paid tax. Efforts to re-establish equal Negro suffrage were defeated in 1846 and 1860. Wisconsin rejected a

Negro suffrage amendment in 1848, but the state supreme court ruled in 1866 that the action had been ratified. Ohio also defeated a Negro suffrage amendment in 1851. The slavery issue was used by the reformers in some of the slave states, who argued that the extension of suffrage to all white males would unite the whites in support of the institution of slavery. Slavery advocates championed the continued use of the federal ratio for apportioning representation in the legislatures on the ground that it would strengthen the South in its defense against abolitionism.

There is little evidence that sectionalism, north or south, east or west, had any material influence on the advance of democracy. Of the original states, South Carolina, generally conceded to have been controlled by the planter aristocracy, was the first to amend her constitution to establish adult white male suffrage, whereas Rhode Island was the last to abolish the freehold requirement. North Carolina, less dominated by a planter aristocracy than any southern state, was the last state to abolish the dual suffrage requirement for the two houses of the legislature. The new western states consciously drew the more liberal suffrage qualifications from eastern states. They also followed the eastern states in setting up different requirements for voting in local and general elections. New states north of the Ohio River did not seem to move any more rapidly forward in establishing adult manhood suffrage than those south of it. Mississippi abolished property qualifications for suffrage in 1817, whereas Illinois retained a taxpaying requirement until 1837. Furthermore, the new upper western states excluded Negroes as well as Indians from the suffrage. One recent scholar has concluded that "In view of the extent to which western suffrage history was a recapitulation of the suffrage history of the eastern seaboard, it is difficult to believe that the New

[11] *Milledgeville* Southern Recorder, *May 31, 1832.*

[12] *See Arthur M. Mowry,* The Dorr War: or, The Constitutional Struggle in Rhode Island (*Providence, 1901*).

West was unique or that it made any new contribution to the growth of suffrage democracy."[13]

By 1860 the states had practically completed their campaign for political democracy as the term was then understood. Property qualifications for voting and officeholding had been abolished. Popular elections of governors, other state officials, and in many cases the judiciary, prevailed; and every state, with the exception of South Carolina, now chose presidential electors by popular vote. The written ballot had been provided in all states except Virginia and Illinois. Polling places had been brought near the voter, an improvement that has been characterized by one scholar "as important as the prior abandonment of the freehold qualification for voting." Primogeniture and entail had been abolished and imprisonment for debt had been drastically restricted. Church and state had been separated and religious tests for voting and officeholding had been abolished. Representation had been more equitably reapportioned, rotten boroughs had been abolished, and the larger urban centers had been given greater representation.

Having established political democracy the people began to use their power for their greater good. Banks and other corporations were brought under regulation, and, of far greater importance, the states began to implement the provisions in their constitutions which provided for state-supported public schools. Varying from state to state, this movement got under way north, south, and west. Along with public schools came funds for internal improvements. One North Carolina farmer expressed a general feeling when he wrote that such state support would provide "a large fund to be laid out in the improvement of roads and rivers; in the creation of schools for the education of the children . . .; in ameliorating our penal code by the establishment of a penitentiary, and in various other ways for the state as the wisdom of the people may, from time to time prescribe and direct."

Alexis de Tocqueville wrote in the first edition of his *Democracy in America* that "the gradual development of the principle of equality is a providential fact. . . . It is universal, it is durable, it constantly eludes all human interference, and all events as well as all men contribute to its progress." Fifteen years later he concluded that his prophecy, at least for the United States, had been fulfilled. Democracy was an established and going concern.[14] The states had played the lead role in this successful enterprise, but their major task had been completed. Democracy was soon to shift its concern to minority groups—Negroes, women, and Indians—whose political rights had been largely ignored and neglected. This shift was accompanied by another, which was to place major emphasis on civil rights and economic democracy. The United States government was to lead in this new venture.

The American Civil War was fought, according to official statements of President Lincoln and the Congress, to save the Union. The Union was saved, but the war transformed it from a federal into a national government, and the victorious North determined that the new Union should use its national power not only to free itself from the

[13] *Chilton Williamson*, American Suffrage from Property to Democracy, 1760–1860 (*Princeton, 1960*), *221–22. For an older and conflicting view see John D. Barnhart, Valley of Democracy: The Frontier Versus the Plantation in the Ohio Valley, 1775–1818 (Bloomington, Ind., 1953*).

[14] *Alexis de Tocqueville*, Democracy in America, *ed. by Phillips Bradley (Vintage Books edition, 2 vols., New York, 1957*), *I, ix.*

sinful stain of slavery but also to further the cause of political democracy. The states were to be shorn of much of their power and to become, as time went on, more and more the mere administrative units of national authority, until today little is left of the federal system as established in 1789.[15] Looking at the problem from the vantage point of the present, one might make a good case for the view that the nation would have been better off if Alexander Hamilton's program for a national state had been accepted by the Constitutional Convention.

The changes wrought by the war in the nature and spirit of the Union were accompanied by another significant change—the shift in the attitude of the people toward government. A large part of the American people no longer accepted the Jeffersonian view that that government is best which governs least. They wanted more and more services from their government. Furthermore, the development of transportation and communication, the expansion of industry and commerce, and the rise of cities contributed to the growth of a large industrial labor class that looked to the national government for economic equality as well as political democracy.

The advocates of freedom for the slave and suffrage for the Negro still looked back to the Revolutionary philosophy of natural rights and human equality. Negroes, like white men, were created equal and possessed unalienable rights to life, liberty, and the pursuit of happiness. President Lincoln had taken the first steps toward this goal during the war but, since his authority was based upon the exercise of war powers of doubtful constitutionality, control shifted to a more radical group in Congress which determined to destroy

the institution, root and branch, and to give the freedmen full citizenship rights. By special acts Congress liberated the slaves in the District of Columbia and the territories in 1862, and required gradual emancipation of West Virginia as the price of her admission into the Union. In 1865 congressional leaders decided on the bold plan of abolishing slavery everywhere in the Union by an amendment to the United States Constitution. This "was the first example of the use of the amending process to accomplish a specific reform on a nation-wide scale,"[16] and it aroused considerable opposition even in the northern states. Of the thirty-six states, three fourths were necessary for ratification. Five of the states failed to ratify. The eleven former Confederate states, constituting more than one fourth of the total number, were not yet back in the Union, but they were required to ratify the Thirteenth Amendment as a prerequisite to re-admission. Secretary of State William H. Seward included eight of them in the proclamation which declared the amendment in force. This was only the first instance of what Thomas Reed Powell has called "complete coercion" by the national government "to secure ratification . . . [of amendments] by the unreconstructed states."[17]

The slaves having been freed, Congress moved to secure suffrage for the Negro. The Reconstruction Act of 1867 required the secession states to "permit all male citizens . . . of whatever race, color, or previous condition of servitude" to vote for delegates to the conventions, which, in turn, were required to incorporate a provision into the constitution guaranteeing the "elective franchise . . . to all such persons as have qualifications herein

[15] See Roy F. Nichols, "*Federalism Versus Democracy*," in Federalism as a Democratic Process (*New Brunswick, 1942*), *49, 74–75.*

[16] *James G. Randall*, The Civil War and Reconstruction (*Boston, 1937*), *508.*
[17] *Thomas Reed Powell*, Vagaries and Varieties in Constitutional Interpretation (*New York, 1956*), *215.*

stated for electors." Finally, the state was required to pledge that its constitution should "never be so altered as to deprive any citizen or class of citizens of the United States of the right to vote who are entitled to vote by the constitution herein ratified."

The Congress had concern for the political rights of Negroes in states other than the secession states. In 1867 it bestowed suffrage on the Negroes in the District of Columbia and the territories. Likewise Congress required Nebraska and Colorado, whose constitutions confined voting privileges to whites, to amend their organic laws so as to permit Negro suffrage. More sweeping was the action of Congress in proposing the Fourteenth and Fifteenth Amendments. The first made of the freedmen citizens of the United States and forbade any state to make or enforce any law "which would abridge the privileges of citizens"; the second declared that "The right of citizens of the United States to vote shall not be denied or abridged by the United States or by any State on account of race, color, or previous condition of servitude." It should be remembered that only six states had permitted Negro suffrage in 1860. That Negro suffrage was advocated by the Radical Republicans for partisan purposes detracts not at all from the importance of the enfranchisement of the Negro. It still stands as one of the most significant steps in the development of political democracy in America. There may be some truth in the statement of a well-known scholar that "In the United States, suffrage came to the Negro like a bolt from the blue sky, confusing both friend and foe as to its meaning. The law did not fit the social system. It was a façade concealing a hollow interior so far as any real freedom for the Negro was concerned."[18] There are explanations for the failure of Negro suffrage not mentioned by the

author. Among them were the fact that the Negro was thrown into the sea of politics before he had been taught to swim; that misguided southern whites threw stumbling blocks in the path of the unlettered, newly enfranchised voter, and illegally prevented him from exercising his rights; and that unscrupulous politicians everywhere deliberately exploited the Negro voter.

Under congressional Reconstruction the southern states added other democratic provisions to their constitutions. Among the more important were the prohibition of imprisonment for debt, a homestead exemption from seizure and sale for debt, the guarantee of married women's property rights, the requirement that taxes should be levied for public schools open to Negroes as well as whites, albeit most of them provided for segregated schools, and the admission of Negroes to the militia. South Carolina provided for the popular election of presidential electors, and Louisiana for the first time included a separate bill of rights in her constitution. Congress also influenced some revision in states outside the South. It required all new states to establish and support public schools free from sectarian control; required Arizona to drop from her constitution a provision for the recall of judges but, like the southern states and their pledge on Negro suffrage, she later violated the pledge; and Indiana dropped the provision from her pre-Civil War constitution that forbade Negroes to settle in the state. Without pressure from Congress other states completed the democratic reforms begun before the Civil War. Among such changes were the popular election of the judiciary; the final dropping of the Protestant religion as a requirement for holding state office, and the remnants of property requirements for officeholding. The over-all significance of congressional influence on political democracy in the last half of the nineteenth century constitutes one of the great landmarks in the history of

---

[18] *Harold F. Gosnell*, Democracy the Threshold of Freedom (*New York, 1948*), 28.

democracy. In 1915 one constitutional historian wrote that "So powerful has been the democratic influence of Congress in reconstruction and in the formation of states out of territories, that one might almost wish that the New England and smaller middle states would attempt to secede from the Union, so that Congress might have the pleasure of reconstructing them on democratic lines."[19]

Congress played a rôle in the successful campaign for direct election of United States senators and suffrage for women similar to that it played in the abolition of slavery and the enfranchisement of the Negro, namely, by drafting and proposing constitutional amendments to be ratified by the states. The system of electing senators by state legislatures, originally provided by the United States Constitution, was subject to many criticisms, chief of which was that it violated a basic concept of American democracy—the popular election of governmental officials. Conservatives generally opposed any change, and southerners opposed popular election of senators for fear that it might interfere with white supremacy in the South. Some states began to hold perferential primaries for senators and the movement gained favor. Finally, in 1912 Congress passed a resolution that was ratified in 1913. Other than conforming to, and satisfying the demand of, the democratic concept of popular elections the change has been of little significance on American democracy.

The demand for woman suffrage had its roots deep in natural rights philosophy. From the beginning of our nation there had been a continuing demand for a broader suffrage. Religious, property, and race or color qualifications fell by the way, but sex, which barred a larger number than either of these, was last to fall. New Jersey had inadvertently permitted women to vote under her constitution of 1776, which gave the suffrage to "all inhabitants of full age worth fifty pounds." Few women took advantage of the opportunity and the constitution was soon changed so as to limit suffrage to males. In 1838 Kentucky gave widows with children of school age the right to vote in all school elections, and Kansas extended this right to all women in 1861. The enfranchisement of Negroes by congressional action shortly after the Civil War gave renewed strength to the woman suffrage movement, and in 1878 a resolution for a constitutional amendment was introduced in Congress. It gained little headway at first. The early victories came in the states, chiefly in the West. Finally, in 1916 the two major parties endorsed woman suffrage in their platforms, and in 1918 President Woodrow Wilson gave his support to the proposed amendment as a war measure. Both houses of Congress passed a resolution in 1919 which declared that "the right of citizens to vote shall not be denied or abridged by the United States or by any State on account of sex." Ratified by the necessary states in 1920, it became the Nineteenth Amendment to the Constition. Chief opposition came in the southern states which were about equally divided on the issue. The southern argument against the change was that it would interfere with white supremacy control of elections. Constitutional historians hold that woman suffrage has not greatly affected either the course of legislation or political practices. Women seem to vote in about the same proportion and for similar reasons as men.[20] Progress has been made, however, in that the number of women who go into active politics

---

[19] *Dealey,* Growth of American State Constitutions, *110–11.*

[20] *Carl B. Swisher,* American Constitutional Development *(2nd edition, Boston, 1954), 702.*

has been gradually increasing, and in recent years they have occupied high positions in both state and national government.

Congress made vigorous efforts during the Reconstruction period to enlarge and secure equal rights of all citizens through legislation and constitutional guarantees. These efforts were closely related to the liberation and enfranchisement of the Negro and were aimed chiefly against state discrimination. Speaking for a civil rights measure, Lyman Trumball frankly said, "if a man is discriminated against under . . . state laws because he is colored then it becomes necessary to interfere for his protection." These measures, however, were broad enough to include all people who were discriminated against, although some were specifically designed for the protection of the Negro.

A broad civil rights act of the latter class was enacted in 1866 but doubt of its constitutionality led Congress to incorporate its major provisions into Section 1 of the Fourteenth Amendment where its protection was guaranteed to all citizens. The Amendment for the first time defined citizenship and also for the first time gave national protection to rights that might be invaded by a state. In doing so it reversed the traditional relationship of the citizen to the two governments. This amendment was followed by several other civil rights acts, one of which, that of 1875, was designed to protect the Negro's social rights, or to establish his social equality, by guaranteeing his admission to hotels, theaters, restaurants, public conveyances, places of amusement, and other semi-public establishments.

This broad program of civil and social rights and equal opportunities was largely thwarted by the decisions of a conservative Supreme Court. In a series of decisions from 1876 to the well-known Civil Rights cases of 1883, the Court found that the rights which the acts were attempting to protect were social rather than civil and that the national government had no jurisdiction over such matters.

By 1890 the southern states came to the conclusion that the national guarantees of Negro suffrage, like those of civil and social rights, might safely be ignored, and they devised constitutional provisions—educational tests, good moral character, poll tax payments, and registration procedures—which almost entirely disfranchised the Negro. They safeguarded white suffrage by various *or* clauses, including property ownership, ability to read or understand the Constitution when read, and the grandfather clauses. At first the national courts upheld the new constitutional provisions, but in 1915 the grandfather clause was held unconstitutional. By that time, however, its benefits to whites had expired in all states except Oklahoma. The exclusions against the Negro were still enforced. By the end of the century Congress had largely lost its enthusiasm for democratic leadership. A new cycle was ready to begin.

During the Progressive era the states temporarily reassumed their former position as leaders in liberal democratic reforms. Various schemes were devised to regain power that had slipped into the hands of the political bosses and interests. They were more numerous and popular in the western states where Populism had been strong. Most notable of these new devices or programs were the initiative, referendum, recall, and the direct and preferential primaries. The initiative and referendum enabled the voters to propose legislation which the interest-controlled legislatures had refused to consider, and the referendum placed laws on the ballot for approval or rejection by the voters. Oregon was the leader in this program. It might be noted that some states in the pre-Civil War period utilized this principle in constitutional revision. The direct primary, first used in Wisconsin, became widespread in state and local elections. Those in the South were restricted to white voters in the Democratic primaries. The preferential primary was used in some states to give the voter a chance to express his preference for senatorial candidates before they had become elective by popular vote and his choice for the presidency. The recall was used in various states to recall officials, both local and state, who were thought to have failed the people. During the latter part of the nineteenth and in the early twentieh century many states adopted educational qualifications for voting. Generally they were designed to improve popular government, but southern states used them as they did their primaries to restrict Negro voting. These state reforms constituted no major revolution in the American democratic system. They merely buttressed the long-accepted idea that the people had the right to govern themselves and should participate in the making of legislation and elect officials who were responsible to the people.

A new era, or cycle, in the development of American democracy, involving social, economic, political, and civil rights, got under way in the second quarter of the twentieth century. Working together as a team to effect the new measures were the states, the President, the Congress, and the Supreme Court. The efforts of the first three were somewhat sporadic, and for the first time the Supreme Court assumed the leadership in effecting democratic advances. This was the more interesting because the Court had heretofore been a conservative check on the more liberal and democratic branches of government. In the period following the Civil War it had limited some congressional legislative action, disallowed in toto some of the more promising provisions of the civil rights acts, and had interpreted the section of the Fourteenth Amendment which prohibited a state to "deprive any person of life, liberty or property" so as to give protection to business interests rather than human rights. The personnel of the Court changed rapidly in the New Deal period and the Court's philosophy became much more liberal. The Court shifted from support of laissez faire in regard to freedom of contract and rights of property, began to sanction legislation designed to regulate economic life in terms of human and national interest, and to apply "due process of law" as a protection to persons rather than corporations.

State action varied from state to state and region to region. Southern public opinion had been partially awakened to the evils of a restricted electorate and to discrimination against the lower economic class, whites and Negroes. In urging the abolition of the poll tax Chief Justice Grafton Green of the Tennessee Supreme Court said: "Universal exercise of the right of suffrage must be regarded as the ideal support of democratic institutions. . . . Elections were designed to put into effective operation the underlying principle of democracy which makes the will of an unfettered majority controlling. So it is that restraint upon plenary participation in a primary election, as well as a regular election, is destructive of the basis of either system."[21] Unfortunately Green's state did not heed his plea, and along with other southern states it continued to require payments of poll taxes for voting. Influenced by the call of eighteen-year-old boys into the armed services during World War II, two southern states have given the franchise to qualified citizens eighteen years of age.

Eastern and western states have been more concerned with individual rights than political action, and many have enacted civil rights and anti-bias legislation. Some forbid "religious or

21 *Jennings Perry*, Democracy Begins at Home (*Philadelphia, 1944*), *flyleaf.*

racial discrimination" in the sale or rental of dwelling and apartment houses; others guarantee "full and equal service and treatment" to persons of any race or color in hotels, restaurants, barber shops, swimming pools, skating rinks, theaters, and public conveyances.[22]

Presidents Franklin D. Roosevelt, Harry S. Truman, and Dwight D. Eisenhower gave support to civil rights. Roosevelt popularized the idea of equal rights to all regardless of race or color, but his accomplishments were not notable. Truman, opposed by a hostile Congress, accomplished more than Roosevelt. He appointed a committee on civil rights that, after much study, prepared a report which revealed widespread discrimination against minority groups in all parts of the country. The committee recommended a series of measures designed to curb the evils, but Truman was unable to get any action from Congress. Eisenhower, less vocal on the issue than either Roosevelt or Truman, accomplished more in the field of civil rights than either. He abolished segregation in the armed services, in schools on army posts, and in institutions maintained by the Veterans' Administration. His administration was instrumental in breaking the color line in hotels and theaters in Washington. And he, very hesitantly, sent troops to Little Rock to preserve order in the integration of the public high schools of that city.

In 1957 Congress enacted a Civil Rights Act, the first since Reconstruction, which provided for a Bi-Partisan Commission on Civil Rights with power to investigate the denial of suffrage and equal protection of the law because of race, color, or religion. An assistant attorney general was given power to initiate suit by injunction where there was evidence of interference with voting rights. Federal judges were empowered to enjoin

[22] See *New York* Times, *February 18, 1961, for recent enactments.*

state officials from refusing to register qualified voters, and punish them with fine and imprisonment, if guilty, without jury trial. This measure promises to be a major victory for racial equality at the polls.

The Supreme Court decisions since 1925 have worked what might be called a democratic revolution in the United States. The Court has accepted the basic principles of the civil rights acts and the Fourteenth Amendment and translated them into reality. At last it has given the American people the assurance that they will have their day in court. It has found that freedom of speech, press, teaching, and learning are included in the liberty which the state may not take from a citizen without due process of law. After half a century it learned that separate accommodations for the Negro on trains, pullman and dining cars, and other common carriers, isolating a Negro student from his fellows in a state university, and denial of Negro citizens the use of public owned parks and swimming pools was a denial of equal protection of the law. In *Smith v. Allwright* (1944) it discovered that party primaries are instruments of the state, and as such are limited by constitutional provisions with respect to due process and equal protection of the laws. Finally, in 1961 it learned that the Civil Rights Act of 1871 is constitutional and valid. Most important of all, in *Brown v. Board of Education* (1954) it found that the decision in *Plessy v. Ferguson* (1896) was in error. It discovered that segregation of children in public schools solely on the basis of race, even though physical facilities and other tangible factors were equal, deprived children of the minor group of equal protection of the laws. In other words segregation per se is unconstitutional. This decision heralded a new epoch in the search for equality. In short, it is a lesson in democracy directed to all United States citizens. And, as Federal Judge Irving R. Kaufman recently said, the lesson is to be learned and applied in the North as well as the South, in the East and in the West.[23]

The present cycle of democratic development, concerned chiefly with the recognition, implementation, and attainment of political and civil rights of minority groups already guaranteed by law and constitution, in which the Supreme Court has played the leading role, has not yet run its course. The courts are continuously broadening and strengthening these rights. And it is not inconceivable that it might yet reverse the decision in the Civil Rights cases of 1883, as it has already reversed that of *Plessy v. Ferguson*, so as to secure the Negro and other minority groups equal rights in hotels, theaters, and all places of amusement and entertainment.

Democracy has been tested in the United States longer than in any other country but, while the United States has gone farther down the democratic road than most countries, much remains to be done before complete democracy can be achieved. For example, the poll tax in five southern states still prevents the lower economic class,

both white and Negro, from voting. The urban centers are discriminated against in many states in regard to representation. And the people of the District of Columbia are denied both the suffrage and representation. These political evils are already under attack and may be eliminated in the not too distant future.[24] But other evils will appear, and it is as true today as when first expressed by Patrick Henry that "Eternal vigilance is the price of liberty." Furthermore, since democracy is progressive in nature, ever growing, ever changing, it may never be completed. Like the mirage, the goal when approached may recede into the future.

[24] *Since the above was written three significant developments have taken place. First, an amendment to the United States Constitution giving suffrage to the citizens of the District of Columbia has been ratified; second, a United States District Court judge has ordered the registration officials of Macon County, Alabama, to register forthwith a group of Negro citizens and has issued an injunction prohibiting future discrimination against any prospective Negro voters; and, third, the United States Supreme Court has agreed to hear a suit from citizens of Tennessee requiring the state legislature to redistrict the state for representation.*

[23] Ibid., *January 25, 1961.*

John Lewis Krimmel "Fourth of July"   Historical Society of Pennsylvania

PART 8

THE NATIONAL CHARACTER

Introduction

As intellectual history matured as an academic field during the first half of the twentieth century, an increasing number of scholars became fascinated by the American national character. They were convinced that Americans, as well as America, were definitely unique. No other people had experienced, in the same way, the transplantation of civilization from Europe, the conquest of a vast wilderness, the organization of a democratic government, and the establishment of an industrial nation. Unwilling to accept forever the interpretations of foreign visitors such as Tocqueville, Bryce, and Brogan, American historians believed it was time to interpret the national character for themselves.

The article by Arthur M. Schlesinger was first presented as a presidential address at the 1942 meeting of the American Historical Association. He claimed that the American character had been molded by the influences of both Europe and America—by Old World traditions and New World conditions. In defining the true American

he discussed numerous characteristics which included such traditional traits as agrarianism, the gospel of work, boastfulness, and mobility.

William G. McLoughlin examines a specific concept, pietism, to determine what has influenced the development of the American character. He emphasizes the role of pietism, defines his concept, and applies it to politics, literature, and the visual arts. He is particularly concerned with the reform spirit and the desire of Americans to create a perfect society.

Like McLoughlin, George W. Pierson discusses a specific concept, mobility, to explain the national character. "Mobility," he writes, "has been one of the oldest and most continuous themes of the American experience. . . ." This constant movement—the "restless temper"—of people has affected all of our basic institutions and the American mind.

The essay by Perry Miller denies that there actually is an American national character because Americans are always in a state of change. He seriously questions whether we even have strong national traditions despite the efforts of the Puritans, the Revolutionary leaders, the Romantics, and the Darwinians. His conclusion is that anyone who attempts to label a set of standards as "American" is perhaps himself "Un-American." Being an American is not something inherited but something to be achieved.

"WHAT THEN IS THE AMERICAN, THIS NEW MAN?"[1]

*Arthur M. Schlesinger**

This question, posed in the last years of the Revolution by a Frenchman long resident in America, has never ceased to be of challenging interest. It lies at the heart of every inquiry into the national past and of every attempt to understand the present or peer into the future. It concerns specialists in economics, political science, and sociology no less than historians; students of religion, literature, and the arts no less than social scientists; statesmen no less than scholars. If we can once learn why the American has come to be as he is, what his instinctive reactions are to life,

[1] *Presidential address prepared for the Columbus meeting but delivered on the evening of the annual business meeting in Washington, December 30, 1942.*

[2] *J. Hector St. John* [*de Crèvecœur*], Letters from an American Farmer (*new ed., London, 1783*), *especially pp. 51–53.*

*ARTHUR M. SCHLESINGER (1888–1965) was the Francis Lee Higginson Professor of American History at Harvard University. In 1922 at the State University of Iowa he taught a course on the "Social and Cultural History of the United States," the first of its kind in any college. His publications include New Viewpoints of American History (*1922*), The Rise of the City, 1878–1898 (*1933*), *and* The American as Reformer (*1950*). *Reprinted by permission of the* American Historical Review, *Vol. 48, No. 2 (January, 1943), 225–244.*

how he differs from the people of other lands, we shall have gained a deep insight into the springs of national thought and action.

Crèvecœur's own answer to his question can still be read with profit.[2] He was, of course, one of a long procession of Europeans who have tried to describe and appraise the American character. Their writings, though of varying merit, possess the common advantage of presenting an outsider's point of view, free from the predilections and prepossessions which blur the American's vision of himself. Viewing the scene from a different background, they are also sensitive to national divergences of which most Americans are unaware. Though bias may influence the individual observer's judgment, the total number of visitors has been so great as to render far more significant their points of agreement.

The composite portrait that emerges deserves our thoughtful consideration. The attributes most frequently noted are a belief in the universal obligation to work; the urge to move about; a high standard of comfort for the average man; faith in progress; the eternal pursuit of material gain; an absence of permanent class barriers; the neglect of abstract thinking and of the aesthetic side of life; boastfulness; a deference for women; the blight of spoiled children; the general restlessness and hurry of life, always illustrated by the practice of fast eating; and certain miscellaneous traits such as overheated houses, the habit of spitting, and the passion for rocking chairs and ice water.

This inventory, so far as it goes, reveals qualities and attitudes recognizably American. Moreover, the travelers express no doubt as to the existence of a distinctive national character. Americans looking at their fellow countrymen readily identify them as New Englanders or Middle Westerners or Southerners, as products of old native stock or newcomers of immigrant origin, and they re-member that at one period of their history the differences between Northerner and Southerner sharpened into a sword, causing a tragic civil war. But the detached observer from Europe has always been less impressed by these variations than by the evidences of fundamental kinship, even in slavery times. James Bryce, most perspicacious of the commentators, goes so far as to say: "Scotchmen and Irishmen are more unlike Englishmen, the native of Normandy more unlike the native of Provence, the Pomeranian more unlike the Wurtemberger, the Piedmontese more unlike the Neapolitan, the Basque more unlike the Andalusian, than the American from any part of the country is to the American from any other part." His conclusion is that "it is rather more difficult to take any assemblage of attributes in any of these European countries and call it the national type than it is to do the like in the United States."[3] The preoccupation of American historians with local and sectional diversities has tended to obscure this underlying reality.

But the particular assemblage of attributes recorded by the travelers leaves much to be desired. Not only is the list incomplete, but it fails to distinguish the significant from the trivial. Since the typical European covered as much ground as possible in a limited stay, his attention was caught by externals. Annoying mannerisms assumed undue importance, as dust in the eye of a wayfarer keeps him from perceiving the main features of the landscape. Thus the gospel of work is hardly to be equated with the addiction to spitting. Some visitors actually prided themselves upon learning

[3] *Bryce,* The American Commonwealth (*London, 1888*), *III, 628. Alexis de Tocqueville expressed a similar view some fifty years before in* Democracy in America (*Henry Reeve, trans., Francis Bowen, ed., Cambridge, 1862*), *I, 215, 505.*

much from seeing little.[4] More thoughtful ones sought to correlate what they observed with the avowed ideals of the people, such as equality, individualism, and democracy; but except in a few conspicuous instances they lacked sufficient knowledge of the profounder trends in American society to understand either the true inwardness of the ideals or how they manifested themselves in action. Finally, the traveler gave little attention to the crucial problem of why the special combination of traits and attitudes had become endemic within the borders of the United States.

Hence the judgment of these onlookers, though often clear-sighted and frequently valuable as a corrective, leaves ample room for the student of United States history to venture an answer to Crèvecœur's question. If the native-born historian be suspect as a party in interest, he may at

least strive to observe that counsel of objectivity which his professional conscience reveres. What, then, is the American from the historian's point of view—or at least from one historian's point of view? The answer, briefly expressed, is so simple as to be a truism. This "new man" is the product of the interplay of his Old World heritage and New World conditions. Real understanding dawns only when the nature of these two factors is properly assessed.

The Old World heritage consisted merely of that part of European culture which the people who settled America had shared. The great bulk of the colonists, like the immigrants of later times, belonged to the poorer classes. Whether in England or on the Continent, they and their ancestors had been artisans, small tradesmen, farmers, day laborers—the firm foundation upon which rested the superstructure of European cultivation. Shut out from a life of wealth, leisure, and aesthetic enjoyment, they had tended to regard the ways of their social superiors with misgiving, if not resentment, and, by the same token, they magnified the virtues of sobriety, diligence, and thrift that characterized their own order. Even when many of them, notably in England, improved their economic position as a result of the great growth of commerce and industry, in the sixteenth and seventeenth centuries, they continued to exalt the ancient proprieties. This attitude found its classic spiritual expression in Calvinism. As Professor Tawney has said, Calvinism was "perhaps the first systematic body of religious teaching which can be said to recognize and applaud the economic virtues."[5] It neatly fitted the glove of divine sanction to the hand of prudential conduct, thus giving a sense of personal rectitude to the business of getting ahead in the world. But

[4] *Count Hermann Keyserling in his widely read volume* America Set Free *(New York, 1929), p. 5, boasts: "During my travels about the country, I guarded myself with almost old-maidish precaution against information. I looked at none of the obvious sights if I could help it; I asked few questions. . . . I went out little; I read hardly any papers." By this procedure he believed he utilized his four months' visit (which he regarded as needlessly long) for maintaining "contact almost exclusively with the subconscious side of American life." This may explain why he found "a good deal of truth" in Dr. Carl G. Jung's psychograph of the American as "a European with the manners of a negro and the soul of an Indian" (pp. 34, 36). Crevecœur, on the other hand, published his book after more than twenty years' residence in America, and Bryce wrote his masterly commentary following a succession of leisurely sojourns. "When I first visited America eighteen years ago," he says in* The American Commonwealth, *I, 5–6, "I brought home a swarm of bold generalizations. Half of them were thrown overboard after a second visit in 1881. Of the half that remained, some were dropped into the Atlantic when I returned across it after a third visit in 1883–84: and although the two later journeys gave birth to some new views, these views are fewer and more discreetly cautious than their departed sisters of 1870."*

[5] *R. H. Tawney,* Religion and the Rise of Capitalism *(New York, 1926), p. 105.*

whether in Britain or elsewhere, whether in the religious groups directly affected or those more remotely influenced, Calvinism merely intensified a pre-existing bent. It is similarly true that the stringent code of morals often attributed to Calvinism, and more particularly to Puritanism, represented a lower-middle-class mentality long antedating the Geneva teachings.

This, then, was the type of human breed upon which the untamed New World exerted its will. It has often been observed that the plants and animals of foreign lands undergo change when removed to America. These mutations arise from differences in climate and geography. But other influences also affected the transplanted European man. One was the temperament of the settler, the fact that he was more adventurous, or more ambitious, or more rebellious against conditions at home than his fellows who stayed put. It is not necessary to believe with William Stoughton that "God sifted a whole Nation that he might send Choice Grain over into this Wilderness,"[6] but undoubtedly the act of quitting a familiar life for a strange and perilous one demanded uncommon qualities of hardihood, self-reliance, and imagination. Once the ocean was crossed, sheer distance and the impact of novel experiences further weakened the bonds of custom, evoked unsuspected capacities, and awakened the settler to possibilities of improvement which his forebears had never known.

The conditions offered by an undeveloped continent fixed the frame within which the new life must be lived, the mold within which the American character took form. Farming was the primary occupation. At first resorted to by the settlers to keep from starvation, it quickly became the mainstay of their existence. The Revolution was fought

by a people of whom nineteen out of twenty were farmers. With good soil easily obtainable for over a century more, agriculture continued, though with gradually diminishing effect, to provide the pervasive atmosphere of American life and thought. "The vast majority of the people of this country live by the land, and carry its quality in their manners and opinions," wrote Emerson in 1844.[7] Even when the hosts from Continental Europe began to swell the population in the nineteenth century, the rural temper of the nation continued unaltered, for most of the immigrants also turned to farming. This long apprenticeship to the soil made an indelible impress on the developing American character, with results which the modern age of the city has not wholly effaced.

The agriculture of the New World, however, differed from the agriculture of the Old. This was the initial lesson which the colonial newcomers were compelled to learn. Those who had been bred to husbandry in their homelands found many of the traditional methods unsuitable. Those who had worked at urban occupations suffered from an even greater handicap. Densely forested land must be cleared, the wildness taken out of the soil, a knowledge gained of indigenous plants and of the best means of growing them. The settlers of Jamestown were barely able to struggle through the early years. "There were never Englishmen left in a forreigne Country in such miserie as wee were in this new discovered Virginia," wrote one of them.[8] "Unsufferable hunger" caused them to eat horses, dogs, rats, and snakes, and instances even of cannibalism are

[6] Stoughton, New-Englands True Interest (*Cambridge, 1670*), p. 19.

[7] *Ralph Waldo Emerson, "The Young American,"* Works (*Boston, 1883*), I, 349.

[8] *George Percy, "Discourse of the Plantation of the Southern Colony in Virginia," abridged in Samuel Purchas,* Hakluytus Posthumus, or Purchas His Pilgrimes (*Glasgow, 1905–07*), XVIII, 418.

recorded.[9] As is well known, the Plymouth colonists experienced similar trials. Yet in both cases the woods abounded with native fruits, berries, roots, and nuts; wild game was plentiful; and the near-by waters teemed with fish.

Had these Englishmen been more readily adaptable, they could have enjoyed a gastronomic abundance beyond the reach of even the nobility at home. But reversion to a stage of civilization which the white man had long since outgrown was not easy. At the very first, all the early settlements actually imported food supplies. The Swedish colony on the Delaware did so for twenty years. A knowledge of self-sufficient farming came slowly and painfully, with untold numbers of men, women, and children perishing in the process. In the long run, however, the settlers learned to master their environment. Utilizing native crops and Indian methods of tillage, they abandoned the intensive cultivation required by the limited land resources of the Old World. It was simpler to move on to new fields when the fertility of the old was exhausted. The typical farm was a small one, worked by the owner and his family. Even when the system of staple production emerged in the South, the small independent farmers considerably outnumbered the great slave-holding planters.

Though the colonial agriculturist owed much to the Indians, his European heritage restrained him from imitating them more than he must. Unlike the aborigines, he thirsted for the simple mechanical aids and other amenities which he and his kind had enjoyed in the Old World, and, lacking other means, he proceeded as best he could to reproduce them for himself. Besides wrestling with the soil, every husbandman was a manufacturer and every home a factory, engaged in grinding grain, making soap and candles, preparing the family meat supply, tanning skins, fabricating nails, harness, hats, shoes, and rugs, contriving tools, churns, casks, beds, chairs, and tables. Occasionally he did some of these things for his neighbors for hire. Such activities were supplemented by hunting, trapping, and fishing. As cold weather closed in, the men used their spare time in getting out rough timber products, such as shingles and planks, or spent the long winter evenings before the open fireplace carving gunstocks or making brooms while the women-folk knitted, spun, or wove.

Under the pressure of circumstances the farmer became a Jack-of-all-trades. As Chancellor Livingston later wrote, "being habituated from early life to rely upon himself he acquires a skill in every branch of his profession, which is unknown in countries where labour is more divided."[10] Take the case of an undistinguished New Englander, John Marshall of Braintree, early in the eighteenth century. Besides tending his farm, he was painter, brickmaker, and carpenter, turned out as many as three hundred laths in a day, bought and sold hogs, and served as a precinct constable.[11] The primitive state of society fostered a similar omnicompetence in other walks of life, as the career of Benjamin Franklin so well exemplifies. Lord Cornbury, the governor of New York, characterized Francis Makemie as "a Preacher, a Doctor of Physick, a Merchant, an Attorney, or

---

[9] *"A Briefe Declaration of the Plantation of Virginia duringe the First Twelve Yeares. . . . By the Ancient Planters nowe Remaining Alive in Virginia,"* *Thomas H. Wynne and W. S. Gilman, eds.,* Colonial Records of Virginia *(Richmond, 1874), p. 71.*

[10] *Robert R. Livingston's remarks on American agriculture in* Edinburgh Encyclopaedia *(1st Am. ed., Philadelphia, 1832), I, 338.*

[11] *Charles Francis Adams, Jr., "John Marshall's Diary,"* Massachusetts Historical Society, *Proceedings, 2d ser., I (1885), 148–64.*

Counsellor at Law, and," he added for good measure, "which is worse of all, a Disturber of Governments."[12]

The pioneer farmer of later times was the colonial farmer reborn. Up and down the Mississippi Valley he faced the same difficulties and the same opportunities as his forefathers, and he dealt with them in much the same way. As time went on, he managed to secure from independent craftsmen and factories certain of his tools and household conveniences; he took advantage of newly invented laborsaving appliances, such as the iron plow and the reaper; and more and more he raised crops for sale in a general market. Along the Atlantic seaboard similar alterations occurred. But whether in the older or the newer communities, these innovations affected the surface rather than the substance of the traditional way of life. Nor did the advent of towns and cities at first do much to change the situation. Mere islands in a sea of population, they long retained marked rural characteristics and depended for a large part of their growth on continued accessions from the countryside.

What qualities of the national character are attributable to this long-persistent agrarian setting? First and foremost is the habit of work. For the colonial farmer ceaseless exertion was the price of survival. Every member of the community must be up and doing. If a contrary spirit showed itself, the authorities, whether Anglican, Puritan, or of a different faith, laid a heavy hand upon the culprit. The Virginia Assembly in 1619 ordered slothful individuals to be bound over to compulsory labor.[13] A few years later the Massachusetts Bay Company instructed Governor John Endecott that "noe idle drone bee permitted to live amongst us . . . ," and the General Court followed this up in 1633 with a decree that "noe prson, howse houlder or oth[r], shall spend his time idlely or unprofitably, under paine of such punishm[t] as the Court shall thinke meete to inflicte. . . ."[14] Such regulations had long existed in England, where it was hoped, vainly, that they might combat the unemployment and vagrancy of a surplus laboring class; in America their purpose was to overcome a labor shortage, that exigent problem of every new country. Of course, the vast bulk of settlers, inured to toil in the homeland, required no official prodding. They were the hardest-working people on earth, their only respite being afforded by strict observance of the Sabbath as required by both church and state.

The tradition of toil so begun found new sustenance as settlers opened up the boundless stretches of the interior country. "In the free States," wrote Harriet Martineau in 1837, "labour is more really and heartily honoured than, perhaps, in any other part of the civilised world."[15] Henry Ward Beecher voiced the general opinion of his countrymen when he asserted a few years later, "It would be endless to describe the wiles of idleness—how it creeps upon men, how secretly it mingles with their pursuits, how much time it purloins. . . . It steals minutes, it clips off the edges of hours, and at length takes possession of days."[16] Even when the usual motives for working did not exist, the social compulsion remained. As William Ellery Channing put it, "The rich man has no

[12] *Hugh Hastings, comp.,* Ecclesiastical Records, State of New York (*Albany, 1901–05*), III, 1670.

[13] *"The Proceedings of the First Assembly of Virginia," Wynne and Gilman, eds.,* Colonial Records, *p. 20.*

[14] *Nathaniel B. Shurtleff, ed.,* Records of the Governor and Company of the Massachusetts Bay in New England (*Boston, 1853–54*), I, 405, 109.

[15] *Martineau,* Society in America (*New York, 1837*), II, 99.

[16] *Beecher,* Lectures to Young Men, on Various Important Subjects (*2d ed., Boston, 1846*), p. 23.

more right to repose than the poor," for no man should so live as to "throw all toil on another class of society."[17] One source of Northern antagonism to the system of human bondage was the fear that it was jeopardizing this basic tenet of the American creed. "Wherever labor is mainly performed by slaves," Daniel Webster told his fellow members of the Senate, "it is regarded as degrading to freemen"; and the Kentucky abolitionist David Rice pointed out that in the South "To labour, is to *slave; to work, is to work like a Negroe. . . .*"[18] After the Civil War, General W. T. Sherman found public occasion to thank God that the overthrow of involuntary servitude enabled the Southern whites at last "to earn an honest living."[19]

Probably no legacy from our farmer forebears has entered more deeply into the national psychology. If an American has no purposeful work on hand, the fever in his blood impels him nevertheless to some form of visible activity. When seated he keeps moving in a rocking chair. A European visitor in the 1890's found more fact than fiction in a magazine caricature which pictured a foreigner as saying to his American hostess, "It's a defect in your country, that you have no leisured classes." "But we have them," she replied, "only we call them tramps." The traveler's own comment was: "America is the only country in the world, where one is ashamed of having nothing to do."[20]

This worship of work has rendered it difficult for Americans to learn how to play. As Poor Richard saw it, "Leisure is the Time for doing something useful"; and James Russell Lowell confessed,

> Pleasure doos make us Yankees kind o' winch,
> Ez though 't wuz sunthin' paid for by the inch;
> But yit we du contrive to worry thru,
> Ef Dooty tells us thet the thing's to du. . . .[21]

The first deviations from the daily grind took the form of hunting, fishing, barn-raisings, and log-rollings—activities that contributed directly to the basic needs of living. As the years went on, the great Southern planters developed rural diversions into a sort of ritual, but their example, like that of the fashionable circles in the cities, made the common man all the more self-conscious when he sought recreation. Nor did the spontaneous gaiety that marked the idle hours of the Germans and Irish who came in the mid-nineteenth century have any other effect than to reinforce suspicions of them formed on other scores. "The American," wrote a New Yorker of his compatriots in 1857, "enters into festivity as if it were a serious business. . . ."[22] And a serious business it has continued to be ever since. Into it goes all the fierce energy

---

[17] *Quoted in William H. Channing*, The Life of William Ellery Channing, D. D. *(Boston, 1880), p. 510, from a letter written in 1839.*

[18] *Webster*, Works *(Boston, 1851), V, 310; Rice*, Slavery Inconsistent with Justice and Good Policy *(Philadelphia, 1792), p. 11.*

[19] *Society of the Army of the Tennessee*, Report of Proceedings at the Fifteenth Annual Meeting, 1882 *(n.p., n.d.), p. 369.*

[20] *Serge Wolkonsky*, My Reminiscences *(Alfred E. Chamot, trans., London, n.d.), p. 219. "In England a man*

who does nothing goes by the name of 'gentleman;' in Chicago he goes by the names of 'loafer'," *wrote Paul Blouët (Max O'Rell, pseud.) and Jack Allyn in* Jonathan and His Continent *(Madame Paul Blouët, trans., New York, 1889), p. 237. In a speech at Milwaukee in 1910 Theodore Roosevelt expressed this sentiment in the American way: "I pity the creature who doesn't work—at whichever end of the social scale he may be." Henry L. Stoddard*, It Costs to Be President *(New York, 1938), p. 164.*

[21] *Lowell*, The Biglow Papers *(1846) in his* Works *(Boston, 1890–92), VIII, 331.*

[22] *[H. T. Tuckerman], "Holidays,"* North American Review, *LXXXIV (1857), 347.*

that once felled the forests and broke the prairies. We play games not for their own sake but in order to win them. We attend social gatherings grimly determined to have a "good time." Maxim Gorky said of Coney Island, "What an unhappy people it must be that turns for happiness here."[23] The "rich gift of extemporizing pleasures," of enjoying leisure leisurely, has, for the most part, been denied us.[24] It is significant that the English *Who's Who* lists hobbies while the American still excludes them.

The importance attached to useful work had the further effect of helping to render "this new man" indifferent to aesthetic considerations. To the farmer a tree was not a symbol of Nature's unity but an obstacle to be reduced to a stump and then quickly replaced with a patch of corn or vegetables. In the words of an eighteenth century American, "The Plow-man that raiseth Grain is more serviceable to Mankind, than the Painter who draws only to please the Eye. The Carpenter who builds a good House to defend us from the Wind and Weather, is more serviceable than the curious Carver, who employs his Art to please the Fancy."[25] The cult of beauty, in other words, had nothing to contribute to the stern business of living; it wasn't "practical." The bias thus given to the national mentality lasted well into America's urban age. One result has been the architectural monotony and ugliness which have invariably offended travelers accustomed to the picturesque charm of Old World cities.

On the other hand, the complicated nature of the farmer's job, especially during the first two and a half centuries, provided an unexcelled training in mechanical ingenuity. These ex-Europeans and their descendants became a race of whittlers and tinkers, daily engaged in devising, improving, and repairing tools and other things until, as Emerson said, they had "the power and habit of invention in their brain."[26] "Would any one but an American," asked one of Emerson's contemporaries, "have ever invented a milking machine? or a machine to beat eggs? or machines to black boots, scour knives, pare apples, and do a hundred things that all other peoples have done with their ten fingers from time immemorial?"[27] As population increased and manufacturing developed on a commercial scale, men merely turned to new purposes the skills and aptitudes that had become second nature to them. Thus Eli Whitney, who as a Massachusetts farm youth had made nails and hatpins for sale to his neighbors, later contrived the cotton gin and successfully applied the principle of interchangeable parts to the making of muskets; and Theodore T. Woodruff, a New York farm boy, won subsequent fame as the inventor of a sleeping car, a coffee-hulling machine, and a steam plow. In this manner another trait became imbedded in the American character.

The farmer's success in coping with his multitudinous tasks aroused a pride of accomplishment that made him scorn the specialist or expert. As a Jack-of-all-trades he was content to be master of none, choosing to do many things well enough rather than anything supremely well. Thus versatility became an outstanding American attribute. In public affairs the common man agreed with President Jackson that any intelligent person could

[23] Quoted in Irwin Edman, "On American Leisure," Harper's Magazine, *CLVI* (1928), 220.

[24] *The quoted phrase is from Adam G. de Gurowski,* America and Europe *(New York, 1857), p. 378.*

[25] *From a pamphlet of 1719 quoted in James Truslow Adams,* Provincial Society, 1690–1763 *(New York, 1927), pp. 141–42.*

[26] Emerson, "Resources," Works, *VIII, 137.*

[27] *Thomas L. Nichols,* Forty Years of American Life, 1821–1861 *(New York, 1937, first published in 1864), p. 63.*

discharge the duties of any governmental office. He had an abiding suspicion of the theorist or the "scholar in politics," preferring to trust his own quick perceptions and to deal from day to day with matters as they arose. In his breadwinning pursuits the American flitted freely from job to job in marked contrast to the European custom of following permanent occupations which often descended from father to son. The most casual scrutiny of the *Dictionary of American Biography* discloses countless instances reminiscent of John Marshall and Francis Makemie in colonial times. Thomas Buchanan Read, born on a Pennsylvania farm, was in turn a tailor's apprentice, grocer's assistant, cigar maker, tombstone carver, sign painter, and actor before he became a portrait painter, novelist, poet, and Civil War officer. Another personage is listed as "ornithologist and wholesale druggist"; another as "preacher, railway president, author"; and still another as "physician, merchant, political leader, magazine editor, poet, and critic." The wonder is that, despite such a squandering of energies, they could yet gain sufficient distinction in any phase of their activities to be recalled by posterity.

Even in his principal occupation of growing food, the farmer encountered harsh criticism from foreign visitors because of his practice of wearing out the land, his neglect of livestock, and his destruction of forest resources. But Old World agriculture was based on a ratio of man to land which in the New World was reversed. It was as natural for the American farmer to "mine the soil" and pass on to a virgin tract as it was for the European peasant to husband his few acres in the interest of generations unborn. Not till the opening years of the twentieth century, when the pressure of population dramatized the evils of past misuse, did the conservation of physical resources become a deliberate national policy.

Meanwhile the tradition of wasteful living, fostered by an environment of abundance, had fastened itself on the American character, disposing men to condone extravagance in public as well as in private life. Even official corruption could be winked at on the ground that a wealthy country such as the United States could afford it. In their personal lives Americans were improvident of riches that another people would have saved or frugally used. One recent arrival from England in the early nineteenth century wrote that the apples and peaches rotting in Ohio orchards were more "than would sink the British fleet." Another immigrant said of her adopted countrymen that she wished "the poor people in England had the leavings of their tables, that goes to their dogs and hogs."[28] A national crisis like the present reveals the ravages of this proclivity. By a sudden inversion of time-honored values the salvaging of kitchen fats, waste paper, abandoned tools, and other discarded materials has become a mark of patriotism.

Toward women the American male early acquired an attitude which sharply distinguished him from his brother in the Old World. As in every new country, women had a high scarcity value, both in the colonies and later in the settling West. They were in demand not only for reasons of affection but also because of their economic importance, for they performed the endless work about the house and helped with the heavy farm labor. "The cry is everywhere for girls; girls, and more girls!" wrote a traveler in 1866. He noted that men outnumbered women in thirty-eight of

[28] *Quoted in Marcus L. Hansen,* The Atlantic Migration, 1607–1860 *(Cambridge, 1940), pp. 157–58. The* Short Guide to Great Britain, *prepared by the War Department for the American soldiers now in England, cautions them that the British "won't think any better of you for throwing money around; they are more likely to feel that you haven't learned the common-sense virtues of thrift" (p. 4).*

the forty-five states and territories. In California the ratio was three to one; in Colorado, twenty to one.[29] "Guess my husband's got to look after me, and make himself agreeable to me, if he can," a pretty Western girl remarked—"if he don't, there's plenty will."[30] In the circumstances men paid women a deference and accorded them a status unknown in older societies. European observers attributed the high standard of sex morals largely to this fact, and it is significant that the most rapid strides toward equal suffrage took place in those commonwealths where the conditions of rural life had lingered longest.

Since the agriculturist regarded his farm only as a temporary abode, an investment rather than a home, he soon contracted the habit of being "permanently transitory."[31] Distances that would have daunted the stoutest-hearted European deterred "this new man" not at all. Many an Atlantic Coast family migrated from place to place across the continent until the second or third generation reached the rim of the Pacific and the next one began the journey back. "In no State of the Union," wrote James Bryce in 1888, "is the bulk of the population so fixed in its residence as everywhere in Europe; in many it is almost nomadic."[32] But for this constant mingling of people and ideas the spirit of sectionalism would have opened far deeper fissures in American society than it did, for the breadth of the land, the regional diversification of economic interests, and the concentration of European immigrants in certain areas were all factors conducive to separatism and disunity. Instead of one great civil war there might have

been many. Apart from the crisis of 1860, however, it has always been possible to adjust sectional differences peaceably. The war between North and South might itself have been avoided if the slave-centered plantation system of agriculture had not increasingly stopped the inflow of persons from other parts of the country as well as from Europe. Denied such infusions of new blood, the Southerners lived more and more to themselves, came to value their peculiarities above the traits they shared with their fellow countrymen, and, in the end, resolved to strike for an independent existence.

As the country grew older and its institutions assumed a more settled aspect, the locomotive tendencies of the Americans showed no signs of abatement. The wanderlust had entered their blood stream. According to a study of population redistribution in 1936, "over the last few decades mobility has been increasing rather than decreasing."[33] The Department of Agriculture reports that the average farm family remains on the same farm for only five or six years and that nearly half the children ultimately go to the towns and cities.[34] Urban dwellers take flight with equal facility. On the principle of the man biting the dog, the New York *Times*, June 14, 1942, reported that a resident of the California town of Sebastapol had lived in the same house for fifty years, although it admitted he was the only one of eleven children who had not gone to other parts. With the advent of the cheap automobile and the passion for long-distance touring, the rippling movement of humanity came to resemble the waves of the ocean. In 1940 the American people owned more motorcars than bathtubs. The pursuit of happiness

[29] *William H. Dixon*, New America (*9th ed., London,* [*1869*]), pp. 233–35.

[30] *Dixon*, White Conquest (*London, 1876*), I, 166.

[31] *Van Wyck Brooks's phrase in* Opinions of Oliver Allston (*New York, 1941*), p. 84.

[32] *Bryce, III, 59.*

[33] *Carter Goodrich and others*, Migration and Economic Opportunity (*Philadelphia, 1936*), p. 503.

[34] *Henry A. Wallace, "National Security and the Farm,"* Atlantic Monthly, CLX (*1937*), 288, 289.

was transformed into the happiness of pursuit. Foreigners had earlier expressed amazement at the spectacle of dwellings being hauled by horses along the streets from one site to another, but by means of the automobile trailer more than half a million Americans have now discovered a way of living constantly on wheels. The nation appears to be on the point of solving the riddle of perpetual motion.

Geographic or horizontal mobility was the concomitant of a still more fundamental aspect of American life: social or vertical mobility. The European notion of a graded society in which each class everlastingly performed its allotted function vanished quickly amidst primitive surroundings that invited the humblest persons to move upward as well as outward. Instead of everybody being nobody, they found that everybody might become somebody. In the language of James Russell Lowell, "Here, on the edge of the forest, where civilized man was brought face to face again with nature and taught mainly to rely on himself, mere manhood became a fact of prime importance." This emancipation from hoary custom was "no bantling of theory, no fruit of forethought," but "a gift of the sky and of the forest."[35] In this manner there arose the ingrained belief in equality of opportunity, the right of every man to a free and fair start—a view which in one of its most significant ramifications led to the establishment of free tax-supported schools. This belief was far from being a dogma of enforced equality. The feeling of the American was "I'm as good as you are" rather than "I'm no better than anyone else." To benefit from equality of opportunity a man must be equal to his opportunities. The government existed principally as an umpire to supervise the game with a minimum of rules.

The upshot was a conception of democracy rigorously qualified by individualism.

This individualistic bias sometimes assumed forms that defied vested authority. The colonists in their relations with the mother country evaded unwelcome governmental regulations and, assisted by their theologians and lawyers, made the most of the doctrine that acts of parliament contrary to their "unalienable rights" were void. Within the colonies those who dwelt remote from the centers of law enforcement adopted a similar attitude toward the provincial governments. The Scotch-Irish who squatted on vacant Pennsylvania lands in the early eighteenth century justified their illegal conduct on the score that "it was against the laws of God and nature, that so much land should be idle while so many Christians wanted it to labor on and to raise their bread."[36] The Massachusetts farmers who followed Daniel Shays later in the century were moved by a similar spirit. As a substitute for constituted authority, the settlers oftentimes set up their own unofficial tribunals, which adjudicated land titles and punished offenders against the public peace. In other instances they resorted to the swifter retribution of individual gunplay or of mob action and lynch law. To use a familiar American expression, they "took the law in their own hands," thus fostering a habit of violence which survived the circumstances that produced it and has continued to condition the national mentality to the present time.

As a result, Americans tend to act on the principle that men should be equal in breaking the law as well as in making it, that they should enjoy freedom *from* government as well as freedom *under* government. Thoreau, the great philosopher of individualism, knew of no reason why a citizen

[35] Lowell, *"The Independent in Politics,"* Works, *VI,* 205, 206.

[36] *Charles A. Hanna,* The Scotch-Irish *(New York, 1902), II, 63.*

should "ever for a moment, or in the least degree, resign his conscience to the legislator." He declared, "I think that we should be men first, and subjects afterward."[37] A similar conviction undoubtedly inspired William H. Seward's flaming declaration to the proslavery senators in 1850 that "there is a higher law than the Constitution . . . ,"[38] just as it actuated the thousands of churchgoing Northerners who secretly banded together to defeat the Fugitive Slave Act. But generally it has been self-interest or convenience, rather than conscience, that has provided the incentive to law defiance, as in the case of the businessman chafing against legislative restrictions or of the motorist unwilling to obey the traffic regulations. Sometimes this attitude has paraded under such high-sounding names as states' rights and nullification. This lawless streak in the American character has often been directed to wrong purposes, but it has also served as a check on the abuse of governmental powers and as a safeguard of popular rights.

In still another aspect the individualism of the pioneer farmer accounts for the intense cultivation of the acquisitive spirit. In the absence of hereditary distinctions of birth and rank the accumulation of wealth constituted the most obvious badge of social superiority, and once the process was begun, the inbred urge to keep on working made it difficult to stop. "The poor struggle to be rich, the rich to be richer," remarked an onlooker in the mid-nineteenth century.[39] Thanks to equality of opportunity with plenty for all, the class struggle in America has consisted in this struggle of Americans to climb out of one class into a higher one. The zest of competition frequently led to sharp trading, fraud, and chicanery, but in the public mind guilt attached less to the practices than to the ineptitude of being caught at them. Financial success was popularly accepted as the highest success, and not until the twentieth century did a religious leader venture to advance the un-American doctrine that ill-gotten wealth was "tainted money" even when devoted to benevolent uses.

It would be a mistake, however, to think of the American merely as a mechanism set in motion by dropping a coin in the slot. When President Coolidge made his famous remark, "The business of America is business," he quite properly added, "The chief ideal of the American people is idealism. I cannot repeat too often that America is a nation of idealists."[40] This dualism puzzled foreign commentators, who found it difficult, for example, to reconcile worship of the Almighty Dollar with the equally universal tendency to spend freely and give money away. In contrast to Europe, America has had practically no misers, and one consequence of the winning of independence was the abolition of primogeniture and entail. Harriet Martineau was among those who concluded that "the eager pursuit of wealth does not necessarily indicate a love of wealth for its own sake."[41] The fact is that, for a people who recalled how hungry and ill-clad their ancestors had been through the centuries in the Old World, the chance to make money was like the sunlight at the end of a tunnel. It was the means of living a life of human dignity. In other words, for the great majority of Americans it was a symbol of idealism rather than materialism. Hence "this new man" had an instinctive

[37] Henry D. Thoreau, "Civil Disobedience," Writings (Walden ed., Boston, 1906), IV, 358.

[38] Seward, Works (George E. Baker, ed., New York, 1853–84), I, 74.

[39] Nichols, p. 195.

[40] William Allen White, Calvin Coolidge (New York, 1925), p. 218. "They are capable of an ideality surpassing that of Englishmen or Frenchmen," said Bryce, III, 59.

[41] Martineau, II, 143.

sympathy for the underdog, and even persons of moderate wealth gratefully shared it with the less fortunate, helping to endow charities, schools, hospitals, and art galleries and providing the wherewithal to nourish movements for humanitarian reform which might otherwise have died a-borning.

The energy that entered into many of these movements was heightened by another national attitude: optimism. It was this quality that sustained the European men and women who with heavy hearts quit their ancestral firesides to try their fortunes in a strange and far-off continent. This same trait animated the pioneer farmers confronted by the hardships, loneliness, and terrors of the primeval forest and served also to comfort their successors who, though toiling under less dire conditions, were constantly pitted against both the uncertainties of the weather and the unpredictable demands of the market. When Thomas Jefferson remarked, "I steer my bark with Hope in the head, leaving Fear astern," he spoke for all his compatriots.[42] To doubt the future was to confess oneself a failure since the life history of almost any American documented the opposite view. A belief in progress blossomed spontaneously in such a soil. If it made some men tolerant of present abuses in the confident expectation that time would provide the cure, it fired others with an apostolic zeal to hasten the happy day. As a keen observer in the middle of the last century said of his fellow countrymen, "Americans are sanguine enough to believe that no evil is without a remedy, if they could only find it, and they see no good reason why they should not try to find remedies for all the evils of life."[43] Not even

fatalism in religion could long withstand the bracing atmosphere of the New World. This quality of optimism sometimes soared to dizzy heights, causing men to strive for earthly perfection in communistic societies or to prepare to greet the return of Christ in ascension robes.

It attained its most blatant expression in the national love of bragging. At bottom, this habit sprang from pride in a country of vast distances and mighty elevations and from an illimitable faith in its possibilities of being great as well as big. The American glorified the future in much the same spirit that the European glorified the past. Both tended to exalt what they had the most of, and by a simple transition the American also found it easy to speak of expected events as though they had already happened. Oftentimes the motive was to compensate for an inner feeling of inferiority. This frame of mind prompted statesmen to cultivate spread-eagle oratory, a style which a writer in the *North American Review* in 1858 defined as "a compound of exaggeration, effrontery, bombast, and extravagance, mixed metaphors, platitudes, defiant threats thrown at the world, and irreverent appeals flung at the Supreme Being."[44]

For the same reason the ordinary citizen was encouraged to tell the truth hyperbolically. In the thinly settled sections this manner of speech went by the name of tall talk, causing the backwoods to be known as a "paradise of puffers."[45] A Frenchman, however, referred to a national, not a regional, trait when he said Americans seemed loath to admit that Christopher Columbus had not been an American, and it was an Easterner writing in an Eastern magazine who solemnly averred, "It is easier, say the midwives, to come into this world of America . . . than in any other world

[42] *Letter to John Adams, April 8, 1816, Thomas Jefferson,* Writings (*Andrew A. Lipscomb, ed., Washington, 1903*), *XIV, 467.*

[43] *Nichols, p. 46.*

[44] North American Review, LXXXVII, 454.

[45] *Timothy Flint*, Recollections (*Boston, 1826*), p. 185.

extant."[46] In business life this indulgent attitude toward veracity lent itself to deliberate attempts to defraud and made the land speculator with his "lithographed mendacity" the natural forerunner of the dishonest stock promoter of recent times.[47] Boastfulness is an attribute of youth which a greater national maturity has helped to moderate. Still the War Department in its manual of etiquette for the American soldiers now in England has seen fit to admonish them: "Don't show off or brag or bluster—'swank' as the British say."[48]

This facility for overstatement has given a distinctive quality to American humor. In the United States humor has never been part of a general gaiety of spirit. It has had to break through a crust of life thick with serious purpose. Hence it has had to be boisterous and bold, delighting in exaggeration, incongruities, and farcical effects, and reaching a grand climax in the practical joke. Out of a comic mood so induced arose such folk heroes as Mike Fink, Paul Bunyan, Pecos Bill, and the myth-embroidered Davy Crockett, whose fabulous exploits flourished in oral tradition long before they were reduced to print. In deference to the national sobriety of temperament the most successful professional humorists have been those who preserved a decorous gravity of expression while telling their incredible yarns.

If this analysis of American characteristics is well founded, then certain modifications might be expected as the primacy of rural life yielded to the rise of urbanism. In the latter decades of the nineteenth century a rapidly increasing proportion of the people found themselves dwelling under conditions different from those of earlier times. In 1860 only a sixth of the nation lived in towns of 8,000 or more, but by 1900 a third resided in urban communities, and today well over half do. Moreover, throughout these years, places of 25,000 or more attracted a majority of the city dwellers.[49] Paralleling this urban growth occurred a remarkable development of new means of communication and transport that carried city ideas and ways to "the very fingertips of the whole land": the telephone, rural free delivery, good roads, interurban electric transit, the automobile, the movie, the radio.[50] In this changed environment of American society many of the historic national traits flourished; others were tempered or transformed. The period of urban and industrial predominance is short as compared with the long impact of ruralism upon the American mind, but already several reversals of older attitudes are apparent.

One is the importance which Americans have come to attach to cultural achievement. The ancient prejudice against "useless" accomplishments could not long withstand the compelling opportunities offered by the city. In such centers were to be found the best schools, the best newspapers, the best churches, and virtually all the bookstores, libraries, publishing houses, concert halls, art galleries, and theaters. There, too, America made closest contact with the vital thought of Europe. The leveling upward of popular taste insured encouragement and financial support for

[46] Jean Jacques A. *Ampère*, Promenade en Amérique (*Paris, 1855*), I, 7–8; anon., "*Are We a Good-Looking People?*" Putnam's Monthly, I (1853), 312.

[47] *The quoted phrase is from John J. Ingalls, "Some Ingalls Letters," Kansas State Historical Society*, Collections, XIV (1915–18), 95.

[48] *War Department*, A Short Guide to Great Britain [1942], p. 28.

[49] *Warren S. Thompson and P. K. Whelpton*, Population Trends in the United States (*New York, 1933*), pp. 20, 24.

[50] *The quoted phrase is from Josiah Strong's preface to Samuel L. Loomis*, Modern Cities and Their Religious Problems (*New York, 1887*), p. 6.

persons who wanted to cultivate their brains rather than their biceps. Who can ever know how dreadful a toll the two and a half centuries of agricultural existence exacted in terms of possible creative advances of the mind and spirit, how many a "mute inglorious Milton" succumbed to the unending struggle with Nature? For persons like these the city meant a glad release. It gave them a chance to mature their powers, to commune with kindred spirits, and to enter the lists for fame and fortune. Even in earlier times cultural stirrings had centered in the towns and cities. Now, as the urban influence became uppermost, Americans commenced to make contributions to scholarship, science, literature, and the fine arts that challenged comparison with the best Europe could offer.

As a necessary consequence, some of the old aversion to specialization of talent vanished. In a civilization rapidly growing more complex, men began to learn to place a higher value on thoroughly mastering a skill or conquering a particular branch of knowledge. The business of making a living tended to fall into compartments, with the men best equipped by training or experience reaping the greatest rewards. This trend characterized not only the arts and sciences but also the upper ranges of industry and trade. Even in public life expertness of knowledge steadily played a larger part, notably in the administrative services of city, state, and nation. The derisive references to a "Brain Trust" several years ago came from partisan critics who did not, however, intend to abandon the device if or when they should return to power.

A further result of the changed aspect of American society has been the great impetus given to voluntary associational activity. In an agricultural environment the gregarious instinct was constantly thwarted by the dearth of neighbors. The hunger for companionship could find only an occasional outlet, as at the county fair or in the tumultuous crowd gathered from far and near for a camp meeting. To the rural birthright of liberty and equality the city added the boon of fraternity. In a crowded community like could find like. The reformer, the businessman, the wage earner, the intellectual worker, the sports lover, the ancestor worshiper—all these and many others drifted together into special groups to foster interests held in common, and these local societies seldom failed to expand into nation-wide federations. Soon the population was divided between the organized and those who organized them, until, if the late Will Rogers is to be believed, "Americans will join anything in town but their own family. Why, two Americans can't meet on the street without one banging a gavel and calling the other to order."[51] Thus the passion for associational activity became a sovereign principle of life.

Quite as noteworthy has been another effect of city growth: the renouncing of individualism as the automatic cure of human ills. As the nineteenth century advanced, the increasing domination of the national economy by the urban magnates of business and finance caused the farmers to demand that the government intercede to protect their right to a decent livelihood. In the cities the congested living quarters, the growing wretchedness of the poor, and the rise of difficult social problems also created doubts as to the sufficiency of the laissez-faire brand of democracy. Only the rich and the powerful seemed now to profit from the system of unbridled individualism. Though the solid core of ancient habit yielded stubbornly, the average man came gradually to believe that under the altered conditions it was the duty of the government of all to safeguard equal opportu-

51 *From a speech quoted in the Boston* Herald, *January 29, 1927.*

nity for all. After the American fashion it was a doctrineless conviction, the product of an adjustment to new times for the sake of preserving the traditional spirit of self-reliance and free competition.

In this modern age the gospel of work retained its grip upon the American mentality, but the assurance of permanent remunerative work no longer existed, particularly for the army of city toilers. Every sudden jar to the national business structure cast large numbers of them out of employment. The wage earner through no fault of his own was being denied an essential part of his natural heritage. As early as 1893 the American Federation of Labor resolved that "the right to work is the right to life," and declared that "when the private employer cannot or will not give work the municipality, state or nation must."[52] But it was not until the Great Depression of 1929 destroyed the livelihood of people at all levels of society that this novel view became an article of American faith. The New Deal assumed the obligation not merely of saving the destitute from hunger but of creating jobs for the idle and guarding against such hazards in the future by means of unemployment compensation, retirement payments for aged employees, and special provisions for farmers. Thus what had begun as the community's need for everyone to work became transformed into a doctrine of the right to work and then into the responsibility of government to provide the means of work.

The national character, as we at present know it, is thus a mixture of long-persistent traits and newly acquired characteristics. Based upon the solid qualities of those Europeans who dared to start life anew across the Atlantic, it assumed distinctive form under the pressure of adaptation to a radically different environment. "Our ancestors sought a new country," said James Russell Lowell. "What they found was a new condition of mind."[53] The long tutelage to the soil acted as the chief formative influence, removing ancient inhibitions, freeing latent energies, revamping mental attitudes. The rise of the city confirmed or strengthened many of the earlier attributes while altering others. Probably none of the traits is peculiar to the American people; some of them we may regard with more humility than pride; but the sum total represents a way of life unlike that of any other nation.

Just as the American character has undergone modification in the past, so it will doubtless undergo modification in the future. Nevertheless, certain of its elements seem so deeply rooted as to defy the erosion of time and circumstance. Of this order are the qualities that made possible the occupying and development of the continent, the building of a democratic society, and the continuing concern for the welfare of the underprivileged. These are attributes better suited to peace than to war, yet every great crisis has found the people ready to die for their conception of life so that their children might live it. Today the nation is engaged in its mightiest struggle for survival. Let none despair. The American character, whatever its shortcomings, abounds in courage, creative energy, and resourcefulness and is bottomed upon the profound conviction that nothing in the world is beyond its power to accomplish.

[52] *American Federation of Labor*, Report of the Proceedings of the Thirteenth Annual Convention (*New York, 1894*), p. 37.

[53] Lowell, "*The Independent in Politics*," Works, *VI*, 205.

PIETISM AND THE AMERICAN CHARACTER[1]

*William G. McLoughlin**

The purpose of this essay is to offer a personal hypothesis for what may be unique, if anything is, about the American character. And if I can demonstrate that the quality of pietism (or, in its broader formulation, pietistic-perfectionism) offers at least as many useful insights into the nature of the American experience as, say, the quality of pragmatism or of democratic liberalism or the influence of the frontier, then I will have made my point. While I am aware that in offering such a "key" I am in danger of explaining so much as to explain nothing, I prefer to leave the inevitable qualifications and exceptions to another time. I will say for this generalized approach only that the present stage in the renascence of the history of religion[2] in America seems to me to merit its consideration.

American pietism had its origin in the protest of Protestantism against the ecclesiastical corrup-

tions of the Christian church in the sixteenth century. Ernst Troeltsch, the German historian of religion, defined this dissenting spirit in terms of the sect-type versus the church-type of Christianity. And he listed as the salient features of the pietistic temper, its anti-institutionalism, its voluntarism, its exaltation of the individual's direct relationship with God, its aspiration "after personal inward perfection," its hostility to worldli-

[1] *This paper was read at the annual meeting of the New England American Studies Association at Amherst College, October 24, 1964.*

[2] *I use the term "religion" here not only in its narrow sense but in the broader sense as defined by J. L. Talmon: "The concrete elements of history, the acts of politicians, the aspirations of people, the ideas, values, preferences and prejudices of an age, are the outward manifestations of its religion in the widest sense."* The Rise of Totalitarian Democracy *(Boston, 1952), p. 11.*

---

*WILLIAM G. McLOUGHLIN (1922–   ) is a Professor of History at Harvard University. His publications include Modern Revivalism *(1959),* Billy Graham: Revivalist in a Secular Age *(1960), and* The American Evangelicals, 1800–1900 *(1968). Reprinted by permission of the author and the* American Quarterly, *Vol. 17, No. 2 (Summer, 1965), 163–186. Published by the University of Pennsylvania. Copyright, 1965, Trustees of the University of Pennsylvania.*

ness and the kinds of compromise which the established church-type systems have to make with the state, and its doctrine of the priesthood of all believers. Pietism, said Troeltsch, disliked the relativistic aspects of the natural law as taught by the medieval scholastics, and substituted for it "the plain Law of Christ or the Sermon on the Mount." To the pietist, "God's Being and Will constitute His Natural and Revealed Law; the Bible is the Law-book of revelation, identical with the Law-book of Nature."[3]

Troeltsch pointed out that there were several types of pietism, and he made a sharp distinction between the mystical or quietistic pietism of Continental Europe and the activistic, aggressive, reform-minded temper of English Puritanism. The mystical pietism of the Continent left the world up to the State and so tended to remain static and agrarian; it was a religion of withdrawal. The activistic pietism of the Puritans gave to the Church the duty of reforming the world and so launched into liberalism in politics and capitalism in economics; it was a religion of commitment. Puritan pietism in England took many forms, but all of them (including the Separatist, Baptist and Quaker varieties which played so important a role in America) were animated by perfectionist ideals:

> Its 'Perfectionist' aim of separating 'converted' Christians . . . from the rest in order to form them into smaller groups of real Christians, its stress on the need for 'converted' preachers, its emphasis upon lay religion and upon the pure apostolic primitive Church, revealed a spirit which was still inwardly hostile to the spirit of ecclesiasticism . . . the greatest impulse towards reform lay in the idea of the coming Kingdom of God and the approaching world transformation.[4]

[3] *Ernst Troeltsch*, The Social Teachings of the Christian Churches, *trans. Olive Wyon (London, 1931), I, 344, 347; II, 677, ff.*

[4] Ibid., II, 716.

As H. Richard Niebuhr put it in *Christ and Culture*, American Puritans, Separatists, Quakers, Methodists and Baptists believed in Christ as "the transformer of culture" and "as the regenerator of man in his culture."[5]

Now my hypothesis (and I want to make it clear that it is mine only as a gloss upon that other seminal work of Niebuhr's, *The Kingdom of God in America*) rests upon the contention that it was this dynamic, sectarian form of pietistic-perfectionism which lies at the basis of American civilization, although since 1776 the orthodox Christian version of this pietism has been challenged by various post-Christian versions. From the beginning of our history the New World attracted those who shared the basic assumptions of this outlook and who crossed the ocean in a quest for a new start, a more complete freedom, in a land where perfection itself seemed possible. Frederick Jackson Turner no doubt exaggerated the environmental contribution when he talked of American democracy's coming out of the forest to greet and transform the immigrant. But he was correct in seeing the virgin land and uncorrupted social order as a prime catalytic agent in shaping the pietistic-perfectionism brought by the immigrant, into genuinely new and different institutional forms.

It was not the forest or the free land, however, which broke down those remnants of the European civilization which the pietists brought with them. What broke down the stratified class system, the established church, the mercantile economic practices, the corporate concept of society, was the internal dynamic of pietistic-perfectionism itself. For there is an inherent tension within pietism, as well as between the varieties of pietism that came to America, which has generated a continual spirit of reformation, a constant search for a more perfect union between God and man

[5] *H. R. Niebuhr*, Christ and Culture *(New York, 1951)*, *p. 220.*

in America from the outset. As Richard Niebuhr pointed out in 1937, and as Edmund S. Morgan recently emphasized in *The Puritan Dilemma*, this inherent tension or conflict within the pietistic-perfectionist outlook may be phrased (as Niebuhr generally put it) in terms of the conflict between the Puritan and the Quaker or (as Professor Morgan put it) between the Non-Separatist Congregationalist and the Separatist. For my purposes it is clearer to see it as a conflict between the conservative and the antinomian aspects of pietism—between those whose primary concern is to maintain perfect moral order and those whose primary concern is to attain perfect moral freedom. This tension was central to the attempt to found a nation dedicated to the proposition that the moral law of God and Nature is supreme, and that all men owe their first and fundamental allegiance to that law rather than to their families, their community or to the state. And the dilemma posed for the pietists who sought to construct the New Jerusalem in America's green and promised land had two sides: first, how do I get myself into harmony with the moral law, and second, how do I translate that law into action without curtailing the freedom of others? Or, in other words, the dilemma of personal responsibility for purity and social responsibility for order, for transforming myself and my society into that state of perfection which God requires on earth even as it is in heaven.

The pietistic dilemma was posed in classic terms by the confrontations which Anne Hutchinson and Roger Williams posed to John Winthrop and John Cotton: Hutchinson, the antinomian true to the Spirit of God within her heart, and Williams, the Separatist and Seeker for absolute conformity to God's law, both refused to compromise with the Non-Separatist and restrictive regulations of the Bible Commonwealth, which, as they saw it, enforced conformity to a corrupt social and ecclesiastical order. The solution to such pietistic confrontations was simple in the 1630s. Williams and Hutchinson, and those who rebelled with them, simply were told that if they did not like the civilization of Massachusetts Bay they could make their own lively experiment in pietistic-perfectionism in the wilderness. For two and a half centuries thereafter a host of antinomian pietists in America continually moved out to the greater freedom of the frontier whenever, like Natty Bumppo or Huck Finn, they felt the restrictions of civilization encroaching upon their moral freedom.

But not all of them moved. By the end of the seventeenth century the Quakers and Baptists had broken down the rigid exclusionist conformity of the religious establishments North and South and maintained their uncompromising attitudes toward a corrupt system in a mild state of siege called toleration. For more than a century the two wings of American pietism remained in constant tension over their differing views of a Christian society. The conservative pietists insisted, for example, that a Christian state required some official recognition of and support for the Christian churches. The Separatists, led by the Baptists, argued that for the state to support Christianity, even by a general assessment tax which aided all Protestant denominations, was infringing upon the freedom of the churches and of the individual conscience. And the Baptists repeatedly refused to obey the laws in this matter. Eventually the conservatives yielded the point, though not without first claiming that the supporters of disestablishment were subversives, agents of the Bavarian Illuminati, seeking to overthrow republican government in order to set up Jacobinical atheism and mob rule.

It is a basic difference between European and American civilizations that disestablishment was not engineered in this country by atheistic *philosophes* shouting *"Ecrasez l'infame!"* but by evangelical pietists shouting "Freedom of religion!" The defenders of the establishment, like Lyman

Beecher, eventually realized to their great surprise, that disestablishment had been undertaken to free America *for* religion and not *from* religion. By the middle of the nineteenth century Roman Catholics in America recognized too the great benefits which derived to their church from the principle of separation of Church and State, though Cardinal Gibbons had to explain again and again to a puzzled Vatican that disestablishment was not secularism in the European sense.

Apart from the tensions over disestablishment, the two wings of pietism (Puritan and Separatist, or Conservative and Antinomian) which constituted the vital core of the American temper, managed to work together toward the implementation of their mutual ideals. Together they fought against the outworn, corrupt, man-made restrictions upon freedom which were associated with the decadent civilization and corrupt churches of the Old World. Having thrown off the shackles of an Erastian, hierarchical state-church system by the very act of coming to America, they proceeded to attack the economic and political tyranny of hereditary monarchy; at the same time they gradually abolished the restrictions of a static corporate society with its fixed class system and its state-controlled economy. And ultimately, having erected both state and federal constitutions which imbedded the moral law into the written law of the land, they gradually established the complete equality of all white men under God through universal manhood suffrage and rotation in office. The concept of the omni-competent, self-governing, self-reliant common man was really the final triumph of the first stage of American pietistic-perfectionism. In the Age of Jackson the two interacting components of pietistic-perfectionism flowered in unison: inner perfection or holiness as personal union with God and the perfectability of the world through the regeneration of everyone in it. America had at last thrown off all the shackles of Satan and all the carnal corruptions of this world and was now ready for the ultimate confrontation with God. In 1836 Charles Grandison Finney, the foremost evangelist of his day and later president of Oberlin College in its perfectionist era, predicted that it would be possible to convert "the whole land in two years."[6] At the same time a Baptist layman named William Miller was persuading thousands of Americans that the millennium would begin on March 21, 1843. Both predictions were premature.

The triumph of Jacksonian democracy marked a new crisis in American pietism just when the millennium seemed at hand. Alexis de Tocqueville pointed out the danger to moral freedom lurking in the potential tyranny of the majority which Jacksonian democracy made possible. Had the pietists recognized the logic of their striving for complete equality under God they might have foreseen this threat. Instead, they had cast aside the cautious checks and balances which the conservative pietists who founded the federal system had set up to prevent such a possibility.[7] They cast it aside not only by expanding the electorate and creating political parties directly responsible to it, but also by changing the theological rationale

6 Letters of Theodore Weld, Angelina Grimke Weld, and Sarah Grimke, *eds. G. H. Barnes and D. L. Dumond (New York, 1934), I, 318–19.*

7 *See the opening chapter in Richard Hofstadter's* The American Political Tradition *in which he points out that "there is a serious dilemma in the philosophy of the Fathers" of the Constitution: "They thought man was a creature of rapacious self-interest and yet they wanted him to be free." Like the Puritans, they tried to balance man's freedom as a moral agent against his depravity as a sinner. They did it by granting the principle of government by consent of the governed and then checking its majority will. They did it also by placing moral absolutes in the Bill of Rights against which the majority might not act. They rejected Thomas Paine's radical pietistic notion that the people has a right to do whatever it chooses to do because its voice is the voice of God.*

for rule by the elite. It is significant that the most radical of the revolutionary state constitutions were written in places like Pennsylvania and Vermont where antinomian pietists predominated, while the most conservative state constitutions were established in Connecticut and Massachusetts where Calvinistic pietists predominated. The gradual triumph of Arminianism over Calvinism in the latter half of the eighteenth century and early part of the nineteenth century was the theological side of the political shift toward democracy. The First Great Awakening began this shift in a pietistic revolt against the declining fervor of a decadent Calvinism and the corrupting influence of the rising Enlightenment. But by emphasizing immediate, crisis conversion through emotional itinerant preaching, the Awakening shifted the whole emphasis of Calvinism in the direction of Separatist pietism. Not only did the Awakening seriously undermine the established church system throughout the colonies but it also undermined the conception of a learned clergy and of rule by the predestined elect. In the evangelistic fervor engendered by the Awakening, pietists of all kinds gradually abandoned the emphasis on a limited atonement and worked their way toward the doctrines of free will, free grace and immediate salvation open to all men. By the end of the eighteenth century the unique American systems of itinerant evangelism and mass revivalism had evolved to provide the techniques for regenerating a whole society (and through missionaries, the whole world).

During the Second Great Awakening the conservative pietists of the East gradually merged with the more radical pietists of the frontier in the efforts to get all of the unwashed masses washed in the Blood of the Lamb before deism, Unitarianism and Jacobinical mob rule put an end to the concept of a Christian commonwealth. This theological merger of Congregationalists, Presby-

terians, Baptists, Separatists and Methodists produced Evangelical pietism; and evangelical pietists believed that a Christian commonwealth could be achieved through the massing of the votes of the regenerate to make "a Christian Party in politics." These voters would elect only converted Christians to office and these legislators in turn would enact and enforce Christian morality throughout the nation. Thus revivalism replaced the establishment as the American method of maintaining moral order without (it was thought) abandoning moral freedom. Or, to put it another way, the evangelical Protestant denominations became a kind of national church dedicated to enforcing the moral law upon everyone in the nation either by revivalistic religion (which produced voluntary obedience) or by a majority vote of the regenerate (which compelled obedience of the unregenerate). However, in their zeal to make America a Christian country the evangelicals began to equate the moral absolute with their own narrow set of Protestant, middle-class, rural virtues. They wanted to outlaw the Masons and the Mormons, to enact nativist laws, to enforce prohibition, to censor immorality, to prevent birth control, to maintain a Christian Sabbath, and eventually to restrict immigration and pass laws preventing the teaching of evolution.

With this transformation of the radical pietism of the Separatists or antinomians into the narrow conformity which eventually became Fundamentalism, a new form of pietism emerged to offset it. And this we may call the post-Christian form of American pietism. But it is important to note that post-Christian pietism is by no means anti-Christian. The anti-Christian or anticlerical thought of Thomas Paine was never a significant force in American life. The real basis of post-Christian pietism in America was the Jeffersonian adaptation of the moral sense philosophy of the Scottish Realists. Thomas Jefferson made Scottish intuitionalism, the innate moral faculty in all men, the basis of his faith in democracy. He did so as a means of preserving the moral freedom of the individual against what he considered the theo-centric authoritarianism of the established priest-craft.[8] He saw the evangelical Calvinism of Timothy Dwight and Lyman Beecher as the spiritual arm of the political paternalism of the Federalist Party, and he was not far wrong. Jefferson, in my view, qualifies as the first post-Christian pietist not only because he joined the movement for disestablishment and opposed the moralistic pretensions of the evangelicals, but also because he did so in the name of preserving the teachings of Jesus against those who would pervert them into their own ideological blueprint for a conformist society. His attack upon the authoritarianism of the Calvinist Federalists was carried on by Emerson's fight against the paternalistic pretensions of the Unitarian Whigs. And just as Timothy Dwight of Yale saw Jeffersonianism as Jacobinical atheism, so Andrews Norton of Harvard saw Emersonian Transcendentalism as "the latest form of infidelity."

The post-Christian pietism of Jefferson differed from that of Emerson more in degree than in quality. Both men were equally committed to moral freedom through adherence to moral law; both believed in the trustworthiness of the heart and conscience of the average man. Everyone is familiar with Jefferson's famous statement concerning the moral equality, if not superiority, of the plowman ("Nature's nobleman") in comparison with the professor. Let me quote a less well-known statement which Jefferson made to his nephew, Peter Carr, in 1787, on the same subject:

Give up money, give up fame, give up science, give up the earth itself and all it contains, rather than do an immoral act. . . . An honest heart being the first blessing, a knowing head is the second.

What is this but a paraphrase of the Biblical injunction, "For what is a man profited if he shall gain the whole world, and lose his own soul?" I wonder too whether Orestes Brownson had not been reading Jefferson when he wrote in the *Democratic Review* in 1840 against Andrews Norton's learned attack upon Transcendentalism:

All are capable of judging of the doctrine [of the New Testament] itself, whether it be of God or not. The unlettered ploughman by this is placed, so far as the evidences of his religious faith are concerned, on a level with the most erudite scholar or the profoundest philosopher. Christianity by this is adapted to the masses. . . . It recognises a witness within the soul that testifies for God. . . . It paves the way for universal freedom, for every man to become a priest and a king. . . .[9]

This then is the Jeffersonian-Jacksonian-Emersonian reformulation of the pietistic doctrine of the priesthood of all believers. By this exaltation of the moral sense, conscience or intuition, democracy could be based upon the universal suffrage of the common man. And thus there was a new pietistic counterpoise, or countervailing power, to the Christian party in politics; i.e., post-Christian pietism. While this reliance upon the voice of the people as the voice of God was as liable to majority tyranny as the combined vote of the evangelical saints, it offered a more viable alternative for the rebellion of the individual heart. It became the basis of a new form of antinomianism.

[8] *For Jefferson's use of the Scottish Realists see Adrienne Koch,* The Philosophy of Thomas Jefferson *(New York, 1943), pp. 15–22, 45–53.*

[9] *Quoted in* The Transcendentalists, *ed. Perry Miller (Cambridge, 1950), p. 246.*

And it was to this iron string of self-reliant individualism that Emerson, Thoreau and Whitman tuned their message. It was to "the honest heart" that the reformers, the utopians, the abolitionists of the day offered their manifold panaceas and received a response which made the era the most nonconformist in our history. Except insofar as the abolition movement captured the American people, it may be said that the individualistic antinomian perfectionists and the evangelical conservative perfectionists fought each other to a stand-off in the years 1830–60.

After the Civil War the second stage of American pietistic-perfectionism commenced. The pendulum had swung as far as it could go toward individual freedom through self-reliant anti-institutionalism. Now it had to go back to the social ethic of the general welfare in order to preserve the moral law and individual freedom. In the industrial revolution following 1860, self-reliance and equal opportunity hardened into the rigid determinism of Spencer's social Darwinism (though it was a characteristically American optimistic and melioristic determinism). The pietistic individualism of Emerson was perverted into a defense of rugged individualism behind which the self-made plutocrats could hide their new form of oligarchic control. Reformation was baffled by a dogmatic insistence upon the Jeffersonian doctrine of laissez faire. The evangelical denominations, now firmly entrenched as a national establishment, even appropriated Darwin's evolutionary hypothesis to the service of a Christian conservatism under the phrase, "Evolution is God's way of doing things."

The new danger of institutionalized tyranny in the complexities of urban industrialism, personified as "Big Business" and "Big Labor," offered the countervailing pietist no alternative but to invoke the power of a benevolent government to smash or regulate the new threats to moral freedom. In the third of America's great awakenings, pietism was reformulated in the churches by the Social Gospelers in the ideals of Christian socialism. They awakened American consciences to the moral evils of the industrial system by calling upon them to apply "the social teachings of Jesus" to free those crushed by "the malefactors of great wealth." However, the Populist, Labor and Progressive reformers, taking a different tack, utilized Hamiltonian means to achieve Jeffersonian ends. Just as Jacksonian pietists crushed "the monster bank" in order to destroy a monopoly which was denying freedom of opportunity to the common man, so the Progressives attacked "the vested interests," "the soul-less corporations," "the demons of Wall Street" with a fervor that was often as heedless of consequences as the abolition movement. And as Richard Hofstadter has shown, these pietistic reformers revealed their evangelical origins by their support of the Fundamentalist William Jennings Bryan and of the Prohibition movement in the rural areas, as well as by their support of Woodrow Wilson, the most pietistic of all our Presidents, in the urban areas.

Shortly after the Social Gospel triumphs of the New Deal, it became apparent that government bureaucracy itself was now an institutional threat to liberty—especially when "Big Government" became the partner of "Big Business" and "Big Labor." The tension between the desire for moral order and moral freedom reached a state of desperation after World War II and unleashed a new pietistic revival which has been with us ever since. Conservative pietists not only judged "Bigness" wrong in itself, but they found evidence of atheistic Communism (like the Bavarian Illuminati) in all aspects of our huge and complicated social structure—in our State Department, in our labor unions, in our philanthropic foundations, in our army, even in our Supreme Court and our churches. In order to save our souls and our society these conservative (usually ultra-conservative) pietists urged a complete dismantling of Bigness in order to return America to the days of free labor, free enterprise and laissez-faire government.

At the other extreme, the antinomian pietists in the postwar awakening emphasized that Big Government and Big Labor had forgotten their original purpose—social justice for the weak; instead they were crushing individual liberty by failing to uphold the moral absolutes of the Bill of Rights and by putting institutional goals above personal needs and rights. The institutions of government and labor had become as corrupt and overbearing as Big Business or the old established church system of the past. Some religious leaders, discouraged by the results of the Social Gospel and inspired by the European theology called neo-orthodoxy, evolved a new form of pietistic radicalism which combined the old moral absolutes with a new sociological relativism. This sophisticated neo-pietism, of which Reinhold Niebuhr was the foremost exponent, revitalized the churches and spilled over to recall the post-Christian nonchurchgoers to their traditional values. One group of neo-pietists looked to the Supreme Court to challenge Bigness in the name of the moral law imbedded in the Bill of Rights; and they filled the ranks of organizations like the American Civil Liberties Union and the A.D.A. Another group, aroused by the moral implications of the atom bomb, formed organizations to crusade for disarmament and a sane nuclear policy. And in the midst of this new concern for freedom the Negro Revolution exploded, producing movements like Martin Luther King's Southern Christian Leadership Conference, James Farmer's Congress of Racial Equality, and the Student Non-Violent Coordinating Committee where Christian and non-Christian pietists demonstrated anew the depth of the antinomian tradition of civil disobedience in America. Simultaneously the creation

of the Peace Corps awakened again the dedicated fervor and personal commitment of the nineteenth century foreign missionaries among a younger generation thought to be lost in ennui or the search for security. Faced with the most fearful and baffling difficulties of their history, Americans took courage from their pietistic faith that he who would save his life must lose it in a cause beyond himself.[10]

What I am trying to say in this rather awkward and cursory glance at American history and the pietistic awakenings and reformulations that have shaped it, is that the dialectic of pietism is a continuous spiral around the moral core of our

[10] *It is possible to make out a case for the continuity of the tension between the Puritan concept of the organic or corporate state as opposed to the antinomian concept of Christian anarchy throughout our history. One can cite the Whig concep of a Christian party in politics, the theocratic belief in stewardship through benevolent societies and even the utopian experiments in communal living as evidence for this before the Civil War. It is even easier after 1865 to point to the concept of Christian socialism and ultimately of the welfare state as embodying this organic view of society in opposition to the increasingly atomistic view of society. But while this form of the dialectic between moral order and moral freedom is in some ways more consistent than the one I offer here, it also involves a serious shift or inversion of the respective roles of the anti-institutional antinomian reformer and the conservative defender of institutionalized order. One can claim that through men like Bushnell and Munger and Gladden the Puritan and Edwardsian conception of the Christian commonwealth carries through logically into the twentieth century. But this makes the Social Gospeler the defender of institutionalized organic order instead of a radical reformer interested primarily in individual freedom; it ignores the direct line "from Edwards to Emerson" which Perry Miller has described. It ignores too the equally distinct line from, say, Endicott to the Mathers to the Beechers and to the Fundamentalists whose conception of a Christian commonwealth was repressive and conformist and the very opposite of the "liberal" aspects of the Social Gospel and the New Deal.*

cultural ethic. What is to the left of the core from one angle of vision or in one generation is at the right in the next. In any given period there are conservative and antinomian pietists striving to apply the values of this moral core to maintain the balance between personal integrity and social justice, between the maintenance of moral order and the attainment of moral freedom, as God or an honest heart gives them to see the right. But what is always central to the quest for perfection in America is the proper interpretation of "the moral law" which, as Emerson said, "lies at the center of nature and radiates to the circumference."

While generalizations about such a variable tradition as pietism are hazardous, nevertheless I will venture this definition of its essential characteristics: American pietism is the belief that every individual is himself responsible for deciding the rightness or wrongness of every issue (large or small) in terms of a higher moral law; that he must make this decision the moment he is confronted with any question in order to prevent any complicity with evil; and having made his decision, he must commit himself to act upon it at once, taking every opportunity and utilizing every possible method to implement his decision not only for himself and in his own home or community, but throughout the nation and the world.[11]

Any attempt to define precisely the moral law or to enumerate Americans' moral absolutes either in terms of the revealed will of God or the natural rights of man is not only impossible but really beside the point. Pietism is a state of mind and not a fixed ideology, which explains why America has been spared the more baneful consequences of European totalitarian democracy. No one man, no group and no ideology has the blueprint for our society—not even the Bible has been a blueprint though some groups have tried to make their interpretation of it into one. It is the heart of American pietism that the individual is considered the single most competent judge of moral truth and that his judgment is to be respected even if it leads him into civil disobedience. The pietists who framed the Constitution organized this nation and its institutions as an open and not a closed society. True pietists (the pietists of the vital center, whether conservative-Puritan or antinomian-Separatist) have never claimed to know the complete will of God. In fact, it is one of their fundamental tenets that God is continually revealing himself in new ways and shedding yet "further light" upon his will: I Corinthians 4:5, "Therefore judge nothing before the time, until the Lord come, who both will bring to light the hidden things of darkness, and will make manifest the counsels of the hearts."[12] The self-righteous, rightwing fanatic (not to be confused with the Puritan conservative pietist) who equates the

---

11 *I do not want to imply here that the pietistic quality of American life produces only honest and straightforward moralistic appraisals or rationales for our actions. On the contrary, our pietism forces us to make (or enables us to indulge in) moralistic defenses of even the most immoral actions: slavery was God's will and a positive good; imperialism on the American continent or abroad was "manifest destiny" and "the White Man's burden." It would probably be fair to say that because of its intense pietism America has produced more hypocrisy per square soul than almost any other civilization in Christendom. The classic example of this was the inversion of the Protestant ethic into the success myth which concluded*

that the poor were poor because they deserved to be poor—they lacked industry, sobriety, thrift and piety. Similarly, labor unions were attacked in the name of "freedom of contract" or "the right to work," and fair housing laws for Negroes are voted down in the name of "the sanctity of private property." But to point out the extent of American hypocrisy is not to deny the prevalence of American pietism but to confirm it.

12 *See also John 16:12–13: "I have yet many things to say unto you, but ye cannot bear them now. Howbeit when he, the Spirit of truth, is come, he will guide you into all truth."*

moral law with "the American way of life" is just as heretical to the true spirit of pietism as the leftwing fanatic (not to be confused with the antinomian pietist) who equates it with Marxian socialism. Neither of these is really seeking further light either for moral order or moral freedom. They have in fact closed their minds to it. Or, as Reinhold Niebuhr put it, they have "absolutized the relative." Yet even these potential totalitarians in America, whether of the left or right, are still more appropriately described as aberrant pietists rather than as atheistic Marxists or proto-Fascists.

But if pietism is the key to the American character, what about the many claims that America is a materialistic and secular civilization? Despite the fact that Americans seem to have devoted as much of their talent, wealth and energy to perfecting their means of production and distribution of creature comforts as they have to perfecting their personal or social morality, the charge that we are a materialistic nation simply will not hold water. Almost all intelligent European observers who have come to know America have perceived this. The philosopher George Santayana, who lived here during the height of the Gilded Age, characterized Americans as "extreme idealists in the region of hope." The average American, he said, is "an idealist working on matter." The American does not respect or admire money as the Europeans do simply in and for itself; money to them is to be used, not hoarded. Wealth is important not for itself but for what it can do to improve the world:

> The American talks about money, because that is the symbol and measure he has at hand for success, intelligence, and power; but as to money itself, he makes, loses, spends, and gives it away with a very light heart.[13]

[13] *George Santayana*, Character and Opinion in the United States (*Anchor paperback, 1956), pp. 108, 109, 115.*

Americans have always maintained a pietistic dislike for the idle rich, for conspicuous consumption, for the spendthrift or the man who wastes either his money or his talent. We have admired those businessmen most who have given their money away most freely for philanthropic ends; we have made social work a profession. And our willingness to support such international charity as Lend-Lease, the Marshall Plan, Point Four, foreign aid and the Peace Corps indicates a similar sense of stewardship toward the world. Our cynicism about money and philanthropy is only a veneer to hide our do-goodism. I once heard the president of Brown University say when he was seeking money from a wealthy businessman, *"Pecunia non olit";* but he would never have said it had he not recognized that Americans still fear, as Washington Gladden feared Rockefeller's gift to his denomination, that money ("filthy lucre") may be "tainted" by the manner in which it is earned. It is fortunate for our own sense of stewardship that the nations of the world which accept our gifts do not feel as Gladden did about how we made our money.

It is just as inaccurate to say that America is a "secular" culture as it is to say that it is materialistic. The United States Supreme Court (in the person of Justice William O. Douglas) has told us, and we have no higher authority on earth to justify ourselves, that America is a religious nation founded upon a belief in God. We exempt our churches from taxation as we do our philanthropic and educational enterprises because we wish to encourage them. And if we take Bible reading and prayer out of the public schools, it is from the same desire to protect the spiritual freedom of our children and churches from the compromising power of the State which motivated disestablishment, though most Americans are still fearful lest public education become "irreligious" or "amoral." We will no doubt find a method (through "released time" or "shared time" or some other plan) to inculcate religion and morality concurrently with the so-called secular subjects.

The same moralistic and pietistic temper has always inspired our political life. There has scarcely been an election in American history since 1796 which was not conducted as a fight between good and evil for the power to steer the ship of state toward the millennial harbor. If the Jeffersonians were considered atheistic Jacobins, the Federalists were considered power-hungry monarchists and defenders of a corrupt established-church system. If the Whigs were monopolistic plutocrats defending a monster bank, the Jacksonians were barbarian demagogues wrecking the economy. The South saw Lincoln as the tyrant of the North and Republicans saw the South as betrayers of the rights of man. In the 1880s the liberal Republican Mugwumps campaigned against the corruptions of the Grant administration; in the 1890s the Democrats thought they were about to be crucified upon "a Cross of Gold," and in 1912 Theodore Roosevelt said of the Bull Moose Party, "We stand at Armageddon and battle for the Lord." Franklin Roosevelt called his "New Deal" a crusade for human dignity, while Herbert Hoover called it the road to serfdom. Dwight D. Eisenhower and Barry Goldwater campaigned against a corrupt mess of men in Washington who were soft on Communism, while Stevenson and Johnson have insisted that only their party is able to maintain the peace and to care for the poor.

Now it may be argued that regardless of campaign slogans the American two- (or four-) party system is essentially a compromise system and that most of the professional business of politics either in the smoke-filled room or the cloakrooms of the state and federal capitals is done on a very hard-headed basis of lobbying, logrolling and political back-scratching. It might even be argued

that the doctrinaire politics of the multi-party systems of Europe are more morally rigid than American politics. But the weight of these arguments is really the other way around. Doctrinaire political parties are immoral by American pietistic standards because they insist that all politicians and party members vote not as their consciences tell them but as their party line tells them. American political parties, while resting upon compromise between the pietistic extremes of right and left, are nevertheless dedicated to the belief that the compromise itself is the only right and just course toward the millennium. Once the party conventions are over, the party platforms (no matter how they were hammered out) become the voice of God and of the people whose will they represent. We believe that it is the conscience of the people which makes our party platforms and not any doctrinaire party dictator hewing to a rigid political ideology. The logrolling and lobbying and back-scratching in Washington are grimly tolerated as the only apparent means in this corrupt world of getting the nation to move forward without trampling too heavily on someone's freedom (the virtue of the filibuster). Nevertheless, there are strict limitations upon "politicking" beyond which the politician moves only at the risk of being "exposed" for corrupt and immoral betrayal of his "public trust." The business of politics in America is conducted on the razor-thin edge of public moralism and scarcely a month goes by that some politician does not fall off that edge into permanent ruin and disgrace. (Has there ever been an election without a Sherman Adams, a Harry Vaughan or a Bobby Baker?) In fact, the essential characteristic of all American political campaigning, whether for dog-catcher or for the presidency, is the fact that the voter is, or ought to be, disgusted with the rascality of the incumbent. "The professional" is simply the man who can get the most done without staining his moral image sufficiently to fail of re-election. We respect but do not love the political "pro" because we think "politics is dirty."

European observers have shuddered at the religious fervor of American election campaigns only slightly less than they have shuddered at what George Kennan rightly called our "legalistic-moralistic approach" to foreign policy. This approach, said Kennan, is "the carrying over into the affairs of states of the concepts of right and wrong, the assumption that state behavior is a fit subject for moral judgment." And because Americans pietistically believe that there is a moral law which is binding for nations in the same way as for individuals, they also believe in punishing to the fullest extent the criminal nation which breaks that law. Hence our conception of total war, total surrender, total victory. We clothe our "military efforts in the language of idealism," said Kennan, and refuse "to admit the validity and legitimacy of power realities and aspirations, to accept them without feeling the obligation of moral judgment."[14]

And so the defeat of the Southern rebellion in 1861 was a moral question, the repayment of Allied war debts in the 1920s was a moral question, the admission of Communist China to the United Nations is a moral question, the defense of Formosa, Quemoy, Matsu, Viet Nam is a moral question, the granting of foreign aid to Yugoslavia, Poland, India, is a moral question, the whole problem of coexistence with "criminal," atheistic, promise-breaking Communism is a moral question. And any president who fails to see matters in this light, who acts on the ground that more is at stake than making a moralistic

judgment about right and wrong in such affairs, runs the risk, as Lincoln and Kennedy did, of producing profound distrust, fear, anger and hatred among Americans.

In short, there is no area of American life which is free from our pietistic concern; none in which the pietistic attitude is not a significant factor.

So much for the exposition of my hypothesis. Now let me conclude by making a few brief applications of it. If we are a nation of pietists, then, this hypothesis must apply to Roman Catholics and Jews as well as to Protestants. It must also apply to our arts and letters as well as to our politics. It must apply to the daily life of the average man as well as to our thinkers and doers.

In regard to the Roman Catholics and Jews, I have already intimated that the measure of their Americanism or acculturation in their own eyes, as well as in that of historians and sociologists, has been the extent to which they have imbibed the temper of American pietism. Or perhaps it would be more fair to say that America has heightened in these more recent immigrants the pietistic-perfectionism inherent in our shared Judeo-Christian tradition. Will Herberg, while he seems to me to underestimate American pietism, rightly sees very little difference today between the outlooks of the three major groups, Protestant, Catholic, Jew; their growing ecumenical fraternalism bears this out. For example, a few months ago Cardinal Cushing gave his hearty endorsement to Billy Graham and urged all Roman Catholics to attend his meetings. And it would be difficult to find much basic disagreement among the messages presented by Joshua Liebman in his book, *Peace of Mind*, by Billy Graham in *Peace with God* or Fulton Sheen in *Peace of Soul*. All three of them bear striking resemblances also to that other recent best-seller, Norman Vincent Peale's *Power of Positive Thinking*.

[14] *George F. Kennan,* American Diplomacy (*Mentor paperback, 1951), pp. 55, 66, 73, 93–94, 98.*

It is not strange that the Reform movement in Judaism found such compatible surroundings in America in the latter part of the nineteenth century and that Rabbi Stephen S. Wise became one of the leading figures in the Social Gospel movement. I should guess too that the strength of the Zionist movement in this country owes something to the millennial and utopian tradition of American perfectionism, though on its own terms Zionism belongs more nearly to the conservative pietism of the Puritan Bible Commonwealth or Brigham Young's Mormon Zion than to the antinomian pietism of the Oneida Community or Brook Farm.

The liberal wing of the Roman Catholic Church in America is comparable to Reform Judaism in its adoption of American Progressive and Social Gospel ideas and in its commitment over the years to education, labor reform and religious toleration. In the late nineteenth century American pietistic principles so far invaded the Catholic Church here under the evangelistic impetus of Isaac Hecker and Orestes Brownson (aided and abetted by Cardinal Gibbons and Archbishop Ireland) that the Pope felt obliged to condemn what he considered the heresy of "Americanism" though he was as wrong as Lyman Beecher had been to see a threat to religious faith in Hecker's pietistic principles.[15] Catholic liberals have tried to make some compromise with the American public school system and today it is possible to find Catholics working in the American Civil Liberties Union to prevent federal aid to private schools

[15] *Archbishop Ireland once characterized Hecker's views in these pietistic terms: "His was the profound conviction that in the present age, at any rate, the order of the day should be individual action—every man doing his fair duty and waiting for no one else to prompt him." Quoted in Clifton E. Olmstead*, History of Religion in the United States (*Englewood Cliffs, N. J., 1960*), p. 431.

out of the conviction that it will compromise the freedom of the Catholic Church. The line from John Ireland and John A. Ryan to Cardinals Cushing and Ritter seems perfectly clear, and the American election of a Roman Catholic to the presidency confirmed the fact that Catholicism is operating here within the accepted limits of our pietistic frame of reference. Even Cardinal Spellman, whose attachment to the conservative wing has dimmed his lustre in recent years, has tolerated in his diocese the existence of Dorothy Day's anarchistic and perfectionist *Catholic Worker*, than which no magazine and no enterprise in America could be more pietistic.

Here again it is necessary to avoid associating pietisim simply with progressivism or the welfare state ideals. Stephen Wise and Dorothy Day are clearly in the antinomian camp of American pietism. But we have also seen a strong movement among Catholics to associate with conservative and even rightwing fanatical pietism since the days of Father Coughlin. During the McCarthy era rightwing pietistic politics became very appealing to a large number of Roman Catholics. I would certainly put William F. Buckley and the *National Review* in the same rightwing pietistic camp with the Protestant journal called *Christian Economics*, which numbered Billy Graham among its board members. Ralph Lord Roy in his book, *Apostles of Discord*, noted that it was no longer uncommon to see Roman Catholic priests sitting on the same platforms with Fundamentalist ministers in various rallies designed to make America safe for the cross and the flag against Communism. In this respect there is little to choose between the conservative revivalism of Fulton Sheen and that of Billy Graham. You can compare the sermons of this Catholic bishop and this Southern Baptist evangelist and find them virtually identical in their pietistic denunciations of atheistic Communism and their blatant equation of Christianity with American patriotism and the free enterprise system. And on the other side of the fence, it is often hard to tell the politically liberal editorials of the Catholic magazine *Commonweal* from those in the Jewish *Commentary* or the Protestant *Christian Century*. What the Protestants, Catholics and Jews all share, whether conservative or liberal, is the acute sense of personal responsibility to make our system work, an urgency to remake the world in conformity with the ethical absolutes we hold in common from the Judeo-Christian tradition, and the sense of guilt at our own good fortune in the midst of a world of underprivilege. Perhaps the most striking feature of America's fourth Great Awakening has been the fact that for the first time Roman Catholics and Jews shared fully in it. "To be a Protestant, a Catholic, or a Jew," Herberg concludes, "are today the alternative ways of being an American."[16]

Turning to the field of American literature, where I speak only as an amateur, I can merely suggest some of the many ways in which I think it can be described as pietistic. The most obvious, though the least satisfying to us today, is in its relation to "the Genteel Tradition"—the view that all true literature is and must be morally pure and spiritually uplifting. This outlook dominated our literary aesthetic in the nineteenth century and it is epitomized in the pietism of Bryant's "To a Waterfowl," Longfellow's "Excelsior," and Holmes' "The Chambered Nautilus." This moralistic quality also inspired Cooper's Leatherstocking Tales and most of William Dean Howells' "smiling" realism. If this soul-perfecting aesthetic did not produce our best literature, it certainly produced our most popular and most characteristic.

The second and almost equally popular pietistic strain in our literature has been in our novels of righteous indignation, social satire and muckraking reform. Characteristic of the best-selling novels in this vein are *Uncle Tom's Cabin*, *Looking Backward*, *In His Steps*, *The Jungle* and *The Grapes of Wrath*. Among this group of pietists striving by one means or another to goad Americans to reform their corruptions and to get on with perfecting the world, we would also have to include novelists of a somewhat higher rank like John Dos Passos, Theodore Dreiser, Frank Norris, Sinclair Lewis and Hamlin Garland. Their muckraking was less direct but their criticism and implicit idealism was no less compulsive.

But our best poets and writers belong in the third category of literary pietism. They are the ones who, like the Puritans, are not sure they are among the saved but who want desperately to establish some rapport with the absolute. They are pietists because, as Paul Tillich puts it, they face the ultimate concerns of the human situation. R. P. Blackmur, in an illuminating essay on "Religious Poetry in America," has characterized this group of American writers as belonging to "the great wrestling tradition" of western Christendom—those who, like Jacob wrestling with the Angel, are "wrestling with God, with the self, with the conscience, and above all in our latter day with our behavior." In this tradition belongs the poetry of Edward Taylor, of Emily Dickinson and of Walt Whitman's "When Lilacs Last in the Dooryard Bloomed." In the post-Christian era of American pietism this tradition includes the poetry of T. S. Eliot, Robert Lowell, Robert Frost and Wallace Stevens. "All of these poets," says Blackmur, "write poetry which can be understood only if it is taken as religious." But

[16] *Will Herberg*, Protestant, Catholic, Jew (*New York*, 1955), p. 274.

since there is no seal upon us in this post-Christian time, our religious like our other emotions come out of Pandora's box; . . . as religion takes new forms and changes the nature and scope of its interventions, so the poetry associated with religion supervenes differently upon our reading lives. . . . We are likely to be concerned with the excrucation (as Jacob was not); with Jacob's wrestling with the Angel, Man, or God; with the dark night of the soul which never ends . . . with the great sweep of rival creations since . . . we can accept God but not his Creation.[17]

This same statement applies with equal force to our novelists, most of whom belong in the post-Christian tradition despite Randall Stewart's attempt to fit them into the category of Christian orthodoxy. It is certainly this wrestling tradition which informs Melville's quarrel with God—as Blackmur says, "he sought the God he fought." This is the essence of Hawthorne's probing of the human heart. It inspired Mark Twain's desperate longing for the certainty of St. Joan and his conclusion that between Mary Baker Eddy and "The Man Who Corrupted Hadleyburg" there was no moral truth left in modern man. It lies at the heart of William Faulkner's message in *The Fable*. The temper of our best literature can be stated in pietistic-perfectionist terms as anguish, frustration, despair, anger, intensity—anguish over the impurity of man in an impure world; anger at the corruptions and corrupters of human conscience; frustration at man's inability to come to terms with himself or the universe. No doubt all great writers are fundamentally concerned with such wrestlings, but I am convinced that this concern has been more pervasive and more consistent in American literature than in that of any other culture in modern Christendom or post-Christen-

dom. It is not just *one* theme of our literature, it is *the* theme.

The peculiarly American approach to the wrestling tradition has been described in many ways. R. W. B. Lewis in *The American Adam*, argues that our literature has been permeated by "the Adamic ideal," the search for innocence in the New World's second Garden of Eden. And even men like Fitzgerald, Faulkner, Ellison and Salinger who know, in the twentieth century, that the quest for perfection is bound to fail because it is based upon false premises, nevertheless write on in search of it. The heroes and nonheroes of contemporary American fiction (and drama too), Lewis concludes,

> share in their common aloneness that odd aura of moral priority over the waiting world which was a central ingredient in the Adamic fictional tradition [of the nineteenth century]. Each of them struggles tirelessly, sometimes unwittingly and often absurdly, to realize the full potentialities of the classic figure which each represents: the Emersonian figure, 'the simple genuine self against the whole world.'[18]

Which is really not only the classic Emersonian figure but the classic pietistic figure of the Christian man who is in the world but not of it because he will not, must not, compromise with evil lest he fall again like Adam.

Another approach to the pietistic temper of our literature is offered in A. N. Kaul's *The American Vision*. Kaul points out that the absence of a realistic tradition in mid-nineteenth-century American fiction and the failure of our novelists in this period to be concerned with pragmatic or practical social reform (as say Dickens or Balzac

[17] *R. P. Blackmur, "Religious Poetry in the United States," in* Religious Perspectives in American Culture, *eds. J. W. Smith and A. Leland (Princeton, 1961), p. 285.*

[18] *R. W. B. Lewis,* The American Adam *(Phoenix paperback, 1958), p. 198.*

were) was the result of a more basic concern among our novelists to create a perfect or an ideal society:

> The most significant novelists of the first sixty years of the 19th century . . . shared the general feeling that America was the land of social experimentation, and while practical men battled over new political and economic institutions, they sought in their work the moral values necessary for the regeneration of human society. Exploration of existing society led them repeatedly to the theme of ideal community life.

That is, they were concerned not with the mere palliatives of reform but with "a fundamental social ethic." Hence, says Kaul, those books which ostensibly deal with an escape from civilization, like the Leatherstocking Tales, *Huckleberry Finn, Omoo, The Blithedale Romance,* and even Henry James' books about Americans in Europe, are not stating a rejection of our society but rather are posing for their readers the ultimate questions about the essential qualities of an ideal society. "Separation from Europe was the great fact of the American experience even as the creation of a regenerate society was its highest ideal," writes Kaul. Therefore the theme which American writers posed for themselves and their readers "can be described as separation from established society and search for ideal community."[19] And by community Kaul means not merely some political Utopia but the kind of communion of free individuals which the pietist finds in a separated church of regenerate believers. It is a moral and not a pragmatic search for Utopia.

A third approach to the pietistic quality of American literature is put forward by Barry Marks in his study of E. E. Cummings as a classic example of the American idealist in revolt against a bourgeois culture. Marks concludes his discussion of Cummings' peculiar and difficult stylistic devices by comparing his style to the difficult styles adopted by so many other American writers—Thoreau, Whitman, Melville, James, Faulkner. Thoreau, Marks says, "had undergone a profound spiritual renewal" in his experience at Walden Pond, and "he was satisfied with nothing less than a book which might induce readers to share the same experience." The most characteristic writers from Thoreau to Cummings write out of what is to them the same kind of "world-shattering" religious experience. And rather than explain it in what would be only feeble expositions, they purposely adopted a difficult, even disorderly and obscure style hoping thereby "to shake readers from the expectation of being *merely* entertained, of *merely* reading a book [about an experience], into a readiness to participate with their whole beings in a deep encounter with life itself."[20]

A similar pietistic interpretation can be made of American art and architecture where a direct personal confrontation of the visual image is designed to uplift the viewer (as in the Hudson River School of painting) or to shock him (as in the Ashcan, abstract, or Pop Art schools) into a new awareness of himself and his world—an awareness which always has moral overtones. I might also point to the moralistic qualities of Jefferson's architectural theory or Horatio Greenough's "functionalism," and suggest that the essentially pietistic quality of American architecture lies in its perennial and deep-seated urge to place man in harmony with the supernatural through establishing his proper relationship to Nature. Our most characteristically American architects from An-

[19] *A. N. Kaul,* The American Vision *(New Haven, 1963), pp. 5, 35, 67.*

[20] *Barry A. Marks,* E. E. Cummings *(New York, 1964), pp. 134, 136.*

drew Jackson Downing to Frank Lloyd Wright have agreed with Emerson's view that "Nature is the expositor of the Divine Mind" and that we must, in Horace Bushnell's phrase, go "through Nature to God."

This is essentially what Wright means by "organic Architecture," and by his phrase "Every true aesthetic is an implication of nature." "Reality," he wrote, "is spirit—essence brooding just behind aspects." His pietism, like Emerson's, can be seen in his reliance upon the intuitive communion between the artist and the moral law. It is this, he says, which produces "the harmony of the whole" in any true work of art.[21]

As for the pietistic-perfectionism which abounds in our everyday life, it takes two forms: one, the quest for perfectionism as itself a kind of pious obligation, and the other, a gnawing fear or guilt (sometimes described by sociologists as "the self-hatred of the middle class") that there is more to life than we are making of it, and that we must do better in the future.

However, while Americans think pietistically on moral questions, they are by no means so perfectionist as, say, the Germans or the Japanese are in the realm of craftsmanship, art or dedication to detail. No doubt some of the old Yankee craftsmen had this quality (like those who built the wonderful one hoss shays or the clipper ships) and the Shakers displayed it in their furniture and architecture. But by and large Americans have not been interested in creating perfect or even careful craftsmanship. They are in too much of a hurry to get on to the millennium to work patiently over any details. Craftsmanship is incompatible with shorter work hours and mass production; moreover it smacks of an exploited lower class and a wealthy aristocracy. Our perfectionism in work or in leisure (like our plastic sailboats that never need painting, caulking or scraping) lies in the realm of efficiency and easy functioning rather than in lasting quality, thoroughness or artistry of detail. There is no denying that American haste in construction is characteristically slipshod, makeshift, jerrybuilt. We build only for the short term, not for eternity. Only God can build for eternity and we have too far to go to reach perfection to waste time trying to perfect the imperfectible. Fearing the sin of pride in our own artistry or craftsmanship we righteously pretend to disdain the things you can't take with you.

American perfectionism lies in movement, in action and in the future. We believe a regenerate man is capable of "growing in grace" but pure grace exists only in heaven or in the millennium. We change our styles in clothes, home furnishings and automobiles almost yearly because change itself is good—it prevents the hardening of anything into custom, tradition or institutionalism, which are by definition bad. They impede the pursuit of happiness by seeking to retain too much of the imperfect present or past. We sometimes regret the shoddiness of American workmanship and the wastefulness of built-in obsolescence (as Thorstein Veblen did) but on balance our distrust of institutionalism is stronger than our love of thrift. David Potter has pointed out that a "people of plenty" finds it difficult to maintain the Old World's faith in thrift as the Protestant ethic defined it. We see in those who hold up the ideals of perfect craftsmanship and art, reactionaries who would lead us back to the static class and craft system of medieval society—the Ralph Adams Crams, the T. S. Eliots, the Nashville Agrarians.

This is what gives the pietistic-perfectionist

21 *Frank Lloyd Wright*, An Autobiography (*London, 1932*), *pp. 144–54.*

tone to American pragmatism despite the unfortunate slip of William James in defining it as "the cash value of ideas." Americans pietistically mistook James to mean that pragmatism was materialistic and concerned only with the expedient or profitable in the mercenary sense. But by using (as Santayana said) the only measure Americans have for values, James meant only to say that the value of pragmatism was in helping us get on with the job of perfecting our society and solving those institutional problems which impeded progress. The key to "the pragmatic revolt" like "the Transcendentalist revolt" was its pietistic antiformalism, its dislike for a block universe, its openness to new experiments in thought and action. Despite John Dewey's apparent commitment to naturalism and behaviorism, his real motivating force was his desire to break the hold of the past and to reconstruct philosophy so as to facilitate change without, as he insisted, limiting freedom. Dewey's own inherent pietism, set forth in his Book *A Common Faith*, lies in his belief that "shared experience" will lead to a common set of values dedicated to the forward-looking experiment and to ever-widening freedom.[22] When an American says he is pragmatic or empirical he means that he is willing to try anything new which promises to get himself or the world a little further along toward perfect freedom and perfect order.

Because we find it so difficult to reconcile our contradictory ideals, like thrift and change, pragmatism and absolutism, moral freedom and moral order, we carry on within our own hearts the terrible anguish of the Puritan conscience. We feel perpetually guilty because we do not live up to our own ideals and because our country does not live up to its ideals. Our sense of guilt is apparent in our high consumption of alcohol and our high rate of divorce, ulcers, heart attacks and colitis. I would contend that it is not the fierce pace of the American pursuit of "the Almighty dollar" which produces these results so much as our pietistic conscientiousness which makes us dissatisfied with ourselves. We drive ourselves to drink not for pleasure but to forget our failures. We even feel that our leisure is wasted and our pleasures are superficial though we work terrifically hard at them.

Out of this self-disgust and guilt, of course, comes much of what is most characteristically worthwhile about American life. We are not just flagellating ourselves by reading *Babbitt*, *The Status Seekers*, *The Organization Man*, *The Crack in the Picture Window*, *The Group*. We are engaging in healthy self-criticism and self-examination. We want to know where we have failed and we take our failures very seriously. We set up all sorts of societies and groups to improve ourselves and our society. We may laugh at the foibles of the P.T.A., the Women's Clubs, the Great Books clubs, the Boy Scouts, Adult Education and the League of Women Voters, but they are the essence of our social system. It is from this self-doubting and guilt-ridden middle class that the more radical pietists of the right and left draw their strength for periodic national reformations. We are too pietistic to like politics—politics requires too many compromises for an "honest" man—but we recognize the compromises we ourselves make in

22 *Dewey's "common faith" is post-Christian pietism in its rejection of the supernatural absolutes of revealed religion. But in its anti-institutionalism, its claims for "natural piety" and its "Faith in the continued disclosing of truth," it is, as Dewey said, "more religious in quality than is any faith in a completed revelation." "Any activity pursued in behalf of an ideal end against obstacles and in spite of threats of personal loss because of conviction of its general and enduring value is religious in quality." "It is this active relation between ideal and actual to which I would give the name 'God.'" It would be difficult to find a clearer statement of post-Christian pietism. See* A Common Faith *(New Haven, 1934), pp. 25–26, 27, 51.*

our everyday lives. We consider it our duty to vote and to make our political parties toe the line or to "throw the rascals out" if they are as forgetful of their campaign promises as we are of our New Year's resolutions. We are still perfectionists underneath our veneer of sophistication and still reformers despite our neo-orthodox awareness of original sin.

No final estimate of the value of the pietistic and perfectionist streaks in the American temper is possible until historical judgment can be passed upon the whole American experiment. These elements have produced some of the worst aspects of American self-righteousness, bigotry and naive stupidity. They have also inspired most of America's dynamic generosity, self-awareness and social concern. I do not contend that everything in American life can be traced to, or explained by, these qualities, but I do believe that by and large they have played a major role in shaping our decisions and given a distinctive coloration to our attitudes. For better or for worse America is, and always has been, a nation *engagé*—committed to a moralistic approach to life—a nation of pietists.

"A RESTLESS TEMPER..."

George W. Pierson*

In 1954, in two international conferences under the aegis of UNESCO, a group of European intellectuals devoted themselves to the discussion of *Le Nouveau Monde et l'Europe*. Characteristically, several of the participants dropped quickly into attacks on United States civilization in its more deplorable manifestations. American materialism (our mechanization and technocracy, the gadgetry

GEORGE W. PIERSON (1904–   ) is the Larned Professor of History at Yale University. His publications include Tocqueville and Beaumont in America (1938), "The Frontier and Frontiersmen of Turner's Essay" (1940), Yale College (1952), "The Obstinate Concept of New England" (1955), and "The M-Factor in American History" (1962). Reprinted by permission of the author and the American Historical Review, Vol. 69, No. 4 (July, 1964), 969–989.

and "emptiness" of our lives), American infantilism and conformism, and the sad state of American arts were arraigned with such mordant fervor that the three Americans present, and the generous and illuminating André Maurois, must have been troubled to keep their calm.

Now and again, but without systematic connection, allusions were made to our mobility: to the *manie itinerante* which was perhaps becoming a national characteristic; to the decline of genuine regionalism under the assaults of invading students, old people, and tourists; to the mournful interchangeable towns; to the nomadism even within our cities; and to the piercing need to conform so as to obliterate an immigrant background. Only this conformity, warned Maurois, was not *immobilisme* but rather conformity to change and improvement, hence an instinct for adaptability carried to extremes. Maurois also said:

> La ville, comme la maison, est un instrument de travail. Dès que la journée active est terminée, on s'évade. Aucun peuple n'éprouve plus que celui-ci le besoin de voyager, de prendre des vacances, de se replonger dans la nature. L'état normal de l'Américain c'est le mouvement. C'est lorsqu'il part dans sa voiture avec sa femme et ses enfants, comme jadis ses ancêtres dans leur wagon de pionnier, pour quelque ranch dans le désert ou pour un campement de montagne, pour une cabane au bord d'un lac où il pourra pêcher et chasser, que l'Américain se sent vivre.[1]

Regrettably, these fragmentary perceptions were not linked together, or pursued toward a deeper understanding, as Thornton Wilder had recently tried to do, with brilliant intuition, in his Norton Lectures at Harvard.[2] By way of preface to his study of the peculiar language of American writers, Wilder had insisted on a certain "disequilibrium of the psyche which follows on the American condition." Specifically, "From the point of view of the European an American is nomad in relation to place, disattached in relation to time, lonely in relation to society, and insubmissive to circumstance, destiny or God." The American's relations were not with the past but with the future: his life was one of becoming (like the characters in his Bible, he had hung "suspended upon the promises of the imagination"). Again, said Wilder, the American was "differently surrounded"; for he had no fixed abode, but carried his "home" with him; his relations were not to place but "to everywhere, to everyone, and to always." The American was the independent, the lonely man. And he was still engaged in inventing what it is to be an American.

If Wilder was right that a process of invention has been going on—or if Americans have practiced any such extreme adaptiveness as Maurois referred to—then some challenging possibilities confront us. For it would appear that, consciously or unconsciously, we Americans have perhaps been engaged in reconstructing the entire gamut of relations for Western (or mobile) man! This would mean (1) new institutions patterned in part on free movement; (2) new relations with the physical environment based on a view of nature differing from the European; (3) a new concept of human fellowship or a decalogue of social conduct in some ways deviant from the Greco-Christian tradition; (4) even possibly a new attitude toward the self.

This is a large order, indeed a new order too vast to be comprehended and described, the more

[1] Le Nouveau Monde et l'Europe (*Neuvièmes Rencontres Internationales de Genève: Premières Rencontres Intellectuelles de Sao Paulo*) (*Neuchatel, 1955*), *173 et passim*.

[2] *Thornton Wilder, "Toward an American Language,"* The Atlantic, CXC (*July, 1952*), *29 ff.*

so as these inventions or ventures in adjustment must be still in process, and far from concluded. The new society, if such it is, has not quite crystallized out. Robert Moses to the contrary notwithstanding, it is too early for some latter-day prophet to codify the commandments of mobility, or make straight the highway for our culture.

Yet are there not signs?

By way of experiment, we might glance first perhaps at some of our *basic institutions* and ask ourselves a question. The family and the home, the city and the industrial corporation, the government whether local, state, or federal: are not all of these institutions being shaken, changed, even visibly restructured by the American habits of movement?

It can be no secret, for example, that under the strains of modern living the American family has been showing signs of coming apart. The progressive weakening of the household as an institution, the loosening of the ties of marriage, the seemingly casual ease of desertion and divorce, the all too obvious decline of parental authority, the quick escape of the children; clearly these derive from no one sickness, no single social cause. Yet clearly they have all been facilitated and increased by our ready mobility.

Home? We move from address to address with an almost frightening carelessness and ease. A few of us have gone so far as to put our homes on wheels for towing between trailer parks. And if finally we take off the wheels and block up our home-mobiles in someone's back yard, is it not in some sort a symbol of defeat, or at least of retirement? Meanwhile the rest of us sell and buy houses with a greater freedom than we used to rent. Wilder likes to think that we Americans have learned to take our homes with us and enjoy "making" new homes, or impressing a new apartment with our "home-making" ability. But can "home" be altogether divorced from "place"?

In this grasshopper existence, have we not converted "home" into "domicile"? And are we not now faced with the disappearance of domicile? How many of us reside in the houses where our grandfathers were born, or even in the same county or state? How many maintain a family seat, which three generations have known and loved? Some of us somehow do manage to stay in one spot for the years our children are in school. Yet others do not, and the educational difficulties engendered by such restlessness are becoming notorious, not to speak of the moral losses as well.[3]

Again, within the past twenty years especially, the spectacular refusal of the young-marrieds to

[3] *Some of the consequences of mobility for the American "home" have been more fully developed in my essay "Under a Wandering Star," Virginia Quarterly Review, XXXIX (Autumn, 1963), 621–38; and one or two hints of the political impact may be found in "The Moving American," Yale Review, XLIV (Autumn, 1954), 99–112, and "The M-Factor in American History," American Quarterly, XIV (Summer 1962, Suppl.), 275–89. On a converging line of thought, Everett S. Lee of the University of Pennsylvania has called attention to the significance of spatial mobility for the family life, social psychology, love of change, economic development, and employment opportunities of the American experience: "The Turner Thesis Re-examined," ibid., XIII (Spring, 1961), 77–83. No adequate bibliography on spatial mobility can be cited, but the most interesting and effective large-scale attempt to relate mobility to the structure and history of American institutions is that of Frank Thistlethwaite in* The Great Experiment: An Introduction to the History of the American People *(New York, 1955). My own fascination with the theme goes back to the unpublished American diaries and letters of Alexis de Tocqueville (which I had the good fortune to encounter in 1928), to subsequent re-examination of Turner's frontier hypothesis, to conversations with Ellsworth Huntington, and to readings in seminal works by Pitirim Sorokin, Isaiah Bowman, Rudolf Heberle, R. H. Gabriel, A. M. Schlesinger, H. S. Commager, and Oscar Handlin.*

live any longer with parents or in-laws has produced not only skyscraper suburbs but endless villages of ranchtype or split-level houses, plastered in dreary monotony across mile on mile of once smiling countryside. Viewed from the air, or from abroad, the tents of our people cut a strange pattern. Better incomes, higher standards of privacy, and a certain restive independence on the part of the younger generation have perhaps triggered this rush outward from our urban centers. Yet such large-scale "developments" would never have been possible but for expressways and commutation tickets, *and the habits* that make their use possible. As a rather obvious corollary, it proves hard now to give to these Levittowns any pride of place or community life of their own. As with the family and the home, no little vitality and moral force have been siphoned out of the American village or town.

At the other end of the scale, the decline of localism, the paring away of states' rights, and the steady enlargement of the sovereignty and activity of the national government have been stimulated by many strong forces, and not least by the dangers of the world situation. Yet have they not had a more than casual connection with the ever-mounting movement of people from state to state? with the long inflow of immigrants whose aim was to be Americans not Pennsylvanians or New Yorkers? with our astonishing interstate commerce and its regulation? with the siphoning of tax monies, industries, and employment from one section to another, and most recently with the channeling of defense orders into places whither the plants can be moved or where the labor and voting forces have already arrived? People have been moving too much to allow of an effective regionalism.

Looked at in the large, our empty continent was supposed to foster individualism of action and belief. And, in retrospect, space-plus-mobility may

have begun with dispersion and freedom to differ, that is, with decentralization. But in the long run mobility overruns space, and the circulation and recirculation of people induces conformity. As once the nineteenth-century utopian colonists and the Mormons learned to their sorrow, wherever they could flee others could follow, and in a surprisingly short time there were no hiding places left. Nor ought there to be, in the eyes of our vigilant moralists. As once the abolitionists and Radical Reconstructionists demonstrated, and then the prohibitionists and child labor crusaders learned, and now the freedom riders have rediscovered, space-plus-mobility may begin by offering escape and freedom for peculiar institutions, but ultimately it brings on the need for federal intervention and big government. You cannot quarantine personal liberties, they say; you cannot prevent the desire for equality from crossing state lines; and you cannot forever segregate schools and public places. Why not? Because ideals speak to the heart; because free speech will carry their message across regional barriers; and finally because people are moving so much back and forth. The Bill of Rights and interstate commerce will prevent.[4] Thus, from anarchy to conformity, from home rule to centralization, has been the story. And where once the idealist might

---

[4] *In President Kennedy's message to Congress on civil rights (as printed in the New York* Times, *June 20, 1963) one reads: "In a society which is increasingly mobile and in an economy which is increasingly interdependent, business establishments which serve the public—such as hotels, restaurants, theaters, stores and others—serve not only the members of their immediate communities but travelers from other states and visitors from abroad. Their goods come from all over the nation. This participation in the flow of interstate commerce has given these business establishments both increased prosperity and an increased responsibility to provide equal access and service to all citizens."*

have founded a utopian colony, now he asks for a constitutional amendment.

We Americans move about so much that many of our intermediate institutions are likewise being geared directly to the expectation. Witness chapels on wheels and drive-in churches, or the circulation of ministerial talent and the growing homogenization of the Protestant believers. To speak merely of the dissenting churches, in the eighteenth and nineteenth centuries the unprecedented American freedom of movement undoubtedly encouraged sectarianism and accelerated the splintering of congregations, but lately interdenominational communication, based on an intensified interchange both personal and intellectual, seems to be promoting consolidation. How powerfully the cooperative movement among the Protestant sects may derive from a fear of Roman Catholicism—or the ecumenical movement among all Christians from the menace of Marxism—should not be underestimated. Yet when one hears on Sunday in a village Congregation a "letter" (of transfer) read—or when twelve people stand up before the minister to be received into membership, and not one enters by confession but all twelve turn out to be communicants from other churches—at that moment the traditional substance seems to leak out of the word Congregation. And the individual church becomes merely one cell in a church universal, a standardized unit for us pilgrims, not unlike a service station for the convenience of the passers-by.[5]

If we turn next to the vast area of the American economy, the Pennsylvania Turnpikes and the New York Thruways, the Holland Tunnels and Golden Gate Bridges, Greyhounds and vista domes, the drive-it-yourself services, and the U-Hauls, and the Teamsters Unions: these may seem too practical and familiar, or too directly tied to transportation, to have any larger implications for our culture. Yet, in the impressions of a visiting Frenchman, symbolically entitled *La Grande Parade Américaine*, one might recall what was said not so very long ago about our railroads:

> pour l'Européen, ce n'est qu'un moyen de transport; mais l'Américain éprouve un sentiment voisin de l'amour patriotique pour le train qui est à la fois un ami, un témoin unique, un champion aimé et un lien national. . . . Sans le chemin de fer, il n'y a pas d'Etats-Unis.

> . . . les villes sont nées sur ses bords, comme en Europe le long des rives des fleuves. Cette rivière de metal amenait avec elle la vie et deposait sur ses verges des alluvions: campements, puis cités.[6]

To H.-J. Duteil, the railroads helped express the grandeur of American conceptions, and he went on to quote from Freeman Hubbard's *Railroad Avenue . . .* , the C & O prose poem:

> Listen . . . From across the sleeping countryside
> Comes the steady, rhythmic rumble of the trains,
> The great, husky trains of America.
> They've talked to you since childhood,
> They've told you, in the lonely silence of the night,
> Of far-off places, of romance and adventure!

Sadly, our own generation has had to watch the demise of the steam engine, the ossification of railroad management, and the threatened ruin by featherbedding. Those old arteries celebrated by

---

[5] *A few Sundays after these lines were penned, the minister in our local Congregational Church stated that because of moving away fifteen members had left the choir within the year.*

[6] *H.-J. Duteil,* La Grande Parade Américaine *(Paris, 1949), 55 ff.*

Duteil have hardened and deteriorated. And so today it is the automobiles and planes that breathe of romance and adventure, that speak to us of distant lands, that carry the mystic numbers and the names from interstellar space: Starfire and Nova, Comet and Galaxie, Riviera and Bonneville, Constellation and Astrojet. Yet even now the threat of a national railroad strike can shake President and Congress.[7]

Going beyond transportation, let us consider for just a moment that extraordinary flat-topped do-it-yourself store which car-minded Californians sold to the nation and which recently has had our continental scholar-critics goggling and almost speechless: the SUPERMARKET. Even with its satellite shopping center, the supermarket may not be so very unprecedented in its concentration of possibilities: one senses a modernized version of Old World market squares; one is reminded of the crowded bazaars which go back to prehistory. Inside this American sales factory

[7] *Twenty-eight years ago Philip Guedalla, in reviewing American development, ventured his celebrated declaration: "The true history of the United States is the history of transportation . . . in which the names of railroad presidents are more significant than those of Presidents of the United States."* (The Hundred Years [London, 1936].) *Then came Henry Ford; and what his system of production and his tin lizzie did to the transport, the roads, the work habits, and the lives of Americans, has become part of the American legend. Yet, as Simeon Strunsky so paradoxically observed, "the more things Americans change under the impact of the automobile, the more they remain American. . . . The automobile embodies a vigorous restatement of basic national principles. The automobile cannot undermine the old American way of life because it is the product of that way of life and of the spirit that shaped it. It incorporates the aims and impulses that guided our older history. The throb of its engine is the beat of the historic American tempo."* (The Living Tradition [New York, 1939], 172.)

there is self-service, which to a European does have some revolutionary implications. But what is it we drop into our wheeled baskets? Why, nothing special: just canned goods, bottled beverages, packaged cereals, and frozen foods—almost all with common names or standard brands. Some of the articles come from a long way off, hardly any from the immediate neighborhood, but that is an old story in the American market. We could buy these articles as well five hundred miles away. In fact we have brought them across the continent, and with time many of the newest brands will seep into the remotest settlements. Why? Because they are cheaper and better? It may be. Because the American production line, with automatic machinery, interchangeable parts, mass production, and high-pressure salesmanship in the mass media, inevitably undersells and replaces the local or regional product? Quite probably. With press and radio and television to back up *Good Housekeeping* and a Sears-Roebuck catalogue, what might one not sell?

Yet I wonder a little about local pride or prejudice, and the proverbial sectional antagonisms, not to mention ingrained habits or man's immemorial dislike of accepting things from outsiders. Did our Californians cheerfully take their steel from Pittsburgh? Did traditions of taste and individual workmanship set no limits to the spread of "Grand Rapids"? Do we really like the western Golden Delicious as well as the New England apples of our boyhood? What standard brand I want to know, can possibly match the bite and aroma of a Broadleaf Connecticut cigar? And how did those insipid "fifteen-centers" get to New Haven in the first place? Because they were advertised and brought in by salesmen? No doubt, in due course. But first one suspects they came in men's pockets. And then they were asked for, and slowly offered, in the corner drugstores. In my book, it was sometimes the obvious superiority of the mass product that persuaded. But at other times it was the man who helped bring the article. Or, coming in from outside, and not finding what he was used to, he asked to have it brought in.[8]

So if the standard brands find their way into the remotest settlements, and soon come to dominate the lonely crossroads, may it not be in part because they are what the travelers asked for? When frozen chickens first invade the village grocery, do they not know that an old customer has already been in, or will drop in tomorrow?

Advertising and word of mouth are immeasurably powerful. Ideas can carry packages no less well than men. But things are surer if the man has been by, too. So our cans chase our consumers about the country—and vice versa. In a sense we are in a circular argument. Standard brands make moving from region to region less painful to the traveler, while at the same time the traveler makes it easier for standard brands to cover the whole nation. Take away the moving consumer, and the standard brand will not "move" so well either. *C'est fou? Eh bien, monsieur.* Which are your favorite chain stores in France?[9]

No doubt this seems a long way around to a simple fact, but that fact is worth pondering. Whether as cause or coincidence or consequence, mobility is built into our social economy. And if we have achieved not only a certain uniformity of speech, but a generalization of consumer taste and an agreed on vocabulary of comfort across the nation, it is because *both* men and ideas have been in almost constant motion everywhere.

One would, of course, like to know much more about the impact of mobility on our institutions. For example, what barriers are there? What happens when free mobility threatens to injure the public welfare? Obviously any government must try to impose restraints. Thus for presumed reasons of social, physical, moral, or financial health, we have restricted immigration, excluded the criminals and the diseased, imposed national origins quotas, and made movement into this country not a little unpleasant as well as far from free. The import of plants and animals into the country or across some state boundaries (for example, California) is controlled and to a degree restricted by agricultural quarantines. For like reasons there are laws against the carriage of firearms across state lines.

Taking advantage of the interstate commerce laws, the federal government has prohibited the carriage from one state to another of kidnaped persons, strikebreakers, or women or young girls for immoral purposes. The United States has also forbidden the shanghaiing of sailors, or any moving or traveling in interstate commerce to avoid prosecution, confinement after conviction, or giving testimony in a criminal case. On a lower plane, tax reasons have acted to inhibit the personal transport of alcohols into one state from another, and when the New York commuter carries city earnings into the suburbs of Connecticut or New

---

[8] *A few days after writing these words, I came on the story of how in 1844 the first wholesale pie factory in New England got its start. It appears that a homesick son in New York, with other New Haven lads who longed for "old-fashioned pies," gave Amos Munson back in New Haven the idea of setting up a pie factory and shipping his "Connecticut pies" via steamboat to New York. Within five years Munson's firm was producing one thousand pies a day, and the freight bills by steamboat became so large that Munson opened a plant in New York City. Eventually three of his workers "started their own pie-making factories after learning the trade. They were H. H. Olds who stayed in New Haven; Elisha Case who went to Chicago; and J. E. Perry who settled in Providence." (*New Haven* Register, Feb. 3, 1963.)*

[9] *In the matter of chain stores the British have come closer to the American practice, as they have also in personal mobility.*

Jersey, two states may try to tax him. Yet all this adds up to little.[10]

Altogether there seem to be few "cattle-guards" sunk into the boundaries of our states to keep their human herds from straying. Instead these sovereign entities find themselves helpless to block the invasion of Okies or freedom riders, to prevent the passage of strangers across their territories, or even to impede the exodus of their own citizens with their votes, their capital, and their businesses. We must conclude that the interstate commerce in persons knows few impediments. Lately the State Department has on occasion withheld passports from its own citizens, to prevent their traveling abroad, reviving that old prerogative and personal power of the kings of England which, from Magna Carta onward, John and his successors were gradually forced to surrender.[11] Yet there is something so arbitrary and tyrannical in this power that only the intense fears of Russia and China perhaps warrant its temporary exercise.

Aside from such restrictions on travel, how has mobility entered into our common or statute law? What changes has it produced in the laws governing real estate? of movable possessions? of domiciliary rights or estate taxes? It would be astonishing if even that tough and resistant mountain complex of accumulated decisions which we call the Law did not show the parallel grooves and occasional water gaps scoured by the slow drifts and sudden freshets of our population within the past two centuries. But, in all candor, I have been able to find few examples.[12] In our legislatures we

---

[10] *C. Vann Woodward, to whom I owe many useful suggestions, has recalled that before the Civil War some states in the Midwest had laws prohibiting the immigration of free Negroes; until 1886 South and North used different railroad gauges; and the southern freight rate structure still perpetuates the design to restrict competition. In a degree the same could be said of the basing point system in industry.*

[11] *In 1215 King John was forced to give up the writ of* Ne Exeat Regno *when it was stipulated that except for criminals, outlaws, alien nationals, and briefly in times of war,* liceat unicuique de cetero exire de regno nostro, et redire, salvo et secure, per terram et per aquam. . . . *Because this permission gave the clergy opportunities to appeal in person to Rome, thereby undermining the King's authority, it was omitted from the second issue of Magna Carta in 1216, and Henry III required all persons going abroad to secure a royal license or be fined. But gradually his successors found they could control or arrest only special classes, the rest presumably being free to come and go. In 1606, to accommodate the Scots, Ne Exeat Regno was presumably abolished, later to be taken over by the Court of Chancery to prevent parties to a suit in equity from withdrawing to a foreign land. One is reminded of our extradition of criminals, and of the piecemeal American prohibitions by the Mann Act and other legislation. (See*

W. S. McKechnie, Magna Carta *[2d ed., 2 vols., New York, 1958], 473–78; P. A. Freund et al., Constitutional Law: Cases and Other Problems [2d ed., Boston, 1961], 390–97.) For guidance and suggestions on these legal and constitutional matters I am indebted to Dean Eugene V. Rostow and Professor Alexander M. Bickel of the Yale Law School, and to my colleagues in history, Professors William H. Dunham and Archibald S. Foord.*

[12] *When Hetty Green died, several states struggled ravenously for the privilege of calling her a legal resident, for in the law she could belong to but one. Will not this someday have to be changed?*

In the world of farm animals (which also moved) it is instructive to observe how the English laws of fencing did have to be changed. For where the common law had required each stock raiser to enclose his animals with a legal fence, in the New World, with so much wilderness and free land available for both domesticated cattle and domesticated plants—man's animal and vegetable slaves—it soon came to seem more sensible, in fact necessary, to require farmers to put the fences around their crops. That is, the costs of fencing (and the more mobile four-footed slaves!) got the upper hand. And it was only with the disappearance of the open range in any given area that the agriculturists began to have a chance to restore the balance in their own favor. (See Earl W. Hayter, "Livestock-Fencing Conflicts in Rural America," Agricultural History, XXXVII [Jan., 1963], 11–20.)

even still cling to the local residence requirements and the district delegate idea rather than shift to the more fluid "virtual representation" long practiced in England and now made possible by our automobile-airplane age.

With our Constitution and the Supreme Court, however, the matter is otherwise. What cognizance has the Supreme Court given to motion? It has struck down taxes and other impediments to interstate circulation. And clearly the equal application of the Constitution to all regions and states, whether humid or dry, whether English, French, Spanish, Indian, or African in origin or prevailing culture, constitutes an implicit assumption and endorsement of free movement. As early as the days of the founding fathers, free movement seemed necessary to the making of the nation. And in Article IV, Section 2 of the United States Constitution (as also in the Constitution of the Confederate States of America!) it was emphatically stated that "citizens of each state shall be entitled to all the privileges and immunities of citizens in the several states." The Constitution should make it safe for a man to go. Disunity through the inhibition of movement must be discouraged.

But let us shift the spotlight from institutions to a second major category: our relations with things. The elite of Europe accuse us of materialism in many forms, from a childlike delight in shiny gadgets to a willing slavery to laborsaving machinery, from engrossment with creature comforts to a worship of the almighty dollar, from an obsession with material possessions to the debasement or total neglect of the finer arts. One vivid image of the American home is that of a procession of new dishwashers, freezers, mixers, and other mechanical devices going in the front door, while out the back door comes another procession of the barely used and still serviceable machines of

yesterday, on their way to the discard heap.[13] This picture says that we are rich, but also wasteful, not to say careless with our things.

Are all rich peoples so enamored of new things or so careless of the old? The question has only to be asked in the context of the European aristocracy, or of privileged classes anywhere, to suggest that something else must be involved here besides "plenty." And I would propose that this something may lie in the American experience. As a part of that experience, traveling hither and yon, even moving his family from year to year, the American has been subjected to a bombardment of new situations, stimulated by the unexpected, taught to accept and value new things. Yet if he seems to keep chasing new possessions, it has been noticed also that his relations with the things themselves do not go very deep. In part for the very reason that he has seen so much that is new and handy and has grown used to changes and improvements, he will be quick to pick up new games and the latest fashions, yet as quick to discard them for something different or better. I find it hard to believe that a sedentary population would show any such gay abandon.

If we now bring into view that category of things we call "nature," or the physical environment, have not Americans once again proved

[13] See Ann Hightower, *"French Myths about America"* in *New York* Times Magazine, *Feb. 27, 1949:* "*take the mattress story* [*that in the US mattresses are thrown away every two years*]. *If only confirms what the Frenchman already 'knows' to be true—that the American home is a reverse assembly line to convert the products of whirring factories back to basic rubble. He still imagines a solid stream of gadgets, clothes, and household materials being delivered to the front door to be tossed out the back when slightly used. If Americans admit that there was a widespread practice of buying a new car every year and turning in the old one, no other tale is too fabulous for belief.*"

themselves avid yet careless of their resources? On landing, our forefathers found the wild continent more terrible than beautiful: a savage wilderness to be feared, brutally fought, and mastered as the price of survival. Once conquered, however, or on the way to subjection, the continent began to fascinate both curiosity and cupidity. The novelty and sheer size of its wonders excited national pride; its wealth drew us on. Our forebears had never seen so much timber or so much virgin land. They ravaged both. Scenically, the Hudson River Palisades were but the curtain raiser to the grand landscapes of the interior. With patriotic fervor we sent foreigners to view Niagara Falls and the Great Lakes, to steamboat down the Ohio and Mississippi, to ride out over the Great Plains to the Rockies, to admire the Bad Lands and Monument Valley, perhaps, but certainly the Grand Canyon and the giant redwoods of California. We have streamed there ourselves, stopping off en route to see the falls of the Yosemite and the fumaroles of the Yellowstone.

Yet on the way, unfortunately, the face of nature soon began to show signs of dissipation or neglect. The magnificent white pine stands of Michigan were decimated; the prairie soils were so abused that they are not what they used to be; while beyond the Great Divide the ghosts of abandoned mining towns haunt the dry gulches and arroyos. Happily, it will be observed, some of the most spectacular resources have now been wrested in some part from commercial exploitation and "saved for the nation" (along with the modest sand dunes of Cape Cod). Yet this in itself is a curious grand concourse kind of salvation. At best our natural wonders we first admire, then exploit, then reluctantly turn into national parks, not to be lived with but to be visited with, not to become the basis for a distinct and colorful regional society but to be experienced superficially by just about everyone.[14] There is no privilege of locality, no priority for the natives. There is even very little of that intimacy with the soil, or that interdependence of man with living nature, which we call love of the land. Hence our regionalisms have been surprisingly superficial. William Faulkner and Robert Frost to the contrary notwithstanding, one encounters too rarely that feel for locality which generations of occupancy should nourish. In a sense, after 350 years in this country,

[14] *It is revealing to read the recent advertisement of* The American Heritage Book of Natural Wonders (*Feb. ?, 1963*):

"As Robert Frost remarked recently, 'What makes a nation in the beginning is a good piece of geography.'

"That, for certain, we've had in these United States. A land so whopping big and wild and varied that even now—when we can span it in four hours, or scar its remotest corner with a beer can—it can awe and dazzle us.

"You've probably seen a lot of America, because the lovely and barrier-free country has conditioned us all to be easy travelers. And surely you have had the thrill, more than once, of imagining what it was like to be the explorer who saw some great vista for the first time—a Henry Hudson, a Captain John Smith, a Meriwether Lewis.

"View the land as they saw it (and you can still, here and there) stretching westward without end, and it is easy to comprehend why America forged a new kind of man. The primitive continent called for a new way of life, and a new point of view, that marks us all to this day.

"No doubt of it, the American land has been the anvil that has shaped a lot of your belief and character. And no doubt at all, much of the American land is a spectacular sight to see. So. . . ."

One wonders if American Heritage *really meant to emphasize that this vast continent, without barriers, has shrunk to a mere four hours, with its beauties considerably spoiled, its natural wonders scarred by beer cans, and its grand vistas only here and there still visible. At all events, the uneasy conscience and the commercial instinct both come through.*

we are sojourners still. (Robert Lee Frost, New England's poet laureate, was himself born in San Francisco, the son of an Indiana "copperhead," who named him after "Marse" Robert.)

Nor has the story been so different with our seasons and our climates. By dint of winter vacations and travel holidays Americans have pretty thoroughly scrambled their seasons. Even the New England Yankee and the Minnesota farmer have broken out of their winter prisons. Having, on some such journeys, encountered the stimulus of desert or mountain air, the thought then occurs of packaging it, resort fashion, for rent to later comers. At the same time Americans have learned to simulate their climates by air conditioning at home. And the denizens of a great metropolis can live for weeks together without once exposing themselves to the weather.

All this, of course, is nothing more extraordinary than the conquest of nature. And Americans take that conquest for granted. Yet, as has so often been hinted by puzzled Europeans, the American's relations with nature are neither human nor natural. For where the classical tradition had given nature a soul, and even endowed each element with a guardian spirit—a god of the sea or of the winds, a goddess of the earth or some wood nymph for the trees—to Americans, somehow, nature's elements were merely things, and things were to be mastered, exploited, manipulated. And where the hunters and tillers of old Europe had painfully worked out a kind of symbiosis, a man-land and crop-game balance of living, we upset the balance. From the first settlements the record of our conquest of the continent became one of destruction and exploitation. Somehow the settlers and their successors, the pioneers, did not really want to live with the land and cultivate its soils or make the most of its natural beauties, but rather slaughtered the wildlife, burned the

forests, mined the soils, desecrated the landscape—and moved on. The story is an old one, and sad. Why take time to repeat it? Because it suggests a haunting might-have-been. Might not our pioneers have been more careful if they had had to stay put?

Today we still manipulate the physical environment in ways that would have horrified Louis XIV and even staggered the Romans. Soils are changed by chemistry, clouds seeded, distances annihilated, or the balance of nature upset by massive applications of sprayed poison. The needed snowfall for skiers a Vermonter accepts from heaven, or else manufactures with a blower. If the home golf course seems too flat and uninteresting, now that the club members have played the Mid-Ocean and Pebble Beach, the greens committee has the old terrain bulldozed into seaside shape. In a strange juxtaposition each "ranch house" for a rising young executive must now have a swimming pool. In our real-estate "developments" we first skim off the topsoil and cut down the trees; then we plant little bushes and saplings in artificial symmetry. So here again one finds us first admiring then abusing nature's varieties. We are not beholden to nature. Neither time nor place must have us in their power. All of which brings even the friendly interpreter face to face with this paradox: that the people who in many regards had the most natural environment to adapt to have yielded to it the least. Perhaps they have moved too much to let it really capture them, or they ate up space too fast to enjoy it?

In a less friendly review, it may be argued that we have become toughened by exposure, hardened to physical environment, superficial in our relations with nature as well as with things. No doubt some pretty careless or indifferent parties came here in the first place, and that might have been a substantial part of the explanation. Yet the American experience of moving and moving again has increased rather than qualified the "detachment."

Turning now to the third and fourth categories, those of his relations to society and to himself, we may ask: has the American really been working out a new decalogue of social conduct and human fellowship?

Thornton Wilder proposed that Americans (living separately and independently, and finding in the environment "no confirmation of their identity") may engage in a hollow gregariousness, but they only really come alive through action: "There is really only one way in which an American can feel himself to be in relation to other Americans—when he is united with them in a project, caught up in an idea and propelled with them toward the future. . . ."

Another way to describe the same uncertainties and arrive at cooperative activism is to see American social relations as essentially those of friendly strangers. Without ancestry or family tradition, without estates or credentials of place, without privileges of authority or gentility of person, each citizen necessarily has had to stand on his own feet and reciprocally accept his fellow Americans as equal integers, at face value. Knowing little or nothing about his fellows because he had not grown up with them, it seemed wise not to discount them in advance, the more so as, having just arrived in town oneself, one hoped to be accepted on equal terms. Living in an unstable community, with new faces appearing continuously and old faces disappearing before one had really come to know them, a smile had come to seem the required greeting, a handshake and perhaps a clap on the back the best welcome, and the use of first names a brotherly and quite sufficient identification.

Our intimacy with strangers can be an engaging experience, yet ultimately disillusioning, even

dangerous for the foreigner. The Englishman, it has been remarked, is notoriously shy, and builds around his personal privacy all sorts of barriers and reserves of manner. The American smiles and invites you in. Yet once you have penetrated the Englishman's defenses, all his aloofness disintegrates, his reserve melts, and he takes you into his heart. Whereas with the American you find yourself only in an antechamber, and the deeper you go the harder the going, the stiffer the barriers to real intimacy.

Others have pointed out how surprised, even overwhelmed, Asian students can be by the friendly welcome of the dean or admissions officer in an American university, but how bitterly disillusioned they become when it turns out that this welcome is standard, not a personal and exclusive concern for the particular soul and body of the visiting student. Never trust a stranger!

Such misunderstandings call attention to the rather peculiar character of the "person" in this country, or at least of the work relations of one person with another, or of one individual and the many. It is a commonplace that we pride ourselves on our individualism, but limit it. Individualism, American style, insists on personal liberty to act, but aims at progress by competition *and* cooperation. No peonage for us. Our hero is the free individual. At the same time no man acts alone. Sooner or later even the lone wolf finds that sheer ruthlessness defeats its own ends; there are too many against him. Over here the rugged individualist learns to compromise, and to be cooperative, too—at which point he may discover how much he can get done with the help of others if he trusts them, and even how satisfying it is to be able to make his own personal "contribution."

By contrast, individualism, French style, demands recognition of a unique personality—is ever jealous and full of "moi"—instinctively suspects fellow employees and depreciates the outsider. Cooperation with the other fellow is limited. Advancement is sought by inside channels. The great slogan of the French Revolution may have been *Liberté, égalité, fraternité*, but when, by American standards, did the French ever learn the first thing about *fraternité*?

Once again, the relative equality of opportunity —the very absence of inherited privileges and established handicaps, or the ability to walk away from such containments into new and neutral communities—enlarges the field of ambition to John Doe, who soon learns that with luck he may even come to call himself Horatio Alger. In a word, lateral fluidity encourages upward mobility. Just how "open" our society still is, by comparison with what it used to be, or just what the ratio may be between lateral and vertical mobility may be questions for heated argument. What seems unarguable is the absolute necessity of much lateral movement if there is to be any appreciable vertical mobility, too. Without other places to go—and those places occupied by strangers—there would be much less opportunity and no second chance.

Altogether, I suggest, no inconsiderable fraction of today's social and economic life can be understood better if it is seen as geared to the stubborn fact that the average American must live and work among a quasi-anonymous and constantly shifting population. Ask how a stranger might introduce himself and protect himself among fellow strangers, and how he might then employ himself, enrich himself, amuse himself, or organize his social occasions, and one will come surprisingly close to some American norms. (In such communities, for example, will charity be interpersonal, spasmodic, and secretive, or cooperative, regularized, and publicly conducted as through some community drive?)

All this will seem commonplace, yet immensely confusing. Is movement cause or consequence or merely coincidence? It may be one or the other or even all three. Is movement coherent in its action and uniform in its results? Anything but. It is full of paradoxes and contradictions, confusions and uncertainties. There are many motives for moving and many kinds of movers and of movement, and at best they overlap rather than coincide.[15] Nor are all our movements, put together, sufficient to explain American peculiarities. Far from it. Freedom of movement is but one freedom; it takes many others to make a free society. Yet let us not make the contrary mistake of regarding free movement as merely neutral. It may either heal or hurt, atomize or restructure our civilization. Rarely is it just coincidental. Every day of our lives it affects you and me.

Perhaps most important of all, let us note that mobility is *not new*, not an accident nor a temporary state of affairs. As demonstrated by much of the evidence already cited, this moving business, in most of its forms, has been going on here for a long time. Movement has always been a major ligament in our culture, knit into the bone and sinew of that body of experiences which we call our history.

Thus in the field of transportation, we may be now perhaps just past the peak of the automobile age. But before that was the age of steam, of the railroad and the paddle-wheeler, and before that the day of canalboat and prairie schooner, and before that the generations of stagecoach and wilderness trail.

As for personal movement, looking backward we can see that in the nineteenth century the westward movement provided a spectacular (though not unique) series of experiments in displacement. For a little more than a hundred

15 *See Pierson, "The M-Factor in American History," and "Under a Wandering Star."*

years the rough-and-ready frontiersmen, the leap-frogging pioneers, the land speculators and back-woods evangelists kept surging relentlessly toward the westward horizons.[16] The expedition of Lewis and Clark, the great Mormon migration, the sudden rushes of the forty-niners or the Sooners into Indian Territory, the sifting of voters across state lines in the battle for Kansas, the Conestoga wagons and the barges drifting down river, the ox trains and pony express—all these played a part not only in the conquest of the continent but in the forging of an "American" character.

Yet even before the Erie Canal had been dug or the Mississippi had been reached Europeans were commenting on a psychology that owed much to movement: on our friendliness and hospitality, our casual informality and lack of deference, our inquisitiveness and our helpfulness with strangers. Already our feverish restlessness and activity, our boastfulness and psychological insecurity, our mental and emotional instability were a familiar story, noticed by foreigners, commented upon by many. And even those who never caught the frontier itch showed a predilection for mobility. They would not stay put.

The moving of houses awed the Swedish observer, Mr. Klinkowström: "What is it that Americans will not try?"[17] The record shows that we tried moving churches and whole towns; schools, colleges, and "universities"; museums, libraries, and judges; printing presses, newspapers, and factories up and down the country and into

the Mississippi Basin. Where other nations had known their little people of the roads—their vagabonds and beggars, their gypsies and strolling players, their friars and minstrels, their tinkers and knife grinders—the Americans developed not merely their fur traders and pioneers, their land scouts and timber cruisers, and their soldier-explorers and their geologist-surveyors, but their frontier lawyers and territorial politicians, their circuit riding teachers and preachers, their Yankee peddlers and traveling salesmen, their lyceum lecturers and the whole Chautauqua movement.

More than a century ago Domingo Sarmiento, the South American reformer and statesman, noticed particularly our Yankee propensity for travel:

> The large number of passengers reduces the cost of the fares and low fares in turn tempt people to travel, even though they have no precise object in view. The Yankee leaves home to enjoy a change of air, or just to take a trip, and he travels a hundred and fifty miles by steamboat or train before returning to his work.

Sarmiento even went so far as to see a connection between travel and other peculiarities of American civilization, in particular our "monstrous hotels," our appalling eating habits, and the explosion of the American population. A little mischievously he noted that it was the custom for young honeymooners "to take the next train to parade their happiness through woods, towns, cities, and hotels. In the coaches these enchanting couples of twenty summers are to be seen in close embrace, reclining very affectionately against one another to the edification of all the travelers." Hence two effects. All the crusty old bachelors decided to get married: the birth rate became phenomenal. And "... I attribute to these ambulant amours in which American flirting ends, the mania for travel which

[16] In *"The Turner Thesis Re-examined,"* 80, 83, Lee makes the point that the true safety valve was not the frontier but migration, while Turner's frontier theory was but "a special case of an as yet undeveloped migration theory." I find myself in substantial agreement with this suggestion.

[17] F. D. Scott, *"Mr. Klinkowström's America,"* Swedish Pioneer Historical Quarterly, III (Winter, 1952), 1–16.

is so characteristic of the Yankee that he is called a born traveler. The rage for traveling is increasing year by year."[18]

Thus, already by the 1840's we were exploring the sensations of peregrination and enjoying them with ill-concealed enthusiasm. Yet if a twentieth-century American should wish to assure himself that mobility had always been a large and meaningful factor in the American way of life and in the making of the American character, he could do no better than to consult our most discerning judge and commentator, Alexis de Tocqueville.

Tocqueville was astonished by our propensity for movement, by the stagecoaches that went everywhere at breakneck speed over bone-breaking roads, by the phlegmatic way in which Americans took the hardships of travel, and by the extraordinary sight of Americans building roads into the wilderness even ahead of their settlers. While traveling through backwoods Tennessee, Tocqueville got to speculating about some of the effects of such movement for the economy and arrived at the by no means inconsiderable discovery that volume of communications and speed of interchange (that is, turnover) had perhaps as much to do with prosperity as anything else.[19]

Again, on his nine months' journey through the country Tocqueville noted how the English Puritans had planted their institutions and their faith in New England, and how the Connecticut Yankees had then sent their lawmakers, their teachers, and their clocks across the continent. Yet in the process the laws changed, the institutions became simpler, more democratic, and freer from ancestral prejudices. The destruction was piecemeal and not complete: it took at least three migrations to destroy or renovate an old English law. But necessarily, he suggested, there was much loss of ancestral baggage on the march. It was almost as if he had said that Europeans could become Americans only by repeatedly moving.

Once again Tocqueville noted the beneficial effects of the continent and of movement in assuring political stability and in preventing revolution. Why were there not more political plots and conspiracies? And how could the state survive, being so weak? Because there was so much land, because careers were all open, because there were so many other avenues to power than the channel of politics, because younger sons could go west, because the frontier was a safety valve for the adventurous and the irresponsible as well as for the ambitious.

Notwithstanding all these advantages and opportunities, the Americans seemed to Tocqueville at once feverish and sad. And in a striking chapter in his *Democracy in America* he finally asked himself "Why the Americans are so restless in the midst of their prosperity."

> In the United States a man builds a house in which to spend his old age, and he sells it before the roof is on; he plants a garden and lets it just as the trees are coming into bearing; he brings a field into tillage and leaves other men to gather the crops; he embraces a profession and gives it up; he settles in a place, which he soon afterwards leaves to carry his changeable longings elsewhere. . . . Death at length overtakes him, but it is before he is weary of his bootless chase of that complete felicity which forever escapes him.[20]

[18] "*The United States in 1847,*" *A Sarmiento Anthology, tr. S. E. Crummon and ed. A. W. Bunkley (Princeton, N. J., 1948), esp. 209–17.*

[19] *G. W. Pierson,* Tocqueville and Beaumont in America (*New York, 1938), 189, 192–93, 239–40, 286, 573, 579, 589–92. For subsequent references, see 370, 399, 420, 440, 567–69, 602.*

[20] *Alexis de Tocqueville,* Democracy in America, *III, Chap. XIII; I used the Phillips Bradley ed. (2 vols., New York, 1945), II, 136–37.*

How account for this strange unrest of so many "happy" men? The taste for physical gratifications, and the hurry to enjoy them because of the shortness of life, seemed to Tocqueville one obvious source. A social condition in which neither laws nor custom retained any person in his place was a great additional stimulant to this restlessness. Still a third was the "equality of conditions" and opportunity, which engendered a feverish competition and ambitions never quite satisfied.

Such passages are informative and suggestive, not least of our physical instability. Yet if one were to seek even sharper insights into what Tocqueville called the "national character" of the Americans, one should read again the intuitions that he confided to his diary, after only a month in America (June 7, 1831), and before he had seen the frontier, or talked to J. Q. Adams about the West, or come to attribute too much to an all-pervasive egalitarian *démocratie*.

A restless temper (l'inquiétude du caractère) seems to me one of the distinctive traits of this people. . . . We have been told that the same man has often tried ten estates. He has appeared successively as merchant, lawyer, doctor, minister of the gospel. He has lived in twenty different places and nowhere found ties to detain him. And how should it be otherwise? In a word, here man has no settled habits, and the scene before his eyes prevents his adopting any. (1) Many have come from Europe, leaving their customs and traditions behind. (2) Even those long established in the country have preserved this difference. There are no American *moeurs* as yet. Each accepts what he likes from the group, but remains a law unto himself. Here the laws vary continuously, magistrates succeed each other, nature itself changes more rapidly than man. Through a singular inversion of the usual order of things, it's nature that appears to change, while man stays immovable. The same man has given his name to a wilderness that

none before him had traversed, has seen the first forest tree fall and the first planter's house rise in the solitude, where a community came to group itself, a village grew, and to-day a vast city stretches. In the short space between death and birth he has been present at all these changes, and a thousand others have been able to do the same. In his youth he has lived among nations which no longer exist except in history. In his life-time rivers have changed their courses or diminished their flow, the very climate is other than he knew it, and all that is to him but the first step in a limitless career. . . .

Born often under another sky, placed in the middle of an always moving scene, himself driven by the irresistible torrent which draws all about him, the American has no time to tie himself to anything, he grows accustomed only to change, and ends by regarding it as the natural state of man.[21]

May we not deduce that what we feel today our grandfathers and their grandfathers felt before us? We have been pilgrims and pioneers from the beginnings; we were and still are restless almost beyond measure. Has this been a superficial trait? Hardly. Has it done something considerable to shape the American character and society? No matter how uncertain we may feel about the precise character of the results, I do not see how one can question this. Perhaps the strongest effect has been our very unsettlement: our culture of endless change. In 1831 Tocqueville said there were "no

---

[21] *Pierson,* Tocqueville and Beaumont in America, *118–19. The original text has now been established and printed, with variations and some slight differences of sentence order and paragraphing, by J.-P. Mayer [and A. Jardin] in* Alexis de Tocqueville, Oeuvres Complètes *(Paris, 1957),* V, Voyages en Sicile et aux Etats-Unis, *208–209. Cf. the new translation by George Lawrence, in* Alexis de Tocqueville, Journey to America, *ed. J.-P. Mayer (New Haven, Conn., 1960), 182–83.*

American *moeurs* as yet"—while Wilder in 1952 thought we were still engaged in inventing what it is to be an American!

In any reading, what remains inescapable is this: mobility has been one of the oldest and most continuous themes of the American experience, and its meaning is still to be fully understood.

Of course movement, restlessness, and change are not unique to Americans. And the conquests of time and of space: these are not American inventions but the conquests of modern man. Perhaps all we ought to say, therefore, is that in this movement, and in their relations with time and space, Americans have been ahead of Europeans: the first modern automobiles? Americanism, after all, can be in part just a matter of timing: for example, a society behind in the arts but ahead in its gadgets.

Yet does one not feel just a little uneasy about the adequacy of such an explanation? The mobility that America has today, Europe will have tomorrow? Not quite. For it is hard to escape the conviction that somehow, for some strange reason, Americans have had a special affinity for mobility, have known it, used it, enjoyed it, and suffered its agonies, with a devotion and an intimacy no other people has experienced. We are, and will remain, a more fluid society. In times past we have been so swept along in the vast currents of movement that we have taken movement itself for granted. Now it is in our institutions and our economy, in our actions and our attitudes, in our expectations, in our bones. As Tocqueville so shrewdly observed 133 years ago, *a restless temper seems to me one of the distinctive traits of this people.*

THE SHAPING OF THE AMERICAN CHARACTER

*Perry Miller**

In 1867 Walt Whitman brought out a revision of *Leaves of Grass*. He was constantly revising; this was the fourth version. The first had been in 1855, the second in 1856, the third in 1860. Virtually all approved and respectable critics of the time who even bothered to consider Whitman were hostile; they believed a "poetry" that could be so recklessly revised to be obviously no poetry at all. Nowadays there are many who regard him as our greatest poet; when Lucien Price asked Alfred North Whitehead what, if anything, original and distinctively American this country has produced, the philosopher answered without hesitation, "Whitman." I suspect that Whitman, at this moment, is not so popular as he was thirty years ago; if I am right, then this is a sign of the times, one which I must consider ominous. But be that as it may, Whitman's successive revisions, Whitman

being what he was, are apt to come not from a heightened sense of form or from a quest for more precise language, but simply out of his constantly changing sense of the American destiny. He could never make up his mind, though at each point he had to pretend that he did and so declaim with a finality whose very flamboyance betrays the uncertainty.

In 1856 he printed one of his most interesting songs, the one called in the collected works, "As I Sat Alone by Blue Ontario's Shore." In this version, and again in 1860, the poem is an exaltation of the rôle he assigned himself, the poet-prophet of democracy. But by 1867 he had lived through the central ordeal of this Republic, the war we call variously "Civil" or "Between the States." Something profoundly disturbing had happened to Walt Whitman; it is expressed not only in poems writ-

*PERRY MILLER (1905–1963) was Professor of American Literature at Harvard University. His publications include "The Half-Way Covenant" (1933), Orthodoxy in Massachusetts (1933), The New England Mind (1939), "Jonathan Edwards to Emerson" (1940), and Errand into the Wilderness (1956). Reprinted by permission of the New England Quarterly, Vol. 28, No. 4 (December, 1955), 435–454.

ten directly out of his experience, like "Drum-Taps" and "When Lilacs Last in the Dooryard Bloom'd," but in the revisions of previous utterances. In 1856 and 1860, for instance, one line of "By Blue Ontario's Shore" had gone, "Give me to speak beautiful words! take all the rest." In 1867 this became "Give me to sing the song of the great Idea! take all the rest." After the war, he would celebrate the democracy itself, not merely the poet. These changes, commentators theorize, record a chastening of Whitman's egotism; they indicate his belated realization that this country is bigger than any man, even a Whitman, and from the realization he learned humility.

However, the sort of humility one acquires only from discovering that his nation is large and he himself small is by definition suspect. In Whitman, there are some curious additions to the postwar announcement of self-abnegation. This couplet for example:

> We stand self-pois'd in the middle, branching
> thence over the world;
> From Missouri, Nebraska, or Kansas, laughing
> attack to scorn.

Or, still more striking, this verse:

> America isolated I sing;
> I say that works made here in the spirit of other
> lands, are so much poison in The States.
> (How dare such insects as we assume to write
> poems for America?
> For our victorious armies, and the offspring fol-
> lowing the armies?)

Recently a French critic, commenting on this passage, has called it the tirade of a narrow and contemptuous isolationism. Perhaps a Frenchman at this point in history has a reaction different from ours to a boast about the offspring following our victorious armies!

In the light of M. Asselineau's opinion, it is of some significance that Whitman himself, in the 1881 revision of *Leaves of Grass*, suppressed these pieces of strident isolationism. By then he had received further lessons in humility, not from victorious armies but from the stroke that paralyzed him; the last poems, as has often been remarked, show an aspiration toward universality with which the mood of 1867 was in open opposition. However, of one fact there can be no doubt: Walt Whitman, self-appointed spokesman for America, found himself responding in a fashion which may, indeed, be characteristic of the patriot in any country, but has been most conspicuously characteristic of the American: exulting in military victory, he proclaimed that an isolated America has nothing and should have nothing to do with the rest of the world.

This episode in the history of the text is only one out of a thousand which underscore that quality in *Leaves of Grass* that does make it so peculiarly an American book: its extreme self-consciousness. Not only does Whitman appoint himself the poet-prophet of the nation, and advertise to the point of tedium that he sings America, but in the incessant effort to find out what he is singing, what America is, he must always be revising his poems to suit a fluctuating conception. As Archibald MacLeish wrote in 1929 (he as much as Whitman shows how acutely self-conscious about nationality our artists must be), "It is a strange thing—to be an American":

> This, this is our land, this is our people
> This that is neither a land nor a race.

Whether the American public dislikes Whitman or is indifferent to him, still, in this respect he is indeed the national poet Mr. Whitehead called him. So, if we then examine closely this quality of Whitman's awareness, even though we do not pretend to be professional psychologists, we are bound to recognize that it emanates not from a mood of serene self-possession and self-assurance, as Whitman blatantly orated, but rather from a pervasive self-distrust. There is a nervous instability at the bottom of his histrionic ostentation—an anxiety which foreign critics understandably call neurotic. In fact these critics, even our friends, tell us that this is precisely what Americans are: insecure, gangling, secret worriers behind a façade of braggadocio, unable to live and to let live.

Some of the articles in the massive supplement on *American Writing To-Day* which the *Times* of London brought out in September, 1954, are by Americans, but one called "A Search for the Conscience of a People" sounds as though of English authorship; either way, it declares an opinion I have frequently heard in England and on the Continent. Americans, particularly from the early nineteenth century on, have been in search of an identity. "The Englishman," says the writer "takes his Englishness for granted; the Frenchman does not constantly have to be looking over his shoulder to see if his Frenchiness is still there." The reason for this national anxiety is that being an American is not something to be inherited so much as something to be achieved. This, our observer concludes, is "a complex fate."

Surely it is, as complex for a nation as for a person. Yet what compounds complexity is that all the time we are searching for ourselves we keep insisting that we are a simple, uncomplicated people. We have no social classes, our regional variations are not great compared with those of France or Germany, no weight of tradition compels us to travel in well-worn ruts. From coast to coast we all buy the same standard brands in chain stores built to a standard pattern, we see the same television shows, laugh at the same jokes, adore the same movie stars, and hear the same singing commercials. How, then, can we be complex? Europe is complex—it is civilized, old, tormented

with ancient memories; but we are as natural as children. Then, why are we so nervous? Why do we so worry about our identity? One can imagine an English college setting up a conference on the constitutional principles of the Cromwellian Protectorate, or on the issues of the Reform Bill of 1832, but never, I am sure, one entitled, "On Values in the British Tradition." At Oxford and Cambridge those would be so much taken for granted that even to mention them aloud would be bad form, and to insinuate that they needed discussion would become indecent exposure.

As far as I read the history of the West, I find only one other great civilization that faced an analogous predicament, and that was the Roman Empire. Not the Republic: the original Rome emerged gradually, as have the modern nations of Europe, out of the mists of legend, mythology, vaguely remembered migrations of prehistoric peoples. The Republic had traditions that nobody created, which had been there beyond the memory of mankind, atavistic attachments to the soil. But after the murderous Civil Wars and wars of conquest, the old Roman stock was either wiped out or so mixed with the races of the Mediterranean that the Empire had become as conglomerate a population as ours, the social cohesion as artificial. As with us, there was not time to let the people fuse by natural and organic growth over several centuries: Rome was no longer a country but a continent, no longer a people but an institution. The aggregation would have fallen apart in the first century B.C. had not somebody, by main force, by deliberate, conscious exertion, imposed unity upon it. Julius Caesar attempted this, but his nephew and ultimately his successor, Augustus Caesar, did it.

This analogy, as I say, has often struck me, but I should be hesitant to construct so seemingly far-fetched a parallel did I not have at least the authority of Alfred North Whitehead for entertaining it. Actually, it was a favorite speculation with Mr. Whitehead, and I may well have got it from him in some now forgotten conversation. However, it comes back to us, as though Whitehead were still speaking, in Lucien Price's *Dialogues*. Augustus Caesar's foundation of an empire would not, Whitehead agrees, satisfy our ideal of liberty, yet it saved civilization. It is, in the very deliberateness of the deed, a complete contrast to the unconscious evolution of the English constitution. Nobody here, Whitehead remarks, can say at exactly what point the idea of a limited monarchy came in; the conception originated with no one person nor at any specific time, and even today no scientifically precise definition is possible. Though the Roman Empire was not the result of any long-range plan, once it existed, it was recognized as being what it had become, and systematically organized; the British acquired their empire, as the saying goes, in a fit of absence of mind, and have never quite found a way to administer the whole of it. So they surrender to nature and let irresistible forces guide it into forms that are not at all "imperial."

Now Whitehead's point is that the only other creation of a nation and an administration by conscious effort, the only other time statesmen assumed control of historic destinies and, refusing to let nature take its course, erected by main force a society, was the American Revolution and the Constitutional Convention. To read the history of the first sessions of the Congress under President Washington in 1789 and 1790 is to be driven either to laughter or to tears, or to both. Even more than in the first years of Augustus' principate, I suspect, it presents the spectacle of men trying to live from a blueprint. The document prescribed two houses of legislators, a court, and an executive; as men of cultivation they had some knowledge of parliamentary procedure, but beyond such elementary rules of order they knew not how to behave. They

did not know how to address the President, and nobody could figure in what manner a cabinet officer was related to the Congress. That is why, although certain customs have been agreed upon, such as "Senatorial courtesy," we do not have the immemorial traditions that govern, let us say, conduct in the House of Commons. Hence, when one of our customs appears to be violated, we behold a Select Committee of Senators trying to find out what the Senate is. We can do nothing by instinct.

As a matter of historical fact, Professor Whitehead might have pushed that moment of conscious decision further back than the Constitutional Convention. Settlers came to the colonies for a number of reasons that were, so to speak, in the situation rather than in their minds, yet none came without making an anterior decision in his mind. They may have been forced by famine, economic distress, a lust for gold or land, by religious persecutions, but somewhere in their lives there had to be the specific moment when they said to themselves or to each other, "Let's get out, let's go to America." The only exception to this rule is, of course, the Negroes; they came not because they wanted to but because they were captured and brought by force. Maybe that is why they, of all our varied people, seem to be the only sort that can do things by instinct. Maybe that is why Willie Mays is the greatest of contemporary outfielders.

Also, the Indians did not come by *malice prepense*. They are the only Americans whose historical memory goes back to the origin of the land itself; they do not have to look over their shoulders to see if their Indianness is still there. So, they astonished the first Americans by acting upon instinct. One of the most charming demonstrations of this native spontaneity was Pocahontas' rush to the block to save Captain John Smith from having his brains beaten out. Later on, Indian rushes were not so charming, but even in warfare they exhibited a headlong impetousity that bespoke an incapacity to make deliberate plans. They could never construct an assembly line or work out a split-second television schedule.

As for Captain John Smith himself, we may doubt that this impetuous adventurer came at first to America out of the sort of conscious decision Whitehead had in mind. To begin with, America meant no more to him than Turkey, and Pocahontas no more than the Lady Tragabigzanda, who inspired his escape from slavery in Constantinople—at least, so he says. But even he, who became a temporary American by accident, after a brief two-years' experience of the land, realized that here lay a special destiny. The initial disorders at Jamestown—which were considerable—convinced him that God, being angry with the company, plagued them with famine and sickness. By the time he was summoned home, the dream of an empire in the wilderness was upon him, and he reviewed these afflictions not as merely the customary and universal rebukes of Providence upon sinners, but as ones specially dispensed for the guidance of Americans. He spent twenty-two years selflessly propagandizing for settlement. By 1624, after he had digested the lesson of his intense initiation, he had thoroughly comprehended that migrating to America was serious business, much too strenuous for those he called the "Tuftaffaty" gentlemen who had come along, as we might say, only for the ride, in the expectation of picking up easy gold from the ground. No: mere tourists, traveling nobles, would not build an empire; it needed people who, having decided to remove, would as a consequence of decision put their backs into the labor. In 1624 he reprinted and emphasized a cry he had written to the company back in 1608, when the lesson was just beginning to dawn upon him:

> When you send againe I intreat you rather send but thirty Carpenters, husbandmen, gardiners, fisher men, blacksmiths, masons, and diggers up of trees, roots, well provided; then a thousand of such as we haue: for except wee be able both to lodge them, and feed them, the most will consume with want of necessaries before they can be made good for any thing.

Smith was more prophetic than even he comprehended: America has not time to make people good for anything; they have to be good for something to start with.

The outstanding case of the conscious act of decision was, we all know, the Puritan migration to New England. Whenever we find the religious incentive strong among immigrating groups, something of the same history can be found, but the New Englanders were so articulate, produced so voluminous a literature in explanation of their conduct, and through the spreading of the stock across the continent have left so deep an impress on the country, that the Puritan definition of purpose has been in effect appropriated by immigrants of other faiths, by those who in the nineteenth century left lands of a culture utterly different from the English. The act was formally committed to paper by the "Agreement" signed and ratified at Cambridge in the summer of 1629. The great John Winthrop, the Moses of this exodus, was able to give full expression to the idea even before he set foot ashore; he did it by preaching a lay sermon aboard the flagship of the fleet, on the deck of the *Arbella*, when still in mid-ocean. It was published under the title "A Modell of Christian Charity," in 1630. Chronologically speaking, Smith and a few others in Virginia, two or three at Plymouth, published works on America before the "Modell," but in relation to the principal theme of the American mind, the necessity laid upon it for decision, Winthrop stands at the beginning of our consciousness.

We wonder whether, once Southampton and

Land's End had sunk beneath the eastern horizon, once he had turned his face irrevocably westward, Winthrop suddenly realized that he was sailing not toward another island but a continent, and that once there the problem would be to keep the people fixed in the mold of the Cambridge Agreement, to prevent them from following the lure of real estate into a dispersion that would quickly alter their character. At any rate, the announced doctrine of his sermon is that God distinguishes persons in this world by rank, some high, some low, some rich, some poor. Ostensibly, then, he is propounding a European class structure; but when he comes to the exhortation, he does not so much demand that inferiors remain in pious subjection to superiors, but rather he calls upon all, gentlemen and commoners, to be knit together in this work as one man. He seems apprehensive that old sanctions will not work; he wants all the company to swear an oath, to confirm their act of will. This band have entered into a Covenant with God to perform the specific work: "We have taken out a Comission, the Lord hath giuen vs leaue to drawe our owne Articles, we haue professed to enterprise these Accions vpon these and these ends." Because this community is not merely to reproduce an English social hierarchy, because over and above that, more important even than an ordered way of life, it has a responsibility to live up to certain enumerated purposes. Therefore this society, unlike any in Europe, will be rewarded by Divine Providence to the extent that it fulfills the Covenant. Likewise it will be afflicted with plagues, fires, disasters, to the extent that it fails. Profound though he was, Winthrop probably did not entirely realize how novel, how radical, was his sermon; he assumed he was merely theorizing about this projected community in relation to the Calvinist divinity, absolute sovereign of the universe. What in reality he was telling the proto-Americans was that they could not just blunder

along like ordinary people, seeking wealth and opportunity for their children. Every citizen of this new society would have to know, completely understand, reckon every day with, the enunciated terms on which it was brought into being, according to which it would survive or perish. This duty of conscious realization lay as heavy upon the humblest, the least educated, the most stupid, as upon the highest, the most learned, the cleverest.

There is, I think all will acknowledge, a grandeur in Winthrop's formulation of the rationale for a society newly entered into a bond with Almighty God to accomplish "these and these ends." However, enemies of the Puritans even at the time did more than suggest that the conception also bespeaks an astounding arrogance. Who was Winthrop, critics asked, and who were these Puritans, that they could take unto themselves the notion that the Infinite God would bind himself to particular terms only with them while He was leaving France and Germany and even England to shift for themselves? One can argue that coming down from this Puritan conception of America's unique destiny—"Wee must consider," said Winthrop, "that wee shall be as a Citty vpon a Hill, the eies of all people vppon us"—has descended that glib American phrase, "God's country," which so amuses when it does not exasperate our allies. But the important thing to note is that after a century or more of experience on this continent, the communities, especially the Puritan colonies, found the Covenant theory no longer adequate. It broke down because it tried, in disregard of experience, in disregard of the frontier and a thriving commerce, to stereotype the image of America, to confine it to the Procrustean bed of *a priori* conception. Not that the theology failed to account for empirical phenomena; only, the effort to keep these aligned within the original rubrics became too exhausting. The American mind discarded this notion of its personality because the ingenuity required to maintain it was more than men had time or energy to devise.

The little states suffered many adversities—plagues, wars, crop failures, floods, internal dissension. According to Winthrop's reasoning, the communities could not accept these as the normal hazards of settling a wilderness or augmenting the wealth; they had to see in every reverse an intentional punishment for their sins. By the time they had undergone several Indian wars and frequent hurricanes, a tabulation of their sins would obviously become so long as to be crushing. We can imagine, for instance, what Cotton Mather would have made in his Sabbath sermons, morning and afternoon, each over two hours in duration, of the fact that New England was struck by not one but *two* hurricanes, and that the first, proceeding according to divine appointment, carried away the steeple of his own church, the Old North. He would perfectly understand why, since the population did not immediately reform their criminal habits, even upon such a dramatic admonition, another storm must come close upon the other. Were we still livingly persuaded that we actually are God's country, we would not now be arguing with insurance companies or complaining about the Weather Bureau, but would be down on our knees, bewailing the transgressions of New England, searching our memories to recall, and to repent of, a thousand things we have contrived to forget. We would be reaffirming our Americanism by promising with all our hearts to mend the evil ways that brought upon us the avenging fury of Carol and Edna.

In pious sections of America at the time of the Revolution some vestiges of the Covenant doctrine remained. Historians point out how effective was the propaganda device employed by the Continental Congresses, their calling for national days of fasting and humiliations. Historians regard these appeals as cynical because most of the leaders, men of the Enlightenment, were emancipated from so crude a theology as Winthrop's. Certainly you find no trace of it in the Declaration of Independence. Yet I often wonder whether historians fully comprehend that the old-fashioned religious sanction could be dispensed with only because the Revolutionary theorists had found a substitute which seemed to them adequate to account for a more complex situation. Being classicists, they read Latin; while nutured on authors of Republican Rome, they were as much if not more trained in the concepts of the empire, not only in writers like Tacitus and Marcus Aurelius, but in the Roman law. Which is to say, that the imperial idea, as Augustus made it manifest, was second nature to them. Whether Madison appreciated as keenly as Whitehead the highly conscious nature of Augustus' statesmanship, he had no qualms about going at the business of constitution making in a legal, imperial spirit. The problem was to bring order out of chaos, to set up a government, to do it efficiently and quickly. There was no time to let Nature, gradually, by her mysterious alchemy, bring us eventually to some such fruition as the British Constitution; even so, had time not been so pressing, Madison and the framers saw nothing incongruous in taking time by the forelock, drawing up the blueprint, and so bringing into working operation a government by fiat. Analysts may argue that separation of powers, for instance, had in practice if not in theory come about by historical degrees within the colonial governments, but the framers did not much appeal to that sort of wisdom. They had a universal rule: power must not be concentrated, it must be divided into competing balances; wherefore America decrees its individuality through a three-fold sovereign, executive, legislative, and judicial, and then still further checks that authority by an enumerated Bill of Rights.

The Revolutionary chiefs were patriots, but on

the whole they were less worried by the problem of working out an exceptional character for America than the spokesmen of any other period. Patriotism was a virtue, in the Roman sense, but one could be an ardent American without, in the Age of Reason, having to insist that there were special reasons in America, reasons not present in other lands, why citizens must inordinately love this nation. Franklin, Jefferson, Madison were as near to true cosmopolitans as the United States has ever produced. But on the other hand, in order to win the war, pamphleteers for the patriot side did have to assert that the Revolution carried the hopes not only of America but of the world. The immense effectiveness of Thomas Paine's *Common Sense*, for example, consisted not so much in its contention that independence of England made common sense but that only America was close enough to Nature, only these simple people were so uncorrupted by the vices of decrepit civilizations, that only here could common sense operate at all.

It is a fanciful speculation, but suppose that the intellectual world of the late eighteenth century had persisted unchanged from 1776 to the present. In that case, through one and three-quarters centuries we should have had a steady and undisturbing task: merely refining on and perfecting the image of ourselves we first beheld in the mirror of the Declaration of Independence. Had there been no Romantic poetry, no novels by Scott, no railroads and steam engines, no Darwin, no machine gun, no dynamo, no automobile, no airplane, no atomic bomb, we would have had no reason to suppose ourselves other than what we were at Concord and Yorktown. We would remain forever formerly embattled farmers listening complacently from our cornfields to the echoes rolling round the world of the shot we fired, without working ourselves into a swivet worrying

about whether we should again shoot. However, even before Jefferson and Adams were dead in 1826, the mind of America was already infected from abroad with concepts of man and nature which rendered those of the patriarchs as inadequate as the Covenant theology, while at the same time the nation itself was being transformed by an increase of population and of machines, and so had to rethink entirely anew the question of its identity.

The French Revolution and the Napoleonic Wars, it is a truism to say, aroused all over Europe a spirit of nationalism which the eighteenth century had supposed forever extinct. One manifestation of the new era was an assiduous search in each country for primitive, tribal, barbaric origins. Germans went back to medieval legends, to the Niebelungen Lied, to fairy tales. Sir Walter Scott gave the English a new sense of their history, so that the ideal British hero was no longer Marlborough or Pitt, but Ivanhoe, Rob Roy, and Quentin Durward, while the yeomen suddenly gloried in having come down from Gurth the Swineherd. Realizing that the evolution of English society was well as of the constitution had been organic, natural, spontaneous, illogical, the English renounced reason; they challenged America to show what more profound excuse for being it had than a dull and rationalistic convention. All at once, instead of being the hope of the enlightened world, America found itself naked of legends, primitive virtues, archaic origins. It might be full of bustle and progress, but romantically speaking, it was uninteresting, had no personality.

Americans tried to answer by bragging about the future, but that would not serve. In the first half of the nineteenth century many of our best minds went hard to work to prove that we too are a nation in some deeper sense than mere wilfulness. At this time Europeans began that accusation which some of them still launch, which drives us to a frenzy: "You are not a country, you are a continent." Not at all, said James Fenimore Cooper; we too have our legends, our misty past, our epic figures, our symbolic heroes. To prove this, he created Natty Bumppo—Leatherstocking the Deerslayer, the Pathfinder, the embodiment of an America as rooted in the soil, as primordial as the Germany that gave birth to Siegfried.

Professor Allan Nevins recently brought out a selection from the five Leatherstocking volumes of the portions that tell the biography of Natty Bumppo, arranged them in chronological order instead of the sequence in which Cooper composed them, and thus reminded us that Cooper did create a folk-hero, achieving in his way a success comparable to Homer's. Modern readers have difficulty with Cooper's romances because they do seem cluttered with pompous courtships and tiresome disquisitions; these were not annoyances to readers in his day (though I must say that even then some critics found his women rather wooden), so that they had no trouble in appreciating the magnificence of his Scout and of Chingachgook. Mr. Nevins says that when he was a boy, he and his companions played at being Natty and Chingachgook; children nowadays do not read Cooper—I am told that if they can so much as read at all, they peruse nothing but comic books—and they play at being Superman and space cadets. But for years Cooper more than any single figure held up the mirror in which several generations of Americans saw the image of themselves they most wished to see—a free-ranging individualist, very different from Winthrop's covenanted saint or from Paine's common-sensical Revolutionary.

Cooper persuaded not only thousands of Americans that he was delineating their archetype but also Europeans. One does not readily associate the name of Balzac with Cooper, but Balzac was an enthusiastic reader of Leatherstocking and in 1841 wrote a resounding review, praising the mighty figures but explaining what was an even more important element in Copper's achievement:

> The magical prose of Cooper not only embodies the spirit of the river, its shores, the forest and its trees; but it exhibits the minutest details, combined with the grandest outline. The vast solitudes, in which we penetrate, become in a moment deeply interesting. ... When the spirit of solitude communes with us, when the first calm of these eternal shades pervades us, when we hover over this virgin vegetation, our hearts are filled with emotion.

Here was indeed the answer to the problem of American self-recognition! We may have come to the land by an act of will, but despite ourselves, we have become parts of the landscape. The vastness of the continent, its very emptiness, instead of meaning that we are blank and formless, makes us deeply interesting amid our solitudes. Our history is not mechanical, calculated; it is as vibrant with emotion as the history of Scott's Britain.

On every side spokesmen for the period between Jackson and Lincoln developed this thesis; by the time of the Civil War it had become the major articulate premise of American self-consciousness. Let us take one example. George Bancroft's *History of the United States* had a success with the populace at large which no academic historian today dares even dream of. When he came to the Revolution, he recast it into the imagery of nature and instinct, so that even Jefferson became as spontaneous (and as authentic a voice of the landscape) as Natty Bumppo:

> There is an analogy between early American politics and the earliest heroic poems. Both were spontaneous, and both had the vitality of truth.

Long as natural affection endures, the poems of Homer will be read with delight; long as freedom lives on earth, the early models of popular legislation and action in America will be admired.

So, for Bancroft and his myriad readers, the lesson of the Revolution and the Constitution was precisely opposite to what Whitehead sees in the story. Prudent statesmanship, Bancroft says, would have asked time to ponder, "would have dismissed the moment for decision by delay." Conscious effort "would have compared the systems of government, and would have lost from hesitation the glory of opening a new era on mankind." But the common people—the race of Natty Bumppo—did not deliberate: "The humble train-bands at Concord acted, and God was with them."

We can easily laugh at such language. We may agree that Cooper and Bancroft were noble men patriotic Americans, but to our ears something rings terribly false in their hymns to the natural nation. Perhaps the deepest flaw is their unawareness of, or their wilful blindness to, the fact that they are constructing in a most highly conscious manner an image of America as the creation of unconscious instinct. They apply themselves to supplying the country with an archaic past as purposefully as General Motors supplies it with locomotion. They recast the conception of America into terms actually as *a priori* as Winthrop's Covenant, and then do just what he did: they say that these spontaneous and heroic terms are objectively true, fixed and eternal. Within them and only them America shall always make decisions, shall always, like the train-bands at Concord, act in reference to their unalterable exactions. We are what we have always been, and so we are predictable. He who acts otherwise is not American.

Behind the Puritan, the Revolutionary and the Romantic conception of social identity lies still another premise; in all these formulations it is *not*

articulated. I might put it roughly like this: they all take for granted that a personality, a national one as well as an individual, is something preexisting, within which an invariable and foreseeable pattern of decision reigns. If, let us say, a man is brave, he will always act bravely. If a nation is proud, chivalric, religious, it will be Spanish; if it is frivolous, amatory, cynical, it will be French. I need hardly remind you that a powerful movement in modern thought has, in a hundred ways, called in question this "deterministic" method. There may be, and indeed there are, physical conditions, such as sex or size, such as climate or mineral resources; but these are not what make the personality we deal with, the nation we must understand. What constitutes the present being is a series of past decisions; in that sense, no act is spontaneous, no decision is imposed, either by the Covenant, by common sense, or by Nature.

In the later nineteenth century, as Romantic conceptions of the universe died out, another determined effort was made to recast the image of America in the language of Darwinian evolution. In this century, as the faith weakened that evolution would automatically carry us forward, we have, in general, reformulated our personality into a creature preternaturally adept in production—the jeep and the know-how. Each successive remodeling retains something of the previous form: we echo the Covenant not only in the phrase "God's country," but when we pray for the blessing of Heaven upon our arms and our industries, we invoke Revolutionary language in our belief that we, of all the world, are preeminently endowed with common sense; we also imagine ourselves possessed of the pioneer virtues of Natty Bumppo, by calling ourselves "nature's noblemen," yet simultaneously suppose ourselves evolving into an industrial paradise, complete with television and the deep freeze. When we try to bundle up these highly disparate notions into a single definition, we are apt to come up with some such blurb as "The American Way of Life."

I am attempting to tell a long story into too short a compass, but I hope my small point is moderately clear. As a nation, we have had a strenuous experience, as violent as that Walt Whitman records; he spent a lifetime trying to put America into his book, to discover himself bedevilled by changing insights, buffeted by unpredicted emotions, rapid shifts, bewildered by new elements demanding incorporation in the synthesis. He who endeavors to fix the personality of America in one eternal, unchangeable pattern not only understands nothing of how a personality is created, but comprehends little of how this nation has come along thus far. He who seeks repose in a unitary conception in effect abandons personality. His motives may be of the best: he wants to preserve, just as he at the moment understands it, the distinctive American essence—the Covenant, common sense, the natural grandeur, the American Way of Life. But he fools himself if he supposes that the explanation for America is to be found in the conditions of America's existence rather than in the existence itself. A man *is* his decisions, and the great uniqueness of this nation is simply that here the record of conscious decision is more precise, more open and explicit than in most countries. This gives us no warrant to claim that we are higher in any conceivable scale of values; it merely permits us to realize that to which the English observer calls attention, that being an American is not something inherited but something to be achieved.

He says this condemns us to a "complex fate." Complexity is worrisome, imparts no serenity only anxiety. It keeps us wondering whether we might now be something other, and probably better, than we are had we in the past decided otherwise, and this in turn makes decision in the present even more nerve-wracking. Trying to escape from such anxiety by affixing our individuality to a scheme of unchanging verities is a natural response. Yet our national history promises no success to the frantic gesture. Generalizations about the American character can amount to no more than a statistical survey of the decisions so far made, and these warrant in the way of hypotheses about those yet to be made only the most tentative estimates. However, if my analysis has any truth in it, a backhanded sort of generalization does emerge: he who would fix the pattern of decision by confining the American choice to one and only one mode of response—whether this be in politics, diplomacy, economics, literary form, or morality itself—such a one, in the light of our history, is the truly "Un-American."